The Comple
Internationa
Jewish Cookbook

To my husband, Myer, and our children,
David, Alan and Judi, with whom it is
my joy to share 'la vie en Rose'.

Evelyn Rose

The Complete International Jewish Cookbook

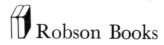

Robson Books

FIRST PUBLISHED IN GREAT BRITAIN IN 1976 BY ROBSON BOOKS LTD., 28 POLAND STREET, LONDON W1V 3DB.

ISBN 0 903895 66 8

First impression August 1976
Second impression September 1976
Third impression November 1976
Fourth impression May 1977
Fifth impression July 1978
Seventh impression March 1984

Illustrations by Ilana Richardson
Designed by Harold King

Printed in Hungary

Contents

Acknowledgements

I have been collecting the material for this book ever since I started writing about food and cookery more than twenty years ago. During that time, I have received more help than I can possibly acknowledge here. I can only express my deepest gratitude to all those who have shared their culinary knowledge with me, including my parents, my husband's parents, my relations, friends, professional colleagues, readers, listeners, viewers, shopkeepers—even strangers met by chance on trains and planes.

However, several people gave me special assistance during the preparation of this book. Sula Leon helped me to collate and retest the recipes; Rabbi F. F. Carlebach and Rabbi Michael Boyden gave me guidance on religious matters; and several of my friends were involved in typing the manuscript as well as testing and tasting the recipes and menus. In addition, many of my fellow home economists in both education and industry have given generously of their expertise and experience.

But the deepest debt of gratitude I owe to my immediate family: my husband has not only taste-tested every one of my recipes for over twenty-five years, but has also given me immense practical help in preparing the book for publication, whilst my children have been my sternest critics—and most faithful fans. To them all, I offer my most sincere thanks.

1976 EVELYN ROSE

How to Use the Recipes

Solid measures are first given in spoons, pounds and ounces.

Liquid measures are first given in spoons, pints or fluid ounces. In the parenthesis, the first figure given is the metric equivalent and the second figure given is the American equivalent measured in cups,

e.g.	**3 oz (75g/$\frac{1}{3}$ cup)**	—	solid measure
	$\frac{1}{4}$ pint (125ml/$\frac{2}{3}$ cup)	—	liquid measure

American equivalent ingredients are given in parentheses,

e.g. **glacé (candied) cherries**
double (heavy) cream

Temperatures are first expressed as a gas number and then in degrees Fahrenheit and degrees Celsius,

e.g. **Gas No. 3, 325°F, 170°C**

Measurements are first given in inches and then in centimetres,

e.g. **2 in (5 cm)**

Spoon measures are level. As the difference in volume is so small, I have assumed British and American spoons to be interchangeable. However, some adjustment in the quantity of seasonings may be necessary to suit individual tastes.

Note on metric equivalents used in the book:
For weights under a pound, 1 ounce = 25g
For liquid measures under 1 pint, 1 fluid oz = 25ml
For weights over a pound, 1 ounce = 30g
For liquid measures over 1 pint, 1 fluid oz = 30ml

As all the recipes have been developed using imperial (traditional) weights and measures it may be necessary in certain dishes to use an extra 25g or 25ml to achieve the texture or the consistency specified.

Jewish Food

One can almost pinpoint the exact occasion, in the second millennium before this era, when the art of Jewish cookery was born. On that day the course of world history was changed when the matriarch Rebecca, by the judicious use of herbs and spices, gave the savour of wild venison to the insipid flesh of a young kid, and established a culinary philosophy of 'taste with economy' which has been followed by her descendants ever since.

At the time that Rebecca made her kid casserole and her son Esau sold his birthright for a bowl of lentil soup, the everyday food of those early Jews was primitive in the extreme; except on special occasions, the staple diet consisted of boiled vegetables such as leeks, garlic and onions, and salads of raw herbs, with boiled meat cooked only on a holiday. During the following two thousand years, the Jews became in turn the subjects of the four civilizations in which the art of the kitchen was first evolved. When the empires of these Egyptians, Persians, Greeks and Romans had faded into history, their cooking methods survived—in the kitchens of their former subjects.

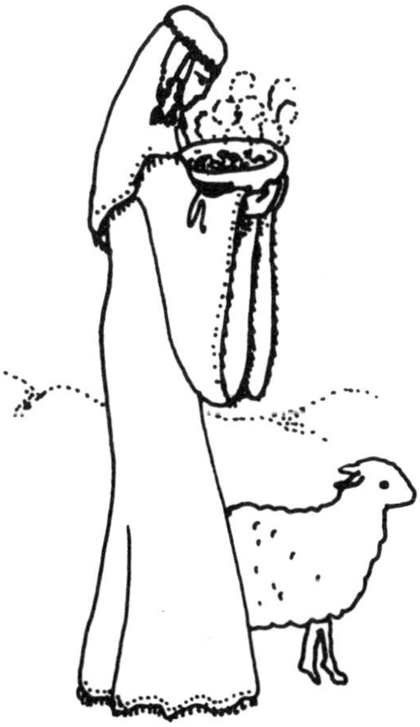

To this day Jewish housewives, during the Feast of the Passover, make a sweetmeat of dried apricots which their ancestors learned when they were slaves in Egypt; they make a stuffed strudel with the same filling of poppy seeds and honey that was used to garnish the fattened dormice at Trimalchio's famous Roman feast; and during Shavuot (the Feast of Weeks) they bake honey and cheese cakes which are a legacy of the many years of Seleucid rule.

If these 'remembrances of foods past' were the sum total of Jewish cooking, it is doubtful if it would have survived to the present day. Jewish tradition teaches that when Moses descended from Mount Sinai he gave the waiting Jewish women the code of culinary practice by which they have conducted their kitchens ever since, and which has been responsible, to a large extent, for the unique flavour and character of their food.

In the Jewish Dietary Laws, there are the prohibitions: no shellfish; no pig; no carrion; no birds of prey; no thing that crawls upon its belly. Then there are the categories of permitted foods: only those fish that have fins and scales; only those beasts that chew the cud and have cloven hooves; only those birds that have been slaughtered according to the Law.

Then there are the cooking and serving instructions for these permitted foods: foods of animal and dairy origin not to be combined either during the cooking or the serving; dairy foods to be served after meat foods only when a specified number of hours has elapsed; meat to be purged of its blood before use.

However, it was in the Ten Commandments themselves that there appeared those instructions which have resulted in the development of some of the most typical of Jewish foods—those dishes which can be cooked one day and served the next. 'On the seventh day thou shalt do no work, neither thy maidservant nor thy manservant,' said the Law, and so Jewish housewives would spend all day Thursday and most of Friday before dusk, making herring salads, liver pâté, soups, fruit pies, yeast cakes and, in particular, those meat and vegetable casseroles which could be left in a low oven overnight.

In nineteenth-century Russia, after the Synagogue service on the Sabbath, the children of the household would be sent to the baker's to collect their family's dish in time for Saturday lunch. Should a child stumble and spill his dish of 'cholent', then the whole village would dip into its own pots to make up a meal for the unfortunate family. A layered fruit and pastry pudding that was often cooked in this way was probably of early French origin, for it was called 'shalet' from the medieval French word for hot: 'chauldt'.

The need to differentiate between meat and milk meals encouraged the development of many delicious dairy dishes made from velvety 'kaese', a soft cheese made from naturally soured milk. These dishes include cheese 'kreplach' (a form of ravioli), 'lokshen' and 'kaese' (noodle and cheese casserole), and the 'blintze'—a paper-thin pancake, stuffed with slightly sweetened cream cheese, which is the most famous Jewish dish to be accepted into the international cuisine.

The shortage of kosher meat in the ghettos of medieval Europe forced the housewife to find ways of stretching her meagre supply. Usually, she would mince it and use it as a stuffing for a variety of different doughs and vegetables. In Russia the housewife would stuff the meat into a 'varenike' (potato dough) or a 'piroshke' (yeast dough); in Hungary, she would stuff a pepper ('gefüllte paprika'); in Austria she would use a strudel dough; in Poland a chicken's neck ('gefüllte helzel') or a noodle dough ('kreplach').

Those Jews who lived in the Middle East stuffed carrots, aubergines (eggplant), tomatoes and even leeks, using an ingenious metal 'excavator' to remove the vegetable flesh. When meat became more plentiful, other methods of cooking it were adopted, but all were based on braising or casseroling, for kosher meat is used only a few days after it has been killed and tends to be tough when it is dry-roasted.

Some of the most interesting Jewish foods are those which are cooked in celebration of a Festival. In biblical times, these Festivals were the occasions for the family to make a pilgrimage on foot to the Temple at Jerusalem, where they would offer the first ripe fruits from their fields, as well as bread and cakes made from the new season's wheat. The delicious meal pancakes that were offered in the Temple on these occasions are still eaten at Passover to this day.

No artificial leavening may be used in Passover baking, so whisked sponges and meringues are the most popular confectionery. As ordinary flour may not be used, ground nuts, matzo meal and potato starch are substituted. There are coconut pyramids and almond macaroons, whisked sponges and ground nut torten, and cinnamon balls made of ground almonds and sugar—many of them made from recipes dating from the Middle Ages. At the harvest festival of Succoth (or 'Tabernacles') everyone makes strudels and stuffed vegetables, as symbols of the bounty of harvest time.

Perhaps the finest Jewish cooks of Western Europe were those who lived in the old Austro-Hungarian Empire. To these women, Friday was 'strudel day'; they would rise at 6 a.m. to stretch the tissue-paper-thin dough onto a cloth laid on the kitchen table, and to make yard-wide tins of yeast cake, topped with cherries ('kirschen kuchen'), plums ('zwetschen kuchen'), or cheese ('kaese kuchen') that would last the family until after the Sabbath on the following day.

The cooking that is done in the majority of Western Jewish households, however, owes much of its inspiration to the fish and fowl of Poland, Czechoslovakia, and the States that border the Baltic Sea. In the freshwater lakes of these countries swam the carp and the bream which were used to make the famous 'gefüllte fish'. Today, Western Jews use haddock, hake, cod and halibut flap to make this delicious fish dish, which has a close affinity to the 'quenelles de brochet' of France. If you visit Israel, you will have this mixture served in a pepper and tomato sauce, or as an appetiser, formed into little balls that are fried and served with pickled cucumbers. Gefüllte fish apart, the new generation of Israeli Jews has discarded many of the traditional dishes of those families who came from the colder lands of Europe, and now enjoys a far lighter diet of vegetables, dairy foods and fish, albeit spiced with many traditional dishes of the Middle East.

Food of an entirely different nature from that prepared by Western Jews is cooked by those Jews who were expelled from Spain by Ferdinand and Isabella in 1492, and who settled in many of the countries that border the Mediterranean. The cookery of the 'Sephardim' as they are known, is spicy and aromatic, and their cakes, flavoured with rose-water and almond oil, seem to have come straight from the Arabian nights. These cakes include the 'gereybes'—crisp shortbread 'bracelets' fastened with a split almond; 'kahks'—light bread rolls topped with sesame seeds; and pastries stuffed with dates and almonds. But perhaps their most delicious concoctions are the 'kibbes'—slender cases of meal pastry moulded on the finger, and then filled with minced lamb, and the ‘cheese cakes’ of ‘fila pastry (the strudel paste of the Middle East), filled with a savoury mixture of grated cheese and egg.

Today the young Jewish housewife can buy prepacked the traditional foods of the past. Chicken soup in a can; gefüllte fish in a jar; even the Sabbath chicken is offered her ready roasted in a plastic bag. The fish her ancestors learned to fry in Egypt she can buy from the refrigerated counter of the delicatessen, and the delicate noodles that her grandmother dried on the tea-towel-draped back of the kitchen chair she can shower direct from packet to pan.

But I, for one, hope that what the women of Israel learned from the Egyptians, the Persians, the Greeks and the Romans will not be forgotten too easily.

Adapting Recipes for the Jewish Kitchen

Many recipes published in general cookery books must be adapted in some way before they can be used in an orthodox Jewish kitchen.

This may be for any of the following reasons: They contain non-kosher ingredients; they combine meat and dairy products in the same dish; or they include a dairy ingredient in a recipe one wishes to use in a meat meal.

To make such recipes acceptable, substitute ingredients must be used which, while they satisfy the requirements of the dietary laws, do not radically alter the flavour and texture of the original dish.

Here are some of the more common 'forbidden' ingredients and the most satisfactory substitutes.

Butter

To fry meat or poultry: Substitute for each 1 oz (25g/2 tbsp) butter: 1 tablespoon rendered chicken fat and 2 teaspoons oil; or 2 tablespoons oil or a pre-packed chicken fat substitute.

To sauté vegetables for a meat casserole or soup: Substitute an equal amount of margarine.

To fry or roast potatoes: Substitute an equal amount of oil, plus a nut of margarine to give flavour.

In a pudding after a meat meal: Substitute an equal amount of margarine and use water instead of milk to mix.

In pastry after a meat meal: Substitute 4 oz (100g/ ½ cup) margarine and 1 oz (25g/2 tbsp) white fat for each 5 oz (125g/⅔ cup) of butter.

With vegetables in a meat meal: Substitute an equal amount of margarine, and flavour with a squeeze of lemon juice before serving.

In a chicken soup or sauce: Substitute an equal quantity of chicken fat (preferably) or margarine.

To fry pancakes after a meat meal: Substitute white cooking fat.

Milk

In a batter for pancakes or Yorkshire pudding: Substitute an equal quantity of water, plus 1 tablespoon of oil for each ¼ lb (100g/1 cup) of flour. Use two eggs instead of one. Yorkshire pudding made with water is crisper and has less 'body' than when made with milk. Pancakes are thinner and lighter, with a less 'cakey' texture.

Cream

To thicken a chicken sauce, soup or casserole: Either: Whip parve synthetic cream with a squeeze of lemon juice, then substitute for an equal quantity of double cream, add just before serving.

Or: Substitute $\frac{1}{4}$ pint (125ml/$\frac{2}{3}$ cup) chicken stock, 1 egg yolk and 1 level teaspoon cornflour (cornstarch) for each 5 fl oz (125ml/$\frac{2}{3}$ cup) double cream. Mix the cornflour to a liquid with the cold stock and then stir in the yolk. Pour on the hot mixture slowly, stirring well. Return to the pan and reheat until steaming.

Or: Substitute this nut cream (however, it will not whip): Melt $\frac{1}{2}$ oz (15g/1 tbsp) margarine in $\frac{1}{4}$ pint (125ml/$\frac{2}{3}$ cup) hot water. Add $\frac{1}{2}$ level teaspoon sugar and 2 oz (50g/$\frac{1}{2}$ cup) cashew nuts. Blend for 1 minute at maximum speed. Pour into a basin and refrigerate for several hours until thickened. It can also be frozen. To use instead of milk (e.g. in a bechamel sauce), thin down with water. *Do not allow to boil.*

To lighten a cold sweet: If the sweet has a pronounced flavour of its own, parve synthetic cream (whipped) can be substituted for whipped cream. In a dessert set with jelly (gelatin), a similar texture (but not taste) to the original can be achieved by using a meringue of 2 egg whites and 2 level teaspoons caster (superfine) sugar for every 5 fl oz ($\frac{2}{3}$ cup) double cream.

Chicken Stock

In a milk soup or sauce: Substitute an equal quantity of water, flavoured with bottled vegetable extract, vegetable bouillon cubes, or a monosodium glutamate product. Add an extra nut of butter or a tablespoonful of cream to enrich the soup before it is served.

Shellfish

In a fish cocktail: Substitute an equal weight of a firm white fish (such as halibut or sole) poached and cut into bite-sized pieces.

In a cream dish or filling for vol au vent cases: Substitute an equal quantity of flaked cooked salmon, halibut or haddock.

In a batter-coated dish: Substitute an equal weight of raw sole, cut into bite-size strips. Coat with batter and fry as directed in deep fat.

Smoked Meat (Bacon or Ham)

In a savoury flan such as **Quiche Lorraine:** As the meat is used mainly for flavour, use a savoury substitute, such as black olives, sautéd onions, finely-diced anchovies or sautéd mushrooms.

In mixed grills: Substitute kosher smoked sliced veal or beef.

In a meat or chicken casserole: The flavour of smoked meat in a casserole is strange to the Jewish palate, and it is best not to use a substitute, but to omit it altogether. (For example, in **Boeuf Bourguignon.**)

How to Substitute Meat Cuts

The following kosher cuts from the forequarters of the animal can be satisfactorily substituted for hindquarter cuts mentioned in specific recipes:

First cut shoulder steak or sliced bola (chuck) for any braising or stewing cut such as round steak
Corner bola—chuck—(for braising) for topside or silverside of beef
Pickled brisket for pickled silverside (it is nicer as well)
Boned and rolled wing rib (short rib) for sirloin
Boned eye of wing rib (short rib) (sometimes known as 'fairy steak') for rump, sirloin or point steak. (The rib steak is in fact entrecôte.)
Shoulder of lamb for leg of lamb
Boned shoulder of lamb for lamb fillet
Boned shoulder or breast of lamb for boned leg (for kebabs)
Boned and sliced veal shoulder for escalopes
Boned and cubed shoulder or breast of veal for leg of veal (in casseroles such as **Sauté de Veau Marengo**)

Double lamb shoulder chops for chump or loin chops or lamb steaks
Minced bola (chuck) for minced beefsteak (in grilled hamburgers)

Note: All meat which is to be grilled, spit-roasted or baked in an uncovered dish (using dry rather than moist heat) should be koshered, then hung in the butcher's cold room, or kept in a commercial or domestic freezer for 10 days before use. This helps to tenderize it.

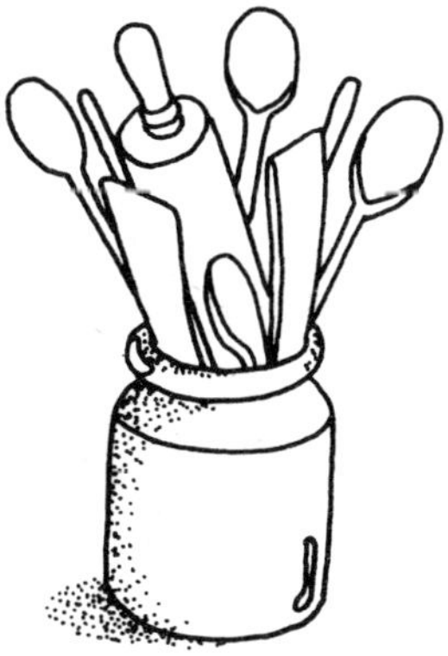

Hors d'oeuvres

To start a meal with a tasty dish has been considered an aid to appetite and digestion since Roman times. Yet whilst the elaborately-dressed dishes as exemplified by the French hors-d'œuvres were based on food available only to the rich, in the Jewish cuisine the humblest peasant in the Pale of Settlement expected to start his meal with a plate of schmaltz herring dressed with oil and vinegar, or a salad of salt herring, sweetened with apple and garnished with egg. These 'forspeise' or tasty starters are enjoyed by Jews in every country of the world, though more recently the traditional chopped liver and pickled herring have been augmented by smoked salmon and trout, as well as by the dressed avocados, aubergines (eggplant) and artichokes grown in Israel.

Pâté As You Like It

It is said that the Jewish poultry breeders of Strasbourg were the first to devise pâté de foie gras. But the pâté or chopped liver of the traditional Jewish Saturday lunch is an altogether more plebeian affair, invented as a means of using the giblets of the Sabbath fowl to make a cheap and tasty 'starter' that could be made on Friday for lunch after the synagogue on the following day.

Chopped Liver

Calf and ox liver may both be used to make chopped liver, but the flavour is sweeter and the texture softer when calf liver is used. This, however, is only available occasionally. It is also much more expensive than ox liver.

½ lb (200g) liver
2 hard-boiled eggs (simmered for 12 min then plunged in cold water till required)
1 medium onion
½ level teasp salt
10 grinds black pepper
Rendered chicken fat to bind (about 1 rounded tbsp)

The liver must be koshered beforehand (see **How to Kosher Meat and Poultry** p. 53). Put the koshered liver into a saucepan with half the onion. Cover with cold water. Bring slowly to the boil, cover and simmer for 10 minutes over very gentle heat. Drain the liver thoroughly and discard the half onion. Remove the outer skin. Put through the medium blade of the mincer the cooked liver, the raw half onion, the whole of one egg and the white of the other. Put in a basin with the salt and pepper and add the chicken fat to bind it together. If the mixture looks crumbly, add a little more soft fat. Turn into a shallow dish and smooth the surface flat. Refrigerate covered with foil (chopped liver will keep in the coldest part of the refrigerator for two days). Just before serving push the remaining hard-boiled egg yolk through a metal sieve on to the surface of the liver. Serve with sliced challah or matzo crackers. This makes enough for 4 portions as an appetiser, or will serve 6 when spread on biscuits (crackers).

Chicken Liver Pâté in the Jewish Fashion

The onion is fried to sweeten it and prevent its flavour from overpowering the delicate chicken livers.

½ lb (200g) grilled chicken livers
1 medium onion
2 hard-boiled eggs
Approx 2 tbsp chicken fat
Salt and pepper

Cook the sliced onion in the chicken fat in a covered frying pan until tender and golden (about 10 minutes). Remove from the pan and add to the livers. Put onions and livers through the fine blade of the mincer, together with the hard-boiled eggs. Blend well, adding the pan juices and a little extra chicken fat if necessary to make a smooth pâté. Season to taste with salt and pepper. Pack into a small earthenware dish and chill for several hours. Serves 6 spread on fingers of toast or challah.

Pâté Maison

This is a pâté in the French style which I have adapted for the Jewish kitchen. It gets even better after a few days under refrigeration. I have sometimes made it with chicken livers alone, but I find the spicing tends to overwhelm them. If allspice (also known as 'piment' or 'quatre épices') is not available, make up the quantity with ground nutmeg, cloves and cinnamon.

1 oz (25g/2 tbsp) chicken fat or margarine
½ onion
½ lb (200g) calf liver; or ¼ lb (100g) each of chicken and calf liver (sliced)
1 tbsp brandy
1 egg
1 clove garlic
1 level teasp salt
10 grinds black pepper
½ level teasp ground allspice
1 bayleaf
Sauce made with ¼ pint (125ml/⅝ cup) chicken stock, ½ oz (15g/1 tbsp) margarine, and 2 level tbsp flour

Grill livers to kosher. Sauté sliced onion gently in fat. Add grilled livers and stir till they have absorbed fat.

To make sauce: Dissolve ½ chicken bouillon cube in ¼ pint (125ml/⅝ cup) boiling water (or use soup). Melt margarine and add flour, cook for a minute, then whisk in hot liquid. Simmer 2 minutes, turn off heat and drop in egg. Beat well.

Combine onion, liver, brandy, sauce, garlic, salt, pepper, spice and liquidize until smooth. Turn into 1 lb (½kg) loaf tin. Smooth level. Place bayleaf on top. Cover tightly with foil. Put in baking tin filled with 1 inch (2 cm) very hot water. Cook for 1 hour (Gas No. 2, 300°F, 150°C) or until pâté is shrinking away from sides of tin. Refrigerate for 2 days if possible. Serve as spread, or hors-d'œuvre. If you wish to serve it in one portion, line the tin with foil. The refrigerated pâté can then be dished and garnished with tomatoes, cucumber and stuffed olives. Alternatively, if you have an attractive French fireproof terrine, scoop the pâté out of the terrine at the table and serve with crisp lettuce and a slice of lemon. Serves 8.

Smoked Salmon Pâté

An exquisitely flavoured pâté that can be made with a cheap quality smoked salmon—the frozen packs are excellent. Allow it to mature overnight.

3 oz (75g/⅓ cup) cream cheese
Finely-grated rind of ½ lemon
1 egg yolk
5 fl oz (125ml/⅝ cup) single (light) cream
⅓ small clove garlic
½ level teasp salt
Few grinds black pepper
3 oz (75g/⅓ cup) smoked salmon
Handful of parsley
1 medium-thick slice bread (1 oz/25g)

Put the cheese in the top of a double saucepan (or heatproof basin) then stir in the lemon rind, yolk and cream. Cook over boiling water until thickened to a pouring sauce consistency (5 minutes). Put into the blender goblet, followed by the sliced smoked salmon, crushed garlic, salt, pepper, parsley, and slice of bread, torn in four. Blend until absolutely smooth. Spoon into 6 tiny soufflé dishes or cocottes. Chill. Serve with cucumber or lemon twist, with hot toast. Serves 6.

Buckling Pâté

The golden buckling is a smoked herring with a similar, if slightly more robust, flavour than smoked trout.

1 large buckling (whole smoked herring which needs no further cooking)
3 oz (75g/$\frac{1}{3}$ cup) soft butter
1 tbsp lemon juice
1 clove garlic, crushed
10 grinds black pepper

Plunge the buckling into boiling water for one minute to facilitate the skinning and boning. Mash the flesh well with a wooden spoon, then work in the softened butter. Add the garlic and lemon juice and season to taste with the black pepper (no additional salt is needed). Pack into a little earthenware pot and refrigerate for 12 hours. Serve with hot toast, or as a biscuit (cracker) spread. Serves 4–6.

Smoked Salmon and Other Delights

A freshly-smoked side of salmon has a shelf life of only twelve days (one reason why the price is so high), before it starts to lose its delicate flavour. To avoid the need for such urgent handling a very large proportion of the smoked fish now leaves the factory already sliced, trimmed, weighed and packeted, and in this condition it will keep for months in a deep freeze.

There is really no better way to enjoy smoked salmon than in thin slices hand-carved from the flesh of a 'fresh' side of the fish, and eaten with a squeeze of lemon juice, a grind of black pepper and a plateful of fine-textured brown bread, spread with cool butter. There is also a lot to be said for a sandwich of smoked salmon on fresh black bread, or on an oven-fresh bagel buttered and spread with the best cream cheese. Allow 1½–2 oz (40–50g/3–4 tbsp) per serving or 1 oz (25g/2 tbsp) per serving if part of a mixed hors-d'œuvre, such as canned asparagus tips, stuffed egg and black olives.

Egg Mayonnaise

This is a dish that can be varied according to the contents of the larder. It is important to have a really well-flavoured home-made mayonnaise (*see section on* **Salad Dressings** *p.* 111).

For each serving:
1 hard-boiled egg
Leaves of crisp lettuce
Mayonnaise
Garnish—which may be anchovy fillets, tomatoes, black olives, avocado

For each serving arrange the leaves of the heart of a cos (iceberg) lettuce in a fan shape on a plate and place two halves of egg at the bottom; cover with mayonnaise which has been diluted to coating consistency with soured cream or yoghourt. It may also be flavoured with a pinch of curry powder or a teaspoonful of French mustard. Arrange 3 or 4 slices of very ripe tomatoes in the 'fan' of lettuce. Sprinkle with a little French dressing. If none is made drip a little oil on the tomatoes then squeeze some lemon followed by a sprinkle of black pepper, salt and a pinch of sugar. Finally decorate the egg with chopped chives and the tomatoes with chopped parsley and put 2 or 3 plump black olives at the side. For a more elaborate finish criss-cross egg with anchovy fillets and arrange two slices of ripe peeled avocado with the tomatoes.

Baked Eggs with Chicken Livers

4 chicken livers
Little chicken fat or oil
4 eggs
Salt and pepper
4 tbsp chicken jelly or gravy (from braised bird); or 1 tbsp sweet sherry and 3 tbsp chicken soup

Grill the livers to kosher, then cut each in four and put into a small frying pan with 2 teaspoons of chicken fat or oil. Simmer for a minute to absorb the fat, then add the chicken jelly (or gravy) or the sherry and soup. Cook gently for 3 minutes. Well grease a shallow casserole just large enough to hold the eggs. Put in oven for 5 minutes (Gas No. 4, 350°F, 180°C) to heat the dish, then break the eggs into it side by side. Season with salt and pepper. Cook for 10 minutes until just set. Add the livers and juices, then return to oven for 2 or 3 more minutes. Serves 4.

Herring Hors-d'œuvres

Chopped Herring Salad (Gehackte Herring)

This delicious mixture is made from herrings which are preserved by salting in wooden casks between layers of rock salt. The salt herring was a staple food of the Ashkenazi Jews of Russia and Poland—indeed, two herrings of any kind will provide an adult man with his full daily requirement of protein.

The seasoning of chopped herring is very much a matter of taste. You may, for instance, use fresh lemon juice instead of vinegar, and crumbled sweet biscuits (crackers) in place of fine meal. If you start with the balance of flavours I suggest below you can then adjust it as you wish. For chopping use a 'hackmesser' or 'hâchoir' (double-handed chopping knife).

4 salt herrings
2 hard-boiled eggs (simmered for 12 min in water to cover)
1 small tart dessert apple
1 medium onion, finely grated
1 level tbsp caster (superfine) sugar
2 level tbsp fine matzo meal
4 tbsp vinegar
¼ teasp white pepper

The day before, cut the heads off the herrings, slit the belly and remove the entrails. Place in a glass casserole and put under the cold water tap, with the water running in a gentle trickle. After an hour, turn off the tap and leave the herrings covered in cold water overnight. Next day, lift them out of the water and drain well. Put on a board and slit the skin down the centre back, when it can be peeled off easily from both sides. Flatten the back of each herring with the palm of the hand, turn it over and lift out the centre bone. Remove any other bones which may be sticking out. Cut the fish up roughly, and put on a chopping board kept specially for the purpose. Add the egg, the apple and the grated onion, and chop until all the ingredients are very fine. Now sprinkle on the meal, vinegar, sugar and pepper, mixing well. The meal should be sufficient to soak up excess juice. If not, add a little more. Taste, and add a little more vinegar or sugar if necessary. Spoon the herring into a shallow dish, smooth level, cover with foil and chill. Just before serving, the herring can be garnished with the sieved hard-boiled yolk of another egg. Chopped herring can be served on a plate, garnished with a lettuce leaf and a slice of tomato and gherkin, or on crisp biscuits or crackers (but in this case, do not spread it until ten minutes beforehand, or the biscuits will go soggy). Serves 4 people as an appetiser, but, spread on biscuits, will make enough for 8.

Pickled Herrings

Sometimes called 'Bismarcks' or 'rollmops'. Although these can now be bought in jars, the home-pickled variety are especially delicious, and their acidity can be varied to suit the family's taste. If salt herrings are not available, soak fresh cleaned and boned herrings in a salt-and-water brine (2 oz/50g/3 tbsp salt and 1 pint/500ml/2½ cups of water to 6 herrings) for 2 hours, then put in the spiced vinegar as directed for the salt herrings.

6 salt herrings
1 pint (500ml/2½ cups) white vinegar; or 7 fl oz (175ml/1 cup) acetic acid diluted with 14 fl oz (350ml/1¾ cups) water
2 medium onions, thinly sliced
1 large unpeeled lemon, sliced
1 level tbsp pickling spice
2 bayleaves and a chili pepper
2 level tbsp brown sugar
White pepper

Behead the herrings, slit the belly and remove the entrails. Put the fish in a glass casserole (so that the smell will not linger) and put under the cold water tap. Leave the water running in a gentle trickle. After an hour, turn off the tap, and leave the herrings overnight covered in cold water. Next day, lift them out of the water and drain well. Put on a piece of paper: scrape with a blunt knife to remove loose scales. Wash again under the cold water tap and put on a board. Open the front, then turn over and press the back with the flat of the hand. Turn over again and you will find that the backbone can be lifted out easily. Remove any other loose bones. Sprinkle each herring very lightly with white pepper, add two or three thin rings of onion, then roll up from tail to head. If the herrings are very large, you may find it easier to split them lengthwise before rolling. Skewer each herring closed with a wooden cocktail stick. Put in a glass jar in alternate layers with the sliced lemon, the onion and the spices. Put the vinegar and sugar into a pan and bring to the boil. Immediately the liquid bubbles, turn off the heat and leave until it is lukewarm. Pour over the herrings. Cover and refrigerate for 4 days before using. The herrings will keep under refrigeration for several weeks, but they do tend to become more acid as the weeks go by. Enough for 4 people on three occasions. Serve in ½ in (1 cm) slices, either speared on a cocktail stick with a drink or as an hors-d'œuvre garnished with the pickled onion slices, tomato and cucumber.

Schmaltz (Matjes) Herrings

Schmaltz herrings are prepared by smoking young fat spring herrings using a process originated by Dutch fishermen. When in season, they make a most tasty, if thirst-making, hors-d'œuvre. A great favourite at Jewish wedding receptions, served with a chaser of 'schnaps', schmaltz or matjes herrings can now be bought ready-filleted from many delicatessen shops. Otherwise, the whole fish has to be skinned and filleted at home.

2 whole schmaltz (matjes) herrings or 4 fillets
Spring onions (scallions) or Spanish onions
Tomatoes
Fresh cucumber
Lemon juice or wine vinegar
Black pepper

Fillets need not be soaked, but whole fish should be beheaded and slit down the belly and the entrails removed, then covered in cold water and soaked for 2 hours. Drain thoroughly, press down on the back to flatten, then remove the centre bone. To skin, slit down centre back, and then peel skin off on either side. Half an hour before dinner, cut the fillets into 1 in (2½ cm) slices and arrange in a narrow shallow dish, surrounded by alternate slices of tomato and fresh cucumber. Over the fish squeeze just enough lemon juice or vinegar to moisten it and point up the flavour. Sprinkle with several grinds of black pepper, and then some finely-sliced spring onions or raw Spanish onions. Serve with black bread or challah. For cocktails, spear the herring portions on toothpicks. Serves 4–6.

Soused Herrings

A favourite Jewish dish quite different from the Scottish dish of the same name.

6–8 medium herrings, filleted
1 medium onion, finely sliced
½ pint (250ml/1¼ cups) vinegar
¼ pint (125ml/⅔ cup) water
Few peppercorns
Blade of mace
Bayleaf
Salt and pepper
2 teasp sugar
1 tbsp golden (corn) syrup

Wash and scale herrings, split lengthwise, sprinkle with salt and pepper and a little onion, roll up from tail. Pack side by side in a shallow casserole. Sprinkle with remaining onion then with vinegar, water and seasonings. (Liquid should just come to top of herrings but not cover them.) Sprinkle dish with sugar then golden syrup. Cover loosely with foil. Put in moderate oven till simmering, then reduce to Gas No. 2, 300°F, 150°C, for 3 hours, or until a rich brown, with liquid reduced by half. Do not allow liquid to boil, or herrings will be hard. Serves 6–8.

Savoury Fruits

It is an American idea—more particularly from California—to serve a starter of fruit, usually in a sweet and sour dressing. The only care one must exercise is to ensure that the sour predominates over the sweet so that the dish stimulates rather than deadens the appetite.

Pineapple and Cucumber on the Half Shell

3 small ripe pineapples
1 medium cucumber
Dressing:
8 fl oz (200ml/1 cup) soured cream
1 tbsp lemon juice
2 level teasp caster (superfine) sugar
1 level tbsp fresh chopped mint; or 1 level teasp freeze-dried mint
½ level teasp salt

Combine the dressing ingredients several hours beforehand and refrigerate. An hour before serving split each pineapple lengthwise right through the tufts, scoop out the flesh and discard centre core. Peel the cucumber, then cut it and the pineapple into ¼ in (½ cm) cubes. Combine with the dressing and pile back into the shells. Garnish with a sprig of fresh mint. Serves 6.

VARIATION
Orange and cucumber: Substitute 3 large oranges for the pineapple. Peel, section and cut each piece in half. Combine with the cucumber. Add the dressing, to which should be added either a pinch of garlic salt or half a small clove of garlic, crushed to a paste. Serve the salad in a shallow dish, or in individual bowls, lined with endive leaves. This can be served as part of a mixed hors-d'œuvre or as a course in itself.

Melon Hors-d'œuvres

The melon is reputed to have been developed in the gardens of the Emperors of Persia and, like the grape, takes its flavour from the soil of its birthplace. To swell and sweeten, it needs a wet winter and a hot summer, the exact climatic conditions to be found in the Negev desert in Israel. A few years ago Israeli agriculturists took the sweet and subtly-flavoured Charentais melon and naturalized it in Kibbutz Ogen, where the conditions of soil and sun were similar to its birthplace on the West Coast of France.

The Ogen Melon

The Ogen melon has a flavour identical to that of its French cousin, but the flesh is greenish rather than orange. I find it reaches its peak after two days in the larder.

A perfect Ogen melon needs no embellishment. Simply chill it for half an hour, cut in half, remove the pips and serve it on the half shell. For gala occasions, however, it can be filled with slightly sweetened fresh or frozen raspberries, liberally sharpened with lemon juice.

The Honeydew Melon

The honeydew melon must be tested for ripeness at the neck (or blossom end), which gives gently when the fruit is ripe. Again, the simplest method of serving is the best.

Melon
Lemon juice
Caster (superfine) sugar
Optional garnish of pineapple, grape and glacé cherry or twists of orange

Cut the melon in half and scoop out the seeds. Cut each half into two, three or four segments according to size. Take each slice in turn, and with a sharp knife cut between the flesh and the skin. Leave the flesh on the skin, but cut into 1 in (2½ cm) slices, each just large enough for a mouthful. The slices can then be pushed to alternate sides to make the melon look attractive. Arrange them on a serving plate, sprinkle lightly with caster sugar and generously with lemon juice. Leave uncovered in the refrigerator for not more than an hour, by which time they will be bathed in a delicious lemon syrup. *To garnish:* Thread a pineapple cube, half a grape and a glacé cherry onto a cocktail stick and spear in the centre of the melon slice; or spear an orange twist and glacé cherry on the stick instead.

VARIATION

Melon with ginger sauce: For 6 wedges of melon cut as above, mix 4 level tablespoons caster (superfine) sugar with 2 level teaspoons ground ginger. Sprinkle on the prepared fruit, but omit the lemon juice. Refrigerate for 1 hour. Garnish with black grapes.

Melon and Grape Cocktail

This can be made with either honeydew or Ogen melons; citrus juices are used to draw out the natural juices from the other fruits.

1 large honeydew; or 2 Ogen or canteloupe-type melons
1 lb (480g) seedless grapes or halved and pipped black grapes
Juice of 1 large orange and 1 large lemon
2–3 oz (50–75g/$\frac{1}{3}$ cup) caster (superfine) sugar (depending on the sweetness of the melon)

Cut the melon in half, remove the pips, then scoop out the flesh in balls using a melon cutter or deep-bowled spoon. Put in a bowl. Put the orange and lemon juice with the sugar into a small pan and dissolve over gentle heat without boiling. Pour over the melon. Add the grapes, but leave them on top of the mixture (for if they are mixed with the juices too soon they will lose their crispness). Cover and leave in the larder or a cool place for several hours to allow the fruit juices to flow. One hour before serving, mix the fruit thoroughly. Arrange in grapefruit glasses and chill. Serve garnished with a sprig of mint. Serves 6–8.

Very Special Vegetables

The Avocado

The skin may be a rich green or almost black, the surface dimpled or smooth. But you can really only judge the ripeness of an avocado by the feel. The fruit cannot be ripened on the tree, and as the crop is exported under refrigeration, the chances are that the avocado you buy will still be hard and under-ripe. Take it home and leave it at room temperature—or in the airing cupboard for speed—for at least two days. When it is ripe enough to use, the fruit will give slightly all over when pressed between the palms. This is the best condition for eating 'on the half shell' with a well-flavoured French dressing or a stuffing of tartly-flavoured citrus, fish or chicken salad replacing the stone. If, however, it is to be used for a dip or spread, then it should be used when very soft all over so that the flesh has a creamy consistency when it is scooped out.

Overchilling will ruin the texture (the avocado cannot be successfully frozen), but if the fruit ripens too soon, it can be stored whole for several days in the bottom of the refrigerator. Once cut, the flesh soon oxydizes and discolours, but this can be prevented by mixing it with a lemon or mayonnaise dressing, or covering the cut surface closely with foil.

Avocado with Vinaigrette Dressing

Make the dressing several hours before dinner to allow the flavours to mature.

3 fat avocados
Dressing:
4 tbsp wine or cider vinegar
2 tbsp lemon juice
$\frac{1}{4}$ pint (125ml/$\frac{2}{3}$ cup) mild olive oil or other salad oil
1 clove garlic
2 level teasp caster (superfine) sugar (optional)
1 teasp prepared mustard
2 heaped teasp chopped fresh mixed herbs—parsley, chives, tarragon or chervil
1 level teasp salt
10 grinds black pepper
1 tbsp very finely chopped onion
1 chopped pickled red pepper (optional)

Put the vinegar, lemon juice and all the seasonings into a screw-top jar and shake until well blended.

Then add the oil and shake again until thickened. Leave at room temperature until required. About half an hour before dinner, cut avocados in half and remove the stones, spoon a little dressing into each cavity, and spread a little more over the cut surface to prevent discolouration. Refrigerate. Serve either in special oval containers or on a bed of flat leaves. Serve the remaining dressing at the table. The flesh is scooped out with a teaspoon. Serve with brown bread and butter. Serves 6.

Avocado and Anchovy on the Half Shell

3 avocados
1 can anchovies
1–2 canned pimentos, depending on size
Dressing:
1 tbsp lemon juice
2 tbsp wine vinegar
4 tbsp mild olive oil
½ fat clove garlic
Pinch of sugar and black pepper
½ teasp each of prepared mustard and salt
2 teasp each of finely-chopped onion and parsley

Put all the ingredients for the dressing into a screw-top jar and shake till thickened. Leave whilst you cut the avocados in half, remove the stone, then carefully scoop out the flesh in one piece. Keep the skins. Cut the flesh into ⅜ in (1 cm) cubes. Put into a bowl with the diced pimento and the anchovies cut in ¼ in (½ cm) lengths. Remove garlic from dressing then spoon over the avocado mixture to moisten it thoroughly. Chill till required. Just before serving, spoon back into the shells. Serve with brown bread and butter. Serves 6.

Avocado Cream

A lovely dish to serve with a cold fish buffet.

1 very ripe avocado
2 teasp lemon juice
1 tbsp thick (heavy) cream
Good pinch of salt and pepper
1 level teasp prepared mustard
Tomato and cucumber slices

Scrape the pulp from the avocado with a stainless steel spoon; mash with all the seasonings, or put in the blender until smooth and creamy. Arrange overlapping slices of cucumber and tomato on individual plates. Pipe or spoon some of the avocado cream in the centre. Serve cold with brown bread and butter. Serves 6.

Artichokes

It is not so much the taste for artichokes that needs to be acquired as the manner of eating them! Not for inclusion in the menu of a formal banquet (unless the heart alone is served), they make the most blissful of hors-d'œuvres at a friendly family meal. Choice artichokes feel weighty in the hand and the stalk should look green and fresh. They may be stored raw for several days under refrigeration. The preparation is simple, if precise. Bend the stalk so that it breaks off and pulls out the coarse filaments at the base, which may need to be trimmed level with a knife. Turn the artichoke on its side and cut off the top ¾ in (2 cm) using a sharp knife. Trim off the points of the remaining leaves with a pair of scissors. Wash well, and put into a very large pan of salted, boiling water, simmering with the lid half-on for 35–40 minutes or until a leaf can be plucked out with ease.

By now, the artichokes will have acquired their typical dark green colour. Drain thoroughly and serve warm with melted butter slightly acidulated with lemon juice, or cold with this dressing:

Vinaigrette dressing for artichokes (sufficient for 6)

In a screw-top jar put:
4 tbsp wine vinegar
2 tbsp lemon juice
¼ pint (125ml/⅔ cup) mild olive oil
1 teasp prepared mustard
1 teasp caster (superfine) sugar (optional)
1 tbsp very finely chopped raw onion
1 cut clove garlic
½ teasp salt
2 teasp each of chopped chives and parsley
Pinch of paprika
10 grinds black pepper

Shake for 2 minutes until thickened, then leave for 1 hour for the flavours to blend.

To serve hot or cold: Put each artichoke on a large plate. The leaves are plucked out one at a time, dipped in sauce, then sucked to remove the flesh at the base. When all the leaves have been pulled out, the thistle-like 'choke' will be revealed. This must be cut off with a sharp knife to reveal the tender heart. This is then cut up with a knife and fork and dipped into the dressing.

Asparagus

Choice asparagus has a brief, expensive season, so it is worth taking great care in its selection and preparation, which is well repaid by its exquisite flavour and texture.

Choose a bundle with thick, green-tipped stalks, firm and fresh-looking. Untie the bundle and wash it, tips down, in a bowl under cold running water, then gently scrub it with a soft brush to remove the sand which clings to the tips. Break off the woody lower 2 in (5 cm) of the stalk—it seems to snap at just the right place, about 2 in (5 cm) below the green stem.

Scrape away the last inch ($2\frac{1}{2}$ cm) of scales on the lower stem using a small sharp knife, then re-tie the asparagus into a bundle of even length, using soft string. If you have no asparagus pan, leave a loop of string to make it easy to lift the cooked bundle from the pan. Asparagus must be cooked 'al dente'—that is, it must have a tender head with a slightly chewy stalk, so that one can almost suck the juices out of it. To achieve this, it is necessary to steam the tender heads, whilst boiling the tougher stalks.

The pan: You can buy a special asparagus pan—a cylindrical pan with a perforated inner section that lifts out like a double boiler. But for most households, a percolator without the coffee container works just as well and is far cheaper to buy (for heaven's sake keep it only for asparagus!).

To cook: Put 4 in (10 cm) of boiling water into pan, add bundle of asparagus, tips to the top, close lid and simmer for 15 minutes. To test whether done, taste one stalk—the tip should be tender without being mushy.

The sauce: While the asparagus is cooking, it is as well to get ready the sauce and the dish. The simplest sauce, and I think the best, is plain melted butter, although Hollandaise Sauce is also often served.

Melted Butter Sauce:
3 oz (75g/$\frac{1}{3}$ cup) butter (preferably unsalted)
Few grains cayenne pepper
Squeeze of lemon juice

Put the butter into a sauce boat and leave in a warm place (the warming oven or the side of the stove) so that the butter becomes liquid without oiling. Just before serving add the cayenne and lemon juice.

The asparagus dish: This can be as elaborate as a specially-designed entrée dish with a built-in tray on which the cooked asparagus is placed to drain; or it can be as simple as a flat platter with a linen napkin liner to hold excess moisture. Lay the steaming bundle of asparagus on the dish, untie the string and serve at once. Tepid asparagus is horrid. Six to seven flat stalks are quite sufficient for one serving, with a slice of challah for mopping up the combined juices and butter sauce. And—fingers, please. That is the only way to eat asparagus.

Note: 1 fat bunch of asparagus will serve 6.

Imam Bayeldi—Whole Aubergines (Eggplant) in Tomato

This is rich, luscious and full of flavour. This is how the Turks make it, though versions of the dish are served all over the Middle East.

6 medium oval aubergines (eggplant)
2 tbsp currants
1 level teasp ground allspice; or a pinch of cinnamon
½ level teasp salt
10 grinds black pepper
1 tbsp chopped parsley
2 large onions
3 tbsp oil
Whole tomatoes drained from a 15 oz (375g) can
Sauce:
Olive oil and water to half cover the aubergines (eggplant)
Juice of a large lemon
2 teasp sugar
1 clove garlic
1 bayleaf

Cut a deep slit lengthwise in the centre of each aubergine, sprinkle inside with salt and leave for one hour. Squeeze out any black juices, rinse under the cold tap and dab dry. Chop the onions finely, then sauté gently in the 3 tablespoons of oil until golden. Add the tomatoes, currants, allspice, salt and pepper and simmer gently until the mixture is thick but still juicy. Add the parsley. Cool, then use to stuff the slits in each aubergine. Arrange the aubergines side by side in a shallow casserole, slit side up. Add oil and water to half cover the vegetables (use half and half of each). Pour over the lemon juice and sprinkle with the sugar, adding the garlic and bayleaf to the liquid. Cover the dish and simmer very gently, either top-of-stove or in the oven (Gas No. 3, 325°F, 170°C) for 1 hour, or until quite soft. Chill, preferably overnight. To serve, lift from the sauce, spoon a little of it over each aubergine, and serve with bread or toast. Serves 6.

Anchovy and Tomato Hors-d'œuvre

This is a simple recipe from the Charente Maritime region of France. It needs really ripe and sweet tomatoes.

6 large, very ripe tomatoes
1 can anchovy fillets
Black olives
½ onion, sliced as thinly as possible
Parsley dressing:
2 tbsp wine or cider vinegar or lemon juice
1 level teasp sugar
Salt, paprika and mustard
10 grinds black pepper
1 tbsp chopped parsley
½ clove garlic (left whole)

Shake all the dressing ingredients together in a screw-top jar. Leave for several hours in the cool. Just before serving, slice the tomatoes and remove the woody core. Arrange 3 or 4 slices on each serving plate and criss-cross with anchovy fillets, filling the gaps with black olives. Top with a few shavings of onion. Just before serving remove the garlic then sprinkle the hors-d'œuvre with the dressing. Serve with fresh challah or black bread. Serves 6.

For other hors-d'œuvres see **The Dinner Party,** p. 254.

Soups and Garnishes

Jewish cooks have been making soup of some kind since the beginning of our recorded history—after all, Jacob diverted the very course of our destiny when he tempted Esau with his savoury 'mess of pottage'. And it was the soups of pulses and cereals which did so much to nourish the immigrant families who could not afford enough meat in the early years of this century. It is certainly worth restating the basic concepts of soup making, in terms of our modern way of eating. Besides, soup is so delicious!

To store soup: All soups improve in flavour if they are allowed to mature overnight. However they should always be stored, covered, under refrigeration, and will keep sweet for up to three days.

To freeze soup: Store in containers of plastic or glass, with an inch headroom to allow for the expansion of the liquid when frozen. Alternatively the soup can be frozen in a plastic bag shaped to fit a container. When the liquid has frozen, lift out the bag, and store in the freezer.

To defrost soup: In a hurry, soup can be reheated from the frozen state—most satisfactorily in the oven. Generally it is better to allow it to defrost in the refrigerator overnight and then pour it into the soup pan to reheat. This avoids any chance of burning, particularly with a thick soup. For instructions on storing cream soups, see p. 32.

Soup Stocks

Stock is quite simply a flavoured liquid from which soups and sauces are made. The more flavourful the stock, the tastier will be the soup or the sauce. In Jewish cookery, meat stocks are made by simmering the coarser parts of root vegetables with herbs and koshered bones, enriched if desired with a piece of shin beef or a portion of fowl. To extract the flavour from these ingredients, the stock must be simmered very slowly for many hours, preferably in the oven. However, with a pressure cooker, one can make excellent stock in only an hour. If stock is made the day before the soup, it is easy to lift off any fat that has congealed on the surface overnight. Stock is an excellent way of using up odds and ends of vegetables that have a good flavour but are too coarse to use in the soup itself.

Here are some different ways to make stock for soup.

Bone Stock

Koshered bones
Green part of a fat leek
Leaves from a head of celery
½ white turnip
½ onion
2 squashy tomatoes
Bayleaf
10 peppercorns
Large sprig of parsley
2 level teasp salt

Put the bones and the coarsely cut vegetables into a pressure cooker, and cover with cold water. Add the seasonings. Pressurize at 15 lb for one hour. Alternatively the ingredients can be put in a soup pan, brought to simmering point, then simmered top-of-stove for 3 hours; or in the oven (Gas No. 2, 300°F, 150°C) for the same length of time. Strain out all the vegetables. If the stock is not to be used at once, it can either be refrigerated until next day, or boiled down to concentrate it, then poured into a plastic container and frozen.

Note: It is not necessary to cut fresh vegetables for stock, but any left-over ends of carrot, half-onions, squashy tomatoes, etc., can be used. In fact, the coarser the vegetables, the more flavour they will add.

Beef and Bone Stock

Proceed as above, but add ½ to 1 lb (200–480g) shin beef to the vegetables. The cooked meat can either be served in the soup, or used to make kreplach or other minced meat pastries.

Cooked Bone Stock

The bone left from a roast rib makes excellent stock. Proceed as above. Use the stock for barley soup.

Cooked Chicken Bone Stock

Break up the carcase of a braised or roast fowl and put it into the pressure cooker, together with the following:

1 large onion
2 large carrots, sliced
1 stalk celery
2 squashy tomatoes or 1 teasp tomato purée
2 level teasp salt
¼ teasp white pepper

Proceed as for bone stock. *Note:* If you are not using a pressure cooker, simmer the stock in a covered pan for 3 hours.

Bouillon Cube Stock

For the small family, it is probably a more economical proposition to use commercial bouillon cubes, which are diluted with water according to the manufacturer's instructions. Excellent beef and chicken cubes are available in a kosher pack.

Note: If a soup requires a long cooking time—for instance, barley soup and split pea soup—the bones and meat (if used) can be cooked simultaneously with the soup ingredients. In that case, the bones should be put into the pan, covered with the amount of water specified in the recipe, and the mixture brought to the boil. The scum from the bones should then be carefully removed with a wet spoon before the soup cereals and vegetables are added.

Rich and Clear

Clear soups depend almost entirely on the flavour from the stock or bouillon with which they are made. I like to cook them in the oven, as the heat that completely surrounds the soup pan seems to give its contents an extra depth of flavour.

Chicken Soup

Chicken soup is traditionally made by simmering a fowl (or part of one) in water flavoured with a variety of vegetables. However, if the fowl is to be casseroled rather than boiled, or a younger bird roasted or fried, then the soup can be made with the feet and giblets alone, and the flavour strengthened by the addition of a chicken bouillon cube. Chicken soup should always be made the day before it is served, as the flavour is incomparably better on the second day.

The feet, the last joint of the wings and the giblets of a young fowl (4 lb/2kg dressed weight) or roasting chicken, plus a chicken bouillon cube; or the whole bird or half-bird with the feet, wings, and giblets
3 pints (1½ litres/7½ cups) water
1 whole onion
2 carrots, peeled and cut in 4
Leaves and top 2 in (5 cm) of 2 stalks celery
1 sprig of parsley
1 squashy tomato
2 level teasp salt
Pinch of white pepper
Any soft eggs from the fowl

Put the water, salt and pepper into a large, heavy soup pan, add the feet, wings and giblets, and the bird or the bouillon cube. Cover and bring to the boil. Uncover and remove any froth with a large, wet metal spoon. Add all the remaining ingredients. Bring back to the boil, then reduce the heat so that the liquid is barely bubbling. Cover and continue to simmer for a further 3 hours, either top-of-stove or in a slow oven (Gas No. 2, 300°F, 150°C), or until the fowl (if used) feels very tender when the leg is prodded with a fork. Strain the soup into one bowl and put the giblets and the carrots into another. The fowl, if used, should be put in a separate container. Refrigerate. Next day remove any congealed fat, and return the soup to the pan. (If there is a thick layer of fat, it can be heated in a pan to drive off any liquid and then, when it has stopped bubbling, cooled and stored like rendered raw fat.) Add the cooked giblets and the carrot (cut into small dice), and reheat slowly before serving. The soup may be garnished with cooked lokshen (vermicelli or egg noodles), mandlen or knaidlach (matzo balls). Serves 4–6. Second-day chicken stock can be made by simmering the stripped carcase of a casseroled bird for 2 hours with vegetables using the same mixture as for fresh chicken soup. This stock makes an excellent basis for borscht, and tomato and vegetable soups, and can be strengthened if necessary with chicken or beef bouillon cubes.

Beetroot Borscht

1 small carrot
1 small onion
2 bunches young beets; or 1½ lb (700g) raw old beets (according to season)
2 pints (1 litre/5 cups) meat or chicken stock; or stock made from Israeli bouillon cubes
Juice of large lemon; or 1 level teasp citric acid crystals (sour salt)
2 level tbsp sugar
2 level teasp salt
Pinch of white pepper
2 whole eggs

Strained beet juice will keep for several days in the refrigerator. The eggs can be added the day the borscht is needed, and any left-over soup will then keep for a further two days. Scrape the skin off new beets with a blunt-bladed knife, or peel old ones with a potato peeler (be sure to keep the beets on a piece of kitchen paper to avoid staining the counter or chopping board). Peel the onion and carrot. Put the sugar, salt, pepper and stock into a soup pan and add the vegetables, coarsely-grated. Bring slowly to the boil, cover and simmer for 45 minutes. Pour the contents of the pan through a coarse sieve into a bowl. Discard the vegetables. Return the liquid to the pan (or refrigerate until required).

To thicken the soup: Beat the eggs in a basin until the yolks and whites are thoroughly blended. Bring the soup to the boil and add the lemon juice or citric acid. Gradually pour a cupful of the hot beet juice on to the beaten eggs, whisking all the time, then return this mixture to the soup pan. Whisk vigorously and reheat until the soup is steaming, but do not let it boil, or it will curdle. Taste and, if the flavour is not equally sweet and sour, add extra sugar or lemon juice. Serve with a boiled potato. Makes 4–6 generous servings.

VARIATIONS

Blender Borscht: Do not grate the peeled vegetables; instead, cut them up roughly and half fill the blender with them. Cover with some of the measured liquid, then blend until mushy. Put in the soup pan and repeat with remaining vegetables. Add remainder of stock and proceed as for recipe.

Milchik Borscht: Use water instead of stock, and chill the soup overnight after it has been thickened.

To serve, stir 5 fl oz (125ml/$\frac{2}{3}$ cup) of sweet or sour cream into the soup and serve chilled in soup cups or wine glasses.

Borscht on the rocks: Make in the same way as milchik borscht but do not stir in the soured cream. Instead serve the chilled soup over ice cubes in individual soup bowls. Just before serving garnish each bowl with a tablespoonful of soured cream.

Cabbage Borscht

This might be called the Jewish version of 'pot au feu', for a 2 lb (1kg) slice of brisket can be cooked in the soup, both to flavour it and to turn it into a simple main course. However, for serving simply as a meal starter, the amount of meat specified in the recipe is sufficient, though a large quantity will add to the flavour (and, alas, to the cost). I give a quantity for 8 as it is really not worth making a smaller amount. Cabbage borscht improves in flavour overnight and solidified fat can then easily be removed.

$\frac{1}{2}$–1 lb (200–480g) piece of brisket
1 marrow bone
3 pints (1$\frac{1}{2}$ litres/7$\frac{1}{2}$ cups) water
1 onion, finely chopped
1 medium can (approx 15 oz/375g) whole peeled tomatoes
2 level teasp salt
Pinch of white pepper
1 small head of white cabbage
4 level tbsp sultanas (white raisins)
Juice of 2 lemons; or 2 level teasp citric acid crystals (sour salt)
4 level tbsp sugar

In a large soup pan put the brisket, bone, salt and water. Bring slowly to the boil, then skim the surface using a wet metal spoon. Add the onion, tomatoes, sugar and pepper. Bring to the boil, reduce the heat until the soup simmers, cover and cook for a further 2 hours, or until the meat is almost tender. Discard the bone. Whilst the soup is cooking, finely shred the cabbage, put it into a colander and sprinkle with some coarse salt. When the meat is almost tender, pour a kettleful of boiling water over the salted cabbage to take away any undue cabbagey flavour. Drain the cabbage and add to the soup. Simmer for a further 30 minutes or until the cabbage is tender. Add the sultanas and the lemon juice or citric acid and simmer for 5 minutes to blend the flavours. Serve plain or with a boiled potato. Serves 8.

Oxtail Soup

As oxtail is very fatty it is essential to prepare the stock the day before the soup is required and refrigerate it in order to facilitate the removal of the fat.

1 oxtail and 1 lb (480g) shin (or 2 bouillon cubes)
2 oz (50g/4 tbsp) margarine and 2 teasp oil
6 pints (3 litres/15 cups) cold water
1 large onion
1 large carrot
2 sticks celery or 2 teasp dried celery
$\frac{1}{2}$ turnip
$\frac{1}{2}$ teasp powdered bouquet garni
3 level teasp salt
$\frac{1}{4}$ teasp ground black pepper
2 tbsp dry sherry
Handful of fine lokshen (vermicelli or egg noodles)

Cut the koshered oxtail into joints. Put in a saucepan and cover with cold water. Bring to the boil, then strain and dry on paper towels. In a large soup pan, melt half the margarine and a teaspoonful of the oil. Fry the oxtail until brown on all sides, then add the shin, cut in cubes, and cover with the cold water. Add the salt, bring to the boil, skim, then cover and simmer for 3 hours (preferably in the oven—Gas No. 2, 300°F, 150°C). Melt the remaining fat and oil in a small pan and fry the onion gently until it is a rich golden brown, adding a good pinch of brown sugar to hasten the process. Add this to the soup together with the other vegetables (diced), the bouquet garni and the pepper. Simmer a further 2 hours. Strain the stock and refrigerate overnight for the fat to set. Take the meat from the soup, remove the oxtail from the bones, and press all the meat between two plates. Next day, remove the fat from the stock, bring to the boil, and add the handful of vermicelli. Simmer for 10 minutes. Add the meat cut in fine shreds and the sherry. Reseason if necessary, then serve piping hot. Serves 8.

Tomato Rice Soup

2 pints (1 litre/5 cups) stock, made from chicken or beef bouillon cubes, bone stock, left-over chicken soup or a stock made from a casseroled chicken carcase—see recipes for stocks, pp. 27–8.
1 medium can (15 ozs/375g) peeled plum tomatoes
Juice of a large lemon
2 level tbsp sugar
4 level tbsp canned or tubed tomato purée
2 level tbsp short grain (Carolina) rice

Put the soup or stock into a soup pan and add all the remaining ingredients, pushing the tomatoes and their juice through a coarse sieve into the pan if you prefer a smooth soup. Bring the soup gently to the boil, then add the rice. Reduce the heat so that the soup barely bubbles, cover and cook very gently for half an hour, or until the rice is tender (bite a grain) and has slightly thickened the soup. Taste. The soup should be slightly sweet and sour. Add a little more sugar or lemon juice if required. Serves 4–6.

Soups for a Winter's Night

Note: In all these recipes, water plus bouillon cubes (in proportion recommended on packet) can be substituted for stock or water plus bones.

Barley Soup

Scottish in origin, but Jewish by adoption, this soup is especially delicious when the stock has been made from a roast rib bone. If ordinary bone stock is used, a little (½ lb) shin beef will greatly improve the flavour.

3 pints (1½ litres/7½ cups) stock
4 level tbsp pearl barley
2 carrots
1 onion
1 small white turnip
White part of a fat leek
1 level tbsp chopped parsley
Salt and pepper to taste

Put the barley into a bowl and add boiling water to cover, then immediately turn into a sieve and rinse well under the cold tap. Cut the carrots, turnip, onion and leek into small dice. Put the stock (and meat if used) into the soup pan and add the salt and pepper, the barley, parsley and all the vegetables. Bring to the boil, skim with a wet metal spoon, then cover, reducing the heat until the mixture is barely bubbling. Simmer for 3 hours, by which time the barley will have thickened the soup. Taste and re-season. There should be plenty of pepper in it. Add some parsley just before serving. Serves 4–6.

Hobene Gropen Soup

This is a thick 'creamy' soup, rich in Vitamin B. Hobene gropen (a form of groats grown in Russia and Poland) can be bought from a Jewish or Polish grocer.

4 pints (2 litres/10 cups) stock
6 level tbsp hobene gropen
½ lb (200g) or more shin beef
2 level teasp salt
½ level teasp white pepper
1 large potato
1 carrot
1 onion
1 fat stalk of celery
Good sprig of parsley

Put the hobene gropen into a small basin and cover with boiling water. Leave to settle while you add the meat, with the salt and pepper, to the stock. Bring to the boil and skim off any froth with a wet metal spoon. Add the strained hobene gropen, reduce the heat so that the soup is barely bubbling, then cover and simmer in this way for one hour. Meanwhile, cut the potato into ½ in (1 cm) cubes, and dice the onion, carrot and celery into ¼ in (½ cm) cubes. Add these vegetables to the soup, together with the parsley sprig. Cover again and simmer for a further 2 hours, when the soup should be creamy and the meat tender. Remove the sprig of parsley, taste, and add more salt and pepper if required. Sprinkle with chopped parsley and serve piping hot. To serve on the second day, add half a cup of water and reheat gently. Serves 8, or 4 people twice.

Haimishe Winter Soup

The proportions of the soup cereals can be varied to taste, but the total amount of the split peas and lentils together should remain the same.

½ lb (200g/1 cup) green split peas
¼ lb (100g/½ cup) red lentils
2 level tbsp pearl barley
4 level tbsp haricot (dried white) beans
½ lb (200g) soup meat (optional but nice)
3 pints (1½ litres/7½ cups) stock; or 3 pints water and 1 soup bone
2 level teasp salt
10 grinds black pepper
1 level teasp 'bouquet garni for soup'
2 large carrots, diced into ¼ in (½ cm) cubes
1 large carrot, coarsely grated
2 stalks celery, diced into ½ in (1 cm) cubes
White part of a fat leek, well washed and thinly sliced
Large sprig of parsley

The day before making the soup, put the split peas, lentils, barley and beans into a large bowl, cover with twice their depth of cold water and leave to soak and swell overnight. Next day, put the meat and the stock (or the water and bone) with the salt into a large soup pan and bring to the boil. Skim with a wet metal spoon. Tip the cereals into a fine sieve to remove any excess soaking-water, then put under the cold tap and rinse thoroughly until the water that drains from them is quite clear. Add to the soup pan with the seasonings and all the vegetables except the grated carrot. Bring back to boil, then reduce heat until the mixture is barely bubbling. Cover and simmer for 2 hours. Uncover and add the grated carrot. Continue to cook for a further hour, stirring the pan occasionally to make sure the soup does not stick to the pan as it thickens. When the soup is ready, the lentils and split peas will have turned into a purée. Taste and add more seasonings if required. Remove the sprig of parsley. Left-over soup can have a tablespoon of tomato purée added, together with ½ cup of water to thin it down before reheating. Serves 4 twice.

Split Pea Soup

12 oz (300g/1½ cups) green split peas
2 carrots
1 onion
2 level tbsp margarine
½ cup of butter beans (dried lima beans)
2 stalks celery
White part of a leek
3 pints (1½ litres/7½ cups) stock; or equivalent made from bouillon cubes
Salt and pepper

Soak split peas and butter beans overnight in cold water to cover generously. Finely dice the carrots and the celery, chop the onion and finely slice the leek. Put in the soup pan with fat, cover and cook gently for 10 minutes, or until fat is absorbed. Pour on the stock and add the rinsed cereals. Simmer for 2½–3 hours, seasoning to taste. If preferred, the vegetables can be only roughly chopped and the soup sieved or liquidized before serving. Serves 6–8.

VARIATION

Milchik Split Pea Soup: Use water instead of stock and sauté the vegetables in butter instead of margarine. Add a knob of butter or 4 tablespoons cream before serving.

Piquant Tomato Soup

1 tbsp rendered chicken fat; or 1 oz (25g/2 tbsp) margarine
1 large onion, sliced
1 small carrot, sliced, and a stalk of celery
2 level tbsp brown sugar
2 level teasp salt
1 clove garlic, crushed
Thinly-peeled rind of ½ lemon
A few black peppercorns
1 large bayleaf
1 level teasp dried oregano
1 can (15 oz/375g) whole peeled plum tomatoes with their juice
2 tbsp canned tomato purée
2 pints (1 litre/5 cups) meat, bone or chicken stock or bouillon made with cubes
Optional:
1 level tbsp cornflour (cornstarch) mixed with 2 tbsp cold water
A handful of fine vermicelli

Melt the fat over gentle heat in a heavy soup pan, add the finely-sliced vegetables, cover and cook with an occasional shake for 10 minutes, when the fat will have been absorbed and the vegetables softened a little without browning. Add tomatoes with the remaining ingredients, cover and simmer for 45 minutes until the vegetables are tender. Remove the bayleaf then push through a sieve or blend until smooth. Return to the pan. Taste and add a little more tomato purée if necessary. To thicken the soup, add the cornflour and water and simmer for 5 minutes. The vermicelli can be cooked in the soup (nicest but a little extravagant as some of the soup is absorbed by the pasta) or cooked in water according to the packet instructions and added to the soup just before serving. Serves 6–8.

Smooth and Creamy

When freezing cream soups it is most convenient to freeze the vegetable purée only, then defrost when required and dilute with the milk, adding the cream and herbs according to the recipe.

Crème du Jour

I give this delicious soup a rather nebulous name because the vegetables, although they always include potato (which acts as the thickener), may be varied according to the season or family preference.

2 large potatoes, peeled (about 1 lb/480g)
1 large carrot
White part of a fat leek
1 medium onion
1 pint (500ml/2½ cups) milk
1 blade mace or pinch powdered mace
1 bayleaf
1 oz (25g/2 tbsp) butter
4 tbsp single (light) cream
2 level teasp salt
¼ level teasp white pepper
1 tbsp finely-cut chives or parsley for garnish

Slice all the vegetables finely but grate the carrot (you will need about 3 cupfuls of vegetables in all). Melt the butter in a heavy pan, put in the vegetables, toss to coat in the butter, cover and 'sweat' for 10 minutes. Uncover, add water to cover the vegetables, the seasonings and the mace. Cover and simmer until absolutely tender—about 45 minutes. Uncover and remove the blade of mace (if used), then add the bayleaf. Push through a sieve or blend until smooth and creamy. In the same pan, bring the milk up to simmering point. Add the purée and heat together. Taste and add more salt or pepper if necessary. Just before serving, stir in the cream and chopped herbs. This soup is greatly improved if it is allowed to stand for several hours before reheating and serving. Serves 6.

VARIATION

Omit the potatoes. When the milk and purée are simmering add sufficient instant potato to thicken the soup to the consistency of pouring cream. Any dieter can be served his portion before the potato thickening is added.

Golden Vegetable Soup

¾ lb (300g/2 cups) young carrots
White part of 2 fat leeks
½ onion
2 stalks celery
1 level teasp salt
Pinch of sugar
4 tbsp cream
1 level tbsp finely-chopped parsley
A little instant potato
½ clove garlic, crushed to a paste with a little salt
¾ pint (375ml/2 cups) water
1 pint (500ml/2½ cups) milk
2 oz (50g/¼ cup) butter
8 grinds black pepper
¼ teasp powdered bouquet garni (if available)

Melt the butter in a heavy pan, add the sliced leeks and onion, toss to coat in the fat, cover and 'sweat' for 10 minutes, until the onion is golden. Uncover and add thinly-sliced carrots, then cover and cook for a further 5 minutes. Uncover and add water. (Vegetables should be barely covered.) Season with salt, pepper, sugar and garlic, cover and simmer until vegetables are absolutely tender (about 40 minutes). Liquidize till smooth or put through a food mill. In same pan, heat milk until steaming, then stir in the vegetable mixture. If not thick enough, add a little instant potato. Allow to simmer for 10 minutes. Just before serving, stir in the cream and parsley. Serves 6.

Minted Cream of Green Pea Soup

1½ oz (40g/3 tbsp) butter
½ large onion
1 fat stick of celery
2 lb (1kg) garden peas (weight before shelling); or 1 lb (480g) packet frozen peas
2 level teasp salt
Pinch of white pepper
Pinch of sugar
1 pint (500ml/2½ cups) water
1 teasp dried mint and powdered fines herbes
1 level tbsp cornflour (cornstarch) mixed with ½ pint (250ml/1¼ cups) milk
4 tbsp single (light) cream
1 tbsp snipped chives; or 2 tbsp chopped parsley

Melt the butter and cook the finely-chopped onion until soft but still golden (keep the lid on), then add the finely-chopped celery and cook a further 3 minutes. Add the peas and stir well, then add the water, seasonings and herbs. Cover and simmer until tender (20–30 minutes). Push through a sieve or put in the blender until smooth. Return to the rinsed pan. Add the cornflour and milk, and simmer for 3 minutes. Just before serving, stir in the cream. Serve with croûtons. Serves 6.

Cream of Mushroom Soup

A most subtly-flavoured soup sparked with the additions of garlic and parsley. I have given large quantities because half can be frozen for the small family.

2 pints (1 litre/5 cups) milk
½ carrot, sliced
Bayleaf, few peppercorns, blade or pinch of mace
4 oz (100g/½ cup) butter
½ lb (200g/3 cups) very fresh mushrooms, chopped
1 small onion, finely chopped
½ large clove garlic, crushed
2 level tbsp chopped parsley
2 oz (50g/½ cup) flour
White pepper and salt
½ pint (250ml/1¼ cups) vegetable water
1 glass dry sherry
4 tbsp single (light) cream

Put sliced carrot, bayleaf, peppercorns and mace in large soup pan with milk and leave steaming and covered for 15 minutes. Melt 2 oz (50g/¼ cup) butter in saucepan and add finely-chopped onion; cook for 5 minutes until soft and golden, then add mushrooms, cover and 'sweat' for 10 minutes. Uncover and add vegetable water, garlic and parsley. Strain infused milk into basin. Rinse out soup pan, then melt remaining butter, add flour and simmer for 3 minutes. Add hot milk off heat and whisk until bubbly. Simmer for 5 minutes, then add mushroom mixture. Taste and adjust seasonings. Just before serving add sherry and cream. Serves 8–9.

Cream of Watercress Soup

1 medium onion, finely chopped
1 oz (25g/2 tbsp) butter
$\frac{1}{2}$ pint (250ml/1$\frac{1}{4}$ cups) water
1$\frac{1}{2}$ pints (750ml/4 cups) hot milk
Bunch of watercress, washed and chopped
Plenty of salt and pepper
2$\frac{1}{2}$ oz (65g) (small packet) instant potato
Nut of butter

Melt the butter, add the onion, cover and 'sweat' for 10 minutes. Uncover, add the water and seasonings. Simmer for 10 minutes, then add the milk. Bring to the boil, then whisk in the potato. Finally add the chopped watercress and the nut of butter. Serves 4–6.

Mother's Milchige Soup

This soup was made to herald summer in the villages of the Pale of Settlement. It is fresh and simple, with the flavour of young vegetables.

2 oz (50g/$\frac{1}{4}$ cup) butter
1 onion, finely chopped
4 new potatoes, cubed
8 oz (200g) shelled peas; or 1 lb/480g pack mixed frozen vegetables together with the potatoes
1$\frac{1}{2}$ pints (750ml/4 cups) water
$\frac{1}{2}$ pint (250ml/1$\frac{1}{4}$ cups) milk
1 grated carrot
1 level teasp salt and sugar
Pinch of pepper

Melt the butter in a heavy pan, and 'sweat' the onion in the covered pan until soft and golden. Add the potatoes, carrot and peas (or the packet of frozen mixed vegetables). Cover with the water, add the salt, pepper and sugar. Simmer covered for 30 minutes or until all the vegetables are tender. Stir in the milk and heat without boiling. Some families make tiny knaidlach with butter instead of chicken fat and serve them in this soup. Serves 6.

Some Interesting Soup Garnishes

Many people consider that what goes into the soup as garnish is the best part of the dish. Certainly kreplach, gefüllte helzel, knaidlach and piroshke are all delicacies in their own right, and when served with a deeply-flavoured soup, they combine to make what can only be described as a 'mechaieh' or very special dish. Many garnishes once made in the home kitchen can now be bought ready made; but with the exception of lokshen (noodles), I would say that the home-made variety wins every time.

A Quartet for Meat Soups:

Gefüllte Helzel (Stuffed Neck)

I know of no other cuisine which treats a hen's neck in this delectable way. When you intend to stuff a helzel you will need to tell the butcher, so that he will send you a fowl with the neck intact. The neck of a chicken is too small to be practicable.

1 fowl's neck, untorn
2 oz (50g/$\frac{1}{2}$ cup) plain flour, minus 1 rounded tbsp (replace this with a rounded tbsp semolina or fine matzo meal—it gives the helzel a better texture)
3 level tbsp raw chicken fat, finely chopped
1 level tbsp coarsely grated raw onion
Good pinch of salt and white pepper

Mix all the stuffing ingredients together with a fork. The mixture should look slightly moist. If it is too dry add a little more fat: if too loose, a little more semolina or meal. With a coarse sewing needle and strong thread, sew up one end of the neck, and fill it with the stuffing mixture. It should be only loosely packed, as it swells during cooking. Carefully sew up the other end. Rinse the stuffed neck with cold water, then pour boiling water over it, to make the skin smooth. If the bird is to be boiled, cook the helzel with it in the soup pan, then brown it with the bird for half an hour in the oven. If the bird is not to be browned after boiling, the helzel can be browned in the oven by itself for half an hour, or in the roasting pan with a joint of meat. If the bird is to be casseroled, and only its giblets used for the soup, then the helzel can be put in the casserole with it and cooked at the same time; in this case it does not need to be boiled in the soup. A stuffed helzel will serve 4, but can easily be eaten by 2.

Mandlen (Soup Nuts)

These are delicious served with chicken or tomato soup. Put a dish on the table and let each person add his own to his bowl of soup. Mandlen may be baked or fried, whichever you prefer.

3 oz (75g/¾ cup) plain flour
½ level teasp salt
2 teasp oil
1 large egg

Sift the flour and salt into a bowl. Make a well in the centre of the flour, and drop in the egg and the oil. Gradually work in the surrounding flour to make a soft dough that you can roll between your fingers into a 'sausage'. If too stiff, add a drop more oil; if too soft, add a teaspoonful more flour. Work the dough into a ball with your hands, then divide it into three. On a floured board, roll each piece into a pencil-thick length, and cut it into ½ in (1 cm) pieces.

To bake: Arrange the mandlen on a greased, flat baking sheet, leaving room for them to puff up. Bake in a moderate oven (Gas No. 5, 375°F, 190°C) for 20 minutes, or until golden brown. After 10 minutes, open the oven and shake the tray, so that the mandlen will brown evenly. When quite cold, store them in an airtight tin until needed.

To fry: Leave the uncooked mandlen for half an hour on the pastry board, for the surface to dry out a little. In a frying pan put oil to a depth of ¾ in (2 cm). After oil has been heating gently for 5 minutes, drop in one mandel as a 'tester'. If gentle bubbles appear round it, the oil is hot enough. Put more mandlen into the oil, but do not overcrowd the pan, or the oil will become too cool. Allow them to cook at a steady bubble, turning them so that they brown on all sides. When golden brown, lift out with a slotted spoon, and drain on crumpled tissue paper. When quite cold, store in an airtight tin. Mandlen may be frozen, then reheated when required.

To reheat: Put in a small heatproof casserole, and leave for 10 minutes in a moderate oven (Gas No. 4, 350°F, 180°C). Serves 4–6.

Quick Mandlen

These are excellent to make at the last moment before a Yomtov lunch, or as a garnish for left-over chicken soup. They are very crisp and puffy, but soften very quickly in soup.

2 large eggs
4 oz (100g/1 cup) self-raising flour; or 4 oz (100g/1 cup) plain flour and 1 level teasp baking powder
1 level teasp salt
Few grinds black pepper
1 tbsp cold water

Beat the eggs, the water and the seasoning with a rotary egg beater, until the mixture is thick and frothy. Sift the flour into the egg, and beat with a fork until a batter-like consistency is obtained (about 2 minutes). In a 9 in (23 cm) frying pan, pour enough oil to come to a depth of ½ in (1 cm). After 5 minutes of heating, drop a little of the mixture from a teaspoon. If bubbles appear round it, the oil is ready. Drop teaspoonfuls of the mixture into the oil, leaving room for them to swell. Reduce the heat until the oil is bubbling gently round each soup nut. When bubbles appear on their surface, turn the mandlen over and continue to cook until both sides are a rich brown. Drain on crumpled tissue paper. Put in a heatproof dish and leave in the oven until required. They are not suitable for storing. Makes about 30 mandlen, enough for 6–8 people.

Knaidlach

These are sometimes called 'halkes' or 'matzo balls'. The secret of success is to use sufficient fat to make them tender yet firm. Providing the specified amount of fat is used, the amount of matzo meal may be increased if you prefer a firmer (though equally tender) texture. Ground almonds greatly enhance the flavour and texture, but an equal quantity of medium matzo meal can be used instead.

1 slightly rounded tbsp soft rendered chicken fat (do not melt it)
1 large egg
2 tbsp chicken soup or warm water
½ level teasp salt
Pinch of white pepper
2 level tbsp ground almonds
2 oz (50g/approx 6 level tbsp) medium matzo meal

Beat the egg with a rotary whisk until fluffy, then stir in the fat, tepid soup or water, seasonings, matzo meal and ground almonds. It is a good idea to keep one level tablespoon meal in reserve and add it only if necessary, when the ingredients have been well mixed and you can see the texture. The mixture should then look moist and be stiff but still stirrable, yet not stiff enough to form into balls. Refrigerate or chill in a cold larder for at least one hour. (The mixture may be left overnight if convenient.) Wet your hands under the cold water tap, take a walnut-sized piece of the now stiffened mixture, and roll it into a ball between your palms. Have ready a large pan half full of boiling water. Add 1 teaspoon salt, then drop in the balls. When the water is barely bubbling, put on the lid, and simmer gently for 40 minutes, without looking at the contents of the pan during that time. Uncover, lift out the knaidlach with a slotted spoon, and lower them gently into simmering chicken soup. Serve with the soup. Left-over balls can be allowed to remain in the soup overnight. Makes 8 knaidlach, enough for 4 people.

VARIATION

Knaidlach with margarine: Substitute 1½ oz (40g/3 level tbsp) soft margarine for the chicken fat. Make in exactly the same way. The flavour is better if the knaidlach are simmered in the chicken soup rather than in water.

For **Kreplach** see **Festival Foods,** p. 255.

Home-Made Lokshen (*Egg Noodles*)

1 recipe **Kreplach Dough** (see p. 225).

Make dough as directed, cover with a large bowl and leave for 20 minutes to relax. Divide dough in two. Roll each piece out on floured board until paper-thin and transparent. Each piece will then measure about 14 in (35 cm) square. Place a dry teatowel on kitchen counter and sprinkle lightly with flour. Lay dough squares on top and sprinkle again lightly with flour. Leave for 20 minutes or until surface no longer feels sticky. Roll each sheet up loosely, then cut into strips each ½–¾ in (1–1½ cm) wide, using a sharp knife. Unwind and hang noodles over same teatowel, this time draped across a chair back or horizontal broom handle. When dry and brittle (about 1 hour), either use fresh or store in jars. Makes approx 12 oz (350g).

Shpaetzlen (Bow Knots): Cut dough 1 in (2½ cm) squares. Pinch each square into tiny bow shape and leave to dry, then cook in salted water. Serve in chicken or tomato soup.

Plaetschen (Noodle Squares): Cut dough into ½ in (1 cm) strips. Stack strips on top of each other and cut into ½ in (1 cm) squares. Dry and store, then boil till tender for a soup garnish.

Fingerhuetchen (Thimble Noodles): Roll out dough, leave to dry for 15 minutes only, then fold over in 2 layers. Using a floured thimble, cut through both layers, making little circles. Drop into hot fat to cover and fry until lightly browned—about 1 minute. Drain on paper towel. Serve in chicken soup.

A garnish for Cream Soups:

Buttered Croûtons

The garnish for a cream soup must be light yet crisp. Use slightly stale bread to get the crispiest results.

3 thin slices bread cut into ¼ in (½ cm) cubes
2 oz (50g/¼ cup) butter
2 teasp oil

To fry: Heat the butter and oil in a heavy frying pan. As soon as foaming stops, put in the bread and fry gently until crisp and golden on all sides.

To bake: Put the oven on Gas No. 4, 350°F, 180°C. While it is heating melt the butter and oil in a tray about 9 × 7 in (23 × 18 cm) and 1 in (2½ cm) deep. Add the croûtons, shake well to coat them with the fat, then bake for 10–15 minutes, shaking once, until crisp and golden brown. Drain on crumpled paper. Serve in little pottery dishes or a sauce boat. Left-overs may be frozen. Serves 4–6.

Fish

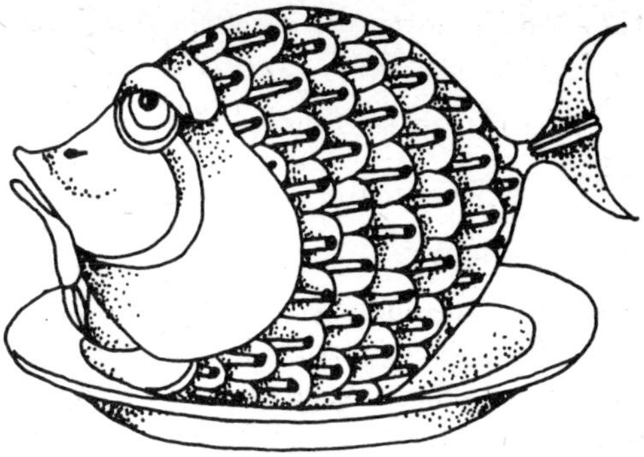

Maybe it is because Jewish housewives have been cooking fish for about three and a half thousand years—ever since their ancestors were slaves in Egypt—but there can be little doubt that the Jewish ways with fish are some of the most practical and tasty in the whole repertoire of cookery.

Perfect Fried Fish

In most Jewish households fried fish means cold fish; for, properly prepared, it is one of the best dishes to cook on Friday for service on the Sabbath. The frying of fish in oil (the only fat which remains palatable when cold) is a method adopted by Eastern European Jews from those (originally from Spain and Portugal via Holland) who had lived in England since the resettlement of the Jews in 1657. It is probably the most popular method of preparing fish used by British Jews.

Fried fish which is still palatable two days later depends on three main factors: the frying pan, the coating and the temperature of the oil.

The pan: The ideal fish-frying pan can be made either of heavy cast aluminium or of iron, but in both cases it must have a thick base that sits evenly on the cooker. The sides should be at least 2 in (5 cm) high, to prevent the bubbling oil from spattering over the cooker. It should be at least 10 in (25 cm) in diameter. After each frying session, the cool oil is poured through a sieve into a screw-top glass or plastic jar, and the pan wiped out with tissue paper and newspaper. The base of an aluminium pan needs cleaning with a damp, detergent-filled pad, but that of an iron pan can be wiped clean with newspaper and a damp cloth. A little new oil is added to the old oil each time fish is fried. If the oil smells acrid after it has been used, it has been overheated and has started to decompose, and should then be thrown away. So should any oil which has become dark and smelly. However, a little of this old oil added to a panful of fresh oil will help the fish to brown more quickly. I like to fry fish in corn oil, as I think it gives it a crisper, more digestible coating.

The coating: I prefer to use stale bread, which has been dried in the oven without browning until it becomes crisp enough to mince or grind into crumbs. They form an even coating which fries to a rich brown and keeps the fish crisp when it is cold Or one can use medium matzo meal.

The oil temperature: It will take about 4 minutes for a layer of oil 1 in (2½ cm) deep to reach the right temperature for fish frying—375°F, 190°C—that is, when a cube of bread browns on one side in 30 seconds. A thermostatically controlled hot-plate should be set at this temperature. An oil thermometer takes the guess-work out of frying.

Fried Fish Fillets or Steaks

Steaks of sole, hake, haddock, cod, halibut or large plaice should be cut ¾–1 in (2–2½ cm) thick. Fillets should be 1 in (2½ cm) thick. Fillets of plaice, sole or baby halibut should be cut from fish not less than 1½ lb (700g) in weight.

6–8 fillets or steaks of fish
1 egg
2 tbsp flour
Coating crumbs

Wash the fish under cold running water, arrange round the sides of a colander, sprinkle lightly with cooking salt and leave to drain. Beat the egg with a fork to blend the yolk and the white, then put into a shallow oval dish. Beside this dish put a piece of greaseproof paper, with a cupful of coating crumbs. Next to it put another piece of greaseproof paper with the flour. Heat the empty pan for 3 minutes over medium heat, then put oil into it to a depth of 1 in (2½ cm) and heat steadily for 4 minutes. Then test to see that a cube of bread browns in 30 seconds, or the thermometer registers 375°F, 190°C. Dip the fish in and out of the flour, patting off any surplus. Next dip it in and out of the egg, and finally lay it in the crumbs and pat them on in an even layer. Lift up the fish on a slotted spoon and lower it into the hot oil. Do not overcrowd the pan, or too much cold fish put in too soon will lower the temperature drastically, and the fish will be soggy. Cook the fish over medium heat with the oil bubbling steadily, until the first side is a rich brown. This will take about 4 minutes for a fillet, 5–7 minutes for a thick steak. Turn it carefully, using a slotted spoon and a fork, and cook until the second side is brown. Have ready a shallow casserole filled with crumpled tissue paper. Lift out the fish to drain. If the fillets are not stiff and crisp when they are lifted out, turn up the heat and return them to the pan for a further minute's cooking in hotter oil. Perfect fried fish should look dry and crisp. As soon as it has drained completely, lift it on to a platter and store in the larder until required.

Fried Fresh Herrings

Have them either filleted, or gutted without being split. (Fish on the bone is more fiddly to eat but the flavour is more pronounced.) Scrape well with a knife to remove the scales, wash, salt and leave to drain in a colander. Dip in flour and egg, but finish with a coating of medium oatmeal or sieved porridge oats. Fry as above. Serve warm or cold. Allow 2 medium herrings per person.

Fried Fish in Butter

Use steaks cut ¾–1 in (2–2½ cm) thick, or fillets from a 1½ lb (700g) fish. This is a practical mid-week method of cooking fish for two. There is no need to coat the fish in anything other than flour, and the smell of oil is kept out of the kitchen. However, the fish must be eaten hot off the pan, as the butter which is so delicious when the fish is hot, congeals and makes the fish greasy when it is cold. Any filleted or steaked fish that is fried in oil can also be fried in butter, but this is a particularly suitable method for frying a small whole fish, like trout.

Fish Meunière

4 fillets, steaks or small whole fish
2 oz (50g/¼ cup) butter
2 teasp oil
2 oz (50g/½ cup) plain flour
Juice of a lemon
Chopped parsley
Salt and black pepper

Wash the fish under cold running water, and leave it to drain in a colander, sprinkled lightly with salt. Put flour onto a sheet of greaseproof paper. Dip each piece of fish into the flour, using the hands, then pat it all over so that only a thin coating of flour remains. Heat a heavy frying pan without fat for 3 minutes, then put in the butter and oil. The minute the butter starts to foam (but has not changed colour at all), put in the fish. Cook steadily for 5 minutes, by which time the underside will be brown. Carefully turn over the fish and continue to cook for a further 5 minutes. Lift out onto a warm serving dish. Into the butter in the pan put the lemon juice, a pinch of salt and a sprinkle of black pepper. Swirl the sauce round the pan, then pour the juices over the fish. Sprinkle with parsley and serve with thick wedges of lemon.

Oven-Fried Fish

This is a most useful way to serve hot 'fried' fish for a large number without being tied to the cooker at the last minute or permeating the house with the odour of hot oil.

6–8 fillets or steaks of any white fish
1 egg
4 tbsp oil; or 2 oz (50g/¼ cup) melted butter and
  1 tbsp oil
Dry breadcrumbs or matzo meal
1 teasp salt

Wash and salt the fish and leave to drain. Beat the egg with the fat and a teaspoon of salt. Have ready a piece of greaseproof paper with a pile of the coating crumbs. Dry each piece of fish thoroughly with kitchen towelling, then brush with the egg mixture and coat with the crumbs. (Use another egg and 4 more tablespoons of oil if necessary, but this quantity should be sufficient for 12 fillets.) Arrange the coated fish side by side on flat oven baking trays (no need to grease them). Leave in a cool place till required.

To cook: Set the oven at Gas No. 6, 400°F, 200°C. Put the fish in and allow to cook, without turning, for 20–25 minutes, depending on the thickness. Serve hot.

Grilled Fish

Unlike meat, fish does not need a fierce heat, as it is unnecessary to 'sear' the outside to contain the juices. Indeed, too high a heat will make the fish dry. Instead, it needs plenty of butter to keep it moist and flavoursome.

Use steaks cut ¾–1 in (2–2½ cm) thick, or fillets from a 1½ lb (700g) fish. Put 1½ oz (3 tbsp) butter in the grill pan or in a flat, cast-iron dish just large enough to contain the fish. Put it under a gentle heat to melt without browning—the melted butter should make a thin layer on the bottom of the dish. If not, add a little more butter. The minute it has melted, put the washed and salted fish into the hot butter, then turn it over onto the other side. In this way both sides of the fish will be coated with the butter. Sprinkle each piece of fish with salt and pepper and dust very lightly with flour. Grill gently but steadily without turning, allowing ten minutes for a piece ¾ in (2 cm) thick, and twelve minutes for one that is 1 in (2½ cm) thick. Two or three minutes before the fish is done sprinkle with a further dusting of flour, or a light sprinkling of dry breadcrumbs. Baste with the butter twice while the fish is cooking. When the fish is done, the fillets will be a rich golden brown. Steaks will be the same colour, and the centre bone will move easily when pulled. Serve the fish with the pan juices poured over them, and thick wedges of lemon.

VARIATION

Savoury fish steaks: Use steaks of hake, haddock or halibut. Omit the second dusting with flour. Instead, spread each steak with a thin coating of mayonnaise, then sprinkle with salt and pepper and finally with a thin layer of dry breadcrumbs. Baste with the pan juices and continue grilling for a further 3 or 4 minutes until the topping is crisp and brown.

Gefüllte Fish

Gefüllte fish was originally a fish 'forcemeat' made from a variety of chopped or minced freshwater fish, which was used to stuff the skin of a carp. The whole fish was then poached in a flavoured fish stock, which jellied when it was cold.

Today we make a similar mixture but (at least in Britain and the U.S.) use mainly sea fish, and put balls of this mixture directly in the stock to poach instead of stuffing it into the fish. The same fish balls can also be fried in the same way as fish fillets or steaks, or poached in a sweet and sour tomato sauce in the Sephardi fashion. Many fishmongers now sell mixtures of ready minced fish and one can also buy ready-to-fry frozen fish packs. But if the mixture is made at home it is really not worth using less than 1½ lb (700g) fish (weighed when filleted and skinned).

The fish: This is a matter of personal preference—and price. When hake is reasonable I use 50 per cent hake, 50 per cent haddock; otherwise I use 50 per cent haddock, 50 per cent cod.

To freeze gefüllte fish: Boiled gefüllte fish balls should be covered with the stock in which they were cooked and frozen in a plastic container; add a little more onion than usual as the flavour tends to fade in the freezer. To defrost, thaw in the refrigerator overnight.

Fried gefüllte fish balls should be individually wrapped then stored in plastic bags. To recrisp, put the frozen balls uncovered in a quick oven (Gas No. 6, 400°F, 200°C) for 10 minutes. Allow to cool and serve the same day.

Savoury gefüllte fish balls should be left in the tomato sauce and frozen in bags or containers. Thaw in the refrigerator overnight.

Gefüllte Fish Mix

For 18–20 *balls* (allow 1–2 balls per serving)
2 lb (1kg) filleted hake and 1 lb (480g) filleted haddock; or 2 lb (1kg) filleted haddock and 1 lb (480g) filleted cod
1 large onion
3 tbsp oil
3 level teasp each of sugar and salt and ½ teasp white pepper
3 large eggs
5–6 tbsp medium matzo meal
2 level tbsp ground almonds (optional)

For 9–10 *balls*
1 lb (480g) filleted hake and ½ lb (200g) filleted haddock; or 1 lb (480g) filleted haddock and ½ lb (200g) filleted cod
½ large onion
6 teasp oil
1½ level teasp each of sugar and salt and pinch of white pepper
1 large egg plus ½ egg shell water
3 tbsp medium matzo meal
1 level tbsp ground almonds (optional)

Ask the fishmonger to fillet and skin the fish. At home wash it under cold water, drain in a colander for half an hour, lightly sprinkled with salt. Cut it into chunks that will slide easily into the mincer (grinder) and remove as much as you can of the white connective tissue or it will wind itself round the mincer cutter and jam it. Put the fish through the coarse blade of the mincer. In the blender goblet put the egg, seasonings, oil, onion and water. Blend for 1 minute or until a smooth mush.

Note: Without a blender, the onion should be minced with the fish and a half egg shell of cold water per egg used should be added to the mixture. Put the minced fish into a large bowl and add the egg mixture followed by the ground almonds (if used) and enough matzo meal to produce a mixture that can just be formed into patties. If too stiff, add a little water; if too sloppy add a little more meal. Only experience will teach you the exact texture as fish and eggs do vary in their performance. I have found the most satisfactory way of mixing the ingredients together is either by hand or by turning the fish onto a chopping board, adding the wet ingredients and the meal gradually and blending together with a 'hackmesser' (hand chopper). At this stage the mixture can either be shaped and cooked or it can be foil-covered and left in the bottom of the refrigerator overnight. Fish chilled in this way will need to be left at room temperature for half an hour before shaping.

Poached Gefüllte Fish

Fish Stock:
1 cleaned hake or haddock head (ask the fishmonger to do this) with the skin and bones from the fish
1 medium onion, sliced
2 medium carrots, sliced
2 level teasp sugar
2 level teasp salt
Water to cover the bones

Put the fish head, the skin and the bones into a wide-based pan. Add the salt and cover with cold water. Bring slowly to the boil, cover and simmer for half an hour, while you are shaping the fish into balls the size of small apples. Remove the skin and bones, but leave in the head (which helps the stock to jell when it is cold). Add the carrots, the onion and the sugar, and put the fish balls into the stock.

Bring to the boil, reduce the heat until the stock is barely simmering, then cover and simmer for 1½ hours. Uncover and continue to simmer for a further half hour to reduce the stock. Lift out the fish balls and put them on to a platter at least 1 in (2½ cm) deep. Strain the stock over and round the fish and garnish it with the carrot. Cover and chill overnight. The same amount of ingredients will make enough stock for up to 3 lb (1½kg) of fish. Just add sufficient water to cover the fish. Many people, however, like to poach half the fish balls and fry the remainder. Alternatively all the fish may be fried, according to the recipe below.

Chopped Fried Fish

With wetted hands shape the gefüllte fish mixture into balls the size of small apples, then flatten into patties and roll in a bowl full of crushed cornflake crumbs or fine dry breadcrumbs, patting the crumbs on evenly. Leave on a fish board. In a heavy fish-frying pan, put oil to a depth of 1 in (2½ cm) and start to heat. When the oil is hot enough to brown a cube of bread in thirty seconds (375°F, 190°C on an oil thermometer) carefully lower in the first batch of fish balls. They should just be submerged in the oil, with plenty of room between them for turning when necessary. Allow the oil to bubble gently until the fish balls are a rich brown on both sides—about 6 minutes in all. Lift them out with a slotted spoon, and drain on crumpled tissue paper. When quite dry, arrange them on a platter and leave in a cool larder until required.

Gefüllte Fish Provençale

The fish is poached in a delicious tomato and pepper sauce. This dish can be served either warm or chilled. It improves with keeping.

8 raw fish patties

Sauce:
1 can (15 oz/375g) Italian tomatoes, sieved or liquidized
2 tbsp tomato ketchup
1 tbsp oil
1 green pepper, seeded and thinly sliced
1 onion, finely chopped
1 level teasp each of salt and sugar
Squeeze of lemon juice
Pinch of pepper

Heat the oil and sauté the onion until transparent then add all the remaining ingredients and bubble until reduced to a thick coating consistency. Arrange the raw fish patties in a shallow ovenproof dish, cover with the sauce and loosely cover with foil. Bake in a slow oven (Gas No. 2, 300°F, 150°C) for 1½ hours, basting once or twice. Serves 6–8.

VARIATION

Omit the canned tomatoes; instead substitute an 8 oz can tomato sauce; sauté the onion as directed then add all the remaining ingredients and pour over the fish. Cook as directed.

Stove-top Fish Casserole

1½ lb (700g) filleted tail of hake; or 6 steaks
½ grated carrot
½ grated onion
1–1½ oz (25–40g/2–3 tbsp) butter
2 level teasp cornflour (cornstarch)
Small bayleaf
2 teasp parsley
¼ pint (125ml/⅔ cup) top milk or single (light) cream

Melt the butter; when it stops foaming, add vegetables; cook a minute or two, stirring well, then put in the salted fish turning it in the butter. Cover bottom of dish with water, add bayleaf, salt and pepper. Cover pan and cook very gently till fish is creamy (about 20 minutes). Mix milk or cream and cornflour and add to pan, simmer 3 minutes, add parsley and serve. Serves 5–6.

Poached Fish Fillets in Wine Sauce (Sauce Bercy)

2½ lb (1¼kg) skinned filleted sole, plaice or baby halibut (8 good fillets)
8 fl oz (200ml/1 cup) dry white wine such as Graves
2 tbsp finely-chopped shallots or spring onions (scallions)
Salt
Pepper
Few peppercorns
Small bayleaf
Sprig of parsley

Take a 10–12 in (25–30 cm) fireproof baking dish, 1½ in (3½ cm) deep, butter it generously, and scatter in chopped shallots. Place on top skinned and filleted (salted) fish (either flat and slightly overlapping or rolled). Pour in wine, together with bayleaf, peppercorns and parsley. Fish should be barely covered; if not, add a little water. Cover with buttered paper and bake in a quick oven (Gas No. 6, 400°F, 200°C) for 20 minutes, or until fish flakes easily with fork. Drain all liquid from fish and strain into a small pan. Keep fish hot in a low oven whilst sauce is made.

Sauce:
½ pint (250ml/1¼ cups) poaching liquid (boil down to this amount if necessary)
1½ oz (40g/3 tbsp) soft butter blended into 1 oz (25g/¼ cup) flour (beurre manié)
6 fl oz (150ml/¾ cup) double (heavy) cream
1 tbsp lemon juice
1 oz (25g/¼ cup) grated cheese
½ oz (15g/1 tbsp) butter

Off heat, beat beurre manié into liquid in little bits. Return to heat and bubble for 2 minutes. Add squeeze of lemon juice and then the cream. Taste and re-season if necessary; it should be of coating consistency. Pour over fish. (*At this point, fish can be foil-covered and left till needed—from lunchtime till dinner, for example. Put in moderate oven for* 15 *minutes to reheat, then treat as newly cooked.*) Scatter fish with cheese and dot with butter. Put under grill until bubbly. Serves 6–8.

VARIATIONS

With mushrooms: Toss ½ lb (200g) sliced mushrooms in nut of butter over moderate heat for 2 min until butter is absorbed. Arrange over fish before poaching.

With grapes: ¼ lb (100g) peeled seeded grapes. Arrange at each end of dish with cooked fish. Then mask with sauce. Omit cheese.

Fish Baked in Cream

6 thick fillets of plaice or baby halibut (cut from fish weighing approx 1½ lb (700g) each
2 lb (1kg) new potatoes
8 fl oz (200ml/1 cup) whipping cream
1 medium onion sautéd in 1 oz (25g/2 tbsp) butter
Butter for greasing dish
2 tbsp grated cheese (optional)

Cook the potatoes in their skins until barely tender; skin when cool, then slice ⅜ in (1½ cm) thick; wash and skin the fish and salt it; season the cream with salt and plenty of white pepper, gently sauté the chopped onion in the butter until soft and golden. Take a dish about 1½ in (3½ cm) deep and wide enough to hold the folded fillets in one layer. Butter it well, then arrange the sliced potatoes evenly over the bottom; lay the folded fillets side by side on top, and scatter with the onions (in a hurry, I omit the sautéing and simply grate a little onion on top). Finally, pour over the seasoned cream and scatter the dish with the grated cheese. Lay a sheet of buttered greaseproof paper lightly on top. Bake in a slow moderate oven (Gas No. 3, 325°F, 170°C) for 30 minutes until the sauce is bubbling very slightly and the fish has lost its glassy appearance. Take off the paper and grill gently for 3 minutes, then serve at once. Serves 6.

Fillets of Fish Baked in the Provençale Manner

1½ lb (700g) filleted hake, haddock or cod, cut in 5 portions
1 medium onion
½ clove garlic, crushed
1 small bayleaf
3 tbsp white wine
1 teasp sugar
1 can (approx 15 oz/375g) Italian plum tomatoes
Good pinch oregano
½ teasp salt
Pinch of pepper
Chopped parsley
1 oz (25g/2 tbsp) butter
1 teasp oil

Put the skinned fish into a shallow dish and pour over the wine (Graves or Chablis are excellent). Leave to marinate whilst making the sauce as follows: chop the onion finely and cook it gently in a lidded frying pan in the butter and oil until soft but still golden. Add the crushed garlic and then the wine drained from the fish. Allow the mixture to bubble for two minutes, then add the tomatoes, bayleaf, salt, sugar and pepper. Simmer for 5 minutes until slightly thickened, adding a little tomato ketchup if the tomato colour is pale. Arrange the fish in a buttered fireproof dish, pour on the hot sauce and cook (Gas No. 6, 400°F, 200°C) for 20 minutes. Just before serving, sprinkle thickly with chopped parsley. Serves 4–5.

Fish Pie

4 good fillets of smoked or fresh haddock or cod
1 pint (500ml/2½ cups) milk
2 oz (50g/½ cup) flour
2 oz (50g/¼ cup) butter
2 hard-boiled eggs
2 level teasp dry mustard
2 oz (50g/½ cup) grated cheese
2 tbsp double (heavy) cream
Salt, pepper and good pinch of mace
Generous 1 lb (480g) potatoes, mashed, or large packet instant potato

If using smoked fish proceed as follows: cover the fish with water in a large frying pan. Bring slowly to the boil then discard the water. Proceed with both smoked and fresh fish as follows: cover with milk and a nut of butter. Leave under boiling point for 10 minutes. Drain, reserve milk, then skin and flake fish.

Sauce:
Melt butter, stir in flour and bubble for 2 minutes. Whisk in hot milk and allow to bubble 2 more minutes. Stir in white pepper, mace, dry mustard, and cheese. (Add only a pinch of salt if fish is salted). Stir in 2 generous tablespoons cream (optional but a vast improvement). Pour sauce over flaked fish and mix gently. Stir in sliced eggs. Pour into shallow ovenproof casserole. Cover with well-whipped mashed potatoes (done with plenty of butter and boiling milk to consistency of thick whipped cream). Bake in a hot oven (Gas No. 6, 400°F, 200°C) for 20 minutes until brown and bubbly. Serves 6.

Herrings and Mackerel

These two fish, so flavoursome and so rich in Vitamin A and D, have special seasons when they are in their prime. Consult the fishmonger before you buy.

Piquant Grilled Herrings or Mackerel

4 fish, filleted
Topping:
2 oz (50g/¼ cup) very soft butter
1 tbsp vinegar
1 teasp dry mustard
1 tbsp grated onion
Good pinch of salt
10 grinds black pepper

Wash, trim and salt the fish, then leave in the colander for 30 minutes. Dry with paper towels, beat all the topping ingredients together and spread evenly on the surface of the fish. Well butter the grill pan and put it under moderate heat for 2 or 3 minutes. Place the fish side by side in the hot pan then grill gently, for 10 minutes in the case of herrings, 12 minutes for mackerel. This dish needs no other sauce, as the topping makes its own and gives the fish a rich brown colour. Serves 4.

Grilled Mackerel with Mustard Butter

The mustard butter counteracts any heaviness of the fish.

4 medium mackerel, filleted
3 tbsp oil
Juice of half a lemon
Salt

Mustard butter:
2 oz (50g/¼ cup) butter
1 level tbsp French mustard
1 tbsp chopped parsley

First make the mustard butter by creaming the butter with the mustard and stirring in the chopped parsley. Chill in a neat tubular shape.

To grill the fish: Rinse thoroughly under the cold tap, sprinkle with salt and leave to drain in a colander. Dry with paper towels, and place in a greased grill tray. Mix the oil and lemon juice and brush thoroughly over the fillets. Sprinkle lightly with salt. Grill slowly for 10–12 minutes, without turning, but basting twice, until the fillets are a rich brown. Serve at once with a slice of the mustard butter. Serves 4.

Halibut

This is one of my favourite fish; its flesh is firm without being woody like so many Mediterranean fish, and the flavour of the freshly-landed fish when simply grilled with butter can hardly be bettered.

Grilled Halibut in Almond Butter

1–1½ lb (480–700g) halibut, cut from centre, in one ¾ in (2 cm) steak
2 oz (50g/¼ cup) butter
A little flour
Salt and pepper
1 oz (25g/¼ cup) blanched almonds
Juice of half a lemon

Salt and pepper the fish. Melt the butter in the grill pan, put in the fish and turn to coat it. Cook for 2 minutes under moderate heat on one side, turn, sprinkle with flour and grill very gently, basting once, for 10–12 minutes, depending on thickness. Lift out onto a warm plate; add a further nut of butter to the grill pan, together with the almonds. Cook until the almonds turn pale gold, add the lemon juice and seasonings, pour over the fish and serve at once. Serves 4.

Grilled Halibut on a Savoury Bed

1½ lb (700g) halibut, cut ¾ in (2 cm) thick in one slice; or 4 steaks
2 oz (50g/¼ cup) butter
3 canned tomatoes
1 small onion, finely chopped
¼ lb (100g/1½ cups) mushrooms, thinly sliced
2 tbsp dry white wine
Salt and pepper
A little flour
1 can creamed corn
Parsley

Melt half butter in saucepan, add onion and cook for 2 minutes, stir in the sliced mushrooms and tomatoes and cook a further 2 minutes. Season with salt and pepper. Place down the centre of shallow baking dish. Brush the halibut steaks with the rest of the melted butter (surface only), season with salt and pepper, sprinkle with flour and place on top of the tomato mixture. Pour 2 tablespoons dry wine round fish. Grill for 10 minutes, basting 2 or 3 times with the liquid. The fish is cooked when the bone lifts easily from the flesh, and the skin can be removed from round fish. Heat a can of creamed corn with a sprinkle of pepper and a nut of butter. When piping hot, garnish fish with it, sprinkle with parsley and serve. Serves 4.

Baked Halibut Creole

This dish has its own built-in sauce which prevents the fish drying-out in the oven. It can be prepared in the morning and then baked just before dinner.

$1\frac{1}{2}$–2 lb (700g–1kg) halibut cut into 4–6 steaks
4 large tomatoes, skinned and chopped (or the equivalent canned)
1 oz (25g/2 tbsp) butter
1 large green pepper, seeded and diced
Good pinch of dried oregano
1 clove garlic, crushed
1 small onion, finely chopped
1 level teasp salt
10 grinds black pepper
4 heaped tbsp dry breadcrumbs, tossed in 2 oz (50g/$\frac{1}{4}$ cup) melted butter, mixed with 2 tbsp grated cheese

Melt the butter and in it cook the onion till golden, then add the tomatoes, green pepper and cook for 2–3 minutes until the butter has been absorbed. Well butter a shallow oven-to-table casserole and arrange the steaks in it. Add the seasoning to the buttered vegetables and divide them evenly between the fish steaks. Cover with a layer of the crumb mixture. Refrigerate until half an hour before dinner. Bake in a quick oven (Gas No. 6, 400°F, 200°C) for half an hour, till the fish flakes easily with a fork and the topping is golden. Serves 4–6.

Fresh Salmon

It is rare indeed to find salmon cooked to perfection —the flesh silky and moist on the tongue. I put it down to the old cook's theory of so many minutes to the pound and so much over. Result: salmon that is overcooked. No matter how large the portion of fish, if it is to be served cold it should not be at simmering point for longer than 10 minutes; the cooking is continued as the fish cools in the cooking liquor. Salmon keeps its delicate colour better if neither lemon nor vinegar is added to the cooking liquor.

To Freeze Salmon

Raw Salmon must be of superb quality and guaranteed freshness if it is to be frozen in the domestic freezer. The salmon can be frozen whole or in cuts or steaks. The viscera should be removed, but do not wash the fish. Wrap in film and then in foil or a plastic bag. Thaw completely before cooking.

Cooked Salmon freezes to perfection, and its texture often improves in the freezer.

To Poach a Whole Salmon

Ask the fishmonger to scale the fish, clean out the viscera (without slitting the belly too far) and remove the eyes but leave on the head (if it will fit into your cooking utensil). Lay the fish on the drainer of a fish kettle and cover with cold water. To each $\frac{1}{2}$ pint (250ml/$1\frac{1}{4}$ cups) water used, add 2 level teaspoons salt and a little white pepper. Cover the fish kettle and bring the water very slowly to the boil—this should take at least half an hour. Allow to simmer for 1 minute to the pound (5 minutes minimum).

To serve the whole salmon hot: Turn out the heat but leave the salmon in the covered fish kettle for half an hour. Drain on its strainer, covered with a paper towel for 5 minutes, then skin and serve whole or in portions.

To serve the whole salmon cold: Remove from the heat and leave to cool in the cooking liquor. Do not refrigerate if to be served the same day. Skin and dish in the same way as hot salmon.

To Bake a Whole Salmon in Foil

Wrap the scaled and washed fish in well-greased foil (oil if the fish is to be served cold, butter if to be served hot). Wrap securely so that no juices escape but not so tightly that the heat cannot penetrate the fish. Bake in a moderate oven (Gas No. 4, 350°F, 180°C) for 1 hour. Salmon steaks will take 25 minutes at the same temperature.

To serve foil-baked whole salmon hot: Leave for 15 minutes in the foil, then unwrap.

To serve cold: Leave to cool in the foil package.

To Poach a Cut of Salmon

Take a double piece of greaseproof paper and butter generously. Place on it the washed and salted fish, then fold into a parcel, securing with loosely-tied string. Put in a pan just large enough to hold it and cover with cold water. Add 2 level teaspoons salt. Bring slowly to the boil (this should take not less than 30 minutes) then simmer for 5 minutes.

To serve a cut of salmon hot: Allow to stand in the covered pan for 30 minutes. Lift out, skin and portion.

To serve a cut of salmon cold: Allow to cool in the covered pan for at least 12 hours (though it can be left up to 48 hours under refrigeration). Skin, portion, and foil-cover until required. It looks particularly attractive on a bed of lettuce, garnished with cucumber slices and stuffed eggs, or with the entire skinned fish covered with overlapping slices of cucumber.

To poach salmon steaks: Wrap in buttered greaseproof paper, lower into boiling salted water to cover, bring back to the boil, cover and simmer (with the water barely bubbling) for 10 minutes. Unwrap and serve.

To Grill Salmon

Grilled salmon must be served as soon as it is cooked, or the flesh may become dry and heavy.

4–6 centre steaks salmon, ¾–1 in (2–2½ cm) thick
2 oz (50g/¼ cup) butter
Juice of a whole lemon
Salt and pepper
Flour or dry breadcrumbs

Wash and salt, then dab dry the salmon. In the grill pan melt the butter until it stops foaming, then place each steak in it, and immediately turn over. Grill for 3 minutes only, turn and grill a further 7 minutes, until the flesh begins to shrink from the bones. At this stage you can dust the fish with a little flour or a few dry breadcrumbs, baste with the butter and turn up the heat for a further minute to brown the fish. Lift the fish onto a warm dish, add the juice of the lemon to the pan juices, together with a little salt and black pepper. Stir well and pour over the fish. Serves 4–6.

VARIATION

Quick sour-cream sauce: Lift the cooked fish onto a serving dish. Add 5 fl oz (125ml/⅔ cup) soured cream and the juice of half a lemon to the juices in the grill pan. Stir under a gentle grill until warm, then pour over the salmon. Serves 4–6, depending on number of steaks used.

Sauce for Salmon to be Served Warm

5 fl oz (125ml/⅔ cup) soured cream
4 oz (100g/½ cup) unsalted butter
2 egg yolks
1 teasp lemon juice
Salt and pepper
1 level tbsp chopped parsley or chives

Put the soured cream and cut-up butter into a double saucepan and whisk with a balloon whisk over simmering water until the mixture has blended in and the sauce has thickened slightly. Whisk in the egg yolks and continue whisking till the mixture has a pale, thick appearance. Stir in seasonings and lemon juice. (The sauce can be kept warm over hot water until required.) Serves 6. For a 'hot' tartare sauce add 2 teaspoons chopped gherkins and 2 teaspoons chopped capers.

Salmon Steaks in White Wine Sauce

A superb dairy dinner dish for 6.

6 salmon steaks, $\frac{3}{4}$ in (2 cm) thick
3 oz (75g/$\frac{1}{3}$ cup) butter
1 level teasp salt
2 shallots, finely chopped, or the bulbs from 4 spring onions (scallions)
1 tbsp lemon juice
2 bayleaves, crumbled
8 fl oz (225ml/1 cup) dry white wine such as Graves or Chablis
2 level tbsp flour
$\frac{1}{4}$ pint (125ml/$\frac{2}{3}$ cup) double (heavy) cream
Chopped parsley

Preheat the oven (Gas No. 6, 400°F, 200°C). Wash salmon steaks then drain in colander. Smear half of butter over the bottom and sides of a baking dish wide enough to hold the fish in one layer. Arrange the steaks in it side by side and sprinkle with the salt, shallots, lemon juice and bayleaves. Add the wine. Cover with foil and bake for 15 minutes. Uncover, baste, then continue to cook covered for a further 10 minutes or until the fish flakes easily with a fork.

Note: In a suitable flameproof dish, this first stage can be done top-of-stove, but make sure the liquid barely bubbles. Lift the cooked fish from the baking dish then pour the liquid into a small pan. Skin the fish (but leave in the bone) and return to the baking dish or put on a serving platter. Keep warm. Work the flour and remaining ounce of butter together with a fork. Bring the fish liquor to the simmer, then add the butter/flour mixture, whisking all the time. Finally stir in the cream. Taste, then pour over the salmon steaks, masking them completely. Grill for 3 minutes until golden brown, sprinkle with parsley and serve. Serves 6.

For a dinner party: An hour before dinner cook salmon and mask with sauce. Cover with foil. Whilst first course is being eaten reheat fish in moderate oven for 15 minutes, uncover and grill as in the recipe.

For **Salmon in Sour Cream Sauce** see p. 261.

Rainbow Trout

The ideal fish weighs between 8 and 10 oz (200–250g). A larger fish tends to be coarse, a smaller one bony.

Fried Trout (Truite Meunière)

To fry the fish: You will need a large heavy frying pan, wide enough to hold 3 to 4 fish side by side; an oval plate containing 2 oz (50g/$\frac{1}{2}$ cup) seasoned flour; butter and oil for frying, lemon juice, parsley, and perhaps almonds and cream for saucing—and just 15 minutes of time. For family eating, it's simple to serve the fish at its best—straight from the pan to table; but when more fish are needed than can be fitted into the pan at once, keep the fish hot in a moderate oven on a heatproof serving dish, or use two pans.

To coat the fish: Use seasoned flour, which gives a light yet crisp coating. Wash and salt the fish, allow them to drain for 10 minutes, then lift them by the tail, one at a time, and roll quickly in the flour, making sure each fish is coated thinly but completely. Place the coated fish side by side, and get your frying pan ready. Heat it gently for 2 minutes, then put in 2 oz (50g/$\frac{1}{4}$ cup) butter and 2 teaspoons oil for each 3 to 4 fish. Butter is the only fat whose delicate flavour will enhance rather than mask that of the trout, whilst the oil will prevent the butter overbrowning without impairing its flavour.

Trout needs to be cooked the whole time over a moderate heat. Put the butter and oil into the pan and the minute it begins to foam, but before it changes colour, lower in the fish, side by side, making sure the underside of the fish is lying flat in the bubbling butter. Cook steadily at a gentle bubble for 5 minutes; have a peep to make sure the bottom is a rich crisp brown, then carefully turn each fish, making sure you do not pierce the flesh. After another five minutes of frying, lift the trout onto a warm serving dish. The fish can be served plain with a wedge of lemon to squeeze over it, but an almond or cream sauce makes it even more special.

VARIATIONS

Truite aux Amandes (*For* 3 *to* 4 *fish*)

When the fish is cooked, pour away any over-browned butter, wipe out the pan with tissue paper, and put another 2 oz (50g/¼ cup) butter into it. Allow the butter to heat and foam, then throw in a handful (about 2 oz/50g/½ cup) of split almonds. Let them cook for 2 or 3 minutes until golden then add the juice of a lemon and plenty of black pepper. Swirl round the pan, pour over the trout and serve at once.

Truite Père Louis (*For* 3 *to* 4 *fish*)

Comes from the heart of provincial France where the trout is fished from its tank, stunned and gutted to your order. After the fish is cooked, pour off most of the butter, leaving the buttery juices at the bottom of the pan. Add 2 tablespoons brandy, and 8 fl oz (200ml/1 cup) double (heavy) cream, and stir well with a wooden spoon. Simmer for 2 or 3 minutes to thicken the sauce, then add a good squeeze of lemon juice, salt and pepper, and pour over the fish. Serve, scattered with flaked almonds, and a dish of parsleyed new potatoes topped with a pat of butter.

Oven Fried Trout with Anchovy Sauce

This is an excellent dish to serve if you do not wish to stand over the frying pan. It is Italian in origin.

6 trout (½ lb/200g each)
1 egg
2 oz (50g/¼ cup) melted butter
Coating crumbs (dry breadcrumbs)
Sauce:
2 oz (50g/¼ cup) unsalted butter
4 anchovy fillets
4 fl oz (100ml/½ cup) white wine or Cinzano Bianco
Juice of ½ lemon
2 level teasp fresh or dried chopped mint

Beat the egg and butter together, then brush on the washed and salted trout (beheaded and cleaned). Roll in dry crumbs and arrange, not touching, on a flat oven sheet. Bake for 20 minutes (Gas No. 6, 400°F, 200°C). Meanwhile, melt the butter (unsalted if possible) in a small pan and add the chopped anchovy fillets. Stir until dissolved (about 3 minutes), then add the wine or Cinzano and simmer for 5 minutes. Stir in the lemon juice and herbs. Serve hot with the trout. Serves 6.

Fish Dishes From the Larder

Salmon au Gratin

Left-over fresh, boiled salmon can be used in season instead of canned salmon.

½ small onion, finely chopped
1½ oz (40g/3 tbsp) butter
1½ oz (40g/⅓ cup) flour
½ pint (250ml/1¼ cups) milk
4 tbsp dry white wine
Pinch of salt and white pepper
¼ teasp oregano
4 tbsp cream or evaporated milk
2 sliced hard-boiled eggs
½ lb (200g) can salmon with bones removed; or the same amount of flaked cooked salmon
Topping:
2 tbsp dry breadcrumbs
1 oz (25g/¼ cup) grated cheese
Nut of butter

Bring the milk to the boil then pour into a jug. Rinse out the pan and melt the butter. Add the onion and cook gently until soft and golden, then stir in the flour. Take off the heat. Add the hot milk and whisk hard till smooth. Return to the heat and add the wine, juice from the canned salmon, salt, pepper and herbs. Bring to the boil and simmer for 5 minutes, then stir in the cream. Carefully stir in the salmon and eggs and turn into a well-buttered shallow casserole. Mix the crumbs and cheese and scatter on the top, then dot with butter. Bake in a hot oven (Gas No. 7, 425°F, 220°C) for 15 minutes or until brown and bubbly. Serves 4.

Salmon Soufflé

1 tbsp finely-chopped onion or spring onion (scallion)
2 oz (50g/¼ cup) butter
½ pint (250ml/1¼ cup) liquid made up of juice drained from salmon can and milk
1½ oz (40g/⅓ cup) flour
1 level tbsp canned tomato purée
½ teasp dried oregano
½ teasp salt
8 grinds black pepper
4 egg yolks
5 egg whites
½ lb (200g) can top quality salmon, skinned, boned and finely shredded (cooked fresh salmon can be used in season)
2 oz (50g/½ cup) finely-grated mature cheese

Preheat oven before putting in the soufflé (Gas No. 6, 400°F, 200°C). Butter a soufflé dish of 3 pint (1½ litres) capacity (about 8 × 3 in/20 × 8 cm), and sprinkle with some finely-grated cheese. Heat the liquid to boiling then pour into a jug. Rinse out the pan and in it melt the butter, add the onion and cook gently for 2 or 3 minutes until soft and golden. Then stir in the flour. Allow to bubble without colouring for 2 minutes. Take off the heat and whisk in the boiled liquid, add seasonings, tomato and herbs. Put back on heat and bring to the boil for a further minute then take off. Beat in the yolks one by one, then finally add salmon and all but a tablespoon of cheese. Add pinch of salt and whisk whites until they form stiff, glossy peaks. Stir one quarter of the mixture into the warm sauce, then *fold* in the rest, cutting through and lifting the mixtures to blend them without flattening the whites. Sprinkle the top with the remaining cheese. Turn the preheated oven to Gas No. 5, 375°F, 190°C, and cook in the middle of the oven for 35 minutes. When ready it should be puffy and golden brown and firm to the touch. Serves 4 for a main dish and 6 for an entrée.

Salmon Fritters

These fritters should be thinner than chopped fried fish. They are delicious with a parsley sauce.

1 lb (480g) can salmon, skinned, boned and flaked, plus the salmon liquor
½ small onion, grated
2 large eggs
4 tbsp medium matzo meal
½ teasp salt
Pinch of pepper
1 teasp grated lemon rind
Breadcrumbs

Beat the eggs with the liquor from the can and the seasonings. Add the well-flaked fish, onion and the matzo meal; the mixture should be just firm enough to form into patties. Leave for half an hour. With wetted hands, take spoonfuls of the mixture and form into balls, then using a spatula, pat into patties ⅜ in (1 cm) thick. Drop into a bowl of dry breadcrumbs and coat evenly. Fry in hot oil until a rich brown on both sides. If the patties are to be served hot, fry in 2 oz/50g/¼ cup) butter and 2 teaspoons oil. As the patties are ready, transfer them to a heatproof dish and keep them hot in a moderate oven until dinnertime. Makes 10 large patties.

Salmon or Tuna Fish Cakes

½ lb (200g) can salmon or finest tuna
¾ pint (375ml/2 cups) cold mashed potato
1 teasp salt
⅛ teasp pepper
1 level tbsp grated onion
1 egg
2 level teasp chopped parsley
Flour for coating

Flake fish, and remove all skin and bones. Potatoes should have been mashed with milk and butter. Combine with potato, egg, onion and seasonings. If mixture is too soft, add 1 tablespoon medium matzo meal. If fresh potatoes have been used, chill mixture before shaping into 6–8 patties. Dip in flour, then fry gently in ¼ in (½ cm) oil, with 1 tablespoon butter. Cook until crisp and brown on both sides. Serves 4–5.

Tuna and Corn Casserole

½ green pepper, finely diced
2 hard-boiled eggs
1 medium can whole kernel corn
1 can (7½ oz/200g) tuna fish
1 tbsp chopped onion
4 oz (100g/1 cup) short cut macaroni
1 pint (500ml/2½ cups) milk
1 tbsp grated cheese
2 oz (50g/¼ cup) butter
2 rounded tbsp flour
1 teasp lemon juice
1 teasp prepared mustard
1 teasp salt
Pinch of white pepper
2 tbsp dry crumbs

Drain corn, flake tuna, slice eggs, cook and drain the macaroni. Arrange in well-buttered gratin tin about 1½ in (3½ cm) deep. Heat milk until steaming. Pour into jug. Rinse out pan and melt butter in it. Put in onion and pepper and cook gently for 5 minutes until softened but unbrowned. Add flour and bubble 2 minutes, take off heat, add hot milk all at once, and whisk till smooth. Return to heat and bring to boil. Add salt, pepper, mustard, and lemon juice. Simmer 2 minutes, then pour over contents of casserole. Mix crumbs and cheese and sprinkle evenly on top. Bake in moderate oven (Gas No. 4, 350°F, 180°C) for 30 minutes. Serves 5–6.

Tuna and Macaroni Bake

8 oz (200g/2 cups) short cut macaroni
½ small chopped onion
2 oz (50g/¼ cup) butter
1 oz (25g/¼ cup) flour
2 oz (50g/½ cup) grated cheese
¾ pint (375ml/2 cups) milk
2 teasp parsley
1 can (7½ oz/200g) tuna fish, flaked
Salt, pepper and grated cheese for topping

Cook the macaroni in boiling salted water until tender. Meanwhile, heat the milk until steaming then pour into a jug. Rinse out pan, melt butter and onion and sauté for 5 minutes until soft and golden, stir in flour, then whisk in hot milk, salt and pepper. Whisk until bubbling. Cook for 2 minutes, then stir in the flaked fish, cheese, macaroni and parsley. Turn into a well-buttered casserole, sprinkle with grated cheese. *Either* reheat in a quick oven (Gas No. 6, 400°F, 200°C) for 15–20 minutes until brown and bubbly *or* put under a gentle grill and brown until crunchy. Serves 4–5.

Meat

The classic meat dishes of the Jewish cuisine include no roasts at all; rather they are casseroles and braises, rich in flavour, and meltingly tender.

Because of the dietary laws which lay down that meat must be koshered within three days of slaughter, it was impossible to hang kosher meat before the days of refrigeration, so that it was too fresh to roast well. Now, however, it is possible to tenderize it either by hanging in a butcher's cold room, or by freezing at home before use. This means that the prime cuts—such as wing rib (short rib) and shoulder of lamb—can be roasted most successfully, whilst the eye of the rib can be grilled or fried.

Because of the relative scarcity and high price of kosher meat, minced (chopped) beef has always been the main standby of the Jewish cook, because of the ease with which it could be extended, either with fillers such as rice, bread or matzo meal, or by using it as a filling for pastry or vegetables. In this chapter, whilst due attention is paid to the meat dishes of tradition, the majority of the recipes are of more modern origin, suitable to the new conditions under which kosher meat is now marketed and cooked.

A Guide to Kosher Meat Cuts and How to Cook Them

The best kosher butchers now cut and prepare their meat to suit all modern methods of cooking. Of course, the number of different cuts available in a kosher butcher shop is limited because they do not include any meat from the hindquarters of the beast. However, a huge variety of dishes can be made with the parts that are permitted, provided each part is used in the most suitable way.

NOTE:

Freezing meat helps to tenderize it, thus making it suitable to fry or grill. To conform to the laws of kashrut, it must first be koshered, and it can then be stored in the freezer for any length of time.

Hanging meat helps to tenderize joints used for roasting, such as rib or bola (chuck) (see note below on roasting bola). The meat must first be koshered and then loosely wrapped (to prevent drying), before hanging at a temperature of between 32°F and 34°F (0°C–1°C) for 7–10 days. As this is colder than the temperature of the normal domestic refrigerator, it should be hung by the butcher before the meat is delivered to your home.

Beef

Fresh beef is bright red when first cut, but darkens on standing in the air.
Tender beef is usually flecked with fat, rather like marble, and is surrounded by a creamy layer of it. Fatless meat cannot be tender. The inside of the

bones should be rosy, and the meat firm and moist to the touch, and very smooth.

1. *Shin beef:* Soup and beef tea; makes a flavoursome, if rather fibrous, pressure cooker stew.
2. *Brisket:* (a) *Thin end.* For tsimmes—used sliced, with a marrowbone. (b) *Point.* Covered roasting—in fat without liquid, 40 minutes to the pound ($\frac{1}{2}$kg). Only economical in a 4 lb (2kg) joint or over. Meaty but fatty (middle brisket has thinner layer of fat). *Note:* Brisket is really too thick to roll. Excellent for pickling.
3. *Flank:* Needs rolling. Cheap. Sweet when pot roasted, but must be pressed and served cold, or it falls to bits. Also for pickling.
4. *Neck steak:* Mincing (grinding) or stewing—has plenty of 'body'.
5. *Chuck or back steak:* Stew, mince (grind) or cook with wine.
6. *Shoulder steak:* First-cut for braising, cut $\frac{1}{2}$ in (1 cm) thick, or for casseroles—excellent for goulash or **Boeuf Bourguignon,** cut in 1 in ($2\frac{1}{2}$ cm) cubes. If hung for ten days, it can be fried.
7. *Blade steak:* Braise in slices, or pot roast in one piece. The thin gristle running through can be nicked out before serving.
8. *Alki or round bola* (part of shoulder steak), also known as chuck: Braise, cooked with plenty of its own fat (dice fat then use to brown meat). Good, hot or cold.
9. *Top rib:* Similar to flank. For borscht, cabbage soup, cholent.
10. *Wing rib* (*standing rib*)*:* Roasting, can be boned out for spit roasting, or shortened rib on bone can be spitted—keeping bone in adds to flavour.
11. *Lid of rib* (*top of back rib*)*:* Rolled, then roasted or spitted. Excellent cold for sandwiches.
12. *Rib steaks:* Boned out and cut $\frac{1}{2}$–$\frac{3}{4}$ in ($1\frac{1}{2}$–2 cm) thick for grilling or frying.
13. *Bola* (*chuck*)*:* (a) *Corner.* Braising, with plenty of its own fat. Hung bola can be open-roasted very slowly, loosely foil-covered for half the time, allowing 40 minutes to the pound. (b) *Slice.* Braising (Swiss steak, or cooked in tomatoes). Bola, frozen, then cut paper-thin can be used for Steak Diane.
14. *Liver:* Chopping. Young beasts' liver need only be grilled; older animals' liver should be grilled to kosher, then simmered in salted water for half an hour.
15. *Knuckle and shin beef:* For soup.
16. *Oxtail:* For soup.
17. *Minced* (*ground*) *beef* should always be used as soon after mincing as possible, as the number of cut surfaces makes it deteriorate more quickly than other meat.

All meats should be completely cooked before storage; partially cooking meat raises the internal temperature just enough to encourage the growth of bacteria, without being sufficiently high to kill them.

Veal

Good veal is between 6 and 8 weeks old, the flesh milky rather than pink in colour. An older animal which is too young to be classified as beef is called a 'sterk'.

1. *Shank of veal:* In thick soups such as barley and hobene gropen; for calves-foot jelly or meat casseroles, such as osso bucco. It must be cut with an electric saw.
2. *Shoulder:* The thick part of the shoulder can be plain roasted, the blade end boned out, stuffed and braised. Use plenty of fat, flavour with bayleaf and onion, cook in a covered casserole.
3. *Breast:* Have it boned and pocketed or boned and rolled, then stuffed. Braise.
4. *First-cut chops:* Braise. Also for kebabs, and veal escalopes in wine.
5. *Shoulder chops:* Boned out, koshered, frozen and sliced for schnitzel.
6. *Calf liver:* Grill to kosher, then slice and smother with onions in frying pan. Or use for chopped liver.

Lamb

Good lamb joints have plenty of light pinkish meat, creamy fat, and very little bone.

1. *Neck and scrag:* For Scotch broth.
2. *First cut chops* (cutlet): For grilling. There are twelve in each beast.
3. *Middle neck:* For casseroling.

4. *Breast:* Casserole with spring vegetables. Can also be stuffed.
5. *Shoulder:* Roast. Can also be boned and rolled.
6. *Kidneys:* To sauté and stew where available.

How to Kosher Meat and Poultry

It is now possible to buy pre-packed meat and poultry which has been koshered under rabbinical supervision and can therefore be cooked without any further ritual preparation. (Butcher's lean minced—or ground—beef is always prepared from pre-koshered meat.)

However, when the food has to be koshered at home, the following procedures should be followed for all kinds of meat, bones, poultry and giblets, with the exception of liver and grilling steaks (see special instructions below).

1) *Meat and Poultry* (including bones and giblets): All poultry must be drawn before it is koshered.

a) As soon as possible after the food has been delivered, put it into a deep plastic or enamel bucket and cover it completely with cold water.

b) Leave it to soak for half an hour.

c) Take it out and place it on a wire or plastic draining grid, tilted so that the liquid can easily drain away. Leave it to drain for 5 minutes.

d) Thoroughly sprinkle every surface with koshering salt. (This can be obtained from a kosher butcher or grocer.)

e) Leave for one hour.

f) Rinse the food three times in cold water, to remove all traces of salt and blood.

Meat and bones should then be well dried with a paper towel and cooked at once, or stored until required in the refrigerator or freezer.

Poultry and giblets must be scalded as follows:

a) Stand the fowl in a bowl and pour boiling water over it from a kettle.

b) When cool enough to handle, scrape the skin of the bird with a blunt knife, to remove any feathers or coarse bits of skin; remove the skin from the feet. Look inside the body cavity to make sure it is absolutely clean, and that no traces of the entrails remain. Trim off any loose skin from the giblets. Dry thoroughly, cook at once, or store in the refrigerator or freezer.

In an emergency, to ensure that food can be cooked before the commencement of Sabbath, the koshering time may be reduced by half. In this case, the food is soaked for 15 minutes only, and then left in salt for half an hour.

2) *Liver:* As liver contains too much blood to be effectively koshered by soaking and salting, the following method is used instead:

a) A thick piece of liver should be cut open, thinner slices should be cut across the surface to facilitate the removal of the blood.

b) Wash the liver thoroughly in cold water, then sprinkle it on both sides with cooking salt (koshering salt is too coarse for the purpose).

c) Place the liver on a sheet of foil and lay it in the grill pan. Grill gently until it changes colour, turn and grill on the second side in the same way. *Alternatively*, the salted liver can be placed in a wire basket or on a wire grid over a gas flame and cooked in the same way, until it has changed colour on both sides. (The foil on which the liver was grilled should be discarded after use. If a wire basket or grid is used, it should be held over the flame to burn off any residue, then washed, wiped and stored.)

d) Calf liver can now be served without further preparation, or it can be put in a frying pan and smothered with fried onions. Ox liver must be tenderized by simmering in salt water for half an hour. It can then be used for chopped liver.

3) *Steaks:* Steaks which are to be grilled do not need to be soaked and salted. The grilling process draws out the blood from the meat, and this is considered to satisfy the requirements of Kashrut.

Note: All utensils used to kosher food should be kept exclusively for that purpose. After use, they should be washed and wiped with a special cloth, then stored separately from other kitchen equipment.

Braised Joints

Braised Bola (or Chuck)

Bola or 'chuck' comes from the shoulder of the animal; it is solid meat, with very little fat flecking the muscle, so it responds best to moist heat. It is, therefore, a very suitable joint to braise, when it is first seared to seal it, and then cooked on a bed of vegetables in a covered casserole. Braised bola is delicious either hot or cold, provided it is cooked very slowly, as follows:

3–4 lb (1½–2kg) corner of bola (chuck), with 1 level teasp salt, 1 level teasp dry mustard and 2 level teasp flour rubbed into the raw surface
2 tbsp cooking fat or oil
Salt and black pepper
2 small onions, 2 stalks celery, 2 carrots, ½ green pepper — all coarsely sliced
1 clove garlic
1 bayleaf
A sprig of parsley
3 fl oz (75ml/⅓ cup) water

Set the oven (Gas No. 3, 325°F, 170°C). In a heavy-based casserole, melt the fat and brown the floured meat quickly on all sides. Lift it out onto a plate. Into the same fat put the sliced onions, cooking them until soft and golden (this is important as it helps to colour the sauce). Add all the remaining vegetables and stir them well to absorb any remaining fat. Sprinkle with a little additional salt and 10 grinds of black pepper. Add the bayleaf, parsley, garlic and water. Stir the contents of the casserole thoroughly, then replace the browned meat on the savoury vegetable bed. Put on the lid and put in the oven. When the liquid starts to bubble (after about 15 minutes) turn the oven down to Gas No. 2, 300°F, 150°C, and cook for 2½–3 hours, depending on the weight of the meat. Allow 40 minutes per pound (½kg) plus 40 minutes for the piece. Ten minutes before serving, take off the lid, and allow the surface of the meat to dry off.

To serve: Put the meat on a hot dish. Push all the vegetables and juices through a sieve into a small pan, or blend in the liquidizer until smooth. Skim off any excess fat, heat to boiling, season with salt and pepper and serve with the meat cut into thin slices. Serves 6–8, or 4 people twice.

Braised Brisket

As the fat that melts off brisket is so tasty, it makes an ideal medium in which to cook potatoes and carrots. Left-over brisket should be forced into a basin, covered with a saucer and a 2 lb (1kg) weight and then refrigerated. Next day it will cut to perfection.

3 lb (1½kg) corner of brisket
1 tbsp meat fat
6 pickling onions
2 large potatoes
2 medium carrots
1 bayleaf
6 peppercorns
2 level teasp salt
10 grinds black pepper
3 fl oz (75ml/⅓ cup) boiling water

Brown the meat quickly in the hot fat. Sprinkle with the seasonings. Put in a casserole surrounded with the onions and the boiling water. Cover and cook in a slow oven (Gas No. 2, 300°F, 150°C) for 3 hours. One hour before the meat is ready, surround it with thick slices of potato and carrot. Serve the brisket cut in thick slices, together with the potatoes and carrots in the delicious meat juices. Serves 4–6, with some left for sandwiches.
(For **Beef Braised in Wine (Daube Marseillaise),** see p. 264.

Minced (Ground) Beef

Always ask for minced (ground) shoulder steak. This is more expensive than plain 'mince', but is far meatier with less gristle content.

The Basic Minced (Ground) Beef Mixture

1 lb (½kg) minced shoulder steak (ground beef)
2 teasp chicken fat or soft margarine
2 level teasp salt
10 grinds black pepper
2 eggs
½ onion
1 thick slice white bread
1 level tbsp medium matzo meal

In the blender: Put the eggs, onion, fat, bread and seasonings in the blender goblet and blend till smooth. Pour onto the meat, add the matzo meal and stir well until blended. Leave for half an hour.

By hand: Beat the eggs, and put the bread to soak in them until soft, then beat with a fork until smooth. Grate the onion, and add to the egg mixture together with seasonings, fat and the matzo meal. Add to the meat and stir thoroughly until blended. Leave for half an hour.

Note: For 2 lb (1kg) minced (ground) beef, use double quantities, but only 3 eggs.

Recipes using Basic Minced (Ground) Beef Mixture

Meat Ball Casserole

1 lb (½kg) basic minced (ground) beef mixture
1 large onion, sliced or chopped
2 tbsp oil
½ pint (250ml/1¼ cups) meat bouillon or thin left-over gravy
1 small bayleaf
1 tbsp flour mixed with a pinch of salt and pepper

Wet the hands under the cold water tap. Take large spoonfuls of the raw meat mixture and form into balls the size of small apples, then flatten slightly into patties. There should be six. Put the seasoned flour onto a piece of paper, and dip each patty into it. Shake off any excess flour. Heat the oil in a heavy frying pan for 4 minutes, put in the meat balls, and fry steadily until they are a rich brown on both sides. Remove the meat, and in the same fat fry the onions until they are soft and golden, but not crispy. Add the bouillon or gravy to the pan with a further sprinkle of salt and pepper and the bayleaf. Stir the pan well to release any meat juices which may have stuck to the bottom. Arrange the patties in a shallow uncovered casserole, in which they can fit side by side. Pour the gravy round them, and cook slowly (Gas No. 2, 300°F, 150°C) for 45 minutes. Alternatively, the meat can be put back into the frying pan surrounded by the onions and gravy, and left to cook very gently for the same time, turning the meat once or twice. Serves 4.

VARIATIONS

Meat Balls in Wine and Mushroom Sauce

1 lb (½kg) basic minced (ground) beef mixture
2 tbsp oil
Mix and fry the meat balls as for Meat Ball Casserole.
Cook the meat balls in this sauce:
½ lb (200g/3 cups) mushrooms, thinly sliced
¼ pint (125ml/⅔ cup) dry red wine such as Burgundy
¼ pint (125ml/⅔ cup) thin gravy or beef bouillon
Salt and pepper
Chopped garlic

To make the sauce: Remove the fried meat balls, and in the same fat, sauté the mushrooms until limp (about 3 minutes). Add the gravy (or bouillon) and wine. Season with salt and pepper and a sprinkle of chopped dried garlic. Stir the contents of the pan well to release any meat juices which may have stuck to the bottom. Cook exactly as for **Meat Ball Casserole**. Serves 4.

Meat Balls in Barbecue Sauce

1 lb (½kg) basic minced (ground) beef mixture
2 tbsp oil
Mix and fry the meat balls as for Meat Ball Casserole.
Cook the meat balls in this sauce:
1 onion, finely chopped
2 level teasp salt
10 grinds black pepper
4 level tbsp fine dark brown sugar
2 teasp prepared mustard
2 teasp Worcestershire sauce
2 tbsp lemon juice
5 oz (125g/½ cup) can tomato purée, diluted with 2 cans water

To make the sauce: Remove the fried meat balls, and in the same fat sauté the onion until golden, add all the remaining ingredients and simmer for 5 minutes. (This sauce can be used with grilled hamburgers as well.) Place meat balls in a casserole, pour over sauce and cover. Simmer either top-of-stove for thirty minutes, or bake in a slow oven (Gas No. 2, 300°F, 150°C) for ¾ hour. Serves 4–5.

Minced (Ground) Beef Mixture for Grilling or Frying

This mixture contains no 'filler' of bread or meal, and is therefore particularly suitable for frying or grilling.

1½ lb (¾kg) minced shoulder steak (ground beef)
1 oz (25g/2 tbsp) soft margarine or white fat
1½ level teasp salt and plenty of black pepper
1 egg
Pinch of thyme (if liked)
1 small onion, very finely chopped and softened in 1 oz (25g/2 tbsp) chicken fat or margarine (optional)

Combine thoroughly all the ingredients, form into 6 cakes ¾ in (1½ cm) thick. Chill or freeze till required.

To fry: Toss in flour, then sauté for 3–4 minutes each side in 1 tablespoon oil. Remove. Pour off oil. Add ¼ pint (125ml/⅔ cup) stock or wine. Bubble for 3 minutes, season with salt and pepper. Serve with meat.

To grill: Put on hot greased grill tray about 2 in (5 cm) from source of heat. Grill for 4 minutes either side or until a rich brown. Serve in hot buns, or with a green salad. Serves 4–5.

Meat Loaf

2 lb (1kg) minced shoulder steak (ground beef)
3 large slices bread
2 eggs
1 medium onion
1 teasp dry mustard
1 tbsp tomato ketchup
2 tbsp bottled brown sauce
2 level teasp salt and pinch of black pepper
1 level tbsp medium matzo meal

In blender put: bread (in chunks—no need to crumb); eggs; onion, cut in four; mustard; sauces and seasonings. Blend for one minute or until smooth. Combine with meat and matzo meal in large bowl. Blend thoroughly. Arrange in loaf shape about 2 in (5 cm) high and 3 in (7½ cm) wide in roasting tin just big enough to leave margin round. Put in quick oven (Gas No. 6, 400°F, 200°C) for 15 minutes, then turn to Gas No. 4, 350°F, 180°C for a further 45 minutes.

Whilst meat is cooking, fry a small, finely-chopped onion in 1 tablespoon chicken fat or margarine until golden brown, then stir in 1 cup beef stock mixed with 2 level teaspoons cornflour. Bring to boil, then pour over and round meat loaf 15 minutes before it is cooked.

Serve loaf with gravy in slices. *Note:* If meat loaf is to be served cold, there is no need for gravy. Serves 6 with left-overs.

VARIATION

Burgundy Meat Loaf: Make exactly as for Meat Loaf, but with the following ingredients:
2 lb (1kg) minced shoulder steak (ground beef)
3 thick slices bread
2 eggs
2 level teasp dry mustard
1 medium onion, cut in 4
Large sprig parsley
2 teasp Worcestershire sauce
2 level teasp Italian seasoning (herbs) or mixed herbs such as basil and oregano
3 fl oz (75ml/⅓ cup) red wine
1 tbsp medium matzo meal
Small green pepper, seeded and cut in 6

Serves 6 with left-overs.

Minced (Ground) Beef Casseroles

Raw lean minced (ground) beef combines extremely well with rice, or pasta, to make tasty and satisfying casseroles that also have the virtue of economy. Below are a selection of some of these dishes. These casseroles all freeze and reheat well.

Mexican Rice

2 oz (50g/¼ cup) margarine
1 chopped onion
1 green pepper, diced
4 stalks of celery, diced (or 2 teasp dried celery)
1 lb (½kg) minced shoulder steak (ground beef)
1 large can whole tomatoes (about 20 fl oz/500ml/ 2½ cups)
2 tbsp canned tomato purée
½ level teasp chili powder; or few drops Tabasco sauce
2 level teasp salt and sugar
10 grinds black pepper
1 level teasp paprika
1 clove garlic, crushed
Juice of ½ lemon

In a heavy frying pan or casserole, melt the fat, then gently brown the onion, green pepper and celery. Add the meat, cook until it loses its red colour, then cover with tomatoes and seasonings. Cover and simmer on top of stove or in oven for 1 hour (Gas No. 3, 325°F, 170°C).

The rice:
¾ pint (375ml/2 cups) chicken or meat stock (or plain water plus 1 teasp chicken fat)
6 oz (150g/¾ cup) long grain rice; or 3 cups cooked left-over or frozen rice

Bring liquid to the boil, add the rice, stir until simmering, then cover and cook for 20 minutes. Add the rice to the meat sauce and simmer for 15–20 minutes, or longer, until thick and juicy. Serves 4 as a main course, 6 as an accompaniment.

Beef and Rice Western Style

¼ lb (100g/1 cup) black olives, stones removed
1 lb (½kg) raw minced (ground) beef
4 tbsp oil
1 medium onion, finely chopped
4 stalks celery, finely sliced (about 1 cupful)
½ green pepper, seeded and finely chopped
8 oz (200g/1 cup) long grain rice
1 large can peeled plum tomatoes (approx 28 fl oz/700ml)
2 level teasp sugar
1 teasp salt
10 grinds black pepper
2 teasp Worcestershire sauce

Cut the olives into large pieces. Brown minced (ground) beef in half the oil in a heavy frying pan. When it has lost its redness remove it from the pan, add a further 2 tablespoons oil (or chicken fat) and add the onions, celery, green pepper and rice. Cook, stirring until the onions are soft and golden and the rice has turned yellow, about 5 minutes. Add the tomatoes, seasonings, meat and olives and bring to the boil. Pour into a casserole. Put in a moderate oven (Gas No. 3, 325°F, 170°C) for 1 hour, stirring once. Serves 6 generously.

Noodle and Meat Ring

½ lb (200g/3 cups) broad noodles (lokshen)
1 tbsp chopped parsley
2 tbsp pine kernels (pine nuts) (optional)
¼ lb (100g/2 cups) mushrooms
½ lb (200g) minced (ground) beef
½ large onion
Stock
1 beaten egg
1 level teasp salt and plenty of black pepper
Oil

Cook noodles according to package directions. Drain well. Cover bottom of frying pan with thin layer of oil. Carefully fry pine kernels (if used) until golden. Drain on tissue paper. In same oil, fry onions until golden, then add mushrooms and meat. Continue to cook until meat has lost its redness. Just cover with stock and simmer for 20 minutes. Add to noodles, together with all the remaining ingredients. Turn into greased casserole or ring mould. Cover with greaseproof paper. Bake for 40 minutes (Gas No. 4, 350°F, 180°C). Turn out, or serve from dish, plain or with tomato sauce. Serves 6.

Spaghetti Bolognese

1 onion
1 carrot
2 stalks celery
$\frac{1}{2}$ green pepper
1 tbsp parsley
1 lb ($\frac{1}{2}$kg) raw minced (ground) beef
1 koshered chicken liver (if available)
2 tbsp oil
1 tbsp chicken fat
1 clove garlic, crushed to a paste with a little salt
4 fl oz (100ml/$\frac{1}{2}$ cup) red wine (optional)
8 fl oz (200ml/1 cup) chicken stock
1 can (15 fl oz/375ml) tomatoes
2 tbsp tomato purée
1 bayleaf
$\frac{1}{2}$ teasp each of basil and oregano
2 level teasp sugar and a few grinds black pepper
1 teasp salt
1 lb ($\frac{1}{2}$kg/5 cups) cooked long spaghetti, tossed with a little oil

Chop the onion and parsley, grate the carrot, finely dice the celery and green pepper (use dried pepper flakes when peppers are not in season), sauté gently in the oil and chicken fat until a rich brown, then add the minced (ground) meat (and liver, if used) and keep stirring with a fork to break up the minced (ground) meat until it loses its redness. Then add the wine (if used) and stock and bubble another 5 minutes. Finally add the tomatoes and juice and the purée together with all the seasonings. The meat should just barely be covered by the liquid; if not, add a little hot water, cover and simmer very gently for 3 hours, if possible. Long, slow cooking is the important thing with a bolognese sauce if it is to have a rich flavour. When it is cooked, the sauce part should be the consistency of pouring cream, so that it is thick enough to coat the strands of spaghetti without being stodgy. If too thin, add one level tablespoon cornflour, mixed with 2 tablespoons cold water—bubble for 3 minutes.

To cook the spaghetti: Bring water to the boil in an 8 pint (4 litre/20 cups) pan together with 4 heaped teaspoons salt; when the water is bubbling, lower in the spaghetti and allow to coil round the pan without breaking it. Cook with the lid partly off, at a fierce bubble for 14 minutes, then test. It should be tender without being sloppy; if not quite soft enough, continue cooking a little longer. When the spaghetti is ready, take it to the sink and immediately pour in a little cold water to stop the cooking, then strain through a colander. Put into a very large bowl or dish, in which you have already put 2 tablespoons olive oil or the same amount of margarine. Toss the two together until the spaghetti is coated with the fat. Keep warm in a low oven until you are ready to serve it.

Note: Many people prefer their spaghetti to be cooked 'al dente', or chewy. In this case the spaghetti should be cooked for no more than 8 minutes, then served at once.

To serve: Heap a mound of spaghetti on each plate and top with ladlefuls of sauce. Serves 4–5.

Spaghetti alla Napolitana

This Southern speciality is made with meat balls, which are browned then cooked in a rich tomato sauce.

2 tbsp oil
1 large onion, chopped
White part of a fat leek and small handful of parsley, chopped together
1 clove garlic, crushed to a paste with a little salt
$\frac{1}{2}$ teasp dried basil or oregano
5 oz (125g/$\frac{2}{3}$ cup) can of Italian tomato purée
4 fl oz (100ml/$\frac{1}{2}$ cup) red wine
1 tbsp red wine vinegar
2 level teasp sugar
1 teasp salt
$\frac{1}{2}$ pint (250ml/$1\frac{1}{4}$ cups) chicken or meat stock
1 can (15 oz/375g) Italian tomatoes
1 lb ($\frac{1}{2}$kg/5 cups) cooked long spaghetti, tossed in a little oil

Cook the chopped vegetables and herbs in oil until golden brown, then add all the remaining ingredients. Simmer very gently, uncovered, for 30 minutes. Then add the meat balls and simmer, covered, a further 45 minutes.

Meat Balls: 1 recipe **Basic Minced (Ground) Beef Mixture** (see p. 54) formed into golf balls then fried.

To serve: Put a serving of spaghetti on each plate and top with a ladleful of sauce and meat balls. Serves 5.

A Variety of Meat Stews

Meat cooked in a savoury sauce can be one of the most delectable of dishes, if certain rules are followed:

1. Always brown the meat to develop its flavour and to seal it, thus preventing the total escape of the meat juices into the cooking liquid.
2. Use only enough liquid to cover the meat, so that the meaty flavour does not become diluted.
3. Make sure that the liquid never boils, but 'shivers' all the time, so that the cooked meat is soft without being stringy.

Savoury Goulash

This basic recipe can be varied in any of the following ways:

1. *Canned tomatoes can be substituted for all the liquid.*
2. *Red wine can be substituted for half the liquid.*
3. *The bayleaves can be omitted and 2 level teasp paprika pepper sprinkled on the meat as it is browning in the fat.*

2 lb (1kg) stewing or braising steak, cut into 1 in (2½ cm) cubes
2 oz (50g/4 tbsp) meat fat; or 2 tbsp oil
Plenty of black pepper
2 large onions, sliced wafer-thin
1 level tbsp brown sugar
2 level teasp salt
2 bayleaves
1 pint (500ml/2½ cups) water or meat stock made with a bouillon cube
2 level tbsp cornflour (cornstarch) dissolved in 4 tbsp cold water

Heat the fat or oil in a heavy frying pan or oven casserole, sprinkle with the black pepper, then put in the meat and brown briskly on all sides (make sure the meat is well dried beforehand on a kitchen paper towel, or it will not brown). Add the onions, sprinkle with the brown sugar and continue to cook until the mixture is a really rich brown. Pour in the water or stock, the bayleaves and the salt. Cover and simmer for 1½ hours on the top of the stove or 2 hours in a slow oven (Gas No. 2, 300°F, 150°C). Adjust the temperature so that the liquid is barely bubbling all the time. Add the dissolved cornflour and continue to cook for a further three minutes. Taste and add more seasonings, if necessary. Serves 4–6.

Belgian Beef Stew (*Carbonnade de Boeuf Flamande*)

The beer in this recipe adds flavour, but it also helps to tenderize the meat.

1 oz (25g/4 tbsp) flour
2 level teasp salt
½ level teasp pepper
2 lb (1kg) braising or stewing meat, cut into 1 in (2½ cm) cubes
4 tbsp salad oil
2 large onions, thinly sliced
1 clove garlic, crushed
1 can light beer
2 teasp soy sauce
1 teasp Worcestershire sauce
2 teasp bottled brown sauce
2 bayleaves
2 lb (1kg) potatoes
1 tbsp chopped parsley

In a large bowl, mix salt, pepper and flour. Toss the cubes of meat in it to coat them. Heat half the oil in a heavy casserole, then sauté the onions and garlic for 8 minutes or until soft. Remove. Add the remaining oil. Put in meat, brown well on all sides. Add onions and garlic, then put in beer, soy, Worcestershire and brown sauces and bayleaves. Bring to boil, cover and simmer for 2 hours top-of-stove or in oven (Gas No. 2, 300°F, 150°C). Boil potatoes, cut in slices, until tender. Toss in parsley. Put stew in dish and serve surrounded by potatoes. Serves 4–6.

Sweet and Sour Beef

1½ oz (40g/3 tbsp) margarine
1 tbsp oil
2 lb (1kg) braising or stewing steak cut into 1 in (2½ cm) cubes
2 level teasp salt
A few grinds black pepper
1 medium onion, coarsely chopped
3 sticks celery, chopped
1 medium can (14 oz/350g) pineapple chunks
½ pint (250ml/1¼ cups) beef stock made with a bouillon cube
2 level tbsp cornflour (cornstarch)
1 tbsp soy sauce
1 tbsp tomato ketchup
2 tbsp vinegar

Put the oil and margarine in a heavy pan and brown the well-dried meat on all sides. Add the onion and celery and continue to cook for a further 5 minutes, until the vegetables have wilted and absorbed most of the fat. Drain the juice from the pineapple and make it up to 10 oz (250ml/1¼ cups) with water. Add with the stock and seasonings to the meat. Bring to the boil, cover and simmer for 2 hours, or until the meat is tender. Blend the cornflour with the soy sauce, ketchup and vinegar, stir into the meat with the pineapple chunks. Simmer for 3 minutes. Serve piping hot. If preferred, this dish can be transferred to the oven and allowed to simmer at Gas No. 2, 300°F, 150°C for 2½ hours. Serves 6.

Spring Beef Casserole

1 tbsp each oil and chicken fat
1½ lb (¾kg) first-cut shoulder steak
2 tbsp flour
1 teasp salt
Plenty of black pepper
2 level teasp mustard
1 level teasp ginger
1 large onion
2 large carrots
1 pint (500ml/2½ cups) hot water with beef bouillon cube

Dumplings:
4 oz (100g/1 cup) self-raising flour or
4 oz (100g/1 cup) plain flour with 1 level teasp baking powder
1 oz (25g/2 tbsp) margarine
1 egg
2 tbsp water
2 teasp chopped parsley
1 pkt frozen peas

Trim any gristle off the steak and cut into 1 in (2½ cm) cubes, then toss in seasoned flour. Brown meat in fats, then add diced onion and carrots and continue to cook until the meat is a rich brown. Now add water and meat cube (and any squashy tomatoes you have), bring to boil, then simmer either top-of-stove for 1½ hours or in a slow oven (Gas No. 2, 300°F, 150°C) for 2 hours. After 1½ hours put in dumplings made by rubbing fat into the flour, adding parsley, then mixing to a sticky dough with the egg and water. Using a wet spoon, drop tablespoons of the mixture on to the simmering stew, cover and continue to cook for a further half an hour. The gravy will be juicy but on the thin side. If you prefer it thicker, mix a level tablespoon of cornflour with a little water, add to the casserole and allow it to bubble a few minutes before serving. The frozen peas should be dropped into the casserole 15 minutes before the end of the cooking time. Serves 4–6.

American Stew de Luxe

2 lb (1kg) sliced bola (chuck) or first-cut shoulder steak, cut into 1 in (2½ cm) cubes
2 large sliced onions
White part of a fat leek
1 large carrot, diced
2 level teasp each brown sugar and flour
3 level teasp salt
Few grinds of black pepper
Pinch of ginger
2 tbsp of oil
2 teasp dry mustard
5 tbsp red wine
Hot water

Heat the oil in a heavy pan, put in the meat and brown quickly, stirring all the time, then add sliced onions and brown sugar, the diced carrot and leek and continue to cook until a rich brown juice flows from the mixture—about 5 minutes. Sprinkle in the flour, mustard and ginger, stir well, then add the wine and just enough hot water to barely cover the mixture. Simmer on top of the stove or in the oven (Gas No. 2, 300°F, 150°C) making sure the liquid only shivers rather than bubbles, for 2–2½ hours, or until the meat is bite-tender. Serves 6.

Meat and Herb Stew

2 lb (1kg) braising or stewing steak, cubed
2 level teasp salt
1 teasp basil leaves
1 large onion, finely chopped
4 celery stalks, chopped, or pinch celery salt
1 bouillon cube and water to cover meat
1 large bayleaf
2 carrots, diced
2 oz (50g/½ cup) flour
White and black pepper
4 tbsp oil
1 clove garlic, crushed
1 level teasp thyme
2 teasp brown sugar

Dredge meat in flour seasoned with salt, pepper and basil. Heat oil and brown meat then remove. Add onion, garlic, carrot and celery and continue to cook until onion is soft and golden, sprinkling with 2 teaspoons of brown sugar to help the process. Return all meat to casserole and add any remaining flour. Cook a minute, then add crumbled cube, thyme, bayleaf and enough hot water barely to cover the meat. Cook, stirring until thickened. When simmering, cover casserole and transfer to oven. Cook at Gas No. 2, 300°F, 150°C for 2 hours or until meat is tender. Serves 6.

Meat Pies

To be perfect, a meat pie must be made with care; the meat first simmered till tender in a succulent sauce, the crust baked crisp on the outside, yet within, moist and juicy from the filling.

The crust can be made from either puff or short-crust pastry, the meat cubed or minced before cooking; but in either case, the filling must be quite cool before it is covered, or the crust will be soggy.

To Make a Meat Pie with a Single Crust

1 recipe **Goulash,** or **Spring Beef Casserole**
½ lb (200g) puff pastry or ½ recipe **Rough Puff Pastry** made with margarine (see p. 140)

Cook the meat mixture according to the recipe, but allow it to cool; then spoon it into a pie dish 2 in (5 cm) deep with a ½ in (1 cm) rim all the way round. Roll out the pastry until it is the thickness of a penny and ½ in (1 cm) larger all the way round than the top of the pie dish. Trim off this extra ½ in (1 cm) and lay it on the dampened rim of the dish. Dampen the strip of pastry in turn, then carefully transfer the remaining pastry to the dish, pressing it down well onto the pastry rim that is already in position. A pie funnel helps the pie-crust to keep its shape. Use a fork to crimp the edges of the pie. If you have a little beaten egg, use it to paint the top of the pie, otherwise leave it plain. Bake in a hot oven (Gas No. 8, 450°F, 230°C) for 20 minutes. Serves 6.

To Make a Meat Pie with a Double Crust

1 recipe **Goulash** or **Spring Beef Casserole**
½ lb (200g) puff pastry or ½ recipe **Rough Puff Pastry** made with margarine (see p. 140)

Divide the pastry in half, and roll one half to fit the bottom of a 7 in (18 cm) or 8 in (20 cm) pie dish. Spoon in the cooled meat mixture. If there is too much gravy, omit it and serve separately. Dampen the edges of the pie, then cover with a second crust rolled from the remainder of the pastry. Crimp the edges firmly with a fork, brush with egg or leave plain, and bake for ten minutes at Gas No. 8, 450°F, 230°C, then for a further 15 minutes at Gas No. 7, 425°F, 220°C. Serves 6.

To Make a Meat Pie with a Dumpling Crust

In this recipe the meat **must** *be hot when the crust is put on, as it needs the steam to cook it.*

1 recipe **Goulash** or **Spring Beef Casserole** or **Meat and Herb Stew** or **American Stew de Luxe.**

4 oz (100g/1 cup) self-raising flour and 1 level teasp baking powder; or 4 oz (100g/1 cup) plain flour and 2 level teasp baking powder
½ level teasp salt
2 oz (50g/¼ cup) margarine
2 teasp chopped parsley
2 tbsp (approx) cold water

Mix the flour, baking powder and salt, then rub in the margarine until the mixture resembles coarse crumbs. Stir in chopped parsley and sufficient cold water to make a stiff dough. Gently roll out the dumpling on a floured board to fit the top of the casserole in which the meat is bubbling. Three-quarters of an hour before the meat is done, uncover the casserole, top with the dumpling crust, cover and continue to cook. When the meat is ready, the crust will have become puffy and brown. Serves 6.

Cottage Pie

1 lb (½kg) minced shoulder steak (ground beef)
1 onion, finely chopped
1 oz (25g/2 tbsp) margarine or 2 tbsp oil
1 level tbsp flour
2 teasp tomato purée
¼ pint (125ml/⅔ cup) water
1 tbsp Angostura bitters; or 2 teasp Worcestershire sauce

Grease an ovenproof dish approximately 7 in (18 cm) square and 2 in (5 cm) deep. Heat the fat then add the onion and cook gently until soft and golden; add the meat and continue to cook until it loses its redness. Sprinkle with the flour and bubble for 2 minutes, then add the water and bubble gently for 5 minutes. Stir in the purée, salt, pepper and flavouring sauce. Put the meat into the casserole.

Potato topping:
2 lb (1kg) potatoes
2 level teasp salt
¼ teasp white pepper
3 oz (75g/⅓ cup) margarine

Peel the potatoes, cut them into quarters and put them in a pan containing sufficient boiling water to cover them. Add the salt, bring back to the boil, cover and cook at a steady boil for 15 minutes, or until a piece feels tender when pierced with a thin vegetable knife. Drain the water from the potatoes, return them to the stove in the same pan and shake over gentle heat until all the moisture has evaporated. Add the margarine in small pieces and start whisking either with a balloon whisk or a portable electric mixer. Continue to whisk on a very low heat until the potatoes lighten in colour and look fluffy. Pile on top of the meat and fork into a design. Bake for 30 minutes in a moderate oven (Gas No. 4, 350°F, 180°C) or until golden brown. Serves 4–5.

Shepherd's Pie

This is made with left-over meat, mixed with a savoury sauce. Because the meat is already cooked, the pie is baked for a shorter time at a hotter temperature than the cottage pie.

1 lb (½kg) (minimum) coarsely-minced, cooked braised or roast meat
½ large onion, minced
2 stalks celery, finely cut
Small crushed clove garlic
1 level tbsp chicken fat; or 1 oz (25g/2 tbsp) margarine
2 level tbsp flour
¾ pint (375ml/2 cups) thin gravy or stock
2 teasp chopped parsley
Salt and black pepper
1 recipe mashed potatoes (as in Cottage Pie)

Melt the fat, fry the celery and onion gently for 5 minutes; stir in the flour and cook a further 2 minutes, then add the liquid and garlic and cook until bubbly. Add parsley, salt and black pepper to taste. Stir the sauce into the minced meat. The mixture should be moist but not soggy. Well grease an oven dish, approximately 7 in (18 cm) square and 2 in (5 cm) deep and put in the meat mixture, smooth the potatoes over the top and ridge with a knife into a design. Finally brush with a little melted margarine. Put in hot oven (Gas No. 7, 425°F, 220°C) for 20 minutes until crisp and golden. Serves up to 6.

Take a Slice of Steak

One of the most versatile of meat dishes available to the Jewish cook is braised steak. The original 'braising' dish had a shallow lid into which hot charcoal could be placed. This meant that a dish cooked on top of the stove could have both moist and dry heat applied to it so that it developed a flavour quite different from a stew. Today we use a similar dish, but without the charcoal, for the modern oven can supply the all-round heat more efficiently.

The meat: One can either use blade steaks, or slices of bola (chuck) or first-cut shoulder steak; but in all cases, the meat must be at least ¾ in (1½ cm) thick otherwise it just dissolves into the sauce. If slices of steak are used, cut them into servings before they are cooked.

The braising liquid: One can use tomatoes, paprika-flavoured liquid, or a variety of vegetables to provide the flavour.

The cooking: Always brown the meat quickly but thoroughly to seal the surface; then use just enough liquid barely to cover it—it isn't a stew, remember.

Swiss Steak

1½–2 lb (1¾-kg) first-cut shoulder steak, trimmed of gristle and cut into individual portions ¾ in (1½ cm) thick
1 oz (25g/¼ cup) flour
1 level teasp salt
Pinch of pepper
½ teasp paprika
1 tbsp oil
1 can (15 oz/375g) plum tomatoes
2 onions, finely sliced
2 stalks celery, diced
1 clove garlic, mashed
2 teasp bottled brown sauce

Mix together the flour and seasonings, then, using an old saucer, pound into both sides of the meat using the saucer edge. (This helps to break down the tissues and tenderize the meat.) Heat the fat in a heavy frying pan, quickly brown the pieces of meat on both sides, then put into an oven casserole. Spoon over the remaining ingredients, cover and bake slowly, first at Gas No. 3, 325°F, 170°C for half an hour, then for a further 2 hours at Gas No. 2, 300°F, 150°C. If the sauce is too thin, uncover for the last half-hour. Serves 4–5 generously.

Braised Steak with Mushrooms

2 lb (1kg) bola (chuck) or first-cut shoulder steak (cut ¾ in/1½ cm thick in 2 slices)
2 tbsp flour
1 teasp paprika pepper
3 tbsp oil
1 large onion, sliced
¼ lb (100g/2 cups) button mushrooms
8 fl oz (200ml/1 cup) left-over gravy, or stock cube plus water
2 level teasp salt
¼ teasp ground black pepper
1 level teasp fines herbes or Italian seasoning
1 crushed clove garlic

Have the meat left in two slices. Taking each slice in turn, pound a quarter of the seasoned flour into into each side, using the edge of an old saucer. In a heavy pan or casserole, heat the fat and quickly brown the floured meat on both sides until a rich brown. In the same fat, put the onions and cook until soft and golden, add the whole mushrooms and cook a further 2 minutes. Pour off any unabsorbed fat (but not the sediment). Lay the meat on top of the onions, together with any juice that has oozed out while waiting. Pour on the left-over meat gravy (or stock plus water), and add the garlic, herbs, salt and pepper. Bring to the boil, cover and transfer to a very slow oven (Gas No. 2, 300°F, 150°C) for 2½ hours or until meat is meltingly tender. Serves 4–5 generously.

Blade Steak Braised in Wine

6 blade steaks, beaten well
1 large onion
2 level teasp tomato purée
4 fl oz (100ml/½ cup) red wine
4 fl oz (100ml/½ cup) thin gravy or stock
1 clove garlic
Salt, pepper, sugar
Oil

Heat oil ⅛ in (¼ cm) deep in heavy pan or casserole, then fry the steaks quickly until a rich brown on both sides. Remove. In same fat put thinly sliced onion and cook until limp and golden, then stir in red wine, allow to bubble for a minute, then add liquid, purée, garlic and seasonings. Stir well, then put steaks back on top. Cover and put in slow oven (Gas No. 2, 300°F, 150°C) for 2 hours, until meat is tender, and gravy is thick. Serves 6.

Steak Braised in the Italian Manner

2 lb (1kg) first-cut shoulder steak, trimmed of gristle and cut into individual portions ¾ in (1½ cm) thick
1 oz (25g/¼ cup) flour
1 level teasp salt
10 grinds black pepper
2 tbsp oil
The sauce:
1 large can (20 oz/500g) whole plum tomatoes
1 tbsp olive oil
1 plump clove garlic
2 teasp oregano or basil (fresh if possible, otherwise use dried leaf)
1 tbsp parsley
1 bayleaf
2 level teasp salt and sugar
10 grinds black pepper

Put the drained tomatoes in a small pan with all the remaining sauce ingredients except the herbs. Simmer uncovered for 10 minutes or until it is as thick as ketchup; stir in the herbs. Meanwhile, heat the 2 tablespoons oil and fry the meat (coated in the seasoned flour) until a rich brown on both sides. Put into a casserole and pour over the sauce. Cook at Gas No. 3, 325°F, 170°C, until it starts to bubble (about ½ hour), then turn down to Gas No. 2, 300°F, 150°C, for a further 1½ hours, or until tender. Serves 6.

Steak in the Hungarian Manner

6 blade steaks or 1½–2 lb (¾–1kg) first cut shoulder steak, cut in serving portions ¾ in (1½ cm) thick
Oil
2 lb (1kg) thickly-sliced potatoes
The sauce:
1 large sliced onion
¼ lb (100g/1½ cups) mushrooms, sliced
8 fl oz (200ml/1 cup) boiling liquid (stock, vegetable water or thin gravy)
1 level tbsp tomato purée
2 level teasp paprika pepper
2 level teasp salt
10 grinds black pepper
1 green pepper, seeded and sliced

In a frying pan put oil to a depth of ⅛ in (¼ cm). Heat till very hot, then put well-dried pieces of meat into it, one by one. Cook until a rich brown, turn and cook the other side (do this quickly). Lift from the pan, and leave on a plate. Turn down the heat to moderate, and in the remaining oil, gently cook the onion for 10 minutes, until limp and golden. Add the mushrooms and green pepper and cook a further 5 minutes, then arrange on the bottom of a casserole, and place the meat (with any juices that have oozed out) on top of it. Stir the purée and seasonings into the boiling liquid, then pour on top of the meat. Cover and simmer, either on top of the stove, or preferably in the oven (Gas No. 2, 300°F, 150°C) for 1½ hours. Uncover, add potato slices, then cover and simmer for a further hour. Serves 4–6, depending on amount of meat used.

How to Cook Kosher Steak

Kosher steaks can be grilled successfully under a really efficient grill, but I think they are more satisfactory, particularly for new cooks, when they are sautéd on top of the stove.

Steak Sauté

4 × ½ lb (200g) portions of rib steak, koshered then frozen for 10 days before use
2 tbsp oil
1 tbsp rendered chicken fat (if available); or 1 oz (25g/2 tbsp) margarine
The sauce:
¼ pint (125ml/⅔ cup) dry white or red wine or white vermouth; or the same amount of gravy left over from a roast or a braise; or stock made from a beef bouillon cube
2 teasp Worcestershire sauce
Few grinds black pepper
1 level teasp salt
1 tbsp chopped parsley

Put the defrosted steak on a chopping board and nick it with a sharp knife wherever there is a layer of gristle between the fat and the meat; this stops it from curling in the pan and cooking unevenly. Dry the steak thoroughly, using a paper towel. Choose a frying pan with a good solid machine-ground base. Heat the oil and chicken fat (used for its flavour) for 4 minutes; test the heat by lowering the steak into the fat. As the first corner touches the oil, it should sizzle encouragingly. If it merely makes a sad 'plop', wait a little longer. The fat should cook the first side of the steak to a rich brown in 4 minutes. Remember that the cooking of a steak does not tenderize it—it merely browns the outside appetizingly and cooks the inside to the colour you prefer. Overcook a steak and it gets progressively tougher. Turn the steak when it is browned, using a slotted spoon or spatula rather than a knife, which might pierce it and cause the escape of the juices. After another 4 or 5 minutes the steak should be '*à point*'—that is, pale pink inside and a rich brown outside. To test, press it with your finger. It should resist slightly instead of being soft like a fresh steak. But perhaps more surely, nick it with a knife and have a look. Allow a total of ten minutes, depending on the thickness of the steak. And remember that it will cook a little more in the few minutes it is in the oven, while you are making the sauce. Transfer the cooked steak to a heated platter and turn your attention to the sauce. Pour off all the cooking fat, except for a teaspoonful or two. Turn the heat down and add the liquid. Swirl this liquid round in the pan to loosen the sediment sticking to the bottom. Allow it to simmer for a minute to concentrate the flavour. Add the Worcestershire sauce and the seasonings. Pour over the steak and sprinkle with the chopped parsley. Serves 4.

Minute Steak

6 'minute' steaks (cut by the butcher ¼ in/½ cm thick from frozen shoulder)
2 tbsp oil
1 tbsp chicken fat or 1 oz (25g/2 tbsp) margarine
French mustard (for thinly coating steaks)
The sauce:
2 tbsp finely-chopped onion
2 teasp oil
2 tbsp canned tomatoes, drained; or 4 fresh tomatoes, skinned
2 tbsp chopped parsley
1 tbsp Worcestershire sauce
2 tbsp dry white wine (optional)
4 tbsp meat jelly or good gravy, or ½ crumbled bouillon cube
Salt and black pepper

First prepare the sauce in a small pan. Heat the 2 teaspoons oil for 3 minutes, then add the onion and cook gently until soft and golden—about 5 minutes. Add the tomatoes and cook till amalgamated with the onions, then stir in the Worcestershire sauce, the jelly, gravy or bouillon cube (add a little water if the bouillon cube is used). Leave this mixture to simmer very, very gently whilst you cook the steaks. As these are very large, you will probably need to do them two at a time. Get the oil and margarine or fat very hot, then add the mustard-coated steaks and cook for no more than 1–2 minutes on each side, until just brown. Remove to a hot platter, and fry the remaining steaks. Into the frying pan put the wine (if used), add the sauce and allow to bubble and blend with the pan juices. Add the fried steaks and mix well, then turn on to a hot platter and serve at once. Serves 4–6.

Bistecca alla Pizzaiola (*Steak with Herb and Tomato Sauce*)

For steak which isn't quite so tasty or tender, this is an excellent Italian recipe.

4 rib steaks
2 tbsp oil
1 tbsp chicken fat; or 1 oz (25g/2 tbsp) margarine

The sauce:
1 can Italian peeled plum tomatoes (approx 20 oz/500g); or 1½ lb (680g) fresh tomatoes, skinned
1 tbsp olive oil
2 plump cloves garlic
2 level teasp oregano or basil leaves; or plenty of scissor-cut parsley
1 level teasp salt
1 level teasp sugar
10 grinds black pepper

Put the drained tomatoes or the skinned cut-up fresh ones into a pan with the olive oil, the crushed garlic, salt, pepper and sugar. Simmer with the lid off until thick (5–10 minutes). Stir in the herbs, then keep the sauce hot whilst cooking the steaks. Cook the steaks as described in **Steak Sauté** (see p. 65). Season the cooked steaks in the frying pan with a sprinkle of salt and plenty of ground black pepper, then cover each one with a thick layer of the sauce. Cover the frying pan and allow the steaks to steam in the sauce for 5 minutes, without bubbling. Serves 4.

To Roast a Standing Wing Rib

4–5 lb (2kg) wing rib (standing rib) of beef (about 2 ribs)
2 level teasp dry mustard
1 medium onion, sliced
2 tbsp oil
8 fl oz (200ml/1 cup) cold water

Have the rib at room temperature for 2 hours before cooking. Rub with the dry mustard. Choose a roasting tin just large enough to contain it. (A meat thermometer will take much of the guesswork out of roasting.)

To sear the meat on top of the stove: Heat the oil until almost smoking in a heavy frying pan, then sear the cut sides of the meat until a rich brown. Stand the meat in the roasting tin.

To sear the meat in the oven: Have the oven preheated as high as it will go (Gas No. 10, 500°F, 260°C). Brush the meat all over with the oil, then allow to brown for 20 minutes.

To cook joint seared in either way: Arrange the sliced onion round the meat and pour over the cold water. Cook at Gas No. 4, 350°F, 180°C, allowing 20 minutes per pound (½kg) and 20 minutes over. When the rib is cooked, it will be brown and crisp outside and slightly pink in the centre. If a well-done joint is preferred, allow another 20 minutes. Season the joint with salt and pepper when it is cooked.

Thermometer readings: Medium—160°F (71°C), Well done—170°F (76°C).

To serve: The meat will carve much more easily if left to stand a little, so it is as well to take it out of the oven whilst the first course is being eaten, and leave it in the warming drawer.

The gravy:
2 teasp fat from the roasting tin
Salt and pepper
2 level teasp flour
½ pint (250ml/1¼ cups) bouillon
3 fl oz (75ml/⅓ cup) red wine (optional)

Remove the onion from the roasting tin, together with all but the two teaspoons fat. Stir in the flour and leave to brown a little, then add the bouillon and wine (if used) and stir really well to incorporate the meat juices into the gravy. Season to taste and leave to simmer gently until required. Serves 6 generously.

Yorkshire Pudding

As the batter for Yorkshire pudding—the traditional accompaniment to roast beef—must be made with water instead of milk, it should be enriched with a little oil and extra egg. I find it cooks most satisfactorily in individual deep patty tins—the non-stick variety are especially good.

Individual Yorkshire Puddings

2 oz (50g/½ cup) plain flour
1 level teasp salt
1 large egg
¼ pint (125ml/⅔ cup) water
2 teasp oil

To mix in the blender: Put all the ingredients in the blender goblet and blend for 1 minute.

To mix by hand: Sieve the flour and salt into a bowl, make a well in the centre, and add the whole egg, the oil and a little of the water. Stir in the flour gradually from the sides, making sure the mixture is kept smooth and free from lumps. Add about half the liquid gradually. Beat well for 5 minutes, then stir in the remaining liquid, cover and leave in a cool place for 30 minutes.

To bake: Turn oven to Gas No. 7, 425°F, 220°C—do this while the meat is resting in warming drawer. Put a little nut of meat fat or ½ teaspoon oil into 12 individual patty tins. When fat smokes, half fill each patty tin with the batter. Return to the oven and bake for 15 minutes or until a rich brown. Serves 6.

Lamb en Casserole

Lamb is an all-the-year meat because although we usually associate it with the spring, the mature lambs of autumn make equally good eating, provided good quality meat is used.

Know your lamb: Lamb should have pinkish meat, creamy yellow fat and bone that is faintly purple tinged. Flinty white bone means mutton! Shoulder chops, which are not tender enough to grill, make an excellent casserole dish for a family meal. The following dishes are particularly succulent.

Lamb Chops in Wine

6 large shoulder chops
1 heaped tbsp flour
2 level teasp salt
Good pinch of pepper
1 oz (25g/2 tbsp) margarine
1 teasp oil
12 small onions, peeled; or 1 large onion, finely chopped
Pinch of dried rosemary
¼ pint (125ml/⅔ cup) dry white wine such as Graves
¼ lb (100g/2 cups) sliced mushrooms
1 large pkt frozen peas
12–18 new potatoes (pre-cooked if fresh)

Wipe the chops with a paper towel and trim off all fat except a thin edging. Coat the chops in the flour seasoned with salt and pepper. Melt the margarine and oil in a heavy frying pan, put in the chops and brown slowly on both sides, until a rich brown (15 minutes). Remove to a casserole as they brown. In the same pan put the peeled onions and cook gently for 5 minutes. Then add the rosemary and white wine (the same amount of chicken stock may be substituted). Stir and scrape to mix the sediment into the sauce. Pour the sauce over the chops, cover and simmer in a moderate oven (Gas No. 3, 325°F, 170°C) for 1 hour. Take off the lid, add the mushrooms, peas and potatoes and baste well with the sauce. Cover and cook for another 15–20 minutes. Serves 6.

Lamb in the Provençale Fashion

6 shoulder chops or 2 lb (1kg) middle neck of lamb, boned out and cubed
1 tbsp oil
1 can (7 oz/175g) tomatoes or 4 fresh ones, skinned
1 fat clove garlic or ¼ teasp chopped garlic
1 medium onion, cubed
1 large carrot, cubed
1 teasp brown sugar
2 teasp chopped parsley
½ pint (250ml/1¼ cups) chicken stock
4 fl oz (100ml/½ cup) white vermouth or white wine such as Graves
2 level teasp salt
10 grinds black pepper
Good pinch ground nutmeg
¼ lb (100g/2 cups) mushrooms
1 level tbsp cornflour (cornstarch)
2 tbsp cold water

Heat the oil in a heavy frying pan (or oven-to-table casserole), and fry the meat quickly until evenly browned. Remove the meat and add the onion and carrots, sprinkling them with 1 teaspoon brown sugar to hasten the browning. Replace the meat on top of the vegetables, and pour in the chicken stock and vermouth (or wine). Season with salt, pepper, and nutmeg and sprinkle with the parsley. Top with the fresh or canned tomatoes, cover and simmer gently for 1½ hours top-of-stove, or transfer to the oven (Gas No. 2, 300°F, 150°C) for 2 hours. Add the mushrooms during the last half-hour. Ten minutes before serving, stir in 1 level tablespoon cornflour, mixed with 2 tablespoons cold water. This serves 6, and is best with plain boiled potatoes or rice to mop up the delicious sauce.

Lamb and Aubergine (Eggplant) Casserole
(*Patlican Kebabi*)

2 lbs (1kg) boned lamb shoulder cut into 1 in (2½ cm) cubes, or 6 shoulder chops
2 medium onions
1 fat clove garlic, crushed
½ pint (250ml/1¼ cups) stock from meat cube
4 tbsp oil
1 heaped tbsp tomato purée
2 level teasp each sugar and salt
½ level teasp oregano
10 grinds black pepper
2–3 aubergines (eggplant), approx 1½ lb/¾kg

Peel aubergines and cut into ½ in (1 cm) cubes. Put in salted water for half an hour, then squeeze dry in the palm of the hand. Fry in the oil until golden brown, then lift from pan with perforated spoon and reserve. To the pan add the trimmed chops or cubed meat and brown lightly to seal the meat. Lift meat out with perforated spoon and put into casserole. To same fat, add the thinly-sliced onions and sauté gently until golden brown, then add the tomatoes, seasonings and stock. Pour the onions and sauce over the meat, transfer to oven and cook (Gas No. 2, 300°F, 150°C) for 1½ hours. Uncover and add the aubergines, cover, cook for a further 30 minutes until meat is tender. Serves 4–5.

To freeze: Cook meat 1½ hours, cool, add sautéd aubergines and freeze. To use—defrost and reheat for 30 minutes.

To Grill Lamb Chops

Herbed Lamb Chops

This is the basic method for grilling first-cut chops. The herbs can be omitted, but they do give added piquancy to the meat.

8 first-cut lamb chops, ¾ in (1½ cm) thick
1 oz (25g/2 tbsp) margarine (melted)
1 tbsp oil
1 cut clove garlic
1 level teasp each of dried basil, rosemary and salt
1 tbsp lemon juice

An hour before the chops are to be grilled, put the oil and melted margarine into a shallow dish, wide enough to hold the chops in one layer. Add the garlic, herbs and lemon juice. Put the chops into the dish and turn to coat them with the oil. Leave for an hour, turning once or twice, during this time, so that they are well and truly steeped in the flavoured fat.

To grill: Fifteen minutes before serving time, heat the grill for 3 minutes. Arrange the chops on the grill pan, pouring over any excess oil. Put the grill pan 4 in (10 cm) below the source of heat and grill the chops for 5 minutes on each side, or until the chops are a rich brown. Serves 4.

To Grill Skewered Lamb

Boned shoulder of lamb can be cubed and grilled on skewers in the Middle Eastern manner. It is, however, essential to soak it in a marinade in order to tenderize it. The resulting 'Shish Kebab' has crunchy brown cubes of meat that remain juicy inside. Serve with a pilaff and a green salad.

Shish Kebab

2 lb (1kg) boned shoulder of lamb
12 mushrooms (optional)
Few bayleaves
Marinade:
$\frac{1}{4}$ pint (125ml/$\frac{2}{3}$ cup) olive oil
4 tbsp white wine vinegar
1 onion, finely grated
2 level teasp salt
Small bunch parsley
1 teasp oregano

Have the boned lamb cut in $1\frac{1}{2}$ in ($3\frac{1}{2}$ cm) squares. Put in a bowl (with the mushrooms) and pour over the marinade. Leave at least 2 hours, but overnight will do no harm. Drain well. Thread on 4 skewers, alternately with the marinated mushrooms (if used) and an occasional bayleaf. Cook under a fierce grill for 15–20 minutes, until crunchy outside and just done inside. Baste frequently with the marinade. Serves 4.

To Roast a Shoulder of Lamb

A thick shoulder of lamb is the prime kosher roasting joint of lamb. Care in the cooking will ensure that the roast has a savoury, crunchy skin, whilst the meat itself is juicy and tender.

4 lb (2kg) thick-cut shoulder of lamb
1 large onion
Salt, pepper
Flour
1 clove garlic (optional)
1 tbsp fat

For glazing: 1 tablespoon of any of the following—honey, marmalade, redcurrant or cranberry jelly.

Rub the meat all over with flour, salt, pepper and seasoning. Slice the onion and put it with 1 tablespoon fat into the bottom of the roasting-tin. Put in a small wire rack and place the meat on that (thus allowing the air to circulate and preventing the meat getting greasy). If you like garlic, put slivers of the peeled clove in between the bone and the flesh, but don't overdo it, or the delicate lamb flavour will be lost. Roast at Gas No. 4, 350°F, 180°C, for 30 minutes to the pound ($\frac{1}{2}$kg), allowing 15 or 20 minutes extra.

There is no need to baste the meat. Fifteen minutes before the joint is ready, drain off most of the fat and spread the meat with any of the conserves I have suggested. This will not only add a gorgeous flavour, but also help to achieve a really crispy skin.

To make the gravy: Lift out the meat and keep warm (a stainless steel carving dish is ideal for cutting the meat on). Drain off all the fat and stir into the sediment 1 teaspoon sugar and 1 teaspoon flour. Then add 1 cup vegetable water or stock made from a cube and seasoning. Boil vigorously for 2–3 minutes. This makes a thin, meaty gravy, which tastes of lamb, without being greasy. A fruity gravy can be made by omitting the conserve and instead pouring $\frac{1}{2}$ cup orange juice, and when in season, $\frac{1}{2}$ cup chopped mint over the joint, *after* the fat has been discarded. Baste several times during the last 15 minutes, then pour the pan juices as gravy. Serves 6.

VARIATIONS

Roast Lamb with Orange and Wine Sauce: Roast the lamb as described. Halfway through the cooking time, pour over 4 fl oz (100ml/½ cup) each of orange juice and cooking wine. Do not brush the meat with conserve; instead sprinkle the meat with demerara sugar 15 minutes before it is done. Use the pan juices for gravy.

Roast Lamb with Redcurrant Sauce: Roast the lamb as described, but omit the conserves. Fifteen minutes before the lamb is cooked, sprinkle it with demerara sugar. Make this sauce:

Redcurrant sauce:
2 level teasp flour
2 level teasp dry mustard
2 tbsp redcurrant jelly
¼ pint (125ml/⅔ cup) meat stock or vegetable water

Put the meat on a dish to keep warm. Pour off all but 2 teaspoons of the fat and stir the flour into it and the sediment from the roast. Add the mustard, redcurrant jelly and stock. Stir vigorously and allow to bubble until the sauce has become slightly thickened and glossy; serve with the lamb. Serves 6.

A Joint of Veal

High quality veal is always expensive in relation to beef and lamb because it must come from an animal between 16 and 24 weeks old. Coming from a young animal, veal is delicate in flavour and extremely tender when correctly cooked. I do not think that one can truly dry-roast kosher veal as the only suitable joint—the shoulder—is without any fat whatsoever. Therefore, I think it should be braised—that is, browned to seal in the flavour, then cooked in moist heat on a bed of aromatic vegetables. Cooked in this way, it is one of the most delicious of kosher meat dishes.

Braised Stuffed Shoulder of Veal

Ask the butcher to bone out the blade end of a shoulder of veal—this bone makes superb barley soup, or it can be frozen to use in a veal casserole.

3–4 lb (1½–2kg) shoulder of veal
1 large carrot and onion, finely diced
2 bayleaves
3 tbsp oil
1 oz (25g/2 tbsp) margarine
2 teasp brown sugar
Salt
Flour
Stuffing:
2 oz (50g/¼ cup) margarine
1 small onion, finely chopped
5 oz (125g/1½ cups) fresh breadcrumbs
1 level tbsp chopped parsley
1 level teasp mixed Italian dried herbs
1 level teasp salt
Pinch of paprika and pepper
1 egg

First make the stuffing: Melt the margarine and gently fry the onion until soft and golden. Put the crumbs into a large bowl with the herbs and seasonings, then moisten with the onion and fat. Beat the egg to blend, then stir that into the crumb mixture; the stuffing should be moist, but not 'cloggy'. Salt the pocket of the meat, and sew up if necessary to make a neat aperture. Loosely fill with the stuffing, then sew or skewer closed. In a heavy oven-to-table casserole, melt the oil and margarine, put in the stuffed meat, lightly dusted with flour. Brown steadily on all sides, adding the chopped vegetables when the meat is turned, and sprinkling with the brown sugar to ensure even browning. Add the bayleaves and cover.

To braise: Cook in a slow moderate oven (Gas No. 3, 325°F, 170°C) for 2 hours, until the veal is a rich brown and absolutely tender.

To make the gravy: Remove the meat to a serving dish and keep warm. To the casserole, add 10 fl oz (250ml/1¼ cups) beef bouillon and simmer on top of the stove for 5 minutes. Mix 2 level teaspoons cornflour with 2 tablespoons cold water or sherry. Take off as much fat as possible from the casserole, stir in the cornflour and bubble for 3 minutes. Serve with the veal, cut in thick slices.

To press remainder of the veal: When sufficient veal to serve hot has been sliced, force the remainder of the joint into a small basin, covering it first with a saucer and then with a 2 lb (1kg) weight. When cold it can be turned out and will slice thinly.

Serves 8 hot—or 4 with one hot meal and one cold.

VARIATION

Stuffed Breast of Veal: Flatten the breast with a cutlet bat or saucer, spread with stuffing. Roll up and tie in four places. Brown and braise as for **Stuffed Shoulder of Veal.**

Veal Chops

Savoury Veal Chops

It is important to brown the chops thoroughly to develop the best flavour in this tasty dish.

6 large first-cut veal chops, cut 1 in ($2\frac{1}{2}$ cm) thick
1 tbsp chicken fat; or 1 oz (25g/2 tbsp) margarine and 1 teasp oil
3 tbsp spring onions (scallions), sliced
1 teasp salt, pinch of pepper
1 clove garlic, crushed to a paste
$\frac{1}{4}$ pint (125ml/$\frac{2}{3}$ cup) dry white vermouth or white wine
2 teasp tomato purée
$\frac{1}{4}$ pint (125ml/$\frac{2}{3}$ cup) rich gravy or stock
Chopped parsley

Dry the chops with paper towels (this facilitates browning), then fry the chops in the hot fat, 3 at a time (allow about 4 minutes each side). As they are browned put in a shallow, lidded casserole, sprinkling well with salt and pepper. Now remove all but 3 tablespoons of fat from the pan. Put in the garlic and spring onions and cook for a minute, then add the wine and tomato purée, and allow to bubble for a few minutes, scraping any residue from the bottom of the pan into the liquid. Pour over the chops, cover and put in a slow to moderate oven (Gas No. 3, 325°F, 170°C) for 1–$1\frac{1}{2}$ hours, or until they feel tender. Don't allow the liquid to boil, or the meat will be tough. For family eating, the bouillon or gravy can now be added, and the meat served from the casserole. For a dinner party, remove the chops to a serving dish. Add the juices from the casserole to the gravy and bring to the boil, cooking until slightly thickened, then pour over the meat and sprinkle with chopped parsley. Serves 6.

Veal Chops with Mushrooms

4–6 first-cut veal chops, about $1\frac{1}{4}$ in (3 cm) thick
3 tbsp oil
1 level tbsp chicken fat or margarine
1 oz (25g/$\frac{1}{4}$ cup) flour
1 level teasp salt
Pinch black pepper
Pinch dried tarragon
$\frac{1}{4}$ pint (125ml/$\frac{2}{3}$ cup) dry white wine
$\frac{1}{4}$ pint (125ml/$\frac{2}{3}$ cup) strong beef bouillon
$\frac{1}{2}$ lb (200g/4 cups) fresh mushrooms sliced in 4
1 tbsp lemon juice
1 oz (25g/2 tbsp) margarine
1 medium onion, finely chopped
$\frac{1}{2}$ clove garlic, crushed

Mix flour, salt and pepper, coat chops thinly with this mixture. Heat oil and chicken fat in heavy pan and sauté chops until a rich brown on both sides. Lift out of pan. Whilst chops are browning, sprinkle the sliced mushrooms with lemon juice, then toss quickly in the margarine for 5 minutes. Leave for the moment. When the chops are brown, add onions to same fat and cook for a further 5 minutes, or until golden. Now stir in any remaining flour and cook for 3 minutes, then pour in the wine and the stock, and stir in the crushed garlic and the tarragon, together with the mushrooms and their juices. Cover and simmer for $\frac{3}{4}$ hour or until tender; or transfer to an oven casserole and simmer, covered, for 1 hour (Gas No. 2, 300°F, 150°C). Serves 4–6, depending on the number of chops. May be reheated.

Veal Escalopes or Schnitzels

These make extremely speedy (if expensive) main dishes, so it is useful to have a stock of frozen escalopes in the freezer. It is advisable to beat them with a metal cutlet bat to flatten and tenderize them.

Veal and Chicken Livers Sautés

6 schnitzels
6 chicken livers, cut in 3 then grilled to kosher
$\frac{1}{4}$ pint (125ml/$\frac{2}{3}$ cup) drained Italian tomatoes; or equal quantity of good gravy
4 tbsp oil
Salt and pepper

Mix 1 level tablespoon flour with 1 level teaspoon salt and plenty of black pepper. Pound schnitzels as thinly as possible, then toss in seasoned flour. Put 4 tablespoons oil in a heavy frying pan. Cook the schnitzels on both sides quickly until a pale gold. As each cooks, remove to a casserole and keep hot. Add livers, cook quickly for 3 minutes, stir in tomatoes or gravy and cook for another few minutes, blending well with the pan juices and seasoning highly. Transfer to casserole with veal. Cover and keep hot (without bubbling any further) until required.

To serve with parsleyed noodles: Cook $\frac{1}{2}$ lb (200g) broad noodles in boiling salted water until tender. Rinse with cold water to remove excess starch. Put 2 oz (50g) margarine in heavy pan or stove-proof casserole, and add a generous tablespoon chopped parsley and several grinds of black pepper. Add the noodles and toss thoroughly until well coated with parsley and steaming hot. Serves 6.

Escalopes de Veau Basquaise

4–6 escalopes of veal, $\frac{3}{8}$ in ($\frac{3}{4}$ cm) thick
2 tbsp olive oil
Seasoned flour
1 clove garlic, finely chopped
3 skinned tomatoes
2 teasp tomato purée
4 tbsp dry white or rosé wine
Vegetables:
1 large onion, sliced
1 large green pepper, diced
1 small aubergine (eggplant), cut into $\frac{1}{2}$ in (1 cm) cubes
Pinch of chopped rosemary
$\frac{1}{4}$ lb (100g/1 cup) stoned black olives
2 teasp chopped parsley
4 fl oz (100ml/$\frac{1}{2}$ cup) chicken or veal stock
3 tbsp olive oil

To cook the vegetables: Heat the oil gently in a wide, heavy casserole or frying pan, then fry the onion, the pepper and the aubergine until golden brown. Then add the cut up tomatoes, the purée, black olives and herbs. Stir in the stock and leave to bubble gently (covered), whilst the meat is cooked—this can be done early and reheated.

To cook the meat: Dip the meat briefly in the seasoned flour, then fry slowly in the olive oil until golden brown. Add the wine, cover and simmer for 3 minutes. Uncover, add the vegetables and leave on a low heat (without further bubbling) until required. Serves 4.

Veal Escalopes with Vermouth (*Scallopine alla Vermouth*)

4 escalopes, pounded thin, or the equivalent in scallopine—little bits of escalope veal
4 tbsp oil
1 oz (25g/2 tbsp) margarine or chicken fat
1 onion, finely chopped
3 fl oz (75ml/$\frac{1}{3}$ cup) sweet vermouth
1 teasp tomato purée
Pinch of mace
Seasoned flour

Roll the thin pieces of veal in seasoned flour; in the oil cook the finely-chopped onion until soft and golden, then brown the meat in the same pan. Lift onto a plate, and to the pan juices add the vermouth, tomato purée and the mace. Simmer to reduce until syrupy (about 3 minutes), then return the meat to the pan, heat through in the sauce. Serve from the pan. Serves 4.

Veal en Casserole

Stewing veal can be treated either in the French manner (see **Sauté de Veau Marengo,** p. 273) or in the Italian style, when it is simmered in a concentrated tomato and herb sauce. This is one of my favourite stews.

Veal Stew in the Italian Style

2 lb (1kg) stewing veal, cubed
1 tbsp chicken fat or 2 tbsp oil
1 level teasp salt
10 grinds black pepper
1 can (14 oz/350g) peeled Italian plum tomatoes
2 level teasp sugar
2 level teasp leaf basil
1 bayleaf
1 clove garlic, crushed
¼ pint (125ml/⅔ cup) hot water and ½ beef bouillon cube (or gravy)
1 tbsp parsley

Put the stock (or gravy), tomatoes, salt, pepper, sugar, crushed garlic, bayleaf and basil into a small pan and simmer gently until almost as thick as ketchup. Melt chicken fat in a heavy casserole and brown the meat on all sides (1 teaspoon brown sugar sprinkled in as it cooks will hasten the process). As it browns, sprinkle the meat with a further level teaspoon salt and a few grinds of pepper. When a rich brown, add the tomato sauce. Cook very gently in oven for 2 hours (Gas No. 2, 300°F, 150°C) or until absolutely tender. If the sauce seems a little too thin, take the lid off for the last 10 minutes. Just before serving, sprinkle in 1 tablespoon parsley. Serves 6.

Veal in Wine Sauce

Cold roast veal has an almost chicken-like texture that takes kindly to careful reheating in a well-seasoned sauce. Served with a pilaff of rice, flavoured with crushed cardamon seeds.

2 cups left-over roast veal, diced
1 pkt (8 oz/200g) frozen peas, cooked
¼ lb (100g/2 cups) mushrooms
½ onion, chopped
¼ pint (125ml/⅔ cup) white wine
½ pint (250ml/1¼ cups) chicken or veal stock (made with left-over gravy jelly if possible, or use cube)
1 tbsp chicken fat
1 oz (25g/¼ cup) flour
1 egg yolk

Melt chicken fat, add onion and cook for a minute; add sliced mushrooms and cook 2 more minutes. Stir in flour, then bubble for a further minute. Add wine and cook for 2 minutes, then take off heat and whisk in hot stock. Return to heat to cook for 2–3 minutes. Season with salt and pepper. Pour sauce onto egg yolk and stir well, then blend in veal and cooked peas. Keep hot in top of double saucepan till needed or leave in low oven.

Pilaff:
12 oz (300g/1¾ cups) rice
½ large onion
2 oz (50g/¼ cup) margarine
6 crushed cardamon seeds
1 bayleaf
1 teasp paprika
1½ pints (750ml/4 cups) chicken stock

Fry onion till golden in margarine; add rice and continue to cook for 3 minutes. Add hot stock and seasonings. Cover and cook either in moderate oven or over low heat top-of-stove for 18 minutes. Serves 6.

Sausages and Other Preserved Meats

While the Jews learned to fry fish from the Ancient Egyptians, it is certain that they learned to salt meat and make sausages from their later masters, the Greeks and the Romans.

As far back as the 9th century B.C.E., one can read of this first 'convenience food', the sausage, in Homer's *Odyssey*. Later Greek writers wrote frequently of it, and the playwright, Epicharmis, even wrote a play in 500 B.C.E., with the title of 'Sausage' or 'Orya' as the Greeks called this favourite food.

The Greek generic term has not survived (though in 14th-century France, the sausage-maker was still known as 'cuisiner-oyer'), but some of the recipes—and certainly the name of one variety, salami (named after the Greek city of Salamis), have not only survived, but are used almost unchanged to this very day.

Basically a sausage consists of minced lean meat and fat, flavoured variously with spices and curing salts. The permutations of these mixtures are almost without number. In particular, the 'filler' or meat extender, varies according to the era and the locality.

As times grow hard, and the meat content of a sausage decreases, the filler often becomes the predominating ingredient. Thus 'gefüllte kishke'—the homemade sausage made in every European Jewish household a generation or so ago, consisted of beef casings, stuffed with a meatless mixture of fat, onions and flour, almost identical to the 'white puddings' made by farm workers in the West Country of England.

However, to most people, it is the spicing of the sausage to which they owe their allegiance, and which is the one common denominator (no matter how varied) that distinguishes the sausage from any other culinary concoction.

Today, the main sausage seasoning is allspice or Jamaica pepper, which has the aroma and properties of pepper, cloves, cinnamon and nutmeg, and which the French most logically call 'quatre épices'. Basil, pennyroyal and marjoram are the favoured English herbs. As to salami, that which comes from Milan is flavoured with ginger, nutmeg and white wine; that from Sardinia with red pepper; and that from Hungary with garlic, paprika and white wine; Mortadella is flavoured with crushed coriander. All of these sausages can be bought in a kosher version.

The Varieties of Kosher Sausage

Even in Roman times, some sausages were sold uncooked and some were boiled, some were made from fresh meat and some were smoked. Over the centuries, these different varieties have been divided into three main classifications.

1. *Fresh sausages:* These are made from fresh, uncured meats, and are known in the delicatessen as 'frying sausages'. They are highly perishable and should be kept under refrigeration for no more than a day or two before they are used.

2. *Cooked sausages:* These are also made principally from fresh uncured meats, though a little cured meat may be added to the mixture. However, they are always cooked after they have been filled, and are sometimes smoked as well before they are sold. In this category are the liver sausages, as well as the bolognas, frankfurters and viennas. These are usually artificially coloured pink.

3. *Dry sausages:* This is the category into which fit all the salamis. These sausages have 20 per cent or more of their natural moisture removed when they are dried; the higher the percentage the longer their 'shelf life'.

Salami is made with fresh meat and saltpetre which is then cured for two or three days. After the sausages have been encased they are either cooked in a smokehouse at a high temperature and then dried in air (as, for example, the cooked salamis) or they may be dried without smoking, as with the majority of those salamis of Hungarian and German origin. These are the sausages that are used on the hors-d'œuvre tray, or as part of the cold table. Some are eaten raw as an appetiser; others, such as the saveloy, are first gently poached, then eaten hot or cold.

Wurst

Perhaps the best known Jewish sausage is this German version of Italian salami, which is made in countless varieties. Frying wurst is pink and lightly spiced and makes an excellent addition to a mixed grill, or to fried eggs. It will keep for a week under refrigeration and makes a most delicious alfresco supper with chips.

Wurst Pfannkuchen (*Sausage Pancake*)

½–¾ lb (200–300g) frying wurst (enough slices to cover the bottom of an 8 or 9 in/20–23 cm frying pan)
4 large eggs
2 teasp cold water
Pinch of salt
Few grinds of black pepper
2 teasp margarine or oil

Heat the empty pan over medium heat for 3 minutes, then put in the fat, and as soon as it is melted, lay the slices of wurst (cut ¼ in/½ cm thick) side by side. Cook steadily on one side only for several minutes until browned. Meanwhile, beat the eggs with the water and seasonings until barely blended, then pour over the wurst. Cook the mixture without stirring over low heat, until the underside is golden brown, then put it 6 in (15 cm) from a gentle grill, and cook until the top is set and puffy—about 2 minutes. Slide onto a heated platter (or serve straight from the pan) in wedges. Serves 4.

Wurst Frittata

1 large potato, raw or cooked, cut in ¼ in (½ cm) cubes
1 fat green or red pepper
1 medium onion, finely chopped
Oil or chicken fat to fry
4 oz (100g) wurst, sliced and cut in strips
2 tomatoes, peeled and chopped
6 eggs
Salt and black pepper

Cut the pepper in half and remove the bitter seeds and white pith 'ribs'. In a frying pan about 9 in (23 cm) in diameter, put oil or chicken fat to a depth of ⅛ in (¼ cm). Cook the onion and potato until both are soft and golden. (If the potato is raw, do this with the lid on for 5 minutes, then take off to brown the ingredients.) Add the pepper (cut in thin shreds) and the wurst and continue to cook for another 3 or 4 minutes, then stir in the tomatoes and mix well, simmering until they are softened. Beat the eggs with the salt and pepper, then pour over the vegetables. Cook as an omelette, lifting cooked mixture to allow uncooked to flow underneath. Finally, put under the grill to brown the top. Serves 4 generously.

Home-Pickled Meats

Hot salt beef, sandwiched between Sunday-morning-fresh rye bread, is surely the quintessence of the Jewish cuisine; yet the Irish pickle beef in almost exactly the same fashion! The main difference lies in the cut of meat. The Jewish cook uses a thick slice of brisket—that humble but tasty cut; the Irish cook uses a hindquarters cut such as topside or round.

Many butchers will sell you a piece of their own pickled raw meat to cook at home, but if you want to enjoy the genuine article with all the nuances of flavour found only in a home pickle, it's worth preparing the pickling solution oneself. It is, however, not worth using a piece of meat smaller than specified. If there is no room in the refrigerator, the meat can be left to pickle in a cool shed or larder—the warmer the temperature, the more quickly will the pickle work. Ideally the temperature should be about 40°F, 4°C (as in a cool cellar). At a refrigeration temperature of 34°F, 1°C it will take 7 to 10 days. You can tell when the meat is ready to cook, because it will be pink right through to the centre.

Pickled Brisket (*Corned Beef*)

Warm boiled pickled brisket (called 'corned beef' in America) is delicious with boiled potatoes and quartered hearts of cabbage; or with chipped potatoes or latkes, or served in sandwiches.

Lightly pressed and cold, it is superb on a buffet or in white-bread sandwiches, served with a crisp heimishe pickled cucumber. In the recipe I give what I have found makes a pleasant but not overspiced or over-salty pickle.

5–6 lb (2½–3kg) brisket (not rolled)
6 oz (150g/½ cup) coarse salt
2 level teasp saltpetre
3 oz (75g/½ cup) demerara (brown) sugar
1 fat clove garlic
1 teasp mixed pickling spices
1 level teasp crushed peppercorns
2 crumbled bayleaves

I find it convenient to pickle and cook the meat in the same dish—a cast-iron enamelled casserole, such as one would use to braise a fowl. Otherwise, an earthenware dish can be used for the pickling. Mix the sugar and salt together, and rub into the meat on all sides. Put the meat into the chosen dish and scatter with all the remaining ingredients and the rest of the salt/sugar mixture. Add cold water to come just to the top of the meat (liquid will also ooze out of it as the days go by.) Refrigerate for 7–10 days, turning the meat daily.

To cook: Take from the liquid and wash well. Pour out the liquid from the dish and put back the meat. Cover with cold water and bring slowly to the boil on top of the stove. Remove all the scum with a spoon dipped in cold water. Now add a large onion and 2 bayleaves. Cover and simmer very gently for 4 hours. You can do this top-of-stove (though I find it easier to keep it at the right temperature in a very slow oven, as one would cook soup).

Lift the meat out onto a board. Part of it can now be carved rather thickly and served hot. After dinner, fit the rest into a basin, cover with a plate and several weights. Leave under pressure until cold. Foil wrap and refrigerate. Use as required. Can be frozen. Serves 8–10.

Home Pickled Tongue

6 lb (3kg) tongue (pickle as for Pickled Brisket)
To cook:
1 pickled tongue
1 onion
2 cloves garlic
2 bayleaves

Lift the tongue from the pickle and wash thoroughly in cold water. Put in a deep soup pan with all the remaining ingredients. Cover with cold water. Bring slowly to the boil, then simmer for 3½ hours or until absolutely tender. Add extra boiling water to keep the tongue covered. Let the tongue cool in the stock, then remove the root and the skin. Coil the tongue round itself in a casserole or tin into which it will barely fit. Weight down with a plate and weights and leave until quite cold. Unmould and slice. Serves 8–10.

Potatoe Latkes

You will need:

6 medium - sized potatoes
1 small onion
1 teaspoon salt
1 egg
3 tablespoons flourm matza meal or bread crumbs

Wash, pare and grate raw potatoes. Strain but not too dry, and use juice for soup or sauce. If juice is retained, a little more flour will be needed for thickening. Grate and add the onion; add salt and the egg. Beat well. Mix remaining ingredients and beat into potatoes; mix well. Drop by spoonfuls into hot fat that is deep enough to almost cover the cake. Brown on both sides. Drain on absorbent paper. Serve with applesauce, if desired. Serves 4 or 5.

Pizza Rollies

1 cup grated kosher cheddar cheese
1/3 cup canned tomatoe sauce
pinch of dried oregano or chili powder
1/2 cup chopped ripe olives
3 tablespoons melted butter or margarine
14 thin bread slices (fresh and easy to roll)

Blen cheese, tomatoe sauce, oregano and olives. Trim crusts from bread; spread slices with mixture. Roll up each slice like a jolly roll; fasten with pick (each may be cut in half if preferred). Brush roll-ups with melted butter; place on baking sheet; refrigerate a half hour before baking. Heat oven to 400 degrees. Bake about 15 minutes or until brown. Serve hot.

Potatoe Latkes

You will need:

6 medium - sized potatoes
1 small onion
1 teaspoon salt
1 egg
3 tablespoons flourm matza meal or breat crumbs

Wash, pare and grate raw potatoes. Strain but not too dry, and use juice for soup or sauce. If juice is retained, a little more flour will be needed for thickening. Grate and add the onion; add salt and the egg. Beat well. Mix remaining ingredients and beat into potatoes; mix well. Drop by spoonfuls into hot fat that is deep enough to almost cover the cake. Brown on both sides. Drain on absorbent paper. Serve with applesauce, if desired. Serves 4 or 5.

Pizza Rollies

1 cup grated kosher cheddar cheese
1/3 cup canned tomatoe sauce
pinch of dried oregano or chili powder
1/2 cup chopped ripe olives
3 tablespoons melted butter or margarine
14 thin bread slices (fresh and easy to roll)

Blen cheese, tomatoe sauce, oregano and olives. Trim crusts from bread; spread slices with mixture. Roll up each slice like a jelly roll; fasten with pick (each may be cut in half if preferred). Brush roll-ups with melted butter; place on baking sheet; refrigerate a half hour before baking. Heat oven to 400 degrees. Bake about 15 minutes or until brown. Serve hot.

Poultry

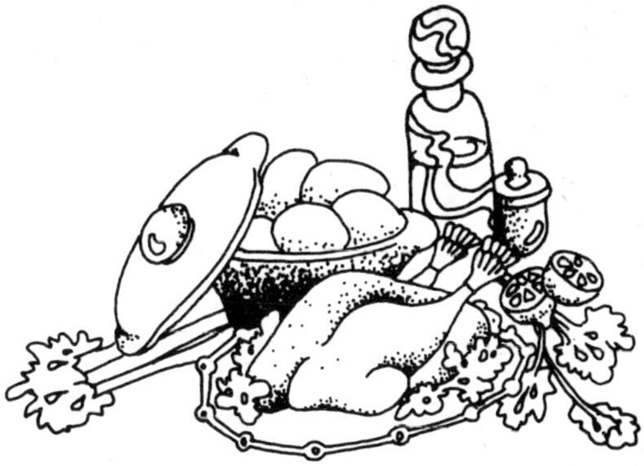

Poultry is a weekend regular in almost every Jewish household, particularly with those families who originally hailed from Poland—the home of the fowl. Cleaning and koshering the bird used to be one of the more onerous jobs involved in preparing for Shabbat; but nowadays most birds come ready-koshered, scalded and trussed.

Be Fair to the Fowl

The most popular bird for the kosher table—for which it is specially bred—is about 12 months old; mature enough to make excellent soup, yet still young enough to be tender and flavoursome *en casserole*. A top quality bird should have a full round breast and white skin, and if it is to be braised rather than boiled, it should be free of excessive subcutaneous fat. However, the slow cooking in liquid that is necessary to make a good pot of soup will tenderize even an over-fat grandmother hen. Fowls should weigh between 4½–6 lb (2–3kg) ready dressed, and besides the main dish, they provide such 'extras' as soup, stuffed helzel and chopped liver—the true 'package' meal!

To Render Chicken Fat

Before a fowl is boiled or casseroled, the excess fat and the fat-impregnated skin at the back should be removed so that it can be rendered down for use in dishes such as chopped liver and knaidlach.

Chicken fat
Fat-impregnated skin
1 onion, roughly chopped

Cut up the fat with the skin into 1 in (2½ cm) squares, and add the onion. Put into a small earthenware dish—add no water—and leave in a low oven until the fat has melted (this may take an hour or two). Strain and store in the refrigerator.

To Boil a Fowl

Follow the instructions for boiling a fowl for **Chicken Soup** (see p. 27).

To Brown a Boiled Fowl

If you wish to cook the bird in the soup, but prefer to have it hot and brown rather than cold and boiled, proceed as follows:

Cut the legs off the raw fowl before boiling—this makes the bird easier to handle. Cook the bird and legs in the soup until barely tender (about 2 hours) or when the flesh of the leg feels soft when prodded with a fork. Lift the bird from the soup and leave covered until needed.

Next day, place the bird and legs in a casserole. Skim the fat off the soup, put it in a frying pan and cook a large sliced onion in it until soft and golden. Sprinkle the bird with a light dusting of paprika and flour, then pour over it the fried onions and the fat in which they were cooked. Cover and cook for 40 minutes (Gas No. 5, 375°F, 190°C) or until the bird looks brown and juicy. Uncover and add half a cup of the chicken soup. Cover and reheat for a further 10 minutes. Serve the bird in joints with the pan juices.

To Casserole a Fowl—Heimishe Style

A fine plump fowl has, perhaps, more flavour than any other kind of bird. However, as its flesh tends to be dry, it must be cooked in gentle, moist heat. The best way is to braise it slowly on a bed of lightly-fried vegetables, in a covered casserole just large enough to contain it. The bird can be whole or jointed, stuffed (with helzel or breadcrumb mixture) or left plain. The vegetables used can be varied with the season, but the basic method is always the same:

1 fowl, 4½–6 lb (2–3kg) net weight, koshered and scalded
1 tbsp oil
1 large onion, thinly sliced
1 carrot, thinly sliced
2 soft tomatoes or 2 tbsp tomato purée
1 bayleaf
2 level teasp flour
2 level teasp paprika
1 level teasp salt
10 grinds black pepper
1 clove garlic, crushed
4 fl oz (100ml/½ cup) chicken soup or chicken stock made with a cube
Any or all of the following may be added if they are available:
½ green pepper, seeded and cut into strips
3 stalks of celery, diced
2 oz (50g/1 cup) mushrooms, sliced

Turn the oven on to Gas No. 4, 350°F, 180°C. Mix together the salt, pepper, flour and paprika, then rub into the skin of the bird. In a heavy casserole, heat the oil and fry the onion until it is soft and golden, then add all the remaining vegetables and stir over gentle heat, until they have absorbed most of the fat. Put the bird in and turn it in the hot fat until it has turned pale gold. Pour the stock or soup down the side of the casserole. Cover and transfer to the oven. After 15 minutes, turn the oven down to Gas No. 3, 325°F, 170°C, and cook for 3 hours, or until the bird is a rich golden brown and the leg can be moved easily in its socket. During cooking, the liquid should be bubbling very gently. It if is too violent, turn the oven down to Gas No. 2, 300°F, 150°C. Baste twice with the pan juices. If dinner is delayed, the oven can be turned down to a 'keep hot' or minimum setting, and the bird will come to no harm.

To serve: Lift the bird onto a warm platter. Skim off as much fat as you can. The gravy can be served as it is, or it can be pushed through a sieve into a pan containing 2 level teaspoons cornflour, mixed with 2 tablespoons cold water. Bring the gravy mixture to the boil, then simmer for 3 minutes. Taste, reseason if necessary and serve.

To reheat a casseroled fowl: Remove some of the jelly in which it will be resting and put this in the soup to enrich it. Put the bird, still covered in the casserole, in a moderate oven (Gas No. 4, 350°F, 180°C) for 30 minutes, or until piping hot. Serves 4 to 6, depending on the size of the bird.

Helzel Stuffing

Use this to stuff a casseroled bird; it will not cook sufficiently in one that is roasted.

3 oz (75g/¾ cup) plain or self-raising flour plus
1 oz (25g/3 tbsp) semolina or fine matzo meal
3 tbsp raw chicken fat, finely chopped
½ medium onion, coarsely grated
½ level teasp salt
Pinch of white pepper

Mix all the ingredients together with a fork. (If raw fat is not available, use 3 rounded tablespoons rendered fat. Use this to cook the onion gently for 2 minutes, then pour onto the dry ingredients and blend well.) The mixture should look slightly moist in appearance—add a little fat if too dry; if too moist, add a little more semolina or meal. Stuff lightly into the body cavity of the bird.

Chickens of Every Size

Roasting chickens are relatively recent arrivals on the Jewish culinary scene, for in comparison with a fowl they make expensive family eating and they have a less satisfying flavour. However, they make up for this in the delicacy of the flesh and the speed with which they become tender when cooked.

Roasting chickens should have pliable breastbones (an indication of youth) and have a dressed weight of between 3½–4½ lb (1½–2kg).

Frying chickens should have full compact bodies and breasts and a dressed weight of between 1½–3½ lb (¾–1½kg).

Grilling chickens should have a dressed weight of not more than 2½ lb (1kg) and are then usually split by the butcher to make two portions.

To Roast a Chicken

This method keeps a kosher bird moist and juicy.

1 roasting chicken, about 3½–4½ lb (1½–2kg) net weight
½ pint (250ml/1¼ cups) chicken stock or soup
2 oz (50g/¼ cup) margarine
Stuffing
½ onion
½ carrot

Set the oven at Gas No. 7, 425°F, 220°C. Sprinkle the inside of the scalded and koshered bird with salt and pepper. Stuff with Savoury Bread Stuffing (see below) or insert a nut of margarine and a large sprig of parsley into the body cavity. Spread the bird all over with the soft margarine, and cover the breast lightly with greasepaper or greased foil. Tie the legs together with string, so that the bird is a compact shape. Put on a wire rack (to allow the heat to circulate freely) set in a roasting tin just large enough to hold it. Strew half a sliced onion and carrot round it, and pour in the stock. Put the bird in the oven for 10 minutes, then open the door quickly, baste well, turn the heat down to Gas No. 4, 350°F, 180°C and continue to cook for a further hour. Open the oven again, take off the paper or foil and baste the bird well. Add a little extra water if the stock has dried up and no longer covers the base of the tin. Continue to cook for a further half-hour, until the leg can be moved easily in its socket and the flesh feels very soft when prodded. If possible, leave the bird in a warming oven for ten minutes before it is carved.

To serve: Put the bird on a serving dish, and pour off the juices into a measuring cup. Make up to 10 fl oz (250ml/1¼ cups) with chicken stock or left-over gravy. Return the juices to the baking tin and scrape it well, to release any sediment stuck to the base. Boil the juices down rapidly until they are rich and syrupy. Season with salt and pepper and serve with the roasted bird. Serves 4–6.

Savoury Bread Stuffing

4 oz (100g/1⅓ cups) stale breadcrumbs (put in blender or pull out of crust with a fork)
3 oz (75g/⅓ cup) margarine
2 teasp oil
1 small onion, finely chopped
Pinch each of salt, paprika, black pepper and dried oregano
2 tbsp finely chopped parsley

Put the crumbs and the seasonings into a bowl. Heat the margarine with the oil in a small frying pan, and add the finely-chopped onion. Cook gently until the onion is soft and golden, then pour the contents of the pan onto the seasoned crumbs. Toss lightly until all the crumbs are coated with fat. Stuff lightly into the salted cavity of the bird.

VARIATION

Stuffing English Style: Fry the onion in 2 oz (50g/¼ cup) margarine and 2 teaspoons oil. Moisten the fat and breadcrumb mixture with a small beaten egg. This makes a firmer stuffing.

To Roast a Bird to be Served Cold

The bird is foil-wrapped and roasted at a very high temperature for a shorter time. Cooked this way, the bird is particularly succulent when cold.

Use a roaster weighing between $3\frac{1}{2}$–$4\frac{1}{2}$ lb ($1\frac{1}{2}$–2kg) net weight. In the body cavity, put half an orange or a lemon, then spread the whole of the carcase (especially the legs) with a thin, even layer of soft margarine. Season well with salt and pepper and wrap *loosely* in foil. Put in a very hot oven (Gas No. 8, 450°F, 230°C) for 1 hour. After 45 minutes, open the foil parcel and allow the bird to brown. Serves 4–6.

Deep-Fried Chicken

If you have a large, deep fryer and basket, this is an exceedingly easy way to fry chicken for serving hot or cold.

1 chicken between $3\frac{1}{2}$–$4\frac{1}{2}$ lb ($1\frac{1}{2}$–2kg) net weight, cut into 6 or 8 joints, according to size
3 oz (75g/$\frac{3}{4}$ cup) flour
1 level teasp salt
Plenty of black pepper
Pinch of paprika
(Mixed in a plastic bag)
1 beaten egg in a shallow dish
4 oz (100g/$1\frac{1}{3}$ cups) dried breadcrumbs (in a plastic bag)

Toss each joint of chicken in the seasoned flour, then paint with the beaten egg (using a pastry brush) and finally toss to coat in the breadcrumbs. Do not start frying until all the joints are coated. Have a pan one third full of oil, heated to a temperature of 350°F, 180°C (when a day-old cube of bread will brown in one minute). Put in as many pieces of chicken as will comfortably fit into the basket at one time, and lower the basket into the oil. Fry gently for 20 minutes, until a rich golden brown. Drain on absorbent kitchen paper and keep hot in a warm oven until all the chicken joints have been fried. This chicken is also delicious cold. Serve with pineapple or banana fritters (see p. 119) or corn fritters (see below). Serves 4–6.

Corn Fritters

1 can (11 oz/275g) corn or equivalent frozen
2 eggs
Salt and pinch of sugar
2 level teasp baking powder
3 rounded tbsp fresh breadcrumbs

Beat yolks, add to corn with seasonings then stir in whisked whites. Fold in baking powder and enough crumbs to make stiff enough to handle. Form into little flat cakes and fry in fat to a depth of $\frac{1}{4}$ in ($\frac{1}{2}$ cm) until a rich brown on both sides. Keep hot until required. Makes 20–24 cakes.

Oven-Fried Chicken

This is an excellent method if a large quantity is to be fried. It avoids any smell of oil in the kitchen. Joints can be coated and frozen, then cooked as required.

2 young chickens, each $3\frac{1}{2}$ lb ($1\frac{1}{2}$kg) net weight, each cut into 4
1 egg
4 tbsp oil
Salt, pepper and paprika
Cornflake crumbs or fine meal

Blend the crumbs with a level teaspoon of salt and paprika and about ten grinds of black pepper. Beat the egg and oil together. Dry the joints thoroughly, then dip first into the egg mixture then into the seasoned crumbs. Arrange the joints on flat ungreased tins, and bake in a quick oven (Gas No. 5, 375°F, 190°C) for 45 minutes or until the chicken is a rich golden brown, and feels tender when gently pressed. The chicken can be kept hot by turning the oven to slow (Gas No. 2, 300°F, 150°C), then turn up for 2–3 minutes just before serving if the coating has gone at all limp. Can be served cold with salad. Serves 6–8.

Mushroom and Wine Sauce

2 level tbsp chicken fat; or 1 oz (25g/2 tbsp) margarine and 1 tbsp oil
1 heaped tbsp (1 oz/25g) flour
$\frac{1}{4}$ lb (100g/2 cups) button mushrooms
1 level tbsp chopped parsley
Small wineglass (3 fl oz/75ml) white wine
2 teasp grated onion
Salt and pepper
$\frac{1}{2}$ pint (250ml/$1\frac{1}{4}$ cups) chicken stock (made from a cube) or chicken soup

In a small, heavy saucepan, heat the oil for 2–3 minutes, then cook the onion and the mushrooms (sliced if too large) for 5 minutes, shaking the pan briskly. Add the wine. Put into a bowl. In the same pan, melt the chicken fat or margarine and add the flour. Simmer for 2 minutes, then whisk in the chicken stock and the mushroom wine mixture. Season with salt and pepper and stir in the parsley. Taste and add more seasonings—or wine—if necessary. Serve the chicken on a platter and pass the sauce separately. To complete the meal, serve savoury rice and petits pois. Serves 6–8.

Grilled Chicken

1 koshered spring chicken, 1¾–2 lb (¾–1kg) net weight, split down the back and then cut in two halves
Black pepper, coarse salt, fresh thyme or marjoram (if available)
Olive oil
1 oz (25g/2 tbsp) melted margarine
Juice of 1 lemon

At least 2 hours beforehand, put the halved chicken into a grill-pan or heat-proof dish just large enough to hold it. Use a pastry brush to paint the bird all over with the lemon juice, then sprinkle generously with freshly-ground black pepper. Sprinkle a light covering of the herbs over the bird, then use the brush to paint all sides with olive oil. Leave the chicken in a cool place until 20 minutes before you intend to serve it. Heat the grill. Arrange the bird on the wire rack of the grill-pan (or on a cake rack kept specially for meat cookery if an ordinary dish has been used), but leave the remainder of the oil in the bottom of the dish. Pour over half the melted margarine, and start to grill, skin side up, about 4 in (10 cm) away from the heat, for 5 minutes, or until the skin begins to brown. Turn the chicken, pour over the remaining margarine, and continue to cook for 5 minutes more until the second side is brown. Now slip the bird off the rack into the pan itself, sprinkle with coarse salt, baste well with the pan juices, and finish off the cooking with 5 more minutes on either side. By this time, the chicken will be a rich brown and very tender. Don't overcook or the flesh may become stringy. Serve with the pan juices poured over the bird. A fleshy bird will serve four, as each half can be cut in two before serving, though hearty eaters may find they can easily polish off a half by themselves. (It's better to cook the bird in halves rather than quarters, as this keeps the flesh juicy.) Serves 2–4.

Chicken by the Joint

Dishes in which the chicken is jointed before it is cooked are especially convenient to serve, as no carving is required at the table. It is also useful to double quantities and freeze half in the sauce which always accompanies this type of dish. All chicken dishes with sauce reheat well. In fact, their flavour is often improved after 24 hours' refrigeration.

Chicken Hawaii

1 chicken, 3½–4 lb (1½–2kg) net weight, cut in 4–6 joints
1 tbsp flour
2 teasp salt
Pinch of white pepper
4 tbsp oil and 1 tbsp chicken fat
Sauce:
1 can crushed pineapple
2 teasp soy sauce
½ large onion
1 large green pepper
2 teasp demerara (brown) sugar
2 level teasp cornflour (cornstarch), mixed with 2 tbsp chicken stock

Put seasoned flour in bag and shake chicken joints in it one at a time to coat. Fry in the fat until a rich brown on both sides. Transfer to a casserole, cover and cook for 45 minutes (Gas No. 4, 350°F, 180°C) in own juices. Meanwhile, make the sauce in the same pan. Sauté the onion in the remaining fat together with the pepper cut in thin strips. When well softened (after about 5 minutes) add all the remaining ingredients. Simmer for 3 minutes until thick and clear, then pour over the bird in the casserole. Cook a further 10 minutes, until the bird is quite tender. Serves 4–6. Reheats well.

Country Captain

A most delicious curry sauce accompanies this chicken dish.

1 chicken, 3–3½ lb (1½–1¾kg) net weight, cut into 4
1 oz (25g/¼ cup) flour
1 level teasp salt
¼ teasp pepper
4 tbsp oil
½ onion, finely chopped
½ green pepper, finely diced
1 clove garlic, crushed
1 level teasp curry powder
Pinch of dried thyme
1 can (14 oz/350g) tomatoes pushed through a sieve
3 level tbsp currants
Some blanched toasted almonds
6 oz (150g) rice, boiled
Chutney

Coat the chicken joints in the flour mixed with the salt and pepper. Heat the oil in a large frying pan, add the chicken and brown well on all sides. Remove. To the same fat, add the onion, green pepper, garlic, curry and thyme. Stir well to amalgamate the drippings at the bottom of the pan. Cook for 3–4 minutes until the onion has softened, then add the tomatoes, including the liquid. Put the chicken back in the pan, skin side up. Cover and cook very slowly for 30 minutes. To cook in the oven, transfer to an ovenproof casserole and cook in a moderate oven (Gas No. 4, 350°F, 180°C) for 45 minutes. Stir in the currants just before serving. Put boiled rice in the centre of a platter, spoon some of the chicken sauce over it, surround with the chicken joints, and serve the remaining sauce in a dish. Serve browned almonds and chutney separately. Serves 4.

Poulet Sauté Marengo

1 koshered roaster, 3½ lb (1¾kg) net weight, cut into 4; or a 4 lb (2kg) bird, cut into 6
4 fl oz (100ml/½ cup) dry white wine such as Graves
1 level tbsp tomato purée
8 fl oz (200ml/1 cup) chicken soup or bouillon made with a cube
1 clove garlic, crushed with a little salt
1 bayleaf
1 level teasp sugar and salt
10 grinds black pepper
½ onion, finely chopped
¼ lb (100g/2 cups) mushrooms
1 tbsp oil
1 rounded tbsp chicken fat; or 2 level tbsp margarine
Sprig of parsley
2 tbsp flour

Put 2 tablespoons flour, 2 level teaspoons salt and 10 grinds black pepper into a plastic bag. One at a time, shake each chicken portion in the flour until it has an even coating of seasoned flour clinging to it. Heat the oil and the chicken fat in a heavy frying pan and fry the coated chicken on all sides over moderate heat until it is golden brown. Lift out. In the same fat, fry the onion gently until golden brown. Add all the remaining ingredients (except the mushrooms), and bring gently to the boil. Transfer to an oven casserole and add the browned joints. Cook in a moderate oven (Gas No. 4, 350°F, 180°C) for no more than 45 minutes, when the chicken will be tender but still moist. If the bird must be kept hot, simply turn the oven down to the lowest temperature and turn up again 5 minutes before serving. Ten minutes before the chicken is cooked, add the raw sliced mushrooms. Serves 4 generously.

Poulet Basquaise

2 chickens, each 3¼ lb (1½kg) net weight, each cut into 4; or 1 capon or large chicken cut into 8
1 tbsp chicken fat
2 tbsp oil
3 tbsp flour seasoned with 2 level teasp salt
10 grinds black pepper
The sauce:
2 medium onions
1 fat clove garlic, crushed
1 fat green pepper
2 large canned pimentos
1 can (8 oz/200g/1 cup) whole tomatoes, drained
½ pint (250ml/1¼ cups) chicken stock
4 oz (100g) green Queen olives
1 level tbsp cornflour (cornstarch)

Whilst the fats are heating gently in a wide frying pan, roll the chicken in the seasoned flour. Brown well in the hot fat on all sides, then remove to a wide casserole or baking tin. Chop the onions finely, slice then dice the peppers, cut the pimentos into wide strips, cut the green olives into little bits and discard the stones. Put all the vegetables (except the pimentos) into the fat and cook steadily for 10 minutes until a rich golden brown. Add the stock, tomatoes, garlic, and a little salt and pepper. Bring to bubbling point, then pour over the joints, cover with a lid or foil and put in a slow oven (Gas No. 2, 300°F, 150°C) for 1½ hours, or until the chicken is very tender. Arrange the chicken in a serving dish. To the sauce add the pimentos, olives and cornflour mixed to a cream with a little cold water. Bubble for 5 minutes top-of-stove, then pour over the chicken. Serves 6–8.

Note: For 1 chicken weighing 3¼ lb (1½kg), use all the same ingredients, but only ¼ pint stock.

Ginger Chicken

8 chicken joints
2 oz (50g/½ cup) flour
2 level teasp salt
½ level teasp pepper
6 tbsp oil
2 tbsp margarine
1 level teasp ground ginger
¾ pint (375ml/2 cups) chicken stock
¼ pint (125ml/⅔ cup) sherry

Mix the ginger, seasonings and flour and coat the bird. Fry in the mixed fat and margarine until a rich brown. Have the chicken stock and sherry heating at the side. Remove the browned joints and put in a casserole, add to the pan any remaining seasoned flour and cook for 3 minutes until pale brown. Add the hot liquids and whisk until smooth. Pour over the joints, cover and cook in a moderate oven (Gas No. 4, 350°F, 180°C) for 45 minutes, until tender when pierced with a fork. Serves 8.

Chicken Hunter Style

1 chicken, 3½ lb (1½kg) net weight, cut into 6; or a 4 lb (2kg) chicken cut into 8
4 tbsp oil
1 tbsp seasoned flour
2 green peppers
¼ lb (100g/2 cups) mushrooms
1 medium onion
1 can (14 oz/350g/2 cups) peeled plum tomatoes
2 teasp tomato purée
Pinch of oregano
1 teasp salt
1 teasp sugar
½ teasp pepper
2 bayleaves
1 clove garlic, crushed
¼ pint (125ml/⅔ cup) dry white wine such as Chablis or Graves
Chopped parsley

Heat the oil in a heavy frying pan or casserole. Shake the joints with the seasoned flour in a paper bag till very lightly coated. Fry in the oil till a rich brown (10–12 minutes). When you turn the joints over, add chopped onion and cook together, and after a minute or two, add sliced peppers. Add wine to the casserole and bubble for 2 minutes then add tomatoes, purée, and seasonings and blend well. Simmer gently top-of-stove for half an hour, then uncover and allow to thicken for a further 10 minutes, or put into a casserole and simmer in oven (Gas No. 3, 325°F, 170°C) for 45 minutes, uncovering for a further 10 minutes to thicken sauce. Put sliced mushrooms in when the dish is uncovered. Serve well sprinkled with parsley. The cooking time will depend on the age of the bird and once it feels tender the dish can either be kept hot in a low oven or refrigerated and reheated when needed. Serves 4–6.

Chicken Sauté in White Wine and Mushroom Sauce

1 chicken, 4 lb (2kg) net weight, cut into 6 or 8
¼ lb (100g/2 cups) button mushrooms
1 very large onion
½ bottle dry white wine
Salt and pepper
2 oz (50g/¼ cup) margarine; or 2 tbsp chicken fat
1 tbsp oil
1 level tbsp flour

Joint, then skin the bird and dry well. Slice the mushrooms and onion finely. In a large heavy frying pan or casserole (must be very wide), melt the chicken fat (or margarine) and oil. Add the onion and cook uncovered for 10 minutes until soft and really golden brown. Add the mushrooms and mix well to coat with onion and fat, then add the chicken joints. Turn well in the mixture and cook for 10–15 minutes until a golden brown on both sides. Sprinkle with the flour and blend in well, then add the wine. Bring to the boil, season well with salt and black pepper, stir sauce, cover and simmer until chicken is tender. This will probably take about 45 minutes (1 hour in the oven, Gas No. 3, 325°F, 170°C). However, the dish reheats very easily. Serves 4–5. (*Note:* Before serving, the chicken can be lifted out and the sauce thickened by bubbling for a few moments.)

Paprika Chicken

The true Hungarian recipe. I give the quantities for 8–10, *half of which can be frozen or kept for another day.*

3 chickens, 3–4 lb (1½–2kg) each, jointed
3 Spanish onions
2 tbsp oil or 1 oz (25g/2 tbsp) margarine
1 large can Letcho (tomato and green pepper) and 1 medium can tomatoes; or 2 fresh green peppers and enough canned tomatoes to almost cover birds
2 level tbsp paprika
2 level teasp salt
Pepper
12 oz (300g/1¾ cups) long grain rice

Chop the onions finely and sauté in the fat till golden. Remove. Brown chicken joints in same pan. Put onion back and add Letcho and tomatoes—they should almost cover chickens. (*Note:* If fresh green peppers are used, add them, finely shredded, 15 minutes before chicken is tender, to keep their colour.) Add paprika, pepper and salt. Simmer, covered, for 25 minutes. Add 12 oz long grain rice and continue to cook, till all the liquid is absorbed and the rice is tender (about 20 minutes). Serves 8–10.

Coq au Vin

1 chicken, 4 lb (2kg) net weight, cut into 6–8 joints
⅓ bottle burgundy
1 clove garlic
¼ teasp dried leaf marjoram or oregano
3 tbsp flour, seasoned with 1 level teasp salt and ¼ level teasp ground black pepper
4 tbsp oil
3 tbsp brandy (optional)
1 bayleaf
Sprig of parsley
12 whole baby mushrooms
12 small onions
2 level teasp arrowroot or cornflour (cornstarch)
1 tbsp water

Cut the bird into 6 or 8 pieces and put into a bowl. Cover with the wine. (Leave the remainder of the bottle well-corked in the refrigerator, where it will keep for cooking purposes for at least two weeks.) Add the garlic mashed to a paste with a little coarse salt and the marjoram or oregano. Leave the bird in this marinade for 2 hours, turning the joints once or twice. Take them out, drain well, and dab dry with a kitchen towel. Roll in the seasoned flour. Brown the joints well in the hot oil and arrange in a casserole. Heat the brandy (if used) in a small pan or a soup ladle held over the flame. Set it alight and pour over the chicken. To the bird now add the bayleaf, parsley, mushrooms, onions and finally the marinade. Cover and simmer either top-of-stove or in a slow oven (Gas No. 2, 300°F, 150°C) for 1½ hours or until the chicken is very tender. Mix the arrowroot with 1 tablespoon water and add to the casserole. Simmer until clear (about 3 minutes). Serves 6.

Winter Barbecued Chicken

The chicken is cooked in a sweet and sour tomato sauce.

1 roasting chicken, about 4 lb (2kg) net weight, cut into 6 joints
Oil to cover frying pan to depth of ¼ in (½ cm)
4 level tbsp fine brown sugar (Barbados is nice)
2 teasp prepared mustard
1 onion, finely chopped
2 level teaspoons salt
¼ teasp freshly-ground black pepper
½ large lemon (about 2 tbsp)
½ teasp Worcestershire sauce
1 can (5 oz/125g) tomato purée, diluted with 2 cans water

Fry chicken joints (do not skin) in hot oil until golden on all sides, then remove to casserole.

The sauce: Sauté onion in remaining fat until golden, then add all the remaining ingredients. Simmer 5 minutes, then pour over the chicken. Cover and bake in a slow oven (Gas No. 2, 300°F, 150°C) for 1½ hours. Freezes well. Better after 1 or 2 days in refrigerator. Serves 4–6.

Chicken Salads

Chicken and Celery Salad

For chicken salad, use either a steam roaster (young fowl) simmered as for soup; or a chicken roasted in foil, as in **To Roast a Bird to be Served Cold** (p. 79).

1 steam roaster, 5 lb (2½kg) net weight
Heart of a celery
4 oz (100g/1 cup) walnut halves, roughly chopped
Salt and pepper
8 fl oz (200ml/1 cup) mayonnaise, slightly thinned with chicken soup and a squeeze of lemon juice
Crisp lettuce
Black olives
Slices of canned red pimento

Boil the fowl as for soup, but only barely cover with water. Leave to cool in the stock. Take all the flesh from the bones, cutting it into ¾ in (1½ cm) chunks. Blend with the finely-sliced celery, the walnuts and the mayonnaise. Arrange in a bowl lined with shredded lettuce, and garnish with the olives and pimentos. Serves 6 as a main dish or 8 as part of a buffet.

Chicken and Chicory Salad

Fruit is blended with the chicken in a curried dressing.

2 cups cooked chicken, cut into bite-sized pieces (about half a boiled or casseroled fowl)
3 fat heads chicory
½ lb (200g) seedless green grapes
Half a honeydew melon, cut into balls
Heart of celery, finely diced
1 cup mayonnaise
Juice of ½ lemon
1 level teasp curry powder
Pinch of salt and white pepper
Shredded lettuce

Slice the chicory across into ½ in (1 cm) rings, then cut each ring in half. Mix with the chicken, grapes and celery. Combine all the dressing ingredients together and gently mix into the chicken mixture. Finally stir in the melon balls. Chill for 1 hour, then serve on a bed of shredded lettuce. Serves 6.

Chicken and Almond Salad

The flesh from 1 cooked chicken (see To Roast a Chicken to be Served Cold, p. 79)
2 celery hearts or 2 medium green peppers
½ lb (200g) grapes or melon balls from one small melon
2 oz (50g/½ cup) salted almonds or peanuts, coarsely chopped
French dressing:
6 tbsp oil
2 tbsp wine or cider vinegar or lemon juice
1 teasp prepared mustard
1 level teasp each salt and sugar
10 grinds black pepper

Put the chicken (cut in strips), the diced celery hearts (or finely-sliced pepper), the pipped grapes (or melon balls) into a bowl and toss with enough of the dressing to moisten. Put into a serving dish and cover with the chopped nuts. Serve with mayonnaise thinned slightly with a little extra lemon juice or parve cream. Serves 6.

Polynesian Chicken Salad

2 oz (50g/½ cup) blanched almonds
Small can of pineapple titbits
4 spring onions (scallions), sliced in ¼ in (½ cm) lengths
2 cups of cubed cooked chicken
½ cup mayonnaise
½ teasp soy sauce
½ cup sliced celery
Good pinch of salt
Crisp salad greens, including watercress

Fry the almonds in a little oil for 3 or 4 minutes, then split them. Drain the pineapple, saving 2 tablespoons of the syrup. In a large bowl toss together the almonds, pineapple, spring onions, celery and chicken. Blend together the mayonnaise, pineapple syrup, soya sauce and salt, then stir in the salad. Toss lightly, and mound into a salad bowl lined with the crisp greens. Incidentally, the salad looks more effective in a shallow oval salad dish. Serves 4–6.

The Second Time Round

Besides using cooked chicken in a salad, it can also be used as the foundation of a variety of réchauffé dishes usually folded into a sauce made with the stock in which it was cooked. Here are a variety of such recipes:

Chicken Plate Pie

Remains of fowl and giblets (half a fowl serves 5 amply)
1 pkt puff pastry (8 oz/200g size) or ½ recipe Rough Puff Pastry made with margarine
Small pkt frozen peas
The sauce:
½ pint (250ml/1¼ cups) chicken soup or stock
3 level tbsp flour
2 level tbsp chicken fat
2 teasp parsley
1 tbsp finely-chopped onion
Seasonings

Remove all skin and gristle from the fowl and cut into bite-sized strips. Cook peas. Melt the chicken fat and cook the onion for 3 minutes, then stir in the flour and cook till bubbly for 2–3 minutes. Take off the heat and add the hot chicken stock all at once, then whisk hard. Return to the heat and whisk till boiling, then simmer for 5 minutes. Season well with salt, pepper, pinch of nutmeg, and stir in the parsley. Fold in the chicken and peas and leave to cool. Cut the pastry in half and roll out to fit the base of a 9 in (23 cm) shallow pie plate. Roll the second half slightly larger to fit the top. Spoon the chicken filling into the crust and cover with pastry lid, pressing the edges firmly together. A little beaten egg (or yolk) brushed on the top will give a beautiful glaze. Bake pie in hot oven (Gas No. 8, 450°F, 230°C) for 20 minutes. Serve hot.

Chicken Blintzes

Blintzes Batter:
4 oz (100g/1 cup) plain flour
2 eggs
2 teasp oil
8 fl oz (200ml/1 cup) water
2 level teasp salt

In blender: Blend all the ingredients together for 30 seconds.
By hand: Sift flour and salt into bowl. Make a well. Drop in eggs, and start stirring in surrounding flour. Add oil and water gradually, to make a smooth batter. When mixture is thin, beat with a rotary whisk until covered with tiny bubbles. Put aside for 1 hour.
To fry: Put a pea-sized piece of white fat in a 6 in (15 cm) frying pan and heat until it smokes. Wipe out with tissue paper. Put back on heat and smear very lightly with oil. Put batter in a jug. Pour a thin coating into frying pan, then immediately pour excess back into jug—there should be just a thin layer in the pan. Cook quickly, until sides curl from pan and underneath is golden. Turn out on greaseproof paper. Smear again with oil and repeat frying until batter is used. Don't stack pancakes on top of each other until they have cooled, then stack and cover with foil till needed.

Chicken filling:

6 oz (150g/1 cup) left-over fowl, diced
1 oz (25g/2 tbsp) rendered chicken fat or margarine
2 oz (50g/1 cup) sliced mushrooms
2 level tbsp flour
8 fl oz (200ml/1 cup) chicken soup or gravy
Salt and pepper
2 teasp parsley

Melt fat, and add sliced mushrooms, cook 3 minutes. Stir in flour, then liquid, whisk till boiling, then add seasoning and chicken.
To fill: Take a pancake, with the brown side uppermost. Put a spoonful of filling on it, fold over the bottom and then the two sides like a parcel and roll it over, sealing it with the edge at the bottom. Ten minutes before dinner, fry the pancakes till golden brown, in a pan covered to a depth of ¼ in (½ cm) with hot oil. Makes 12 blintzes. Serves 4 as a main dish, 6 as an entrée.

VARIATION

Meat Blintzes: Mix together: 2 cups minced (ground) meat (boiled or braised), 1 tbsp grated onion, 1 beaten egg, 1 level teasp salt, few grinds black pepper, 1 tbsp parsley (mixture should be moist, not wet). Makes 12. Fill and fry as for Chicken Blintzes.

Note: To avoid last-minute frying when cooking for a crowd, set oven at Gas No. 7 (425°F, 220°C); arrange blintzes side by side on greased trays, leaving ½ in (1 cm) between them. Pour over 3fl oz (75ml) hot oil; bake till crisp and golden.

Sherried Chicken (or Turkey)

2 cups cold chicken or turkey breast, cut in small cubes
1 oz (25g/2 tbsp) margarine or chicken fat
3 level tbsp flour
½ level teasp salt
Pinch of paprika pepper
½ pint (250ml/1¼ cups) chicken or turkey stock
1 egg yolk
¼ lb (100g/2 cups) button mushrooms
2 tbsp sherry or white wine
2 oz (50g/½ cup) toasted almonds

Melt the fat and stir in the flour. Whisk in the hot stock and seasonings and allow to bubble for 3 minutes, then stir in the meat, the sherry, the almonds and the mushrooms (which have been sautéd in a nut of margarine for 5 minutes). Turn off the heat and drop in the egg yolks, stirring vigorously. Serves 4–6 as entrée, or will fill 12 medium patty cases.

Chicken Risotto

6 oz (150g/1 cup) packeted parboiled long grain rice
4 tbsp oil
1 medium onion, finely chopped
1 pint (500ml/2½ cups) rich chicken stock (can be made from cubes)
2 fl oz (50ml/4 tbsp) dry white wine
1 clove garlic, crushed
½ level teasp powdered ginger
¼ lb (100g/2 cups) mushrooms, finely sliced
2 level tbsp currants
2 level tbsp pine kernels (pine nuts), if available
1 oz (25g/2 tbsp) margarine
Half a cooked fowl; or the flesh from one roasted chicken, cubed; or ½ lb (200g) koshered chicken livers

In a heavy stove-to-oven casserole, heat the oil and sauté the chopped onion gently until softened and golden (about 5 minutes), then add the unwashed rice and continue to fry until the rice begins to colour. Add the garlic, ginger and the hot stock, in which a pinch of saffron has been steeped (optional but gives a lovely golden colour). Put in a moderate oven (Gas No. 4, 350°F, 180°C) for 25 minutes. Meanwhile, melt the margarine and fry the pine kernels till golden. Remove. In same fat sauté the mushrooms and the currants for 5 minutes. Add the wine and the chicken and stir briskly to incorporate all the pan juices. Stir into the rice and serve. Serves 4–6.

Roast Duck

A duckling should be less than 6 months old; older birds are better casseroled. As the duckling has a higher ratio of bone to flesh than a chicken, a bird weighing 4½ lb (2kg) oven-ready weight will only serve 4. The duckling is a water bird, and therefore has a lot of fat beneath the skin, so no additional fat is required for roasting.

1 bird, 4½–5½ lb (2–2½kg) net weight
Salt, pepper and small onion (for the body cavity)
1 medium sliced carrot and onion (for the roasting tin)

Season the body cavity with the salt and pepper and put in the onion. Tie the legs, wings and neck skin to the body. Prick the skin round the wings, back and breast to allow excess fat to escape. Dry the bird with paper towels. Place the duck, breast up, in a roasting tin just large enough to contain it and arrange the sliced carrot and onion around it. Roast at Gas No. 6, 400°F, 200°C for 15 minutes. Reduce the heat to Gas No. 4, 350°F, 180°C and continue to cook so that the fat is gently sizzling round the bird all the time. As fat collects in the tin, remove it with a spoon. Half-way through the cooking period turn the duck over. Fifteen minutes before it is ready, turn breast up once more and salt lightly. The duck is done when the juices that run from the thigh when it is pricked with a fork are almost colourless.

Time-table

Weight of bird	*Cooking time*
4½ lb (2kg)	1½–2 hours
5½ lb (2½kg)	2¼–2½ hours

When the duck is ready, remove trussing strings and place on a serving dish. Put the duck in a warming drawer, or leave in the oven at 'warm' until required.

Duck gravy:

½ pint (250ml/1¼ cups) stock (made from the giblets); or ½ pint (250ml/1¼ cups) beef bouillon (made from a cube)

Pour off all but 1 tablespoon fat from the roasting tin. Add the stock or bouillon and stir thoroughly to incorporate the sediment and the vegetables in the tin. Simmer until well reduced, then season to taste. Add 3 tablespoons kosher wine (optional) and serve. Serves 4–6.

Let's Talk Turkey

The turkey, a relative new-comer to the Jewish menu, makes an excellent alternative to casseroled fowls or roast chickens for a Yomtov menu, or for a large family for the Sabbath.

First choose your bird: Unless you're a devil for martyrdom, buy a bird that is already cleaned, koshered and trussed. If such oven-ready birds are not available, then allow an extra third poundage in calculating the weight of the bird you will need. Thus, if you want a 12 lb (5kg) oven-ready bird, you will have to buy an 18 pounder (8½kg) 'on the hoof'. All the calculations I give below are based on the weight of the oven-ready bird.

How big shall it be?: Allow ¾ lb–1 lb (300–480g) per serving, the higher figure referring to the smaller bird (to allow for the higher ratio of bone to flesh). Thus, an 8 lb (4kg) bird will provide 8 to 9 servings, a 12 lb (5½kg) bird about 16. From a 12 lb (5½kg) bird, a family of 4 adults and 4 children could well get one hot meal, one cold meal and one réchauffé dish such as turkey pie or blintzes.

But, wait a moment—will the chosen bird fit your oven? Too large a bird in too small an oven produces uneven browning. There should be 1 in (2½ cm) clearance of the sides when the roasting tin is put in position.

How to thaw: If the bird is frozen, it is important to allow sufficient time for it to thaw before cooking. A large bird—15 lb (7kg) or over—may take up to 48 hours in a cool larder or outhouse; a smaller bird—up to 12 lb (5½kg)—will take 20–30 hours. If the bird thaws before it is time to cook it, refrigerate it, and treat it as a fresh bird.

How to stuff: Stuffing the neck end (or crop) gives the breast a good shape. Stuffing the body cavity helps to keep the flesh of the bird moist. However, if you do not wish to stuff the body cavity, put an onion, a bunch of parsley and a good knob of margarine inside it instead, and season well with salt and pepper. Use a firm, sliceable helzel stuffing for the crop and a fluffy breadcrumb-based stuffing for the body. The amount of helzel stuffing given in the recipe will be sufficient for all but a monster bird (when half as much again should be prepared). For the body cavity, allow ½ lb (200g) stuffing (approximately) per 5 lb (2½kg) oven-ready weight. When the bird has been stuffed, sew or skewer the crop securely to the breast; skewer or sew up the vent.

Turkey Helzel Stuffing

This makes a firm, savoury and easily-sliced stuffing for the crop.

3 oz (75g/¾ cup) plain flour
1 oz (25g/¼ cup) fine matzo meal or semolina
6 level tbsp raw chicken or turkey fat, cut or chopped in tiny pieces, or 2 oz (50g/¼ cup) chopped firm margarine
Good pinch each of salt and sugar
½ medium onion, finely grated

Mix all the ingredients together with a fork; the mixture should be moist, neither 'cloggy' (it needs more flour) nor crumbly (add a little more fat). Stuff the mixture loosely into the crop of the turkey, and sew the neck skin to the backbone. Enough for a 10–15 lb (5–7kg) bird.

Parsley Stuffing

A fluffy, light stuffing for the body cavity.

2 level teasp salt
¼ level teasp white pepper
4 oz (100g/½ cup) margarine
1 level teasp dried mixed poultry seasoning or Italian herb mixture
½ lb (200g/2½ cups) breadcrumbs
2 level tbsp finely-chopped parsley and celery
1 large onion, finely chopped

Put the breadcrumbs in a bowl and blend with the herbs and seasoning. Melt the margarine in a large frying pan, add the onion and simmer until tender. Add the seasoned breadcrumbs to the pan, and stir thoroughly to moisten. If the breadcrumbs appear dry, add another 2 oz (50g/¼ cup) margarine at the side of the pan, melt and stir in. Enough for a 10–12 lb (5–6kg) bird (approx.).

Chestnut Stuffing

2 lb (1kg) fresh chestnuts or 1 lb (½kg) dried chestnuts or 1 large can (approx 15 oz/375g size) whole chestnuts
4 oz (100g/1⅓ cups) fresh breadcrumbs
Grated rind of an orange and a lemon
1 large egg
2 oz (50g/¼ cup) melted margarine
Little salt, pepper and paprika

If using fresh chestnuts, make a slit in the skin and simmer for 10 minutes in boiling water. Drain, and whilst still hot, remove the inner and outer skins with a sharp knife. Simmer in chicken or giblet stock to cover, until quite tender (about 30 minutes). (Soak the dried chestnuts overnight, then simmer in stock until tender. Drain the canned chestnuts.) Chop the chestnuts coarsely with a knife. Blend all the dry ingredients together and bind with the fat and the egg. Use this stuffing for the body cavity. Enough for a 10–15 lb (5–7kg) bird.

To Prepare the Bird for the Oven

Make sure the stuffed neck end is securely sewn or skewered to the breast; sew up or skewer closed the vent. Brush the bird all over with a mixture of 4 oz (100g/½ cup) melted margarine (or 4 fl oz/100ml/½ cup oil) seasoned with 1 level teaspoon salt and paprika, 10 grinds black pepper, and 1 level teaspoon mustard. When oiling the bird, pay special attention to the legs, which tend to dry out in the cooking. Tie the legs together and tie the wings close to the breast. (*Note:* For convenience, stuff, oil, truss and cover the bird the night before it is to be cooked. Refrigerate, and cook the next day.)

How to Cook the Bird

I have cooked turkeys by both methods I give below and have come to the conclusion that, provided the bird is of a good quality and kept well basted with fat, a succulent flavourful bird can be produced by either. It is merely a question of which method is most convenient—slow cooking for a long time at low temperature, or hotter temperatures over a shorter period.

Note: The cooking should be timed so that the bird is ready 15 minutes before dinner. This allows the flesh to firm up so that the bird can be easily carved.

To test whether done, pierce the deepest part of the thigh. The juice should be almost colourless.

Moderate Oven Method

Wrap the bird *very* loosely in foil. Set the oven at Gas No. 6, 400°F, 200°C.

For a bird weighing 14 lb (6½kg) or under: Cook for 1 hour at Gas No. 6, 400°F, 200°C, then turn down to Gas No. 4, 350°F, 180°C, for the rest of the time.

For a bird weighing 15 lb (7kg) or over: Cook for 1 hour at Gas No. 6, 400°F, 200°C, then turn down to Gas No. 2, 300°F, 150°C, for the rest of the time.

Time-table

Weight of bird	*Cooking time*
6 lb (3kg)	2 hr 20 min
8 lb (4kg)	3 hr
10 lb (4½kg)	3 hr 40 min
12 lb (5½kg)	4 hr 10 min
14 lb (6½kg)	4 hr 50 min
16 lb (7½kg)	5 hr 10 min

For all sizes: For the last half-hour of cooking time, uncover the bird, pour off the juices and reserve for gravy. Allow to brown.

Hot Oven Method

The bird is set on a rack in the roasting tin and covered with a 'tent' of foil, sealed to the edges of the tin. This is a useful method if the bird is to be served cold, as it produces a very juicy bird in a short time.

Set the oven at Gas No. 7, 450°F, 230°C (25° higher are needed in an electric oven).

Time-table

Weight of bird	*Cooking time*
6–7 lb (3–3½kg)	2¼ hr
8–9 lb (4–4½kg)	2½ hr
10–11 lb (4½–5kg)	2¾ hr
12–13 lb (5½–6kg)	2 hr 50 min
14–15 lb (6½–7kg)	3 hr
16–18 lb (7½–8kg)	3¼–3½ hr

For all sizes: For the last half-hour, uncover the bird, pour off juices and reserve for gravy. Allow to brown.

Turkey Gravy

In either case, proceed as follows: Pour off the fat from the baking tin and reserve for other use. Add 1 pint (500ml/2½ cups) stock or turkey juice to the tin, and stir round with a wooden spoon to release the flavourful residue clinging to the base. A small glass of sherry or Madeira can be poured into the tin. Mix 2 level teaspoons arrowroot or cornflour (cornstarch) with a little water and add to the mixture. Bring to the boil, and simmer until thickened and clear (about 3 minutes). Taste, season and serve.

To carve a turkey:

1. Cut off the legs and wings.
2. Separate the drumstick from the leg, using poultry shears or the point of a knife.
3. Carve slices of meat from the legs, beginning at the boney end.
4. Carve slices of meat from the breast, starting at the neck end. Wrap left-over turkey in foil and refrigerate.

Vegetables and Main Dish Accompaniments

You can tell the geographical origins of a Jewish family by the way it prepares its vegetables. Jews of Russian and Polish origin have a limited repertoire of dishes as the main vegetable crops in that part of the world are root vegetables and cabbages; but as you move into a warmer climate, you find delectable recipes for such exotica as peppers and aubergines (eggplant), whilst in Israel not only do they market some of the finest luxury vegetables in the world, but they also have recipes to use them to their best advantage. In this chapter, therefore, I give the basic lore of family vegetable cookery as well as recipes for a wide range of speciality dishes.

Instructions for cooking vegetables for a party (as in the French manner) are given on p. 255.

To Cook Fresh Green Vegetables

To conserve their colour and food value, all green vegetables should be cooked as rapidly as possible in the minimum of boiling water, then served as soon as they are barely tender.

Prepare the vegetables according to the variety (see below). Have ready a heavy-based saucepan with a tight-fitting lid, in which is boiling $\frac{1}{4}$ pt (125ml/$\frac{2}{3}$ cup) water seasoned with 1 level teaspoon salt. Put in the prepared vegetables, bring the water back to the boil, cover and then boil rapidly for 10–15 minutes, or until the vegetables feel barely tender when pierced with a slim knife. Pour off any liquid that is left and use it in soups and gravies, as it will be rich in mineral salts. Put the vegetables into a serving dish and top with a knob of butter (or margarine for a meat meal) and serve at once.

Sprouts: Remove any discoloured outer leaves, and examine each sprout closely for maggots. If any are seen, discard the sprout. Make two little nicks in the stalk end (to hasten the cooking) then leave in water to cover, plus 1 level teaspoon salt, for half an hour. Rinse well, and cook as above.

Cauliflower: Cut the flowerets free from the stalk end. Soak as above and cook.

Spring cabbage: Remove the coarse outer leaves and discard. Rinse the tender inner leaves under the cold tap, one at a time. Put on a chopping board and shred finely. Cook as above. When tender, drain well, put on board and chop till fine. Mix with a nut of butter or margarine.

White cabbage: Cut in quarters and remove the stalk. Cut each quarter into thin shreds and soak in salted water as for sprouts. Add 1 oz (25g/2 tbsp) margarine to the cooking water, then proceed as above. When the cabbage is tender, strain, turn onto a board and chop until fine.

Young green cabbage (usually in season in July): Quarter the cabbage head, then shred finely, discarding any tough outer leaves and the stalk. Half fill a bowl with cold water and add 2 level teaspoons salt. Put in the cabbage and leave for half an hour. Melt 2 oz (50g/$\frac{1}{4}$ cup) butter (or margarine for a meat meal) in a heavy-based 8 in (20 cm) saucepan. Lift the cabbage from the water and put it into the hot fat, seasoning with black pepper. Cover and simmer, in its own juices, shaking occasionally, until the cabbage is bite-tender (about 15 minutes). Uncover and shake over a low light to remove any excess moisture. Turn into a dish and add a squeeze of lemon before serving. Serves 4–6.

French beans (string beans): Remove strings, rinse under cold tap, cut in diagonal slices and cook as above.

Broad beans (kidney or shell beans) and peas: Shell and cook as above.

To Cook Frozen Vegetables

Explicit instructions for basic cookery techniques are given on most packs of frozen vegetables. However, a little extra attention to the cooking method can greatly enhance their enjoyment.

Perfect Frozen Peas

(The quantities are sufficient for any size pack between 10–16 oz (250–500g).)

10 oz (250g) pkt frozen peas
Knob of margarine (or butter for a milk meal)
1 tbsp chopped spring onions (scallions); or $\frac{1}{4}$ mild onion
Pinch each of salt, pepper and sugar
$\frac{1}{4}$ pint (125ml/$\frac{2}{3}$ cup) chicken soup (or water for a milk meal)

Bring the butter or margarine, the seasonings, onion and liquid to the boil. Add the frozen peas, cover and simmer for 5–6 minutes. Uncover and boil away any remaining liquid. The peas will be bathed in a delicious glaze. Serves 4–6, depending on size of the packet.

Perfect Green Beans (Whole or Sliced)

$\frac{1}{2}$ medium onion, finely chopped
2 oz (50g/$\frac{1}{4}$ cup) butter (or margarine for a meat meal)
10–16 oz (250g–$\frac{1}{2}$kg) pkt green beans
1 level teasp salt
Plenty of black pepper

Soften the onion in the butter over a low heat with the lid on the pan. After 5 minutes put in the frozen beans, add the seasonings and heat till the butter bubbles again. Cover and cook over a low heat, until beans are just tender (about 10 minutes). Serve piping hot. Serves 4–6, depending on size of the packet.

Vegetable Specials

The recipes that follow are the ones I cook when I want to serve something other than 'plain boiled'. They're tasty without being too demanding on time and effort.

Aubergines (Eggplant)

The aubergine is a favourite vegetable of the Sephardi Jews who came from the Middle East via the Iberian Peninsula. Today it is widely grown—and eaten—in Israel. Many of the best recipes are of Turkish, Rumanian or Hungarian origin. A choice aubergine may be either egg-shaped or elongated, but it should always be glossy, plump and firm, for shrinkage, dullness and softness herald decay. For stuffing, the boat-shaped kind are best; for cubing, the egg-shaped; and unless it is to be cooked whole, the flesh should first be salted for an hour to draw out the bitter juices. A fresh aubergine can be stored in the refrigerator for up to a week without deteriorating in any way.

Aubergine (Eggplant) Sauté

This is the best way to taste the characteristic flavour in its simplest form, and a good recipe to serve with grilled steaks or chops.

2 large plump aubergines (eggplant)
Coarse salt
4 tbsp oil
1 level tbsp parsley
2 level teasp dried leaf oregano
½ clove garlic, crushed
10 grinds black pepper

Peel, then cut the aubergines into ½ in (1 cm) cubes. Put into a colander, sprinkle with coarse salt, cover with a weight and a plate and leave for an hour for the juices to drain away. Rinse with cold water, then dab dry with paper towels. Heat the oil in a heavy frying pan (it should be ⅛ in/½ cm deep), put in the cubes and cook gently, shaking the pan occasionally until they are meltingly tender (about 15 minutes). After 10 minutes, add the crushed garlic. Just before serving add the parsley and oregano, and sprinkle with the black pepper. The dish can be reheated, and comes to no harm if made early and left to stand. Serves 4 generously.

Aubergine (Eggplant) Meunière

A rather more sophisticated dish. The aubergines should be freshly cooked or the coating may go soggy.

3 long aubergines (eggplant)
Oil and butter for frying or oil alone
Lemon juice
Chopped parsley and oregano
Coarse salt
Flour

Peel the aubergines with a potato peeler, cut in ½ in (1 cm) slices crosswise and sprinkle lightly with coarse salt. Cover with a plate and a weight, and leave to 'sweat' for half an hour, then rinse under the cold tap and dry well. Have ready a square of greaseproof paper with 2 or 3 tablespoons flour. For a milk meal, melt enough butter to a depth of ¼ in (½ cm) in the pan. Add 1 tablespoon oil and heat until the butter starts foaming. Dip each slice into the flour, brush off the surplus and then cook gently on both sides until the aubergine is soft and golden, and the coating is crisp. (For a meat meal, fry in oil.) The frying will take about 10 minutes. Put the slices into a serving dish, sprinkle with lemon juice and the herbs. Serves 6.

Aubergines (Eggplant) Stuffed in the Mediterranean Fashion

These stuffed aubergines are used as an accompaniment rather than as a dish in their own right, as when stuffed with meat or chicken livers. Serve with hot fried fillets of sole or plaice (classic name, Filet de Sole Alphonse XIII).

6 small or 3 plump aubergines (eggplant)
6 tbsp oil
1 oz (25g/2 tbsp) butter
1 large onion, finely chopped
½ large green pepper
6 large tomatoes, peeled and chopped, or well-drained canned ones
2 level teasp oregano
2 level teasp chopped parsley
1 clove garlic, crushed
Salt, pepper, pinch of sugar
3 tbsp browned crumbs
2 tbsp melted butter
1 tbsp grated cheese

Cut aubergines in half, lengthwise, make deep criss-cross cuts into the flesh and sprinkle lightly with coarse salt. After half an hour rinse off the surface and dry well, squeezing out any free juice. Heat oil gently, put aubergines face down and fry gently on both sides till flesh feels soft. Remove and allow to cool, then scrape out the flesh and put the skins in an oven casserole. Meanwhile, sauté the chopped onion in butter till soft and golden then add the pepper and tomatoes and cook for a few minutes longer. Add mashed or chopped aubergine flesh and seasonings and simmer altogether until mixture is thick but still juicy. Divide the mixture evenly between the skins, mix 3 tablespoons dry crumbs and 1 oz (50g/2 tbsp) melted butter, then mix with 1 tablespoon grated cheese and sprinkle on the aubergines. Put under a moderate grill for 5 or 6 minutes, or bake in quick moderate oven (Gas No. 6, 400°F, 200°C) for 15 minutes. Serves 6.

Glazed Carrots

1 lb ($\frac{1}{2}$kg) new carrots
1 level tbsp sugar
1 level teasp salt
Good nut of margarine (or butter for a milk meal)

Scrape the carrots, then slice as thinly as possible. Put in a deep narrow pan; add fat; sprinkle with seasonings. Cover completely with water, then bring to the boil. Simmer uncovered until the water has evaporated, the carrots are tender and coated in a shiny glaze (about 30 minutes). For a party, the carrots can be cooked until almost dry earlier in the day. Then they can be reheated for a minute or two to drive off the remaining liquid while the meat is being sliced between courses. Carrots cooked this way can also be mixed with peas, and make a most delicious and colourful vegetable. Serves 6.

Carrot Ring

This is a recipe from the Pacific coast of the United States which I first tasted in Seattle. It makes an unusual accompaniment to a dairy meal, served either at Shavuoth or Succoth.

6 oz (150g/$\frac{3}{4}$ cup) butter or margarine
3 oz (75g/$\frac{1}{3}$ cup) fine brown sugar
1 egg
8 fl oz (200ml/1 cup) finely-grated raw carrot
1 tbsp lemon juice and 1 teasp lemon rind
6 oz (150g/1$\frac{1}{2}$ cups) plain flour mixed with 1 level teasp each of baking powder and bicarbonate of soda (baking soda) and $\frac{1}{2}$ level teasp salt
Dry breadcrumbs or cornflake crumbs

Cream the fat and sugar until fluffy, then beat in the well-whisked egg followed by all the remaining ingredients. Grease a ring tin, then scatter the bottom with crushed cornflake crumbs. Spoon in the carrot mixture and sprinkle more crumbs on top. Bake in a moderate oven (Gas No. 4, 350°F, 180°C) for 40 minutes or until golden brown and firm to gentle pressure. Turn out onto serving dish and fill centre with cooked peas. Serves 6–8.

Cauliflower Polonaise

1 cauliflower
2 oz (50g/$\frac{1}{4}$ cup) butter
1 heaped tbsp fresh white breadcrumbs
1 chopped hard-boiled egg
Little finely-chopped parsley

Remove the outer leaves from the cauliflower and break it into flowerets. Wash well. Cook gently in boiling salted water for 15 minutes, drain and arrange in a hot serving dish. Melt the butter, fry the breadcrumbs to a golden brown, scatter over the cooked cauliflower and sprinkle with the egg and parsley. Serves 4.

Creamed Corn

Fresh corn is best cooked on the cob, salted and served with firm cool butter and black pepper. Canned corn is most delicious in a cream sauce, as an accompaniment to grilled or baked fish such as halibut.

1 can (12 oz/300g) whole kernel corn or Mexicorn; or 1 pkt (12 oz/300g) frozen corn kernels cooked according to instructions
2 level teasp flour
$\frac{1}{2}$ oz (15g/1 tbsp) butter
4 tbsp double (heavy) cream
Good pinch of powdered mace
Salt and black pepper

Melt the butter, stir in the flour and cook a minute. Remove from the heat and add corn liquor from the can (or 3 tablespoons cooking liquor from frozen ones), simmer a minute, then stir in the fresh cream, the corn, and the mace together with a little salt and black pepper. Heat till steaming. Serves 4–5.

Courgettes (Zucchini) and Tomato

Courgettes are baby marrows, tender and delicate. They can be treated much like aubergines (as in Aubergine Meunière and Sauté).

1 lb ($\frac{1}{2}$kg) small courgettes (zucchini)
3 large canned or skinned fresh tomatoes
1 clove garlic
2 tbsp oil
Salt and pepper
1 level teasp oregano

Peel the courgettes in strips, using a potato peeler. (They will look stripey when peeled.) Cut in slanting $\frac{1}{4}$ in ($\frac{1}{2}$ cm) thick slices, put in a soup plate, sprinkle with coarse salt, cover with another plate and a weight and leave an hour. Drain off all the moisture, and dab dry with a paper towel. Heat 2 tablespoons oil in a heavy pan, put in the courgettes, and cook gently, turning often until soft, cooking the crushed garlic at the same time. Now add the tomatoes, and cook gently together until thick but still juicy. Season with black pepper, salt, and a pinch of oregano.

VARIATION

Courgettes Niçoise: With the tomatoes, add 6 stoned and diced fat black olives and 1 level tablespoon chopped parsley. This is also delicious served cold as a 'starter' or accompaniment to cold meats. Serves 4.

The Mushroom

Because it's grown in the dark and is therefore quite independent of the vagaries of the weather, the mushroom is the one vegetable that is in prime season all the year round. And because it contains a negligible number of calories, and quite a good supply of the B vitamins, it's one of the few 'gourmet' foods that can be enjoyed without a dietetic qualm.

Cultivated mushrooms are grown in sterilized compost so that they do not need to be peeled; if the stalks are used, discard only the last quarter of an inch ($\frac{1}{2}$ cm) of tip, but use all the rest. Rinse only briefly and dry before use. A truly fresh mushroom is plump and clean with a sweet smell, and its gills, whatever the size of the cap, should be a pinky beige, never a murky brown.

Button mushrooms with unopened caps are used for soups and sauces where a creamy colour is required in the finished dish.

Slightly open caps just beginning to show the gills, are ideal for frying and baking.

Fully open caps (called flats) are best for stuffing.

Field mushrooms have darker caps with dark brown gills and are altogether floppier in appearance. Their deeper flavour makes them good accompaniments to robust food such as chops and steaks.

Buy mushrooms if possible the day you intend to use them; alternatively, store in an airtight plastic container under refrigeration for a maximum of 3 days.

To freeze: Either sauté in fat and then freeze, or, if only a few hours old, pack in plastic bags and freeze without more ado.

Grilled Mushrooms

Remove the stalks (refrigerate for other use), Brush the mushrooms all over with melted butter. arrange hollow side up on a grill pan. Sprinkle with salt and pepper and grill under moderate heat for 5 minutes. Turn and grill for another 5 minutes on the second side. Season when cooked. Use as a garnish or to serve on toast.

Mushrooms Fried in Butter

The secret of perfect fried mushrooms lies in having dry mushrooms, fried in butter at the correct temperature, in a pan large enough to brown them without steaming them by overcrowding.

½ lb (200g/4 cups) mushrooms
1 oz (25g/2 tbsp) butter
2 teasp oil

Trim the stalks off at the cap. If the mushrooms are small leave whole, otherwise cut into quarters. Heat the butter and oil in a 10 in (25 cm) frying pan. The butter will foam and as soon as this subsides, immediately put the mushrooms into it. Cook steadily for 5 minutes, tossing them lightly until they are evenly browned. Serves 4.

Mushrooms in Sour Cream Sauce

This makes a very pleasant accompaniment to grilled fish.

½ lb (200g/4 cups) small mushrooms; or large ones, sliced in 4 right through the stalk
1 small onion, very finely chopped
5 fl oz (125ml/⅔ cup) soured cream
1 oz (25g/2 tbsp) butter
1 tbsp sherry
½ clove garlic, crushed
Pinch of mace, salt and white pepper
Squeeze of lemon juice

Melt the butter, then add the onion, cover and cook gently for 5 minutes until soft and golden. Add the mushrooms and toss to coat with the oniony butter. Add the squeeze of lemon juice, cover and cook for 5 minutes until mushrooms are fork tender. Uncover, season with salt and pepper, garlic (optional) and mace and stir in the sherry and the soured cream. Heat till steaming. Serves 4–6. Cooked green beans can be treated in exactly the same way.

The Capsicum (or Sweet Pepper)

The pepper needs sun and warmth to mature and sweeten it—Israel, Spain and Italy grow it with great success. It is a most useful vegetable to have in stock, for even a quarter will add flavour to a stew or salad, and the remainder can be foil-wrapped and refrigerated for up to a week. There is little to choose in flavour between red, yellow or green peppers, but whatever the colour, the vegetable should be glossy and firm and quite free from bruises. Before it is used every scrap of the white ribs and bitter seeds must be discarded.

Fried Peppers

This is excellent with roast beef or grilled steak.

4 large glossy green peppers
2 tbsp salad oil
Small garlic clove, crushed with salt
1 level teasp marjoram or oregano
1 level teasp salt
10 grinds black pepper

Cut peppers in half and remove the seeds and ribs. Wash then slice in strips, 3 to each half. Heat the oil gently, then add the peppers and cook quickly for a few minutes till beginning to soften, stirring frequently. Add the garlic, cover, reducing heat to minimum and cook slowly (15–20 minutes) until tender. Add the herbs and seasonings. Serves 4.

Peperonata

A juicier dish altogether, which can be served either hot or cold. Use green peppers if the red are not available.

6 plump and glossy red peppers
1 medium can (15 oz/375g) tomatoes; or 10 very ripe fresh ones
1 large onion
½ clove garlic
2 tbsp oil
Salt and pepper

Slice the onion and cook it until limp and golden in the oil. Halve peppers, remove seeds and inner pith, then slice finely and add to pan. Toss to coat with oil, sprinkle with salt and cover. Cook gently for 15 minutes to soften, then add the drained canned tomatoes, or the peeled and halved fresh ones, and crushed ½ clove garlic. Continue to stew for another half-hour. Uncover, and if necessary, simmer to ensure a juicy but not watery mixture. Serves 8 or 4 twice.

Ratatouille

This kind of vegetable 'stew' is made all over the Mediterranean, and is particularly popular with Jews who came from the former Ottoman Empire. If aubergines (eggplant) are out of season use a 10 *in* (25 *cm*) *long vegetable marrow, or extra courgettes. Serve with roast veal, or as an appetizer.*

Ratatouille Niçoise

2 long aubergines (eggplant) or 1 fat egg-shaped one
1 large onion
2 large green peppers
1 clove garlic, crushed
Smallest size can tomatoes, without juice; or 6 fresh ones
2 courgettes (zucchini)—optional
5 tbsp oil
1 tbsp lemon juice
1 tbsp wine vinegar
Salt and pepper
1 teasp sugar

First prepare vegetables. Peel and cube the aubergines, seed, and slice then dice the peppers; slice the onion thinly; scrub and slice the courgettes (if used); peel and quarter tomatoes if fresh. Crush garlic with a little salt. Put oil in a heavy-lidded frying pan, and cook onion gently, covered, until soft. Then add the remaining ingredients. Season with salt and pepper, sprinkle with sugar, cover and cook 1 hour. If pan starts to stick, add a little hot water. Finally, mixture should be thick; if too runny, remove lid and allow to thicken. Just before serving, add wine vinegar, and lemon juice. Serves 6.

Stuffed Tomatoes

Choose large, squat tomatoes which are very firm to the touch.

6 large tomatoes
1 oz (25g/2 tbsp) butter or oil
1 medium onion, finely chopped
1 small clove garlic, crushed
3 heaped tbsp fresh breadcrumbs
Salt and pepper
1 level teasp each of chopped parsley, oregano and basil
Good pinch of sugar

Cut a 'lid' off the tomato at the stem end, and scoop out the inside. Sprinkle the insides with salt and turn upside down on a paper towel to drain. Meanwhile, melt the butter or oil, add the onion and cook gently until tender but unbrowned (5–6 minutes). Add the garlic, followed by the tomato pulp and cook until the tomato is soft. Add the breadcrumbs, mixed with the herbs and seasonings. Taste the mixture—it should be highly-seaonsed and herby. Arrange the tomatoes on a greased tin. Fill lightly with the stuffing (don't pack it in), cover with the tomato 'lid', then bake in a moderate oven (Gas No. 4, 350°F, 180°C) for 25 minutes or until just tender. Serves 6.

Perfect Potatoes

When you consider the calories in a potato, it's got to be well-cooked to be worth the expenditure. That's why the recipes in this section are limited, but really good. They're not dishes to 'fill up the gaps' but to add real eating pleasure to a meal.

To Bake Potatoes

This method conserves all the nourishment which lies under the skin and is usually discarded with the potato peelings.

1 medium potato per person
Butter or margarine

Set the oven (Gas No. 6, 400°F, 200°C). Choose potatoes of an even size, so that they will be ready at the same time. Scrub thoroughly with a nylon pan scrub kept for the purpose, then remove any eyes with a potato peeler. Dry thoroughly, and prick all over with a fork (to stop the potato bursting). Rub each potato with a butter or margarine wrapper to give it a light coating of fat. Arrange on a baking tin. Cook for 1–1½ hours (depending on size) until the potato feels tender when it is gently squeezed.

To serve: Squeeze the skin to break it and allow some of the steam to escape from inside. This makes the potato floury and light. Serve in an uncovered dish to prevent the skin going soggy. Hand round the butter, salt and a pepper mill. Soured cream flavoured with 2 teaspoons finely-cut chives makes an excellent accompaniment.

To Mash Potatoes

No packeted potato can match the perfection of home-made mashed potatoes, cooked by the method described below. But don't keep them hot for more than 15 minutes—they lose their flavour and much of their nourishment.

2–3 lb (1–1½kg) potatoes
2 level teasp salt
¼ teasp white pepper
2 oz (50g/¼ cup) butter
4 fl oz (100ml/½ cup) hot milk

Peel the potatoes, cut them into quarters and put them in a pan containing sufficient boiling water to cover them. Add the salt, bring back to the boil, cover and cook at a steady boil for 15 minutes, or until a piece feels absolutely tender when pierced with a thin vegetable knife. (Do not boil vigorously, or they may become 'soupy'). Drain the water from the potatoes, return to the stove in the same pan and shake over a gentle heat until all the moisture has evaporated. Pour the milk down the side of the pan, and when it starts to steam, add the butter, then start whisking together with the potatoes, using either a small balloon whisk or a portable electric mixer. Continue to whisk on a very low heat until the potatoes lighten in colour and look fluffy. Add more milk if the mixture seems too dry—the texture is a matter of taste. Pile into a warm vegetable dish and serve immediately. Serves 4–6.

VARIATIONS

For a meat meal, omit the milk and the butter. Substitute 2 rounded tablespoons chicken fat or 3 oz (75g/⅓ cup) margarine. The mixture won't be as creamy, but will be equally tasty.

Duchesse: Mash the boiled potatoes with 2 fl oz (50ml/¼ cup) milk, 1 oz (25g/2 tbsp) butter and 1 egg yolk. Put into piping bag fitted with coarse rose tube. Pipe onto greased trays. Bake in a quick oven (Gas No. 6, 400°F, 200°C) until golden brown (about 10 minutes). Serves 4–5.

Potato Puff Balls: Mix 4 oz (100g/1 cup) finely-grated cheese with a good pinch of dry mustard. Shape the duchesse potato mixture into balls the size of an egg. Roll in the cheese mixture. Arrange on a greased tray and bake (Gas No. 6, 400°F, 200°C) for 10 minutes until golden brown. Alternatively, brown under the grill. Serves 4–5.

Potato Croquettes

1 lb (½kg) potatoes (weight when peeled)
1 egg yolk
1 oz (25g/2 tbsp) butter
1 tbsp hot milk
Salt and pepper
Dry white crumbs
1 beaten egg

Boil the potatoes, drain, then return to a low heat to dry off thoroughly. Using an electric mixer, beat in the milk, egg yolk and butter—the mixture must be pasty rather than fluffy. Season well. Turn onto a floured board and divide into 8 or 10 pieces. Leave to cool. With floured hands, form into balls or corks, brush with beaten egg and then with the dry crumbs. Fry the croquettes in shallow or deep oil (375°F, 190°C). Serves 4–5.

VARIATIONS

For a meat meal, omit the milk and butter; instead use 2 eggs yolk and ½ oz (15g/1 tbsp) margarine. Fry in oil.

Pommes Berny: Make the croquette mixture and form into small balls the size of a tomato. Brush with beaten egg, then roll in chopped or slivered blanched almonds. Fry in deep hot fat (375°F, 190°C on a thermometer or hot enough to brown a ½ in (1 cm) cube of bread in 40 seconds).

Roast Potatoes

If the potatoes are parboiled before roasting rather than put in the oven raw, they develop a crisp yet tender crust and a deliciously soft inside.

2–3 lb (1–1½kg) potatoes
Oil and margarine
Salt

Peel the potatoes and cut them (if large) into slices 1 in (2½ cm) thick. Put in a pan half-full of boiling water, add 1 level teaspoon salt and bring slowly back to the boil. Cook until the potatoes are almost, but not quite, tender—they will feel slightly hard when pierced with a slim vegetable knife. This will take about 15–20 minutes. Drain the potatoes, then return them to the empty pan and shake over a low heat until they look absolutely dry. Meanwhile put in the oven a shallow roasting tin (just large enough to hold the potato slices in one layer) which has a thin layer of oil covering the bottom. The oven can be set at any moderate temperature (whichever is the most convenient for the main dish cooking at the same time). At Gas No. 3, 325°F, 170°C, it will take the oil 10 minutes to heat; at Gas No. 5, 375°F, 190°C, it will take 7 minutes. Put the tin of hot oil on the cooker, add a nut of margarine, then carefully lay the potatoes in it, and immediately turn them over so that they are coated with the hot fat. Sprinkle lightly with salt and return to the oven. Cook at Gas No. 3, 325°F, 170°C, for 1¼–1½ hours. Cook at Gas No. 5, 375°F, 190°C, for 1 hour. At either temperature, turn the potatoes at half-time. Serves 4–6.

Crisp Chips (French Fries)

For a family it's worth investing in a chip pan (deep fat fryer) with a basket, so that chips can be cooked by the two-stage French method as follows.

4 large potatoes (approx 1½lb/700g when peeled)

Peel the potatoes, cut them into slices ⅜ in (1 cm) thick, then cut the slices into chips ⅜ in (1 cm) wide. Result: chips are of equal width and depth (this is important for even cooking). If you are great chip eaters, you can of course, invest in a chipper. Soak the chips in cold water for half an hour—this will dissolve excess surface starch. Drain and dry thoroughly on a tea towel.

To fry: Fill the chip pan one third full of oil, heat (it should register 375°F, 190°C). To test the temperature of the oil, either use an oil thermometer or: 1. A 1 in (2½ cm) square of day-old bread should brown in 40 seconds. 2. A dry chip should rise to the surface of the oil a few seconds after being dropped in. Put the chips in a frying basket and lower into the oil. Cook for 3–4 minutes, uncovered, or until the chips feel tender when pierced with a knife, but are unbrowned. Lift the basket from the oil, and allow the oil to drain back into the pan. This preliminary process is called 'blanching', and can be done at any time before a meal. When the chips are required, reheat the oil to its former temperature (375°F, 190°C or use the bread test), put the chips back in and fry for a further 1 minute, until crisp and golden. Shake gently to remove excess oil and serve in a hot dish at once. (*Note:* It is better to do the final crisping in small batches, for if the frying basket is too full, the oil will be cooled and the chips will take much longer to brown.) Serves 4–6.

VARIATIONS

Chips for 2: For a small number of chips good results can be obtained by frying only once in a large saucepan as follows:

2 large potatoes (¾ lb/300g)

Fill the pan (it can be a saucepan or deep frying pan) one third full of oil, and heat to 375°F, 190°C or until a dry chip sizzles gently when put into it.

Carefully lower the remainder of the chips into the oil and cook at a steady but busy bubble for 7–10 minutes, or until they look a rich crisp brown. Lift out with a slotted spoon, drain briefly on crumpled tissue paper and serve at once.

Crisps: Peel small potatoes and cut into paper-thin slices with a mandoline (vegetable cutter). Soak for half an hour, dry thoroughly and then fry at 375°F, 190°C for 5–6 minutes.

To Fry Potatoes

To achieve a really crisp, flavourful result, the potatoes should be fried slowly at first to absorb the fat, and then more quickly when they are almost ready, to make them crisp. Cold left-over potatoes can be used, but the finest results are achieved with potatoes freshly cooked in their skins.

2 lb (1kg) potatoes (boiled in their skins)
2 oz (50g/¼ cup) butter
2 tbsp oil
Salt and black pepper

Scrub the potatoes, then cook them whole in their skins, covered with boiling salted water for 25–40 minutes, depending on their size. Drain the potatoes and return to the empty pan to dry off on a low heat. Leave until cool enough to handle, then skin and cut into thick slices or cubes.

To fry: Put the oil and butter in a heavy frying pan. When the butter starts to foam, put in the potatoes and cook very gently, shaking the pan occasionally so that the potatoes absorb the fat rather than fry in it. This will take about 15 minutes. When the potatoes are golden all over, increase the heat to make them crisp. Drain from the fat (there should be very little, if any, left), put in a dish and sprinkle with salt and black pepper. Serves 4–6.

VARIATIONS

To fry in chicken fat and oil: Heat 2 tablespoons chicken fat and 2 tablespoons oil together over moderate heat for 3 minutes. Add the potatoes—they should sizzle slightly. Continue to cook as above.

Savoury Fried Potatoes (Pommes Lyonnaise): After 10 minutes, add 1 finely-sliced or chopped onion to the pan. Continue to cook until the onion is soft and golden as well as the potatoes. Sprinkle with chopped parsley before serving.

Golden New Potatoes (*Pommes de Terre Château*)

These make a beautiful garnish for a milk meal—they are not successful if fried in oil alone. Use small new potatoes measuring about 2 × 1 in (5 × 2½ cm). The waxier they are the better. Peel, but do not wash—merely wipe with a dry cloth.

2 lb (1kg) new potatoes
1½ oz (40g/3 tbsp) butter
1 tbsp oil
Salt
Butter and herbs for serving

Put the butter and oil in a frying pan wide enough to hold all the potatoes. Immediately the butter stops foaming, put in the potatoes and leave for 2 minutes over gentle heat. Now shake the pan so that the topside of the potatoes gets a chance to brown. Continue shaking the pan and browning the potatoes for 5 minutes, until they are evenly coloured, then sprinkle them with a little salt, cover with a tight lid and allow to steam for 15 minutes, shaking occasionally so that they continue to brown evenly. Test to make sure that a knife will pierce them easily, then pour off any remaining fat. If required, the potatoes can be kept hot with the lid partially on for half an hour, then reheated just before serving. To serve, turn off the heat, add a large nut of butter and 2 tablespoons mixed chopped fresh herbs such as parsley and chives. Roll in this mixture until glistening and then serve. Serves 6.

Danish Candied Potatoes

Canned new potatoes can be used.

1½ lb (700g) small new potatoes
1 oz (25g/2 tbsp) butter
1 oz (25g/2 tbsp) sugar

Boil the potatoes in their skins until just tender.

Skin when cool enough to handle. Put the sugar in a heavy dry frying pan, and heat until it begins to melt, and turns a pale gold. Add the butter and stir until melted. Rinse the peeled potatoes quickly, in cold water, then gently lay them in the caramel. Cook gently, shaking frequently, until evenly glazed. Serves 4–6.

Rice is Nice

Rice is one of the most ancient of foods—the first record of its cultivation dates from the reign of the Chinese Emperor Shen Nung about 3,000 B.C.E. Yet it is still popular, not only in those Eastern countries where it is the staple food, but all over the Western World. Sephardi Jews are great rice cooks, using it both as a main dish accompaniment and as an ingredient in many of their most delicious dishes.

Until twenty years ago, most rice came in hessian sacks, with a full quota of stones, dirt and rubbish—the 'picking over' of rice to remove these impurities was a traditional chore of Sephardi Jewish housewives before the Passover. The cooking quality of the grain also varied from one country to another, and indeed from one crop to the next. So a major part of the preparation of rice for cooking used to be in the cleansing, whilst the cooking process itself had to be varied according to its quality and country of origin.

Today it is a very different story. Most of the rice sold in the Western world is pre-cleaned and pre-packeted. The quality is standardized and so therefore is the cooking method. If you cannot buy packeted rice, then the best advice I can give is to cook it according to the traditional method of the country where you buy it.

Although botanists have recorded no less than 7,000 different varieties, to most Western cooks, buying rice has meant shopping by name for but two of them: 'Carolina' for puddings and 'Patna' for curries, pilaffs and other savoury dishes. Today the 'Carolina' rice one can buy has never seen Carolina, and little if any of the Patna rice comes from Bengal. Rice sold under these names has in fact been grown from seed descended from the original varieties and is now successfully cultivated in many other parts of the world. In addition, small quantities of 'wild rice' are marketed in the United States, and in the Po valley of Italy is grown the 'risotto' rice, which cooks creamily while still retaining its chewiness.

Rice for cooking: You can cook rice according to the customs of the Chinese, Persians, and Turks, the Egyptians, the Sephardim or indeed of the English and, if you've the time and the patience you will get consistently good results. For savoury cookery however, I use packeted parboiled long grain rice, cooking it in a measured amount of water, so that the cooked rice needs no draining or steaming, but becomes fluffy and separate with the minimum of cookery. It is this type of rice that is used in the recipes below.

To refrigerate rice: Store in an airtight container for up to a week if it has been cooked in water, for up to 3 days if cooked in stock.

To freeze rice: Pack in plastic bags or containers for up to six months. Defrost before reheating. (If the rice must be heated from the frozen state use the oven method below, but allow 30 minutes.)

To reheat rice: Cover the bottom of a pan or casserole to a depth of ¼ in (½ cm) with boiling water or stock, then add the rice. Cover and re-heat until steaming, stirring once (top-of-stove—about 5 min; oven—15 min at Gas No. 4, 350°F, 180°C).

Quantities: For a main dish accompaniment allow 1½–2 oz (40–50g/3–4 tbsp) raw rice per serving.

Boiled Savoury Rice

To serve in place of potatoes or with curries or other savoury dishes. (*Note:* 1 cup = 8 fl oz)

7 oz (175g/1 cup) pkt parboiled long grain rice
1 pint (500ml/2½ cups) water
1 oz (25g/2 tbsp) butter or margarine or chicken fat; or 1 tbsp oil for a meat meal
1 level teasp salt

Put all the ingredients into a heavy-based pan.

Bring to the boil, stir once, cover and cook for 15–20 minutes when all the water will have been absorbed and the rice is fluffy and separate. Serves 4.

VARIATIONS

1. Replace the water by beef or chicken stock. Use either margarine, oil or chicken fat for the fat.
2. If using regular rice (not parboiled), use only ¾ pint (375ml/2 cups) water.
3. For large quantities it is often more convenient to cook in the oven. Put the rice in a casserole, then put in a moderate oven (Gas No. 4, 350°F, 180°C) for 30 minutes. If a large casserole is not available, use an oven roasting tin, tightly covered with foil.

Oriental Boiled Rice

This is the method used by Sephardi cooks, using the regular (not parboiled) long grain Patna rice.

7 oz (175g/1 cup) long grain rice
Chicken fat
½ pint plus 3 tbsp (300ml/1½ cups) water
1 level teasp salt

Wash the rice thoroughly till the rinsing water is clear. Melt enough chicken fat in a heavy-bottomed pan to cover the bottom to depth of ⅛ in (½ cm). Add the salt and water and bring to the boil. Add the rice, cover and simmer until water has just been absorbed but rice still looks moist. Place the covered pan in a moderate oven (Gas No. 4, 350°F, 180°C) for 20 minutes. Serves 4.

Pilaff

1 medium onion, finely chopped
1 oz (25g/2 tbsp) margarine; or 1 rounded tbsp rendered chicken fat
7 oz (175g/1 cup) parboiled long grain rice
1 level teasp paprika pepper
2 teasp tomato purée
1¼ pints (600ml/3 cups) chicken soup or stock made from bouillon cubes
½ clove garlic
2 level teasp salt
Black pepper

The ideal utensil to use is a cast-iron enamelled casserole that can be used on top or in the stove. Have ready the hot soup or stock. Melt the fat in the casserole, add the onion and cook for 5 minutes until softened and golden. Add the rice and cook a further 5 minutes over gentle heat until most of the fat has been absorbed. Add half the stock and simmer on top of the stove until the stock has been absorbed by the rice, then add the remainder of the stock, together with the garlic and the seasonings. Cover and put in a moderate oven (Gas No. 4, 350°F, 180°C) for 25 minutes until the rice is fluffy and the stock has been absorbed. Serves 4 generously.

VARIATIONS

1. For less hearty appetites use 1 cup rice (7 oz/175g) and 2½ cups stock (1 pt/500ml).
2. Sauté ¼ lb (100g) chopped mushrooms and 3 koshered chicken livers together with the onion.

Pilaff in the Greek Fashion

Excellent to serve with the remains of the chicken or the joint.

7 oz (175g/1 cup) American long grain rice
1 pint (500ml/2½ cups) chicken stock
2 tbsp oil
1 medium onion, finely chopped
1 small clove garlic, crushed with 1 level teasp salt
Good pinch of sugar and ground black pepper
4 frying sausages cut in 4
¼ lb (100g/2 cups) mushrooms
3 canned tomatoes, well-drained and chopped
Small pkt frozen peas
4 level tbsp raisins

Heat the oil and cook the onion until a rich golden brown. Add the rice and cook a further 3 minutes, then add the mushrooms, sausages, garlic and tomatoes. Stir well, then add the boiling chicken stock, the pepper and sugar. Cover and transfer to the oven and cook for a further 30 minutes at Gas No. 4, 350°F, 180°C. Stir in the raisins and peas, and leave covered for 5 minutes. This serves 4–6.

Chinese Fried Rice

An excellent way to use left-over rice.

3–4 cups cooked rice (about 7 oz/175g/1 cup raw)
1 onion, finely chopped
2 tbsp oil or chicken fat
¼ lb (100g/2 cups) button mushrooms, coarsely chopped
1 medium green pepper
2 teasp soy sauce
1 level tbsp snipped chives or chopped parsley
Salt and pepper

Fry the onion in the fat until soft and golden, together with the deseeded and slivered pepper. Add the cold rice and heat gently, stirring the rice till brown. Stir in the soy sauce, salt and pepper to taste and the herbs. Serve very hot.

For more recipes see **Entertaining** p. 253.

Noodles

Savoury Lokshen Kugel (Pudding)

This can be served as a soup accompaniment (to make a more substantial meal on the Eve of the Day of Atonement—Erev Yom Kippur), or in place of potatoes with a main course. The flavour is best when rendered chicken fat is used as well as 'grebenes' —the crackling from the rendered fat.

4 oz (100g/1½ cups) egg noodles
1 large egg
4 level tbsp rendered chicken fat or margarine
2 level tbsp of grebenes
Salt and pepper

Turn the oven to Gas No. 2, 300°F, 150°C. Half fill an 8 in (20 cm) diameter pan with cold water, add 1 level teaspoon salt and bring to the boil. Then add the lokshen, stir until the water comes back to the boil, half cover the pan and allow to boil steadily for 8 minutes. (Do not cover tightly, or the water will froth over the side of the pan.) Taste a piece of lokshen. It should be bite-tender. Turn into a metal sieve, but do not rinse under the cold tap, because the starch on the outside of the lokshen helps to 'set' the pudding. Allow the lokshen to drain completely. Put the chicken fat or margarine into a 2 pint (1 litre/5 cups) casserole and leave in the oven for a few minutes. Meanwhile, beat the egg, add the grebenes, a pinch of salt and pepper, and the drained noodles. Take the hot dish out of the oven, swirl the fat round to coat the sides, then pour it onto the noodle mixture. Stir well, then spoon into the casserole. Bake for 1½ hours or until crispy on top and set within. Lokshen kugel can be cooked in a Gas No. ¼, 200°F, 100°C oven overnight, but double the quantity must be used if the dish is not to be dry. Serves 4–5.

Savoury Lokshen (Noodles)

Serve with grilled or fried steaks and chops.

4 oz (100g/1½ cups) broad egg noodles
¾ pint (375ml/2 cups) boiling water
1 chicken or beef bouillon cube
Nut of margarine
1 tbsp chopped parsley
Black pepper

Bring the water to the boil, add the stock cube and the noodles, partially cover and simmer for 10 minutes. Whilst the noodles are cooking put the margarine in the serving dish in a warm oven. Drain the noodles (reserve the stock for other use), add to the margarine with the parsley and black pepper. Toss well, then serve piping hot. Serves 4–5.

VARIATION

For a milk meal, boil the noodles in water. Heat 2 oz (50g/¼ cup) butter in the serving dish, then blend with the noodles, parsley and black pepper.

For **Pasta** main dishes see p. 58.
For **Home-made Noodles (Lokshen)** see p. 36.

Salads and Their Dressings

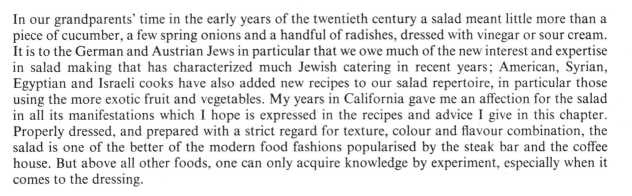

In our grandparents' time in the early years of the twentieth century a salad meant little more than a piece of cucumber, a few spring onions and a handful of radishes, dressed with vinegar or sour cream. It is to the German and Austrian Jews in particular that we owe much of the new interest and expertise in salad making that has characterized much Jewish catering in recent years; American, Syrian, Egyptian and Israeli cooks have also added new recipes to our salad repertoire, in particular those using the more exotic fruit and vegetables. My years in California gave me an affection for the salad in all its manifestations which I hope is expressed in the recipes and advice I give in this chapter. Properly dressed, and prepared with a strict regard for texture, colour and flavour combination, the salad is one of the better of the modern food fashions popularised by the steak bar and the coffee house. But above all other foods, one can only acquire knowledge by experiment, especially when it comes to the dressing.

The Green Salad

The preparation of a green salad needs especial care. As even the best salad baskets don't remove every drop of moisture, one must literally dry each leaf by hand, then put the dried leaves in a pottery bowl and cover. Chill.

For such a salad, I prefer to mix the herbs with the greens rather than with the dressing; so that fresh basil, parsley and chives should be scissored (rather than chopped) into the salad bowl.

As a green salad must always be dressed at table, and I find that a dressing that has been matured for an hour has a deeper flavour than one mixed at the last moment, leave the prepared dressing in a glass-stoppered jar which can be shaken just before it is spooned through the salad at the table.

Mixed Green Salad: A General Guide

1 large lettuce, washed and crisped in the refrigerator (tear leaves into bite-sized pieces)
1 bunch watercress (leaves only)
1 tbsp fresh herbs such as scissored parsley or basil
4 tomatoes, seeded and cut in 4 } optional
4 in (10 cm) cucumber, thinly sliced } optional
6–8 red radishes, thinly sliced } optional

Arrange ingredients in a bowl large enough to allow contents to be tossed with dressing. Cover with film or foil and leave at bottom of refrigerator until required. Serves 4-6.

Chicory Salad in the French Manner

An excellent salad for late winter when lettuces are in poor supply.

4 large or 6 small head of chicory
The dressing:
3 tbsp olive oil
1 tbsp wine or cider vinegar
1 level teasp each of salt and sugar
Plenty of freshly-ground black pepper
1 level tbsp finely-chopped parsley
1 level teasp dried fines herbes (if available)
1 small clove garlic, crushed

Cut off the base of the chicory so that the leaves can be removed whole. Put these in a colander and rinse under the cold tap. Put in a salad bowl, cover with plastic film and refrigerate for a few hours until required. Make the dressing by shaking all the ingredients together in a screw-top jar until they thicken (about 2 minutes), then refrigerate as well. Just before serving, pour the dressing over the chicory, toss thoroughly until all the leaves are coated with the dressing and serve at once. Serves 6.

Cooked Vegetable Salads

Green Bean Salad

Fresh or frozen beans can be used for this refreshing salad.

1 lb ($\frac{1}{2}$kg) French beans, broken into 2 or 3 pieces and boiled
4 tomatoes
$\frac{1}{2}$ large green pepper
Dressing:
4 tbsp olive oil
2 tbsp wine vinegar
1 level teasp each of sugar and salt
Plenty of black pepper
1 level tbsp chopped onion
1 level tbsp chopped parsley
1 level tbsp snipped chives

Boil the beans rapidly in a large pan of boiling salted water with the lid off until just bite-tender. Immediately, turn into a colander and plunge it into a bowl of cold water for 2 minutes. This will set the colour of the beans. Drain thoroughly. Shake all the dressing ingredients together until blended. Cut the tomatoes into 6 or 8, depending on size, and the pepper into very fine dice. Blend with the dressing and serve very cold. Serves 6.

Cauliflower, Black Olive and Pimento Salad

Make this salad when cauliflowers are at their best.

2 small or 1 large very white cauliflower
$\frac{1}{2}$ lb (200g/2 cups) choice black olives
1 small can (3–4) pimentos
Dressing:
$\frac{1}{4}$ pint (125ml/$\frac{2}{3}$ cup) oil
3 tbsp red wine vinegar
1 clove garlic, cut in two
1 teasp sugar
$\frac{1}{2}$ teasp salt
Black pepper

Soak cauliflower in salt water for half an hour. Remove, wash then separate into little flowerets without any tough stalk. Boil for 5–8 minutes, until just tender but not sloppy. Refresh with cold water under tap, drain thoroughly. Put in bowl with olives pipped and cut in pieces, pimento in strips. Shake all ingredients for the dressing in a covered jar 1 hour before needed. Pour over mixed ingredients (discarding garlic). Refrigerate several hours, tossing occasionally to blend in dressing. Serve cold. Serves 6.

Corn Confetti Salad

If you don't like cooked peas, omit them and substitute a double quantity of corn. This salad is ideal with fresh salmon, as the flavour is subtle and delicate.

1 pkt (approx 12 oz/300g) petit pois (frozen)
2 canned pimentos
1 tbsp chopped parsley
1 tbsp mayonnaise
1 large can (12 oz/300g) corn, or pkt frozen corn, cooked
2 teasp chopped onion
2 tbsp garlic French dressing

Cook peas until just tender; drain corn thoroughly. Dice pimentos, chop onion and parsley. Mix all together then blend with French dressing (home or bottled) and mayonnaise. Chill. Serves 6–8.

Perfect Potato Salad

The kidney-shaped, waxy, yellow kipfel potato is ideal for salad. However, if you cook an ordinary new potato with special care, add the oil and vinegar when the potatoes are hot and the mayonnaise when they are cold, I am sure you will agree this is the best potato salad you have ever tasted.

1½ lb (700g) new potatoes
4 tbsp prepared French dressing; or 3 tbsp oil and 1 tbsp vinegar, ½ teasp salt, pinch of pepper, pinch each of sugar and mustard
1 level tbsp finely-chopped onion
1 tbsp scissored chives; or 1 bunch spring onions (scallions)
1 tbsp finely-chopped parsley
¼ pint (125ml/⅔ cup) home-made mayonnaise
1 level teasp French mustard
1 tbsp each of boiling water and lemon juice

Boil potatoes in their skins until almost tender. Drain, return to the heat covered with a tea-towel, then cook gently for a further 3 or 4 minutes until tender and absolutely dry (they will be firm). Spread on a cloth and leave until cool enough to handle, then skin and dice or slice into a bowl. Mix the dressing with onion and herbs, then stir gently through the potatoes. Heap into a shallow bowl. Blend together the mayonnaise, mustard, boiling water and lemon juice. Spoon on top of the potatoes. Leave in a cool place for at least an hour. Just before serving, mix the mayonnaise through the salad and garnish with more parsley. This salad will keep under refrigeration for at least 48 hours, and seems to improve in flavour with the passing hours. Always serve it at room temperature. Serves 6–8.

Tomato Salads

Cyprus Tomato Salad

1 medium cucumber, peeled, cut in ½ in (1 cm) cubes and salted in colander for half an hour
4 large tomatoes, cubed
1 large green pepper, diced
1 tbsp chopped parsley
Black olives for garnish

Dressing:

4 tbsp olive oil
2 tbsp lemon juice
1 teasp each of salt and sugar
Pinch of black pepper
Pinch of garlic salt
} All shaken together

Shake all the dressing ingredients together until blended. Arrange the tomatoes, cucumber, and pepper in a shallow bowl and sprinkle with parsley. Just before serving, sprinkle on the dressing and toss well. Top with calamata (black) olives. Serves 6.

French Tomato Salad

3 large tomatoes (1 lb/½kg)
2 fl oz (50ml/¼ cup) olive or salad oil
1½ fl oz (40ml/3 tbsp) lemon juice
½ teasp salt
Black pepper
1 level tbsp finely-chopped onion
½ clove garlic, crushed
1 level teasp paprika
1 level teasp fresh mint (or, if out of season, parsley)

Put all seasoning ingredients in jar, and shake till thick. Leave 30 minutes. Slice 3 large ripe tomatoes, chill. Pour dressing over, and leave further half-hour in 'fridge. Serves 4.

Salad from the South

Excellent with chopped fried fish.

4 large firm tomatoes
1 Spanish onion
1 green pepper
3 in (7½ cm) length cucumber

The dressing:

2 tbsp corn or olive oil
1 tbsp lemon juice or cider vinegar
Good pinch of salt
Paprika and black pepper
1 teasp sugar
½ clove garlic, crushed
Basil leaves (dried ones can be used)

In a long dish about 1 in ($2\frac{1}{2}$ cm) deep arrange alternate slices of thickly cut tomatoes and cucumber cut very thin. Over top strew the onion (cut wafer thin) and the green pepper (seeded and cut into fine strips). Put all dressing ingredients into a screw-top jar and shake until thickened (about 1 minute). Pour over the vegetables then leave for half an hour for the flavours to develop. Just before serving scatter over a teaspoon of basil leaves. Serves 4–6.

Tomato and Cauliflower Salad

Serve with grilled chops or chicken.

1 small white cauliflower
$\frac{3}{4}$–1 lb (300–480g) firm tomatoes
Chopped chives

Dressing:
1 tbsp cider or wine vinegar
1 tbsp lemon juice
6 tbsp olive or other salad oil
1 teasp tomato ketchup
1 level teasp each of sugar and salt
Good pinch dry mustard
$\frac{1}{2}$ peeled clove garlic

Put all the salad ingredients into a screw-top jar and shake until thickened (about 2 minutes). Wash the cauliflower, then break into flowerets, plunge into a large pan of boiling, salted water. Simmer uncovered for 5 minutes until just bite-tender. Drain into a colander then plunge into a pan of very cold water for 2 minutes. Lift colander out and allow to drain thoroughly. Put cauliflower in bowl, pour over dressing (first discarding garlic), cover and chill for several hours.

To serve: Arrange a ring of sliced tomato on oval platter, then spoon drained cauliflower into centre. Scatter with chopped chives. Serves 4–6.

Relish Salads

The salads in this section all add piquancy to more blandly-flavoured foods, and are therefore more in the Jewish tradition than the green salads. They are especially suitable for a cold buffet.

Danish Cucumber Salad

Particularly delicious with cold boiled salmon. The dressing must be both very sweet and very sour.

1 cucumber
Coarse salt

Dressing:
2 level tbsp caster (superfine) sugar
1 tbsp boiling water
4 tbsp wine vinegar
Plenty of black pepper
1 tbsp finely-cut chives

Peel and slice cucumber thinly in a soup plate, sprinkle with salt, cover with an upturned plate and a 1 lb ($\frac{1}{2}$ kg) weight. Leave half an hour. Pour off water. Dissolve sugar in the boiling water, then add all the remaining ingredients. One hour before serving, pour onto cucumber slices. Serves 6.

Cucumbers in Soured Cream or Yoghourt

A dish popular all over the Middle East. This version, with its garnish of mint, comes from Turkey. Yoghourt is more authentic, soured cream more satisfying. Another good dish to serve with salmon, either boiled or grilled.

1 cucumber
5 fl oz (125ml/$\frac{2}{3}$ cup) soured cream or yoghourt
2 teasp lemon juice
2 teasp wine vinegar
2 teasp sugar
Grind of pepper
Pinch of salt
2 teasp chopped fresh mint or a pinch of dried mint

Peel, then thinly slice the cucumber. Sprinkle with coarse salt, cover with plate and weight. Leave half an hour, then drain off liquid, and pat cucumber slices dry. Arrange in a shallow dish. Beat sour cream together with seasonings. Pour over cucumber slices. Serve very cold, garnished with the chopped mint. Serves 6.

Citrus Salad with Avocado Dressing

This is typical of those salads which originated in Southern California in the 1930s—usually invented by the French chefs imported by the movie moguls. It combines sweet and savoury in a most interesting way, and makes an excellent 'side salad' to serve with roast chicken or grilled steak.

1 grapefruit
3 oranges
Little caster (superfine) sugar
Dressing:
1 small or ½ large avocado, mashed
2 teasp lemon juice
¼ teasp prepared mustard
½ level teasp salt
Dash cayenne pepper
¼ teasp finely-grated onion
2 teasp mayonnaise

Peel and segment the grapefruit and oranges, scatter very thinly with caster sugar, cover and chill. Mix the avocado with all the seasonings (this can be done in the blender) and stir in the mayonnaise to make the consistency of whipped cream. Cover and chill.

To serve: Arrange drained fruit either on crisp lettuce or on Belgian chicory and top with a blob of the avocado mayonnaise. Serve as side salad. Serves 4–6.

Italian Pepper Salad

A superbly-flavoured relish that well repays the time spent in skinning the peppers. The initial grilling is sufficient to soften the peppers and remove their slight bitterness. Allow 1 pepper per person; smaller quantities than those given can be made with equal success when peppers are expensive.

6 large sweet green or red peppers
5 tbsp olive oil
1–2 cloves garlic, crushed
1 tbsp finely-chopped parsley
1 teasp finely-chopped fresh mint
Squeeze of lemon juice
Salt and freshly-ground pepper to taste

Spear the stem end of the peppers with a long fork, and grill until black and blistered. Cool then rub off the skin, then carefully remove the seeds and white ribs. Cut into long strips. Place in a mixing bowl, and cover with the remaining ingredients. Chill well until served. Use as hors-d'œuvre, or as relish with cold meats. Serves 6–8.

Spiced Mushrooms

Serve as part of an hors-d'œuvre, or with cold pickled meats or chicken.

½ lb (200g/4 cups) small mushrooms, cut lengthwise in 4, or if button size, left whole (or 1 drained can of grilling mushrooms)
4 tbsp salad oil
2 tbsp wine vinegar
1 level teasp salt
1 teasp grated onion
1 clove garlic, crushed
10 grinds black pepper
1 level tbsp chopped parsley

Simmer the mushrooms in a squeeze of lemon juice and enough salted water to cover for 5 minutes. Drain well, and mix with the dressing ingredients which have been shaken together to form an emulsion. Cover and leave till quite cold. This amount of dressing will probably suffice for twice the amount of mushrooms. Serves 4–6.

Mushrooms in Wine

½ lb (200g/4 cups) very fresh mushrooms
2 tbsp olive oil
½ clove garlic, cut in slivers
10 grinds black pepper
½ level teasp salt
1 level tbsp chopped parsley
4 fl oz (100ml/½ cup) red wine such as Burgundy

Remove tip of stalk, then slice mushrooms about ⅛ in (½ cm) thick. Heat oil and toss the mushrooms in it until they have absorbed it and are beginning to colour. Add the garlic and wine. Allow to bubble violently for a minute or so, then turn down the heat and simmer, uncovered, for 5 minutes, until most of the wine has evaporated. Stir in the salt, pepper and chopped parsley. Serve cold, as a relish or part of an hors-d'œuvre. Serves 4–6.

Piquant String Beans

I like to serve this with fried filleted plaice or halibut steaks.

10–12 oz (250–300g) pkt frozen beans
1 medium can corn
½ small onion, finely chopped
2 teasp sugar
Grind black pepper
3 tbsp salad oil
4 tbsp vinegar
Chives in season

Cook beans until barely tender. Rinse in cold water. Drain and mix with corn and chopped onion. Beat together oil, vinegar and sugar, with pepper and chives. Blend with vegetables. Serve in a shallow bowl. Serves 6.

A Variety of Rice Salads

Rice for salads must be long-grained, so that it cooks firm yet tender, and keeps its shape whilst it absorbs the flavours of its salad-mates. It should therefore be cooked by the pilaff method, which ensures that it is absolutely separate yet still absorbent to a dressing. Here is the basic method of preparation:

Rice for Salad (Pilaff Method)

Note: 1 cup = 8 fl oz or 7 oz (175g) by weight

1 cup long grain rice and 2 cups water; or 1 cup long grain rice, packeted, parboiled rice and 2½ cups water
2 tbsp oil
½ small onion
1 level teasp salt

Sauté the finely-chopped onion in the oil until soft and golden. Add the rice and cook a further 2 minutes, stirring to blend, then add the hot water and salt. Cover and cook for 20 minutes either on a low heat on top of the stove or in a quick oven (Gas No. 6, 400°F, 200°C), when the rice will be savoury, separate and fluffy. Makes 3 cups. Use as directed in any of the recipes below.

Rice, Tomato and Pimento Salad

Colourful and flavourful—an ideal 'buffet' salad to serve with cold meats.

2 cups cooked rice
4 large tomatoes, each cut in 8
1 small can of pimentos, drained and cut in slivers
Dressing:
4 tbsp salad oil
2 tbsp wine vinegar
1 clove garlic, crushed
1 small onion, finely chopped
1 level tbsp chopped parsley
1 level teasp salt
10 grinds black pepper
½ level teasp sugar

Put all the dressing ingredients in a screw-top jar and shake vigorously until thickened. Blend into the salad ingredients, tossing lightly. Pile into a dish. Serve slightly chilled. Serves 6–8.

Rice Ravigote Salad

A main dish for lunch or supper, served with plenty of crusty bread. Useful for making a meal of the remains of a fowl.

3 cups cooked rice
1 large green pepper, diced
3 canned pimentos, sliced
¾ lb (300g/3 cups) roasted chicken or boiled fowl (½ large bird)
¼ pint (125ml/⅔ cup) mayonnaise blended with ½ level teasp curry powder
1 teasp lemon juice
1 tbsp chopped chives
Dressing:
2 tbsp olive oil
1 tbsp wine vinegar
Pinch of salt
Few grinds of black pepper
} All shaken together

Blend the hot rice with the dressing. Blend the mayonnaise with the curry and lemon juice. Mix the diced chicken with the rice, pepper and pimentos, then stir in the mayonnaise. Garnish with the chives. Serve on a bed of lettuce leaves. Serves 6.

Oriental Chicken and Rice Salad

This salad can be used either as a main dish, or as an entrée before a light main course. The flesh from a boiling fowl is especially juicy.

3 cups cooked rice
1 medium green pepper, finely sliced
4 level tbsp walnuts, roughly chopped
4 level tbsp raisins
Half a cooked boiling fowl, diced (¾ lb/300g/3 cups flesh)
1 tbsp mayonnaise
Dressing:
4 tbsp olive oil
2 tbsp wine vinegar
1 cut clove garlic
1 level teasp salt
10 grinds black pepper
(All shaken together)
Lettuce leaves for serving

Sauté the raisins in a nut of margarine until plump and glossy (about 5 minutes). This greatly enhances their flavour. Blend the dressing ingredients in a bowl whilst rice is cooking. When the rice is cooked, discard the garlic, add the hot rice and coat with the dressing, then stir in all the remaining ingredients. Leave in a cool place for several hours to intensify the flavour. Line a shallow bowl with crisp lettuce leaves and spoon the salad into centre. Serves 4 for a main dish, 6–8 for a buffet.

Tomatoes Stuffed with Curried Rice

This is a beautiful salad both visually and to taste, either on a cold buffet, or served as an hors-d'œuvre with brown bread and butter.

6 large firm tomatoes
2 cups cooked rice
6 level teasp raisins, sautéd for 5 min in a nut of butter (margarine for meat meal)
½ large green pepper, diced
1 canned pimento, diced
Dressing:
4 tbsp olive oil
Juice of a lemon (3 tbsp)
1 level tbsp mango chutney
½ level teasp each of salt and curry powder

Shake or whip the salad dressing together. Blend with the salad ingredients. Cut firm tomatoes in half and remove the seeds and moisture. Salt lightly and drain for half an hour upside down. Fill with the rice salad. Serves 6.

Dressings for all Seasons

To our Jewish grandmothers, dressing a salad meant sprinkling it with a little salt and vinegar; mayonnaise and what is generally known as 'French dressing' were completely unknown. Yet when serving salads in the modern manner, the dressing is an integral part of the whole.

In the recipes and instructions I give below, I hope to simplify what many unreasonably consider a difficult branch of cookery.

Mayonnaise

Given a strong rotary hand whisk (let alone an electric mixer), mayonnaise is literally child's play to make, and it is one food which it is rarely possible to duplicate in the factory. Despite the pessimistic instructions in many cookery books, I find it keeps for 2 or 3 weeks under refrigeration.

Pointers to success: Cream the yolks with plenty of mustard before adding any oil; use a combination of olive oil and corn oil in equal quantity; and at the very end, add a little boiling water to lighten the sauce—and hold the emulsion. The maximum quantity of oil that one egg yolk can absorb is 6 fl oz (150ml/¾ cup).

Whisked Mayonnaise

2 egg yolks
1 level teasp dry mustard
2 level teasp French mustard
1 level teasp each salt and sugar
Pinch of cayenne pepper
2 teasp each of lemon juice and wine or cider vinegar
1–2 tbsp boiling water
12 fl oz (300ml/1½ cups) oil (half olive, half corn oil is good)

If you are using a hand whisk, mix the mayonnaise in a pint measure; with a mixer, use a bowl with the smallest diameter into which the beaters can fit. Have the oil and eggs at room temperature (but not too hot or the mixture will not thicken—in summer, chill the oil for an hour before use). Beat the yolks until creamy, then beat in the seasonings and a teaspoonful of the lemon juice. Now start adding the oil. I find that the best method with an electric mixer is to dribble it down the side of the bowl so that it can be absorbed gradually. With a hand mixer, it is a little more tedious, adding it drop by drop, but as soon as the sauce 'takes'—that is, thickens to the consistency of double (heavy) cream, the oil can be added in a steady stream, thinning the mixture down in between with the remaining lemon juice and the vinegar. Finally, whisk in the boiling water. Store in a screw-top jar in the bottom of the refrigerator. This makes ¾ pint (375ml/2 cups).

Blender Mayonnaise

This may not be the classic method but I find it is the quickest, especially for a quantity sufficient for just one meal. It is also possible to use a whole egg, rather than two yolks (which is not recommended when making a whisked mayonnaise as above).

1 whole egg, or two yolks (whichever is most convenient)
1 tbsp lemon juice
2 level teasp dry mustard
¼ pint (125ml/⅔ cup) corn oil
¼ pint (125ml/⅔ cup) mild olive oil
1 level teasp sugar
Pinch of cayenne and pepper
1 level teasp salt
1 teasp boiling water

Put the whole egg or the yolks into the blender, add the salt, pepper, sugar, mustard and cayenne pepper, and blend at high speed for 30 seconds or until foamy. Add the lemon juice and blend for 10 seconds. Uncover blender and add the corn oil very slowly, trickling it in, with the blender at high speed. When all is in and the mayonnaise has thickened, add the olive oil and blend until it has been absorbed. Finally, add the boiling water to thin the mayonnaise to the consistency of thick cream. Makes ¾ pint (375ml/2 cups). Store in the bottom of the refrigerator in a screw-top jar or plastic container. Do not freeze.

VARIATION
Green Mayonnaise: Add 1 tablespoon each roughly cut chives and parsley and ½ peeled clove of garlic to the egg and seasonings. Proceed as for blender mayonnaise.

Mayonnaise Sauces

Coleslaw Dressing

¼ pint (125ml/⅔ cup) mayonnaise
1 tbsp each of vinegar and caster sugar
1 teasp dry mustard

Mix well together. Sufficient for 1 lb (450g) shredded cabbage, 1 grated carrot and 1 finely-sliced green pepper. Serves 6.

Mustard Mayonnaise Sauce

A Danish version that is excellent with hot or cold fried fish.

1 cup mayonnaise (200ml)
1 teasp French mustard
1 teasp finely-chopped spring onion (scallion)
2 teasp finely-chopped parsley
Few drops of lemon juice

Beat all together. Serves 6.

Tartare Sauce

Put 1 cup of mayonnaise into a bowl and stir in the following ingredients, all finely chopped:

2 tbsp parsley
1 tbsp chives or green onion tops
1 teasp finely-chopped onion (use the white bulb part if you are using spring onions)
1 teasp prepared mustard
Squeeze of lemon juice
1 small pickled cucumber
¼ clove garlic, crushed with a little salt to a paste
2 level teasp capers

Leave for several hours for the flavours to blend. Serves 6–8.

Green Goddess Dressing

A Californian speciality, usually served on quarters of lettuce hearts. I often serve it with fish, or blend it with a cold flaked fish.

1 cup (200ml) mayonnaise
6 anchovy fillets, finely chopped
1 tbsp each of chopped spring onions (scallions) and chives
2 tbsp chopped parsley
A pinch each of salt and dry mustard
2 tbsp each of lemon juice and single (light) or soured cream

Blend all the flavourings into the mayonnaise and leave for several hours. Serves 6.

French Dressings

This covers a wide variety of salad dressings, many of which the French would vigorously repudiate! Basically they consist of some form of acid—lemon juice, wine or cider vinegar in which seasonings are dissolved—shaken into an emulsion with varying proportions of oil (which may be pressed from corn, peanuts, sunflower, olive or even walnuts).

To store French dressing: Leave it in a screw-top jar in the bottom of the refrigerator where it keeps almost indefinitely. Perishable flavourings such as herbs and onions should be added on the day of use.

French Dressing for Green Salads

Add herbs shortly before use.

¼ pint (125ml/⅔ cup) any salad oil
3 tbsp wine or cider vinegar or lemon juice
1 level teasp each of salt and sugar
10 grinds black pepper
Pinch of paprika

Place all the ingredients in a screw-top jar and shake until thickened (about 2 minutes). Makes enough dressing to dress a green salad for 6.

VARIATIONS

Herb Dressing: Add 2 level tablespoons chopped mixed herbs—basil, parsley, chives, tarragon or any combination of two or more of them.

Garlic Dressing: Leave a peeled clove of garlic in the dressing until dinner time. Discard before dressing the salad. For other variations, see specific salad recipes.

Sauce Vinaigrette

A sharper dressing suitable for bland vegetables such as tomatoes, French beans, or artichoke hearts. This is the dressing to serve with avocado on the half shell or chilled artichokes, or to dress a hearty mixed salad such as Salade Niçoise.

¼ pint (125ml/⅔ cup) mild olive oil
4 tbsp wine vinegar
2 tbsp lemon juice
1 clove garlic, peeled
2 level teasp caster (superfine) sugar (optional)
1 level teasp prepared mustard
2 level teasp chopped mixed herbs—such as chervil, parsley, chives
1 level teasp salt
Few grinds black pepper
1 level tbsp finely-chopped onion

Put the sugar, salt, pepper, onion, garlic, herbs and mustard into a screw-top jar and add the oil, vinegar and lemon juice. Shake vigorously for 2–3 minutes, until thickened. Leave for one hour before use. Serves 6.

French Fruit Dressing

For citrus fruit salads and fruit cups served as appetizers.

4 fl oz (100ml/½ cup) oil
2 tbsp each of lemon and orange juice
½ level teasp salt
Pinch of dry mustard
2–3 level teasp caster (superfine) sugar (depending on mixture used)
1 teasp mint, chopped with sugar (optional)

Put seasonings into jar, stir in fruit juices, then oil. Shake until thickened. Serves 6.

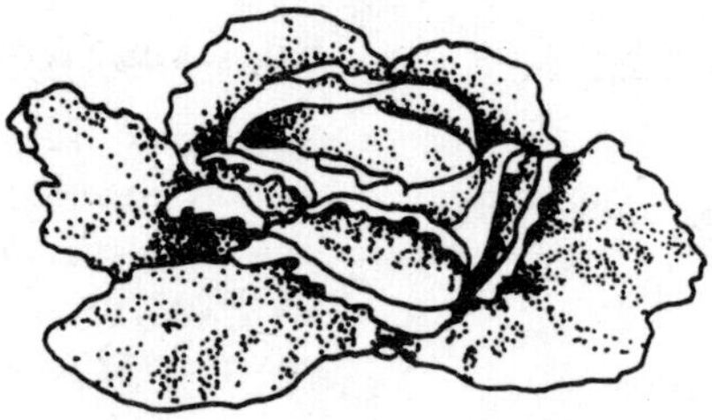

Desserts

The sweet course does not figure large in the Jewish cuisine, though the possibilities are more varied than is generally thought. Here, I have divided my recipes into three main categories: Hot Puddings, Cold Sweets and Frozen Desserts.

Hot Puddings

The repertoire of hot puddings is strictly limited to those of the 'shalet' variety (fruit and pastry, layered and baked) or sweet versions of noodle and rice kugel (pudding). In the early years of this century, however, Jewish immigrant mothers were quick to see in the pudding recipes of their adopted countries a cheap means of satisfying many hungry children; now the pendulum is swinging the other way, and lighter, fruitier recipes are more in favour —when the sweet course is not restricted to fresh fruit alone. However, young families do enjoy their 'afters' and the recipes that follow are all hot and delicious.

Family Sponge Puddings

There is no necessity to cream fat and sugar for a family pudding; the one-bowl method works to perfection as in the recipes that follow.

Steamed Sponge Pudding

4 oz (100g/½ cup) soft parve margarine
4 oz (100g/½ cup) caster (superfine) sugar
4 oz (100g/1 cup) self-raising flour
2 large eggs
Grated rind of ½ lemon

Topping:
2 tbsp golden (corn) syrup, marmalade, raspberry jam or stewed apple

Put a pan on to boil, half-full of water, with a steamer on top. If you have no steamer, the pudding should be 'boiled', that is, stood on a metal trivet or a folded cloth in the bottom of the pan, with water coming half-way up the sides. Put the margarine, sugar, flour, eggs and lemon rind into a bowl and beat for 3 minutes until smooth and creamy. Turn into a greased pudding basin in which you have first put the syrup, jam or fruit. There should be a 1 in (2½ cm) gap between the top of the pudding mixture and that of the basin. Cover with foil. Steam or boil for 2 hours. Turn out onto a warm dish and serve. Serves 6.

VARIATIONS

Apple Butterscotch Pudding: Lavishly spread the inside of the pudding basin with butter and smear thickly with golden (corn) syrup. Put 2 tablespoons stewed apples or 2 baking apples finely sliced and mixed with 1 oz (25g/2 tbsp) sugar in the bottom. Make the sponge pudding as in the recipe above and cook as directed. Serve with warm golden syrup or custard.

Apricot Top: Put 3 tablespoons apricot conserve in the bottom of the basin and fold 1 tablespoon conserve into the pudding mixture. Proceed as directed.

Eve's Pudding

A light, baked apple sponge.

3 oz (75g/$\frac{1}{3}$ cup) very soft butter or margarine
3 oz (75g/$\frac{1}{3}$ cup) caster (superfine) sugar
5 oz (125g/1$\frac{1}{4}$ cups) self-raising flour
Pinch of baking powder
2 eggs
1 tbsp milk or water (for a meat meal)
Fruit mixture:
4 large baking apples
1 tbsp lemon juice
4 tbsp water
3 oz (75g/$\frac{1}{3}$ cup) sugar
Pinch of cinnamon

Peel, core, and slice the apples into a wide, buttered casserole. Pour over the water and lemon juice and sprinkle on the sugar and cinnamon. Put all the pudding ingredients into a bowl and beat together for 1–2 minutes or until quite smooth. Spread thinly over the apple mixture. Bake in a moderate oven (Gas No. 4, 350°F, 180°C) for 45–50 minutes until golden brown and firm to the touch. Serve plain for a meat meal, or with hot custard for a milk meal.

VARIATION
Plum or Damson Pudding: Bring to the boil the contents of a medium can of Victoria plums or damsons or 1 lb ($\frac{1}{2}$kg) fresh fruit lightly stewed in syrup. Pour into a wide ovenproof casserole. Top at once with the pudding mixture and bake in the same way.

Pineapple Upside-down Pudding

Other fruit (such as apricots) can be used, but I don't think they equal the flavour of the pineapple bathed in a butterscotch glaze.

1 medium can (approx 15 oz/375g) pineapple rings, spears or titbits
A few glacé cherries
2 oz (50g/$\frac{1}{4}$ cup) butter (margarine for a meat meal)
2 oz (50g/$\frac{1}{4}$ cup) soft brown sugar

Grease an 8 in (20 cm) round solid-based cake tin. Melt the butter in a heavy saucepan. Add the brown sugar and simmer together until the sugar is dissolved in the butter and the mixture is a golden brown (about 3 minutes). Pour into the cake tin. Arrange the well-drained pineapple and glacé cherries in a design on top.

Pudding mixture:
4 oz (100g/$\frac{1}{2}$ cup) butter or margarine
4 oz (100g/$\frac{1}{2}$ cup) caster (superfine) sugar
4 oz (100g/1 cup) self-raising flour
Grated rind of $\frac{1}{2}$ lemon
2 eggs

Put the soft fat and the other ingredients into a bowl and beat together until smooth and creamy (2–3 minutes). Spoon over the pudding, and level with a knife. Bake in quick moderate oven (Gas No. 5, 375°F, 190°C) for 35–40 minutes or until the pudding is golden brown and firm to the touch. Reverse onto a serving dish and leave for 5 minutes. Lift off the cake tin. Serve plain, with custard, or with this fruit sauce:

Pineapple sauce:
The juice strained from the canned pineapple
1 tbsp orange juice or squash
Juice of $\frac{1}{2}$ lemon
2 level tbsp caster (superfine) sugar mixed with 1 level tbsp cornflour (cornstarch)

Mix the cornflour and sugar in a small pan, then stir in the juices. Bring to the boil. Simmer for 3 minutes. Serves 6.

Peach Pudding

Topping:
5 large peaches
Juice of $\frac{1}{2}$ lemon
3 oz (75g/$\frac{1}{2}$ cup) fine brown sugar
1 level teasp cinnamon
Cake:
6 oz (150g/1$\frac{1}{2}$ cups) self-raising flour
6 oz (150g/$\frac{3}{4}$ cup) caster (superfine) sugar
4 oz (100g/$\frac{1}{2}$ cup) soft butter
2 eggs
4 tbsp milk
Grated rind of $\frac{1}{2}$ lemon

Put all cake ingredients into bowl and beat until smooth and creamy—about 2 minutes. Spread in buttered tin 11 × 6 × 2 in (28 × 15 × 5 cm). Skin peaches by plunging into boiling water for 1 minute then into cold. Slice each into 6 and sprinkle with lemon juice. Arrange on top of cake mixture and sprinkle evenly with brown sugar and cinnamon mix. Bake in a quick oven (Gas No. 6, 400°F, 200°C) for 30 minutes. Serve warm as pudding, cold as cake. Serves 6.

Hot and Crunchy

Apple Crisp

4 large baking apples (Bramleys if possible)
1 tbsp lemon juice
3 fl oz (75ml/6 tbsp) water
2 oz (50g/¼ cup) sugar
½ level teasp cinnamon
Topping:
3 oz (75g/¾ cup) flour
1 oz (25g/3 level tbsp) porridge oats
4 oz (100g/½ cup) soft brown sugar
3 oz (75g/⅓ cup) margarine or butter

Peel, core and slice the baking apples into a shallow baking dish approx 6 × 9 in (15 × 23 cm). Sprinkle them with the lemon juice and water, topped with the 2 oz (50g/¼ cup) sugar, and the cinnamon. Combine the flour, oats and brown sugar, then gently rub in the fat until the mixture is crumbly. Sprinkle in an even layer over the apples. Bake in a quick moderate oven (Gas No. 5, 375°F, 190°C) for 40 minutes or until crunchy and golden brown. Serve plain or with custard or pouring cream. Serves 6.

VARIATION
Damson Crunch: Arrange the fruit from a can of damsons over the base of the dish. Spoon on enough of the juice to cover the bottom to a depth of ¼ in (½ cm). Top with the crunch and bake as directed. A little stewed apple may be mixed with the damsons to add body.

Scalloped Apples

1½ lb (700g) baking apples
4 oz (100g/½ cup) soft brown sugar
2 oz (50g/¼ cup) butter
⅛ teasp cinnamon
Pinch of nutmeg
5 oz (125g/1½ cups) fresh breadcrumbs
Juice of ½ lemon
3 tbsp water

Peel and coarsely chop or thickly grate the apples. Mix the sugar with the spices. Melt the butter and pour over the crumbs, mixing until all are slightly moistened by it. Butter a shallow oven casserole well. Put a quarter of the crumbs on the bottom of the casserole and add half the apples. Sprinkle them with half the sugar mixture and add another quarter of the crumbs. Spread with the remaining apples and sugar and pour over the lemon juice and water. Finally top with the remaining crumbs. Cover and bake for 45 minutes in a moderate oven (Gas No. 4, 350°F, 180°C) then uncover and allow to brown for a further 15 minutes. Serve if possible with custard or pouring cream. Serves 6.

Bread and Butter Pudding

6 thin slices buttered white bread
2–3 tbsp currants or mixed fruit
1 pint (500ml/2½ cups) milk
2 level tbsp custard powder (vanilla pudding mix)
2 level tbsp caster (superfine) sugar
Demerara (brown) sugar

Butter a casserole and sprinkle it with brown sugar. Cut the bread into fingers and arrange in layers, sprinkling demerara sugar and fruit between the layers. Make custard with the powder and 2 tablespoons of sugar (it should be thin pouring custard). Pour slowly into the dish down the side. Allow to stand half an hour for the custard to be absorbed. Bake in a slow moderate oven (Gas No. 3, 325°F, 170°C) for 1½ hours, increasing the heat at the end if necessary to brown the top. Sprinkle with brown sugar. Serves 4–6.

The Perfect Baked Apple

You can't really spoil a baked apple however you cook it (though you can cause it to burst if the oven is too hot); but you can turn it into a dinner party dish, if you cook it with sufficient care. The basic method is easy: even-sized apples are first cored and then slit through the skin around their 'equator' —this stops the flesh exploding. The core cavity is then filled with brown or white sugar, dried fruits or jam, and the apples are set side by side in a buttered baking dish about 2 in (5 cm) deep. The bottom of this dish is covered with water to a depth of ⅜ in (1 cm), and sugar (one tablespoonful for each apple used) is scattered on top. The apples are then cooked in a slow oven (Gas No. 2, 300°F, 150°C) for 2 hours, with frequent bastings of the syrupy juices.

You can take it from there—with a pinch of imagination. For instance, the cavity can be filled with granulated sugar flavoured with a pinch of cinnamon or nutmeg; or with brown sugar blended with a few chopped walnuts and a nut of butter (or margarine); or it can be filled with mixed dried fruit, topped with sugar, with additional dried fruit scattered round to enrich the syrup. If you want to be more ambitious, you can try:

Nutty Apples

For this dish, the apple peel is removed and a crusty coating of sugared nuts is patted on in its place.

6 medium baking apples, peeled and cored
6 level tbsp apricot jam
1 egg white
4 level tbsp each of cornflake crumbs (or dry cake crumbs), soft brown sugar and chopped walnuts
4 level tbsp sugar

Beat the egg white until frothy, then dip each apple first into the egg white and then into a mixture of the crumbs, nuts and sugar. Stand each coated apple in a baking dish and put 2 teaspoons apricot jam into the core cavity. Pour round water to come to a depth of ⅜ in (1 cm). Scatter round 4 level tablespoons sugar. Bake in a moderate oven (Gas No. 4, 350°F, 180°C) for one hour, or until the apples are tender. Slow baking is unnecessary in this case as the apples have been peeled. Serve warm or cold with cream or without. Serves 6.

California Baked Apples

6 medium Bramleys (tart cooking apples)
3 tbsp lemon juice
2 oz (50g/½ cup) chopped walnuts
2 oz (50g/½ cup) raisins
4 generous tbsp golden (corn) syrup
Juice of a medium orange
6 teasp brown sugar

Core the apples and nick the skin through the centre. Arrange in a buttered baking dish. Mix the raisins, lemon juice and walnuts, and use to fill the centre of each apple. Top each apple with 1 teaspoon brown sugar. Dribble the syrup over the apples. Add enough water to cover the bottom of the dish to a depth of ¼ in (½ cm). Add the orange juice. Bake in a slow oven (Gas No. 2, 300°F, 150°C) for 2 hours, basting several times. Serves 6.

Baked Apples in Orange Syrup

4 or 5 baking apples
Currants
Brown sugar
Butter (or margarine for a meat meal)
Juice of 2 oranges

Core apples and make a cut round the circumference. Arrange side by side in baking dish. In each cavity put 1 teaspoon soft brown sugar, then a few currants, then a pea-sized piece of butter or margarine and finally top with a further teaspoonful of sugar. Scatter more currants in the dish and pour over them the juice of 1 or 2 oranges. Scatter another 2 or 3 tablespoons brown sugar onto the juice. Bake in a very low oven (Gas No. 2, 300°F, 150°C) for 2 hours or until absolutely tender, basting with the syrup two or three times. Serves 4–5.

Apricot-Glazed Apples

4 level tbsp raisins
4–5 medium cooking apples
4 tbsp apricot jam
4 tbsp water
4 tbsp sugar
Juice of 1 lemon

Peel and core apples. Cover raisins with water; bring to boil, simmer 1 minute, then drain. Fill apple cores, and reserve the rest. Put the jam, sugar and water in pan, and bring to boil gently, stirring until smooth. Put in apples (use pan large enough to accommodate them side by side), baste with liquid, scatter round remaining raisins, then cover and cook very very gently for 45 minutes, or until apples are tender, or bake in a moderate oven (Gas No. 4, 350°F, 180°C) for ¾–1 hour. Baste frequently so apples are glazed. Carefully put on serving plate, and spoon sauce round. Serve warm or cold with cream. Serves 4–5.

VARIATION

Orange-Glazed Apples: Simmer apples in a saucepan with 4 oz (100g/½ cup) sugar, ¼ pint (125ml/½ cup) water, 1 teaspoon grated orange rind, 4 cloves (optional). When the apples are tender, lift onto serving plate, reduce syrup till of coating consistency, spoon over each apple on individual plates. Garnish with candied orange peel. Serve with whipped cream.

Fritters and Pancakes

Various Fritters

The secret of perfect fruit fritters is a crisp coating batter fried at exactly the right temperature. Add to that fruit that has been marinated in fruit juice or liqueurs and you have a delicious dessert that has to be a family treat—it's really impossible to produce for a dinner party, for a fritter must be eaten hot off the pan.

The batter:
3 oz (75g/¾ cup) plain flour
3 teasp oil
Pinch of salt
8 tbsp tepid water
1 level teasp caster (superfine) sugar
1 egg white

Put the flour and salt into a bowl with the sugar. Make a well, put in the oil and warm water. Gradually draw in the surrounding flour to make a smooth batter. Beat with a wooden spoon for 2 minutes or until the mixture falls in sheets from the spoon. Leave until needed. Just before using, fold in the stiffly-beaten egg white.

To prepare fruit: Allow 4 pieces of fruit per person. (Liqueur is optional.)
Bananas: Peel, then cut in 3 or 4 slanting slices, sprinkle with caster (superfine) sugar and lemon juice or rum.
Oranges: Section choice Jaffas, then sprinkle with sugar and Curaçao.
Fresh pineapple: Peel, cut in slices, take out core and cut slices in two. Sprinkle with sugar and kirsch. Canned pineapple needs acidulating with lemon juice.
Fresh apricots: Choose them slightly under-ripe, halve, stone, then sprinkle with sugar and apricot brandy.
Apples: Peel, core, cut in ½ in (1 cm) thick rings, sprinkle with sugar and brandy. All fruit can of course be simply sprinkled with sugar and lemon juice if necessary.

To fry fritters: Heat a pan one third full of oil until it reaches a temperature of 375°F, 190°C (when a 1 in (2½ cm) square of day-old bread browns in 40 seconds). Lift the fruit pieces from their juices, drain well, spear on a fork, dip in and out of the batter, then lower into the hot fat. Cook, turning often until golden brown (about 3 minutes). Drain on crumpled tissue paper. Arrange on a serving dish and sprinkle well with caster (superfine) sugar. Serves 4.

French Pancakes

The French crêpe or pancake is richer than an English pancake (because it contains more eggs), more 'cakey' than a blintze, because it contains both fat and sugar. It is best made in a 6 in (15 cm) iron crêpe pan, but any frying pan that is rounded between the base and the sides can be used. (*Note:* Pancakes can be kept ready for service in two ways: they can either be laid one on top of the other on the back of a plate over a pan of boiling water, and kept covered with a pan lid until needed; or they can be laid overlapping on a greased dish covered with foil and reheated in a moderate oven (Gas

No. 4, 350°F, 180°C) for 20 minutes. This is the best way to reheat defrosted frozen pancakes.)

Basic Crêpe Mixture:
4 oz (100g/1 cup) plain flour
Pinch of salt
2 eggs
8 fl oz (200ml/1 cup) milk
Grated rind of 1 medium orange and lemon
2 oz (50g/$\frac{1}{4}$ cup) butter

By machine: Put the liquids followed by the solids into the blender goblet. Blend for a few seconds until absolutely smooth.

By hand: Put the flour into a bowl and make a well; add the eggs, rinds and half the liquid, drawing in the surrounding flour to make a smooth paste. Add enough liquid to make a batter that can be whisked well until tiny bubbles cover the surface. Stir in the remaining liquid.

Heat the butter in the pan until it turns a light, nutty brown. Immediately stir into the batter. Leave for half an hour. It should be the consistency of pouring cream. If too thick, add a little water to dilute to the right consistency. Heat the frying pan empty for 3 minutes over a moderate flame. (This prevents sticking later on.) Have ready a pad of tissue paper. Rub this over a block of butter, then lightly smear the hot pan. Immediately pour in 2–3 tablespoons batter, swirling it evenly over the base of the pan. Cook over moderate heat until the mixture sets and detaches itself from the sides of the pan (this should take no more than 1 minute). Turn and cook the other side. Repeat with all the batter. This makes about 18 pancakes. Serves 6.

Crêpes à l'Anglaise

As the crêpes are cooked, toss them on to a piece of greaseproof paper thickly covered with caster (superfine) sugar. Turn over, sprinkle with lemon juice and roll up. Keep hot in a warm oven until all the pancakes are ready.

Crêpes Normandes

Melt 1 oz (25g/2 tbsp) butter in a heavy pan. Add $\frac{3}{4}$ lb (300g) finely-sliced apples, a pinch of cinnamon and 3 oz (75g/$\frac{1}{3}$ cup) sugar. Cover and cook until pulped. As each crêpe is cooked, spread it with the apple purée, roll up, lay side by side and keep hot in a moderate oven.
To serve: Sprinkle with caster (superfine) sugar and put under the grill for 1 minute.

Apricot and Pineapple Pancakes

Put 2 tablespoons apricot jam in a saucepan. Add the contents of a small can pineapple titbits and enough juice to make a thick creamy mixture. Add a squeeze of lemon juice and heat till bubbling. Use to spread on each crêpe. The mixture can be flavoured with 1 tablespoon apricot brandy or kirsch.

Cold Sweets

I cannot claim that there is any influence of the traditional Jewish cuisine to be found in the recipes that follow, unless it be the large number of fruited desserts that are permissible to serve after both a meat and a milk meal. Rather, these are the results of twenty years of travel and study of international cuisine. When I started experimenting with desserts, an electric mixer was a rarity and the blender quite unknown. Now these electrical 'kitchen maids' make it possible for even the inexperienced cook to produce elaborate sweets with ease and speed.

All the recipes are explicit as to methods; the only general advice I can give is to ensure that only the finest quality ingredients are used; many of the recipes depend for their success on the simple but careful preparation of superb raw ingredients. Without them, they are nothing.

Fruit Compotes

A compote is a dish of fresh or dried fruit that is stewed in a sugar syrup to ensure that it keeps its shape and texture.

Sugar Syrup to Store

This syrup can be made in quantity and refrigerated. It is then always available for stewing fruit, glazing tarts, and serving as the foundation of fruit drinks.

4 lb (2kg/9 cups) granulated sugar
2½ pints (1250ml/6¼ cups) water

Warm sugar and water in a thick pan until sugar has dissolved without boiling. Bring to slow rolling boil, reduce to a simmer for 3 minutes. Chill. Store either in refrigerator or larder.

Fresh Apricot Compote

This compote is delicious served plain or with pouring cream or ice-cream. With the addition of drained pineapple titbits and sliced bananas it becomes a fruit salad. Alternatively, the fruit can be halved and stoned before poaching, then drained when cooked and used to fill a flan case. The poaching syrup can then be used to make up part of the liquid for a jelly glaze. (*See* **Sponge Flans,** *p. 125 for quantities.*)

1½ lb (700g) fresh or frozen apricots
6 oz (150g/1 cup) sugar
½ pint (500ml/1¼ cups) water
Juice of ½ lemon

In a wide, shallow, lidded pan dissolve the sugar in the water over gentle heat, then bring to the boil and simmer till syrupy (about 5 minutes). Put in the whole fruit in one layer, cover and simmer very, very gently till fork tender (about 15 minutes). Add the lemon juice and chill well.

Morello (Sour Red) or other Cherries Cooked in their Own Juices

Sugar is used to draw out the natural juice from the fruit, as it cooks slowly in the oven.

1 lb (½kg) cherries (not pipped)
Juice of a large lemon
4 oz (100g/½ cup) demerara (brown) sugar; or ½ lb/200g/1 cup if morello cherries are used

Put cherries in a fairly shallow ovenproof dish. Sprinkle with the sugar and pour over the lemon juice. Cover and cook in a moderate oven (Gas No. 4, 350°F, 180°C) for 35 minutes or until cherries are tender, swimming in juice. Serve warm or cold. Serves 4–5.

Oven-Baked Rhubarb Compote

Rhubarb cooked in this manner will keep its shape and colour and make its own rich syrup. The diced flesh of a small pineapple or three sectioned oranges can be added just before serving (excellent for Passover use).

1 lb (500g) forced rhubarb
6 oz (150g/¾ cup) sugar
1 tbsp water

Put half rhubarb, cut in 1 in (2½ cm) pieces into a casserole. Sprinkle with half the sugar. Add remaining rhubarb and sugar and sprinkle with water. Cover and bake in a moderately hot oven (Gas No. 5, 375°F, 190°C) for 40 minutes, stirring once. Serves 4–6.

Poached Peaches in Apricot Syrup

4 level tbsp apricot jam
1 teasp grated orange rind
3 level tbsp sugar
¼ pint (125ml/⅔ cup) water
4 large peaches
Juice of ½ lemon

Put jam, orange, lemon, sugar and water in a saucepan. Stir over gentle heat until sugar dissolves, then cook gently until mixture looks syrupy. While syrup cooks, pour boiling water over peaches, then skin. Cut into halves or quarters and remove stones. Drop fruit into syrup, cover and cook very gently until just tender (5 minutes). Serve very cold. Serves 4 (or more if mixed with other fruit).

Fruit Salads, Plain and Simple

Sugar, be it scattered over the raw fruit or combined with water and fruit juice to make a syrup, helps to draw the natural juices from cut-up fruit, intensifying the flavour of the fruit salad.

Citrus Fruit Salad

A refreshing winter salad, when the Jaffa oranges are in season.

4 large Jaffa oranges
Juice of 1 lemon
4 oz (100g/$\frac{1}{2}$ cup) sugar
3 firm, ripe bananas
Few black grapes

Peel the oranges with a sharp knife, removing all the pith. Divide into sections, cutting between the pith sections to free the fruit. Put any juice that has come out of the oranges into a pan, together with the lemon juice and sugar and stir over gentle heat until dissolved. Peel and slice bananas. Halve and pip grapes. Arrange the oranges and bananas in a design in a shallow bowl and pour over the sugar syrup. Garnish with grapes. Serve very cold. Serves 4.

Winter Fruit Salad

8 fl oz (200ml/1 cup) water
4 oz (100g/$\frac{1}{2}$ cup) sugar
Juice of 2 lemons
2 tbsp whole fruit apricot jam
$\frac{1}{2}$ lb (200g) very ripe red plums
3 large oranges
1 can ($\frac{1}{2}$kg) sweet black cherries, drained
2 large bananas
Few black grapes

Boil the sugar and water till very thick then stir in the jam, and dilute with the fresh lemon juice and any juice from the oranges. Cut the plums in small pieces; peel the oranges as though they were apples and cut into segments, add the drained cherries (reserve the juice—it's delicious to stew apples or to use as a sauce over ice-cream). Pour over the syrup. Refrigerate for several hours, then add the halved and pipped black grapes and the sliced bananas. Serves 6.

Autumn Fruit Salad

A lovely dish to serve at Rosh Hashanah (New Year) when melons and peaches are both in season.

Syrup:
4 oz (100g/$\frac{1}{2}$ cup) sugar
3 tbsp water
Juice of 1 lemon and any juice from fruit
2 tbsp raspberry jam

Dissolve sugar in water, simmer for 3 minutes, then add lemon juice and raspberry jam and any fruit juice from cut-up oranges, etc.

Fruit:
2 large oranges, peeled and sliced
2 large peaches, peeled and sliced
2 large comice pears, peeled and sliced
4 dessert plums, cut up
1 small, very ripe melon, cubed
$\frac{3}{4}$ lb (700g) seedless or pipped grapes

Pour hot syrup over fruit. Leave in cool place. Just before serving add the grapes. Serves 6–8.

Fruits and Liqueurs

The judicious addition of a small amount of liqueur or wine can greatly enhance a simple fruit dish. Do not be overlavish, however, or the delicate flavour of the fruits will be masked.

Oranges in Curaçao Syrup

It is worth the trouble to candy the cut orange peel in a syrup, as the flavour of the dish is greatly enhanced. Any orange-flavoured liqueur can be used if Curaçao is not available.

6 large oranges
4 oz (100g/$\frac{1}{2}$ cup) sugar
8 fl oz (150ml/1 cup) water
3 tbsp Curaçao
3 large bananas
$\frac{1}{2}$ lb (200g) black grapes (optional)
Juice of 1 lemon

Using a blade-type potato peeler, shave off the peel of one orange. Cut it in 1 in (2½ cm) matchsticks. Dissolve the sugar in the water, add the peel, and simmer, half-covered, for half an hour, or until the peel looks candied. Add the lemon. Peel oranges, using a sharp knife, and cut in segments. Put in a serving dish with any juice that comes out in the preparation. Pour on the peel and syrup, pour on the liqueur, cover and leave several hours or overnight. Just before serving, slice in the bananas and pipped grapes. Serves 6–8.

VARIATION

Pineapple Pyramids: Prepare the syrup as directed. Peel, then slice the oranges across and soak in the syrup.

To serve: Allow one thick slice of fresh pineapple per person, the core cut out and the slice trimmed; one thick slice of soaked orange and 3 or 4 black grapes. Put a slice of pineapple on each plate and top with a slice of orange and a little of the syrup. Garnish with the black grapes. Chill for 1 hour, serve, passing a bottle of kirsch for the guests to sprinkle on their own serving.

Orange and Ginger Salad

4 large Jaffa oranges
3 pieces bottled or preserved ginger
2 tbsp ginger syrup
2 tbsp cherry brandy, Curaçao or Cointreau
2 peeled and sliced bananas

Slice the oranges crosswise, removing pith and core, then cut each half-segment into fan-shaped pieces. Put into a bowl with any juice that has dripped from them. Add the ginger sliced into slivers, with the syrup and liqueur. Mix gently together, then refrigerate for 2 hours. Just before serving add 2 peeled and sliced bananas. Serve with pouring cream or cold custard. Serves 6.

Whole Oranges in Cointreau Syrup

6 oranges
½ lb (200g/1 cup) sugar
¼ pint (125ml/⅔ cup) water
1 tbsp apricot jam
3 tbsp lemon juice
2 tbsp Cointreau or other orange-flavoured liqueur
6 slices fresh or canned pineapple
Few black grapes

Peel the oranges, removing all the pith. Cut a tiny slice off the base so that the orange will sit straight on the dish. Slice each orange crosswise into 4–6 slices, then reassemble into shape and arrange in a shallow casserole. Make a very thick syrup by dissolving the sugar in the water and adding the apricot jam. Simmer for 3 minutes, then remove from the heat, and add the lemon juice and the liqueur. Pour this syrup over the oranges. Put the dish in the refrigerator and chill for several hours, basting the fruit with the syrup three or four times.

To serve: Arrange a slice of fresh or canned pineapple on each serving plate. On it stand a glazed orange and pour over a little of the syrup. Spear pipped black grapes onto a cocktail stick and stick in the top of each orange. Serves 6.

Oranges Vénitienne

This recipe was given to me by a waiter who used to prepare oranges in this manner for Winston Churchill, when he wintered in Marrakesh. It is simple but refreshing after a heavy meal. I often serve it at a Chanucah (Festival of Lights) dinner.

For each person choose a very large orange. Cut a tiny slice off the base so it will balance on the plate. Cut a 'cap' off the orange about a third of the way down. Prepare the fruit itself as if it were a grapefruit, loosening the sections with a grapefruit knife and removing the centre core of pith. Fill this core cavity with caster (superfine) sugar and pour on enough grenadine (pomegranate-flavoured syrup) to saturate the sugar. Sprinkle the fruit itself with a little kirsch or lemon juice. Replace the top of each orange and chill for not more than ½–1 hour. Serve with a grapefruit spoon.

Pêches Cardinale

6 ripe fresh peaches
1 pint (500ml/2½ cups) water
½ lb (200g/1 cup) granulated sugar
Mint leaves or toasted almonds for decoration
¾ lb (700g) fresh raspberries
4 oz (100g/½ cup) granulated sugar
2 tbsp Cointreau or Curaçao

Put the sugar and water into a pan and stir until the sugar has dissolved. Add the unpeeled peaches, bring to simmering point, and allow to stand in the hot syrup, which should be barely bubbling, for 8 minutes. Take the pan off the stove, keep covered and leave for 20 minutes. (Use syrup again for another dish.) Drain peaches on cake rack. Peel whilst warm and arrange in an oval entrée dish. Chill. Sieve the raspberries then place the purée in the blender with sugar. Cover and blend at top speed for about 2 minutes until thick. Add 2 tablespoons Cointreau or Curaçao to the sauce. Chill. Pour chilled sauce over chilled fruit and leave in refrigerator until needed. Decorate either with mint leaves or toasted almonds. Serves 6.

Peaches in Wine

6 large peaches
Syrup:
4 oz (100g/½ cup) sugar
4 tbsp lemon juice
4 tbsp water
¼ pint (125ml/⅔ cup) Sauterne

Choose firm peaches. Plunge in boiling water for 1 minute then put in bowl of cold water. Remove skins. Put syrup ingredients in lidded pan large enough to hold peaches in one layer. Heat, stirring until sugar is dissolved. Put in peaches, baste with syrup, then poach, covered, for about 5 minutes or until just tender. Pour into bowl and chill. At start of meal, pour wine over fruit. Serve with thick cream. (If freestone peaches are used, they may be halved before poaching. If sliced, they tend to go too mushy.) Serves 6.

Strawberry Compote

Although I firmly believe that a choice strawberry needs no other addition than a little caster (superfine) sugar or fresh lemon juice, later in the season, fruit can be embellished, in the French manner, by soaking in boiling syrup then chilling before serving.

2 lb (1kg) firm, fully ripe strawberries; or 1 lb (½kg) strawberries plus
 4 large bananas, sliced
 2 oranges, sectioned
 Small can of drained pineapple titbits
Syrup:
¼ pint (125ml/⅔ cup) water
6 oz (150g/¾ cup) sugar
Juice of 1 lemon
2 tbsp grenadine syrup or maraschino liqueur

Slice the hulled strawberries, if large, and put into a heatproof dish. Dissolve the sugar in the water, boil for 1 minute, add the lemon juice and grenadine syrup or liqueur, then pour at once over the strawberries. Add the other fruits (if used). Cover and chill. Serves 6–8.

Strawberries in Liqueur Sauce

A dish for the height of the strawberry season, when fruit is bought by the trayful rather than by the punnet. I usually make strawberry purée in bulk at this season, and freeze it for the winter. One cartonful I save for this recipe.

First make the purée. Put 1 lb (½kg) strawberries (small jamming ones will do) and 4 oz (100g/½ cup) caster sugar in the blender. Blend for 1–2 minutes until thick and smooth. This makes the 8 fl oz (200ml/1 cup) required in the recipe.

2 lb (1kg) whole strawberries
8 fl oz (200ml/1 cup) strawberry purée
2 level teasp arrowroot or cornflour (cornstarch), mixed with 3 tbsp orange juice
1 teasp orange rind
2 teasp lemon juice
3 tbsp kirsch or Cointreau

Arrange the whole cleaned strawberries in a shallow oval entrée dish. Put the purée in a pan and stir in the cornflour or arrowroot mixed to a cream with the orange juice. Bring to the boil and simmer 3 minutes, then stir in the orange rind, lemon juice and liqueur. Allow to go cold. Just before serving, spoon over the strawberries. Serve at once, plain, or with pouring cream for a milk meal. Serves 6–8.

A Variety of Sponge Flans

A sponge flan consists of a whisked sponge baked in a special hollow tin, which leaves a convenient cavity in which fresh or canned fruit can be arranged and topped either with a jelly or a fruit glaze. As the flan can be a little difficult to ease out of the tin, it is advisable to invest in a non-stick flan tin, from which the flan will drop without trouble.

The Sponge Base

This recipe has the virtues of speed, certain success and flavour. I usually make several at once and freeze the extras for later use. The recipe below is sufficient for one 8 *in* (20 *cm*) *flan tin.*

2 eggs
3 oz (75g/⅓ cup) caster (superfine) sugar
2 oz (50g/½ cup) plain flour
1 tbsp hot water
Nut of butter or 1 tbsp oil

Set the oven at Gas No. 5, 375°F, 190°C, and put the fat and the water in it (in a small container) to heat. Prepare the flan tin according to the manufacturer's instructions, or grease with oil, then dust oil with a mixture of 2 level teaspoons each of caster sugar and flour. Put the whites into a bowl and whisk until they form stiff, glossy peaks. Sprinkle in half the sugar and 1 yolk and continue beating for 2 minutes until a pale gold colour. Add the remaining sugar and yolk and beat again. Pour the hot water and fat down the inside of the bowl and fold in with a metal spoon. Finally, sift the flour over the top of the mixture and fold that in thoroughly but gently. Spoon into the flan tin. Level the top of the mixture by tapping the base of the tin gently on the counter top. Put in the oven for 15 minutes by which time it will be golden brown, and firm to gentle pressure. Leave for 5 minutes then turn out onto a cooling tray. When quite cold put on the serving dish.

Black Cherry Filling

1 can black cherries, pipped and drained
1 kosher lemon jelly (gelatin mix)
Juice of 1 large fresh lemon (3 tbsp)
1 tbsp Swiss black cherry jam (if available)
½ pint (250ml/1¼ cups) water
Whipped cream for decoration

Put the water into a small pan and add the jelly. Heat gently (without boiling) until the jelly is dissolved. Pour into a one pint (500ml/2½ cups) jug. Add the lemon juice and the jam and enough of the cherry syrup to make up to ¾ pint (375ml/2 cups). Pour one quarter of the hot jelly over the sponge. Arrange the drained fruit on top. Chill the remaining jelly until it is beginning to set but is still pourable. Carefully spoon it over the fruit, masking the sponge completely. Leave until set. Decorate with very slightly sweetened whipped cream. Serves 6–8.

Raspberry Filling

Dissolve 1 strawberry jelly (gelatin mix) in ½ pint (250ml/1¼ cups) hot water, then add the juice of 1 lemon (3 tbsp); 1 tablespoon of apricot jam and enough additional water to make up to ¾ pint (375ml/2 cups). Use ½ lb (200g/1 cup) sugared fresh or frozen raspberries and 2 bananas for the filling. Serves 6–8.

Strawberry Filling

Dust 1 lb (½kg) strawberries with caster (superfine) sugar and sprinkle with the juice of an orange. Leave for 1 hour. Dissolve an orange jelly (gelatin mix) in ½ pint (250ml/1¼ cups) water. Add the juice from the strawberries and enough additional water to make up to $\frac{3}{4}$ pint (375ml/2 cups). Proceed as above. Serves 6–8.

Pineapple Filling with Clear Glaze

Peel, core and dice a medium-sized fresh pineapple. Pour over a syrup made by boiling 6 oz (150g/$\frac{3}{4}$ cup) sugar in $\frac{1}{2}$ pint (250ml/1$\frac{1}{4}$ cups) water for 5 minutes. Leave for several hours. Drain the pineapple and arrange in the cooked sponge case. Measure $\frac{1}{4}$ pint (125ml/$\frac{2}{3}$ cup) syrup. Mix 2 level teaspoons arrowroot with a little of the cold syrup, then stir into the remaining syrup, which has been brought to the boil in a small pan. Boil until thickened and clear (about 5 minutes). Add a squeeze of lemon juice, cool until it stops steaming, then spoon over the pineapple. Leave to set. Serves 6–8.

French Sponge

This is an excellent sponge for those sweets in which the sponge is soaked with a flavoured syrup and then filled or topped with fruits.

2 large eggs
3 oz (75g/$\frac{3}{4}$ cup) plain flour
Pinch of salt
4 oz (100g/$\frac{1}{2}$ cup) caster (superfine) sugar
Few drops vanilla essence (extract); or 1 teasp lemon juice

This quantity makes one 8 in (20 cm) fairly shallow cake or one ring tin (filling a 1$\frac{1}{2}$ pint/750ml/4 cups capacity ring tin). First set the oven at Gas No. 4, 350°F, 180°C. Grease the tin with oil, then dust with a mixture of 1 teaspoon each of caster sugar and flour. Sift the flour and salt together. In the mixer bowl put the whole eggs and sugar and beat at high speed until the mixture is so thick that a little dropped from the beaters will remain on the surface for a count of 5 before the surface goes level again. This will take at least 5 minutes. Stir in the essence or juice and finally sift in the flour, using a large metal spoon to fold it thoroughly into the egg mixture. At once turn into the prepared tin, smooth level and bake. A ring tin will take 30 minutes; an ordinary tin about 40 minutes. The sponge is done when it will spring back when gently touched with the finger, and when it has just begun to shrink from the sides of the tin. Turn onto a cooling tray and leave for half an hour, then ease out.

Liqueur Sponge

1 baked French Sponge
Syrup:
8 fl oz (200ml/1 cup) water
4 oz (100g/$\frac{1}{2}$ cup) granulated sugar
2 tbsp orange-flavoured liqueur or brandy or rum

Put the water and sugar into a small pan. Heat and stir until the sugar dissolves, then continue to boil gently until a syrup forms (the mixture will go a little yellow, like canned fruit syrup). Take from the heat and stir in the chosen spirit. Have the lukewarm cake on a serving dish. Spoon over the syrup until it has been absorbed.

Cream:
5 fl oz (125ml/$\frac{2}{3}$ cup) double (heavy) cream
4 tbsp top milk
2 teasp caster (superfine) sugar
1 teasp vanilla essence (extract)
Almonds for decoration

Beat the cream and milk together until thickened, then beat in the sugar and essence. For the most authentic French flavour, beat the cream with half a carton of *soured* cream instead of the milk—this gives it the true 'pâtisserie' flavour. Pipe or spoon the cream on top of the soaked sponge and decorate with slivered almonds which have been browned for 10 minutes in a moderate oven. Chill well before serving. Serves 6–8.

Apricot Sponge Ring

1 baked French Sponge
The apricot compote:
1$\frac{1}{2}$ lb (700g) whole or halved apricots (depending on size)
6 oz (150g/$\frac{3}{4}$ cup) sugar
$\frac{1}{2}$ pint (250ml/1$\frac{1}{4}$ cups) water
Juice of $\frac{1}{2}$ lemon
Apricot jam for glaze
Almonds for decoration (optional)

Put the sugar and water into a shallow, lidded pan wide enough to hold the fruit in one layer. Bring gently to the boil, simmer for 5 minutes, then add the apricots. Cover and simmer for 15 minutes or until barely tender. Add the lemon juice. If possible, bake the sponge in a 1½ pint (750ml/4 cups) capacity ring tin. When cool, turn out onto a serving dish which has room for the fruit as well.

To assemble the sweet: Use 6 tablespoons of the syrup to moisten the cake. To the remainder, add 2 tablespoons apricot jam and heat until dissolved. Spoon a little of this glaze over the sponge, then arrange the remainder with the fruit in and around the ring. The cake can be decorated with toasted almonds scattered on the glaze, or left plain. Serves 6–8.

The Chilled Soufflé

The aim is to use just enough 'gel' to hold together a blend of fruit, custard, meringue and (when used) whipped cream, and still preserve a finished texture that resembles fluffy, flavoured whipped cream, rather than jelly (gelatin).

Whilst these dishes traditionally include powdered or leaf gelatin, I have developed my recipe based on kosher jelly (gelatin), as I find it hard to get a consistent texture with vegetable gelatin.

This type of sweet can be presented in a collared soufflé dish, or set in individual cups; or it may be poured into a loose-bottomed cake tin (previously side-lined with soft sponge fingers), from which it can be eased just before serving.

Banana and Orange Soufflé

3 large ripe bananas, puréed
2 tbsp fresh orange juice
1 tbsp lemon juice
1 teasp each of finely-grated orange and lemon rind
Pinch of salt
2 large eggs, separated
2 oz (50g/¼ cup) caster (superfine) sugar
Orange jelly (gelatin mix)
8 fl oz (200ml/1 cup) double (heavy) cream
1 tbsp kirsch (optional)
Mandarin orange slices (optional)

In the top of a double saucepan put the sieved bananas, lemon and orange juice and rinds, salt, egg yolks and half of the sugar. Whisk over hot water until the mixture thickens to the consistency of a custard. Stir in the jelly. Cool whilst you whip the cream until it barely holds its shape, and beat the whites until foamy, then beat in the remaining ounce of sugar a teaspoonful at a time. If kirsch is used, beat that into the whipped cream. Into the cool custard fold first the cream (save a quarter) and then the meringue. Spoon into any of the containers mentioned above. Foil cover and chill overnight. Just before serving, decorate with the remaining cream and, if liked, mandarin orange slices. Serves 6–8.

Lemon Soufflé

3 fl oz (75ml/⅓ cup) lemon juice (approx 2 large lemons)
Grated rind of 2 lemons
6 tbsp orange juice
3 large eggs, separated
1 kosher orange or lemon jelly (gelatin mix)
3 oz (75g/⅓ cup) caster (superfine) sugar
8 fl oz (125ml/1 cup) double (heavy) cream (optional)
Sponge fingers or sponge cake sufficient to line a 7 in (18 cm) loose-bottomed tin
Fruits or glacé (candied) cherries for decoration

Put the jelly and fruit juices into a pan and stir over gentle heat until the jelly liquifies (don't let the liquid boil). Chill until syrupy (quickest in the freezer). Put the yolks into a basin and beat with a rotary whisk until frothy. Add the sugar gradually, beating continuously until the mixture is thick and mousse-like and falls in a steady 'ribbon' when the beaters are lifted from the bowl. Stir in the lemon rind and the syrupy jelly. Refrigerate whilst the egg whites are whisked until they form stiff, glossy peaks, then beat in 2 level teaspoons caster sugar.

If cream is used, whip it until it hangs from the lifted whisk. Take the lemon mixture from the refrigerator and fold in the cream (if used) followed by the meringue, using a metal spoon. Have ready a greased 7 in (18 cm) loose-bottomed cake tin, lined with sponge fingers or slices of sponge cake. Pour in the mousse, and leave to set.

To serve: Decorate with sugared soft fruits or glacé (candied) cherries. Loosen the sweet from the edge of the tin; stand the tin on a canister of smaller circumference and ease down the sides. Leave on the tin base, but set on a serving dish. Alternatively, the sponge lining can be omitted and the mousse set in a glass serving dish. Serves 6–8 (more with cream).

Berry Liqueur Mousse

This has a marvellous fruit flavour. It is especially good served half-frozen.

1 lb ($\frac{1}{2}$kg) strawberries or raspberries
$\frac{1}{4}$ pint (125ml/$\frac{2}{3}$ cup) water
1 kosher lemon jelly (gelatin mix)
Caster (superfine) sugar to taste
2 egg whites
8 fl oz (200ml/1 cup) whipping cream
4 boudoir or sponge finger biscuits (ladyfingers)
3 tbsp Curaçao, Cointreau or kirsch

Put the water and jelly into a saucepan and heat gently until jelly dissolves; sieve or blend the fruit until smooth (raspberries will need to be sieved). Add to jelly. Take, and if necessary add a little sugar and enough water to make mixture up to $\frac{3}{4}$ pint (375ml/2 cups). Chill until the mixture is the consistency of unbeaten egg white. Beat the whites until they form stiff peaks, then beat in 2 teaspoons caster (superfine) sugar. Beat the cream until it is thick enough to hang on the whisk; reserve a quarter to decorate the mousse. Fold the remaining cream into the fruit mixture followed by the meringue. Crumble the sponge fingers and sprinkle with the liqueur, then fold them into the fruit mixture. Spoon into a glass dish or a soufflé dish and chill for several hours. Decorate with a few strawberries or raspberries coated in caster (superfine) sugar and the remaining cream. Serves 8.

Chocolate Mousse

This recipe uses chocolate rather than jelly (gelatin) to achieve a mousse-like texture. It is particularly useful as it contains no dairy products and can therefore be served after a meat meal.

4 oz (100g) plain dessert chocolate
3 large eggs, separated
2 level teasp instant coffee
1 tbsp brandy, rum, crème de menthe or orange-flavoured liqueur

Break up the chocolate and stand in basin over very hot water (*not* boiling). Heat gently until melted then remove from heat. Immediately, drop in the egg yolks and beat vigorously until mixture begins to thicken. Stir in liqueur. Beat the whites until they just form soft peaks (don't overbeat or mixture may not blend well). Pour chocolate mixture into whites bowl and blend together. Spoon into individual cups or a small soufflé dish. Leave to chill overnight.

VARIATIONS

1. The mousse may be decorated with whipped cream, toasted almonds or chopped walnuts.
2. The mousse is also delicious when approximately 2 oz (50g/$\frac{1}{2}$ cup) chopped walnuts are alternated with layers of the mousse, then allowed to chill; or very well-drained canned white peaches or morello (sour red) cherries may be layered in the same way (drain on absorbent paper).

The basic mousse serves 4–5; with additions it will serve 6.

Fruits and Creams

These sweets all depend for their charm on the blending of fruit with sweet or soured cream. This type of sweet should be chilled for several hours before use to allow it to develop its flavours to the full.

Banana Fool

The secret of a successful fool is to ensure that the fruit purée, the custard and the cream are of a similar consistency when they are folded together, for unlike a mousse, no jelly (gelatin) is used in this type of sweet.

Custard made with ½ pint (250ml/1¼ cups) milk and 2 level tbsp each of custard powder (vanilla pudding mix) and sugar
Juice of 1 large lemon
2 tbsp damson jam
8 fl oz (200ml/1 cup) cream (some can be soured)
2 teasp sugar
2 teasp vanilla essence (extract)
12 little meringues
5 large bananas

Put the lemon juice and jam in the blender for 10 seconds; add the bananas in chunks and blend until smooth; add the cooled custard and blend a further 15 seconds. Turn into a bowl; fold in the whipped cream (save some for decoration), flavoured with the sugar and vanilla essence—taste to see if more sugar is required. Gently fold in the meringues. Divide into 6 or 8 glasses. Decorate with cream. Chill thoroughly—I leave them for 1 hour in the freezer.

Gooseberry Fool

The purée given in this recipe can be made in bulk (most easily in the oven), and stored in plastic cups in the freezer for winter use.

1½ lb (700g) green gooseberries
6 oz (150g/¾ cup) sugar
3 fl oz (75ml/⅓ cup) water
Green colouring optional
Custard made with ½ pint (250ml/1¼ cups) milk, 2 level tbsp custard powder (vanilla pudding mix) and 3 level tbsp sugar
¼ pint (125ml/⅔ cup) cream (more does no harm)

Make the custard, leave to cool covered with damp greaseproof paper. Stew the fruit with the sugar and water until soft; sieve and leave to go cold. Whip the cream. When the custard and the fruit purée are both cold, blend together, then fold in the cream. Turn into individual glasses and leave to go cold. A judicious few drops of green colouring greatly add to the appearance of the dish. Serves 6.

Dulce Zacatecano (*Bananas with Sherried Cream*)

A delicious Mexican way with bananas; the cooked bananas change their texture and combine extremely well with the creamy topping.

6 green-tipped bananas
2 oz (50g/¼ cup) butter
3 oz (75g/⅓ cup) soft brown sugar
8 fl oz (200ml/1 cup) cream
3 tbsp sherry
2 level teasp caster (superfine) sugar
Almonds or coconut for garnish

Peel bananas and cut in two lengthwise. Sauté in the frothy butter until beginning to brown, then sprinkle with the sugar and cook until a caramel is formed. Arrange the bananas and the caramel in a shallow dish. Whip the cream until it stands in soft peaks, then gradually beat in the sugar and sherry. Spoon over the bananas, covering them completely. Chill for several hours. Serve garnished with spiked almonds or browned coconut. Serves 6.

Pêches Brûlées

6 peaches
2 level tbsp caster (superfine) sugar
2 tbsp orange liqueur; or 1 tbsp lemon juice
5 fl oz (125ml/⅔ cup) double (heavy) cream
Custard made with ¼ pint (125ml/⅔ cup) milk, 2 level teasp custard powder (vanilla pudding mix) plus 2 level teasp caster (superfine) sugar
Demerara (brown) sugar

Drop each peach into boiling water for 1 minute; then remove skin; slice the peaches into a soufflé dish or other heatproof casserole. Sprinkle with the sugar, and the liqueur or lemon juice. Whip the cream, then blend it with the cooled custard, and pour over the top of the peaches. Put in the freezer or ice compartment of the refrigerator for about 1 hour. Cover the top of the cream with demerara sugar to a depth of $\frac{1}{4}$ in ($\frac{1}{2}$ cm). Put 3 in ($7\frac{1}{2}$ cm) away from a hot grill for 2–3 minutes, or until the sugar has melted. Chill again. The sugar will have formed a crisp topping. Serves 6.

Summer Fruit and Cream Bowl

Simple but succulent. The fruit can be varied as the season demands.

2 fat bananas
1 lb ($\frac{1}{2}$kg) choice strawberries
2 large peaches
Juice of $\frac{1}{2}$ lemon
3 tbsp grenadine or other bottled fruit syrup
4 level tbsp icing (confectioners') sugar
5 fl oz (125ml/$\frac{2}{3}$ cup) double (heavy) cream
4 tbsp top milk or single (light) cream

Slice the peaches (no need to peel), bananas and washed strawberries, sprinkle with sugar, then the lemon juice and grenadine. Leave in a cool larder for the juices to flow for 2 hours. Drain off the juice. Whip the cream with the top milk (or single cream), then beat in the fruit juice. Blend fruit in gently, then chill thoroughly for 1 hour, preferably in freezing compartment of refrigerator. Serves 8.

Marbled Strawberry Cream

A simple sweet that looks beautiful. The soured cream brings out the flavour of the strawberries in a most subtle manner.

1 strawberry jelly (gelatin mix)
Juice of $\frac{1}{2}$ lemon
1 lb ($\frac{1}{2}$kg) fresh or frozen sliced strawberries, lightly sugared
10 fl oz (250ml/$1\frac{1}{4}$ cups) soured cream

Make up jelly to 1 pint (500ml/$2\frac{1}{2}$ cups) then stir in lemon juice. Allow to chill until syrupy, then stir in sugared strawberries and soured cream—it should have a marbled effect. Leave to chill until set in a glass dish. Serves 6 generously.

Brandied Oranges

The cream sauce which tops this sweet can be used on any fresh or stewed fruit; it can also be frozen to make a liqueur ice.

6 large oranges
Caster (superfine) sugar
Juice of 1 large lemon

Finely grate the rind from one orange and reserve for the sauce; then peel it with the other oranges; section and put into a bowl. Pour over the lemon juice, then sprinkle lightly with the caster sugar. Leave in a cool place (*not* the refrigerator) to allow the juices to flow from the fruit. This will take about 2 hours. About 30 minutes before dinner, divide the fruit and juice between 6 dessert glasses.

Sauce:
1 egg, separated
2 level tbsp caster (superfine) sugar
5 fl oz (125ml/$\frac{2}{3}$ cup) double (heavy) cream
2 tbsp brandy or rum
Grated rind of 1 orange
Almonds for decoration

Separate the egg and put the yolk in one small bowl and the white in another. Whisk the white until it forms stiff peaks, then gradually whisk in 1 level tablespoon caster sugar until a stiff meringue is formed. Whisk the yolk until thick and creamy with the second level tablespoon of sugar. Rinse the beaters and use to whisk the cream until it starts to thicken. Beat in the brandy or rum and the grated orange rind. Fold the yolk mixture into the meringue and that combination into the cream. You will now have a light golden fluff. Spoon this on top of the oranges. Decorate with toasted almonds and chill for half an hour. Serves 6.

Pavlovas

Pavlovas, or 'schaum torten' as they are known on the Continent, are meringue sweets with a difference; for they combine a crisp outer crust with an inside which has the texture of marshmallow. They can be baked as cake layers or piped into the shape of small or large cases for their filling of fruit and cream. Once baked and filled they freeze extremely well. Unlike conventional meringues they do not go soft once they are filled; in fact the texture and flavour is vastly improved after several hours under refrigeration.

4 egg whites
Generous 8 oz (200g/1 cup) caster (superfine) sugar
2 level teasp cornflour (cornstarch)
1 teasp vinegar
1 teasp vanilla essence (extract)
Pinch of salt

Put the whites in the mixer bowl with a pinch of salt and whisk until the mixture forms stiff, glossy peaks. Blend the cornflour and sugar, then add a tablespoonful at a time, beating between each addition until the meringue is quite stiff. This should take 5 minutes even with an electric mixer. Finally beat in the vinegar and vanilla.

To make meringue layers: Grease and bottom line with greaseproof paper, two 9 in (23 cm) loose-bottomed cake tins. Divide the meringue mixture between the two tins and smooth one level. Decorate the other with a fork or a piping bag.

To make a meringue case: Mark a 9 in (23 cm) circle on a piece of greaseproof paper. Grease it and lay it on the base of a greased biscuit tin. Build up a case of the pavlova mixture, using a spoon and a fork or a piping bag, following the pencilled circle.

To bake either shape: Have the oven heated to Gas No. 2, 300°F, 150°C; turn down to Gas No. 1, 275°F, 140°C, when the layers or case of meringue go in. Bake for 45 minutes, or until crisp to the touch. The case is done when it can be lifted easily from the greaseproof paper. Place on wire cooling trays and leave until cold before filling with any of the following mixtures:

Lemon Pavlova

This is perhaps the tastiest and most convenient of all the fillings. The sweet/sour filling makes the perfect contrast to the very sweet meringue and, conveniently, makes use of the egg yolks as well. If soured cream is not available, use the same quantity of sweet cream, whipped until it is thick enough to hang on the whisk.

4 egg yolks
4 oz (100g/½ cup) caster (superfine) sugar
3 tbsp lemon juice
1 teasp grated lemon rind
5 fl oz (125ml/⅔ cup) soured cream
2 layers Pavlova

Put the yolks and sugar into a thick-bottomed pan, and beat with a wooden spoon till creamy, then beat in the juice and rind. Heat gently, stirring constantly until the thickness of mayonnaise (the timid can do this over hot water). Allow to cool completely, then fold in the soured cream. Put one meringue layer on a serving dish, cover with the filling and then put the top layer in position. Chill overnight. Cut in slices to serve. Serves 8–10.

Banana Pavlova

8 fl oz (200ml/1 cup) double (heavy) cream
4 large bananas
1 tbsp lemon juice
2 tbsp sherry, grenadine or maraschino syrup
2 tbsp chopped maraschino cherries
2 level tbsp caster (superfine) sugar
1 Pavlova case
Chocolate or almonds for decoration

Whisk the cream until it begins to thicken, then whisk in the sherry or fruit syrup; sieve or blend bananas, then sweeten with the sugar and flavour with the lemon juice. Fold the flavoured cream into the banana purée. Pour into the cooled shell. Chill thoroughly, if possible leaving for 1 hour in the freezer. Decorate with grated chocolate or toasted almonds. Serves 8–10.

Banana and Apricot Pavlova

2 large bananas
Juice of ½ lemon
4 stewed or tinned apricots with a very little juice
1 tbsp cherry brandy or apricot brandy
5 fl oz (125ml/⅔ cup) double (heavy) cream
2 layers Pavlova

If the cream is very thick, dilute with a quarter its volume of top milk, then beat until thick. Put the other ingredients into the blender and blend until a smooth purée results (otherwise push through a sieve, but it's tedious). Blend the two mixtures together. Chill for an hour, then spoon on top of the first layer and cover with the second. Chill at least overnight (if possible), as the flavours improve with time. Serves 10.

Swiss Chocolate Pavlova

8 oz (200g) plain dessert (semi-sweet) chocolate
3 tbsp water
1 level tbsp instant coffee
2 egg yolks
1 teasp vanilla essence (extract)
5 fl oz (125ml/⅔ cup) double (heavy) cream, whipped and sweetened with 1 level tbsp caster (superfine) sugar
1 Pavlova case
Almonds for decoration

Bring to the boil, stirring constantly, the water and the coffee, remove from the heat and add the chocolate broken into bits. Stir until smooth, then beat in the egg yolks one at a time, and cool. Fold in the sweetened, whipped cream flavoured with vanilla. Spoon into the Pavlova case. Chill overnight. Serve sprinkled with toasted almonds. Serves 8–10.

Pineapple and Kirsch Pavlova

8 fl oz (200ml/1 cup) double (heavy) cream
3 large slices fresh pineapple
2 level tbsp caster (superfine) sugar
2 tbsp kirsch
2 Pavlova layers

Cut the fresh pineapple into pieces, sprinkle with sugar and kirsch and leave for 2 hours, for the juices to flow. Put the cream into a bowl, and beat it until it begins to thicken, then beat in the fresh pineapple syrup. Fold in the fruit and spoon between the layers. Chill at least an hour, preferably overnight. Serves 8.

Crushed Pineapple Pavlova

1 medium can of crushed pineapple; or a can of chunks either finely-chopped or put in the blender for 5 seconds only
10 fl oz (250ml/1¼ cups) double (heavy) cream
8 maraschino cherries and 1 tbsp of the juice
Juice of ½ lemon
1 tbsp kirsch or grenadine syrup
2 layers Pavlova

Put the pineapple, the halved cherries, the liqueur and the juices into a bowl. Leave for 2 hours. Whip the cream until it begins to thicken, then start beating in the pineapple mixture, continuing to whisk until it is of a thick, non-runny consistency. Taste and add more sugar if required. Put one layer of Pavlova on a serving dish, pile on the filling and top with the second layer. Put in the freezer for 1 hour, or leave in the coldest part of the refrigerator for several hours. Cut and serve like a cake. Serves 8.

Frozen Raspberry Pavlova

5 fl oz (125ml/⅔ cup) double (heavy) cream
1 small pkt vanilla ice-cream
½ lb (200g) sweetened semi-thawed frozen raspberries
2 teasp lemon juice
1 Pavlova shell

Have the raspberries half-thawed and the ice-cream as soft as cream. Whip the cream until it holds its shape, then fold in the ice-cream and raspberries. Spoon into the shell and put in the freezing compartment of the refrigerator. Take it out 10 minutes before you intend to serve it. Cut in wedges like a cake. Serves 8.

Fresh Raspberry or Strawberry Pavlova

10 fl oz (250ml/1¼ cups) double (heavy) cream
1 lb (½kg) strawberries or raspberries, crushed and sweetened
1 tbsp grenadine or maraschino syrup (optional)
2 Pavlova layers

Crush berries and sweeten. Beat the cream until it starts to thicken then beat in the grenadine or maraschino syrup. Fold into the berries. Arrange one layer on a serving plate, spread with the filling and top with the second layer. Refrigerate for several hours. Serve in slices like a cake. Serves 10.

Merely Trifles

The trifle is said to have originated in Spain, where the native sherry was poured over a sponge cake, which in turn was covered with a rich custard.

Strawberry Trifle

4 oz (100g) sponge fingers or the equivalent in slightly stale sponge cake
Strawberry or raspberry jam
4 fl oz (100ml/½ cup) wine (port-type or sweet sherry)
1 pint (500ml/2½ cups) custard
1½ lb (700g) fine whole dessert strawberries
8 fl oz (200ml/1 cup) double (heavy) cream
Angelica and almonds for garnish
2 level teasp caster (superfine) sugar

Sandwich pieces of sponge cake with the jam and cover the bottom of a glass dish. Pour over the wine or sherry and leave for an hour to soak well.

Custard:
1 pint (500ml/2½ cups) milk
2 whole eggs
2 oz (50g/¼ cup) caster (superfine) sugar
Few drops vanilla essence (extract)
1 level teasp cornflour

Heat the milk until it steams then blend with sugar, the cornflour and eggs (or add to beaten eggs and whisk by hand). Cook very gently over boiling water until thick enough to coat the back of a wooden spoon. Pour the hot custard over the sponge cake and allow to set. Whisk the cream, sweeten with 2 level teaspoons caster sugar, then spread all over the custard. Stud the entire surface with the dessert strawberries, and decorate with pieces of angelica and almond. Serve very cold, in small portions. Serves 8.

Raspberry and Banana Trifle

4 oz (100g) sponge fingers or the equivalent in slightly stale sponge cake
Raspberry jam
4 fl oz (100ml/½ cup) sherry
1 kosher jelly (gelatin mix), lemon or raspberry flavour
½ lb (200g) pkt frozen raspberries
2 large ripe bananas
1 pint (500ml/2½ cups) custard (recipe as in **Strawberry Trifle**)
5 fl oz (125ml/⅔ cup) double (heavy) cream
1 egg white
1 tbsp orange-flavoured liqueur
2 teasp caster (superfine) sugar
Chopped toasted hazelnuts

Spread the sponge fingers with jam and cut in 4. Arrange in the bottom of a glass dish. Spoon over the sherry. Make the jelly (nicest with fruit syrup substituted for part of the water) and put in the freezer until as thick as unbeaten egg whites. Arrange the raspberries and bananas on top of the sponge, then spoon over the jelly and leave to set. Pour on the cooled custard. Finally, whip the cream and egg white until thickening, then beat in the liqueur and sugar. Spoon or pipe over the custard and decorate with toasted nuts. Chill thoroughly, preferably for several hours. Serves 8–10.

And the Etceteras

Cold Zabaione

This frothy sweet is served warm from the pan in Italy. It therefore demands a very devoted cook. In my version, it is chilled overnight and is equally delicious but far more convenient! If possible, make early on the day it is to be served, though it will keep without separating overnight (foil-covered and refrigerated).

6 large yolks
3 oz (75g/$\frac{1}{3}$ cup) caster (superfine) sugar
3 fl oz (75ml/$\frac{1}{3}$ cup) Marsala or medium sherry; or 2 fl oz (50ml/$\frac{1}{4}$ cup) sherry and 1 fl oz (25ml) of brandy or Grand Marnier
1 egg white
2 level teasp sugar

By hand or machine, beat the yolks and sugar until thick and white, beat in the liquid, then transfer to a basin over a pan of almost boiling water. Continue to whisk vigorously until the mixture fluffs up and has the texture of a whisked sponge or mousse (it should *just* hold the weight of mixture dropped from the whisk). Immediately this stage is reached, take off the heat and stand in a pan of cold water. Keep on whisking gently until it cools. Beat the white until it holds stiff peaks, then beat in the sugar. Fold into the cooled zabaione. Spoon into wine glasses or similar small containers. Serves 6–7 (only a small portion is necessary).

Individual Crème Caramel

This is made in the same way as the classic French sweet, but in individual cocottes, with caramel sauce as a topping. Served topped with pouring cream, it makes a marvellously delicate dessert.

Custard:
1 pint (500ml/2$\frac{1}{2}$ cups) milk
4 whole eggs
2 oz (50g/$\frac{1}{4}$ cup) caster (superfine) sugar
1 vanilla bean or 1 teasp essence (extract)

Heat milk until bubbles appear round edge. Add vanilla bean (or essence), cover and leave to infuse for 10 minutes. Remove bean. Beat the eggs and sugar until frothy, then beat in the hot milk (very easy in blender). Strain into 6 individual cocottes or soufflé dishes. Set the dishes in a baking dish half-full of boiling water. Put in oven at Gas No. 4, 350°F, 180°C. Close oven and immediately turn down to Gas No. 3, 325°F, 170°C, and leave for 40 minutes. Test by inserting knife in centre which should come out clean. Chill thoroughly.

Caramel Sauce:
3 oz (75g/$\frac{1}{2}$ cup) cube sugar
2 teasp lemon juice
2$\frac{1}{2}$ fl oz (60ml/$\frac{1}{3}$ cup) water

Run sugar lumps quickly under cold tap to absorb water, then put in small, heavy-bottomed pan with lemon juice. Cook gently until sugar dissolves, then boil briskly until sugar turns caramel colour—don't overcook or caramel will be bitter. Add water, simmer until smooth. Chill sauce.

To serve: Pour a little chilled caramel sauce on top of each custard, and top with cream. Serves 6.

Lemon Dainty

In the baking a sponge forms at the top while the lemon sauce thickens below it.

6 oz (150g/$\frac{3}{4}$ cup) granulated sugar
Juice and rind of 1 large lemon (3 tbsp)
8 fl oz (200ml/1 cup) milk
3 level tbsp flour
2 eggs, separated
$\frac{1}{2}$ oz (15g/1 tbsp) butter

Mix 4 oz (100g/$\frac{1}{2}$ cup) of the sugar with the flour. Whisk the egg yolks until they start to thicken, then add rind and juice, soft butter and milk. Stir in the sugar mixture and whisk until smooth. Whisk the whites until they hold stiff, glossy peaks, then whisk in the remaining 2 oz (50g/$\frac{1}{4}$ cup) sugar. Fold into the lemon mixture. Pour into individual soufflé dishes or one oven casserole about 2 in (5 cm) deep. Bake in a slow, moderate oven (Gas No. 3, 325°F, 170°C) for 30–40 minutes, or until the sponge is set. Serve chilled to 4 or 5.

Frozen Desserts

With the advent of the freezer or the really efficient freezing compartment of the refrigerator, it is now quite simple to make ice-cream at home. Perhaps the most convenient way is to make a mousse of eggs, cream and flavouring. This mixture sets satin-smooth without the need for stirring, and the flavour can be varied to suit the needs of the menu.

The Master Ice-Cream Recipe

Vanilla Ice-cream

This is the basic recipe for 8.

3 large eggs, separated
3 oz (75g/¾ cup) sifted icing (confectioners') sugar
2 teasp vanilla essence (extract)
8 fl oz (200ml/1 cup) double (heavy) cream

Put the yolks, whites and cream into three separate basins. Beat the whites until they hold stiff, glossy peaks, then beat in the icing sugar 2 teaspoons at a time, beating after each addition. Add the vanilla to the yolks, then whisk this mixture gradually into the meringue. Finally, whip the cream and fold that into the egg mixture. Put in an ice tray or shallow serving dish, cover with foil and freeze. The ice-cream is nicest served creamy rather than absolutely solid, so half an hour before serving, transfer it to the refrigerator itself.

Coffee Ice-cream

Proceed exactly as above, but omit the vanilla; instead add 1 tablespoon strong instant coffee or liquid essence and 2 tablespoons Tia Maria liqueur to the yolks.

Liqueur Ice-cream

This can be made with kirsch (to serve with stewed cherries) or with Cointreau or Curaçao (to serve with peaches or raspberries). Proceed as for vanilla ice-cream but add 2 tablespoons of the chosen liqueur to the egg yolks instead of the vanilla.

Rum and Raisin Ice-cream

Leave 2 tablespoons raisins to soak in 2 tablespoons rum for 2 or 3 hours. Add to egg yolks, then beat into the egg whites as in the previous recipe.

Chocolate Ice-cream

Melt 4 oz plain (semi-sweet) chocolate in a basin standing in a pan of simmering water. Stir into the yolks with 1 teaspoon vanilla essence. Proceed as above.

Chocolate Ripple

Melt 3 oz plain (semi-sweet) chocolate and stir in 2 tablespoons double (heavy) cream or soured cream. Leave to cool. When the ice-cream is half set, run a spoon through it, leaving cracks, through these cracks pour the chocolate mixture. Re-cover and allow to set.

Ice-Cream Specialities

Chestnut Ice-cream (*Plombière alla Torinese*)

½ pint (250ml/1¼ cups) creamy milk (or light cream)
2 eggs
2 oz (50g/¼ cup) caster (superfine) sugar
1 tbsp brandy or rum
5 fl oz (125ml/⅔ cup) double (heavy) cream, whipped
1 can (8½ oz/200g) sweetened chestnut purée (purée de marron)

Heat milk until bubbling around edges, then whisk into beaten eggs. Cook over hot water until of coating consistency. Remove from heat and add the sugar. Stir the brandy or rum into the purée, then blend into the custard. Pour into a large refrigerator tray. Foil-cover and freeze for 1 hour. Then leave another hour after stirring vigorously to blend. When almost set, stir in the whipped cream to give marbled effect. Serve the ice-cream slightly soft. Ideal with chestnuts in syrup! Serves 6 generously.

Nesselrode Pudding

A rich custard-based ice-cream, studded with sultanas (white raisins) and cherries. Freeze in a loaf tin, to make a beautiful dinner party presentation.

10 fl oz (250ml/1¼ cups) double (heavy) and
10 fl oz (250ml/1¼ cups) single (light) cream
4 egg yolks
5 oz (125g/⅔ cup) sugar flavoured with vanilla bean; or 4½ oz (110g/½ cup) sugar and ½ oz (15g/2 tbsp) vanilla sugar
Flavourings:
2 oz (50g/⅓ cup) sultanas (white raisins)
2 oz (50g/⅓ cup) chopped glacé (candied) cherries
4 fl oz (100ml/½ cup) sweet sherry or Marsala
4 oz (100g/½ cup) unsweetened chestnut purée
Whipped cream and glacé (candied) cherries

Heat single cream until steaming, pour on to yolks and sugar in blender and blend for 30 seconds. Cook over hot water until thickened (it is thick enough when bubbles on surface disappear). Stir into the chestnut purée and chill. Put sultanas in pan covered with water. Simmer for 1 minute to plump up, drain and add to sherry and cherries. Leave for 1 hour. Add to custard. Whip the double cream until it is thick, then fold this into custard. Turn into long, narrow 2 lb loaf tin. Foil-wrap and freeze until amost solid. Turn sides to centre and stir well. Re-cover and freeze until solid. One hour before serving, wrap mould in very hot cloth to loosen. Turn pudding out onto oval dish and decorate with whipped cream and glacé cherries. Return to ordinary freezing compartment for 1 hour. Serves 8–10.

Frozen Berry Bombe

An ice-cream 'cake', cut in slices.

2 large yolks
4 tbsp orange juice
3 oz (75g/⅓ cup) caster (superfine) sugar
1 teasp grated orange rind
Pinch of salt
2 large egg whites
8 fl oz (200ml/1 cup) double (heavy) cream
2 level tbsp caster (superfine) sugar
1 lb (½kg) strawberries, raspberries or loganberries, puréed and sieved and lightly sweetened to taste

In the top of a double saucepan, beat the yolks with the sugar, juice, rind and salt, cook over boiling water until of a coating custard consistency. Stand the bowl in another one full of cold water to chill. Beat the whites until they form stiff, glossy peaks, then beat in the 2 level tablespoons sugar. Beat the cream until it forms floppy peaks. Fold first the cream, then the meringue and then the fruit purée into the cooled custard. Spoon the mixture into a 7 in (18 cm) loose-bottomed cake tin. Foil-cover and put in the freezer; or into the freezing compartment of an ordinary refrigerator at the coldest setting. Freeze until firm for several hours. Return the refrigerator setting to normal; or if in the freezer, place on the coldest shelf of a refrigerator for one hour before serving.

To serve: Run a knife round the edge of the tin and pull down the sides. Put thc soufflé (still on the base) onto a serving dish and decorate with sugared fruit. Serves 8.

Presenting Ice-Cream

Fruit, ice-cream and sauce can be permutated endlessly to make exciting presentations. I give but three ideas, each worthy of the effort of preparation.

Pineapple and Ice-cream on the Half Shell

1 pineapple split lengthwise with the pines intact, and the fruit scooped out, the core discarded.
Sauce:
3 oz (75g/⅓ cup) sugar
1 level tbsp cornflour (cornstarch)
8 fl oz (200ml/1 cup) boiling water
Juice and rind of 1 lemon (3 tbsp)
Juice and rind of ½ orange (2 fl oz/50ml/¼ cup)
1 pint (500ml/2½ cups approx) vanilla ice-cream

Mix the sugar and cornflour in a small saucepan, then add the boiling water gradually, stirring constantly with a wooden spoon. Bring to the boil and simmer 3 minutes, then stir in the fruit juices and rind and the diced pineapple. Pile the empty shells with scoops of ice-cream and mask with the sauce. Serve extra sauce at the table. Serves 6–8, depending on the size of the pineapple.

Peach Coupe with Cherries Jubilee

1 large can or jar morello (sour red) cherries; or 1 lb ($\frac{1}{2}$kg) stewed cherries
2 level tbsp caster (superfine) sugar (more if cherries are very sour)
1 level tbsp cornflour (cornstarch)
1 piece (3 in/7$\frac{1}{2}$ cm) lemon peel
2 tbsp cherry brandy
Juice of $\frac{1}{2}$ lemon
6 peach halves
1 large carton vanilla ice-cream

Drain and stone cherries, reserving juice (there should be about 8 fluid ozs). If using fresh cherries, use stewing syrup. Mix sugar and cornflour, then stir in cherry juice and lemon juice and strip of peel. Cook gently until thick and clear (about 3 minutes). Remove from heat, remove peel, and stir in cherry brandy and fruit. Leave to go cold in dish suitable for heating up (either in oven or top-of-stove).

To serve: Put a peach half in each sundae glass and top with ice-cream. Pour over hot cherry sauce and serve at once. Serves 6–8.

Poires Belle Helène

A bed of ice-cream scoops, arranged in a shallow entrée dish is topped with choice William pears, poached in syrup. Mask each serving with:

Bitter-Sweet Chocolate Sauce:
$\frac{1}{2}$ lb (200g) plain dessert (semi-sweet) chocolate
Hot coffee made with 6 fl oz (150ml/$\frac{3}{4}$ cup) water and 2 level teasp instant coffee
1 oz (25g/2 tbsp) caster (superfine) sugar
Nut of butter (or margarine for a meat meal)
2 teasp rum or brandy

Put hot coffee in small, thick-bottomed pan. Add broken chocolate and sugar, then stir over gentle heat until mixture is smooth. Remove from heat and add rum and fat. Serve warm.

To serve later: Store in air-tight container under refrigeration (keeps for weeks). To reheat, put in serving bowl, and stand it in pan of simmering water. Reheat, stirring until warm. Serves 6–8.

Fruit Sorbets

These water ices were featured in formal banquets as a palate-cleanser half-way through the traditional 12-course meal; today we serve them as a refreshing end to a meat meal (though I like them also after a milk meal, masked with pouring cream). A sorbet (or water ice) consists of a sugar syrup, flavoured with fruit juice or purée, partly frozen, then lightened with whisked egg white. It is then frozen until firm. It looks particularly attractive frozen in the hollowed-out shell of an orange or lemon.

Orange Sorbet

4 oz (100g/$\frac{1}{2}$ cup) granulated sugar
$\frac{1}{2}$ pint (250ml/1$\frac{1}{4}$ cups) cold water
6 fl oz (150ml/$\frac{3}{4}$ cup) fresh orange juice; or 3 oz (75ml/$\frac{1}{2}$ cup) frozen orange juice diluted with $\frac{1}{2}$ can (3 fl oz/75ml/$\frac{1}{3}$ cup) water
Juice of a large lemon (3 tbsp)
Grated rind of the oranges (if fresh ones are used)
1 egg white

If a freezer is not available, turn the refrigerator to its lowest setting. Chill a deep ice-tray. Put the sugar and water into a thick-bottomed pan and heat without boiling, stirring with a wooden spoon until the sugar is dissolved. Simmer for 10 minutes, until a thick syrup is formed. Add the rind and leave to go cold. Add the fruit juices and strain into the ice-tray. Foil-cover and freeze until mushy. In one bowl whisk the egg white until it forms stiff, glossy peaks. In another whisk the mushy sorbet until smooth. Fold the white into the sorbet and return to the freezer. After an hour give another stir, then leave until frozen (approximately 30 minutes). One hour before serving put the sorbet on the top shelf of the refrigerator, so that it is creamily soft when served. Serves 6.

VARIATIONS

Citrus Sorbet: A tarter version. Use the rind of the lemon as well as the orange. Use $\frac{1}{4}$ pint (125ml/$\frac{2}{3}$ cup) orange juice to 2 fl oz (50ml/$\frac{1}{4}$ cup) lemon juice.

Grapefruit Sorbet: Use ¼ pint (125ml/⅔ cup) freshly squeezed or bottled grapefruit juice, and the grated rind of 1 fruit, together with 3 tablespoons lemon juice.

Raspberry Sorbet: Add 1 lb (½kg) puréed raspberries and the juice of ½ lemon to the fruit syrup. Freeze as above, but omit the egg white. Delicious with pouring cream.

Ice-Cream Sauces

Fudge Sauce

3 oz (75g/⅓ cup) brown sugar
2 level tbsp golden (corn) syrup
1 oz (25g/2 tbsp) butter
4 tbsp unsweetened evaporated milk

Place all the ingredients in a small, strong saucepan and heat gently for about 5 minutes until they are well blended. *Do not boil.* Serve hot on cold ice-cream. Serves 6.

Florida Orange Sauce

2 oz (50g/⅓ cup) seedless raisins
4 oz (100g/½ cup) butter
4 oz (100g/½ cup) caster (superfine) sugar
3 tbsp orange juice
2 teasp grated lemon rind

Melt butter and sugar in a saucepan and bring to the boil slowly. Stir in orange juice, lemon rind and raisins. Serves 6.

Fresh Raspberry Sauce

The perfect 'melba' sauce for serving with fresh poached peaches and vanilla ice-cream. It freezes remarkably well, and can be kept for a week under refrigeration. It can also be used to flavour milk shakes.

1 lb (½kg) ripe raspberries
½ lb (200g/1 cup) granulated sugar

Push the fresh fruit through a sieve then put into the blender container together with the sugar. Switch on for a total of 3 minutes or until the sauce has thickened and no sugar can be felt. (With a mixer, beat with the whisk for 10 minutes until thickened.) Serves 8.

VARIATION

Fresh Strawberry Sauce: Use only 6 oz (150g/¾ cup) sugar to 1 lb (½kg) fruit, and acidulate with 2 tablespoons lemon juice. There is no need to sieve the fruit; put it straight into the blender with the sugar.

Pineapple Sauce

Rind and juice of 1 orange
2 teasp lemon juice
Juice strained from a 15 oz (375g) can of pineapple to make ½ pint (250ml/1¼ cups) with orange and lemon juices (add little cordial if necessary)
2 level tbsp sugar
1 level tbsp cornflour (cornstarch)
Finely cut-up pineapple
2 tbsp Curaçao or Cointreau (optional)

Mix together sugar and cornflour, then add the juices and rind, blending smoothly. Bring to the boil, simmer for 3 minutes, then add the finely cut-up pineapple and the liqueur. Leave until cold, then spoon over ice-cream. Serves 8.

Pastry

Pastry, whether it be made with oil, margarine or butter, is an integral part of the Jewish culinary scene all over the world, mainly because (when made with a parve fat) it provides the most satisfying dessert that can be served after a meat meal.

The Austrian, Hungarian and German Jews make a sweet and cakey 'muerberteig' pastry, the Sephardim the multi-layered fila pastry; the English make a short crust; the Americans their own version of flaky pastry for pies; the Danes have a superb flan pastry, the French the meltingly-tender puff; whilst every Jewish housewife, wherever she may live, makes some kind of strudel paste, whether it be made with oil or butter, and stretched, pulled or rolled.

In this chapter I give what I consider to be, from long years of experiment, the optimum recipes to use for various kinds of sweet and savoury pastry dishes.

The Basic Principles of Pastry-Making

The phrase 'a light hand with the pastry' is no old wives' tale; for over-vigorous addition of fat to flour (especially in rubbed-in pastry) can result in a heavy dry texture. Whilst I give explicit directions for making the different types of pastry within the recipe itself, there are certain basic principles common to all kinds.

The well-balanced pastry recipe has a high ratio of fat to flour (the fat never weighing less than half the weight of the flour) for it is the fat content that makes pastry tender, and an excess of flour that can make it tough. Too much water makes pastry hard, too little makes it crumbly and dry, so just sufficient liquid to bind the dry ingredients together should be added.

All pastries, unbaked or baked, freeze well.

To Freeze Shortcrust Pastry

Shortcrust pastry frozen in bulk takes 3 hours at room temperature to thaw before it can be rolled and there is little advantage in freezing it this way. Shape into pies, flan cases, tartlets or pie lids before freezing, unbaked or baked.

UNBAKED

To freeze:

Pies, large and small: Make large pies in foil dishes or plates. Make small pies in patty tins or foil dishes. Do not make a steam vent in lid. Freeze uncovered. When frozen leave large and small pies in foil dishes, and seal with foil. Remove small pies from patty tins and pack in heavy duty foil or polythene bags.

Flan cases: Freeze in flan ring or foil case until hard. Remove ring or case, wrap in a polythene bag or heavy duty foil, then in a box for protection.

Tartlet cases: Freeze uncovered in patty tins. When frozen remove from tins, pack in polythene or heavy duty foil, and pack in a box.

Pie lids: Prepare in quantity and cut into shape to fit pie dish. Freeze uncovered. Pack several together separated by foil or polythene sheets and then in a box. Storage time: up to 3 months.

To thaw:
Pies: Unwrap and place in a preheated oven and bake as usual, allowing extra time for thawing. Cut a vent in the pastry when it begins to thaw.

Flan cases: Unpack and place frozen case into flan ring on a baking sheet. Bake 'blind' (Gas No. 6, 400°F, 200°C) for 20–25 minutes.

Tartlet cases: Unpack and place frozen into patty tins and bake at Gas No. 6, 400°F, 200°C, for about 15 minutes.

Pie lids: Dampen edge of filled pie dish and place frozen lid on top. Bake at Gas No. 6, 400°F, 200°C, for 20–25 minutes, reduce oven to Gas No. 3, 325°F, 170°C, and bake for a further 10–15 minutes.

BAKED
To freeze:
Pies large and small: Bake in foil dishes or plates. Cool quickly, leave in the dish and pack in heavy duty foil. Freeze immediately.
Flan and tartlet cases: Pack cooled cases in sealed polythene containers or into polythene bags or heavy duty foil and then into a box.

Storage times:
Meat pies 3–4 months.
Fruit pies up to 6 months.
Unfilled pastry cases up to 6 months.

To thaw:
Pies: Leave at room temperature for 2–4 hours depending on size of pie. Reheat in oven if required hot.
Flan and tartlet cases: Leave at room temperature for about 1 hour.

To Freeze Flaky and Puff Pastry

UNBAKED
To freeze:
Bulk pastry: Prepare up to last rolling. Pack in polythene bags or heavy duty foil.
Pies: Freeze as for shortcrust pastry pies.
Pie lids: Freeze as for shortcrust pastry.
Vol-au-vent cases: Prepare in quantity. Freeze uncovered on a baking sheet or tray. When frozen pack in sealed polythene containers or wrap in polythene bags or heavy duty foil and pack in a box. Storage time 3–4 months.

To thaw:
Bulk pastry: Leave 3–4 hours at room temperature or overnight in the refrigerator.
Pies: Unwrap and place frozen in oven. Bake flaky pastry at Gas No. 7, 425°F, 220°C, for 25 minutes. Bake puff pastry at Gas No. 8, 450°F, 230°C, for 15–20 minutes. Reduce both oven temperatures to Gas No. 5, 375°F, 190°C, if filling requires longer.
Pie lids: Dampen edge of filled pie dish and place frozen lid on top. Bake as above for pies.
Vol-au-vent cases: Place frozen on a baking sheet in a hot oven at Gas No. 8, 450°F, 230°C, for 15 minutes.

BAKED
To freeze:
Pies and vol-au-vent cases: Can be frozen baked but are fragile to store and take up more room than when frozen unbaked. Pack carefully in sealed polythene containers.
Storage time: up to 6 months.

To thaw:
Pies: Leave at room temperature for 2–4 hours depending on size. Reheat, if required.
Vol-au-vent cases: Leave at room temperature for 1 hour or place frozen cases uncovered in a hot oven (Gas No. 8, 450°F, 230°C) for 5–10 minutes.

Rough Puff Pastry

This is the easiest kind of puff pastry for the home cook to make. Pointers to success: Use a 'strong' (bread) flour and a firm, plastic butter or margarine. Soft fats will not incorporate properly with the flour.

½ lb (200g/2 cups) plain flour
7 oz (175g/1 cup) butter or margarine
1 level teasp salt
7 tbsp cold water
1 tbsp wine or wine vinegar

Cut the fat into 15 ½-in (1 cm) cubes. Put the flour and salt into bowl, then add the butter or margarine and mix very gently to coat with the flour. Add the water and wine gradually, stirring with a spoon until the mixture leaves the sides of the bowl clean and no dampened flour remains. Gather into a ball.* Roll into a rectangle 6 × 8 in (15 × 20 cm), using sharp, firm rolls rather than long, squashing ones. Fold the bottom two-thirds of the pastry over, cover with the top third, seal on all sides by pressing edges firmly with rolling pin. Make one quarter turn of the pastry rectangle and repeat from *. Wrap in film or foil, and chill for at least half an hour, or until firm. Repeat once from * to * (4 rolls in total). Chill covered until required, or freeze for later use.

This pastry can be used in any recipe calling for puff pastry (see **Apple Strudel** p. 179, **Puff Pastry Strudel,** p. 228, etc.).

Meat Strudel

(*to make* 2)

1 lb (½kg) frozen puff pastry, thawed; or 1 recipe Rough Puff Pastry made with margarine
3 tbsp oil
1 medium onion
1 large green pepper, finely chopped
1 beaten egg
1 heaped tbsp tomato purée or ketchup
Salt and pepper
Pinch of nutmeg
2 teasp finely-chopped parsley
1 teasp Worcestershire sauce
1 lb (480g) minced beef

Heat the oil, and add the onion and pepper. Cook until the onion softens (about 3 minutes), then add meat and stir with fork until it loses its redness; add purée, seasonings and parsley. Simmer gently for 10 minutes until thick but still juicy. Allow to cool. Divide pastry in half. Proceed with each half as follows: Roll first half into a rectangle 10 in (25 cm) wide—it must be so thin that you can see the board through it. Spread half the cooled meat mixture over the pastry, leaving a 1 in (2½ cm) margin all the way round. Turn ends in to seal, then roll up like a Swiss roll. Brush with beaten egg, and decorate if liked with sesame seeds for crunchiness. Bake in a hot oven (Gas No. 7, 425°F, 220°C) for 10 minutes then at Gas No. 6, 400°F, 200°C, for a further 20 minutes until crisp and brown. Serve warm. Serves 4–6. May be reheated. Delicious for a buffet.

Minced (Ground) Beef Puff Pie

1 lb (½kg) frozen puff pastry; or 1 recipe Rough Puff Pastry made with margarine
1 lb (½kg) minced shoulder steak (ground beef)
1 large egg
1 minced onion
1 teasp salt and good shake of pepper
1 tbsp tomato ketchup
1 teasp dry mustard
1 oz (25g/2 tbsp) melted fat or schmaltz (rendered chicken fat)
1 clove garlic, minced
1½ oz (40g/½ cup) soft breadcrumbs

Line a 1 in (2½ cm) deep pie dish with half the pastry. Fry the onion gently in the fat, then mix with all the remaining ingredients. Spoon into the crust and carefully fit on the top crust. Brush with a little reserved egg and decorate with a few slits. Cook in a hot oven (Gas No. 7, 425°F, 220°C) for 15 minutes, then reduce the heat and cook for a further 45 minutes in a moderate oven (Gas No. 5, 375°F, 190°C). If the pie seems to be over-browning, lay a piece of foil loosely on the top. Serves 5–6.

Coffee Puffs

Enough Rough Puff Pastry rolled ⅛ in (½ cm) thick, to make 12 tartlet cases
Filling:
1 small egg (or ½ large egg)
3 oz (75g/⅓ cup) ground almonds
3 oz (75g/⅓ cup) caster (superfine) sugar
2 level teasp instant coffee dissolved in 2 tbsp hot water
1 oz (25g/2 tbsp) melted butter
Almond nibs for decoration

Mix all ingredients together. Line tartlet or patty cases with the chilled pastry. Prick the pastry all over with a fork, then fill three-quarters full with the filling. Scatter almond nibs on the top. Bake in a hot oven (Gas No. 7, 425°F, 220°C) for 12 minutes or until a rich golden brown. Serve cold. Makes 12.

Quick Flaky Pastry

Traditional flaky pastry is made by a similar method to rough puff, but the butter is incorporated in flakes rather than in cubes. It is rather tedious. This recipe achieves very similar results with much less effort.

10 oz (250g/1¼ cups) butter or firm margarine
1 lb (480g/4 cups) plain flour
6 fl oz (150ml/¾ cup) boiling water

Cut the butter into small pieces and put into a bowl. Pour over the boiling water. Stir until dissolved. Add flour, mix to a dough, and chill overnight. Use as for flaky pastry cooking at Gas No. 7, 425°F, 220°C.

Eccles Cakes

A traditional Lancashire recipe consisting of a buttery dried fruit filling encased in flaky pastry; it is best made with butter pastry. For speed, vegetarian mincemeat can be substituted for the filling. I give a large quantity recipe so that part can be frozen.

1 recipe Quick Flaky Pastry, chilled
Filling:
4 oz (100g/½ cup) butter
½ lb (200g/2 cups) currants
4 oz (100g/½ cup) soft brown sugar
4 oz (100g/¾ cup) chopped mixed candied peel
1 egg white
Caster (superfine) sugar

Melt the butter in a small pan, then stir in the fruit, sugar and peel. Mix well together and leave to cool in a basin. Divide the pastry in two. Work on each half as follows: Roll the pastry to a rectangle measuring 12 × 6 in (30 × 15 cm). Trim the edges to make them quite straight, then cut down the centre so that each piece measures 12 × 3 in (30 × 7½ cm). Divide each section into four 3 in (7½ cm) squares. Put a little filling on each square; dampen the edges with water, then draw them together to enclose the filling, and seal well with the fingers. Turn the filled pastries over and gently press them into a round measuring 3 in (7½ cm) in diameter, using the rolling pin. Make three slashes across the top to allow steam to escape during the baking, then arrange on dampened baking sheets. Leave in the refrigerator for 20 minutes.

To bake: Bake at Gas No. 7, 425°F, 220°C, for 15 minutes. Take out, brush with the egg white (whisked till foamy) then scatter with caster sugar. Bake for a further 5 minutes until the glaze is set and golden brown. Leave to cool on a wire tray. Serve fresh, or reheat until warm when required. Makes 16.

Banbury Cakes

Southern pastries from Banbury in Oxfordshire (of 'Ride a Cock Horse' fame).

1 recipe Quick Flaky Pastry, made with butter, chilled
Filling:
2 oz (50g/¼ cup) butter
2 level tbsp flour
½ lb (200g/2 cups) currants
2 oz (50g/⅓ cup) chopped peel
2 oz (50g/½ cup) chopped walnuts
4 oz (100g/½ cup) brown sugar
1 level teasp grated nutmeg
1 level teasp mixed spice
2 tbsp rum or brandy
1 egg white
Caster (superfine) sugar

Melt the butter in a small pan, stir in the flour and bubble without browning for 1 minute. Remove from the heat and stir in the fruit, sugar, spices and rum. Leave to go cold. Divide the pastry in two. Work on each half as follows: Roll out the pastry to a rectangle measuring 12 × 6 in (30 × 15 cm). Divide down the centre lengthwise, then cut each strip into three pieces. Put a small spoonful of filling on each piece of pastry, then gather up the edges to enclose it. Turn it over, and roll in one direction to make an oval measuring approx 5 × 3 in (12½ × 7½ cm). Make three slashes across the top of each oval, then arrange the cakes on a damp baking sheet. Chill for 20 minutes.

To bake: Bake at Gas No. 7, 425°F, 220°C, for 15 minutes. Take out, brush with the egg white (whisked till foamy) then scatter with caster sugar. Bake for a further 5 minutes until the glaze is set and golden brown. Leave to cool on a wire tray. Serve fresh, or reheat until warm when required. Makes 12.

Beef and Aubergine (Eggplant) Pie ·

If canned aubergine is not available, use ½ lb (200g) cubed fresh aubergines, fry in oil for 5 minutes; or omit the aubergine and use an extra ¼ lb (100g) lean minced beef.

½ recipe Flaky Pastry made with margarine; or use Shortcrust Pastry made with 8 oz (200g/2 cups) plain flour, 5 oz (125g/⅔ cup) firm margarine, pinch of salt and icy water to mix

Filling:

½ lb (200g) canned aubergines (eggplant)
1 oz (25g/2 tbsp) margarine
1 medium onion, finely chopped
1 clove garlic, crushed
¾ lb (300g) minced shoulder steak (ground beef)
1 tbsp chopped parsley
2 teasp Worcestershire sauce
1 level teasp salt
10 grinds black pepper
Good pinch of ground mace
1 can (8 oz/200g) tomato sauce; or 2 tbsp tomato purée mixed with 8 fl oz (200ml/1 cup) stock, and a pinch each of sugar and salt

Set the oven to Gas No. 7, 425°F, 220°C (Gas No. 5, 375°F, 190°C, if shortcrust is used). Melt the margarine in a frying pan and sauté the onion and garlic until soft and golden (about 5 minutes). Add the meat together with all the remaining ingredients (except aubergine), and simmer for 5 minutes, giving the mixture an occasional stir. It will be thick but juicy. Stir in the aubergine. Allow to cool for 5 minutes. Roll out half the pastry to fit an 8–9 in (20–23 cm) pie dish approx 1 in (2½ cm) deep. Spoon in the cooled filling. Top with a lattice of pastry strips, cut ½ in (1 cm) thick, and arranged ½ in (1 cm) apart and sealed to the edge of the dish with cold water. Brush with a little beaten egg or leave plain. Bake for 45 minutes until golden brown. Serve hot. Serves 6.

Cream Cheese Flaky Pastry

This is a delicious Austrian pastry that makes a perfect base for pizzas or quiches. It can also be used for sweet or savoury turnovers in place of Rough Puff Pastry.

4 oz (100g/½ cup) dry curd or sieved cottage cheese
4 oz (100g/½ cup) firm butter
4 oz (100g/1 cup) self-raising flour; or 4 oz (100g/1 cup) plain flour with a pinch of salt and 1 level teasp of baking powder

Cream the butter and cheese till well blended. Stir in the flour (and baking powder and salt if used), mixing to a dough. Foil wrap and chill in the refrigerator for at least 1 hour.

VARIATION

Savoury Cheese Pastry: Add 3 oz (75g/¾ cup) finely-grated dry cheese and 2 level teaspoons mustard to the flour, before stirring it into the butter and curd cheese.

Party Pizza

1 recipe for Cream Cheese Flaky Pastry, rolled out to fit two 7 in (18 cm) loose-bottomed flan tins, or one 11 or 12 in (28 or 30 cm) one

Filling:

4 tbsp oil
1 large onion
2 level teasp each of sugar and salt, and plenty of black pepper
½ level teasp basil
1 fat clove garlic, crushed
2 bayleaves
2 medium cans (14 oz/350g each) tomatoes or
1 large can (28 oz/750g)
2 tbsp tomato purée
½ lb (200g/2 cups) cheddar cheese
1 tin anchovies

Heat the fat in a large saucepan, then add the chopped onion and cook gently until soft and golden. Then add all the remaining ingredients except the cheese and anchovies. Simmer gently for about 15 minutes until the sauce is the consistency of ketchup. Spoon the filling into the uncooked crust. Cut the cheese into matchsticks and arrange on top with the flat fillets of anchovy. Bake in a hot oven (Gas No. 7, 425°F, 220°C) for 15–20 minutes. Serve hot. Serves 10.

Jam Puffs (Polster Zipfel)

1 recipe Cream Cheese Flaky Pastry
Jam
A little beaten egg
Caster (superfine) sugar

Roll out the chilled pastry to the thickness of a knife blade, then cut into 2½ in (6 cm) circles with a pastry cutter. Put a tiny spoonful of jam in the centre, dampen the edges with water and fold over to seal into a half-moon. Brush with the egg and bake in a quick oven (Gas No. 7, 425°F, 220°C) for 15 minutes or until golden brown. Sprinkle with caster sugar whilst warm. Makes about 24.

Cheese Straws

Serve as cocktail nibbles or as an accompaniment to a cream soup.

1 recipe Savoury Cheese Pastry

Roll the chilled pastry ¼ in (½ cm) thick and cut into strips, rounds or straws. If liked, anchovy fillets can be wound round the strips. Bake at Gas No. 7, 425°F, 220°C, for 7–10 minutes, or until golden brown.

Salmon and Corn Tart

1 recipe Savoury Cheese Pastry
Filling:
1 lb (½kg) fresh cooked or canned salmon (free of skin and bones and finely flaked with a fork)
1 can (12 oz/300g) whole kernel corn with pimentos
5 fl oz (125ml/⅔ cup) soured cream
Salt and black pepper
1 tbsp snipped chives (if available)

Blend the drained corn and flaked salmon and the chives with the soured cream. Season with salt and pepper, adding a squeeze of lemon juice if necessary. Roll half the pastry to fit a 9 in (23 cm) shallow pie plate. Spread the filling on top and cover with the remaining pastry. Brush with a little beaten egg or milk. Bake at Gas No. 7, 425°F, 220°C, for 30 minutes or until golden brown. Serve warm. Serves 6.

Shortcrust Pastry and its Variations

Shortcrust Pastry for Fruit Pies

This recipe produces a short but slightly flaky pastry with a fine flavour that keeps fresh for 2–3 *days and can be reheated. It is sufficient for a two-crust plate pie* 10 *in* (25 *cm*) *in diameter or an* 8 *in* (20 *cm*) *pie* 1 *in* (2½ *cm*) *deep.*

8 oz (200g/2 cups) plain flour
4 oz (100g/½ cup) butter or margarine
1 oz (25g/2 tbsp) white fat
2 level tbsp icing (confectioners') sugar
Pinch of salt
1 egg yolk
Juice of ½ lemon (1½ tbsp)
3 tbsp icy water
1 egg white for glaze (if used)

Into a large mixing bowl, sift the flour, salt and icing sugar. Cut the fats into 1 in (2½ cm) cubes, then rub gently into the flour mixture with the tips of the fingers of both hands. (An electric mixer at low speed can be successfully used provided the whisk is used, as paddle type beaters tend to crush the fat.) When the fat has been rubbed in enough, the mixture will resemble floury, coarse crumbs, with no particle larger than a small pea. Do not over rub beyond this stage or the mixture will become sticky, and as it will not be able to absorb the correct amount of liquid, the baked pastry will be crumbly and dry. Beat together the egg yolk, lemon juice and 1 tablespoon icy water. Sprinkle this liquid into the bowl, using a cupped hand to turn the mixture over and over, until all the particles are moistened but not wet—add a little more water if necessary. Gather the dampened mixture together and lightly mould it into a ball. Turn it onto a board or counter top sprinkled with a very light layer of flour. Knead it gently with the finger-tips to remove any cracks. Divide it into two portions, wrap each in foil, and put in the refrigerator for at least half an hour. (At this stage it can be frozen, or refrigerated for two days.)

To finish the pie: Get ready a 10 in (25 cm) pie plate or an 8 in (20 cm) pie dish, 1 in (2½ cm) deep. Have the required filling ready in a bowl. Put one of the balls of pastry on a lightly floured pastry board. Lightly flour a rolling pin, and using short, sharp strokes, start rolling the pastry into a circle about 11 in (28 cm) across. Keep making quarter turns of the pastry, so that the circle is kept even and does not stick to the board. Do not turn the pastry over, as raw flour would then be rolled into both sides and the pastry would be toughened. Carefully ease the pastry circle onto the back of the rolling pin then lay it gently into position in the pie dish. Spoon in the filling. Lift up the filled dish in one hand and, holding a sharp knife vertically with the other, cut off the overhanging pastry all the way round. Knead these remains into the second ball of pastry and roll that out in exactly the same way, to fit the top of the pie. With a pastry brush, dampen the edge of the bottom crust all the way round, then gently transfer the top crust via the rolling pin to fit on top. With the side of a finger press the two crusts together. Use a dull-bladed knife to nick the two crusts together all the way round, making 'cuts' every ⅛ in (½ cm). Alternately you can 'scallop' the two edges together with the fingers and thumb.

Beat the white of the egg until it is frothy. Make six cuts in the centre of the top crust (to allow steam to escape), then paint the egg white evenly over the top. Scatter a thin layer of granulated sugar over the pie, and bake as directed. (A sheet of foil on the shelf below is good insurance against any dripping, hot fruit juice.)

Perfect Apple Pie

This produces a very juicy filling in which the slices of cooked apple swim in a cinnamon-sugar sauce.

1 recipe Shortcrust Pastry for Fruit Pies
Filling:
4 large baking apples (about 1½ lb/700g, weight unpeeled)
4 oz (100g/½ cup) granulated sugar
2 level teasp cornflour (cornstarch)
1 level teasp cinnamon
Grating of nutmeg
2 tbsp raisins (optional)

Peel, quarter and core the apples, and cut into slices ⅛ in (½ cm) thick. Put them in a bowl and mix well with all the remaining ingredients. Choose a pie dish 8 in (20 cm) in diameter and 1 in (2½ cm) in depth. Fill the bottom crust with the apple mixture, mounding it into the centre. Cover with the top crust and glaze as directed above.

To bake: Put in a hot oven (Gas No. 7, 425°F, 220°C) for 10 minutes, then reduce the heat to moderate (Gas No. 5, 375°F, 190°C) and bake for a further 40 minutes, or until the apple feels tender when the pie is pierced with a knife, and the pastry is a rich golden brown. Serves 6 generously.

Spicy Apple Pie

The apples are bathed in a spicy butterscotch sauce.

1 recipe Shortcrust Pastry for Fruit Pies
Filling:
1½ lb (700g) cooking apples (weight unpeeled)
2 tbsp lemon juice
½ level teasp each of cinnamon and ground nutmeg
3 oz (75g/⅓ cup) granulated sugar
3 oz (75g/⅓ cup) soft brown sugar
2 level tbsp sultanas (white raisins) or currants
1 level tbsp flour
½ oz (15g/1 tbsp) butter or margarine

Choose a pie dish 8 in (20 cm) in diameter and 1 in (2½ cm) in depth. Peel, core and quarter the apples, and cut in slices ⅛ in (½ cm) thick. Arrange in the lined pie dish, and sprinkle them with the lemon juice. Mix the sugar, raisins, flour and spices and scatter on top. Dot with the butter or margarine. If the apples are dry (particularly at the end of the season), sprinkle over 3 tablespoons water. Put on the top crust and glaze with egg white as directed.

To bake: Put in a hot oven (Gas No. 7, 425°F, 220°C) for 10 minutes, then reduce to moderate (Gas No. 5, 375°F, 190°C) and bake for a further 40 minutes, or until the apple feels tender when the pie is pierced with a knife, and the pastry is a rich golden brown. Serve warm. Serves 6 generously.

Bilberry (Blueberry) Tart

Bilberries are also known as blueberries and whinberries and can be made with fresh or frozen fruit. Choose a shallow pie plate 10 *in* (25 *cm*) *in diameter.*

1 recipe Shortcrust Pastry for Fruit Pies
Filling:
¾ lb (300g) bilberries (blueberries)
4 oz (100g/½ cup) granulated sugar
2 tbsp lemon juice

Mix the fruit, sugar and lemon juice. Mound into the lined pie plate. Put on top crust and glaze with egg white as directed.

To bake: Preheat the oven to Gas No. 6, 400°F, 200°C. Put in the pie, then immediately turn down to Gas No. 5, 375°F, 190°C, and bake for 35 minutes, until golden brown. Serve warm, with cream. Serves 6.

Spicy Damson Tart

1 recipe Shortcrust Pastry for Fruit Pies
Filling:
1 can (15 oz/375g) damsons (plums) in syrup
2 oz (50g/¼ cup) sugar
2 level tbsp cornflour (cornstarch)
Pinch of salt
1 level teasp cinnamon
¼ level teasp ground nutmeg
½ oz (15g/1 tbsp) butter or margarine

Choose a pie dish 8 in (20 cm) in diameter and 1 in (2½ cm) in depth. Drain the syrup from the damsons, measure ¼ pint (125ml/⅔ cup) and mix with the cornflour, sugar and spices. Add the damsons and pour into the lined pie dish. Dot with butter. Put on the top crust and glaze with egg white as directed.

To bake: Preheat the oven to Gas No. 6, 400°F, 200°C, and bake for 35 minutes until golden brown. Serve warm, plain or with cream or thick custard. Serves 6.

Gooseberry Tart

This is most flavourful when young green gooseberries are used.

1 recipe Shortcrust Pastry for Fruit Pies
Filling:
1½ lb (700g) green gooseberries, topped and tailed
7 oz (175g/1 cup) granulated sugar
1 level tbsp cornflour (cornstarch)
3 tbsp water

Choose a shallow pie plate, 9–10 in (23–25 cm) in diameter. Mix together the gooseberries, sugar and cornflour, then mound into the lined pie plate. Sprinkle with water. Put on the top crust and glaze with egg white as directed.

To bake: Preheat the oven to Gas No. 6, 400°F, 200°C. Put in the pie then immediately turn the oven down to Gas No. 5, 375°F, 190°C, and bake for 35 minutes, until golden brown. Serve warm, plain or with pouring cream or custard. Serves 6.

Honey Apple Pie

1 recipe Shortcrust Pastry for Fruit Pies
Filling:
1½ lb (700g) apples (weight unpeeled)
4 oz (100g/½ cup) sugar
2 level tbsp flour
3 fl oz (75ml/⅓ cup) single (light) cream
4 level tbsp thin honey
½ teasp each ground cinnamon and nutmeg
½ oz (15g/1 tbsp) butter or margarine

Choose a pie dish, 8 in (20 cm) in diameter and 1 in (2½ cm) deep. Sprinkle 1 tablespoon of the flour and 2 level tablespoons of the sugar into the pastry-lined dish. Peel, core and quarter the apples, then cut into slices ⅛ in (½ cm) thick and put into a bowl. Combine the remaining sugar, flour, spices, cream and honey and pour over them. Arrange in the lined pie plate. Dot with the butter. Put on the top crust and glaze with egg white as directed.

To bake: Bake in a quick oven (Gas No. 6, 400°F' 200°C) for 45 minutes, or until the apples feel tender when pierced with a knife, and the crust is golden brown. Serve warm. Serves 6.

Old Fashioned Peach Pie

An American recipe, best made with freestone, cling or Hale peaches.

1 recipe Shortcrust Pastry for Fruit Pies

Filling:
4–5 peaches
4 oz (100g/½ cup) light brown soft sugar
2 level tbsp flour
½ level teasp cinnamon
Juice of 1 lemon

Choose a shallow pie plate, 9 in (23 cm) in diameter. Immerse the peaches in boiling water for 1 minute, then turn into a bowl of cold water. Lift off the skin with a knife. Slice them into a bowl, and sprinkle with the lemon juice. Mix the sugar, flour and cinnamon, then gently stir into the peaches. Spread the peach filling in the pastry-lined plate. Put on the top crust and glaze with egg white as directed.

To bake: Bake at Gas No. 7, 425°F, 220°C, for 15 minutes, then turn to Gas No. 5, 375°F, 190°C, for a further 20 minutes, or until golden brown. Serve warm with cold cream. Serves 6.

Rhubarb Pie

This pie has the prettiest colour and most delicate flavour when it is made with forced spring rhubarb, grown under glass.

1 recipe Shortcrust Pastry for Fruit Pies

Filling:
1 lb (½kg) rhubarb
6 oz (150g/¾ cup) granulated sugar
2 level teasp cornflour (cornstarch)
½ oz (15g/1 tbsp) butter or margarine

Choose a pie dish 8 in (20 cm) in diameter and 1 in (2½ cm) deep. Cut off the heel from each stick of rhubarb, but do not peel the fruit. Cut into 1 in (2½ cm) lengths and put into a bowl with the sugar and cornflour, then stir well. Spoon into the pastry-lined pie dish, and dot with the fat. Put on the top crust and glaze with egg white as directed.

To bake: Bake at Gas No. 7, 425°F, 220°C, for 10 minutes, then turn down to Gas No. 5, 375°F, 190°C, for a further 30 minutes, until golden brown. Serve warm or cold, plain or with custard. Serves 6.

Spicy Purple Plum Pie

Use freestone plums, such as the black zwetschen plums, to make this sweet yet tart pie.

1 recipe Shortcrust Pastry for Fruit Pies

Filling:
2 lb (1kg) plums, halved and stoned
Juice of ½ large lemon
6 oz (150g/¾ cup) granulated sugar
2 level teasp cornflour (cornstarch)
½ level teasp each of cinnamon and nutmeg
1 oz (25g/2 tbsp) butter

Choose a pie dish 8–9 in (20–23 cm) in diameter, and 1 in (2½ cm) in depth. Put the plums into a bowl and sprinkle with the lemon juice. Mix together the sugar, cornflour and spices and stir into the plums. Mound into the pastry-lined dish. Put on the top crust and glaze with egg white as directed.

To bake: Bake in a quick oven (Gas No. 6, 400°F, 200°C) for 45 minutes, or until the crust is golden and crunchy. Serve slightly warm, not hot. Serves 6–8.

Spicy Raisin Pie

1 recipe Shortcrust Pastry for Fruit Pies
Filling:
½ lb (200g/1½ cups) raisins
¾ pint (375ml/2 cups) water
3 oz (75g/⅓ cup) brown sugar
3 level teasp cornflour (cornstarch)
½ level teasp each cinnamon and ground nutmeg
1 tbsp rum
1 oz (25g/2 tbsp) butter or margarine

Choose a pie dish 8 in (20 cm) in diameter, and 1 in (2½ cm) deep. Bring the water to the boil in a small pan, then add the raisins and simmer uncovered for 5 minutes. Mix together the sugar, cornflour and spices. Stir into the raisins over low heat, and bubble until thickened and clear (about 3 minutes). Stir in the butter and rum and leave to cool. Pour the cold filling into the pastry-lined pie dish. Put on the top crust and glaze with egg white as directed.

To bake: Bake at Gas No. 7, 425°F, 220°C, for 30 minutes. Serve warm, plain or with cream. Serves 6.

Shortcrust Pastry for Savoury and Sweet Flans and Tarts

There are innumerable recipes for flan pastry, and the following points may help you to choose the right recipe for a particular dish:

Flan pastry made with water is flakier and crunchier than pastry made with egg. It makes excellent savoury flan cases.

Flan pastry made with egg is more biscuity than pastry made with water. It stays crisp, even with a 'wet' filling such as baked custard. It makes excellent sweet flans.

Savoury Flan Pastry

This is splendid for all kinds of quiches, or savoury tarts. The quantity given is sufficient for one 8–9 in (20–23 cm) flan case.

6 oz (150g/1½ cups) plain flour
Pinch of salt
4 oz (100g/½ cup) butter or margarine
Squeeze of lemon juice
1 level teasp icing (confectioners') sugar
About 2 tbsp icy water

Rub the fat into the flour with salt and sugar, until no particles larger than a small pea appear when the bowl is shaken. Mix to a firm dough with the icy water and lemon juice. Foil wrap and chill. Use as directed in the recipe.

Tourte Forestière (*Mushroom Lattice Tart*)

The flavour of this tart depends on the use of the finest quality of mushrooms. These must be firm to the touch, with really pink gills beneath a creamy cap.

1 recipe Savoury Flan Pastry

Use to line an 8 in (20 cm) loose-bottomed flan or sandwich tin. Roll out the trimmings and cut into ½ in (1 cm) strips for the lattice top. Prick the case all over and chill whilst the filling is made.

Filling:
½ pint (250ml/1¼ cups) milk
½ lb (200g/4 cups) pinky mushrooms
1 bayleaf
6 peppercorns
2 blades of mace or a pinch of ground mace or nutmeg
3 oz (75g/⅓ cup) butter
4 level tbsp (2 oz/50g) flour
2 egg yolks
4 tbsp double (heavy) cream
1 large onion, finely chopped
Salt and pepper

Put the milk, bayleaf, peppercorns and mace into a pan, bring to steaming point, cover, turn off the heat and leave for 10 minutes to infuse. Melt half butter and cook the finely chopped onion until soft and golden, then add the flour and cook for a further 2 minutes. Take off the heat and pour on the hot strained milk, then return to the heat and whisk until bubbly and smooth using a small balloon whisk. Season with salt and pepper, then leave on a very low heat. Cut the tips only off the washed mushrooms, but do not peel. Slice thinly through both the cap and the stalk. Cook in the remaining butter until softened (about 5 minutes). Add to the sauce. Beat the yolks, reserving a little for gilding the flan. Stir the remainder into the cream, then stir into the hot sauce. Allow to cool until the filling stops steaming, then pour into the unbaked case and cover with the trellis pastry. Dilute the reserved yolk with a teaspoon of water, then brush over the top of the tart.

To bake: Bake at Gas No. 6, 400°F, 200°C, for 30 minutes, or until golden brown. Slide from the flan tin (leave on the base) and put on a heatproof dish. Serve at once. To reheat, cover the top with foil and leave for 15 minutes in a moderate oven. Makes 6 generous portions.

Cheese and Olive Quiche

1 recipe Savoury Flan Pastry

Use to line a 9 in (23 cm) loose-bottomed flan or sandwich tin. Prick all over with a fork.

Filling:
1 oz (25g/2 tbsp) butter
1 onion, finely chopped
3 eggs
5 fl oz (125ml/$\frac{2}{3}$ cup) single (light) cream
$\frac{1}{4}$ pint (125ml/$\frac{2}{3}$ cup) milk
4 oz (100g/1 cup) sharp cheese, finely grated
4 oz (100g/1 cup) black olives, stoned and sliced
1 level teasp each of salt and prepared mustard
10 grinds black pepper
Pinch of paprika
2 teasp Worcestershire sauce

Melt the butter in a small pan, put in the onion and cook gently until soft and golden. Whisk the 3 eggs until blended, then stir in all the remaining ingredients and seasonings. Put the onion-butter mixture in the bottom of the uncooked flan, and carefully pour the custard on top.

To bake: Bake in a very hot oven (Gas No. 8, 450°F, 230°C) for 15 minutes, to set the pastry then immediately turn down to Gas No. 2, 300°F, 150°C, for a further 30 minutes, or until a knife inserted in the centre comes out clean. Serve warm or cold. Serves 6.

Cheese and Mushroom Quiche

1 recipe Savoury Flan Pastry

Use to line a 9 in (23 cm) loose-bottomed flan or sandwich tin. Prick all over with a fork.

Filling:
1 oz (25g/2 tbsp) butter
$\frac{1}{2}$ lb (200g/4 cups) button mushrooms
3 eggs
5 fl oz (125ml/$\frac{2}{3}$ cup) single (light) cream
$\frac{1}{4}$ pint (125ml/$\frac{2}{3}$ cup) milk
Pinch each of mustard, cayenne pepper and salt
2 oz (50g/$\frac{1}{2}$ cup) grated cheese
Pinch of mace or grated nutmeg
2 level tbsp grated cheese

Trim the tips from the mushrooms; melt the butter and fry the mushrooms gently until softened, tossing them in the pan. Slice half of them in two, keeping the remainder for garnish. Whisk the eggs, then slowly add the cream, milk, seasonings and grated cheese. Add the sliced mushrooms, then pour into the flan case. Sprinkle with the remaining cheese.

To bake: Put in a very hot oven (Gas No. 8, 450°F, 230°C) for 15 minutes, then immediately turn down to Gas No. 2, 300°F, 150°C, for a further 30 minutes, until a knife inserted in the centre comes out clean. Serve warm or cold, garnished with the mushrooms. Serves 6.

Tuna or Salmon Quiche

1 recipe Savoury Flan Pastry

Use to line an 8 in (20 cm) loose-bottomed flan or sandwich tin. Prick all over with a fork.

Filling:
2 eggs
8 fl oz (200ml/1 cup) single (light) cream
1 level teasp salt
1 tbsp Worcestershire sauce
4 oz (100g/1 cup) cheese
1 level tbsp flour
7½ oz (200g) can finely-flaked tuna or salmon
1 tbsp snipped chives or parsley

Whisk together the eggs, cream, salt and Worcestershire sauce. Combine the cheese, flour, fish (drained, skinned and flaked with a fork) and the chives. Arrange this mixture on the unbaked quiche, then pour over the custard.

To bake: Put in a very hot oven (Gas No. 8, 450°F, 230°C) for 15 minutes, then immediately turn down to Gas No. 2, 300°F, 150°C, for a further 30 minutes, until a knife inserted in the centre comes out clean. Serve warm. Serves 6.

Sweet Flan Pastry

This can be used for flan cases that are baked 'blind', or for any recipe which calls for a biscuity pastry.

6 oz (150g/1½ cups) plain flour
Pinch of salt
4 oz (100g/½ cup) firm butter or margarine
2 level tbsp icing (confectioners') sugar; or caster (superfine) sugar if a slightly crunchier texture is preferred)
1 egg yolk blended with 2 tbsp water and 1 teasp vinegar or lemon juice

Rub the fat into the flour and salt until no large particles can be seen when the bowl is shaken. Stir in the icing sugar then moisten with the egg yolk, blended with the water and the vinegar (or lemon juice). Gather into a dough. Chill for at least half an hour.

To bake the flan 'blind': Roll out the chilled pastry to fit an 8 in (20 cm) loose-bottomed flan or sandwich tin. Trim the edges even with the top of the tin by rolling the pin across the top of the tin. Push the dough gently up ⅛ in (½ cm) above the rim, then press down again with the tines of a fork, to form a pattern all the way round. Line with greased foil, heatproof cooking film or greaseproof paper. Weight down with old crusts, rice or beans. (These can be used indefinitely if stored in a plastic bag or container.)

To bake: Put in a hot oven (Gas No. 6, 400°F, 200°C) for 10 minutes, lift out the lining, then continue to bake the flan case for a further 10 minutes, or until golden brown. Carefully ease out of the tin, and allow the flan case to cool on a wire rack. Makes one 8 in (20 cm) flan case.

Glazed Berry Flan

One flan case of Sweet Flan Pastry, baked blind
¾ lb (300g/¾ pint) fine whole berries (strawberries, raspberries or loganberries)
A little redcurrant jelly for spreading on flan case
Whipped cream for decoration

Glaze:
¼ lb (100g/¼ pint) of the less choice or smaller berries
¼ pint (125ml/⅔ cup) water
2 oz (50g/¼ cup) sugar
2 level teasp arrowroot or cornflour (cornstarch)
1 tbsp redcurrant jelly

Put the ¼ lb (100g/¼ pt) berries, sugar, water and redcurrant jelly into the blender and blend until smooth. (Raspberries and loganberries will need to be sieved.) Put in a pan and bring to the boil. Stir in the arrowroot (or cornflour) mixed to a cream with 1 tablespoon water, boil 2 minutes, then cool to lukewarm. Arrange the cooled shell on a serving plate, and spread a thin layer of redcurrant jelly over the surface (if too stiff to spread, warm slightly until semi-liquid). Cover the jelly with the berries arranged in an even layer. Spoon the cooled glaze over the fruit. Chill for 2 hours. Decorate with whipped cream, or serve with pouring cream. Serves 6 generously.

Liqueur Fruit Flan

1 flan case of Sweet Flan Pastry, baked blind
1 medium can choice apricots, pineapple or sweet black cherries
Toasted almonds for decoration
Glaze:
$\frac{1}{4}$ pint (125ml/$\frac{2}{3}$ cup) of the fruit syrup
1 oz (25g/2 tbsp) sugar
2 level teasp arrowroot or cornflour (cornstarch)
1 teasp lemon juice
1 tbsp liqueur (optional)

Put the arrowroot or cornflour with the sugar into a small bowl, and mix to a cream with a little of the fruit syrup. Heat the remainder of the syrup until it is steaming, then stir in the mixture in the bowl. Simmer for 2 minutes, until thickened and clear, stirring all the time. Stir in the lemon juice and liqueur. Use kirsch for pineapple; apricot brandy or Cointreau for apricots; cherry brandy or kirsch for cherries—or the liqueur may be omitted altogether. Allow the glaze to cool whilst the well-drained fruit is arranged in the flan case. Spoon over the glaze and decorate with chopped toasted almonds. Chill until required. Serve plain or with whipped cream. Serves 6.

Lemon Meringue Pie

1 flan case of Sweet Flan Pastry, baked blind
7 oz (175g/1 cup) granulated sugar
3 level tbsp flour
2 level tbsp cornflour (cornstarch)
Pinch of salt
12 fl oz (300ml/1$\frac{1}{2}$ cups) boiling water
2 egg yolks
4 tbsp lemon juice
1 level tbsp grated rind (rind of 2 lemons)

In the top of a double saucepan (or bowl that will fit over a pan of boiling water) thoroughly mix 5 oz (125g/$\frac{2}{3}$ cup) of the sugar, salt, flour and cornflour, then gradually stir in the boiling water. Put over boiling water, and stir constantly until smooth and thick. Cover and leave to cook for 15 minutes to thoroughly cook the starches in it. Whilst this mixture is cooking, beat together the remaining 2 oz (50g/$\frac{1}{3}$ cup) sugar and the egg yolks, then pour on the hot mixture stirring all the time. Return to the pan, and cook over hot water for a further 5 minutes. Stir in the lemon juice and rind, then remove from the heat and cool until steaming stops. Stand the baked flan case on a baking tin. Pour in the filling.

The meringue:
2 egg whites
Pinch of salt
4 oz (100g/$\frac{1}{2}$ cup) caster (superfine) sugar mixed with 1 level teasp cornflour (cornstarch)

Beat the whites with the pinch of salt until they form stiff, glossy peaks. Beat in the sugar a tablespoon at a time, beating well until stiff again after each addition. Swirl or pipe this meringue over the pie, sealing the meringue to the edges of the flan so that the filling is completely covered.

To bake: Put in a slow oven (Gas No. 2, 300°F, 150°C) for 30 minutes, or until crisp and biscuit-coloured. Keep in a cool place (not the refrigerator) until required. Serves 6.

VARIATION
Orange Meringue Pie: Make exactly as for Lemon Meringue Pie, but with this filling:

5 oz (125g/$\frac{2}{3}$ cup) sugar
3 level tbsp flour
2 level tbsp cornflour (cornstarch)
Pinch of salt
2 egg yolks
$\frac{1}{4}$ pint (125ml/$\frac{2}{3}$ cup) boiling water
$\frac{1}{4}$ pint (125ml/$\frac{2}{3}$ cup) orange juice
3 tbsp lemon juice
Grated rind $\frac{1}{2}$ lemon

Aloha Pineapple Pie

1 flan case of Sweet Flan Pastry (made with margarine if for a meat meal), baked blind
3 large eggs, separated
4 oz (100g/$\frac{1}{2}$ cup) caster (superfine) sugar
$\frac{1}{2}$ pint (250ml/1$\frac{1}{4}$ cups) crushed pineapple and juice; or pineapple titbits blended for 5 seconds
Juice of 1 lemon (3 tbsp)
Grated rind of 1 lemon
1 lemon jelly (gelatin mix)

In the top of a double saucepan (or bowl that can stand in pan of boiling water) beat together the yolks and 3 oz (75g/6 tbsp) of the sugar, then add the pineapple, the lemon juice and the rind. Cook over hot water until thickened to a custard consistency. Add the jelly and stir until dissolved. Chill until it begins to thicken (about half an hour). Beat the egg whites until they form stiff, glossy peaks, then beat in the remaining ounce of sugar. Fold this meringue into the half-set jelly mixture, then spoon into the flan. Allow to set. Serves 6.

Custard Flan

The flan case is partially cooked blind, and the custard filling is then added. This prevents the pastry rising to swamp the custard, and yet does not prevent the filling and pastry 'marrying' in a custard flan's inimitable manner.

1 uncooked flan case of Sweet Flan Pastry
1 egg white (left over from pastry)
Filling:
½ pint (250ml/1¼ cups) creamy milk (light cream)
2 eggs
1 oz (25g/2 tbsp) caster (superfine) sugar
½ teasp vanilla essence (extract)
Ground nutmeg

Whisk the egg white until foamy throughout, then paint over the base of the pastry to prevent sogginess. Line with buttered foil, heatproof cooking film or greaseproof paper. Weight down with old crusts, rice or beans. Bake in a quick oven (Gas No. 6, 400°F, 200°C) for 10 minutes, until set but only pale cream in colour. Remove the lining. Whilst the flan is cooking, make the filling by heating the milk until steaming then pouring onto the whisked eggs, sugar and vanilla (most easily done in the blender). Strain into the pastry case (to remove the froth) and sprinkle with grated nutmeg.

To bake: Bake in a slow oven (Gas No. 3, 325°F, 170°C) for 35–40 minutes, or until a knife plunged into the custard comes out clean. Cool before serving. Serves 6.

Tarte Normande

In this simple but satisfying traditional French recipe, first invented by Normandy peasants to help use their prodigal crop of apples, the filling is baked with the partially cooked flan pastry, then glazed with jam when it comes out of the oven.

1 unbaked 8 in (20 cm) flan case of Sweet Flan Pastry (in a loose-bottomed flan or sandwich tin), prepared for baking 'blind'
Filling:
2 lb (1kg) crisp cooking or baking apples
Squeeze of lemon juice
1 oz (25g/2 tbsp) granulated sugar

Peel, core and quarter the apples. Take slightly less than half and cut in slices ⅛ in (¼ cm) thick. Put in a bowl with the sugar and lemon juice. These are for the top of the tart.

The remaining apples:
2 oz (50g/¼ cup) granulated sugar
Good nut of butter
½ level teasp cinnamon
Grated rind of ½ lemon

Put the apples and butter into a wide shallow pan, cover and cook gently in their own juice, giving an occasional stir until tender. Uncover, add the sugar, cinnamon and lemon rind, and cook more quickly until a thick purée. Leave to cool.

To bake: Put uncooked shell in oven at Gas No. 6, 400°F, 200°C. After 9 minutes, take out lining and return to oven for 3 minutes. The flan will now be pale but set. Remove from oven and carefully put on baking tray. Fill with apple sauce mixture. Arrange sugared apples in neat, overlapping concentric circles on top. Turn oven to Gas No. 5, 375°F, 190°C. Bake for 30 minutes, until apples are golden brown. Carefully put flan on cooling tray.

Glaze:
2 generous tbsp smooth apricot jam
2 oz (50g/¼ cup) granulated sugar

Boil jam and sugar until the mixture spreads in a film over wooden spoon. Spoon the hot glaze over the apples. Allow to set. Serve plain or with pouring cream. Serves 6.

VARIATION

Apple Slices: This is the version in every French pâtisserie. Roll out the pastry to fit a shallow tin approximately 12 × 8 × ¾ in (30 × 20 × 2 cm) deep. Arrange the apples in overlapping rows all over the pastry (you will need about 1½ lb/¾kg unpeeled). Sprinkle with 4 oz (100g/½ cup) sugar. Bake at Gas No. 5, 375°F, 190°C for 30 minutes and glaze like **Tarte Normande.** Serve in squares. Serves 6.

Tarte des Demoiselles Tatin—Upside-down Apple Tart

This can be made with left-over pastry from either savoury or sweet flan pastry. The apples become caramelized during the cooking and develop the most beguiling flavour.

½ recipe Flan Pastry
Filling:
2 lb (1kg) crisp baking or eating apples mixed with 1 oz (25g) sugar and ½ level teasp cinnamon
2 oz (50g/¼ cup) granulated sugar
2 oz (50g/¼ cup) melted butter
1 oz (25g/2 tbsp) soft butter

Use an ovenproof, round glass dish or a baking tin, 7 in (18 cm) in diameter and 2 in (5 cm) deep. Spread the soft butter on the bottom and sides, then sprinkle with 1 oz (25g/2 tbsp) sugar. Peel, core and quarter apples, then cut into slices ⅛ in (¼ cm) thick. Divide into three portions. Put one portion of the apples into the tin, sprinkle with half the remaining sugar and half the melted butter. Repeat with the second portion of apples, sugar and butter, and finish with the remainder of the apples, arranging them in a level layer. Roll out the pastry to fit the top of the tin, then place it in position, allowing the edges to fall inside the tin. Bake at Gas No. 5, 375°F, 190°C, for 60 minutes. Tip up the dish—a rich brown caramel should appear. If not, leave a little longer (cover the pastry with foil if it is over-browning). Reverse the hot tart onto a serving dish. Serve warm. The tart can be reheated by covering with foil and heating through in a moderate oven (Gas No. 4, 350°F, 180°C). Serve with cream. Serves 6.

Note: It is not advisable to substitute margarine for butter in this recipe as the flavour of the melted margarine is not satisfactory.

Sweet Tart Pastry

The following pastry keeps its shape merely with fork pricks, and remains crisp for hours even after filling with soft fruits. Empty tarts can be frozen, or they can be stored for up to six weeks in an airtight tin, then briefly reheated and cooled before use.

8 oz (200g/2 cups) plain flour
Pinch of salt
5 oz (125g/⅔ cup) soft butter
3 oz (75g/¾ cup) icing (confectioners') sugar
2 egg yolks; or 1 yolk and 2 teasp water (for economy)

Put all the ingredients into the mixer and mix gently until a dough is formed. Chill for at least 1 hour. Roll out on a board sprinkled with icing sugar instead of flour to a thickness of ⅛ in (¼ cm). Cut to fit patty tins, prick well.

To bake: Put in a moderate oven (Gas No. 4, 350°F, 180°C) for 15–20 minutes until a pale gold in colour. Makes about 40 tartlets.

Danish Strawberry Tarts

20 baked tartlets (recipe above)
1 lb (½kg) strawberries
Redcurrant jelly
5 fl oz (125ml/⅔ cup) whipping cream
1 egg white
2 level teasp caster (superfine) sugar
2 teasp maraschino or grenadine syrup

In the bottom of each cooled shell put a little chopped redcurrant jelly. Melt 4 tablespoons more redcurrant jelly until liquid. Drop the egg white into the unbeaten cream, then whisk together until thickening. Beat in the sugar and flavouring syrup, and continue to whisk until it will hold its shape. Arrange 3 strawberries in each tartlet, and glaze with the redcurrant jelly; when set decorate with a blob of the cream topping. Chill until required. (Don't keep overnight or they will go soggy.)

Strawberry and Cream Cheese Tarts

20 baked tartlets (recipe p. 153)
Filling:
1 oz (25g/2 tbsp) butter
1 oz (25g/2 tbsp) caster (superfine) sugar
6 oz (150g/¾ cup) cream cheese
1 tbsp cream
Few drops vanilla essence (extract)
1 lb (480g/1 pint) whole strawberries
4 tbsp warm redcurrant jelly

Cream the soft butter and sugar until fluffy, then beat in the cheese, cream and vanilla. Line each tartlet with some of the filling, arrange 3 strawberries on top and coat with the warm redcurrant jelly. Chill until required.

Honey Tarts

20 baked tartlet cases or boat-shaped cases (recipe p. 153)
Filling:
3 oz (75g/⅓ cup) butter
3 oz (75g/⅓ cup) caster (superfine) sugar
3 oz (75g/¾ cup) ground almonds
1 tbsp honey
2 level tbsp instant coffee dissolved in 1 tbsp boiling water

Put all the ingredients into a bowl and beat until thoroughly blended. Fill the cases and smooth level with the top. Dredge with icing sugar. Leave in a cool place until the filling is firm.

Lemon Tarts

These delicate little tarts can also be made with Sweet Flan Pastry.

20 tartlet cases (recipe p. 153)
Filling:
2 oz (50g/¼ cup) butter
2 oz (50g/¼ cup) caster (superfine) sugar
1 egg
1 oz (25g/3 tbsp) stale cake or biscuit (cookie) crumbs
Juice (3 tbsp) and grated rind of a large lemon

Put all the filling ingredients into a bowl and beat until smooth and well-blended. Put a heaped teaspoon into each unbaked tartlet.

To bake: Put in a quick moderate oven (Gas No. 5, 375°F, 190°C) for 20 minutes, until the filling is a golden brown. When cool, dust with icing sugar.

Almond Shortcrust Pastry

This meltingly-tender pastry will keep fresh for several days.

9 oz (225g/2¼ cups) plain flour
1 oz (25g/3 tbsp) ground almonds
6 oz (150g/¾ cup) butter
3 oz (75g/⅓ cup) caster (superfine) sugar
Grated rind of ½ lemon
2 tbsp single (light) cream
1 egg yolk

Rub the fat into the flour, almonds and sugar until the mixture resembles dry breadcrumbs. Mix to a dough with the cream, lemon rind and yolk. Divide in two and foil-wrap. Chill for an hour. Use as required.

Apfelschnitten (*Austrian Apple Slices*)

1 recipe chilled Almond Shortcrust Pastry
Filling:
1½ lb (¾kg) peeled baking apples, coarsely grated
5 oz (125g/⅔ cup) sugar
2 tbsp seedless raisins or sultanas (white raisins)
1 egg white, whisked until foamy
Granulated sugar for glazing

Roll one portion of the chilled pastry to fit a shallow tin, approx 12 × 8 × $\frac{3}{4}$ in (30 × 20 × $\frac{1}{2}$ cm) deep. Cover with the grated apples, scattered with the sugar and raisins. Cover with the remaining pastry, rolled out to fit.

Note: If pastry breaks in rolling, lift onto the apple, and pinch together—the join will be mended in the oven. Paint with the foamy egg white, then mark lightly into 2 in (5 cm) squares. Scatter with granulated sugar.

To bake: Put in a moderate oven (Gas No. 5, 375°F, 190°C) for 45 minutes until golden brown. Serve warm or cold. Makes twenty-four 2 in (5 cm) squares.

VARIATION

Brandied Mincemeat Slices: Make in exactly the same way as the **Apfelschnitten** but substitute this filling for the apples:

1 lb (480g) jar vegetarian mincemeat
2 tbsp apricot jam
2 tbsp brandy or rum
1 oz (25g/3 tbsp) ground almonds or fine cake crumbs

Blend all together, and use to fill pastry.

Brown Sugar Almond Pastry

This is a crunchier version, made with whole egg.

6 oz (150g/$\frac{3}{4}$ cup) butter (or margarine for a meat meal)
8 oz (200g/2 cups) self-raising flour
2 oz (50g/$\frac{1}{2}$ cup) ground almonds
4 oz (100g/$\frac{1}{2}$ cup) soft light brown sugar
1 large egg
Juice of 1 lemon

Mix the almonds, flour and sugar, then rub in the fat until the mixture resembles coarse dry bread-crumbs. Mix to a dough by sprinkling with the egg beaten with the lemon juice, then gathering the damp particles into a ball. Divide in two, foil-wrap and chill for at least an hour.

Rhubarb Slice

1 recipe Brown Sugar Almond Pastry (see above)

Filling:

1$\frac{1}{2}$ lb ($\frac{3}{4}$kg) forced rhubarb, cut in 1 in (2$\frac{1}{2}$ cm) pieces
6 oz (150g/$\frac{3}{4}$ cup) granulated sugar
1 level tbsp cornflour (cornstarch)

Mix all filling ingredients together.

Roll one portion of pastry to fit a tin 12 × 8 × $\frac{3}{4}$ in deep (30 × 20 × $\frac{1}{2}$ cm). Spread with the rhubarb filling. Cover with the second portion of the pastry, rolled out to fit.

To bake: Put in a quick oven (Gas No. 5, 375°F, 190°C) for 40–45 minutes or until golden brown. Take from the oven and sprinkle with caster sugar. Serve warm or cold. Makes 10–12 good-sized squares.

VARIATION

Ginger Slices

Make in exactly the same way for **Rhubarb Slice,** but substitute a 1 lb ($\frac{1}{2}$kg) jar of ginger marmalade for the fruit filling. Scatter the pastry with almond nibs or slivers. Makes about 24 small slices.

Cakes

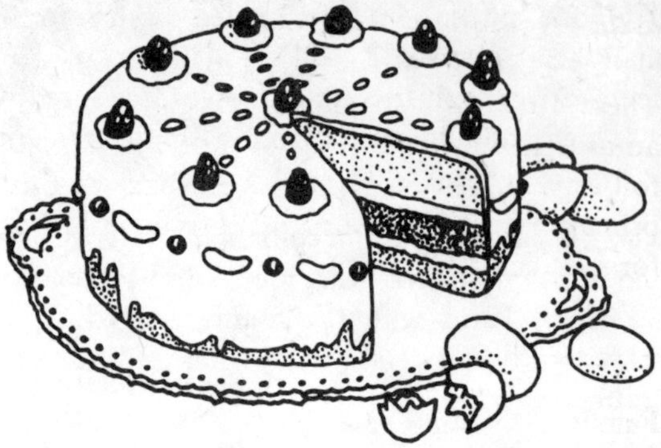

Ginger cakes, sponge cakes, butter cakes and yeast cakes—these are the traditional 'cut and come again' varieties of the Jewish kitchen, ever ready in the cake tin for the unexpected guest or the hungry child. Now the range has been widened by the use of freezer storage, for even the most delicate or perishable cake can be stored, ready for use, or left-over sections safely kept for another day. So in this chapter, besides the familiar family-type cakes, there are more elaborate gâteaux and fruit-and-cream cakes, as well as one-bowl cakes for immediate use and very rich cakes which improve with keeping.

Storage: All cakes need air-tight storage as this retards staling. In addition, cream cakes should be refrigerated, covered in some way to prevent the absorption of 'foreign' flavours from other foods.

Freezing: All cakes freeze exceptionally well, provided they are tightly enclosed in foil or plastic. Iced or cream-topped cakes should first be frozen uncovered until the topping is solid, and then wrapped as usual. Most cakes can be stored for as long as twelve months, though it is inadvisable to store whisked sponges for more than six months. Uncooked cake batter can be frozen for a maximum of fourteen days, but this is only advisable in an emergency as there will be some loss of lightness in the cake when it is finally baked.

Preparing the tin: Unless the tin has a non-stick coating, it must be prepared in some way to prevent the baked cake from sticking to it. Unless specified otherwise in the individual recipe, the tin should always be lightly but thoroughly brushed with a thin coating of oil—butter and margarine may cause the mixture to stick. Richer cakes will also need either bottom-lining with a piece of oiled greaseproof paper or foil, or if they are to spend longer than 1½ hours in the oven, completely lined.

Cooling the cake: Set the cake on a metal cooling rack for 5–10 minutes to allow it to set, then gently ease out of the tin. A spatula may be necessary to loosen the cake from the sides. Gently turn the cake over so that it is right side up. The easiest way to do this is to transfer it on to a second cooling rack. To remove a cake from a tin with a loose bottom, stand the cake on a canister of smaller diameter, then gently ease down the sides of the cake tin. Use a spatula to transfer the cake (still on the base) from the canister to a cooling rack. Remove the base when the cake is cool enough to handle. This method is recommended for fragile cakes or heavy fruit cakes which might not take kindly to being turned upside down to release them.

Cake-Cupboard Insurance

These 'cut and come again' cakes will keep moist in an airtight tin for 7–10 days, longer if wrapped in foil as well. Take care not to overbake as this is a primary cause of dryness. (See individual recipes for specific baking instructions.)

Family Favourite Cake

A superb basic cake mixture, tender and moist, which can easily be varied to suit individual tastes.

3 oz (75g/⅓ cup) soft butter
3 oz (75g/⅓ cup) soft margarine
7 oz (175g/1 cup) caster (superfine) sugar
8 oz (200g/2 cups) plain flour
1 level teasp baking powder
4 tbsp hot water
1 teasp vanilla essence (extract)
3 eggs

Bake the cake in a 9–10 in (23–25 cm) oiled ring tin or an 8 in (20 cm) loose-bottomed cake tin, 3 in (8 cm) deep, which has been oiled and bottom-lined with oiled greaseproof paper. Cream the two fats until they resemble mayonnaise, then add the sugar a tablespoonful at a time, beating thoroughly after each addition, until the mixture has lightened in colour and is fluffy in texture. Beat the essence into the creamed mixture. Whisk the eggs to blend the yolks and whites then beat in a spoonful at a time. Have the flour and baking powder sifted together, then *stir* into the creamed mixture in three portions, alternately with the hot water. The mixture is now ready to be flavoured and baked as required.

Marble Cake

To make a Marble Cake, use half the mixture to fill any of the tins, dropping it by spoonfuls with gaps in between, to leave room for the chocolate half. To the remaining cake mixture, add a level tablespoonful of cocoa and 4 level tablespoons drinking chocolate. Stir well, then drop this mixture into the gaps left by the white portion. Gently smooth the top of the cake level.

Sultana (White Raisin) Cake

Omit the vanilla essence (extract), and instead beat in the rind of half a lemon. Plump ½ lb (200g/1½ cups) sultanas (white raisins) by standing them in boiling water for 5 minutes, then draining and dabbing dry with a tea towel. Stir into the cake mixture with the flour.

Coconut Cake

Fold 2 oz (50g/½ cup) desiccated (dried and shredded) coconut into the cake with the flour.

Almond Cake

Omit the vanilla essence (extract) and add 8 drops of almond essence (extract) instead. Instead of 8 oz (200g/2 cups) plain flour, fold in 6 oz (150g/1½ cups) plain flour and 2 oz (50g/½ cup) ground almonds.

Madeira Cake

Leave the cake mixture plain, as in the basic recipe. Bake the cake in a 7 in (18 cm) diameter cake tin. After half an hour of cooking time, open the oven, lay a 3 in (7½ cm) long sliver of candied orange or lemon peel over the cake and close the oven door again.

If you do not wish to ice the cakes, proceed as follows: Before the cake is baked, paint the uncooked surface of the cake with milk, and scatter with a thin, even layer of caster (superfine) sugar. (This is unnecessary in a ring tin, as the top of the cake will become the underside when it is cooked.)

To bake the cakes: In a square or ring tin, bake (Gas No. 4, 350°F, 180°C) for 50–60 minutes. In a round deep tin, bake for one hour, (Gas No. 4,

350°F, 180°C) then reduce the heat to Gas No. 3, 325°F, 170°C, for a further 15 minutes, if necessary.

To test whether done: Open the oven gently, and press the centre of the cake with the tip of the forefinger. If it is ready, the cake will spring back at once. If not, a faint impression will remain. The sides of the cake will have shrunk slightly from the sides of the tin. When the cake is cooked, remove it from the oven and stand it in the tin on a metal cooling tray. Leave for 5 minutes. If it is in a ring tin, reverse the tin onto a second cooling tray. If it is a loose-bottomed tin, stand it on a canister of smaller circumference and gently ease down the sides. When the cake is quite cool, remove the loose bottom. If it is in a square, solid-bottom tin, reverse on to a second cooling tray. When the cakes are quite cool, wrap in foil, and store in an airtight cake tin.

Almond Feather Cake

Fluffy yet moist, this is a truly delectable cake, at its best when baked in a ring tin, fluted for the prettiest effect.

8 oz (200g/1 cup) butter
8 oz (200g/1 cup) caster (superfine) sugar
5 oz (125g/1¼ cups) self-raising flour
3 oz (75g/¾ cup) ground almonds
4 large eggs
Few drops almond essence (extract)

Cream the butter until it resembles mayonnaise, then beat in the sugar and almond essence, creaming until like whipped cream. Beat in the eggs one at a time, beating vigorously after each addition, and adding a tablespoonful of flour with each egg. Finally fold in the sifted flour and almonds. Spoon into a greased 9–10 in (23–25 cm) ring tin, or 8 in (20 cm) square tin. Bake in the middle of a moderate oven (Gas No. 4, 350°F, 180°C) for approximately one hour, or until the cake has shrunk from the sides of the tin and the centre springs back when gently pressed. The top can be covered with a thin layer of lemon glacé icing, or painted with milk and sprinkled with caster sugar before it goes into the oven.

Sponge Cherry Cake

Light yet fruity, it is improved by a covering of glacé icing.

4 oz (100g/1 cup) self-raising flour
4 oz (100g/1 cup) plain flour
3 oz (75g/⅓ cup) white fat or margarine
3 oz (75g/⅓ cup) butter
6 oz (150g/¾ cup) caster (superfine) sugar
3 eggs
4 oz (100g/⅔ cup) glacé (candied) cherries
Grated rind of a lemon
2 tbsp boiling water

Cream the fats, then beat in the sugar till fluffy. Beat in the eggs, one at a time, adding a little flour with the last egg. Beat in the boiling water, beating till the mixture resembles whipped cream. Cut the cherries in half, then mix with the flour. Add the sifted flour and cherries with the lemon rind to the mixture. Spoon into tin. Bake in a ring tin at Gas No. 5, 375°F, 190°C, for 20 minutes, and then at Gas No. 4, 350°F, 180°C, for 30 minutes. Bake in a 7–8 in (18–20 cm) tin at Gas No. 4, 350°F, 180°C, for one hour.

Mother's Orange Cake

4 oz (100g/½ cup) butter
5 oz (125g/⅔ cup) caster (superfine) sugar
6 oz (150g/1½ cups) self-raising flour
2 large eggs
1 teasp orange rind
2 tbsp hot water

Cream the butter till it is like mayonnaise. Beat in the caster sugar, then the eggs. Finally fold in the flour, orange rind and water. Bake in an 8 in (20 cm) greased sandwich tin at Gas No. 4, 350°F, 180°C, for 45 minutes, or until golden brown. When quite cold, ice with orange glacé icing (see icing recipes), and decorate with candied orange and lemon slices.

Orange Ring Cake

A moist, fruity cake which bakes best in a 9 in (23 cm) ring tin such as a kugelhupf tin (fluted ring tin) with a loose bottom.

9 oz (225g/1⅛ cups) butter
9 oz (225g/1⅛ cups) caster (superfine) sugar
9 oz (225g/2¼ cups) plain flour
1 level teasp baking powder
4 large eggs
3 tbsp orange juice (approx 1 small orange)
Grated rind of ½ orange and ½ lemon
1 tbsp boiling water

Cream the butter until it resembles mayonnaise, then beat in the sugar until the mixture looks like whipped cream. Add the rind, then the egg yolks one at a time. Finally beat in the boiling water and orange juice. Whip the whites until they form floppy peaks. Sift the flour with the baking powder, then sift onto the creamed mixture. Lay the whites on top then fold the whole thing together. It should be of a soft dropping consistency. If not, add a little more water. Turn into a 9 in (23 cm) greased ring tin. Bake in a moderate oven (Gas No. 4, 350°F, 180°C) for 45 minutes. Allow to cool 5 minutes in tin then turn out. When quite cold, either sift with icing (confectioners') sugar or coat with glacé icing, or with orange-flavoured butter icing.

A Trio of Chocolate Cakes

Each of the three cakes below has a true chocolate flavour, but a different texture. Block chocolate should always be melted *over* hot water rather than in a pan set directly on the stove top, as overheating will prevent it becoming liquid.

Milk Chocolate Cake

4 oz (100g/½ cup) caster (superfine) sugar
4 oz (100g/½ cup) butter
5 oz (125g/1¼ cups) self-raising flour
2 oz (50g/½ cup) ground almonds
3 oz (75g/¾ cup) drinking (instant) chocolate
2 tbsp hot water
2 tbsp milk
2 eggs
½ teasp vanilla essence (extract)

Cream the butter and sugar, add the vanilla and then beat in the eggs. Add flour, nuts and drinking chocolate, alternately with the milk and water. Bake in an 8 in (20 cm) loose-bottomed cake tin for 35–40 minutes at Gas No. 4, 350°F, 180°C. Ice when cold with **Milk Chocolate Icing** (see p. 170).

French Chocolate Cake

A rich, tender cake that keeps fresh for days, and needs no icing. The use of potato flour makes it especially soft and the large amount of chocolate gives it a rich dark colour and pronounced chocolate flavour.

6 oz (150g) plain dessert (semi-sweet) chocolate
4 oz (100g/½ cup) butter (unsalted if possible)
2 oz (50g/¼ cup) potato flour
4 oz (100g/½ cup) caster (superfine) sugar
1 level teasp baking powder
4 eggs, separated
1 teasp vanilla essence (extract)

Use an 8 in (20 cm) moule à manqué (shallow tin with sloping sides). Otherwise use an 8 in (20 cm) loose-bottomed tin. In both cases, oil the tin and bottom-line with oiled greaseproof paper. Melt the butter in the top of a double boiler or mixing bowl standing in a pan of very hot water, then add the broken chocolate and stir again until the chocolate too has melted. Take from the heat and stir in the sugar then the yolks, vanilla, baking powder and sifted potato flour. Finally, fold in the egg whites, beaten with a pinch of salt until they form stiff but still glossy peaks. Turn the mixture into the prepared tin and bake at Gas No. 4, 350°F, 180°C, for 45 minutes until well risen and firm to a very gentle touch. Leave on a cooling tray for 5 minutes, then turn out and leave until cold. Sift all over with icing sugar.

Mocha Fudge Gâteau

The basic cake is similar to the Milk Chocolate Cake, but is filled and topped with a luscious frosting.

4 oz (100g/½ cup) caster (superfine) sugar
4 oz (100g/½ cup) butter or soft margarine
1 teasp vanilla essence (extract)
2 eggs
5 oz (125g/1¼ cups) self-raising flour
3 oz (75g/¾ cup) drinking (instant) chocolate
1 level tbsp cocoa
2 tbsp each of hot water and cold milk

Cream the fat until soft, then beat in the sugar a tablespoonful at a time, until the mixture looks fluffy. Beat in the vanilla, and the slightly beaten eggs. Beat in the hot water. Finally stir in the flour (which has been mixed with the cocoa and drinking chocolate) alternately with the cold milk. Spoon into a loaf tin (approx 9 × 5 × 3 in/23 × 13 × 8 cm) which has been oiled and bottom-lined with oiled greaseproof paper. Level with a spatula. Bake at Gas No. 4, 350°F, 180°C, for 50–60 minutes or until firm to the touch. Leave to cool for 5 minutes then gently turn out onto a wire cooling tray.

To finish: Make **Mocha Fudge Frosting** (p. 171) and divide into two portions. To one portion, add 2 oz (50g) each of coarsely-chopped walnuts and glacé (candied) cherries. Split the cold cake in two, and sandwich together with the cherry and walnut mixture. Spread the top with the remaining plain frosting, rough up with a fork into a decorative design and arrange halved cherries and walnuts in a design on the top. To keep the icing fresh, store this cake in a tin in the refrigerator. Leave at room temperature for ¾ hour before serving.

For a fourth chocolate cake, see **One-Bowl Cakes,** below.

One-Bowl Cakes

One-bowl cakes were first developed in the United States in the early 1940s for use with soft white fats. As these shortenings had air introduced during manufacture, it was found that to produce a light-textured cake, it was unnecessary to cream them with sugar in the conventional manner. Later, the same method was adapted for soft margarines, and I have found that results are equally good with soft (but not with waxy) butters. Speed is the main advantage of this method. Most recipes can be adapted, but whilst the fresh product is excellent, staling is more rapid than with the creamed method. Very practical for family use or for the unexpected guest.

One-Bowl Sandwich Cake

4 oz (100g/½ cup) soft butter or margarine
4 oz (100g/½ cup) caster (superfine) sugar
5 oz (125g/1¼ cups) self-raising flour sifted with 1 level teasp baking powder; or 5 oz (125g/1¼ cups) plain flour with 2 level teasp baking powder
2 eggs
Jam for filling
Icing (confectioners') or caster (superfine) sugar for decoration

Place all the ingredients into a mixing bowl and beat with a wooden spoon or electric mixer until smooth (about 2–3 minutes). Place in one 8 in (20 cm) or two 7 in (18 cm) sandwich tins, which have been oiled and then lined with oiled greaseproof paper. Smooth the surface level. Bake in a slow moderate oven (Gas No. 3, 325°F, 170°C) until spongy to the touch. Bake the 8 in (20 cm) cake for 35–45 minutes, the two smaller cakes for 25–35 minutes. Turn out onto a cooling tray. When quite cold, split the 8 in (20 cm) cake to make two layers. Sandwich the cakes with jam, lemon curd, or jam and whipped cream. Sprinkle the top with icing or caster sugar.

One-Bowl Fairy Cakes

4 oz (100g/½ cup) soft butter or margarine
4 oz (100g/½ cup) caster (superfine) sugar
Grated rind of 1 orange or 1 lemon
5 oz (125g/1¼ cups) self-raising flour with 1 level teasp baking powder
2 eggs
Orange or lemon glacé icing
Halved glacé (candied) cherries for decoration

Place all ingredients in a mixing bowl and beat with a wooden spoon, until well mixed and smooth in texture (2–3 minutes). Place heaped teaspoonfuls of the mixture in paper cases. Bake in a fairly hot oven (Gas No. 6, 400°F, 200°C) for 15–20 minutes, until springy to the touch. Cool on a wire tray.

To decorate: Place teaspoons of the icing on top of each cake and smooth evenly. Decorate with halved glacé cherries. The cakes can also be left plain. Makes 20–24 cakes.

Luscious Lemon Cake

A delicate sponge, moistened with a tart lemon syrup. This cake will keep moist for as long as any of it remains uneaten!

4 oz (100g/½ cup) soft butter
6 oz (150g/¾ cup) caster (superfine) sugar
6 oz (150g/1½ cups) self-raising flour
4 tbsp milk
Grated rind of 1 lemon
2 large eggs
Pinch of salt
Lemon syrup:
3 oz (75g/¾ cup) icing (confectioners') sugar, warmed to a syrup with juice of 1½ large lemons (4 tbsp)

Well oil a 2 lb (1kg) loaf tin (9 × 5 × 3 in/23 × 13 × 8 cm) or 6 in (15 cm) square tin and line the bottom with greased greaseproof paper (this is important). Put all the cake ingredients into a bowl and beat by mixer or wooden spoon until smooth (about 3 minutes). Turn into the cake tin and smooth level. Bake for 45 minutes at Gas No. 4, 350°F, 180°C. Remove from the oven and stand the cake, still in the tin, on a cooling tray. Heat the sugar and lemon juice until a syrup is formed. Prick the warm cake all over with a fork, then gently pour the syrup over it. Leave until the cake is cold, then turn out. Serve sprinkled with icing sugar.

One-Bowl Chocolate Cake

4 oz (100g/½ cup) soft butter
4 oz (100g/½ cup) caster (superfine) sugar
4 oz (100g/1 cup) self-raising flour
2 eggs
2 level tbsp drinking (instant) chocolate
1 level teasp baking powder
1 level tbsp cocoa
2 tbsp cold milk
½ teasp vanilla essence (extract)

Lightly grease two 7 in (18 cm) sandwich tins. Put all the ingredients into a bowl and beat by mixer or hand until smooth and creamy—about 3 minutes. Divide the mixture between the two tins and smooth level with a spatula. Bake at Gas No. 4, 350°F, 180°C, for 25 minutes, or until springy to the touch. Turn onto a cooling tray. When quite cold, sandwich together with **Milk Chocolate Frosting** (see page 171), and then spread the remainder on top. Decorate with grated chocolate.

Dutch Apple Cake

This can be served hot as a pudding, cold as a cake. During the baking, the melted butter and sugar form a beautiful glaze over the apples.

6 oz (150g/1½ cups) self-raising flour
½ level teasp baking powder
3 oz (75g/⅓ cup) caster (superfine) sugar
1 egg
¼ pint (125ml/⅔ cup) milk
1½ oz (40g/3 tbsp) melted butter
Topping:
1 lb (½kg) baking apples
4 oz (100g/½ cup) granulated sugar, mixed with 1 level teasp cinnamon
1 oz (25g/2 tbsp) melted butter

Grease a baking tin 12 × 7 × 1 in (30 × 18 × 3 cm) with unsalted butter or oil. Put the flour, baking powder and sugar into a bowl. Put the egg, milk and 1½ oz (40g/3 tbsp) melted butter into a screw-top jar. Shake the liquids until blended then pour into the flour mixture. Mix to a smooth batter then pour into the tin. Smooth the top level, then brush with 1 oz (25g/2 tbsp) melted butter. Peel and core the apples and cut into quarters, then into slices about ¼ in (½ cm) thick. Lay the slices in overlapping rows to cover the cake completely. Mix the sugar and cinnamon and sprinkle evenly over the top. Bake at Gas No. 6, 400°F, 200°C, on a shelf slightly above the centre of the oven for 35 minutes. Cut into squares.

Whisked Sponges, Plain and Fancy

The whisked sponge is surely the archetypal Jewish cake, served with a glass of wine after the synagogue or for Saturday afternoon tea. Old family recipes (such as the Plava given below) usually contain no fat, and though very light and tender when freshly-baked, they tend to stale quickly. Modern recipes are often enriched with either oil or melted butter which help to keep the cake moister longer and also to give it a slightly firmer texture.

The success of any recipe depends mainly on the correct incorporation of the eggs with the sugar—the stage at which the air needed to leaven the cake is beaten in. By hand, this means a long and tedious job, but with an electric mixer, the mixture can be beaten to the correct mousse-like thickness swiftly and efficiently. Once this stage has been reached, it is important to fold in the flour and any liquids with a metal spoon (not a beater), or the lightening air will be beaten out, and the cake will be small and close in texture.

If an electric mixer is not available, use a stainless steel hand whisk or a balloon whisk and speed the thickening process by standing the mixing bowl over a pan of steaming water. There are several methods of beating the sugar and eggs together, and despite exhaustive experimentation, I cannot recommend one more than another. But in the recipes below, the method suggested gives the best results for each particular cake.

Plava

The traditional name of this most typical of Jewish sponge cakes would seem to derive from the Russian root 'plava' meaning that which swims or floats in water. Translate 'plava' as sponge (in the aquatic sense) and you have a fair description of this light, open-textured cake. This is a cake with a sugary crust and a soft, satisfying texture that makes it particularly suitable to serve unadorned by either filling or icing.

5 large eggs
10 oz (250g/1¼ cups) caster (superfine) sugar
6 oz (150g/1½ cups) plain flour
Pinch of salt
1 tbsp orange flower water or lemon juice

Separate the egg yolks from the whites. Divide the sugar into two equal quantities of 5 oz (125g/⅔ cup) each. Put one amount of sugar into a bowl with the egg yolks, whisk with an electric beater till white and thick. If no electric beater is available, stand the eggs and sugar in a bowl over a pan of very hot, but not boiling water and whisk till thick and white. Add the orange flower water or lemon juice. In another bowl, whisk the whites and salt until they hold firm peaks. Gradually beat in the sugar until a firm meringue is formed, then fold into the first mixture. Finally fold in the sifted flour. Put into a deep loose-bottomed 9 in (23 cm) round tin, which has been oiled and lightly sprinkled with sugar. Sprinkle a thin layer of caster sugar over the surface of the cake.

Bake in a moderate oven (Gas No. 4, 350°F, 180°C) for 1 hour, 10 minutes. Leave in the tin until cold, then remove. Store wrapped in foil. Freezes very well. The cake can also be baked in a 12 × 10 × 2 in (30 × 25 × 5 cm) baking tin and will take approximately 50 minutes, when the top will be firm to very gentle pressure and the cake will have shrunk slightly from the sides.

Hot Milk Sponge

This is a recipe which takes the traditional 'Plava' of the Russian Jewish cuisine and Americanizes it, with a method developed in the United States in the 1940s. The result is a sponge of meltingly tender texture, which is extremely good for filling and icing. In the United States, high ratio cake flour is used; other countries with a stronger flour can get a similar result by using a mixture of flour and cornflour.

3 large eggs, separated
6 oz (150g/¾ cup) caster (superfine) sugar
3 oz (75g/¾ cup) plain flour
1 oz (25g/¼ cup) cornflour (cornstarch)
3 fl oz (75ml/⅓ cup) hot milk
Grated rind of ½ lemon
1 level teasp baking powder
Pinch of salt

Put the oven on at Gas No. 6, 400°F, 200°C. Prepare an 8 in (20 cm) cake tin. Brush with oil, fit a round of greaseproof paper into the bottom and oil that. Mix 2 teaspoons each of caster sugar and flour and shake all over the tin to form a fine coating, discarding any excess. Drop the whites into a mixing bowl. Add a pinch of salt and whisk until they hold stiff but glossy peaks. Now start adding the yolks and sugar, a little at a time, whisking well between each addition until all have been added and the mixture is pale and mousse-like. Have the milk ready in a saucepan, heated until the edges of the milk bubble. Have ready also the flour, cornflour and baking powder sifted onto a paper and the lemon rind added. Now sift the flour onto the eggs and pour the milk gently down the side, immediately folding the mixture over and over with a large metal spoon until no flour can be seen. Pour into the cake tin and sprinkle the surface with granulated sugar.

Put the cake into the oven, and immediately turn it down to Gas No. 4, 350°F, 180°C. Bake for 45 minutes until the surface of the cake is firm to a gentle touch and the mixture has begun to shrink from the sides of the tin. Leave in the tin for 10 minutes before turning out carefully away from any draught.

Chiffon Sponge

The main virtue of this cake lies in its easy mixing and surprisingly tender texture. It also keeps extremely well because of its oil content. A good cake to choose if an electric mixer is not available.

3 oz (75g/¾ cup) plain flour, plus 1 oz (25g/4 tbsp) cornflour (cornstarch) and 1 level teasp baking powder; or 3 oz (75g/¾ cup) self-raising flour, plus 1 oz (25g/4 tbsp) cornflour (cornstarch) and ½ level teasp baking powder
5 oz (125g/⅔ cup) caster (superfine) sugar
3 tbsp cooking oil
2 tbsp orange juice or cold water
Grated rind of 1 orange or of ½ lemon
¼ teasp cream of tartar
3 eggs, separated

Into a mixing bowl, put the sifted flour, cornflour, sugar, baking powder, and, if plain flour is used, a pinch of salt. Make a well in this mixture and add the oil, unbeaten yolks, the water or orange juice and the rind. Beat until smooth. In a large bowl, put the whites and the cream of tartar and whisk together until the meringue holds stiff peaks and is so solid that it will stay in the bowl when turned upside down. Pour the yolk mixture onto the meringue and using a metal spoon, cut and fold the two together until the mixture is evenly creamy in colour. Have ready a large ring tin or a deep 9 in (23 cm) diameter cake tin or a deep 8 in (20 cm) square cake tin, but do not grease them. Pour the mixture into the cake tin and bake at Gas No. 3, 325°F, 170°C, for 45 minutes, or until firm to the touch. Leave the tin upside down on a cooling tray. When quite cold, run a knife round the inside edges of the tin and the cake will fall out. Serve the cake plain, as an accompaniment to fruit or ice-cream; or split and fill it with fruit and cream.

South African Sponge Layers

This recipe produces a cake with a fine texture that makes it perfect for filling with fruit and cream, jam and cream, or buttercream. It can be baked either in two separate shallow tins or in the deeper 'moule à manqué', the sloping-sided French cake tin which produces a cake well shaped for easy icing.

3 large eggs, separated
4 oz (100g/½ cup) caster (superfine) sugar
4 oz (100g/1 cup) self-raising flour
Grated rind of ½ lemon
½ oz (15g/1 tbsp) butter, melted in 3 tbsp boiling water

Whisk the whites with a pinch of salt, until they form stiff, glossy peaks, then whisk in the sugar a tablespoonful at a time, until a stiff meringue is formed. Whisk in the yolks until the colour is an even gold. Sift the flour over the surface of the mixture, then gently fold it through and through using a metal spoon. Finally, stir the butter into the boiling water until it melts, add the grated rind and pour it down the side of the bowl. Fold the liquid into the egg mixture until the two are completely amalgamated. Divide the mixture between two lightly-oiled 7 or 8 in (18 or 20 cm) sandwich tins which have been bottom-lined with oiled greaseproof paper; or spoon into an 8 in (20 cm) moule à manqué prepared in the same way. Bake the sandwich tins in a moderate oven (Gas No. 5, 375°F, 190°C) for 20 minutes. Bake the moule à manqué (which is deeper) in a slow moderate oven (Gas No. 3, 325°F, 170°C) for 40 minutes. In both cases, the cake is ready when the surface springs back after gentle finger pressure and the cake has shrunk slightly from the sides of the tin. After 5 minutes, turn the cakes out onto a wire cooling tray. Fill when quite cold.

To fill with jam and cream: Whisk 5 fl oz (125ml/$\frac{2}{3}$ cup) whipping cream with 2 tablespoons caster (superfine) sugar and $\frac{1}{2}$ teaspoon vanilla essence (extract) until it holds its shape. Spread one sandwich cake (or the bottom half of the split deeper cake) with raspberry, strawberry or apricot jam, then top with the cream.

To fill with fruit and cream: Whisk 5 fl oz (125ml/$\frac{2}{3}$ cup) whipping cream with 1 unbeaten egg white and 2 teaspoons caster (superfine) sugar until the mixture forms soft peaks. Add any juice that has come out of $\frac{1}{2}$ lb (200g) sugared raspberries or strawberries which have been standing at room temperature for half an hour. Fold in the fruit.

Other fruit fillings: $\frac{1}{2}$ lb (200g) sliced bananas tossed in lemon juice; 3 rings canned or sweetened fresh pineapple; 4–5 stewed fresh apricots. Spoon onto the bottom layer of the cake.

To assemble either cake: With a sharp knife cut the second sandwich or the top half of the split cake into 6 or 8 even segments, then reassemble into shape on top of the filling (this makes serving easy). Sift icing (confectioners') sugar evenly over the top. Leave at the bottom of the refrigerator until required. Left-over cake should be refrigerated either in an air-tight container or covered with a bowl.

See section on **Cake Icings, Toppings and Fillings** p. 169 for other ideas.

Cinnamon Sponge Layers

A light sponge with a delicately-spiced flavour. The hot milk gives a particularly smooth texture.

3 large eggs, separated
6 oz (150g/$\frac{3}{4}$ cup) caster (superfine) sugar
3 oz (75g/$\frac{3}{4}$ cup) plain flour
1 oz (25g/4 tbsp) cornflour (cornstarch)
1 level teasp baking powder
2 level teasp cinnamon
2 level teasp cocoa
3 tbsp hot milk

Put the oven on at Gas No. 6, 400°F, 200°C. Prepare one 8 in (20 cm) cake tin or two 8 in (20 cm) sandwich tins. To do this, brush the tins with oil, fit a round of greaseproof paper into the bottom and oil that. Mix 2 teaspoons each of caster sugar and flour, and shake over the tin to form a fine coating, discarding any excess. Drop the whites into a mixing bowl, add a pinch of salt, and whisk until they hold firm but glossy peaks. Now start adding the yolks and sugar a little at a time, whisking well between each addition until all have been added and the mixture is pale and mousse-like. Have the milk ready in a saucepan, heated until the edges of the milk bubble. Have ready the flour, cornflour, baking powder, cinnamon and cocoa sieved onto a paper. Sift the flour mixture on the egg mixture and pour the milk gently down the side. Immediately fold in the mixture over and over with a large metal spoon till no flour can be seen. Pour into the cake tin and sprinkle with granulated sugar. Put the cake or cakes in the oven. Immediately turn the oven down to Gas No. 4, 350°F, 180°C. Bake layers for 30 minutes, the deep cake for 45 minutes, or until the surface of the cake is firm to a gentle touch, and the mixture has begun to shrink from the sides of the tin. Leave in the tin for 10 minutes before turning out carefully away from a draught. Fill the layers or split and fill the larger cake with ¼ pint (125ml/⅔ cup) slightly sweetened whipped cream.

Chocolate Sponge Layers

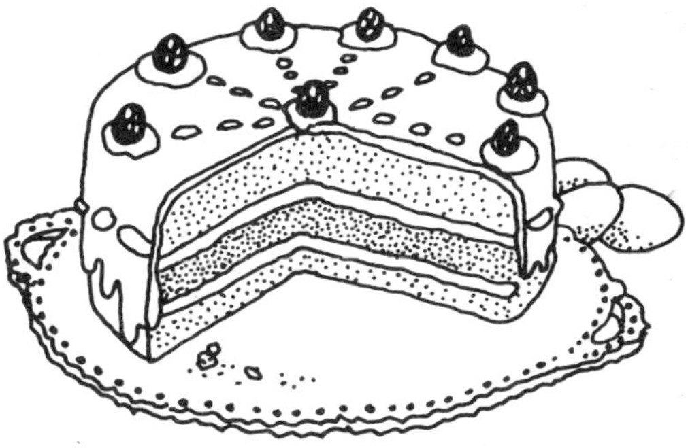

An excellent chocolate sponge to fill with French whipped cream—a subtle combination of sweet and soured creams (See **Liqueur Sponge**; *p. 126*).

3 large eggs
4 oz (100g/½ cup) caster (superfine) sugar
3 oz (75g/¾ cup) self-raising flour
2 level tbsp cocoa
2 tbsp hot water and a nut of butter
½ teasp vanilla essence (extract)

Set the oven to Gas No. 5, 375°F, 190°C, and put in water and butter to melt. Separate eggs, sift flour and cocoa. Whisk whites until they form stiff peaks; beat in each yolk and a third of the sugar, beating until thick again after each addition. By the time all have gone in, the mixture should be mousse-like and hold its shape. Fold in the sifted flour. Finally dribble water, butter and vanilla down side of sponge, folding it in carefully with metal spoon. Have a 7 or 8 in (18 or 20 cm) loose-bottomed sandwich tin (deep) lined with grease-proof paper and greased, then lightly floured. Spoon in mixture and level. Bake at Gas No. 5, 375°F, 190°C, for 25 minutes, or until firm to the touch. Cool for 10 minutes, then turn out. When cold, split and fill with whipped cream and dust the top layer with icing sugar.

Recipes for **Whisked Sponge Flans** can be found in the chapter on Desserts, p. 125.

The texture and flavour of certain rich creamed cakes is actually improved if they are allowed to mature in a tightly-sealed tin before they are eaten. This ripening period varies with the recipe but generally the fruitier the cake the longer it takes to reach perfection. To store during this maturing period, first allow the cake to cool completely, then wrap it tightly in foil and put it in an airtight tin. (For a storage period of more than a month, seal the tin itself with self-adhesive tape.) Do not refrigerate or freeze the cake until it is mature, as very cold temperatures delay the ripening process. Minimum storage times are given with individual recipes.

Sherried Sultana Cake

The fruit must be soaked in the sherry overnight.

3 oz (75g/⅓ cup) butter and 3 oz (75g/⅓ cup) soft margarine
6 oz (150g/¾ cup) caster (superfine) sugar
9 oz (225g/2¼ cups) sifted self-raising flour
Grated rind of ½ lemon
3 large eggs
3 tbsp sherry
½ lb (200g/1½ cups) sultanas (white raisins)
½ oz (15g/2 tbsp) slivered almonds

Put the sultanas in a small plastic container and pour over the sherry, leave overnight. Grease a 2 lb (1kg) loaf tin (9 × 5 × 3 in/23 × 13 × 8 cm) and line the bottom with a strip of greased greaseproof paper (or use an 8 in/20 cm loose-bottomed cake tin). Cream the fats until as soft as mayonnaise, add the sugar gradually, beating till like whipped cream, then add the lemon rind. Beat the eggs until thick, then beat into the creamed mixture a spoonful at a time, adding a little flour if the mixture starts to curdle. Finally fold in the fruit and any unabsorbed sherry, alternately with the flour. Spoon into the prepared tin and level the top. Paint the top lightly with milk and sprinkle with granulated sugar, then scatter with the almonds. Bake for 45 minutes at Gas No. 4, 350°F, 180°C, then turn the oven down to Gas No. 3, 325°F, 170°C, for a further half-hour or until the cake is a rich golden brown. Leave in the tin for 10 minutes, then turn out onto a cooling tray. Store for 3 days before use.

Almond Cherry Cake

8 oz (200g/1 cup) soft butter
8 oz (200g/1 cup) caster (superfine) sugar
4 large eggs
8 oz (200g/2 cups) plain flour
1 level teasp baking powder
4 oz (100g/1 cup) ground almonds
8 oz (200g/1¼ cups) glacé (candied) cherries
2 oz (50g/⅓ cup) angelica or candied lemon peel, finely chopped (optional)
Rind and juice of 1 lemon
Flaked almonds

Put the eggs into a small bowl and beat until fluffy. Quarter the cherries and mix with the chopped peel and ground almonds. Beat the butter until like mayonnaise, then beat in the caster sugar and continue to beat until like whipped cream. Add the beaten eggs a little at a time, beating until like cream again after each addition. Beat in the lemon rind. Stir in the flour sifted with the baking powder, then stir in the lemon juice and finally the cherry and almond mixture. Spoon into an 8 in (20 cm) diameter deep cake tin which has been lined sides and bottom with greased greaseproof paper. Level off the top. Paint with a little milk and scatter with a few flaked almonds and a very little granulated sugar. Bake in the middle of a moderate oven (Gas No. 4, 350°F, 180°C) for 45 minutes, then turn to Gas No. 3, 325°F, 170°C, for a further 45 minutes or until the cake is firm to the touch and has shrunk slightly from the side. Store for one week before use.

Cherry and Ginger Ring

A lightly-fruited cake with a rich flavour. It looks very decorative when baked in a shallow ring tin, though a 9 in (23 cm) round cake tin can also be used.

4 oz (100g/½ cup) butter
2 oz (50g/¼ cup) soft margarine
6 oz (150g/¾ cup) caster (superfine) sugar
3 large eggs
7 oz (175g/1¾ cups) self-raising flour
2 oz (50g/½ cup) ground almonds
2 fl oz (50ml/4 tbsp) milk
4 oz (100g/⅔ cup) quartered glacé (candied) cherries
2 oz (50g/⅓ cup) finely-sliced crystallized ginger
Grated rind of ½ lemon

Cream butter, margarine and sugar until like whipped cream, then beat in eggs together with a little of the sifted flour. Add the lemon rind. Mix the cherries and ginger with a tablespoonful of the flour. Add a third of the flour to the creamed mixture, then half the milk, then the fruit and another third of the flour, the remaining milk and finally the remaining flour mixed with the almonds. Turn into a shallow oiled ring tin 10 in (25 cm) in diameter. Bake at Gas No. 4, 350°F, 180°C, for 40 minutes. In an ordinary 9 in (23 cm) cake tin, bake for 1–1¼ hours or until firm to the touch. Store 3 days before use.

Jewel Fruit Cake

An extravagant golden cake, studded with ruby, emerald and topaz! It can be used quite fresh—after a week if necessary, though a longer period ensures full development of the flavour. This is a suitable cake for weddings, engagements or barmitzvahs as it is firm enough to decorate with royal icing.

8 oz (200g/1 cup) butter
8 oz (200g/1 cup) caster (superfine) sugar
8 oz (200g/2 cups) plain flour
½ level teasp baking powder
4 oz (100g/⅔ cup) glacé (candied) pineapple
2 oz (50g/⅓ cup) angelica
2 oz (50g/½ cup) ground almonds
4 large eggs
Good pinch of salt
Rind of 1 orange and ½ lemon
4 oz (100g/⅔ cup) glacé (candied) cherries
8 oz (200g/1½ cups) sultanas (white raisins)
4 oz (100g/⅔ cup) crystallized (candied) ginger

Cream butter till like mayonnaise, then beat in sugar until creamy and fluffy. Beat 4 eggs together until blended, then beat a tablespoon at a time into the creamed mixture together with the grated peel. Slice the ginger, chop the sultanas and the pineapple, halve the cherries and chop the angelica. Mix with the ground almonds. Add to the cake mixture, alternately with the flour. Pour into a 9 in (23 cm) loose-bottomed cake tin, sides and bottom lined with oiled brown paper or two layers of greaseproof paper or foil. Bake for 1 hour at Gas No. 3, 325°F, 170°C, then for a further half an hour at Gas No. 2, 300°F, 150°C. Test. The top should spring back when touched lightly with the forefinger, and a skewer or knitting needle should come out clean from the centre. Store for a week before use.

Traditional Fruit Cake

The dark fruit cake that usually graces the wedding table. This recipe makes a moist, tender cake. Whilst it is still warm it can be enriched with spirits by pouring 3 tablespoons brandy, rum or whisky slowly over the cake.

10 oz (250g/1¼ cups) butter
10 oz (250g/1¼ cups) soft brown sugar
6 eggs
½ lb (200g/1½ cups) currants
½ lb (200g/1½ cups) seedless raisins
1 lb (480g/3 cups) sultanas (white raisins)
4 oz (100g/⅔ cup) chopped candied peel
2 oz (50g/⅓ cup) chopped angelica
2 oz (50g/⅓ cup) glacé (candied) pineapple
4 oz (100g/1 cup) ground almonds
Grated rind of ½ orange
12 oz (300g/3 cups) plain flour
Pinch of salt
2 level teasp mixed spice

Cream the butter and sugar, and beat in the eggs. Add all fruits and ground almonds alternately with flour, spice and salt. Stir very thoroughly. Put into a brown paper lined 9–10 in (23–25 cm) cake tin. Bake in a slow oven (Gas No. 2, 300°F, 150°C) for 3–$3\frac{1}{2}$ hours. The cake is done when a skewer or knitting needle comes out clean from the centre. Store at least two weeks before use.

Spice is Nice

Spice cakes have always been popular in the Jewish household because when cooking oil (which, unlike butter, adds no flavour to a cake mixture) was the main cooking fat, it was possible to produce a cake of excellent flavour by judiciously blending ginger, cinnamon and mixed spice. The use of treacle (molasses), golden (corn) syrup or brown sugar also gives this type of cake richness of flavour and colour, as well as greatly enhancing the keeping qualities. The cakes below can all be eaten as soon as they are cold, but the flavour does improve after three days.

Wine and Spice Cake

1 lb (480g/$1\frac{1}{3}$ cups) golden (corn) syrup
$\frac{1}{2}$ pint (250ml/$1\frac{1}{4}$ cups) cold water
7 oz (175g/1 cup) granulated sugar
8 fl oz (200ml/1 cup) cooking oil
3 eggs
1 lb (480g/4 cups) self-raising flour; or 1 lb (480g/4 cups) plain flour with 4 level teasp baking powder
$\frac{1}{2}$ level teasp each of ground ginger, cinnamon and baking powder
2 level teasp mixed spice
1 level teasp bicarbonate of soda (baking soda) dissolved in 2 tbsp kosher wine or port

Warm together over gentle heat the syrup, water, sugar and oil, stirring until the mixture is smooth. Beat the eggs until fluffy in a large bowl, then add the syrup mixture, followed by all the dry ingredients sifted together and the bicarbonate of soda dissolved in the wine. Line a baking tin (approx 12 × 9 × 2 in / 30 × 23 × 5 cm) with foil or greased greaseproof paper. Pour in the mixture. Bake at Gas No. 3, 325°F, 170°C, for $1\frac{3}{4}$ hours, or until firm to the touch and golden brown. Turn out onto a cooling tray. After 5 minutes, turn the right way up or the top may stick to the tray. When quite cold, wrap in foil and store. Cut in squares to serve.

Moist Ginger Cake

A good family cake; vary the flavour by substituting treacle (molasses) for half the syrup.

4 oz (100g/$\frac{1}{2}$ cup) soft brown sugar
5 oz (125g/$\frac{2}{3}$ cup) margarine
6 fl oz (150ml/$\frac{3}{4}$ cup) golden (corn) syrup (measured in an oiled measuring cup)
7 oz (175g/$1\frac{3}{4}$ cups) self-raising flour; or 7 oz (175g/$1\frac{3}{4}$ cups) plain flour and 2 level teasp baking powder
2 eggs
Rind and juice of 1 lemon
2 level teasp ground ginger
1 level teasp mixed sweet spice
2 oz (50g/$\frac{1}{3}$ cup) chopped crystallized (candied) ginger (optional)

Warm the margarine, syrup and sugar together over gentle heat. When smooth and melted, pour onto the sifted dry ingredients, followed by the beaten eggs, the lemon rind and juice, and the crystallized ginger (if used). Beat until smooth. Pour into a greased 8 or 9 in (20 or 23 cm) round tin or a 2 lb (1kg) loaf tin (measuring approx 9 × 5 × 3 in/23 × 13 × 8 cm). Bake at Gas No. 4, 350°F, 180°C, for 40 minutes or until firm to the touch. Turn out onto a cooling tray and leave until quite cold. Wrap in foil and store in an air-tight tin.

Gingerbread

This cake really needs to mature for three days before use. It can then be thinly sliced and buttered.

1 lb (480g/4 cups) plain flour
2 level teasp mixed sweet spice
2 level tbsp ground ginger
2 level teasp bicarbonate of soda (baking soda)
½ lb (200g/1 cup) margarine
8 oz (200g/1 cup) soft brown sugar
4 eggs
½ lb (200g/1 cup) golden (corn) syrup
¼ pint (125ml/⅔ cup) milk
½ lb (200g/⅔ cup) treacle (molasses)
½ lb (200g/1½ cups) sultanas (white raisins)—optional
4 oz (100g/1 cup) ground almonds (optional but nice)

Line a tin (approx 12 × 9 × 2 in/30 × 23 × 5 cm) with greased greaseproof paper or foil. Sift together the flour, spices and soda. Put into a pan the margarine, sugar, syrup and treacle and heat until liquid, then stir into the dry ingredients, together with the well-beaten eggs and the milk. Mix thoroughly, then pour into the prepared tin. Bake at Gas No. 3, 325°F, 170°C, for 1½ hours. Serve sliced and buttered.

Cake Icings, Toppings and Fillings

True cake decoration is the province of the craftsman: the recipes that follow lend themselves to more homely use, and have been developed in most cases to go with specific cake recipes. They are easy to prepare and delicious to eat, and give the maximum effect with the minimum of skill. For more specialized advice, it is better to go to a book devoted to this craft alone.

Glacé Icing

This is a simple icing that gives a smooth, flat finish suitable for decorating with glacé fruits or nuts.

8 oz (200g/2 cups) sifted icing (confectioners') sugar
2–2½ tbsp water
Squeeze of lemon juice

Put the icing sugar into a small saucepan (enamel-lined if possible as aluminium may turn white icing grey); add the lemon juice and 2 tablespoons of the water. Beat well with a wooden spoon, meanwhile warming over very gentle heat. Avoid too much heat which may cause the icing to crack or dull on the cake—the base of the pan should never be too hot to touch with the fingers. To test the consistency of the icing, dip the wooden spoon into it—the icing should thickly coat the spoon before running off. If it is too thick, add the further ½ tablespoon of water and reheat again. It is impossible to be specific about the exact amount of liquid required as some sugars absorb more liquid than others. However, it is generally better to have the icing too thick rather than too thin as a thick icing can always be eased over the cake with a hot damp palette knife, whereas too thin an icing will run straight down the sides of the cake, leaving the top naked and forlorn. This quantity will ice the tops of two 7 in (18 cm) sandwich cakes or the top and sides of one 8 in (20 cm) cake.

To ice the cake: Have ready any decorations (such as nuts, glacé fruit or chocolate shot), as these must be applied immediately the icing has been poured onto the cake. Stand the cake on a cooling rack or plate—where it can be left until it has set. Pour the icing over the cake, helping it to spread, if necessary, with a palette knife. Arrange the decoration and leave to set. To coat the top and sides, allow the icing to run down the sides, helping it to spread smoothly by tilting the cake or smoothing the icing with the palette knife.

VARIATIONS

Orange Glacé Icing

8 oz (200g/2 cups) sifted icing (confectioners') sugar
2–2½ tbsp strained orange juice or squash
A few drops of colouring

Coffee Glacé Icing

8 oz (200g/2 cups) sifted icing (confectioners') sugar
2 level teasp instant coffee dissolved in 2–2½ tbsp hot water

Chocolate Glacé Icing

4 oz (100g) plain (semi-sweet) chocolate
½ oz (15g/1 tbsp) butter
2 tbsp water
8 oz (200g/2 cups) sifted icing (confectioners') sugar

Grate or shred the chocolate with a knife and put it into a small thick-bottomed pan with the butter. Add the water and warm over very gentle heat, stirring with a wooden spoon until a smooth cream is formed. Gradually stir in the icing sugar, adding a little more hot water if necessary, to produce a coating consistency. Ideal for chocolate éclairs. For variety, add a few drops of peppermint essence to the melted chocolate.

Milk Chocolate Icing

This sets to give a topping the consistency of a bar of chocolate.

4 oz (100g) milk chocolate
2 oz (50g/¼ cup) butter

Grate or shave the chocolate with a knife and put into a small thick-bottomed pan with the butter. Heat very gently until smooth, then pour over the cake. Sufficient to ice a cake 7–9 in (18–23 cm) in diameter, depending on the thickness required. Half the quantity will thinly ice a 7 in (18 cm) cake.

French Mocha Icing

4 oz (100g) plain dessert (semi-sweet) chocolate
2 oz (50g/¼ cup) butter
1 tbsp rum
1 level teasp instant coffee

Grate or shave the chocolate with a knife and put it into a small, thick-bottomed pan together with the butter. Heat very gently until smooth, then stir in the powdered coffee and rum. Pour over the cake. This amount will ice the same size cake as the **Milk Chocolate Icing.**

Butter Creams

This kind of mixture lends itself to both icing and filling a cake, and to simple piped decorations or designs made with a fork or palette knife. The use of butter accentuates the flavour of ingredients such as chocolate, rum or liqueur. It can be mixed either by hand or machine. To make the addition of the icing sugar easy, cream the butter first until it resembles mayonnaise, and only then beat in the icing sugar in several portions. All the recipes in this section will fill and frost two 8 in (20 cm) layers or one 8 in (20 cm) cake split in two. To spread the icing on the cake use a palette knife or use a piping bag and tube following manufacturers' directions.

Velvet Butter Cream

This makes a rather yellow icing, but it has a delicious flavour and silken texture. Excellent for piping decorating as it holds its shape well.

4 oz (100g/½ cup) butter
8 oz (200g/2 cups) sifted icing (confectioners') sugar
1 egg yolk
1 teasp orange flower water
1 teasp rose water or 2 teasp orange or lemon juice or other fruit syrup

Cream butter, then beat in the egg yolk. Beat in icing sugar, a third at a time, alternately with liquids.

Mocha Butter Cream

This has a very deep flavour; excellent on a chocolate cake.

4 oz (100g/½ cup) butter
1 egg yolk
12 oz (300g/3 cups) icing (confectioners') sugar
2 tbsp cocoa
3 tbsp strong coffee made with 1½ level teasp instant coffee

Cream the butter until like mayonnaise, then beat in the egg yolk. Sift together the sugar and cocoa and beat into the butter alternately with the coffee until the icing is smooth and easy to spread.

Orange and Lemon Butter Cream

The juice and rind are soaked together to draw out the flavouring oils from the rind, which is then discarded.

1 level tbsp grated orange rind
2 level teasp grated lemon rind
1 tbsp lemon juice
2 tbsp orange juice
4 oz (100g/½ cup) butter
10 oz (250g/2½ cups) sifted icing (confectioners') sugar
1 egg yolk

Leave the rinds and juices to stand for 10 minutes, then strain. Beat the butter until creamy, then beat in the egg yolk. Add a little of the sifted icing sugar, then some of the strained juice. Continue beating, adding icing sugar and juice alternately, until smooth.

Mocha Fudge Frosting

This is a cross between glacé icing and butter cream; creamier than a glacé icing, but not as rich as a butter cream.

½ lb (200g/2 cups) icing (confectioners') sugar
2 oz (50g/¼ cup) butter
1 level teasp instant coffee
1 tbsp hot water
1 tbsp top milk or single (light) cream

Sift icing sugar into a bowl. Put butter, coffee, water and milk into a small pan. Heat slowly without boiling until the butter melts. Allow to cool until steaming stops then pour over the icing sugar. Beat well. Spread on top of chocolate cake or use to fill and frost it if preferred.

One-Bowl Frosting

This makes an ideal topping for a family cake; although it does not have the fine texture of a creamed icing, it can have just as much flavour—and it can be made in minutes. Soft margarine can be used if the cake is to be served after a meat meal.

8 oz (200g/2 cups) sifted icing (confectioners') sugar
3 oz (75g/⅓ cup) soft butter or margarine
1 tbsp top milk, single (light) cream, or fruit juice (orange, lemon or blackcurrant)

Put all the ingredients into a bowl and beat by machine or hand until creamy. This makes sufficient to fill and ice the top of an 8 in (20 cm) sandwich cake.

One-Bowl Milk Chocolate Frosting

3 oz (75g/⅓ cup) soft butter
4 oz (100g/1 cup) sifted icing sugar
2 level tbsp drinking (instant) chocolate
2 teasp single (light) cream or strong black coffee
½ teasp vanilla essence (extract)

Put all ingredients into a bowl and beat until smooth and fluffy. Use to decorate the top of the **One-Bowl Chocolate Cake.** (See page 161.)

Toasted Toffee Topping

This toffee mixture can be spread on a plain home-made or bought cake, then grilled until golden. It sets to a butterscotch crunch.

1½ oz (40g/3 tbsp) melted butter
4 level tbsp coconut
4 level tbsp soft brown sugar
6 glacé (candied) cherries, cut in quarters
4 level tbsp chopped walnuts (optional)

Mix all together until blended. Spread on baked sandwich cake, 7–8 in (18–20 cm) size. Grill gently for 3–4 minutes or until golden brown.

To Ice a Rich Fruit Cake with Royal Icing and Almond Paste

Unless one is an expert, my advice is to bake the fruit cake for a special occasion, such as a wedding or barmitzvah, and have a professional pastry cook apply the almond paste and the decoration of royal icing. If, however, a simple finish only is required, perhaps for Chanucah or another festival, a very acceptable result can be achieved at home with little more than a great deal of patience! Below I give the basic instructions for finishing a cake in this way.

When to bake the cake: The cake should be made at least eight weeks before it is required, to allow it to mature. Storing instructions are given with the recipe.

Almond-pasting the cake: At least 10 days before it is required, put the almond paste on the cake. It must have time (48 hours is the minimum) to dry out before the icing is put on, or the almond oil may seep through. If you intend to cover the sides as well as the top of the cake, double these quantities.

Almond Paste

For a 7 in (18 cm) cake:
4 oz (100g/1 cup) ground almonds
2 oz (50g/¼ cup) caster (superfine) sugar
2 oz (50g/½ cup) icing (confectioners') sugar
Few drops almond and vanilla essence (extract)
1 egg yolk

For a 9 in (23 cm) cake:
6 oz (150g/1½ cups) ground almonds
3 oz (75g/⅓ cup) caster (superfine) sugar
3 oz (75g/¾ cup) icing (confectioners') sugar
Few drops almond and vanilla essence (extract)
1½ egg yolks or 1 large yolk

Mix the dry ingredients, then knead with the yolk and essence till the mixture forms a ball. Don't squeeze too hard or the paste will be oily. Using the bottom of the tin as a guide, roll the paste into a round, on a sugared board. Brush your cake to remove any crumbs, then brush again with unbeaten egg white or warm apricot jam. Lay the round of almond paste on top, and roll gently to smooth it. If you wish to cover the sides roll two strips, the depth, and half the circumference of the cake. Press gently into place, then even up by rolling a jam jar round the cake, pressing the paste into place. With a spatula and your hand, make a right angle of the join between top and sides. Now cut a strong strip of paper long enough to go under the cake and come above the sides. Lay the cake on this, and use it as a 'sling' to lift the cake into the tin and out again later. Leave the cake uncovered, for 48 hours at least, to dry out the paste.

Icing the cake: You can do this any time from 48 hours after the almond pasting up to a day or two before it is needed. But I advise you to get it done when your nervous system is still unfrazzled!

Royal Icing

For a 7 in (18 cm) cake:
For top only:
8 oz (200g/2 cups) icing (confectioners') sugar
1 egg white
For top and sides:
1¼ lb (580g/5 cups) icing (confectioners') sugar
2½ egg whites
For a 9 in (23 cm) cake:
For top only:
12 oz (300g/3 cups) icing (confectioners') sugar
1½ egg whites
For top and sides:
2 lb (1kg/8 cups) icing (confectioners') sugar
4 egg whites

Both sizes will need a few drops of acetic acid or squeeze of lemon juice. Sift icing sugar thoroughly. Beat the whites until they are foamy. Make a well in the centre of the sugar, stir in most of the egg white and then beat until the icing is thick, pliable and glossy, at least 15 minutes. The acid goes in with the egg whites.

To apply: Keep the icing covered with a damp cloth as you work. Then any left over can be kept a day or two in a plastic container for the final decorations. Stand the cake on an upturned plate or turntable, and swirl the icing over the top and sides (if they're to be covered). Then, using a deep jug of boiling water, dip a spatula in this, shake dry and smooth the icing. If you want a snow scene, pull the icing up into little peaks. Drawing the spatula right across the top in a sweeping movement is the quickest way of getting a smooth finish. Now put the cake away, covered, to dry thoroughly overnight, before you apply the decorations.

To decorate: For piping, your icing may need a little more beating, to make it really stiff. Tint it if you will, but go easy!

Decide on the outline of your design and prick it out on the top of the cake. For inspiration look in the high-class confectioners, and buy a booklet put out by the icing-tube manufacturers.

If all this sounds too intimidating, and if you've made a plain, rather than a fruit cake, decorate the cake with **Seven-Minute Icing.** It peaks beautifully, and it's soft on the tongue. But only make it two days before it is needed otherwise it gets rather dry.

Seven-Minute Icing

2 egg whites
11 oz (275g/1½ cups) granulated sugar
4 tbsp cold water
A pinch of cream of tartar
1 teasp vanilla essence (extract)

Combine all the ingredients in a double boiler. Beat over boiling water, using a hand mixer, for 7 minutes, until the icing forms peaks. Remove from heat, then beat until thick enough to spread.

Cheese Cakes

These delicacies have been among the glories of Jewish cookery for many centuries; indeed, as cheese cakes are known to have been made in Greece as far back as 350 B.C.E., it is not fanciful to conjecture that they have been part of the Jewish cuisine since the Greek occupation of Palestine in the second century B.C.E.

The best of the early Greek cheese cakes were made on the Island of Samos—Pythagoras's birthplace in the Aegean Sea. You can find some of the recipes in *The Deipnosophists*—the anthology of gastronomic writings compiled by the Egyptian philosopher, Athenaeus, in the third century of this era.

Jews of the pre-Christian era also made some form of cheese cake to celebrate Shavuoth ('the Time of the Giving of the Law'), for they saw in the whiteness of milk cheese a symbol of the purity of the Mosaic Code. But at a time when ordinary flour was as coarse as oatmeal—and baked as brown as gingerbread, it's not surprising that the pale and delicately-textured cheese cake was so often made to mark a special occasion. What is a little surprising is that it has remained in fashion ever since.

Today there are as many cheese cakes as there are cookery books, though they are almost all a variation on the original Greek recipe—curd cheese, sweetenings and eggs, baked in some form of protective crust. Polish cheese cakes are thickened with ground almonds, Swiss ones with semolina, whilst in America it is usual to thicken the mixture with cornflour instead. In Italy, the cheese mixture is blended with glacé fruits or cinnamon, whilst in Germany, brandy or rum is the favoured flavouring.

The Jews who came to England from Russia and Poland at the end of the 19th century continued to make their traditional cheese cake in a rich short-crust case, flavoured with lemon rind and studded with sultanas, quite unaware that the country of their adoption had a long tradition of cheese cake-making itself. For instance, in the East Riding of Yorkshire, they used to make 'Chissicks' with curd blended with butter, cream and brandy; in Melton Mowbray, currants, ginger and lemon peel were preferred; whilst in the Derbyshire Dales, the curd made from the 'beestings'—the first milk of a cow after calving—is so rich that only sugar and currants needed to be added to it to make perhaps the most delicious traditional English cheese cake of all.

Forty years ago, my Lithuanian grandmother made her own cheese for the cakes she made with a rich yeast dough. Today, I usually buy my curd cheese—technically known as 'low or medium fat soft cheese with a 10–20% butterfat content'—to make the delectable cheese cakes which I describe below.

To freeze any recipe of cheese cake: Cheese cakes freeze extremely well with no loss of flavour. Allow the cake to cool in the tin, standing on a cooling rack. Put the uncovered cake still in the tin into the freezer and leave until solid. Ease out of the tin, foil-wrap and label. To defrost, take from the freezer, unwrap and put on a serving dish. Refrigerate until required. (Takes about 3 hours to defrost in the refrigerator.)

The Base for a Cheese Cake

There are three main varieties of crust for a baked cheese cake—sponge, crushed biscuit and pastry. The choice is mainly a matter of taste—and the time you have available.

Sponge Base

This is made of enough ½ in (1 cm) thick slices of slightly stale sponge necessary to cover the bottom of the chosen tin. Use either bought trifle sponges or left-over home-made or baker's whisked sponge.

Crumb Crust

Make crumbs from 4 oz (100g/1 cup) digestive biscuits (graham crackers)—this can be done in the blender or by putting the biscuits in a plastic bag and crushing to crumbs with a rolling pin—then add 1 level tablespoon caster (superfine) sugar and ½ level teaspoon cinnamon. Stir in 2 oz (50g/¼ cup) melted butter until the crumbs are evenly moistened. Press onto the base of an oiled tin.

Sufficient to cover the base of an 8 or 9 in (20 or 23 cm) loose-bottomed round tin.

Pastry Crust

The icing (confectioners') sugar in this pastry ensures a crisp, non-porous texture.

4 oz (100g/1 cup) self-raising flour; or 4 oz (100g/1 cup) plain flour and 1 level teasp baking powder
2½ oz (65g/⅓ cup) butter
1½ oz (40g/⅓ cup) icing (confectioners') sugar
1 egg yolk
Little vanilla essence (extract)

Stir the icing sugar into the butter, then stir in the yolk, essence and flour. This can be done by mixer or by hand. If possible, chill before use, then roll out to fit a loose-bottomed sandwich tin. Sufficient for a tin 8 or 9 in (20 or 23 cm) in diameter.

Traditional Cheese Cake

This is the simple 'cheese cake pie' that Ashkenazi Jews have been making for very many years.

Pastry:
One recipe of Pastry Crust

Reserve quarter of the pastry for the lattice top. Use the remainder to line an 8 or 9 in (20 or 23 cm) loose-bottomed shallow sandwich tin.

Filling:
½ lb (200g/1 cup) curd cheese
1 oz (25g/¼ cup) ground almonds
Grated rind and juice of ½ lemon
½ teasp vanilla essence (extract)
½ oz (15g/1 tbsp) soft butter
2 oz (50g/¼ cup) caster (superfine) sugar
2 level tbsp currants (plumped for 5 min in boiling water then drained)
2 eggs, separated

Blend together all the filling ingredients except the egg whites. Whisk these until they form stiff, glossy peaks, then fold into the cheese mixture. Spoon into the unbaked pastry case and level with a knife. Use the remaining pastry to roll strips $\frac{1}{4}$ in ($\frac{1}{2}$ cm) thick. Dampen the edge of the pie then arrange the strips about $\frac{1}{2}$ in (1 cm) apart, securing their ends to the rim. Beat the egg white left over from the pastry until it is frothy, then paint over the surface of the pie including the strips. Sprinkle lightly with granulated sugar. Bake at Gas No. 4, 350°F, 180°C, for 40 minutes until golden brown. Serve warm or at room temperature. Serves 8.

Velvet Cheese Cake

I permutated thirty different recipes from as many different sources in both America and Europe before I arrived at what I consider the best 'modern' home-made cheese cake of all. This version is creamy, light and smooth on the tongue. Its success depends on a short baking period (which prevents the over-heating of the cheese which often causes the cake to fall on cooling) and the use of a dry curd rather than a rich cream cheese.

Crust base:
Any of the three crusts given can be used. I personally like the sponge base. Use to line a 7 in (18 cm) square tin, or an 8 in (20 cm) loose-bottomed sandwich tin, not less than 2 in (5 cm) deep.

Filling:
1 lb (480g/2 cups) curd cheese
$\frac{1}{2}$ teasp vanilla essence
Juice and rind of $\frac{1}{2}$ lemon
2 oz (50g/$\frac{1}{4}$ cup) melted butter
2 eggs, separated
2 oz (50g/$\frac{1}{4}$ cup) caster (superfine) sugar
2 level tbsp cornflour (cornstarch)
5 fl oz ($\frac{2}{3}$ cup) soured cream

Separate the whites from the yolks and reserve. Put all the other ingredients into a bowl in the order given and beat until smooth and thick. Whisk the whites until they form stiff, glossy peaks, then whisk in 2 teaspoons caster sugar. Fold this meringue into the cheese mixture. Spoon into the tin, previously lined with the chosen base. Smooth level.

To bake: Sponge or crumb linings: Gas No. 4, 350°F, 180°C, for 30 minutes. Pastry lining: Gas No. 4, 350°F, 180°C, for 40 minutes. (*Note:* The cake is done when the inch ($2\frac{1}{2}$ cm) of filling adjacent to the rim of the tin feels firm to the touch. Cheese cakes continue to set as they cool. Leave to cool in a draughtfree place. When cold, refrigerate until required. Serve plain, or topped with sugared soft fruit. Serves 10.)

VARIATIONS

With a topping of sour cream: Make the **Velvet Cheese Cake,** but omit the sour cream from the filling. Instead add 2 tablespoons top milk or single or soured cream. For the topping, beat 10 fl oz (250ml/$1\frac{1}{4}$ cups) soured cream with 1 level tablespoon caster (superfine) sugar and a few drops of vanilla essence (extract). When the cake has cooked, remove from the oven and leave for 10 minutes. Turn the oven up to Gas No. 6, 400°F, 200°C. Spread the sour cream topping over the cake. Return to the oven for 8 minutes to set the topping. When cold, foil-cover and refrigerate until thoroughly chilled.

With a fruit glaze: Make the **Velvet Cheese Cake.** Allow to go quite cold. Drain a can of black or morello cherries, sliced peaches, pineapple rings or apricots. Measure 8 fl oz (200ml/1 cup) of syrup from the can. In a small saucepan put 1 level tablespoon cornflour and 2 oz (50g/$\frac{1}{4}$ cup) granulated sugar. Gradually stir in the fruit juice syrup. Bring to the boil and simmer for 3 minutes. Taste and add the juice of half or a whole lemon according to taste. Arrange the fruit in a design on the cheese cake. Spoon over the cooled glaze. Leave under refrigeration until set.

Chocolate Cheese Cake

The base:
Use enough split trifle sponges or slices of stale sponge cake to completely cover the sides and bottom of a 7 in (18 cm) loose-bottomed sandwich tin.

Filling:
½ lb (200g/1 cup) curd cheese
1 egg
2 oz (50g/¼ cup) granulated sugar
4 oz (100g) dessert (semi-sweet) chocolate such as Menier or Bournville
Pinch of salt
3 fl oz (75ml/⅓ cup) soured or whipping cream
½ teasp vanilla essence (extract)
1 tbsp rum, brandy or Tia Maria liqueur

Whisk the egg with the sugar until creamy, then beat in the cheese, the chocolate (melted in a bowl standing in a pan of hot water), the vanilla, salt, spirit or liqueur and soured cream. Beat until smooth. Turn into the sponge-lined tin. Bake in a moderate oven (Gas No. 4, 350°F, 180°C) for 40 minutes. Chill thoroughly before serving. For a larger cake, double the recipe and bake in a 10 in (25 cm) round spring form tin. Serves 6.

Tutti Frutti Cheese Cake

The chilled cheese cake, set with gelatin or jelly instead of oven heat, is an American invention. It is really a cold soufflé. The flavour is best if vegetable gelatin is used, but as this has varying setting powers (depending on the manufacture), I often use a kosher lemon jelly (gelatin mix) instead, with very acceptable results. (If you find a whole jelly makes too stiff a texture for your taste, use ½ or ¾ until you get the correct set—this cheese cake should just be firm enough to cut into portions, but should not be at all jellyish).

2 eggs, separated
Pinch of salt
2 oz (50g/¼ cup) sugar
Juice and rind of a large lemon (3 tbsp)
2 tbsp orange squash diluted with 4 tbsp water; or 6 tbsp fresh orange juice
1 lemon jelly (gelatin mix) or 1 level tbsp vegetable gelatin
1 teasp vanilla essence (extract)
12 oz (300g/1½ cups) best cream cheese or sieved cottage cheese
5 fl oz (125ml/⅔ cup) double (heavy) cream
2 tbsp caster (superfine) sugar
4 digestive biscuits (graham crackers), crushed
½ oz (15g/1 tbsp) butter
Pinch of cinnamon

Beat yolks, salt, gelatin (if used) and sugar, then gradually add the liquids. Cook in a double saucepan over boiling water (or in a basin standing in a pan of water) until the mixture becomes a thin custard that coats the back of the spoon. Add the jelly and dissolve. Leave until cool. Beat the cream until it thickens but isn't stiff. Beat the whites until they hold stiff peaks, then beat in the 2 tablespoons sugar. Now stir the cooled custard into the cheese followed by the cream, the vanilla and finally the meringue. Spoon the mixture into an 8 in (20 cm) loose-bottomed sandwich tin. Mix the crushed crumbs with the melted butter and cinnamon and sprinkle round the top edge. Chill for several hours, preferably overnight.

To serve: Run a knife round the edge of the cake to loosen it, then lift out, still on the base. Put on a serving dish and spoon a little of the reserved cream in the centre, decorating with sugared soft fruits, or sliced banana. Leave in the fridge until needed. Serves 10 for a snack or 6 for a dinner sweet.

VARIATION
Either top with morello (sour red) cherry conserve or this glaze:

1 can morello (sour red) cherries
Juice of ½ lemon
2 oz (50g/¼ cup) caster (superfine) sugar
1 level tbsp cornflour (cornstarch)
Juice strained from fruit

Arrange drained fruit in design on top of cheese cake. Mix all remaining ingredients. Boil 3 minutes, cool to lukewarm, then spoon on fruit. Chill.

Pineapple Cream Cheese Torte

The sweetness of the pineapple is counteracted by the slight acidity of soured cream used instead of sweet cream; however, if it is more convenient, whipped sweet cream can be used, and a little more lemon juice added to the cheese mixture. Double the recipe for a 10 or 12 in (25 or 30 cm) cake suitable for a celebration.

4 oz (100g/$\frac{1}{2}$ cup) sugar
Pinch of salt
1 egg yolk blended with 4 fl oz (100ml) syrup drained from a medium can pineapple chunks
$\frac{3}{4}$ lemon jelly (gelatin mix) or 1 level tbsp vegetable gelatin
Juice of $\frac{1}{2}$ lemon
$\frac{3}{4}$ lb (300g/$1\frac{1}{2}$ cups) best cream cheese
$\frac{1}{2}$ teasp vanilla essence (extract)
5 fl oz (125ml/$\frac{2}{3}$ cup) soured cream
1 egg white
Topping:
3 digestive biscuits (graham crackers) crushed to fine crumbs, mixed with 1 oz (25g/2 tbsp) melted butter
2 level teasp caster (superfine) sugar
$\frac{1}{4}$ level teasp mixed sweet spice

In the top of a double saucepan or bowl standing in a pan of boiling water put sugar, gelatin (if used) and salt. Stir in the yolk, blended with the pineapple syrup. Cook until the mixture thickens enough to coat the back of a wooden spoon. Add jelly and stir until it has dissolved. Leave to cool whilst you put the cheese into a bowl and stir in the lemon juice and essence. Beat the white until it forms stiff, glossy peaks. Now fold into the cheese first the cooled custard, then the soured cream and the whisked egg white. Finally fold in two-thirds of the pineapple, cut in bite-sized pieces. Spoon this mixture into an 8 in (20 cm) loose-bottomed sandwich tin. Sprinkle the topping in an even band $\frac{3}{4}$ in ($1\frac{1}{2}$ cm) wide round the edge of the cake. Chill, foil-covered, overnight.

To serve: Loosen the torte from the sides of the tin with a sharp knife, then pull down the sides, leaving the torte on the base. Place on a serving plate. Decorate with the remaining pineapple and a few glacé (candied) cherries. If liked, garnish with whipped cream. Refrigerate until required. Serves 6–8.

The Strudel Saga

This fragile rolypoly represents perhaps the greatest triumph of culinary skill over the exigencies of domestic economics. A strudel dough, whether it be stretched or rolled, prepared with yeast, oil or puff pastry is extravagant only in the time needed to make it; for the filling may be as humble as mincemeat, though it can also be as exotic as morello (sour red) cherries or Turkish delight.

Stretched Strudel Dough (Strudel Teig)

This is the feathery, flaky pastry used in the true Viennese Apfel Strudel (allegedly invented, by the way, by the Hungarians). I give below the traditional recipe, but I must admit that I rarely make it myself, but instead rely on the commercial strudel pastry or 'strudelblaetter', or on the Greek 'phyllo' or layered pastry, both of which can be bought in many delicatessens. The authentic method I give was taught me by a Viennese—a natural cook whose graceful yet powerful hands moved in an almost primitive rhythm as she kneaded the puddingy mess of flour and water into the silken dough that is the first step in strudel making.

A note on the flour: In Vienna, special flour or *glattes Mehl* is used. This is high in gluten content and so can be stretched without tearing. Here one must use plain household or bread flour and knead it well to develop the gluten as much as possible.

$\frac{1}{2}$ lb (200g/2 cups) plain flour
2 level teasp sugar
$1\frac{1}{2}$ tbsp oil
1 egg
About 4 fl oz (100ml/$\frac{1}{2}$ cup) water (see method)

Put flour on the table (or a large pastry board) and make a hollow in the centre. Into this put the sugar, oil and egg and mix with a knife to draw in some of the surrounding flour. Add enough tepid water (about 4 fl oz/$\frac{1}{2}$ cup) to make a slightly sticky dough—like a scone dough. Knead dough with palm of the hand until it is silky and smooth. Put on to the table or board, brush lightly with oil, then cover with an inverted mixing bowl and leave to rest for half an hour while the filling is prepared.

To stretch the dough: When the filling is prepared, cover the table with a white cloth or extra-large tea-towel, and rub in a little flour. Roll dough into a 15 in (37½ cm) circle and brush with a little oil or melted unsalted butter. Lift dough and lay it on to the back of the hands, then pull it a little. Put back on the table and start walking round, pulling the dough from underneath with the knuckles until it is as thin as tissue paper. Cut away any thick edges.

Filling:

3 lb (1½kg) baking apples
About 4 oz (100g/1 cup) dried breadcrumbs
6–8 oz (150–200g/¾–1 cup) sugar (depending on tartness of apples)
6 oz (150g/¾ cup) melted butter, margarine or oil

Peel, core and quarter apples, then cut into blade-thin slivers. Sprinkle half the pastry with the dry crumbs, then cover with the apples in an even layer. Dredge with most of the sugar, then sprinkle with almost all the fat. At the far end of the strudel, where there are no apples, brush with fat and sprinkle with remaining sugar. Turn in the edges of the strudel and roll up, holding on to the cloth to facilitate the process. Carefully ease on to a baking sheet, join side down, and curve into a horseshoe shape to fit. Brush with remaining butter. Bake at Gas No. 6, 400°F, 200°C for 30 minutes, turning the heat down to Gas No. 5, 375°F, 190°C after 15 minutes if pastry seems to be browning too quickly. Serve warm in 2 in (5 cm) thick slices. Serves 18.

Apfel Strudel with Ready-to-Use Strudel or Phyllo Pastry

There are several makes of fresh or frozen strudel or phyllo (sometimes spelt filo) pastry on the market. They are most likely to be found in an Armenian, Greek or Polish delicatessen. The raw pastry will keep up to 6 weeks in the freezer.

Getting the pastry, however, is but the beginning of the strudel story, for if you don't handle it the right way, you're liable to end up with tissue paper and stewed apple, instead of the buttery-crisp confection you'd expected. Here is the way to do it.

Apfel Strudel with Bought Pastry

1 lb (½kg) cooking apples (weight peeled and cored)
4 oz (100g/½ cup) granulated sugar
3 oz (75g/½ cup) seedless raisins
4 oz (100g/1½ cups) fresh breadcrumbs
5 oz (125g/⅔ cup) butter

Put a damp tea-towel on a table or counter with the edge overlapping the counter edge. Do not open strudel packet until you are ready to use the pastry as it becomes dry and brittle on contact with the air. Toast the crumbs by mixing them with 2 oz (50g/¼ cup) of melted butter and putting them in the oven at Gas No. 5, 375°F, 190°C as it heats up for the strudel. It should take about 10 minutes for the crumbs to become crisp and golden brown. Put them in a basin. Coarsely grate the apples and mix them with the sugar and the raisins. Melt the remaining 3 oz (75g/⅓ cup) of butter.

(*The instructions below make one strudel using pastry* 16 *in*/40 *cm wide. If, however, you use the* 8 *in*/20 *cm wide pastry, then divide all the filling ingredients in half as you will want to make two separate strudels.*)

Open the packet and carefully take out two sheets of pastry. Lay one piece on the damp tea-towel and brush it liberally with the melted butter, then sprinkle on a few of the toasted crumbs. Lay a second layer of pastry on top and brush with butter in the same way. Sprinkle with crumbs, then arrange apple filling over the half of the pastry nearest to you, leaving 1 in (2½ cm) pastry free of filling all the way round. Turn in the sides of the pastry, then, lifting the tea-towel with both hands, gently roll the pastry into a strudel. Carefully transfer strudel, join side down, on to a greased baking tray and brush all over with remaining butter. Cover with greaseproof paper and bake in a moderate oven (Gas No. 5, 375°F, 190°C) for 40 minutes, uncovering for the last five mintutes to complete browning. This amount of strudel serves 6–8, depending on the size of the serving.

Kirschen (Cherry) Strudel with Bought Pastry

1 pkt commercial Strudel Pastry
Filling:
1 can of pitted morello (sour red) or black cherries, or 1½–2 lb (¾–1kg) raw morello (sour red) cherries (stoned) mixed with 4 oz (100g/½ cup) caster (superfine) sugar
2 oz (50g/½ cup) toasted chopped almonds (optional)
1½ cups fresh breadcrumbs mixed with 2 oz (50g/¼ cup) melted butter then toasted in a moderate oven (Gas No. 4, 350°F, 180°C) for 10 min until golden brown
3 oz (75g/⅓ cup) melted butter

Proceed exactly as for the apfel strudel; if the cherries are canned, additional sugar is not required but a little should be sprinkled on the pastry in the same way as for the apfel strudel. Bake in a quick, moderate oven (Gas No. 6, 400°F, 200°C) covered with greaseproof paper for 25 minutes, until crisp and golden. To gild the lily, serve with chilled, soured cream. Serves 6–8.

Cheese Strudel with Bought Pastry

1 pkt commercial Strudel Pastry
Filling:
12 oz (300g/3 cups) curd cheese
2 oz (50g/¼ cup) butter
2 oz (50g/¼ cup) caster (superfine) sugar
1 egg, separated
3 oz (75g/½ cup) sultanas (white raisins)
½ teasp vanilla essence (extract)
Rind and juice of ½ lemon
1½ cups fresh crumbs with 2 oz (50g/¼ cup) butter
Further 2 oz (50g/¼ cup) butter (unsalted if possible)
Few ground almonds

Cream 2 oz (50g/¼ cup) butter and sugar then beat in the vanilla essence and the egg yolk, followed by the cheese, rind and juice and sultanas. Finally fold in the egg white, beaten to a meringue. Melt the 2 oz (50g/¼ cup) butter and blend with the crumbs. Spread on an oven tray and leave in a moderate oven (Gas No. 4, 350°F, 180°C) for 10 minutes (stirring once), until crisp and golden brown. Melt remaining 2 oz (50g/¼ cup) butter. Wet a large white tea-towel. Cut open the packet of strudel and unfold. Place first 'leaf' on damp cloth. Paint with melted butter and scatter with a few ground almonds. Place on second layer. Paint this with butter and scatter with ground almonds and then the crumbs. Arrange the cheese filling on top quarter of pastry in thick mound leaving 1 in (2½ cm) pastry clear at top and sides. Fold in sides and top, then hold top of tea-towel and roll up, rolling strudel at the same time. Place strudel on tray and paint with the remaining butter. Cover with a piece of greaseproof paper. Bake in quick oven (Gas No. 6, 400°F, 200°C) for 25 minutes. Serves 8. Serve warm. May be reheated.

Apple Strudel with Puff Pastry

This is akin to the French 'jalousie', for with puff pastry I have found it is more successful to roll out two layers and sandwich them with the apple filling, rather than to roll the pastry and apple together. It is extremely successful with frozen puff pastry, though if you prefer, you can make your own.

½ lb (200g) pkt frozen Puff Pastry
Buttered Apple filling:
A generous 1 lb (½kg) cooking apples
1 oz (25g/2 tbsp) butter
6 level tbsp brown sugar
1 teasp grated lemon rind
Apricot jam

Peel, core and quarter the apples then cut each quarter into 4 thick slices. Arrange, overlapping, in a wide ovenproof dish. Dot the butter on the top, then sprinkle with the sugar, lemon and jam. Bake, covered, in a moderate oven (Gas No. 4, 350°F, 180°C) for 30 minutes, turning the apples once. They will cook in their own juice, and will be soft but whole. Allow to go cold before using. Divide the pastry in two and roll each half into a very thin rectangular sheet measuring 11 × 6 in (28 × 15 cm). Place one piece of pastry on a wet ungreased baking sheet (this keeps the pastry in shape), then pile on the cooled apples, leaving a $\frac{3}{4}$ in ($1\frac{1}{2}$ cm) margin all the way round. Dampen this margin with water. Take the second sheet of pastry, fold it lengthwise and make slanting slits down the centre, then unfold and lay in position on top of the filling. Press the edges together all the way round, then flake them together using the edge of a knife. Bake in a very hot oven (Gas No. 8, 450°F, 230°C) for 15 minutes. Take out and sprinkle with caster sugar, then reduce the heat to Gas No. 6, 400°F, 200°C, and continue to bake for a further 10–15 minutes until golden brown. Serve warm. Serves 6.

Cherry Strudel with Puff Pastry

1 lb (480g) can pitted black or morello (sour red) cherries
1–3 level tbsp sugar (more for morellos)
2 level teasp cornflour
Squeeze of lemon juice

Drain the cherries, reserving the juice. Mix the cornflour and sugar then stir in the juice. Bring to the boil and simmer for 3 minutes. Stir in the lemon juice and cherries, then allow to go cold. Spread on the pastry and proceed exactly as for the apple strudel.

Marillen (Apricot) Strudel with Puff Pastry

1 lb (480g) stoned or canned apricots (fresh are nicest)
2 oz (50g/$\frac{1}{4}$ cup) sugar (if fresh fruit used)
2–3 tbsp whole fruit apricot jam

Spread the pastry generously with apricot jam to within $\frac{3}{4}$ in ($1\frac{1}{2}$ cm) of the edge all the way round. Arrange the apricots on top; if raw ones are used sprinkle with the sugar. Proceed as for the apple strudel.

For **Meat Strudel** see p. 141.
For **Other Strudels** see pp. 228–9.

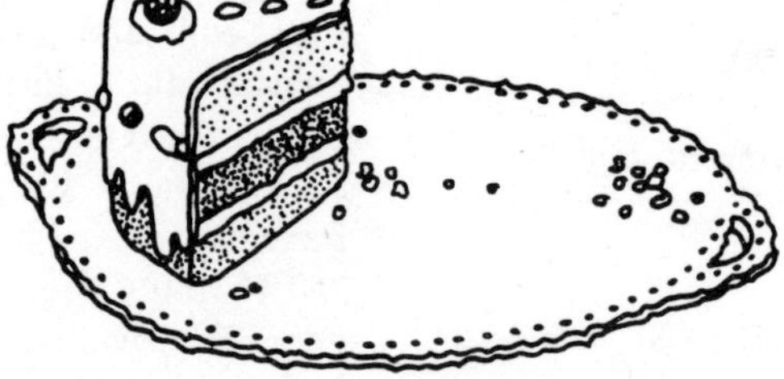

Biscuits (Cookies)

The biscuit (cookie) or 'kichel' served to the visitor with a glass of 'schnapps' or wine, is a very old tradition in Jewish hospitality. In olden days, the biscuit would be made with cooking oil, so that it could be offered to a visitor after either a milk or meat meal. These oil biscuits or 'kichels' are still delicious even to modern palates, but increasingly butter is used for biscuit-making, and the repertoire enriched by biscuit recipes from all over the world.

Whilst biscuits are more time-consuming to make than cakes, their flavour cannot be duplicated in the factory; so, provided the finest ingredients only are used, they are well worth making at home.

The ingredients

For creamed mixtures, use a soft butter; for biscuits made on the board or with the fat rubbed in, use a waxy one. Caster (superfine) sugar will give a finer texture than granulated, and icing (confectioners') sugar makes the crispest, shortest biscuit of all.

Baking the biscuits (cookies)

Bake the biscuits on heavy flat tins kept specially for the purpose. Non-stick tins are the most convenient, but sticking can be prevented by greasing with oil, rather than with butter or margarine.

Watch the biscuits carefully the first time you make them as ovens may vary in baking performance. All biscuits (unless otherwise stated in the recipe) should be treated after baking as follows: Allow to cool on the tray for one minute until firm enough to lift; remove with a spatula and place side by side on a wire cooling tray. Leave until quite cold then store in an air-tight tin.

Freezing

Almost all biscuits freeze well. Fragile biscuits should be stored in a tin which has been sealed with freezer tape. As many biscuits as are required can be taken out, the tin resealed and put back in the freezer. Firmer varieties can be stored in plastic bags. Biscuits take about 30 minutes to defrost.

Reheating

If biscuits have gone soggy in the tin, put them on an ungreased tray and leave in a pre-heated moderate oven (Gas No. 4, 350°F, 180°C) for 10 minutes, take out and treat as though freshly baked.

It's a Tradition

Traditional Jewish biscuits (cookies) are made either with oil or butter, and are really sweetened pastry of the kind used for some forms of strudel or hamantaschen.

Traditional Kichels

Use the minimum amount of flour needed to achieve a rollable dough and the 'kichels' will be light and crisp.

5 oz (125g/⅔ cup) caster (superfine) sugar
2 large eggs
4 fl oz (100ml/½ cup) oil
1 teasp vanilla essence (extract)
Rind of ½ orange
11–12 oz (275–300g/3 cups) flour (use half plain, half self-raising)

Whisk the eggs until thick, then gradually whisk in the sugar, followed by the oil, the orange rind and the essence. Finally stir in enough flour to make a rollable, non-sticky dough. Knead until smooth, then roll out on a floured board to a thickness of ⅜ in (¾ cm). Sprinkle the dough with caster sugar, then roll lightly to press in the sugar. Cut into shapes with biscuit cutters and arrange on oiled trays, leaving room for the biscuits to spread. Bake in a moderate oven (Gas No. 4, 350°F, 180°C) for 20–25 minutes or until a pale gold in colour. Makes about 50, depending on size.

Traditional Butter Biscuits (Cookies)

These should be very thin and very crisp.

½ lb (200g/2 cups) plain flour
½ level teasp baking powder
5 oz (125g/⅔ cup) butter
3 oz (75g/⅓ cup) caster (superfine) sugar
About 2 tbsp beaten egg

Sift together the flour and baking powder, then rub in the butter until the mixture resembles breadcrumbs. Stir in the sugar and add enough of the egg to make a soft, non-sticky dough. Chill for half an hour, if possible. On a floured board, roll out the dough to a thickness of ⅛ in (¼ cm). Cut into rounds or crescents. Brush with the reserved egg diluted with a teaspoonful of water. Decorate with this topping: 4 level tablespoons caster (superfine) sugar mixed with ½ level teaspoon cinnamon and 2 level tablespoons chopped almonds. Bake in a quick moderate oven (Gas No. 6, 400°F, 200°C) for 8–9 minutes, or until golden brown. Makes about 40.

Grandma's Vanilla Biscuits (Cookies)

The use of icing (confectioners') sugar gives this biscuit a meltingly-tender texture. It keeps well.

10 oz (250g/2½ cups) plain flour
Pinch of salt
4 oz (100g/1 cup) sifted icing (confectioners') sugar
8 oz (200g/1 cup) butter
1 egg
2 teasp vanilla essence (extract)
1 oz (25g/¼ cup) finely chopped nuts blended with 1 oz (25g/2 tbsp) caster (superfine) sugar

Mix together the flour, salt, and sugar. Rub in the butter until the mixture resembles coarse crumbs, then mix to a dough with 2 tablespoons of the beaten egg and the vanilla essence. Wrap in foil and chill for 30 minutes. Roll out ⅛ in (¼ cm) thick on a lightly-floured board and cut into shapes with a floured cutter. Transfer to ungreased baking sheets. Paint with the remaining egg and sprinkle with the sugar and nuts. Bake in a quick oven (Gas No. 5, 375°F, 190°C) for 7 minutes. Makes about 60.

Shortbread and Variations

Traditional Scotch shortbread is made on a pastry board in the same way as the French 'pâte sucrée' of which it is a lineal descendant, for it was the chefs who came from France with Mary, Queen of Scots, who introduced this biscuit to Scotland. For speed, it can be made by creaming the butter and sugar together, but the texture is not as delicate on the tongue. Shortbread can be made with all flour, with flour and cornflour, or with flour and rice flour (to achieve a more crumbly texture); and it can be mixed without liquid, with egg yolk or with cream. All methods have something to commend them, and I can only suggest you try the variations for yourself.

Shortbread burns easily, so it must be baked carefully and only long enough to colour it lightly.

Perfect Shortbread

12 oz (300g/3 cups) plain flour; or 10 oz (250g/2½ cups) plain flour and 2 oz (50g/½ cup) cornflour (cornstarch); or 10 oz (250g/2½ cups) plain flour and 2 oz (50g/½ cup) rice flour or fine semolina
8 oz (200g/1 cup) waxy butter
5 oz (125g/⅔ cup) caster (superfine) sugar
1 tbsp double (heavy) cream or 2 egg yolks
Pinch of salt

Sift the flours and salt onto a pastry board and make a 'clearing' in the centre. Into this put the sugar and on top place the butter which should be neither too hard nor too oily. On top of the butter, scatter a handful of flour, then start kneading it into the butter and sugar, adding flour until all but about a cupful has been used. Flatten the dough with the heel of the hand and spread it either with the yolks or with the cream. Fold the dough over to enclose the liquid, then add the remaining flour and knead until the dough is quite smooth and free from cracks. Chill for half an hour to allow the mixture to firm up. Sprinkle the pastry board with caster sugar (no flour). Roll the dough to a thickness of ½ in (1 cm). It can then be cut with fancy biscuit cutters, or using a sharp knife, cut into rectangular fingers; another method is to cut it to fit a shallow sponge tin, lined with greaseproof paper. The traditional 'edging' for fingers or rounds of shortbread is the same as for 'piecrust'—pinching the dough between the thumb and forefinger of one hand and the forefinger of the other. Rounds of shortbread should then be lightly marked into sections like the spokes of a wheel. All shapes must be pricked with a fork or skewer at ¼ in (½ cm) intervals, to prevent the dough from puffing up when it is cooked

Bake the shortbread in a slow moderate oven (Gas No. 3, 325°F, 170°C) until a pale golden brown; biscuits will take about 20 minutes, rounds (protected by the tin) about 35 minutes. Immediately the shortbread comes from the oven, place on cooling trays and scatter with caster sugar. Makes about 30 fingers, 40 biscuits, or 3 rounds.

VARIATION

Divide the dough into three; leave one plain, work 2 oz (50g/⅓ cup) chopped glacé (candied) cherries into one third, and 2 oz (50g/½ cup) chopped almonds or walnuts into the other.

Toffee Shortbread

Half the master recipe can be used for these delectable biscuits, or a batch made from scratch. Children especially enjoy this confection.

Base:
6 oz (150g/1½ cups) plain flour
4 oz (100g/½ cup) butter
2 oz (50g/¼ cup) caster (superfine) sugar

Use a tin 11 × 7 × 1 in (28 × 18 × 3 cm) or one of similar area. Butter lightly. Rub butter into flour and sugar until like breadcrumbs, then knead into a dough. Roll on sugared board to size of tin. Lift off and arrange in base, trimming sides even. Prick all over. Bake at Gas No. 4, 350°F, 180°C, for 20 minutes or until pale gold in colour. Allow to cool.

Toffee:
4 oz (100g/½ cup) butter
4 oz (100g/½ cup) dark fine brown sugar
2 level tbsp golden (corn) syrup
Small tin (6 fl oz/150ml/¾ cup) sweetened condensed milk
½ teasp vanilla essence (extract)

Put all ingredients except essence into thick-bottomed pan and heat, stirring until sugar has dissolved. Bring to boil and cook, stirring every once in a while, for 7 minutes, by which time the mixture will be a golden brown toffee colour. Take from heat, add vanilla and beat for one minute. Pour the toffee mixture on to the cooled shortbread base. Leave till cold.

Topping:
$\frac{1}{4}$ lb (100g) coating milk chocolate
Melt the chocolate over hot water and as soon as it is liquid, pour over the toffee. When almost set, mark lightly into squares. Makes about 20.

Almond Shortbread Meringues

6 oz (150g/$\frac{3}{4}$ cup) butter
10 oz (250g/2$\frac{1}{2}$ cups) plain flour
2 oz (50g/$\frac{1}{2}$ cup) ground almonds
2 oz (50g/$\frac{1}{2}$ cup) sifted icing (confectioners') sugar
2 eggs, separated
4 oz (100g/$\frac{1}{2}$ cup) caster (superfine) sugar
Apricot jam
Flaked almonds

Mix together the flour, ground almonds and icing sugar then rub in the butter until the mixture resembles fine crumbs. Mix to a dough with the two egg yolks, and knead until the mixture is smooth and free from cracks. Cover with foil and chill for half an hour. Roll the dough $\frac{1}{8}$ in ($\frac{1}{2}$ cm) thick and cut into strips 2$\frac{1}{2}$ in (6 cm) long and 1 in (2$\frac{1}{2}$ cm) wide. Arrange the strips on ungreased baking sheets, and prick all over with a fork. Spread with a thin layer of apricot jam. Beat the whites until they hold stiff, glossy peaks, then gradually beat in all the caster sugar until the meringue is stiff and solid. Put into a piping bag fitted with a coarse rose tube and use to decorate the shortbread. Scatter with the almonds. Bake in a very slow oven (Gas No. 2, 300°F, 150°C) for half an hour, or until the biscuits are firm and the meringue crisp. Makes about 40 strips.

The International Collection

The biscuit is a truly international food; though flavours and techniques may vary between one country and another, the basic ingredients—best butter, fine sugar, quality flour remain the same. Here are some of the best examples of their kind.

Raisin Biscuits (*Australia*)

7 oz (175g/1$\frac{3}{4}$ cups) plain flour
$\frac{1}{2}$ level teasp each of cinnamon and nutmeg
Pinch of salt
4 oz (100g/$\frac{1}{2}$ cup) butter
4 oz (100g/$\frac{1}{2}$ cup) fine brown sugar
1 egg yolk
1 tbsp top milk (light cream), mixed with 1 level teasp bicarbonate of soda (baking soda) and 1 teasp vinegar
3 oz (75g/$\frac{1}{2}$ cup) coarsely-chopped seedless raisins

Beat the brown sugar into the butter, then beat in the yolk and the milk, mixed with the vinegar and bicarbonate of soda. Finally stir in the flour mixed with the spices and the raisins. Roll out $\frac{1}{8}$ in ($\frac{1}{2}$ cm) thick and cut into 2 in (5 cm) diameter rounds. Arrange on oiled trays. Bake 12 minutes at Gas No. 4, 350°F, 180°C. Sprinkle whilst warm with caster sugar. Makes 20.

Nut Crescents (*Austria*)

8 oz (200g/1 cup) butter
Bare 3 oz (75g/$\frac{1}{3}$ cup) caster (superfine) sugar
2 teasp hot water
2 small teasp vanilla essence
8 oz (200g/2 cups) sifted plain flour
Pinch of salt
2 oz (50g/$\frac{1}{2}$ cup) chopped walnuts

Cream the butter thoroughly and add the sugar gradually. Then add the water and essence and beat again. Finally stir in the flour, salt and nuts. Wrap the dough in foil and leave to harden for 1 hour. Shape pieces of dough into pencils, then curve into 3 in (7$\frac{1}{2}$ cm) crescents. Arrange on ungreased sheets, leaving room to swell. Bake in a slow moderate oven (Gas No. 3, 325°F, 170°C) for 15 minutes, until firm but still pale. Cool 5 minutes, then dip in sifted icing sugar. Makes about 50.

Vanilla Kipferl (*Austria*)

The famous biscuit served in the Konditorei (coffee houses) of Vienna since the seventeenth century.

8 oz (200g/1 cup) butter
4 oz (100g/½ cup) caster (superfine) sugar
4 oz (100g/1 cup) ground almonds or hazel nuts
8 oz (200g/2 cups) plain flour
Pinch of salt
1 teasp vanilla essence (extract)

Cream the butter, work in the sugar, then the almonds, flour and essence. Foil wrap and chill for half an hour. Take small pieces of the dough and shape into crescents about 2½ in (6 cm) long and ¾ in (1½ cm) thick. Place on ungreased sheets. Bake at Gas No. 3, 325°F, 170°C, for 18 minutes until firm to the touch, but unbrowned. Roll in sifted icing or caster sugar whilst warm. Makes about 50.

Brandy (Ginger) Snaps (*Great Britain*)

The factory-made version cannot equal the delicate taste and texture of these admittedly 'tricky' biscuits. They will bake evenly if you use heavy baking sheets, well greased with oil. My husband made me a 'brandy snap machine' by sticking 4 pieces of ½ in (1 cm) dowelling into a connecting piece of wood, at 4 in (10 cm) intervals.

4 oz (100g/⅓ cup) golden (corn) syrup
3½ oz (90g/½ cup) caster (superfine) sugar
4 oz (100g/½ cup) butter
3½ oz (90g/1 cup less 2 tbsp) plain flour
2 level teasp ground ginger
1 teasp grated lemon rind

Weigh all ingredients very carefully. Put the syrup, caster sugar and butter into a saucepan and heat, stirring, without boiling till melted. Add flour, rind and ginger, and beat till smooth. Grease oven trays, and put out teaspoons of mixture at 3 in (7½ cm) intervals. Bake at Gas No. 3, 325°F, 170°C, for 10 minutes, or until a rich golden brown. Cool a minute, then lift off tray and twist round a stick or wooden spoon handle. Makes approximately 36. Fill with sweetened whipped cream (using a piping bag and coarse rose tube) no more than half an hour before serving.

Vaniljekranse (*Denmark*)

A delicate biscuit to serve with ice-cream or a cold sweet.

8 oz (200g/2 cups) plain flour
½ level tbsp baking powder
8 oz (200g/1 cup) butter
3 oz (75g/½ cup) caster (superfine) sugar
3 oz (75g/¾ cup) ground almonds
About 2 tbsp beaten egg
½ teasp vanilla essence (extract)

Cream the butter until like mayonnaise then beat in the sugar. Add the egg and vanilla essence, then beat in the flour and the ground almonds. Beat well. The mixture should be the consistency of butter icing; if too solid, beat in a little more egg. Place in a forcing bag with a medium star tube, or put in a biscuit press. Pipe into rings or into sticks onto a slightly greased sheet. Scatter with almond flakes or nibs. Bake in a quick moderate oven (Gas No. 5, 375°F, 190°C) for 10–12 minutes. Makes about 48.

Tuiles (*France*)

A special-occasion biscuit to serve with ice-cream or fruit mousse.

2 large egg whites
5 oz (125g/⅔ cup) caster (superfine) sugar
Pinch of salt
3 oz (75g/6 tbsp) butter, melted and cooled until lukewarm
2 tbsp cooking oil
2 oz (50g/½ cup) plain flour
2 oz (50g/½ cup) finely-chopped almonds or almond nibs

Beat the sugar, egg whites and salt with a wooden spoon or electric beater until the sugar has dissolved and the mixture has thickened. Add shortenings and blend well, then stir in flour and almonds. Drop rounded teaspoons of mixture on greased baking sheets, leaving plenty of room in between. Spread the mixture thinly into a round with a fork (doesn't matter how thin—it will join up in the cooking. Bake in a moderate oven (Gas No. 4, 350°F, 180°C) for 12 minutes or until golden brown. Take from oven, cool 30 seconds, then lift off and lay over rolling pin. When set, put on cooling tray. Store in a tin when cold. Makes 24.

Spritz Biscuits (*Scandinavia*)

8 oz (200g/2 cups) plain flour
6 oz (150g/¾ cup) butter
4 oz (100g/½ cup) caster (superfine) sugar
1 egg yolk
1 teasp vanilla essence (extract)
1 teasp water, if necessary

Chill two ungreased biscuit tins until needed. In a large bowl, beat together the sugar, butter, egg yolks and vanilla. When smooth and fluffy, add the flour, sifted with a pinch of salt. If the mixture seems too stiff to pipe, add the teaspoon of water. Put into a large piping bag fitted with a coarse rose tube, pipe out into small biscuits about ¾ in (½ cm) in diameter, leaving 1½ in (3½ cm) between each one. Decorate with little bits of cherry and angelica. Bake for 10 minutes at Gas No. 5, 375°F, 190°C, until a pale golden brown. Alternatively, the mixture may be taken by the teaspoon and dropped into a bowl of chopped walnuts or slightly crushed sugared cornflakes, then formed lightly into a flattened disc and baked in the same way. Makes 40.

Rum and Butter Biscuits (*Sweden*)

A crisp, richly-flavoured biscuit to serve with coffee. These biscuits keep up to three weeks in a tightly-closed tin.

4 oz (100g/½ cup) soft butter
3 oz (75g/½ cup) caster (superfine) sugar
1 tbsp rum
6 oz (150g/1½ cups) plain flour
1 egg yolk
Topping:
3 level tbsp almond nibs
1 level tbsp granulated sugar

Cream the butter with the caster sugar until light and fluffy, then beat in the rum. Stir in the flour. The mixture may be chilled if preferred for ease in handling. Roll out on a floured board to ¼ in (½ cm) thickness. Cut into biscuits using a 1½ in (3½ cm) diameter cutter. Place 1 in (2½ cm) apart on ungreased trays. Mix the almonds with the granulated sugar; beat the egg yolk with a teaspoon of water, brush the biscuits with the egg and sprinkle with the sugar and almond mixture. Bake in a quick moderate oven (Gas No. 5, 375°F, 190°C) for 15 minutes, or until a pale golden brown. Allow to cool. Store in a tightly-covered tin. Makes approx 36.

Child's Play

Any of these delicious biscuits can be made by a child of eight or nine with only minimal adult supervision. Use a large breakfast cup (8 fl oz/200ml size) as a measure when necessary.

Chocolate Peanut Clusters

The roasted peanuts add greatly to the flavour of these biscuits but can be omitted for young children—or if you haven't the patience to skin the nuts!

½ lb (200g) pkt milk chocolate for dipping
¼ lb (100g/1 cup) peanuts, toasted in a moderate oven until golden brown (about 15 min)
3 cups Rice Krispies or similar cereal

Toast the peanuts, then rub in a tea-towel to remove skins. Melt the chocolate in a bowl standing in a pan of very hot water. When melted, stir in nuts and Rice Krispies. Put into little paper cases, and allow to set. Makes about 24.

Cereal Macaroons

2 egg whites
Pinch of salt
1 cup caster (superfine) sugar
1 cup shredded coconut
1 teasp vanilla essence (extract)
2 cups cornflakes or Rice Krispies

Whisk the whites with a pinch of salt until they form stiff, glossy peaks. Carefully fold in the sugar, using a metal spoon so that air is not expelled. Fold in the vanilla, coconut and cereal. Drop in little heaps onto a greased baking sheet. Decorate with a piece of glacé cherry. Bake in a moderate oven (Gas No. 4, 350°F, 180°C) for 10–15 minutes or until golden brown. Remove immediately to a cooling tray. Makes approximately 24.

Gordon's Fancy

Some kind of electric mixer is essential to beat these biscuits, as it is too laborious by hand. They have a delicious marshmallow inside with a crispy outside.

4 egg whites
9 oz (225g/2¼ cups) icing (confectioners') sugar
Few drops of peppermint essence (extract) and green colouring
Approx ½ lb (200g/3 cups) desiccated (dried and shredded) coconut

Beat whites and icing sugar in an electric mixer at high speed until they hold peaks. Stir in essence and enough coconut to make a mixture which, though moist, will just hold its shape in a little pile. Finally stir in enough green colouring to tint the mixture a delicate shade. Two thirds fill little paper cases with the mixture. Bake in a moderate oven (Gas No. 4, 350°F, 180°C) for about 20 minutes, until crisp and pale brown on top, though creamy within.

Meringue Kisses

This recipe is easier to make than the traditional meringue; it produces a crisp outside with a marshmallow interior. As all the sugar must be beaten in, it should not be attempted without some form of electric mixer.

3 egg whites
6 oz (150g/¾ cup) caster (superfine) sugar
1 level teasp cornflour (cornstarch)
1 teasp each of vinegar and vanilla essence (extract)

Make sure that there is no trace of grease in the mixing bowl or mixers, and no trace of yolk in the whites, or the mixture will not achieve its true volume. Mix the cornflour and sugar, and put the vinegar and essence into an egg cup. Whisk the whites until they hold stiff, glossy peaks, then start adding the sugar/cornflour mixture a spoonful at a time, beating until stiff again after each addition. When all the sugar has been added and the mixture is solid, beat in the liquids. Have ready baking trays covered with greased greaseproof paper, or use non-stick trays. Either pipe the mixture onto the tray, using a coarse rose tube, or drop from a teaspoon in little blobs. Bake in a slow oven (Gas No. 1, 275°F, 140°C) for about 40 minutes, or until the meringues feel crisp and lift off the tray without difficulty. Use either as a petit four, or sandwich together with cream. Makes about 36, depending on size.

Biscuits (Cookies) in a Hurry

These biscuits can be made literally in minutes, as the most time-consuming operation—rolling and cutting—has been side-stepped altogether. Instead, the mixture is either dropped from a spoon or rolled into balls which form into perfect biscuits in the heat of the oven.

A word of caution: When the shortening is to be melted, use only butter or oil—margarine is less successful used in this way.

Flapjacks

½ lb (200g/2⅔ cups) breakfast oats or rolled oats
4 oz (100g/½ cup) butter
½ lb (200g/⅔ cup) golden (corn) syrup
4 oz (100g/½ cup) moist brown sugar

Melt the butter in a pan, then add the sugar and syrup and warm together. Stir in oats and mix well. Spoon into a large flat greased baking tin (11 × 15 × ½ in/28 × 38 × 1 cm) or two Yorkshire pudding tins, flattening into a layer ¼ in (½ cm) thick with wetted fingers. Bake in a slow, moderate oven (Gas No. 3, 325°F, 170°C) for 30 minutes until a rich brown. Cut into fingers whilst warm. Remove from the tin when cold. Makes 50.

Golden Buttons

3 oz (75g/¾ cup) self-raising flour
3 oz (75g/½ cup) caster (superfine) sugar
3 oz (75g/1 cup) porridge oats
3 oz (75g/6 tbsp) butter
1 level tbsp golden (corn) syrup
1 tbsp milk with ½ level teasp bicarbonate of soda (baking soda)

Put flour and oats into bowl. Bring sugar, butter and syrup slowly to bubbling point, stirring all the time to dissolve the sugar. Immediately add the bicarbonate of soda and milk, then pour onto the dry ingredients. Leave for 10 minutes. Roll into ¾ in (1½ cm) balls and arrange well apart on greased trays. Bake in moderate oven (Gas No. 5, 375°F, 190°C) for 10–12 minutes or until golden brown. Makes 30.

Butter Crunchies

4 oz (100g/½ cup) soft butter
4 oz (100g/½ cup) caster (superfine) sugar
1 egg
Grated rind of ½ lemon
8 oz (200g/2 cups) self-raising flour
Granulated sugar for rolling

Put all ingredients in bowl and beat until dough is formed. Roll in walnut-sized balls between wetted palms, then roll in granulated sugar. Arrange on buttered trays. Bake in a moderate oven (Gas No. 5, 375°F, 190°C) for 18 minutes until golden brown. Makes approx 48.

Quick Kichlach

A featherweight biscuit which is ideal to serve with stewed fruit or morning coffee.

2 eggs
¼ pint (125ml/⅔ cup) oil
2 small teasp vanilla essence (extract)
1 teasp grated lemon rind
5 oz (125g/⅔ cup) caster (superfine) sugar
8 oz (200g/2 cups) self-raising flour
Pinch of salt
Almond nibs

Beat eggs with fork until well blended. Stir in oil, vanilla and lemon rind. Blend in sugar until mixture thickens. Sift flour and add to egg mixture (dough will be soft). Drop by rounded teaspoons on ungreased biscuit tin, 2 in (5 cm) apart. Using the bottom of a glass which has been dipped in oil and then in sugar, flatten each biscuit into a round. Decorate with nuts. Bake in a quick oven (Gas No. 6, 400°F, 200°C) for 8–10 minutes. Makes 36.

Treacle (Molasses) Crisps

4 oz (100g/½ cup) butter
4 oz (100g/½ cup) caster (superfine) sugar
4 oz (100g/1 cup) self-raising flour
1 rounded tbsp treacle (molasses)
3 oz (75g/1 cup) oats
1 oz (25g/½ cup) coconut
½ level teasp bicarbonate of soda (baking soda)
1 tbsp milk

Bring the sugar, butter and treacle very slowly to the boil, stirring all the time, then stir in the bicarbonate of soda dissolved in the milk. Immediately, pour onto the flour, oats and coconut, and mix well. Leave to cool and firm up (about half an hour). Roll into marbles and arrange on greased trays, leaving room for the biscuits to spread. Bake in a moderate oven (Gas No. 4, 350°F, 180°C) for 15 minutes. Makes about 48.

Bread, Rolls and Yeast Kuchen

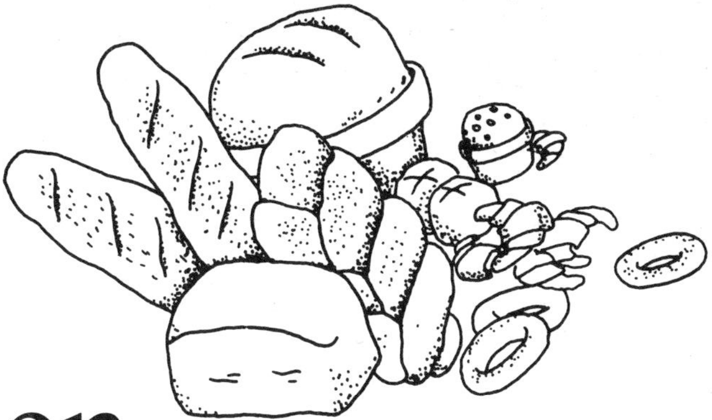

Good Jewish Bread

Every Thursday evening, from teatime to dawn, a dwindling band of Jewish master bakers mixes, shapes and bakes the challahs, twists and tin loaves of 'best bread' which have been part of every Jewish Sabbath for close on 3,000 years.

Into the dough (now mixed and divided by machine but still shaped by hand), these craftsmen put oil, salt and sugar according to the recipe developed for their famous 'Cappadocian' bread by the Macedonian bakers of Perseus II, and leaven it with yeast, whose miraculous raising powers were first discovered in Egypt at about the same period as their ancestors were the slaves of Pharaoh. They even scatter the loaves with poppy seeds by the method described in the third century of this era by gastronomic historian, Athenaeus.

But even when bread was made from the unleavened flour and water mixture described in Genesis XVIII, it was a food highly regarded by the Jews. Indeed, since Sarah mixed her meal-and-water hearth cakes for the visiting angels, it has been the privilege of the Jewish mother to bake this staple food and offer it as a mark of hospitality to family guests. Until the Second World War, it was still the custom for Jewish housewives to take their unbaked loaves to be baked in the more even heat of the professional baker's ovens.

Today, very few women make bread themselves, and it is left to a tiny band of professionals to shape the loaves according to the season. By tradition a challah plait is made for the Sabbath so that bread can more easily be broken without the aid of a knife. For Rosh Hashanah it is round, to symbolise the fullness of the year ahead, whilst on the Eve of Yom Kippur, a ladder sits on top, or a dove—a 'feigele'—to carry one's prayer up to heaven. Comes Hoshanah Rabbah and the loaf is shaped like a key, while Purim is marked by the raisin bread, a descendant of the 'Artologanus' or cake bread the Romans used to bake.

Until the beginning of this century, white or 'best' bread was reserved for the Sabbath and Festivals alone, whilst at other times, black or brown bread, solid and satisfying with its characteristic sour dough flavour, was the rule. Whilst the recipe for Jewish bread is almost universal, the names and the shapes of the loaves made from the dough vary between one community and another; and when it comes to rolls, one would need to be an expert in linguistics to distinguish between bulkes, barches, bobkes and bundes. For one man's zemmel pampalik (onion roll) is another man's tsibbele bonde, and the plaetzel of one country is the mohn kichel (poppy seed roll) of another.

Which brings us, inevitably, to the bagel—one name and shape which remains the same wherever it is eaten. Elaborate attempts have been made to establish the etymology of the word, and to date its origins to the defeat of the Turks before Vienna in 1683. Some food historians trace its origins back to the 'buegels' or stirrup-shaped rolls baked on that occasion in honour of the victorious King of Poland, and suggest that the word was corrupted to 'byegel' and 'bagel' by Galician Jews. I myself think 15th-century France rather than 17th-century Vienna saw the birth of this inimitable confection and that the bagel is a lineal descendant of the 'pain échaudé' (boiled bread) of the medieval French bakery.

Perhaps the best policy would be to forget the whole matter, and be content to buy one's bagels from the baker's on Sunday morning. Then again, you could follow my superb recipe and make your very own!

To Freeze Bread, Rolls and Bagels

Baked Bread

All baked bread, bought or home-baked, freezes well provided it is frozen when freshly baked, but length of storage time varies with the type of bread.

To freeze: Wrap in aluminium foil or polythene bags. If bread is likely to be required quickly, always wrap in foil so that it can be placed frozen in a hot oven to thaw and refresh.

Storage times:
White and brown bread keeps well for up to 4 weeks.
Enriched bread and rolls (milk, fruit, malt loaves and soft rolls) keep up to 6 weeks.
Crisp-crusted loaves and rolls have a limited storage time as the crusts begin to 'shell off' after 1 week. Vienna-type loaves and rolls keep for 3 days only.

To thaw:
Loaves: Leave in packaging at room temperature for 3–6 hours depending on size of loaf *or* leave overnight in refrigerator *or* place frozen loaf wrapped in foil in a hot oven (Gas No. 6, 400°F, 200°C) for 45 minutes.

Toast: Sliced bread can be toasted while frozen. Separate slices carefully with a knife before toasting.

Rolls: Leave in packaging at room temperature for 1½ hours or place frozen rolls wrapped in foil in a hot oven (Gas No. 8, 450°F, 230°C) for 15 minutes.

Note: Crusty loaves and rolls thawed at room temperature should be refreshed before serving. Place unwrapped loaves or rolls in a hot oven (Gas No. 6, 400°F, 200°C) for 5–10 minutes until crust is crisp.

Bread Doughs

All doughs can be frozen but the storage times vary with the type of dough, plain or enriched, and also whether it is frozen risen or unrisen. All standard bread recipes can be frozen but the best results are obtained from doughs made with 50% more yeast than is given in the standard recipes, i.e. ½ oz (15g/1 cake) yeast should be increased to ¾ oz (20g/1½ cakes). Freeze dough in quantities you are most likely to use—i.e. 1 lb 2 oz (540g) dough for a 1 lb (480g) loaf tin. Heavy duty polythene bags, lightly greased, are best. They must be tightly sealed as any air left inside causes skinning on the dough surface, which will crack during handling, and gives the baked dough crumb a streaky appearance. If there is a chance of the dough rising a little before freezing, leave 1 in (2½ cm) space above the dough.

Unrisen Dough

To freeze: After kneading, form dough into a ball. Place in a large, lightly greased polythene bag, seal tightly and freeze immediately.

Storage times: Plain white and brown doughs keep up to 8 weeks. Enriched dough keeps up to 5 weeks.

To thaw: Unseal polythene bag and then tie loosely at the top to allow space for rising. Leave for 5–6 hours at room temperature *or* overnight in the refrigerator. Complete rise, then knock back, shape, rise and bake.

Risen Dough

To freeze: Place dough in a large, lightly greased polythene bag, tie loosely at the top and put to rise. Turn risen dough on to a lightly floured surface, flatten firmly with knuckles to knock out air bubbles, then knead until firm. Replace in polythene bag, tightly seal and freeze immediately.

Storage time: Plain and enriched white and brown doughs keep up to 3 weeks. Dough kept longer than these times gives poor results.

To thaw: See unrisen dough instructions. After thawing, knock back if required, shape, rise and bake.

Part-Baked Rolls and Loaves

Both home-baked white and wheatmeal rolls can be frozen partly baked. This is a very successful way of freezing rolls as the frozen rolls can be put straight from the freezer into the oven to finish baking. It is the best method of freezing rolls to serve for breakfast. Loaves are not so successful as rolls because during part-baking the crust becomes well-formed and coloured before the centre of the loaf is set. Part-baked loaves and rolls available in shops freeze well.

To part-bake rolls: Place shaped and risen rolls in a slow oven (Gas No. 2, 300°F, 150°C) for about 20 minutes. The rolls must be set, but still pale in colour. Cool.

To freeze: Pack cooled rolls in usable quantities in foil or polythene bags. Seal and freeze. As the sides of the rolls are still slightly soft, care must be taken when packing to avoid squashing.

Storage time: Up to 4 months.

To thaw and finish baking: Unwrap and place frozen rolls in oven to thaw and complete baking. Bake white rolls at Gas No. 6, 400°F, 200°C; brown rolls at Gas No. 8, 450°F, 230°C for 20 minutes.

Part-Baked Bought Rolls and Loaves

To freeze: Freeze immediately after purchasing. Leave loaves in polythene bags in which they were sold. Pack rolls in polythene bags and seal.

Storage time: Up to 4 months.

To thaw:
Loaves: Place frozen unwrapped loaf in a hot oven (Gas No. 7, 425°F, 220°C) for 40 minutes. Cool for 1–2 hours before cutting.

Rolls: Place frozen unwrapped rolls in a hot oven (Gas No. 6, 400°F, 200°C) for 15 minutes.

Perfect Challah

This recipe is the result of many hours of experimentation, the object of which was to find the simplest and quickest method of producing a perfect challah under domestic conditions.

The dough is first mixed and kneaded with the dough hook of an electric mixer. It is then left to rise *slowly* overnight in the refrigerator. Next day, it is ready to be shaped and baked as usual. Although the refrigerated doughs have been developed only in very recent years, the method is similar to the old Russian way of leaving the bread dough outside the kitchen door overnight to rise in the winter cold. Bread baked in this way is particularly successful in both texture and taste. The same method can be used for sweet yeast doughs, which are especially easy to handle after refrigeration.

NOTES ON THE INGREDIENTS

A plain flour with a high gluten content is necessary to success. Many bakers will sell you some of their own flour, or you can buy special 'bread' flour from supermarkets or health food stores. You can also use a plain all-purpose flour (but *not* a cake flour).

Fresh yeast looks like putty and should have a fresh 'yeasty' flavour. If it is crumbly and dark it is useless. If tightly foil-wrapped, it will keep in the refrigerator for a month, and in the freezer for 6 months.

Dried yeast is granular and is packed in 1 oz (25g) packs or in tins. It will keep for 6 months in the larder if tightly closed. As dried yeast is concentrated, only half the quantity given for fresh yeast is required.

To make 1 very large plait or 2 medium plaits:

1 lb (480g/4 cups) 'bread' (or enriched white) flour
2 level teasp salt
3 level teasp caster (superfine) sugar
2 tbsp oil
½ oz (15g/1 cake) fresh yeast; or 2 level teasp dried yeast
1 large egg plus 1 yolk; or 2 standard eggs
8 fl oz (200ml/1 cup) warm water

Heat the water until it feels as warm as a baby's bath. Put into the mixer bowl. Add one third of the flour, all the sugar and the fresh or dried yeast. Mix until smooth, cover with a tea-towel and leave for 20 minutes until it looks frothy. Now add all the remaining flour, the salt, oil and egg (saving the yolk or half of one standard egg for glazing the bread). Mix with the dough hook at minimum speed until a dough forms then knead with the dough hook at low speed for 3 min. Tip the dough on to a floured board, and knead with the hands for 30 seconds to shape into a ball—it should have a scone-like texture. (By hand alone, the dough should be kneaded 5–6 minutes or until smooth.) Put this ball into a greased polythene bag (large enough for the dough to double in size). Fasten the bag loosely.

To rise: Put the dough at the bottom of the refrigerator for 12–24 hours, whichever is more convenient.

To shape: Take the risen dough from the refrigerator, and leave in the kitchen for about half an hour or until it loses its chill.

To make one large plait: Divide the dough into 3 or 6 pieces. Knead each piece into a round, then roll into a sausage about 12 in (30 cm) long. Press the strands firmly together at one end, then plait tightly (the six-strand plait makes the best shape, but you need to see how it is done—it is impossible to describe in words). Put the plait on a greased tray.

To make two medium plaits: Divide the dough in two and work on each half in exactly the same way.

To make tin loaves: The ordinary 2 lb (1kg) loaf tin is too small for the whole quantity of dough, so unless you can get a tin as big as those which the bakers use, divide the dough in half and proceed as follows with each half:

Take the portion of dough and divide it into three. Knead two of the pieces of dough into balls and arrange, touching, in the middle of a greased loaf tin (approx 9 × 5 × 3 in/23 × 13 × 7½ cm). Take the third piece of dough, and cut it into half. Knead into two balls and place one on either side of the centre balls.

The next step for both plaits and tin loaves:
Put the loaves into a greased polythene bag and leave until they regain their lightness, springing back when touched with a floured finger—about half an hour in the kitchen. Brush over with the reserved egg, diluted with 1 teaspoon water and 1 teaspoon salt. Scatter with poppy seeds.

To bake: Put in a hot oven (Gas No. 7, 425°F, 220°C) for 15 minutes, then turn down to Gas No. 5, 375°F, 190°C, for a further 30 minutes for the small loaves, and a further 45 minutes for the large loaves.

To test: When the loaves are cooked, they will be a rich brown, and will sound hollow when the base is tapped.

To make rolls: The risen dough can be used to make approximately 16 rolls, depending on the size. When at room temperature, divide into 16 pieces.

Plætzels (Dimple Rolls)

Take each piece of dough and knead into a ball the size of a small apple. Roll into a round about $\frac{3}{8}$ in ($\frac{3}{4}$ cm) thick. Put on a floured tray to rise until puffy as for the bread. Take two fingers and press a 'dimple' firmly into the centre of the dough. Brush with salted egg mixture and scatter with poppy or sesame seeds. Bake in a hot oven (Gas No. 7, 425°F, 220°C) for 15 minutes until a rich brown.

Tsibbele Bondes (Onion Rolls)

Top the dimpled rolls with a teaspoonful of finely chopped raw onion. Brush with salted egg mixture and bake at Gas No. 5, 375°F, 190°C, for 20 minutes.

Knots

Roll each piece of dough into a rope 7 in (18 cm) long. Shape into a coil and put one end through the centre of the coil. Rise till puffy. Brush with egg and bake as for the plaetzels.

Miniature Challahs

Divide each piece of dough into three and roll into a 6 in (15 cm) rope. Plait as for the challah. Allow to rise until puffy. Brush with salted egg mixture and scatter with poppy seeds. Bake like the plaetzels.

Bagels

Once you know that they must be boiled before they are baked, it is surprisingly easy to produce professional-looking bagels at home. As you can make 20 bagels from just over 1 lb (480g) flour, it is worthwhile making a stock for the freezer, particularly if you live far from a Jewish bakery. The method I have developed is adapted from the professional technique used by the craftsmen at a bakery in Manchester, who were my instructors in the art of bagel-making at 2 a.m. one Sunday morning.

The dough: This is identical to that used for challah, with one exception—the flour. As bagels are much firmer in texture than bread, use 1 lb 2 oz ($\frac{1}{2}$kg/4$\frac{1}{2}$ cups) flour instead of 1 lb (480g/4 cups). Mix and refrigerate the dough in exactly the same way as for the challah. The difference in technique starts once the risen dough is taken from the refrigerator.

To shape the bagels: Work with the chilled dough direct from the refrigerator. Divide it into 20 pieces. Shape each bagel as follows:

Knead the piece into a ball, then flatten with the palm of the hand and roll into a rope 7 in (18 cm) long and $\frac{3}{8}$ in ($\frac{3}{4}$ cm) thick. Wind the rope round the knuckles of your hand, and press on the table to seal the joint. Roll the joint gently on the table to seal it firmly, then slip the bagel off the knuckles onto a floured board. Repeat with all the pieces of dough. Leave to rise for an hour until the bagels have increased slightly in size, but are not as puffy as rolls. Have the oven set at Gas No. 10, 500°F, 250°C, and a soup pan of boiling water ready on the stove. Put 5 or 6 bagels at a time into the boiling water and boil for 2 minutes, turning them over with a slotted spoon as they rise to the top. Drain from the water and lay on a board. Repeat with the remaining bagels. Put the boiled bagels on a floured tray and put in the oven for 1 minute to dry the top surface, then turn and bake for a further 15 minutes until a rich shiny brown. Makes 20 bagels.

Refrigerator Rolls

These rich tender rolls have a texture rather like the French brioche (breakfast rolls), yet they are so simple a completely inexperienced cook can make them to perfection. No kneading is required.

1 lb (480g/4 cups) plain (enriched white) flour
$\frac{1}{2}$ pint (250ml/1$\frac{1}{4}$ cups) milk
$\frac{1}{2}$ oz (15g/1 cake) fresh yeast; or 2 level teasp dried yeast and a pinch of sugar
1 large egg
1 oz (25g/2 tbsp) caster (superfine) sugar
2 level teasp salt
3 oz (75g/6 tbsp) soft butter

Warm the milk to blood heat, then pour a quarter of it onto the yeast together with a pinch of sugar and leave for 5 minutes (if fresh), 15 minutes if dried. Stir to blend, then add all the remaining ingredients. Beat vigorously by machine or hand until the dough is smooth and well blended (about 3 minutes). Tip into a large plastic bag (which has been lightly oiled inside), close and leave overnight in the bottom of the refrigerator. Next day, the dough will be of a scone-like texture. Roll out ½ in (1 cm) thick on a floured board and cut into circles 2½ in (6 cm) in diameter, or into fingers measuring about 2½ × 1 in (6 × 2½ cm). Dip the tops of the rolls in melted butter (for a soft, shiny finish) or into beaten egg (for a crisp, brown finish) and arrange well apart on greased trays. Slide the trays into greased plastic bags and leave to rise for ¾ hour or until risen and puffy to the touch. Bake in a quick oven (Gas No. 6, 400°F, 200°C) for 15 minutes until a rich brown. Makes 24–30 rolls.

Bridge Rolls

1 lb (480g/4 cups) strong bread (or enriched white) flour
2 level teasp salt
1 level tbsp sugar
1 oz (25g/2 tbsp) melted butter
2 eggs
8 fl oz (200ml/1 cup) milk
½ oz (15g/1 cake) fresh yeast; or 2 level teasp dried yeast

Heat the milk until it feels as warm as a baby's bath. Put into the mixer bowl. Add one third of the flour, all the sugar and the fresh or dried yeast. Mix until smooth, cover with a tea-towel and leave for 20 minutes, until it looks frothy. Now add all the remaining flour, salt, soft butter and egg (saving one quarter of it for glazing the rolls). Either mix with a dough hook on No. 1 for 3 minutes, then turn out and knead on a floured board for 30 seconds; or turn out onto the floured board and knead for 5 minutes or until smooth. Put the ball of dough into a greased polythene bag (large enough for the dough to double in size). Fasten the bag loosely.

To rise: Put the dough at the bottom of the refrigerator for 12–24 hours, or leave in the kitchen to rise for 2 hours.

To shape: If the dough has been refrigerated, leave in the kitchen for half an hour or until it loses its chill.

If the dough has been allowed to rise at room temperature, shape as soon as it has doubled in bulk.

Divide the dough into four sections, then divide each section into six. Knead each little piece into a ball, then roll with the palm of the hand into a bridge roll shape, tapering at both ends. Arrange the rolls on greased baking sheets—almost touching if soft sides are required; further apart if a crisper finish is preferred. Take the reserved egg and mix with a teaspoonful of cold water. Brush the rolls with this glaze. Leave for half an hour until puffy to the touch, then brush again with egg and bake in a hot oven (Gas No. 8, 450°F, 230°C) for 10–12 minutes, or until golden brown. Makes 24 bridge rolls.

Croissants

These delicious morning rolls, one of the joys of a continental holiday, are made from a yeast-raised flaky pastry. As they freeze extremely well, a large number can be made at once, and when they are reheated they will taste freshly baked.

1 lb (480g/4 cups) strong plain (enriched white) flour
2 level teasp salt
1 oz (25g/2 tbsp) butter
1 egg, beaten
1 oz (25g/2 cakes) fresh yeast, blended with 8 fl oz (200ml/1 cup) cold water; or 1 level tbsp (½ oz/15g) dried yeast, sprinkled onto 8 fl oz (200ml/1 cup) warm water mixed with 1 level teasp sugar
6 oz (150g/¾ cup) waxy butter or margarine
1 egg, beaten with 1 teasp water and 1 level teasp sugar (for glazing)

Mix the fresh yeast with the water until dissolved, *or* sprinkle the dried yeast onto the warm water and sugar and leave for 10 minutes until frothy. Mix the flour and salt and rub in the 1 oz (25g/2 tbsp) butter.

To mix the dough by hand: Put the flour mix into a bowl, make a well in the centre and put in the yeast liquid and beaten egg. Mix to a dough, then turn onto a floured board and knead until smooth and silky (about 10 minutes).

To mix the dough by machine: Put the yeast liquid into the mixer bowl, then add the flour mixture and the beaten egg and beat at minimum speed with the dough hook for 1 minute. Increase speed to No. 2 and knead for 2 minutes. Turn out onto a floured board and knead by hand for 1 minute.

To make the pastry: Roll the dough into a rectangle approximately 21 × 7 × ¼ in (5 × 18 × ½ cm), making sure all the corners are absolutely square. Soften the 6 oz (150g/¾ cup) butter with a wide-bladed knife until it is creamy, then divide into 3 portions. Take one portion of butter. Use a knife to dot the top ⅔ of the dough with this butter (as in flaky pastry), leaving ½ in (1 cm) of the dough clear. Fold the pastry in three by bringing up the bottom third of the dough onto the middle portion, and folding the top third of the dough onto that. Seal the edges of the dough lightly with a rolling pin to prevent a 'leak-out' of butter. Turn the dough so that the fold is to the right hand side. Reshape once more into a rectangle by gently pressing the dough into shape with the rolling pin (do not roll it). Using the second portion of butter, dot the butter in the same way, then fold and turn as before. Repeat with the third portion of butter. If the dough becomes sticky and soft, chill a little between rollings. After the third folding, slip the dough into a polythene bag and chill for 30 minutes.

Shape once more into a rectangular strip, then repeat the rolling and shaping twice; finally fold for the last time, and refrigerate for another 30 minutes (by now the fat will be distributed in 18 layers which will provide the characteristic flakiness when the croissants are baked).

To shape the croissants: Roll the dough to a rectangle about 26 × 11 in (65 × 28 cm). Cover with greased polythene and leave to rest for 10 minutes. Trim the edges with a sharp knife to produce a rectangle precisely 25 × 10 in (63 × 25 cm) and divide in half lengthwise—each strip will now measure 5 in (12½ cm) in width. Cut each strip into 9 triangles, each measuring 5 in (12½ cm) on all three sides (equilateral triangles). Brush with egg wash. Roll up each triangle loosely from the base to the point, with the tip underneath. Curve into a crescent shape and arrange wide apart, to allow for rising, on ungreased baking sheets. Brush the tops with egg wash, cover again with polythene for 30 minutes, and leave at room temperature until light and puffy in appearance. Brush once more with egg. Bake in a hot oven (Gas No. 8, 450°F, 230°C) for 15 minutes. Serve warm.

To freeze: Pack in a single layer in a polythene bag or foil, or place in a foil tray sealed with foil.

Storage time: Up to 8 weeks.

To thaw: Leave in packaging at room temperature for 1½–2 hours, then refresh, wrapped in foil, in a hot oven (Gas No. 7, 425°F, 220°C) for 5 minutes, *or* place frozen, wrapped in foil, in a moderate oven (Gas No. 4, 350°F, 180°C) for 15 minutes.

Kuchens of Many Kinds

Translated literally, kuchen means 'cake', but it has also come to mean a vast variety of yeast-raised confectionery, which was the main kind of sweet mixture baked by European Jewish women until after the First World War. Its main virtue lay in its economy, for few eggs and little sugar or fat were required to make a whole kitchenful of rolls, cakes and fruited desserts. Recipes are legion, ranging from the economical Russian to the prodigal Hungarian ones.

Below I give two basic kuchen doughs—one to bake the same day, the other that can safely be left to rise slowly overnight. Both can be used to make the varieties of kuchens and rolls that I give below:

To freeze kuchens of any kind: For best results, bake, then freeze.

To freeze: Wrap in foil or polythene bags.

Storage time: Up to six weeks.

To thaw: Leave in packaging at room temperature for 2–3 hours, *or* if undecorated, place foil-wrapped in moderate oven (Gas No. 4, 350°F, 180°C) for 15–20 minutes.

Basic Kuchen Dough

This dough can either be risen and shaped on the same day, or if it is more convenient, left to rise overnight.

2 large eggs
Approx 6 fl oz (150ml/¾ cup) milk and water (see method)
1 oz (25g/2 cakes) fresh yeast, or 1 level tbsp dried yeast (½ oz/15g)
3 oz (75g/6 tbsp) soft butter
3 oz (75g/½ cup) caster (superfine) sugar
1 lb (480g/4 cups) plain flour
½ level teasp salt

Break the eggs into a measuring jug, add 3 fl oz (75ml) cold milk, then make up to ½ pint (250ml/10 fl oz) with 3 fl oz (75ml) hot water. Pour into a large mixing bowl and add the yeast. Stir until the yeast is dissolved. (If dried yeast is used, add a teaspoon of the sugar to the liquid with the yeast and leave for 10 minutes to allow the yeast to become active again). Add the butter, sugar, flour and salt. Beat for 5 minutes, either by mixer, wooden spoon or hand until the dough is smooth and stretchy and leaves the bowl and beaters clean when pulled away from them. If it is a little too sticky after this time, add a further rounded tablespoon of flour. Leave in the bowl, but cover with a damp tea-towel or plastic film. Leave in the kitchen for 1 hour, until it has doubled in bulk. Then press the dough down, turn it over and knead it in the bowl for 1 or 2 minutes. This redistributes any large gas bubbles that may have developed.

To rise overnight: Slip the dough into a greased plastic bag large enough to allow it to double in volume. Tie loosely and put on the bottom shelf of the refrigerator. Before use, it should be brought out into the kitchen for 1 hour, to return to room temperature. It can then be treated as newly-risen dough.

To rise in the kitchen: Leave for a further half hour. (This second rising gives the dough a very fine texture.) This dough is now ready for shaping.

Cinnamon Butter Kuchen (*To slice and butter*)

½ the risen dough
2 oz (50g/¼ cup) caster (superfine) sugar
1 level teasp cinnamon
About 2 oz (50g/½ cup) currants or sultanas (white raisins)
About 1 oz (25g/2 tbsp) soft butter

Roll the dough out into a rectangle ½ in (1 cm) thick. Spread with half the butter then sprinkle with half the cinnamon and sugar and a little dried fruit. Roll up tightly, then roll out again ½ in (1 cm) thick, and repeat the process. Tuck in the ends of the dough roll, then place, join downwards in a greased loaf tin measuring 9 × 5 × 3 in (23 × 13 × 7½ cm). Put into a plastic bag and leave until the dough rises level with the top of the tin and feels spongy and light to the touch. This will take about 30 minutes. Put in a quick moderate oven (Gas No. 5, 375°F, 190°C) for 10 minutes, then turn down to Gas No. 4, 350°F, 180°C for a further 30 minutes. When done, the kuchen will sound slightly hollow when tapped on the bottom. Ice whilst still warm with icing made by stirring 2 teaspoons lemon juice into 2 oz (50g) sifted icing sugar, then decorate with glacé cherries and walnuts. Or leave until cold then sprinkle with icing sugar.

Fruited Ring

½ the risen dough
2 oz (50g/¼ cup) caster (superfine) sugar
1 level teasp cinnamon
1 oz (25g/2 tbsp) soft butter
2 oz (50g/½ cup) raisins

Roll the dough out ⅜ in (¾ cm) thick, into a rectangle measuring 11 × 6 in (28 × 15 cm). Spread all over with the softened butter, then scatter with the raisins and the cinnamon and sugar. Roll up by the long side into a tight roll, then twist round and seal the ends into a circle. Place on a greased tray. Using kitchen scissors, make cuts $\frac{2}{3}$ of the way through the ring at intervals of $1\frac{1}{2}$ in ($3\frac{1}{2}$ cm) to show a little of the filling. Slip the tray into a greased plastic bag and leave to rise until puffy (about 30 minutes). Bake in a quick oven (Gas No. 6, 400°F, 200°C) for 25 minutes. Ice like the cinnamon butter kuchen.

Schnecken with Butterscotch Glaze

Schnecken are individual rolls rather like Chelsea Buns.

Proceed exactly as if making the fruited ring, spreading the dough with butter, cinnamon, sugar and raisins and forming into a roll. Cut this roll into 1 in ($2\frac{1}{2}$ cm) thick slices. Have ready a tray of 12 patty tins, each tin spread with 1 teaspoon soft butter and sprinkled with 1 teaspoon of soft brown sugar. Put the rolls, cut side down, into the patty tins, then put the tray of tins into a greased plastic bag. Leave to rise until puffy (about 30 minutes). Bake at Gas No. 5, 375°F, 190°C for 15 minutes or until a rich brown. Immediately turn each schnecken upside down on a cooling tray to allow the glaze to set. Half the dough makes 12 schnecken.

Apfelkuchen (*Apple Cake*)

$\frac{1}{2}$ the risen dough
4 large cooking apples, cord, peeled and sliced $\frac{1}{4}$ in ($\frac{1}{2}$ cm) thick
4 oz (100g/$\frac{1}{2}$ cup) caster (superfine) sugar mixed with 1 level teasp cinnamon
Plum jam or ginger marmalade

Roll out the risen dough to a thickness of $\frac{3}{8}$ in ($\frac{3}{4}$ cm) and use to line a shallow tin measuring approx 14 × 10 in (35 × 25 cm) which has been lightly greased. Allow the dough to rise for $\frac{1}{2}$ hour, then spread with the jam or marmalade and arrange the apple slices in overlapping rows on top. Sprinkle with the cinnamon sugar. Leave for 10 minutes, then bake in a moderate oven (Gas No. 4, 350°F, 180°C) for 40 minutes. This will keep for a week. Serve in squares. Apricots, peaches and plums can be substituted in season.

Kaese Kuchen (*Cheese Cake*)

$\frac{1}{2}$ the risen dough
Cheese Filling:
$\frac{3}{4}$ lb (300g/$1\frac{1}{2}$ cups) cooking cream cheese
1 egg
2 oz (50g/$\frac{1}{4}$ cup) sugar
Pinch of salt
2 level teasp flour
Grated rind of $\frac{1}{2}$ lemon

Blend all the filling ingredients together until smooth. A few sultanas can also be added.

Grease a round, loose-bottomed 9 in (23 cm) tin, about $2\frac{1}{2}$ in (6 cm) deep. Roll out a circle of the risen dough 1 in ($2\frac{1}{2}$ cm) thick and ease into the tin. Allow to rise for 10 minutes. Spoon the cheese filling on top. Roll some of the dough into strips and make a lattice work to partly cover the filling. Leave to rise for $\frac{1}{2}$ hour, brush with milk or a little beaten egg. Bake in a moderate oven (Gas No. 4, 350°F, 180°C) for 40 minutes.

Streusel Kuchen

$\frac{1}{2}$ the risen dough
1 oz (25g/2 tbsp) melted butter
Streusel:
2 oz (50g/$\frac{1}{4}$ cup) butter
2 oz (50g/$\frac{1}{2}$ cup) flour
5 oz (125g/$\frac{2}{3}$ cup) soft brown sugar
1 level teasp cinnamon

Melt the butter, then stir it into the mixed flour, sugar and cinnamon. Mix to a crumble. Roll out the dough to fit a tin approx 14 × 10 in (35 × 25 cm) which has been lightly greased. Allow the dough to rise for $\frac{1}{2}$ hour, then brush with the melted butter and scatter with the streusel. Leave for a further 10 minutes, then bake in a quick oven (Gas No. 5, 375°F, 190°C) for 25 minutes or until a rich brown. Serve in squares.

Quick Kuchens

Man has been eating some form of cake for almost as long as he has been eating bread. The first cakes were in fact a form of bread, sweetened with honey and highly-flavoured with spices.

Quick kuchens, tea breads and scones are all closely related to these primitive 'cake-breads' but instead of being leavened with yeast they rely on chemical reagents to produce the gases which lighten them. Bakers began to experiment with chemical leavening in the late Middle Ages, but the chemicals which were used (such as pearlash and alum) left a distasteful residue even though they helped to lighten the cakes. It was only with the advent of baking powder and self-raising flour in the middle of the nineteenth century that the baking of economical cakes that did not rely on the leavening power of either yeast or beaten eggs became universally popular.

All the recipes in this section freeze extremely well.

Quick Kuchen

'Quick kuchen' is a generic term that covers a wide range of cakes that can be topped either with sweet crumbles (usually called streusels) or with an assortment of seasonal fruits. The cake mixture itself is an economical one, containing a low ratio of eggs and butter to flour, but a high ratio of baking powder. The resulting cake is light, and when it is freshly baked it can also be served as a dessert. This basic cake mixture can be used for both streusel and fruit kuchens.

8 oz (200g/2 cups) self-raising flour and 1 level teasp baking powder; or 8 oz (200g/2 cups) plain flour, a pinch of salt and 3 level teasp baking powder
3 oz (75g/⅓ cup) soft butter
5 oz (125g/⅔ cup) caster (superfine) sugar
1 egg
¼ pint (125ml/⅔ cup) milk

Put all the ingredients into a bowl and beat by hand or machine until a thick, smooth batter is formed. This will take 2–3 minutes. The mixture is now ready to be used as directed in any of the recipes below.

Streusel Kuchen

Turn the batter into an oiled 9 in (23 cm) loose-bottomed cake tin. Sprinkle with Streusel Topping.

Streusel Topping:
1 oz (25g/¼ cup) flour
1 level teasp ground cinnamon
1 oz (25g/2 tbsp) butter
3 oz (75g/⅓ cup) light brown sugar

Mix the flour, cinnamon and sugar. Melt the butter then pour onto the dry ingredients and blend with a fork until evenly moistened. Sprinkle the crumble over the unbaked kuchen. Bake in a quick oven (Gas No. 5, 375°F, 190°C) for 40 minutes, or until well-risen and golden brown. This kuchen is soft and tender for 3 days after it has been baked. When it begins to stale, it can be sliced and buttered like a tea bread. When really stale it is still delicious toasted and buttered.

Apple Kuchen

The cake layer is spread rather thinly, then topped with sliced baking apples and a streusel.

Make the quick kuchen batter and spoon into a greased tin measuring 12 × 9 × 2 in (30 × 23 × 5 cm) or into two 7 in (18 cm) loose-bottomed sandwich tins. Spread the batter evenly with a palette knife.

2 lb (1kg) baking apples (weight before peeling)

Peel, core and quarter the apples, then cut into slices ⅛ in (½ cm) thick. Arrange the apple slices in over-lapping rows so that the kuchen batter is completely covered. Cover with the streusel.

Streusel Topping:
2 oz (50g/¼ cup) butter
2 oz (50g/½ cup) flour
6 oz (150g/¾ cup) soft brown sugar

Mix the flour and sugar. Pour on the melted butter and mix until crumbly. Scatter evenly over the apples. Bake in a quick moderate oven (Gas No. 5, 375°F, 190°C) for 40 minutes, or until the cake has shrunk from the sides of the tin, the apples feel tender when pierced with a knife, and the streusel is golden brown. This kuchen is at its most delicious 1–2 hours after baking, when it should be cut into squares. But it is still very edible for up to 3 days. Store tightly foil-covered in the refrigerator. Freezes well. Makes about 12 portions.

VARIATION

Peach Kuchen: Peel 6 large peaches (by plunging for 1 minute into boiling water, then skinning). Slice and use to cover the kuchen instead of the apples.

Cherry Kuchen

Morello (sour red) cherries are ideal for this recipe. Their tartness combines with the sweet cream custard to make a sweet-sour topping.

Make the quick kuchen batter and spoon into oiled tin, 12 × 9 × 2 in (30 × 23 × 5 cm) or two 7 in (18 cm) round loose-bottomed sandwich tins. Sprinkle with a thin layer of ground almonds (about 2 oz/50g/½ cup).

Topping:

At least 2 lb (1kg) morello (sour red) cherries (weight before stoning)
2 egg yolks
½ lb (200g/1 cup) sugar
3 fl oz (75ml/⅓ cup) thick cream
Juice from cherries when stoned

Cover surface of the kuchen batter with the stoned cherries. Beat together all the remaining ingredients, then pour over the fruit. Bake at Gas No. 5, 375°F, 190°C, for 40 minutes or until golden brown. Makes 12 portions.

Plum Kuchen

A true Viennese speciality. Use the black freestone plums that usually come from Hungary, Poland or Italy.

Make the quick kuchen batter and spread in an oiled tin, 12 × 9 × 2 in (30 × 23 × 5 cm).

1 oz (25g/2 tbsp) melted butter
2 lb (1kg) plums (weight before stoning)
6 oz (150g/¾ cup) granulated sugar
1 level teasp cinnamon

Brush the batter with the melted butter. Arrange the stoned and halved plums flesh side up all over the surface. Sprinkle with half of the sugar. Bake in a quick moderate oven (Gas No. 5, 375°F, 190°C) for 40 minutes, until well risen. Take out of the oven and sprinkle with the remaining 3 oz (75g/⅓ cup) sugar. Allow to cool in the tins. Serve warm or cold, if possible with thick cream. Makes 12 portions.

Tea Breads

These are very like the first cakes, but baking powder has been substituted for yeast as a leavening agent. They originated in farmhouse kitchens as an economical way of providing something sweet for the farm workers. They are best stored for at least a day before cutting, as they tend to crumble when fresh.

Banana Tea Bread

A moist flavourful loaf, of American origin, which can be served plain, buttered or spread with honey, lemon curd or cream cheese. It will keep moist for a week in an air-tight tin. Store in a cool place or refrigerate because of the fruit content.

8 oz (200g/2 cups) self-raising flour
1 level teasp baking powder
¼ teasp (good pinch) bicarbonate of soda (baking soda)
3 oz (75g/⅓ cup) butter
5 oz (125g/⅔ cup) caster (superfine) sugar
2 eggs
3 large ripe bananas, mashed (1 cup pulp)
2 oz (50g/½ cup) chopped walnuts
2 oz (50g/⅓ cup) chopped glacé (candied) cherries
Grated rind of ½ orange or lemon

Put all the ingredients into a bowl and beat by hand or mixer until smooth and creamy (about 2 minutes). Put into a greased 2 lb (1kg) loaf tin. Bake for 1 hour at Gas No. 4, 350°F, 180°C, until golden brown and firm to the touch. When cold, foil wrap and leave overnight before cutting.

Date and Walnut Loaf

½ lb (200g/2 cups) self-raising flour
6 oz (150g/¾ cup) soft brown sugar
8 oz (200g/1⅓ cups) chopped stoned dates
2 oz (50g/½ cup) chopped walnuts
1 oz (25g/2 tbsp) butter
1 level teasp bicarbonate of soda (baking soda)
1 large egg
8 fl oz (200ml/1 cup) boiling water
½ teasp vanilla essence (extract)

Put dates, sugar and butter into a basin, sprinkle with the bicarbonate of soda, and pour on the boiling water. Leave until steaming stops, then add the beaten egg, vanilla essence, walnuts and flour. Pour into a 2 lb (1kg) loaf tin which has been greased then bottom-lined with greaseproof paper. Bake in a moderate oven (Gas No. 4, 350°F, 180°C) for 1–1¼ hours, depending on the depth of the tin. When done, the loaf will be golden brown and the top will spring back when lightly pressed with a finger. Leave overnight and then slice and butter.

Honey and Spice Loaf

5 oz (125g/½ cup) each (by weight) of honey and demerara (brown) sugar
¼ pint (125ml/⅔ cup) milk
1 large egg
10 oz (250g/2½ cups) plain flour and 1 level teasp baking powder; or 6 oz (150g/1½ cups) plain flour and 4 oz (100g/1 cup) self-raising flour
1 level teasp each of mixed sweet spice, ground cinnamon, ground ginger, bicarbonate of soda (baking soda)
2 oz (50g/¼ cup) butter
2 level teasp dry instant coffee
1 oz (25g/¼ cup) slivered almonds or chopped walnuts

Warm butter until melted, then turn off light, and add honey and brown sugar. Allow to cool, then stir in beaten egg, coffee and milk. Sift together the flour, bicarbonate of soda, baking powder (if used) and spices, then pour on the melted mixture. Beat thoroughly until smooth and glossy. Pour into a 2 lb (1kg) loaf tin which has been greased then bottom-lined with greased greaseproof paper. Smooth level and scatter with the nuts. Bake in a moderate oven (Gas No. 4, 350°F, 180°C) for 50 minutes to 1 hour, or until firm to the touch and slightly shrunken from the sides. Turn out on cooling tray. When cool, foil wrap and put in a tin. Do not cut for 24 hours, then slice and butter.

Mother's Fruit Loaf

½ lb (200g/1½ cups) mixed dried fruit
¼ pint (125ml/⅔ cup) tea
4 oz (100g/½ cup) brown sugar
1 egg
1 rounded tbsp ginger or orange marmalade
½ lb (200g/2 cups) self-raising flour; or ½ lb (200g/2 cups) plain flour and 2 level teasp baking powder

Pour the strained tea over the fruit and sugar, in a large basin. Leave overnight. Next day stir in the beaten egg, the marmalade and sifted flour, and baking powder if used. Mix well. Then spoon into a greased 2 lb (1kg) loaf tin. Bake in a slow, moderate oven (Gas No. 3, 325°F, 170°C) for 1¼ hours, or until firm. Turn out, allow to cool completely, then wrap in foil. Store in air-tight tin. Use after 2–3 days, buttered.

Scones

Scones are what the Americans call 'biscuits'. The word is also used to describe slightly sweetened cakes cooked on a girdle, which the Americans call 'hot cakes'. This produces a certain amount of confusion in the minds of cooks on both sides of the Atlantic! But bake it how you wish, and call it what you may, this kind of mixture always contains very little fat, and a great deal of raising agent. This may be baking powder or (in the Scottish fashion) a mixture of cream of tartar and bicarbonate of soda. The liquid may be water, sweet or sour milk or cream. An unsweetened scone mixture can be moulded into a loaf, or shaped into rolls which relate to yeast breads in the same way that quick kuchens relate to yeast kuchens. Scones and their ilk are not traditional in the Jewish kitchen, but they have been made by many Jewish housewives, particularly in the U.S.A., since the beginning of this century, and they are now extremely popular everywhere. All scones should be served the day they are made, though they can be toasted when stale. They freeze extremely well.

Oven Scones

The best scones—with a light, fluffy texture—are achieved by adding the liquid all at once to the dry ingredients, and mixing swiftly to a springy, non-sticky dough. A very hot oven is essential to activate the large amount of chemical raising agent they contain. It is convenient to double the amounts given and store the remainder in a screw-top jar or plastic container, where it will keep under refrigeration for many weeks. It will then only need liquid to turn it into an instant scone dough.

½ lb (200g/2 cups) self-raising flour and 2 level teasp baking powder; or ½ lb (200g/2 cups) plain flour and 4 level teasp baking powder; or ½ lb (200g/2 cups) plain flour and 1 level teasp bicarbonate of soda (baking soda) and 2 level teasp cream of tartar
1 oz (25g/2 tbsp) sugar
1½ oz (40g/3 tbsp) butter
½ level teasp salt
¼ pint (125ml/⅔ cup) sweet or sour milk

Mix together the dry ingredients, then rub in the fat until the mixture resembles fine crumbs. Make a well in the centre, pour in the liquid, and mix to a soft but non-sticky dough with a round knife, cutting through and through the dry ingredients to moisten them equally. Turn out onto a lightly floured board, knead for 30 seconds or until no cracks remain on the underside. Roll the dough ¾ in (1½ cm) thick. Cut into circles 2 in (5 cm) in diameter and place on greased trays. Brush with milk then sprinkle with granulated sugar. Bake at Gas No. 8, 450°F, 230°C, for 12–15 minutes or until golden brown. When cool, split and butter and serve plain, or with jam and unsweetened whipped cream. Makes 12–15.

VARIATIONS

Sultana (White Raisin) Scones: Add 1 oz (25g/3 tbsp) sultanas (white raisins) or other dried fruit before mixing with the liquid.

Brown Scones: Use 5 oz (125g/1¼ cups) wholemeal flour and 3 oz (75g/¾ cup) white flour instead of the 8 oz (200g/2 cups) white flour.

Cheese Scones

Omit the sugar but add 2 oz (50g/½ cup) finely-grated cheese, 1 level teaspoon salt and a pinch of dry mustard with the dry ingredients. Mix to a dough with an egg beaten with 4 tablespoons cold water. (Save a little of the liquid for brushing the scones.) Roll ½ in (1 cm) thick and cut into 2 in (5 cm) rounds. Brush with the egg mixture and put on greased trays. Bake at Gas No. 7, 425°F, 220°C. for 10–15 minutes. Split and butter when cool. Serve plain or with any savoury spread such as cream cheese, liptauer cheese, cheese and chives, or egg butter. Makes 12–15 whole scones.

Girdle (Griddle) Scones

If a girdle (or griddle as it is sometimes known) is not available, use the base of a heavy frying pan, a solid electric hot plate, or an electric skillet. The girdle was the traditional Scottish utensil for scone and bread making and until recent times it was always part of the equipment of the Scottish soldier. Scones cooked on a girdle are especially soft and tender. Baking powder can be used as in the oven scone mixture, but the traditional Scottish recipe is as follows:

½ lb (200g) plain flour
1 level teasp bicarbonate of soda (baking soda)
2 level teasp cream of tartar
½ level teasp salt
1 oz (25g/2 tbsp) butter
1 oz (25g/2 tbsp) sugar
¼ pint (125ml/⅔ cup) milk

Sift the flour, salt and raising agent into a basin. Rub in the butter and stir in the sugar. Mix to a soft but non-sticky dough with the milk, then knead for 30 seconds or until smooth. Heat the oiled girdle, frying pan or electric skillet until the heat can be felt with the hand held 1 in (2½ cm) above it. Another good test is to drop a teaspoon of cold water onto the hot girdle. When it is the right temperature the water will immediately form tiny droplets and 'skitter' across the surface before evaporating. Divide the dough in two portions, and roll each into a circle ¼ in (½ cm) thick. Divide each circle into 6 triangular segments. Cook on the girdle until golden brown (about 5 minutes) then turn and cook the other side. When cool, split and butter.

Drop Scones (or Scotch Pancakes)

These light and tender hot cakes are at their best served as soon as they are cooked, split and buttered, with honey, jam or golden syrup.

½ lb (200g/2 cups) plain flour
½ level teasp salt
1 level teasp bicarbonate of soda (baking soda)
2 level teasp cream of tartar; or ½ lb (200g/2 cups) self-raising flour and 2 level teasp baking powder
2 teasp golden (corn) syrup
1 level tbsp caster (superfine) sugar
1 egg
6 fl oz (150ml/¾ cup) milk (or enough to produce a very thick batter)

Sift the flour, salt and raising agents into a bowl, add the sugar and syrup. Beat the egg then stir in the milk. Add to the dry ingredients and mix quickly to a thick batter which will just pour from the spoon. Drop the mixture from the point of a tablespoon onto a greased girdle heated until one can feel the heat with the hand held 1 in (2½ cm) above it. When the bubbles on the surface of each scone start to break and the under side is a pale gold, turn it over with a palette knife. As each pancake is cooked, slip it inside a folded tea-towel—the steam will keep the surface soft. Serve buttered.

Potato Cakes

How delicious these are on a winter's night! They can be made with fresh potato (1 *lb*/½*kg when mashed*) *but why bother when they're so much more quickly made—and just as tasty—with a packet of instant mash!*

1 large pkt of Instant Potato (5 oz/125g net weight)
Nut of butter (optional—see below)
1 pint (500ml/2½ cups) water
Approx 6 oz (150g/1½ cups) plain flour
2 level teasp salt

Make up potatoes with water according to packet instructions. Cool for 15 minutes. Turn into bowl, add salt, flour and butter (if none in mix). Mix to a scone-like dough—mixture should leave sides of bowl clean. Divide into four. Roll out each piece ⅜ in (1 cm) thick, cut in 2 in (5 cm) rounds. Cook on hot greased griddle or heavy frying pan for 3–4 minutes on each side until golden brown. Serve at once with butter or fry in butter when cold. Makes 36. May be frozen.

Dairy Dishes

Since the separation of meat and milk foods laid down in the Dietary Laws, Jewish cooking has always put a special emphasis on dairy dishes made from butter, eggs, cream and cheese. The first cheese-making tribes in Asia Minor were idol worshippers whose food products the early Jews were forbidden to eat. So from Bible times, the making of soft cheese from naturally-soured milk became a highly-developed craft in the Jewish household, reaching its highest point in the nineteenth-century kitchens of Russia and Poland.

Today, cheese-making is mainly left to the commercial dairyman, but curd cheese of all kinds, as well as soured cream and milk (smetana) are still widely used in the Jewish kitchen. Indeed, Jewish dairy specialities such as cheese blintzes and cheese cake are now eaten in the general as well as the Jewish community.

Soured Cream

Once upon a time, it was called 'smetana' (a word now reserved only for soured milk) and it was skimmed off the milk curds before they were put to drain for cheese. Today, it's called 'soured (sour) cream' and its use is certainly not limited to Jewish households. Even in the commercial dairies, however, it is still made in much the same way, although to speed up the souring process (particularly with pasteurized cream), the cream is 'injected' with some of the same bacteria that the pasteurization process has destroyed. After it has been homogenized (to prevent separation), the cream is 'set' rather like yoghourt with a lactic acid bacillus. Soured cream will keep for seven days on the middle shelf of the refrigerator, and it can be used in almost any dish for which one would use fresh cream. Apart from its delicious flavour, it has one big advantage: although as thick as whipping cream, it contains less than half the butter-fat content. Although it will not whip by itself, it can be blended with sweet cream to give a very rich flavour and texture. One disadvantage: it separates if heated to boiling point, so it must be added to hot sauces with very great care.

Soft White Cheese (Kaese)

Soft cheeses are generally classified by the amount of butter-fat they contain. There are two main categories: *curd cheese* which is similar to old-fashioned home-made cheese and whose richness depends on the amount of cream that is added, and *cottage cheese* which is a granular cheese made from skim milk, sometimes enriched with added cream.

Home-Made Kaese (Milk Cheese)

This is a useful way to use up sour milk; or to produce a delicious cheese if commercial varieties are not available.

3 pints (1½ litres) milk (Jersey milk will give the richest cheese)
1 tbsp yoghourt can be added to each pint of milk to help the milk to sour

A triangular cheese bag is required; this can be made from an old pillowcase or a thin tea-towel or from a piece of butter muslin. A good size has two sides each 18 in (45 cm) long and the third side 12 in (30 cm) long. Put the milk into a tall jug or pottery crock. If it is ice cold, put it in the oven at the lowest temperature until it feels pleasantly warm. Take out and leave to sour for 48 hours. An ideal spot is on a ledge above a heating radiator, or in an airing cupboard. After 48 hours, the cream will have thickened and soured and the milk below will have set to a junket-like clot. Carefully skim off the cream and refrigerate until required. Put the soured milk, still in its container, to heat very gently so that the thin whey will rise to the top. This can be done either in the oven, set at its lowest heat, or on top of the stove, with the container of milk standing on an asbestos mat or wire trivet. Do not overheat or the curds will become toughened. As soon as the whey has separated from the curds (after about 15–30 minutes), remove the milk from the heat. Pour the curds and whey into the bag, and tie it up with string. Hang it up where it can drip freely (an outside clothes line is ideal). Allow to drip for 12 hours or until no whey can be seen dripping from the bag. Turn out the cheese into a bowl. It is now ready to use in a cheese cake.

For table use: Stir in the soured cream which has been skimmed off, and season to taste with salt and a pinch of sugar. Spoon back into the cheese bag, tie into an oval shape, cover with foil and then a weight. Leave for an hour, then carefully turn out onto a platter. If preferred, serve the cream separately and simply turn the cheese into a pottery bowl. Makes 14–16 oz (350–480g) cheese (including soured cream).

Various Omelettes

The traditional Jewish omelette or 'pfannkuchen' is more akin to the Spanish 'frittata' than the French rolled variety, and used to be a favourite for Sunday supper, served with fresh black bread and butter. Sephardi Jews make delicious oven-baked omelettes, whilst in America the 'omelette soufflé' with cream cheese and chives is served in many households. The recipes that follow are capable of infinite variety, but with each one I have given a different method of making omelettes to perfection.

French Omelette with Mushroom Filling

The French omelette is a very 'private' dish, best served to no more than two people at once, as bigger omelettes can be tough. However, for larger numbers, it is possible to double up on the filling, and then make a series of small omelettes to serve hot off the pan.

The pan is of vital importance; it should be thick-based, with rounded sides (to make rolling easier), but the material is not of supreme importance, as I have made excellent omelettes in aluminium, enamelled steel and iron pans.

Cooking secrets are few
To blend the yolks and the whites, beat the eggs with a large fork or small balloon whisk—a rotary whisk makes them too bubbly and spoils the cooked texture. Add this mixture to the butter when it is just changing colour from yellow to fawn; and *don't* turn the omelette—if the pan is the right size for the number of eggs, the top surface will be creamily set by the bottom heat alone.

3–4 eggs, seasoned with a pinch of salt and pepper
1 teasp cold water
Large nut of butter (½ oz/1 tbsp)
Mushroom filling:
4 oz (100g/1½ cups) mushrooms
1 oz (25g/2 tbsp) butter
4 tbsp top of milk or (preferably) single (light) cream
2 level teasp flour
2 teasp brandy (optional)
Pinch of salt and few grinds black pepper
Pinch of ground mace or nutmeg

First cook the mushrooms. Cut off $\frac{1}{4}$ in ($\frac{1}{2}$ cm) from the tip of each stalk and discard. Do not peel the mushrooms, but put into a sieve and rinse quickly under the cold tap. Slice each mushroom into 4 right through the stalk. Melt the butter in a small saucepan. Add the sliced mushrooms and toss to coat them in the butter. Leave to cook gently for 5 minutes, then stir in the flour (to take up any free butter), and add the cream and the seasonings. Bring to simmering point then leave on a very low heat.

Now make the omelette. Put an oval serving dish to heat. Get out a 7 in (18 cm) omelette pan—that is, a frying pan with rounded sides—and put it on the cooker. Break the eggs into a mixing bowl, add the water, salt and pepper, and beat with a fork until the yolks and whites are just blended. (The mixture should not be too frothy.) Turn the heat on under the empty pan and heat for 2 minutes. Have ready a fork and a flexible spatula. Put in the nut of butter, and the minute it turns from yellow to pale fawn, pour in the beaten eggs. Immediately start to tilt the pan with one hand, whilst you push the cooked egg towards the centre with the fork held in the other, so that the uncooked egg can flow to the side. When the top of the omelette is set but still creamy stir the brandy (if used) into the mushroom mixture and spoon it on to one side of the omelette. Fold the omelette over and push another tiny nut of butter underneath it to glaze it. After another 15 seconds, turn the omelette over on to the serving plate. Rush to the table and eat at once!

Serve with brown bread and butter, and fresh watercress. Serves 2.

VARIATIONS

Do not make a filling; instead add any of the following to the beaten eggs: 1 tablespoon mixed herbs (any combination of chives, parsley, tarragon and chervil); or 2 tablespoons grated cheese; or 2 tablespoons tiny bread or cooked potato cubes, fried until crisp in butter.

When the top of the omelette is creamily set, roll up in the pan, slip a nut of butter underneath and glaze for 15 seconds, then serve at once. Serves 2.

Aubergine (Eggplant) Omelette

A delicious flat omelette, served from the pan in which it is cooked. Use a fresh aubergine weighing about $\frac{1}{2}$–$\frac{3}{4}$ lb (200–300g) or a can of aubergines in their own juices which do not require any preparation.

1 medium aubergine (eggplant), cut in $\frac{1}{2}$ in (1 cm) dice
2 tomatoes, peeled and diced
$\frac{1}{2}$ clove garlic, crushed
1 level tbsp chopped parsley
$\frac{1}{2}$ teasp dried oregano
6 eggs
2 tbsp oil
1 tbsp butter

Sprinkle aubergine with coarse salt, weight and cover and leave for half an hour. Rinse well, and dry thoroughly. Heat the oil and butter in an 8 in (20 cm) omelette pan, sauté aubergine gently for 15 minutes until tender, then add the tomatoes. Cook until juice disappears, then season with garlic and herbs. Pour on beaten eggs, stir well then cook until set and golden brown underneath. Put briefly under the grill, then serve from the dish. Serves 3–4.

Omelette Basquaise

2 oz (50g/$\frac{1}{4}$ cup) butter
2 teasp oil
1 small onion, chopped
1 green pepper, diced
3 canned or skinned fresh tomatoes
2 mushrooms, sliced
1 teasp each of oregano and chopped parsley
1 small clove garlic, crushed
Salt and black pepper
2 oz (50g/$\frac{1}{2}$ cup) grated cheese

Melt the butter in an 8 in (20 cm) omelette pan, then add the onions. Sauté gently for 5 minutes, then add the peppers, mushrooms, tomatoes, garlic and seasonings. Cover and cook for 10 minutes until soft. Then pour on the eggs and proceed as for aubergine omelette. Just before putting under the grill, sprinkle with the grated cheese. Serves 3–4.

Baked Omelette in the Sephardi Fashion

This omelette can be served either hot or cold, when it makes an unusual cocktail titbit. Great for dieters!

3 eggs
4 tbsp creamy milk
1 small pkt frozen leaf spinach (approx 4 oz/100g)
1 small onion, chopped
1 oz (25g/2 tbsp) butter
¼ lb (100g/1 cup) mushrooms, sliced
6 oz (150g/1½ cups) grated cheese
1 level tbsp chopped parsley or scissored chives
Salt and black pepper

Sauté the onion in the butter until soft and golden. Add the sliced mushrooms and cook until the butter is absorbed (about 2 or 3 minutes). Beat the eggs until blended, then add the milk, herbs, seasonings, defrosted spinach, onions, mushrooms and cheese. Butter a 9 in (23 cm) diameter oven-proof casserole (about 2 in/5 cm deep) or use a tin of similar depth, measuring about 10 × 7 in (25 × 18 cm). Pour in the mixture, and bake in a quick moderate oven (Gas No. 5, 375°F, 190°C) for 30 minutes until set and golden. Serve in sections when hot, or cut in squares and spear on cocktail sticks to serve cold.

Cheese and Chive Omelette Soufflé

A satisfying omelette which is exceptionally low in calories; for 2 servings, halve the quantities and fry in a 7 in (18 cm) pan.

6 eggs, separated
½ lb (200g/1 cup) cream or cottage cheese
1 tbsp chopped chives or 2 teasp finely-chopped spring onions (scallions)
1 oz (25g/2 tbsp) butter
Salt and black pepper
Pinch of cayenne pepper and mustard

Have ready an 8 in (20 cm) frying pan. Beat the yolks into the cheese then stir in the seasonings and beat until the mixture is thick and smooth. Beat the whites until they hold stiff but still glossy peaks. Pour the yolk mixture onto the whites and cut and fold until evenly blended. Put the butter into the frying pan, and heat until it stops foaming. Pour in the omelette mixture, smooth it level and then cook very gently for 5–6 minutes, until it has puffed on top and the underside is brown when a corner of the omelette is lifted from the pan. Transfer to the oven and grill, very gently, for a further 3 or 4 minutes, until well risen and golden. Serve at once, cut in sections. Serves 4–5.

For **Wurst Pfannkuchen,** see p. 74.

Scrambled to Perfection

A perfect dish of scrambled eggs is set yet still creamy with a good liaison between the butter and the eggs.

Scrambled Eggs

6–8 eggs
3 tbsp top milk or cream
1 level teasp salt
10 grinds black pepper
1 oz (25g/2 tbsp) butter
Optional extras: 1 oz/25g/2 tbsp butter or 2 tbsp double (heavy) cream

Blend the eggs with the top milk or cream and the salt and pepper by beating them for about 30 seconds using a large fork or rotary whisk. Put the butter into a pan approximately 7 in (18 cm) in diameter. Melt the butter over a low heat then add the egg mixture, and start stirring with a spoon. At first nothing will happen—but don't be tempted to turn up the heat. After 2 minutes, the eggs will begin to thicken. Keep on stirring all round the sides and the bottom, lifting the pan off the heat if the mixture seems to be cooking too quickly. When the mixture looks soft and creamily set, it's ready. Now's the time to drop in either the extra ounce (25g/2 tbsp) of butter or the double cream. This immediately stops any further cooking, and helps to achieve the creamy, rich texture that's so delectable. Serve on a hot plate with really fresh, buttered black bread, or on buttered brown toast. Serves 4–5.

VARIATIONS

Chive Scramble: Add 1 tablespoonful scissored chives to the beaten eggs.

Cheese Scramble: Add 4 tablespoons grated sharp cheese to the eggs just before serving; the heat of the mixture will be sufficient to melt the cheese.

Mushroom Scramble: Nicest are the tiny canned 'champignons de Paris', cooked in a nut of butter for 2 minutes, then stirred into the scrambled eggs before serving. Or:
Sauté 2 oz (50g/½ cup) thinly-sliced fresh button mushrooms in the cooking butter. After 3 minutes, add the egg and proceed to cook the scrambled eggs as described in the recipe.

Cottage Cheese Scramble: As soon as the egg mixture begins to thicken, stir in ¼ lb (100g/½ cup) cottage cheese (about 8 tablespoons) and 1 tablespoon snipped chives (if available) and continue to cook until the mixture is the consistency of half-whipped cream. Add no further butter or cream.

Luxury Scrambled Egg (with Smoked Salmon): Blend the eggs with 10 drops Tabasco sauce or a pinch of cayenne pepper. In the ounce of butter, gently sauté 2 tablespoons finely-chopped onion and 1 small green pepper, seeded and diced. When these vegetables have softened (after about 5 minutes), add 4 oz (100g) shredded smoked salmon with the beaten egg mixture and proceed as in the recipe.

Baked Eggs

The French have perfected this method of cooking eggs to the extent of inventing special dishes or 'ramekins'. But there are more homely methods that are just as tasty for family occasions.

Oeufs en Cocotte

For each serving:
1–2 eggs
A nut of butter
2 tbsp thick cream or white sauce
Salt and pepper

The cooking dishes should be about 2½ in (6 cm) in diameter and about 1½ in (3½ cm) deep, of glass, earthenware or heatproof porcelain.

Half fill a rectangular tin (large enough to hold all the ramekins) with boiling water, and put it on a low heat on top of the stove. Use half the butter to grease the dishes and pour in half the cream. Put the dishes in the water and when the cream looks hot (after 2 minutes), add the whole eggs, season with salt and pepper, then cover with the remaining cream and dot with the butter. Transfer the tin and the dishes to the oven. Bake at Gas No. 5, 375°F, 190°C, for 10 minutes, when the eggs will be set, but shiver slightly when the dish is moved. The eggs can be kept hot out of the oven (but still in the water bath) for up to 15 minutes.

VARIATIONS

With herbs with cheese: First make the sauce—into a thick-bottomed pan put 1 tbsp sour cream, 4 oz (100g/1 cup) grated cheese, 1 tbsp sherry and 2 level tbsp of a mixture of as many of the following chopped fresh herbs as are available: parsley, thyme, sage, tarragon, chives, chervil. Stir over gentle heat until smooth and pale green, then season with a pinch of salt and black pepper. Use in place of cream. This mixture stores for weeks in the refrigerator.

With mixed herbs: Add 2 level tablespoons chopped mixed fresh herbs to the cream before use.

Baked Eggs with Sweet Corn and Tuna or Salmon Sauce

6 eggs
8 oz (200g) can tuna or salmon, flaked
½ lb (200g) can whole kernel corn
½ pint (250ml/1¼ cups) milk
1 oz (25g/2 tbsp) butter
1 oz (25g/¼ cup) flour
1 level teasp dry mustard
Pinch salt and white pepper
4 tbsp sweet or sour cream
4 oz (100g/1 cup) grated cheese

First make the sauce: heat the milk until it steams, then pour into a jug. Rinse out the pan, melt the butter then add the flour. Simmer for 2 minutes, then add the hot milk and use a whisk to beat to a smooth sauce. Simmer for 2 minutes then add the seasonings and the cream, followed by 3 oz (75g/$\frac{3}{4}$ cup) of the cheese. Turn off the heat and stir until the cheese dissolves.

Butter a shallow casserole wide enough to hold the eggs in one layer. In a basin combine the flaked fish and the drained corn with half the sauce. Spread on the bottom of the dish then break the eggs on top. Spoon the remaining sauce on top to completely cover the eggs. Bake at Gas No. 5, 375°F, 190°C, for 10 minutes. Immediately sprinkle the top with the remaining grated cheese and place under a hot grill, until golden brown. Serves 4–5.

VARIATION

Eggs in Cheese Sauce: Use the cheese sauce to spoon over halved hard-boiled eggs, allowing 1$\frac{1}{2}$ eggs per serving. Sprinkle with cheese and put under a hot grill until bubbly.

Swiss Eggs

The layer of cheese at the bottom of the dish insulates the eggs from the oven heat, so that they can cook evenly without a water bath. Eggs can be cooked in individual ramekins in the same way. Rub the cooking dish with a cut clove of garlic speared on a fork, before buttering it.

2 oz (50g/$\frac{1}{4}$ cup) butter
5 fl oz (125ml/$\frac{2}{3}$ cup) single (light) cream
Several slices of cheese
8 eggs
2 oz (50g/$\frac{1}{2}$ cup) finely-grated cheese
Nutmeg
Salt, pepper

Spread the butter thickly over the bottom of a wide, shallow, ovenproof dish, then cover it completely with the thin slices of cheese. Onto this carefully break the eggs and sprinkle with seasoning. Over the eggs pour the cream and sprinkle all over with finely-grated cheese. Bake in a quick oven (Gas No. 5, 375°F, 190°C) for 10 minutes. Then pass under a red-hot grill to brown the topping without toughening the eggs. Serves 4–5.

Cheese, Please

Here are three variations on the rarebit (rabbit) theme which owe everything to Lancashire and Wales and nothing to traditional Jewish food. They're delicious!

The Classic Rarebit (Rabbit)

1 oz (25g/2 tbsp) butter
6 oz (150g/1$\frac{1}{2}$ cups) sharp cheese, grated
2 tbsp beer (or milk if not available)
Good pinch of salt and black pepper
1 teasp prepared mustard
$\frac{1}{2}$ teasp Worcestershire sauce
2 level teasp cornflour (cornstarch)

Melt the butter and stir in the cheese, seasonings, and the beer, mixed with the cornflour. Cook slowly till smooth and allow to bubble for one minute. Leave for 5 minutes to thicken slightly. Spread on 4 large or 5 medium slices of buttered toast. Grill gently until golden brown.

VARIATION

Buck Rarebit (Rabbit): Top each slice of rarebit with a poached egg. Serves 4.

Cheese Toast Topping

A useful mixture to make up in quantity and keep under refrigeration.

4 oz (100g/1 cup) strong cheese
1 level teasp prepared mustard
1 oz (25g/2 tbsp) butter
2 level teasp horseradish sauce or fresh grated horseradish
Salt and pepper

Cream the butter with the cheese then beat in all the other ingredients. Use as a spread for buttered toast, spreading on mixture and then grilling until golden. Delicious topped with a poached egg.

Hot Cheese Spread

A more savoury version to go in between rather than on top of slices of bread. It can, however, be treated as a rarebit (rabbit) and spread on toast fingers then grilled.

4 oz (100g/1 cup) sharp cheese, grated
2 level teasp chopped onion
2 level teasp sugar
1 tbsp vinegar
Pinch of salt
Nut of butter and 2 teasp flour
4 tbsp evaporated milk or single (light) cream

Melt the nut of butter, add onion and cook gently for 2 minutes, then stir in the sugar, flour, vinegar and milk. Whisk over gentle heat until thickened. Turn off the heat, add the cheese and stir until melted. Cool. Enough for 8 rounds of bread.

To use as toasted sandwiches: Use 8 rounds of bread to make 4 sandwiches, spreading the bottom with a quarter of the cheese mixture and spreading the top round with a little made mustard. Press the two rounds of bread together, then spread thinly but evenly on both sides with soft butter. Heat a heavy frying pan for 3 minutes then put in the sandwiches. Cook slowly but steadily for 5 minutes until bottom is golden, then turn and cook second side. Cut each sandwich into 4 triangles, and arrange on a platter with pickled onions and cucumbers as garnish. Serves 4–6 as a snack.

Jams

Pointers to Success

The quantity to make: For the occasional jam-maker it is better to make only small batches at one time. The process is less lengthy and it seems easier to make successful jam. Indeed, if you grow your own fruit, it is better to jam it as it ripens, pound by pound, when it is in the optimum condition.

The Equipment

1. *A preserving pan* of cast aluminium, or stainless steel, wide-based and heavy, or a pressure cooker of similar dimensions (copper pans destroy the vitamin C). Too small a pan is useless even for small quantities as the sugar and fruit mixture may froth up to three times its own height, and will boil over. The pan should only be a third full when the sugar and fruit are in it.
2. *A large wooden spoon.*
3. *A soup ladle*, approx 3 in (8 cm) in diameter, to make it easy to spoon the hot jam into jars.
4. *A wooden board* on which to set the warm jars to be filled, to prevent any possibility of cracking.
5. *Jam pot covers* of cellophane or foil with inner covers of waxed papers, and labels.
6. *A sugar thermometer* (optional but useful): If the fruit is in the right condition and the proportions of the recipe are correct, the jam will set at exactly 220°F, 104°C. The use of the thermometer will therefore cut out all the guesswork from the most uncertain part of making jam—testing for the set.
7. *Jars:* At the beginning of the jam-making season (usually the end of June when raspberries, strawberries, loganberries, gooseberries, red and blackcurrants start to ripen), sort out your stock of empty jars. Put them all to soak in very hot detergent. When the water is hand-hot, rinse the jars thoroughly in clear hot water, and leave them to drain and dry, then store them in a dust-free cupboard. When it is time to make the jam, put the required number of jars into a cool oven (Gas No. 1, 275°F, 140°C) and leave them to warm through while the jam is boiling. By the time the jam is ready, the jars will be well heated, and the boiling jam can be poured into them without any danger of cracking the glass.

The ingredients

The fruit: Whether it is from the garden or the greengrocer, the fruit should be slightly underripe (rather than overripe), for its pectin and acid content—both vital to the successful setting of the jam—will then be at their optimum.

The sugar: Preserving sugar is specially prepared for making jam. It is made up of large white crystals, which prevent the sugar settling in a dense layer on the bottom of the pan as is the case with ordinary granulated sugar. This sugar also produces very little froth, so that it is unnecessary to skim the jam (which is rather wasteful) or to butter the pan. If preserving sugar is not available, granulated sugar can be successfully substituted but care must be taken to prevent the jam from burning or from frothing over.

Testing for a set: With any of the recipes that follow you can be sure the jam has set when the temperature on a sugar thermometer reaches 220°F, 104°C. There are two rule of thumb methods—the saucer test and the flake test.

1. *The saucer test:* Before starting to make the jam, put three little saucers into the ice-making compartment of the refrigerator or into the freezer to chill thoroughly. When the correct cooking time has elapsed, take out one saucer and put a teaspoonful of jam on it. Return it to the cold for 2 or 3 minutes, and meanwhile take the pan of bubbling jam off the heat. To test for a set, push the chilled jam back with the finger; if the jam is set, the surface will form a thin skin and wrinkle slightly. If not, continue to boil and test on another saucer.
2. *The flake test:* Catch a little jam in the bowl of the wooden spoon, lift it above the pan, and allow it to cool for a minute. Turn the spoon so that the jam drops from the edge of the spoon. If the jam has reached the setting point, the drops of jam will run together to form a flake which breaks off cleanly and sharply from the spoon. Jam that needs further boiling will run off in a liquid stream.

Blackcurrant Jam

If you don't grow your own fruit, you can still make the jam with bought blackcurrants, making sure you choose fruit which is plump and glossy, never shrivelled or dusty-looking. You may find the skins are tougher than with garden fruit (as the fruit is bound to be slightly less fresh), so it will be necessary to simmer the currants longer. This initial simmering is most important, for once the sugar has been added the fruit will not soften however long it is cooked, and tough fruit will produce a tough jam. This quantity will do nicely in a large, thick saucepan or pressure cooker.

2 lb (1kg/4 cups) blackcurrants
1½ pints (750ml/4 cups) water
3 lb (1½kg/7 cups) granulated or preserving sugar

Remove all stalks and wash the fruit. Put into the pan with the water and simmer gently, uncovered, for 30 minutes, or until the liquid has reduced by a quarter, and a berry, when rubbed between the fingers, is absolutely soft. Have the sugar warming in a bowl, together with jam jars, in a low oven. Tip the sugar onto the fruit, and stir with a wooden spoon until it is boiling vigorously, then allow it to bubble without stirring. After 2 minutes, start testing. (See 'Testing for a set'.) If the jam has not set, boil another minute and re-test. (As blackcurrant jam sets easily, I usually keep testing it with a wooden spoon, and when I think it is set, then put a little in the saucer for confirmation.) Stand the warm jars on a wooden board and using a soup ladle, spoon in the jam to the top of the jars. Immediately put a wax disc on each. Allow to go cold before covering with cellophane or foil. Makes 5 lb (2½kg).

Spiced Cherry Jam

I make this with home-grown morello (sour red) cherries and it is quite superb; occasionally you can buy morello (sour red) or other tart cherries; but do not use a sweet variety as the flavour will be insipid.

2 lb (1kg/4 cups) morello (sour red) or other tart red cherries
Juice of 1 large lemon (3 tbsp)
3¾ lb (1kg 875g/7½ cups) granulated sugar
½ level teasp ground cinnamon
½ level teasp mixed spice
½ bottle liquid pectin (4 fl oz/100ml/½ cup)

Wash jam jars thoroughly, then put in low oven (Gas No. 1, 275°F, 140°C) to dry and warm whilst making jam. Half fill blender with stoned cherries and blend for a few seconds; or chop cherries by hand. In preserving pan, put the cherries (and any juice which comes out when they are stoned), lemon juice, sugar and spice and heat until the sugar is dissolved, stirring all the time. Bring to a full rolling boil, then boil for one minute, stirring constantly. Add the half-bottle of pectin off the heat. Continue to stir for 5 minutes to distribute fruit and skim if necessary. Pour into hot jars and cover with waxed discs. Cover with cellophane or foil when cold. Makes 4½ lb (about 2kg).

Raspberry or Loganberry Jam

This recipe is ideal for jamming each day's crop as it ripens in the garden. If you are making a larger quantity, to save time, heat the sugar in a bowl in the oven whilst the fruit is simmering; but for a small quantity, this is not necessary. The short cooking time gives this jam a marvellous fresh-fruit flavour. If the fruit is not freshly picked, simmer it until it is tender, then add the sugar. After the fruit and sugar have come back to the boil, it will probably take 3 minutes to reach setting point.

1 lb (½kg/2 cups) sugar
1 lb (½kg/2 cups) freshly picked fruit (raspberries, loganberries or a mixture of the two)

Put the fruit in a heavy pan, and mash it with a potato-masher or large fork, to extract some of the juice. Bring to the boil, then tip in the sugar, and stir until it has dissolved. Bring back to a fierce boil (that is, one that cannot be 'stirred out' with the wooden spoon). *Immediately* take the pan off the heat. Ladle the jam into warm jars and cover at once with wax discs. Cover with cellophane tops or foil when cold. Makes almost 2 lb (1kg).

Economical Raspberry Jam

This uses commercial pectin to 'extend' the jam—particularly useful if the fruit has to be purchased. It makes an excellent jam.

4 lb (2kg/8 cups) raspberries
5½ lb (2¾kg/12½ cups) sugar
1 bottle liquid pectin (200ml/1 cup)

Crush the berries. Add the sugar and heat slowly until dissolved, stirring continually. Bring to a full rolling boil quickly. Boil hard for 2 minutes. Remove from heat and stir in the pectin, pot quickly and cover in the usual way. Makes 10 lb (5kg). *Note:* When making half the quantity, 1 minute boiling of the fruit and sugar is enough.

Whole Fruit Garden Strawberry Jam

Strawberries have little pectin or acid, and therefore do not set as easily as raspberries. This recipe is only suitable for garden strawberries which do not need to be washed; instead wipe them with a damp paper towel if at all sandy. (Excess water on the fruit will stop the jam from setting until the fruit has overcooked.)

3½ lb (1¾kg/7 cups) hulled small strawberries
3½ lb (1¾kg/8 cups) sugar
1 level teasp citric acid crystals; or 3 tbsp fresh lemon juice

Put the wiped fruit in alternate layers with the sugar in a large bowl and leave overnight. Next day when the sugar has dissolved in the natural juices from the fruit, add the citric acid or lemon juice, put into the preserving pan and heat gently with constant stirring until the sugar is completely dissolved. Bring to the boil as quickly as possible, then boil without stirring until the setting point is reached; test either with the thermometer (220°F, 104°C) or by the saucer or flake test. Skim the jam, removing any froth that might spoil the clear appearance. Leave the jam in the pan until the surface begins to set and a film appears (this will prevent the fruit sinking to the bottom of the jar). Pot and cover with wax discs, and leave until quite cold before covering with cellophane or foil and labelling. Makes 5 lb (2½kg).

For 10 lb (5kg) jam, use 7 lb (3½kg) whole strawberries; 7 lb (3½kg/16 cups) sugar; juice of 2 large lemons or 2 level teaspoons citric acid crystals.

Whole Fruit Strawberry Jam with Liquid Pectin

This is an ideal recipe if the strawberries have been bought and need to be washed. The jam has a delicious fresh flavour and colour with the whole fruit in a lightly-set jelly.

2¼ lb (2kg 100g/4½ cups) small strawberries
3 tbsp lemon juice (1 large lemon)
½ bottle liquid pectin (100ml/½ cup)
3 lb (1½kg/7 cups) sugar

Hull the fruit and wash quickly. Put in a pan with the lemon juice and sugar. Stand for 1 hour, stirring occasionally. Place over low heat, stirring occasionally. When sugar has dissolved, add a small knob of butter to reduce foaming. Bring to a full rolling boil, and boil rapidly for 4 minutes, stirring from time to time. Remove from the heat, add the pectin and stir very well. Cool for at least 20 minutes, or until a skin begins to form on top. Pot and cover. Makes 5 lb (2½kg) jam.

Uncooked Strawberry Jam

This has the freshest flavour of all. It will keep in the refrigerator for 3 months, and almost indefinitely in the freezer. It cannot be stored in a cupboard as it has not been boiled at all, and will quickly go mouldy at room temperature.

3 lb (1½kg/5 cups) finely mashed ripe strawberries
4 lb (2kg/9 cups) caster (superfine) sugar
1 bottle liquid pectin (200ml/1 cup)

Mix the fruit with the sugar. Let stand for 1 hour stirring occasionally. Add this mixture to the liquid pectin. Stir a further 2 minutes. Pour into dry jars. Cover with foil and leave in the kitchen for 48 hours or until set. Store in the refrigerator for use during the next 2–3 months, in the freezer for wintertime. Makes 7 lb (3½kg) jam.

Etceteras

Mincemeat

This is a flavourful mixture quickly made and always available for making into Brandied Mincemeat Slices (recipe on p. 155), as a filling for baked apples, or little tarts.

8 oz (200g/1½ cups) currants
8 oz (200g/1½ cups) stoned raisins
4 oz (100g/¾ cup) sultanas (white raisins)
2 oz (50g/⅓ cup) chopped candied peel
4 oz (100g/1 cup) coarsely-chopped walnuts (optional)
1 lb (500g) cooking apples
8 oz (200g/1 cup) white vegetable fat or vegetarian suet
1 level teasp ground cinnamon
1 level teasp mixed sweet spice
¼ level teasp ground nutmeg
8 oz (200g/1 cup) soft brown sugar
Grated zest (shiny skin without the pith) of a large lemon and orange
2 tbsp lemon juice
3 fl oz (75ml/⅓ cup) rum or brandy
3 fl oz (75ml/⅓ cup) port wine or sweet sherry

Clean and wash the dried fruit in boiling water, then dry thoroughly by leaving in a thin layer in a very cool oven. Skin and core the apples. Coarsely chop the raisins, sultanas, apples and nuts, mix with currants, candied peel, spices, sugar and fruit zest. If vegetarian suet is used, stir that in as well. If white fat is used, heat until liquid and stir well with the other ingredients. Add the juice, spirits and wine or sherry. Put the mixture into clean, dry jam jars, leaving an inch at the top. Cover tightly with cellophane or foil. Store in a cool place. Before using, stir well. The mincemeat is very digestible and will keep for 6 months. Makes 3½–4 lb (1¾–2kg).

Cumberland Rum Butter

There is no vestige of Jewish influence in this recipe; it was given to me by a friend from Cumberland, and I can only say it's absolutely delicious spread on hot toast or scones, or with a steamed Chanucah pudding.

½ lb (200g/1 cup) butter
½ teasp nutmeg
¾ lb (300g/1½ cups) caster (superfine) sugar
½ teasp cinnamon
1 wineglass (3 fl oz/75ml/⅓ cup) rum

Warm butter until of a thick pouring consistency (not hot). Pour gradually on to caster sugar which has been mixed with the spices. Beat thoroughly until smooth and free from sugar crystals. Add a glass of rum and beat well again. Pour into little glass dishes. When set, dredge with caster sugar. Serve with hot toast or scones, or with steamed fruit puddings. Keeps at least a month in the larder, longer when refrigerated.

International Jewish Dishes

Whilst all Jewish women prepare their family's food according to one common set of dietary laws, the flavour of the food—and the cooking processes they use—naturally reflect the culinary customs of the community in which they live. Thus roast beef and Yorkshire pudding have been made their own by many Anglo-Jewish families; apple pie is now almost as traditionally Jewish as American; whilst in Israel, 'Falafel ve Tahina', the Coptic Christian delicacy of chick peas and sesame seed purée is almost a national dish.

As Jewish communities have moved on, and their children married into families from differing cultural backgrounds, the national origins of many Jewish dishes have been obscured. But it is still possible to talk about 'Rumanische' cookery, or 'Litvak' cookery, to denote a very specialized Jewish cuisine, whilst the Sephardi Jews still cook much as their Middle Eastern—and indeed Spanish—forebears have done for 500 years.

I have chosen these dishes to represent differing national flavours within the Jewish cuisine. They have been adopted—and adapted—by Jewish cooks, either because they are especially delicious, or because they fit in particularly well with the Dietary Laws, or because they express the symbolism of a particular festival. The entire book is, in a sense, a collection of international dishes, but the ones I have included in this chapter retain most strongly the national culinary characteristics of their country of origin.

Austro-Hungary

Zwetschen Plum Tart

The zwetschen plum, black, sweet and freestone, grows all over that part of Europe which once comprised the Austro-Hungarian Empire. Here were developed some of the finest dishes of the Western European cuisine. These plums are sometimes made into a conserve, sometimes used as a topping for a yeast kuchen. In this delicious recipe, they are used as the filling for a one-crust tart made with 'muerberteig', the sweet, cakey shortcrust common to German and Austrian cooking.

Pastry:

6 oz (150g/1½ cups) plain flour
3 oz (75g/⅓ cup) caster (superfine) sugar
3 oz (75g/⅓ cup) butter or margarine
1 teasp lemon juice
1 egg yolk
Ice water if needed

Mix the sugar and flour, then rub in the butter, and mix to a dough with the egg yolk, lemon juice and ice water (if required). Form the dough into a ball, foil-wrap and chill. Roll out to fit a 9 in (23 cm) shallow pie plate or sandwich tin, and flute the edges with the fingers.

Filling:
1½ lb (700g) zwetschen plums
4 oz (100g/½ cup) caster (superfine) sugar
2 teasp lemon juice
1 oz (25g/2 tbsp) butter or margarine
1 level teasp cinnamon

Halve and stone the washed plums, then arrange, cut side up, in a series of concentric circles all over the pastry. Mix together the caster sugar and the cinnamon, then sprinkle half of it in an even layer over the fruit. Pour over the lemon juice and dot with the fat. Bake in a moderate oven (Gas No. 4, 350°F, 180°C) or until the pastry is a golden brown. Take from the oven and sprinkle with the remaining sugar. Serve warm or cold. Serves 6.

Gefüllte Paprika

You may be offered a dish of stuffed vegetables in any Jewish household eastwards from Austria, for when kosher meat was scarce, particularly during the Middle Ages, it was often 'stretched' by mixing it with a 'filler' of rice or meal and stuffing it into a readily-available local vegetable. This recipe is a more sophisticated version than usual, reflecting the 'cuisine soignée' typical of this part of Europe.

The sauce:
1 medium onion
2 tbsp oil
5 oz (125g) can tomato purée and 2 cans water
4 level tbsp demerara (brown) sugar
2 tbsp lemon juice
½ teasp mixed spice (if available)
¼ pint (125ml/⅔ cup) white wine (optional but nice)

If peppers are to be stewed on top of the stove, use same pan to make sauce. Chop the onion finely then sauté in the oil until soft and golden. Add all the remaining ingredients. Simmer uncovered for 20 minutes.

Peppers and stuffing:
4–6 medium green peppers
1 lb (½kg) lean minced (ground) beef
1 onion, grated
1 egg
1 level teasp salt
½ teasp mustard
Pinch of pepper

Slice the tops off the peppers and remove the seeds and ribs. Put into a pan and pour over boiling water. Leave for 5 minutes. Beat the egg, grate the onion, add salt, mustard and pepper. Then mix in the meat. Drain the peppers, and stuff with the meat mixture. Put into a pan where the sauce is simmering. Cover with foil, and then with the lid of the pan. Simmer gently for one hour, basting twice. When done, the sauce will be thick and the peppers tender. To cook in the oven, simmer at Gas No. 3, 325°F, 170°C, for 1½ hours. Serves 4–6.

Germany

Cold Fruit Soup

German Jews who summered, before World War II, in cottages on the shores of the Baltic, made marvellous cold soups from the fruits of high summer—a custom which has now been naturalized in Israel. The choice of fruits depends on the season, but this combination of the sweet and the tart is particularly refreshing.

½ lb (200g/1 cup) stoned plums
½ lb (200g/1 cup) morello (sour red) or other tart cherries
½ lb (200g) sliced peaches
2½ pints (1½ litres/6¼ cups) water
3 oz (75g/⅓ cup) sugar
A pinch of salt
Small stick of cinnamon or 1 level teasp ground cinnamon
2 tbsp cornflour (cornstarch)
5 fl oz (125ml/⅔ cup) soured cream

In a soup pan, put the stoned and sliced fruit, the water, seasonings, and sugar. Simmer, covered, for 15–20 minutes, or until the fruit is tender, then force through a fine sieve or blend until smooth. Mix the cornflour with a little water (or better still, sweet red wine), stir into the soup, and simmer for 10 minutes until thickened and clear. Chill well. Serve in soup cups, topped with soured cream as a refreshing 'starter' to a summer meal. Serves 6–8.

Pflaumen Kuchen

This delicious dish consists of a plum and apple filling in an almond pastry case, topped with a 'streusel' or crumble of butter, sugar and flour. The rich pastry keeps well, and is a favourite Rosh Hashanah dish of Jews of German origin.

Pastry:
2 oz (50g/½ cup) ground almonds
4 oz (100g/½ cup) fine brown sugar
6 oz (150g/¾ cup) butter or margarine
8 oz (200g/2 cups) self-raising flour
1 beaten egg
Squeeze of lemon juice

Mix the ground almonds, brown sugar and flour. Rub in the fat gently, then mix to a soft dough with the squeeze of lemon juice and all but one tablespoonful of the egg. Chill for one hour, wrapped in foil or in an airtight plastic container.

Filling:
1 lb (½kg) cooking apples (weight peeled and cored)
1½ lb (700g) of zwetschen plums, halved and stoned
4 oz (100g/½ cup) granulated sugar
Little extra ground almonds

Peel, core and slice the apples very thinly. Put in a bowl and mix them with the halved and stoned plums. Mix with the sugar. Do this just before the fruit is needed or the juices will run and make the pastry soggy.

Streusel topping:
2 oz (50g/½ cup) plain flour
2 oz (50g/¼ cup) butter or margarine
5 oz (125g/⅔ cup) fine brown sugar

Mix with the fingers until a crumbly mass forms. Roll the chilled pastry to fit the bottom and sides of a 9 in (23 cm) loose-bottomed tin or a spring form tin that opens at the side. If the pastry breaks, don't worry, but patch it up as it is very short. Sprinkle the bottom of the pastry with a thin layer of ground almonds, add the sugared fruit, squeeze a little lemon juice over the top, and finally cover with an even layer of the crumble. Bake in a moderate oven (Gas No. 4, 350°F, 180°C) for 1–1¼ hours, or until the crumble is a golden brown and the filling feels absolutely soft when pierced with a knife. Serve warm or cold. If the zwetschen plums are not available, and juicy plums are used, mix 2 level teaspoons cornflour with the sugar when sweetening the fruit so as to thicken the juice. Serves 8 generously.

Israel

Israeli Cheese Pancakes

Israeli food today conjures up a picture of the exotic fruit and vegetables grown so brilliantly in the Negev and exported to gourmets all over the world. But the fruits of the earth were not so abundant in the years immediately after the founding of the State. Meat and poultry in particular were in extremely short supply. It was then that milk cheese—the 'kaese' of the Eastern European Jews—became the staple protein food. This recipe was originally called 'cheese steaks', and was served like a mock cutlet. If there is less cheese available than specified, a little extra flour may be substituted instead. The mixture should resemble a very thick batter.

½ lb (200g/1 cup) cottage or curd cheese
2 eggs
2 oz (50g/½ cup) self-raising flour; or 2 oz (50g/½ cup) plain flour and ½ level teasp baking powder
1 level teasp each of sugar and salt
2 oz (50g/¼ cup) butter and 1 tbsp oil (or all oil) for frying
Sugar and cinnamon

Put the cheese in one bowl and the eggs in another. Beat the eggs with a rotary whisk until fluffy, then stir into the cheese together with the flour and the seasonings. Put the butter and oil into a heavy frying pan over moderate heat. The minute the butter starts to foam, drop tablespoonsful of the mixture into the pan, flattening slightly with the back of the spoon. Fry gently until risen and golden brown on one side, turn and cook until the second side is brown. Serve hot off the pan with cinnamon sugar. Serves 4.

Israeli Icebox Cake

Like many modern Israeli recipes, I suspect this is really of American origin; however, it was brought back from Israel, and the name has stuck. It is utterly delicious for a party, or half can be eaten and half frozen—it really is not worth making a smaller quantity than specified.

6 oz (150g) semi-sweet dessert chocolate
2 tbsp water
3 tbsp caster (superfine) sugar
16 fl oz (400ml/2 cups) double (heavy) cream
1 tbsp rum
30 boudoir biscuits (ladyfingers)—about 3 pkt
¼ pint (125ml/⅔ cup) hot water with 2 level teasp instant coffee
2 oz (50g/½ cup) toasted, skinned and chopped hazelnuts or walnuts or toasted almonds

The day before, put the chocolate, water and sugar into a pan over low heat. When smooth, add 6 fl oz (150ml/¾ cup) cream and bring to the boil. Immediately remove from the heat and refrigerate. Next day, put the chocolate mixture into a bowl, add 1 tablespoon rum and beat or whisk until fluffy. Make hot coffee. Divide the biscuits into three lots of ten. Prepare a triple layer of foil about 12 in (30 cm) long and 6 in (15 cm) wide. Take the first group of biscuits, dip the unsugared side into the hot coffee, then place side by side, sugared side down, on the foil. Spread with half the chocolate cream. Repeat with the second layer, the remaining chocolate and finally the third layer of biscuits. Beat the remaining 10 fl oz (250ml/1¼ cups) cream until stiff, then pipe or swirl all over the cake. If to be used that day, refrigerate. If not, freeze, uncovered, until the cream is solid, then foil-wrap. Defrost at room temperature for 3 hours, then chill until required. Just before serving, decorate with chopped nuts. Serve in slices. Serves 12.

Poland and Russia

It is as difficult to disentangle the dishes from this part of the world as to define the borders of what we now call Poland and the U.S.S.R. Suffice it to say that the Jewish cooking that originates from this part of Eastern Europe is essentially a peasant one, with a strong emphasis on dishes rich in fat and carbohydrate that could provide a form of 'personal' central heating.

Kolacky (*Yeasted sweet buns*)

Yeast cookery plays an important part in this cuisine, Poland in particular being the home of some of the finest yeast cakes. In this recipe, a soft yeast dough is refrigerated overnight, then topped or filled with a mixture of cheese or apple.

1 lb (480g/4 cups) plain flour
Pinch of sugar and salt
1 oz (25g/2 cakes) yeast
8 fl oz (200ml/1 cup) milk
2 eggs
Rind of a lemon
3 oz (75g/$\frac{1}{3}$ cup) caster (superfine) sugar
3 oz (75g/$\frac{1}{3}$ cup) soft butter

Filling (for half the dough):
$\frac{1}{2}$ lb (200g/1 cup) curd cheese
1 egg
2 level tbsp caster (superfine) sugar
A few drops vanilla essence (extract)
$\frac{1}{2}$ oz (15g/1 tbsp) butter
Beat all together with a squeeze of lemon juice till smooth.

Apple filling (for the other half of the dough):
$\frac{1}{2}$ lb (200g) baking apples
Nut of butter
1 heaped tbsp brown sugar
Squeeze of lemon juice
Melt the butter, add the finely cut-up peeled apples, simmer with the lid on for 15 min, then stir in the sugar and lemon juice. Allow to go cold.

Warm the milk to blood heat (when a drop feels neither hot nor cold on the inside of the wrist), then pour one quarter of it on to the crumbled yeast in a mixing bowl, together with the pinch of sugar. Leave for 5 minutes, then stir to mix. Add remaining milk, lemon rind, eggs, flour, sugar, salt and soft butter. Using either an electric mixer or a wooden spoon, beat this very soft dough until it is smooth and no longer sticky (about 5 minutes). To test, press with a finger—no dough should stick to it. Gather into a soft ball and put into a large polythene bag which has been greased with a little oil. Chill overnight. It will rise slightly in the refrigerator. Next day, take the chilled dough from the refrigerator—if very cold, leave in the kitchen until it is the consistency of a scone dough. On a floured board, roll out $\frac{1}{4}$ in ($\frac{1}{2}$ cm) thick and cut into 3 in ($7\frac{1}{2}$ cm) rounds. Put these rounds on to greased trays, leaving 2 in (5 cm) between each round. Cover with a damp tea-towel. Leave in a warm place (e.g. the warming drawer of the cooker), or put uncovered in the oven at the lowest temperature with a bowl of water to prevent drying out. When the dough has risen to double its size (about 45 minutes) make a deep impression in the centre and put in a spoonful of filling. Leave for another 15 minutes, then paint the uncovered dough with beaten egg and bake the kolacky for 15 minutes in a quick oven (Gas No. 6, 400°F, 200°C) or until golden brown. Serve in wedges that day, or refrigerate till the next, or pack in plastic bags and freeze. This quantity makes about 10.

VARIATION

Cheese Rolls: Take a portion of the refrigerated dough and roll it $\frac{1}{4}$ in ($\frac{1}{2}$ cm) thick into a rectangle about 8 × 4 in (20 × 10 cm). Spread a thick ribbon of the cheese filling down the centre, then fold in the sides and roll over. Place on a baking tray with the join underneath. Leave to rise until double in bulk and puffy in appearance (about 1 hour). Paint with egg. Bake in a quick moderate oven (Gas No. 5, 375°F, 190°C) for 25 minutes.

Chopped Egg and Onion

A simple but delicious appetizer, depending for much of its flavour on the rendered chicken fat used to bind it. Some people substitute spring onions (scallions) for ordinary onions, then bind with butter to make a sandwich filling:

8 hard-boiled eggs
1 medium onion (nice if softened by putting in with chicken fat as it is rendered)
Additional fat to bind together
Salt and pepper

Chop (don't mince) the egg and onion together until fine and without discernible lumps. Bind together with a generous tablespoonful of soft chicken fat. Arrange on a platter or spoon onto lettuce. Serves 6 as an appetizer, 12 on biscuits (crackers).

Roast Herring

This dish was often served with 'eier kichel'—light unsweetened biscuits.

2 salt herrings
2 medium onions
1 teasp acetic acid (vinegar)
2 level teasp sugar
Pinch of pepper and salt

Put the salt herrings in water to cover and leave to soak overnight. Next day, skin, fillet and cut in small bite-sized pieces. Slice the onion into a small casserole, barely cover with water and season with the salt, sugar and pepper. Cover and cook until soft (Gas No. 3, 325°F, 170°C), for about 40 minutes. Add the herrings and the acetic acid. Re-cover and simmer for a further half an hour to develop the flavours. Serve with plain or buttered black bread. Serves 4.

Lokshen Kugel

A generation ago, this dish was made every Friday and cooked overnight for serving hot on Saturday. It is a good-tempered dish that can be cooked at the most convenient temperature without detriment. To achieve the crusty lining which is the best part of a kugel, the fat is first heated in the cooking dish, then swirled round the sides to coat them.

4 oz (100g/1½ cups) broad egg noodles (lokshen)
1 egg
Pinch each of cinnamon and salt
Grated rind of ½ lemon
2 oz (50g/¼ cup) sugar
1 oz (25g/2 tbsp) margarine
2 tbsp currants

Set the oven to the required temperature (see below) and put in a 2 in (5 cm) deep oven casserole with the margarine. Meanwhile, boil the noodles according to packet directions, then put into a sieve and rinse with cold water to remove excess starch. Drain well. Whisk the egg and the sugar, then stir in the flavourings and the raisins. Finally stir in the noodles and the hot fat which has been swirled round the baking dish to coat the sides. Bake either at Gas No. 5, 375°F, 190°C, for 45 minutes or at Gas No. 2, 300°F, 150°C, for 1½ hours. In either case, it should be set inside, crisp and brown on top. Serves 4.

Rice Kugel

6 oz (150g/¾ cup) Carolina (pudding) rice
3 oz (75g/⅓ cup) butter
4 oz (100g/½ cup) caster (superfine) sugar
2 eggs
4 oz (100g/1 cup) raisins or sultanas (white raisins)
½ teasp vanilla essence
½ level teasp cinnamon

Cook the rice in a large pan of boiling salted water until very tender (about 20 minutes), then strain and allow to cool. Meanwhile set the oven at Gas No. 3, 325°F, 170°C, and put the butter in an oven casserole (about 3 in/7½ cm deep) to melt it. Whisk the eggs, add the sugar and whisk to a creamy consistency. Mix in the flavourings and rice. Swirl the butter round the casserole to coat the sides, then pour the surplus into the rice mixture. Stir until thoroughly blended, then pour into the casserole. Cook at Gas No. 3, 325°F, 170°C, for one hour until golden brown. Serve plain or with melted syrup sauce. Serves 6.

Potato Kugel

2 eggs
4 large potatoes (¾ pint/375ml/2 cups when grated)
2 oz (50g/½ cup) self-raising flour; or 2 oz (50g/½ cup) plain flour and ½ level teasp baking powder
1 level teasp salt
2 oz (50g/¼ cup) margarine or 2 tbsp chicken fat or substitute
1 medium onion

Grate the potatoes finely and put in a sieve to drain for 10 minutes. Set the oven at Gas No. 8, 450°F, 230°C, and put the fat in a casserole to melt in it.

Whisk the eggs until fluffy then add the well-drained potatoes, flour, salt and grated onion. Swirl the hot fat round the baking dish to coat the sides, then pour into the potato mixture. Blend thoroughly and return to the dish. Bake in a hot oven (Gas No. 8, 450°F, 230°C) for 15 minutes, then turn to Gas No. 4, 350°F, 180°C, for a further hour, or until crisp, well risen and golden brown. Serves 6.

Schav (*Cold sorrel soup*)

This is a form of borscht, with a sweet and sour flavour.

1 lb (½kg) sorrel or spinach; or ½ lb (200g) pack frozen spinach
½ onion, finely chopped
1½ pints (1 litre/4 cups) water
2 level teasp salt
2 level tbsp sugar
Juice of a large lemon (3 tbsp)
2 eggs
5 fl oz (125ml/⅔ cup) soured cream

If fresh spinach or sorrel is used, rinse well until completely clear of grit. Drain and strip the leaves from the stalks, then shred the leaves finely. Proceed as follows both for the frozen and the fresh vegetables: Put the greens into a soup pan, together with the onion, water and salt. Cover and simmer for 20 minutes. Add the sugar and lemon juice and simmer a further 10 minutes. Have the eggs well whisked in a large bowl. Pour the hot soup slowly on to the eggs. The residual heat will be sufficient to thicken them. Chill overnight. Serve either topped with the soured cream or blended with it. Serves 6.

Cholent

The dish goes by several names—cholent, sholent or shalet to mention but three; and the ingredients, though basically meat, potatoes and fat, are capable of infinite variety according to the whim of the cook and her geographical location. But, as one Jewish cookery writer puts it, this ancient Sabbath concoction is best defined as 'any dish that has the stamina to stand up to 24 hours in the oven'.

The need for a hot dish that would conform to the laws of Sabbath observance was less pressing when the Jews lived in Palestine, though as far back as the time of the second Temple there are records of food being kept hot for Sabbath in special vessels. But in the bitter winters of Europe the need became a necessity and the 'cholent' (to give it its more usual name) became staple Sabbath fare for both the rich city Jew and his poor country cousin alike.

The cholent ritual was an important part of Jewish life in the Polish villages of the nineteenth century. Each family would mark its pot with chalk, tie it with string before sending it to be cooked in the baker's oven. It was a tragedy indeed if a child should drop the hot dish on the way home, and the whole village would give a spoonful to make up the family's meal. In those cholents, potatoes and 'kasha' (groats) were the main ingredients, with a good meat bone to help the flavour. But the richer communities, where kosher meat was more readily available, would put in a good chunk of boneless brisket or top rib. Jews who came to Britain in the latter years of the nineteenth century continued to make their cholent just as they had done in 'der heim', putting in butter beans or barley for variety, and topping the dish with a fluffy 'knaidel' or dumpling; they found it an ideal way of feeding their large families in the days when a joint, as we know it today, was beyond the finance of most immigrants. The cholent cooked to perfection in the coal oven, as it had done in the wood ovens of Russia and Poland.

But as gas and electricity took over in the kitchen the days of the cholent were numbered. Tastes changed, too, and what had tickled the palate on a bitter winter's day in Poland, sat heavily on the Westernized stomachs of the next generation. It didn't taste the same either when cooked in a gas or electric oven at a temperature of 250°F, 130°C.

The Jews who emigrated to America kept on making cholent for the first years, but they were able to buy meat more readily and the recipe soon took on a more lavish look. A typical version includes brisket, onions, butter beans (known as lima beans in the U.S.A.), barley or potatoes.

1 lb ($\frac{1}{2}$kg/2$\frac{1}{2}$ cups) butter (dried lima) beans
3 lb (1$\frac{1}{2}$kg) piece of boneless brisket
Salt, pepper, paprika and ginger
2 tbsp chicken fat; or 2 oz (50g) margarine
3 sliced onions
1 clove of garlic, crushed
1 bayleaf
6 peeled whole potatoes; or $\frac{1}{2}$ lb (200g) pearl barley

Soak the butter beans in water to cover overnight, then drain well. Rub the brisket with the salt, pepper, paprika and ginger, then brown quickly in the chicken fat or margarine, together with the onions and the garlic. Put in a deep earthenware casserole (a hot-pot dish or Dutch oven is ideal). Add the bayleaf, drained soaked beans, and the potatoes or barley. Cover with boiling water, cover the dish and put in a quick oven (Gas No. 6, 400°F, 200°C) for 30 minutes or until the contents start to bubble. Turn the heat right down to Gas No. $\frac{1}{2}$, 250°F, 130°C, and leave overnight. Serve for lunch the next day. If the dish is to be served as an accompaniment, use only $\frac{1}{2}$ lb (200g/1$\frac{1}{4}$ cups) butter beans, $\frac{1}{2}$ lb (200g) meat and a knuckle bone for flavour. Serves 6.

Heimishe Pickled Cucumbers

This is the most delicious pickle I know, traditional to my husband's family and always prepared by the male members of it. The refinement of refrigeration has been added in this generation—and it does maintain the cucumbers at their peak for a far longer period. The cucumbers are usually pickled a month before the New Year, so that they provide a very special treat for the holiday.

10 lb (5kg) firm green pickling cucumbers (4–6 in/10–15 cm long)
2 gal (10 litres/40 cups) water
1 lb ($\frac{1}{2}$kg) coarse salt
Spices:
4 medium pieces root ginger
6 red pickling peppers
6 cloves garlic, peeled
1 level tbsp mixed pickling spice
6 bayleaves
2 teasp acetic acid (vinegar)

Put the water into a large pan and add the salt and all the other ingredients (except the cucumbers). Bring to the boil, stirring until the salt has dissolved. Boil rapidly for 5 minutes. Take off the heat and leave until completely cold. Scrub the cucumbers thoroughly with a small soft bristle nailbrush (kept specially for the purpose), discarding any that have soft or diseased parts. Rinse them in cold water, then use them to fill a plastic or enamel bucket to within 2 in (5 cm) of the top. As each layer is put in the bucket, scatter on it some of the spices strained from the liquid. Cover the cucumbers with a large, upturned plate, then weight it down with a heavy weight such as a clean brick sealed in a plastic bag. Pour the cold pickling solution down the side of the bucket until it covers the plate to the depth of an inch. Cover with a muslin cloth or thin tea-towel, and leave in a cool place such as an outhouse for 10 days. After 10 days, skim off the froth that will have appeared on the surface. Cover and leave for a further week. Skim again, and test by slicing into one cucumber. If the taste is not right, leave them for a further week, or until ready (the speed of the pickle depends on the temperature around them). When the cucumbers are ready, skim again, pack into large plastic containers and fill up with the pickling liquid until the cucumbers are completely submerged. Store in the refrigerator. Makes 10 lb (5kg).

The Middle East

Many books have been written on the cooking of the Sephardim—those Jews of Spanish and Portuguese origin, who were expelled from Spain in 1492, and then made their homes in the countries bordering the Mediterranean. The recipes here are a selection which I have culled from Sephardi friends and which, because of their universal appeal, are now being made in many Ashkenazi kitchens as well.

Pastales

These little meat pastries can be made either with a shortcrust or puff pastry (when they are baked) or with a yeast pastry (when they are fried). The minced (ground) beef filling differs from the Ashkenazi mixture in that the meat is browned before use, contains no egg, is seasoned with piment (allspice) and contains fried pine kernels which give it a most unusual texture.

A Sephardi cook will mould the pastales by hand, sealing the top to the bottom with an intricate edging which cannot be described in words. Unless you can get a Sephardi cook to demonstrate, it is best to use the simple Western method in the recipe below.

Pastry:
8 oz (200g/2 cups) plain flour
1 level teasp salt
3 oz (75g/½ cup) margarine
1 tbsp oil
3 tbsp (approx) warm water

Rub the fat and oil into the salted flour. Mix to a scone-like dough with the warm water. Knead until smooth. Roll out ⅛ in (½ cm) thick. Cut into 24 rounds to fit patty tins.

Filling:
¾ lb (300g) minced shoulder steak (ground beef)
½ large onion
2 tbsp oil
Good pinch of ground black pepper and allspice
1 level teasp salt
2 tbsp pine kernels (pine nuts) if available
Sesame seeds
Beaten egg for gilding

Fry pine kernels gently in the oil until brown then drain. Put the chopped onion into the pan and brown gently, then add the meat and continue to cook until it is a uniform brown all over. Barely cover with water, add the seasonings and simmer uncovered until the moisture has almost evaporated and the meat looks juicy. Stir in the pine kernels. The filling is now ready.

Place circles of pastry in 12 patty tins, add a spoonful of cooled meat mixture, and cover with another round, sealing the edges well together. Just before baking, brush with beaten egg and scatter with sesame seeds. Bake in a hot oven (Gas No. 7, 425°F, 220°C) for 15 minutes. Makes 12.
Note: The unbaked pies can be frozen and cooked as required.

Ouk

This is a flavouring syrup (originally made with pomegranate juice) which gives the characteristic Sephardi flavour to stuffed carrots, cabbage, vine leaves and courgettes.

1 lb (½kg/1⅓ cups) black treacle (molasses)
4 oz (100g/½ cup) demerara (brown) sugar
2 oz (50g) citric acid crystals (sour salt)
2 level tbsp salt

Warm all the ingredients together until blended. Store in a jar.

Stuffed Carrots

As an Ashkenazi housewife prepares for the Sabbath by making a panful of chicken soup and a dish of chopped liver, so the Sephardi housewife cooks a selection of vegetables stuffed with minced (ground) beef. These can be served either hot or cold and reheat to perfection. Leeks and courgettes (zucchini) can both be treated in the same way as the carrots in this interesting recipe.

12 young carrots
2 tbsp oil
Meat stuffing:
1 lb (½kg) lean minced (ground) beef
½ onion (optional)
4 level tbsp raw, well-washed Carolina rice
1 level teasp salt
Pinch of white pepper
½ level teasp piment (allspice) or cinnamon
A little water
1 tbsp ouk

Mix all the ingredients together, binding with a little water. Scrape the carrots and hollow out the centre with an apple corer (it is possible to buy a special instrument for the job), leaving a shell ¼ in (½ cm) thick. Stuff the carrots with the minced beef mixture. Sauté slowly in oil, 5 minutes on each side, until they look slightly glazed and are beginning to soften. Arrange in a baking dish and pour on the frying oil. Add 1 tablespoon ouk (lemon juice could be substituted) and water to cover. Cover and bake in a moderate oven (Gas No. 4, 350°F, 180°C) for 30 minutes, then turn down to Gas No. 3, 325°F, 170°C, and simmer for a further 1½ hours, by which time the sauce will be syrupy and the carrots meltingly tender. Serves 6.

Stuffed Tomatoes

12 fat tomatoes
Meat stuffing as for the carrots
2 teasp oil
1 tbsp lemon juice
2 level teasp sugar
½ level teasp salt
10 grinds black pepper

Slice a 'lid' off the tomatoes and hollow them out, putting the tomato pulp into an ovenproof dish just wide enough to hold the tomatoes when packed tightly side by side. Salt the tomato shells lightly, then fill them with the meat mixture and replace the lid. Add the oil, lemon juice and seasonings to the tomato pulp in the dish then arrange the tomatoes in it. Add sufficient water to ensure that the tomatoes are barely covered. Cover the dish with foil and then with a lid. Bring to the boil on top of the stove, simmer for 5 minutes, then transfer to the oven and cook at Gas No. 5, 375°F, 190°C, for 45 minutes. Serves 6.

Gereybes (*Middle Eastern Shortbread*)

The baking of the Sephardim is of a delicacy and refinement rarely equalled in Western cooking. Craft plays a great part in the shaping of the pastries of which this delicate biscuit is typical.

½ lb (200g/1 cup) butter
5 oz (125g/⅔ cup) caster (superfine) sugar
12 oz (300g/3 cups) plain flour
2 oz (50g/½ cup) blanched almonds

Melt the butter gently, then skim to remove the salt (or use saltless butter). Pour into a bowl and leave to set until creamy. Cream the butter and sugar until almost white, then add the sifted flour a little at a time. Knead thoroughly. Leave to chill for 1 hour. Take pieces of the dough and roll each with the palm of the hand into a pencil shape about 7 in (17½ cm) long. Form into a bracelet (a little like a miniature beigel) and put an almond over the join. Arrange on ungreased trays, leaving 1 in (2½ cm) between each biscuit. Bake in a slow moderate oven (Gas No. 3, 325°F, 170°C) for 20 minutes until a very pale gold and firm to the touch. Makes about 30 biscuits.

Date Cakes

Pastry:
12 oz (300g/3 cups) self-raising flour
6 oz (150g/¾ cup) butter
4–5 tbsp icy water

Rub the fat into the flour until the mixture resembles fine crumbs, then moisten with enough water to gather into a dough. Chill.

The filling:
12 oz (300g/2 cups) stoned dates
2 level teasp cinnamon
Squeeze lemon juice
½ oz (15g/1 tbsp) butter
1 tbsp water

Mix the dates with the water and butter over gentle heat and stir until a smooth paste results. Add a little more water if necessary. Stir in the cinnamon and lemon juice and cool.

Divide the dough into three balls. Roll each ball into a rectangle approximately 10 × 8 in (25 × 20 cm). Spread the date filling to within ½ in (1 cm) of the edge. Roll the pastry over twice as for a flat strudel. Cut into 1 in (2½ cm) thick diagonal slices. Arrange on ungreased tins and bake in a quick oven (Gas No. 6, 400°F, 200°C) for 20 minutes or until risen and slightly golden. Cool 5 minutes, then dredge with icing sugar. Makes about 30.

Festival Foods

To prepare the house and table for each Festival as it occurs in its turn during the year, is one of the most pleasurable responsibilities involved in running a Jewish household.

Although it is permitted to cook on a Festival, most women prefer to get all the special cooking and baking done in advance, so that they too can enjoy the holiday spirit. In earlier generations this meant a great deal of hard work, for every single food had to be made at home, without any mechanical or electrical assistance. Fish had to be chopped by hand—after being carried home in the early morning from the local fish market. Then there was special enriched bread to be kneaded, intricately plaited and gilded with a goosefeather dipped in egg. The fowl had to be plucked and drawn, herrings skinned and filleted, kreplach rolled and boiled, and beetroots hand-chopped for borscht.

Today, frozen gefüllte fish mix can be bought at the supermarket; the baker labours over the bread; the fowl comes scalded and koshered in its polythene bag; borscht comes ready to be poured from a bottle, kreplach to turn out of a tin. Which is all very labour-saving, but just a little sad. I do hope that the tradition of home-making those dishes which recall great moments in our history (and provide a unique social commentary on the life-style of the Jew for the past 3,500 years) will not die out completely. That is why, in the pages that follow, I have modernized the method of making these delicacies, whilst trying to retain the essential flavour of the dish.

For each festival, I give a selection of special recipes; for other dishes traditionally associated with the occasion, recipes will be found in other sections of the book.

Rosh Hashanah

New Year (1st and 2nd Tishri): September/October

Ever since the return from Babylon (where the art of sugar cookery is thought to have originated) Jewish housewives have made all kinds of sweet foods at this festival as a symbol of the sweetness they hope for in the year ahead.

Whilst all kinds of fruit are served at Rosh Hashanah, the apple is the symbolic fruit of the season, expressing in its sweetness the hope for a good and sweet New Year. Besides being used in all kinds of pies, cakes and strudels, it is also served in slices spread with honey after Kiddush has been made on the eve of the Festival. On the second night, it is usual to serve an additional fruit such as pineapple to justify the recitation of the 'Schecheanu' blessing always recited over a new and fresh food.

Even the familiar Sabbath bread takes on a new shape at this season, for it is baked in a round shape instead of a plait, and enriched with extra egg and sugar—and in some cases with raisins—to signify the promise of a rich and full New Year.

Kreplach

These three-cornered pasties are said to symbolise the three Patriarchs, Abraham, Isaac and Jacob. They are also eaten on the Eve of the Fast (Kol Nidre) as well as at Shavuot (Feast of Weeks), when they are served with sour cream in a dairy version. For a special occasion they may be cooked in chicken or meat broth instead of salted water.

The dough:
8 oz (225g/2 cups) plain flour
Pinch of salt
2 large eggs
1 tbsp plus 2 teasp water

By machine: Put flour and salt in bowl, make a well and add eggs and water. Knead with dough hook until a smooth non-sticky dough is formed (3–4 min). *By hand:* Put flour and salt on a board, make well in centre, drop in the whole eggs and water, gradually drawing in the surrounding flour with a knife. Mix with the hand until a firm dough is formed. Knead with heel of hand until like chamois leather in appearance (about 5 min). Cover with a large bowl and leave to relax for 20 min.

Filling:
2 cups cooked minced (ground) shin (used to make soup—about 1 lb/450g)
1 large egg
½ small onion, grated
½ level teasp salt
Speck of pepper

Mix together all ingredients (meat should cling but not be pasty). Add more egg if too dry.

To make the kreplach: Work on half the dough at a time. Roll out on floured board until transparent and thin as a knife blade. Add extra flour if necessary and turn dough over to prevent it sticking (if sufficiently kneaded and rested it won't stick!). Cut into 2 in (5 cm) squares. Put a teaspoonful of filling onto each, fold over into a triangle, pressing the edges firmly to seal. (If necessary, dampen with a little water.) Lay each krepel on a sheet of greaseproof paper as it is completed. Add kreplach to large pan of boiling salted water in two lots, as they swell. Bring to boil, reduce to a simmer, cover and cook for 30 min. Lift out with a slotted spoon and put into colander standing in a bowl. Repeat with second batch. To serve, simmer in boiling chicken or meat soup to heat through for 10–15 min. Makes approx 54.

Lekach (*Honey and spice cake*)

Honey cakes of this kind—like all the spice cakes—were the first to be made with artificial raising agents, for the crude reagents then used left unpalatable by-products which were not readily discernible in a heavily-spiced cake. Honey was the chosen sweetener because cheap refined sugar was not widely available until the end of the nineteenth century, whilst the cooking oil with which this cake is traditionally mixed made it 'parve' so that it could be eaten after either a meat or milk meal. Any kind of honey cake needs to mature for a week in a tightly-closed tin or foil container. When mature it can be frozen, but the spices tend to lose some of their flavour.

½ lb (200g/2 cups) plain flour
6 oz (150g/¾ cup) caster (superfine) sugar
1 level teasp each of cinnamon and mixed spice
10 oz (250g/¾ cup) clear honey
4 fl oz (100ml/½ cup) cooking oil
2 eggs
1 level teasp bicarbonate of soda (baking soda) dissolved in 4 fl oz (100ml/½ cup) orange juice
2 oz (50g/½ cup) chopped walnuts

Mix together the flour, sugar and spices. Make well in centre, then add the honey, oil and eggs. Beat well together until smooth. Dissolve the bicarbonate in orange juice and add nuts. Pour into greaseproof paper lined tin approximately 10 × 8 × 2 in (25 × 20 × 5 cm). Bake (Gas No. 3, 325°F, 170°C) for 1¼ hours or until firm to the touch. Cool out of draught. When quite cold, foil wrap and leave if possible for 1 week before using. Improves with keeping.

VARIATION

Coffee and Spice Honey Cake: Use 2 level teaspoons each cinnamon and ginger. Dissolve bicarbonate in 4 fl oz (100ml/½ cup) hot coffee instead of orange juice.

Tsimmes with Dumpling

This might be called a Jewish hot-pot, for its flavour depends on long slow cooking. What makes a 'tsimmes' unique is that it is sweetened, be it with prunes or dried pears, or, as in the recipe below, with carrots cooked with sugar or golden syrup.

2 lb (1kg) carrots
1½ lb (700g) potatoes
2 lb (1kg) slice of brisket
4 tbsp golden (corn) syrup
2 teasp salt
Pepper
1 tbsp cornflour (cornstarch)
Dumpling:
6 oz (150g/1½ cups) self-raising flour
3 oz (75g/⅓ cup) meat fat or margarine
½ teasp salt
3–4 tbsp water to mix

Trim excess fat off the meat, leaving a thin edging, then cut into 1½ in (3½ cm) chunks. Peel the carrots and cut into ½ in (1 cm) cubes. Put the carrots and meat into a pan, barely cover with hot water, 2 tablespoons of syrup, pepper, and ½ teaspoon of salt, bring to the boil, and simmer for 2 hours either on the top of the stove or in a slow oven. Skim, or if possible, chill so that most of the fat can be removed. Four hours before you want the tsimmes, make the dumpling by rubbing the margarine, or cutting up the fat, into the flour and salt. Mix to a soft dough with the water. Put the dumpling in the middle of a large oval earthenware, enamel or enamelled iron casserole. Arrange the drained meat and carrots around it. Mix a tablespoon of cornflour with enough water to make a smooth cream, then stir into the stock from the carrots and meat. Bring to the boil then pour over the carrots and meat. Peel and cut the potatoes into large cubes and arrange on top, adding extra boiling water if necessary so that they are just submerged. Sprinkle with the remaining teaspoon of salt and 2 tablespoons of syrup. Cover and bring to the boil on top of the stove then transfer to a slow oven (Gas No. 2, 300°F, 150°C) for 3½ hours. Uncover and taste, adding a little more syrup if necessary. Allow to brown for a further half an hour, then serve. The potatoes and dumpling should be slightly brown and the sauce slightly thickened. Serves 6.

Yom Kippur

The Day of Atonement (10th Tishri): September/October

Although Yom Kippur is a Fast Day, the main preparations from the housewife's point of view are concerned with making two special meals—the one before the Fast and the one eaten twenty-five hours later, when it has ended. On the eve of the Fast it is important to serve a meal that is sustaining without provoking thirst. After the Fast, the meal should be light and easily digested after a day of abstinence from food.

Before the Fast

Dinner often starts with a meat or chicken soup garnished with kreplach, matzo balls or savoury lokshen kugel. Poultry makes a lighter main course than meat, and the meal may be finished with a fruit sponge pudding or fruit salad followed by large glasses of lemon tea. The food should be prepared in good time, as the meal must be eaten earlier than usual (between 5 p.m. and 6 p.m. according to the calendar), for the family will need to leave at once for the synagogue and the Kol Nidre service. After the meal, the table is cleared and then reset with the cloth and candles. A special 'yahrzeit' candle is lit if either husband or wife has lost a parent, and then the wife lights the Festival candles, and the Fast has commenced.

Suggested Menu before the Fast

Melon
Chicken Soup with Meat Kreplach, or Savoury Lokshen Kugel or Knaidlach
Braised Stuffed Fowl, Rice Pilaff, Green Vegetables
Stewed Fruit or Fruit Salad or Apple Sponge
Lemon Tea

Suggested Menu for after the Fast

Chiffon Sponge, or Marble Cake, with Tea
Tray of Mixed Hors-d'œuvres, including Smoked Salmon or other smoked fish
Cream of Vegetable Soup

Platter of assorted Fried Fish, Gefüllte Fish, assorted Salads
Buttered Challah
Fruit Mousse or Ice-Cream
More Tea or Coffee

Succot

Tabernacles (15th Tishri): September/October

Succot, the autumn harvest festival which commemorates the years that the Jews had to wander in the wilderness, living out their days in makeshift huts, is a particularly happy occasion in the Jewish calendar. Many families make their own Succah or Tabernacle where they eat their meals, and every house is sweet with the fragrance of fruit and flowers.

To symbolize the richness of the harvest (for Succot is one of the three harvest festivals that used to be celebrated by pilgrimages to the Temple in Jerusalem) stuffed foods of all kinds are served as both savouries and sweets. Cabbages, vine leaves, tomatoes, aubergines (eggplant) and peppers are stuffed with lean minced (ground) beef and braised in a sweet and sour tomato or meat sauce. Holishkes and gevikelte kraut (the stuffed cabbage, respectively, of the Sephardi and Ashkenazi Jews) are the most popular in the West but in Israel, stuffed aubergines ('chatzilim') and peppers ('pilpel mimulad') are in a new tradition. For dessert, strudels are stuffed with apples and dried fruits, and melons of all kinds are served in the Succah.

Holishkes (*Stuffed cabbage in sweet/sour tomato sauce, in the Rumanian tradition*)

According to geographical location this dish may also be called 'Galuptzi' or 'Praakes'. Holishkes taste better if they can be left under refrigeration for two days before they are served—either reheated (which is usual) or cold (for a delicious hors-d'œuvre).

1 firm head winter cabbage
1 onion, finely chopped
2 tbsp chicken fat; or 2 oz (50g/$\frac{1}{4}$ cup) margarine
4 level tbsp patna (long grain) rice
4 fl oz (100ml/$\frac{1}{2}$ cup) chicken stock
1 lb ($\frac{1}{2}$kg) minced shoulder steak (ground beef)
Salt, pepper

Blanch the head of cabbage by boiling for 5 minutes, covered, then plunge into cold water. Strip off at least 12 leaves, removing the tough stalk end.

The filling: Cook onion in chicken fat or margarine till tender, then add rice and cook a further 3 minutes till opaque. Add stock and cook till absorbed. Then stir into meat with seasonings. One by one, put cabbage leaves (destalked) on table, put on a tablespoon of the filling, fold over like parcels, then squeeze gently between palms, to seal. Place in casserole, and cover with this sauce:

Sauce:
5 oz (125g) can tomato purée
3 cans water
4 level tbsp brown sugar
Juice of a large lemon; or $\frac{1}{8}$ teasp citric acid

Sauce should just cover holishkes. Cook at Gas No. 2, 300°F, 150°C, covered for 2 hours, then uncover, turn up to Gas No. 4, 350°F, 180°C, for further half-hour, to brown holishkes and thicken sauce. Serves 6 as an entrée, 4 as a main course. Makes 12.

Gevikelte Kraut

This is the version favoured by Jews of Russian origin. It has a sweet and sour meat sauce, and tastes better if it can be left under refrigeration for two days before it is served either hot or cold.

1 firm head of cabbage

Stuffing:
1 lb ($\frac{1}{2}$kg) minced raw steak (ground beef)
2 level tbsp medium matzo meal
1 level teasp salt
Pinch white pepper
1 beaten egg
$\frac{1}{2}$ onion, grated

Sauce:
2 tbsp wine or cider vinegar
2 generous tbsp golden (corn) syrup
1 bayleaf and 5 peppercorns; or $\frac{1}{2}$ level teasp powdered bouquet garni
1 level teasp salt
Beef stock or thin gravy barely to cover the cabbage
Mix all the ingredients together.

Plunge the cabbage into a pan of boiling water (to cover) and simmer for 5 minutes. Turn into a colander and put under the cold tap until cool enough to handle. Carefully remove the leaves—you will need 12, though several small ones can be overlapped to make a larger one, if necessary. Remove the tough stalk end with a 'V' cut. Stuff each leaf one at a time, by placing a tablespoonful of the stuffing in the centre, turning in the sides and rolling up into a bundle. Lift each bundle and give a gentle squeeze with the palm of the hand to seal it. Lay the bundles side by side in a wide, shallow casserole and cover with sufficient stock (or thin gravy) barely to cover them. Spoon the remaining sauce ingredients over the top. Put in a moderate oven (Gas No. 4, 350°F, 180°C) for half an hour. Then when the sauce is simmering, turn the oven down to Gas No. 2, 300°F, 150°C, for a further 2 hours. Fifteen minutes before the dish is cooked, uncover it and turn the heat back to moderate to brown the tops of the cabbage bundles and thicken the sauce. This will serve 6 an as entrée, 4 for a main course.

Stuffed Aubergines (Eggplant)

This is the way Egyptian Jews prepare stuffed aubergines. It is one of my favourite stuffed vegetable recipes.

3 oval aubergines (eggplant)
Oil for frying
Flour for coating
1 beaten egg
1 level teasp salt
10 grinds black pepper
1 level teasp paprika
Stuffing:
1 lb (½kg) raw minced (ground) beef
4 level tbsp raw rice
Fried aubergine (eggplant) flesh (see method)

Blend all the ingredients with the beaten egg.

Sauce:
½ onion, finely chopped
1 can (15 oz/375g) Italian tomatoes, sieved
3 level tbsp brown sugar
Juice of a large lemon (3 tbsp)
½ level teasp salt
Pinch of white pepper
A little chicken stock or water if necessary

Cut the aubergines in half and scoop out the flesh, leaving a good ¼ in (½ cm) of aubergine all the way round. Roughly chop the scooped-out aubergine then fry till soft in a little oil. Add to the meat. Sprinkle the shells with salt whilst you mix the stuffing ingredients together. Mound the meat mixture into each aubergine, pressing it well in. Dip each stuffed aubergine in flour, then brown it quickly on both sides in a little hot oil. Arrange the browned aubergines in an ovenproof casserole. In the same oil, cook the chopped onion until golden, then stir in all the remaining ingredients for the sauce. When the sauce is bubbling, pour it round the aubergines—they should just be submerged. If not, top up with a little chicken stock or water. Cover the dish and put in a moderate oven (Gas No. 4, 350°F, 180°C) for half an hour (until the sauce is bubbling nicely), then turn the oven down to Gas No. 2, 300°F, 150°C, and cook for a further 2 hours. When the aubergines are ready, they will have absorbed most of the sauce, leaving just enough to pour over each aubergine when it is served. This dish reheats well. Serves 6.

Strudels Stuffed with Dried Fruits

Unlike the stretched strudel dough, this type of strudel is extremely easy to prepare and keeps well in a tin. It is served for afternoon tea rather than as a dessert.

Puff Pastry Strudel

This can be made with frozen puff pastry. To be successful the pastry must be rolled to the thickness of a knife blade.

8 oz (200g) pkt puff pastry
12 oz (300g/2½ cups) mixed dried fruit; or same amount of currants and raisins
Raspberry, blackcurrant or damson (plum) jam
Little stewed apple
4 oz (100g/½ cup) sugar
1 teasp cinnamon
1 egg white or milk

Roll out the defrosted pastry as thinly as possible. Cut in two. Each half should measure 7 × 12 in (17½ × 30 cm); if not, roll again until right size.

To make each strudel roll: Spread jam generously on pastry, leaving 1 in (2½ cm) margin clear all the way round. Arrange dried fruit down centre. Spoon a little drained stewed apple on top (you don't want extra moisture). Sprinkle with half the sugar and cinnamon. Dampen long edges of rectangle. Bring to centre, overlapping each other. Strudel should now be 12 in (30 cm) long and about 3 in (7½ cm) wide. Carefully lift onto a greaseproof paper-lined tray (makes it easier to remove if jam boils out). Seal ends of strudel and mark into slices 1 in (2½ cm) thick without actually cutting through the pastry. Brush with slightly beaten egg white. If inconvenient, use milk. Sprinkle with granulated sugar. Bake at Gas No. 7, 425°F, 220°C, for 10 minutes, then reduce to Gas No. 5, 375°F, 190°C, for 15 minutes or until crisply brown. Makes 2 strudel rolls.

Almond Pastry Strudel

This is made with a melt-in-the-mouth rich short pastry. It has the best keeping qualities of all, but the pastry is a little more difficult to handle. Chill well before rolling it out.

Pastry:

6 oz (150g/1½ cups) plain flour and 6 oz (150g/1½ cups) self-raising flour; or 12 oz (300g/3 cups) plain flour and 1½ level teasp baking powder
7 oz (175g/1 cup) butter (or margarine if preferred)
3 oz (75g/⅓ cup) caster (superfine) sugar
1 large egg
1 teasp grated lemon rind
1 tbsp lemon juice
2 oz (50g/½ cup) ground almonds
2 tbsp cold water

Rub the fats gently into the flour, baking powder (if used) and the ground almonds, until no lumps larger than a small pea can be seen when the bowl is shaken. (Don't over-rub or the pastry will be crumbly and dry.) Stir in the sugar. Beat together the egg, lemon juice and rind plus 1 tablespoon of the water. Sprinkle onto the flour mixture until all the particles are dampened, turning over the mixture with a fork as you do this, or using your cupped hand to ensure even damping. If necessary add the further tablespoon of cold water. Gather the mixture gently into a dough and knead gently into a ball. Divide into 4 portions then wrap each in foil and chill for 1 hour (to make handling easier).

Filling:

1 lb (½kg/3 cups) mixed dried fruits—sultanas (white raisins), raisins and currants (plumped by standing in boiling water for 5 min and then drained and dabbed dry); or 1 lb (½kg/3 cups) mixed raisins, sliced glacé (candied) cherries and chopped dates
Raspberry or apricot jam
6 oz (150g/¾ cup) sugar mixed with 1 level teasp cinnamon
1 cooking apple, grated

Mix the fruit with the cinnamon and sugar, and stir in the grated apple. Roll each ball of dough in turn into a rectangle about 10 × 8 in (25 × 20 cm). Spread thinly with jam. Leaving a ½ in (1 cm) border all round, sprinkle the dough with the sugared fruit. Roll each rectangle over into three or four like a Swiss roll, then place it with the join underneath on a greased baking tray. Brush with milk or beaten egg and then with granulated sugar. With a sharp knife, mark lightly into slices about 1 in (2½ cm) wide, but don't cut through to the base. Bake in a quick, moderate oven (Gas No. 5, 375°F, 190°C) for 35–40 minutes or until golden brown. Lift off the trays immediately onto wire cooling trays. Wrap each roll in foil, and cut into slices when required. Makes 28–30 individual slices.

Suggested Menu for Succot

Ogen Melon Halves filled with Black Grapes
Holishkes or Gevikelte Kraut
Roast Turkey with Cranberry Sauce, Corn and Peas
Apple or Cherry Strudel
Pomegranates
Black Coffee

Chanucah (Chanukah, Hanukkah)

The Feast of Lights (25th Kislev): December

The famous defeat of the Greeks by Judas Maccabaeus and his followers is celebrated during the eight days of Chanucah with parties and presents—particularly for the children. This is the season for potato latkes eaten hot from the pan, and for rich puddings and cakes such as trifle, fruit cake and pudding with wine sauce.

Potato Latkes

Latkes are fritters which were originally made with cream cheese, to celebrate the notorious wine and cheese party with which Judith entertained the Greek general Holofernes. As Chanucah falls in December, Russian Jews substituted potatoes for cheese to make these delectable latkes. It is important to allow the grated potato to drain well before use. Latkes may be served straight off the pan as a special treat; but they are also delicious instead of chips (French fries) with cold meats or poultry.

4 large potatoes (16 fl oz/375ml/2 cups when grated)
2 beaten eggs
4 level tbsp self-raising flour; or 4 level tbsp plain flour and 1 level teasp baking powder
1 level teasp salt
Pinch of white pepper

Grate potatoes so finely that they are almost a pulp. Leave in a sieve to drain for 10 minutes. Put in a bowl and add the remaining ingredients. In a heavy frying pan put enough oil to come to a depth of ½ in (1 cm). When it is hot, put in tablespoons of mixture, flattening each latke with the back of spoon. Cook over steady moderate heat, 5 minutes on each side, until a rich brown. Drain on crumpled tissue paper and serve at once. Serves 5–6.

Chanucah Pudding

The rich fruited steamed pudding has been adopted only in recent years by British and American Jews as a Chanucah dish. This recipe is light and less rich than a traditional English pudding, but the main advantage is that though its keeping qualities are good it can be eaten the day it is made.

4 oz (100g/½ cup) margarine
4 oz (100g/½ cup) soft brown sugar
2 beaten eggs
Grated rind and juice of 1 orange
2 tbsp brandy
4 tbsp (100ml) Guinness (stout)
1 small apple, peeled, cored and grated
4 oz (100g/1⅓ cups) fresh white breadcrumbs
2 oz (50g/½ cup) blanched and chopped almonds
2 oz (50g/⅓ cup) cut mixed peel
½ lb (200g/2 cups) currants
6 oz (150g/1½ cups) sultanas (white raisins)
4 oz (100g/1 cup) raisins
4 oz (100g/1 cup) plain flour
Pinch of salt, nutmeg and mixed spice

Melt margarine and sugar together, sift flour with salt and spices. Place all ingredients in a bowl and beat with a spoon until thoroughly mixed (about 3 minutes). Place mixture in greased 2-pint (1 litre) pudding basins. Cover with double thickness of greaseproof and then with foil. Steam for 6 hours. Makes 2 puddings.

Wine Sauce

This recipe is from Russia. The sauce is a delicate pink.

2 egg yolks
2 oz (50g/¼ cup) caster (superfine) sugar
2 level teasp cornflour (cornstarch)
8 fl oz (200ml/1 cup) kosher wine or port
1–2 tbsp brandy or orange-flavoured liqueur

k together the yolks and sugar until pale, beat in the cornflour, wine and the brandy. over boiling water, whisking until thickened. be left standing in warm water, then reheated before using. Serves 8.

Sabayon Sauce

This is best made by one member of the family whilst another is dishing up the pudding. It is pale gold in colour.

2 egg yolks
4 fl oz (½ cup) sweet sherry or white dessert wine
1 level tbsp caster (superfine) sugar

Put the yolks and sugar in the top of a double saucepan or basin. Whisk well, then gradually whisk in the sherry or wine. Have the water simmering in the bottom of the pan. Put the basin over it, and whisk (with portable beater) until thick and foamy. Don't overcook or it will curdle. This takes only 3 or 4 minutes. Serves 6.

Chanucah Trifle

A delicious trifle that uses kosher (port-type) wine to give its special flavour.

½ large Swiss roll (jelly roll)
1 pint (500ml/2½ cups) custard (see recipes below)
4 tbsp kosher wine
5 fl oz (125ml/⅔ cup) double (heavy) cream
1 cupful (approx) fresh or canned fruit salad
4 tbsp fruit syrup from any canned fruit
Two recipes for custard:
Powder custard:
1 pint (500ml/2½ cups) milk
2 level tbsp custard powder (vanilla pudding mix)
1 level tbsp caster (superfine) sugar
1 egg yolk

Make according to packet instructions.

Egg custard:
1 pint 500ml/2½ cups) milk
2 whole eggs
2 oz (50g/¼ cup) sugar
Few drops vanilla essence (extract)
1 level teasp cornflour (cornstarch)

Heat the milk until it steams. In blender goblet put hot milk, sugar, cornflour and eggs and blend for 10 seconds (or whisk by hand). Cook very gently over boiling water until thick enough to coat the back of a wooden spoon. Add vanilla. Leave to cool.

Slice the Swiss roll ½ in (1 cm) thick and use to line the bottom of a glass bowl. Sprinkle with the kosher wine. Pour custard over the cake and leave to cool. Whisk the cream until it starts to thicken, then add the fruit syrup gradually, whisking again until thick. Fold in the fruit (oranges, pineapple and bananas are especially nice). Spoon over the top. Freeze for one hour to chill thoroughly, or leave in the coldest part of the refrigerator overnight. Serves 6–8.

Suggested Menu for a Night during Chanucah

Avocado Vinaigrette
Haimische Winter Soup
Stuffed Capon, Saveloys, Potato Latkes, Carrots and Peas
Chanucah Pudding with Wine Sauce
Fresh Fruit
Black Coffee

Purim

The Feast of Lots (14th Adar): February/March

Purim occurs exactly one month before Passover—on the 14th of Adar. It commemorates the downfall of Haman, the vizier of King Ahasuerus (Artaxerxes II), who in the fourth century of this era formulated his own 'Final Solution' by planning the massacre of the entire Jewish population of Persia. Haman ended up on the gallows he had prepared for his enemies, and his name is perpetuated in a variety of unusual cakes and sweetmeats. By tradition, these are three-cornered—some say like Haman's ears, others like his purse which he planned to fill with

Jewish gold. There are 'Hamantaschen' (Haman's purses) and 'Haman's Ears' (sugared fritters) as well as 'Little Dutch Hamans' (special gingerbread men).

Hamantaschen

Hamantaschen can be made with a yeast dough, a sour cream dough, a rich shortcrust, or a kichel (biscuit) dough. Each variety is delicious in its own way.

Wine and Walnut Filled Hamantaschen

Filling:
4 oz (100g/1 cup) walnuts
4 oz (100g/⅔ cup) stoned dates and 8 oz (200g/1½ cups) mixed sultanas (white raisins), currants and raisins
1 tbsp kosher wine
1 tbsp warm golden (corn) syrup
Juice and grated rind ½ lemon
1 tbsp apricot jam
½ teasp cinnamon
Pastry:
½ lb (200g/2 cups) self-raising flour
½ lb (200g/2 cups) plain flour
10 oz (250g/1¼ cups) margarine
4 tbsp water
2 egg yolks
2 oz (50g) icing (confectioners') sugar
1 egg white

Mix all filling ingredients together. Mix flour and icing sugar. Rub in fat until mixture resembles coarse breadcrumbs. Sprinkle with blended egg yolk and water and gather into a ball. Chill for half an hour. Roll out pastry ¼ in (½ cm) thick and cut into 3 in (7½ cm) circles. Put a spoonful of filling on dough, then draw up to form a triangle and pinch the edges firmly together. Brush with egg white beaten till foamy, and sprinkle with sugar. Bake at Gas No. 7, 425°F, 220°C, for 15 minutes or till a rich brown. Makes 56.

Kichel Hamantaschen

This recipe produces a cakey pastry which cont well with a fruit filling.

5 oz (125g/⅔ cup) caster (superfine) sugar
2 eggs (reserve a little for gilding hamantasche
4 fl oz (100ml/½ cup) oil
1 teasp vanilla essence (extract)
Grated rind of ½ orange
12 oz (300g/3 cups) flour (half plain, half self-raising); or 12 oz (300g/3 cups) plain flo and 1½ level teasp baking powder

Whisk eggs until thick, then whisk in sugar, oil and seasonings. Finally stir in enough flour to make a rollable dough. Roll out on a floured board, ¼ in (½ cm) thick and cut into 3 in (7½ cm) rounds. Place a spoonful of filling in the centre, then draw up three sides to form a triangle, and pinch the edges firmly together. Brush the tops with a little beaten egg. Bake in a moderate oven (Gas No. 4, 350°F, 180°C) for half an hour. Makes approx 24.

Apple Filling:
1 lb (½kg) peeled, cored and sliced apples
Juice and rind of a small lemon
3 oz (75g/⅓ cup) sugar

Butter a pan, put apple, sugar and juice in layers. Cover and cook gently until tender. Uncover and cook longer to drive off any excess liquid. Cool.

Apricot Filling:
½ lb (200g) apricots
½ cup (150g) honey
2 teasp grated orange rind
Juice of ½ orange

Soak apricots in water to cover overnight. Next day, drain well and put through coarse blade of mincer. Add rest of ingredients.

Prune Filling:
½ lb (200g/1¼ cups) tenderized prunes
3 oz (75g/½ cup) raisins
2 oz (50g/½ cup) walnuts
Juice and rind of 1 lemon
4 oz (100g/½ cup) sugar

Soak prunes and raisins overnight. Remove stones. Chop or mince with remaining ingredients

Sour Cream Hamantaschen

This is a delicious yeast dough, extremely easily made even if you are inexperienced at yeast cookery. The dough is allowed to rise slowly in the refrigerator overnight which makes it easy to handle and also gives a splendid texture.

1 oz (25g/2 cakes) yeast
4 fl oz (100ml/½ cup) lukewarm milk
1 lb (½kg/4 cups) plain bread flour
2 eggs
4 oz (100g/½ cup) caster (superfine) sugar
4 oz (100g/½ cup) melted butter
1 level teasp salt
5 fl oz (125ml/⅔ cup) soured cream
Melted honey or golden (corn) syrup

In a small jug, crumble the yeast into the milk and leave to dissolve for 5 minutes, sprinkling the top with a pinch of sugar to hasten the process. Put the flour and salt into a large bowl. Make a well in the centre and drop in eggs, sugar, melted butter and soured cream. Stir the yeast mixture well and add that. Gradually stir in the surrounding flour and beat until a soft dough is formed. Keep on beating until the dough leaves the beater or the fingers clean (about 5 minutes). Tip the mixture into a polythene bag large enough to allow the dough to expand (the bag should be greased beforehand with a few drops of oil). Close loosely and refrigerate overnight. Next day roll out the dough ¼ in (½ cm) thick and cut into circles 4 in (10 cm) in diameter. Put a spoonful of filling in the middle, and draw the edges together to make a three-cornered shape. Arrange on greased baking trays, brush with melted honey or golden syrup and leave in a warm place until double in bulk (about 1½ hours). At this stage, the hamantaschen will look puffy and feel spongy when poked with the finger. Bake in a quick moderate oven (Gas No. 5, 375°F, 190°C) for 30 minutes, or until a rich brown. Makes approx 24.

Poppy Seed Filling:
4 oz (100g/1 cup) black poppy seed
1 oz (25g/2 tbsp) butter
2 oz (50g/¼ cup) caster (superfine) sugar
2 level tbsp golden (corn) syrup
½ teasp vanilla essence or grated lemon rind
2 oz (50g/½ cup) walnuts, chopped
2 oz (50g/⅓ cup) seedless raisins, chopped
4 fl oz (100ml/½ cup) milk

Put poppy seed through food mill or in liquidizer, then stir in milk, followed by all other ingredients, and cook until thick (about 5 minutes). Taste and add more sugar if necessary. Add vanilla (or lemon rind) when cold.

Apple, apricot or prune filling can be used.

Haman's Ears

Known as Hamansooren in Holand, Orechie de Aman in Italy, Oznei Haman in Israel and as Hojuelos de Haman, the Sephardi name. A fritter-like pastry, deep fried and served sprinkled with icing (confectioners') sugar.

2 eggs
½ level teasp salt
2 level tbsp caster (superfine) sugar
½ lb (200g/2 cups) plain flour
1 level teasp baking powder
1 tbsp tepid water or rose water

Beat the eggs until fluffy, then add the salt, sugar and rose water, beating well. Stir in the flour to make a soft but non-sticky dough (the amount of flour may vary a little with the size of the eggs). Turn the dough onto a floured board and roll out to the thickness of a knife blade. Cut into half-moons using a 2 in (5 cm) round cutter, moving the cutter down the dough to form the crescents. Pinch each crescent in the centre so that it looks like a bow tie with an 'ear' on either side of the centre. Heat a pan of deep oil until it reaches 370°F, 190°C on a fat thermometer or a 1 in (2½ cm) cube of bread browns in a minute. Fry the 'ears' until golden brown, turning over with a slotted spoon so that they brown evenly. Drain on crumpled tissue paper. Serve hot or cold, well sprinkled with icing (confectioners') sugar.

Shavuot

Feast of Weeks or Pentecost (6th Sivan): May/June

In earlier days, Shavuot was celebrated as a great agricultural festival, when the start of the wheat harvest was marked by offerings of newly-baked bread. Every man brought the first fruits of his crops to the Temple in Jerusalem, while his wife ground flour from the new season's wheat, and baked special cakes and bread in honour of the occasion. Today we commemorate those early days by decorating the house with seasonal flowers and plants, and by taking them as gifts to the synagogue. Milk, cheese and honey are the symbolic foods of this festival, and they are made into some of the most delicious dishes of the Jewish cuisine. From milk, cream cheese is made. From cream cheese are made the cheese cakes, the blintzes, the kreplach and the noodle casseroles that so enrich the table on this occasion.

In biblical times, to symbolize the richness of the Torah for both body and soul, honey and milk were used in the same dish—especially in cheese cakes, which were further enriched with Jordan almonds. Today we sweeten cheese cake with sugar and flavour it with vanilla and lemon, but we still put honey into our Shavuot cakes and spread it on our bread. Although most of the traditional dairy dishes have a long culinary history, there are other recipes of more modern origin, which are equally suitable for serving at Shavuot. These include cream cheese dips, salads, uncooked cheese cakes, and sauces made with soured cream. While cooked dairy dishes, such as blintzes and cheese cakes, can be frozen very satisfactorily, uncooked cream cheese should not be frozen, but bought as late as possible before the festival. The rich double-cream cheeses are excellent to serve on bread, but for cooking purposes 'kaese' and cottage cheese are better, because they are drier and lighter in baked and fried dishes.

Yomtov Cheese Cake

A rich, deep cheese cake in a lovely tender crust. It can be frozen well in advance. Serve at room temperature.

Pastry:

8 oz (200g/2 cups) plain flour
Pinch of salt
5 oz (125g/⅔ cup) butter
2 level tbsp icing (confectioners') sugar
1 egg yolk
1 teasp lemon juice or vinegar
2–3 tbsp icy water

Sift together the flour, salt and icing sugar. Cut the butter into 1 in (2½ cm) chunks then rub in gently either by hand or machine until no lumps of mixture larger than a small pea appear on the surface when the bowl is shaken. Beat together the yolk, lemon juice or vinegar, and 2 tablespoons of the water. Sprinkle over the mixture until it is evenly dampened, adding the extra water if necessary. (I usually use my cupped hand at this stage, then gather the dampened mixture together into a dough.) Form into a ball and chill for at least half an hour. Have ready a round, greased, loose-bottomed cake tin, 8–9 in (20–23 cm) in diameter and 2 in (5 cm) deep. Roll the pastry ⅛ in (½ cm) thick and cut a round to fit the bottom of the tin. Roll 2 strips, 2 in (5 cm) wide, each half the circumference of the tin. Fit these round the sides, sealing them well to each other and to the bottom strip. Roll the remaining pastry ⅛ in (½ cm) and cut into strips ¼ in (½ cm) wide for the lattice top of the cake.

Filling:

4 eggs
2 oz (50g/¼ cup) caster (superfine) sugar
Grated rind of 2 lemons and the juice of 1 lemon
½ lb (200g/1 cup) curd cheese or sieved cottage cheese
10 fl oz (250ml/1¼ cups) soured cream
2 level tbsp cornflour (cornstarch)
4 level tbsp sultanas (white raisins)
2 oz (50g/⅓ cup) chopped mixed candied peel (optional)

Whisk the eggs and sugar until thick, then stir in all the remaining ingredients, ending with the dried fruit. Pour gently into the unbaked pastry base. Bake in a hot oven (Gas No. 7, 425°F, 220°C) for 5 minutes. This sets the surface. Take the cake from the oven and lay strips of pastry across the top to form a lattice. Put back in hot oven again for a further 10 minutes, then reduce the heat to Gas No. 3, 325°F, 170°C, for a further 50 minutes. Turn the oven off and leave the cake to cool in it. Makes 8 generous servings.

Cheese Blintzes

These are one of the glories of the Jewish cuisine. A blintze is a paper-thin pancake, which is fried on one side only. After it has been filled, it is fried again on the unbrowned side, and served plain or with soured cream. The secret of the perfect blintze lies first in the batter, and then in the special method of frying which I learned from a Russian cook. Follow the instructions implicitly and you are certain of success.

To freeze: Can be frozen either as pancakes or stuffed and ready for the final browning. Each stuffed blintze can be wrapped in foil and then put with the rest in a plastic bag; or if they are all to be used at once, lay side by side on foil, with a piece of foil between each layer. Make into a firm foil parcel and freeze. Defrost before frying.

The batter:
4 oz (100g/1 cup) plain flour
Pinch of salt
2 large eggs
4 fl oz (100ml/$\frac{1}{2}$ cup) each of milk and water
2 teasp oil
Butter and oil for frying

With a blender: Put the liquids into the blender, followed by the dry ingredients and blend until a smooth batter is formed.

By hand or electric mixer: Sift the flour and salt into a bowl. Make a well, drop in eggs and oil, and start stirring in the surrounding flour to make a stirrable batter. Gradually add the milk and water until smooth. Beat with a whisk until the surface is covered with tiny bubbles. Leave the batter for half an hour, though it can be refrigerated overnight if more convenient.

The filling:
$\frac{3}{4}$ lb (300g/$1\frac{1}{2}$ cups) curd cheese or sieved cottage cheese, mixed with 2 tbsp single (light) cream, top of the milk or an egg yolk (whichever is most convenient)
1 level teasp sugar
Pinch of salt

Blend all the filling ingredients together and leave until required.

To fry the pancakes: Stir the batter well, and pour into a jug. It should be the consistency of single cream; if too thick, add a further tablespoonful of water. Use a 6 in (15 cm) diameter omelette pan (with rounded sides). Put on medium heat for 3 minutes then drop in a teaspoonful of oil, and swirl it round the base and sides of the pan. Take a pad of tissue or kitchen paper and wipe out any excess. Using the pad of paper, smear the entire inner surface of the pan very thinly with butter, then pour in a thick layer of batter, swirling it round so that it covers the sides as well as the base of the pan. The heat will immediately set a thin layer so that the excess can be poured back into the jug. By this means you will get a blintze so thin that by the time the sides of the pancake begin to curl from the pan, the bottom will be brown and the top side dry. Turn the pancake out onto a sheet of greaseproof paper covering a wooden board. Re-butter pan and repeat the process until all the pancakes have been made (there should be 12). As each pancake stops steaming, stack one on top of the other, browned side up. (At this stage pancakes can be frozen, refrigerated overnight, or stuffed.)

To stuff the pancakes: Place a pancake brown side up on a board or counter. Spread a tablespoon of the filling thinly over the bottom half, turn in the sides and roll up into a long thin roll. Repeat with each pancake. The blintzes can now be refrigerated overnight or frozen.

To serve: Heat 2 oz (50g/$\frac{1}{4}$ cup) butter and 2 teaspoons oil in a wide frying pan. The moment the butter stops foaming, put in the blintzes, joint side upwards. Cook gently for 3 minutes until golden brown, turn and cook the second side. Blintzes may be kept hot for 10 minutes in a moderate oven, then served plain, or with a jug of ice-cold soured cream. Makes 12.

For **Meat** and **Chicken Blintzes** see p. 87.

Smetana and Kaese Bowl

Cream cheese and soured cream can be served plain as part of a dairy meal, or they can be combined with herbs and seasonings to make a delicious salad bowl, particularly nice with plain digestive biscuits (graham crackers) or fresh brown bread, or as a stuffing for tomatoes.

1 lb (½kg/2 cups) cottage cheese or curd cheese
5 fl oz (125ml/⅔ cup) soured cream or smetana (thick soured milk)
½ cucumber, peeled and diced
1 green pepper, seeded and finely diced
1 level teasp salt
3 spring onion (scallion) bulbs, finely sliced
1 tbsp mayonnaise
1 level tbsp mixed fresh herbs such as chives, basil, parsley
Crisp lettuce

Line a wide shallow bowl with the torn lettuce leaves. Combine all the other ingredients together and pile on top. Serves 6–8.

Suggested Dairy Meal for Shavuot

Chilled Borscht
Cheese Blintzes
Fresh Salmon, Mayonnaise Sauce, New Potatoes, Garden Peas
Liqueur Fruit Salad and Cream
Coffee

Pesach

Passover (15th Nissan): March/April

Each spring, during the Passover week which commemorates the liberation of the Jews from slavery in Egypt more than 3,500 years ago, the Jewish household takes on an appearance quite different from the one it presents during the rest of the year, or indeed during any other festival. In the kitchen, unfamiliar pots and pans stand on the cooker top and counters; in the larder, matzot, matzo meal and other Passover foods are stacked on the newly-covered shelves, and there is no trace of either bread or flour; whilst in the dining-room, dishes are served that do not appear on the table at any other season.

The Preparation of the Seder Table and its Contents

The Seder meal is unlike any other eaten in a Jewish home, both in the way the table is prepared and in the order of the Haggadah service that precedes it. It is symbolic of the last meal that the Jews ate before they left on their exodus from Egypt.

Setting the Seder Table
Early in the afternoon on the Eve of Passover, the table is laid with a white tablecloth and the freshly-polished candlesticks are put on their tray. As it is traditional to invite guests (especially those who might otherwise be alone on this night), there are usually many chairs to be set at the table. A wine glass is placed for each guest. A special large cup for Elijah the Prophet dominates the centre of the table. (As the glasses will be refilled no less than four times during the meal, it is a good idea to set each glass on a small plate to avoid spilling wine on the tablecloth.) The cutlery for the meal should not be put on the table, but arranged in place settings on a tray at the side, so that the table can be set just before the meal is served. It is traditional for the men to lean back in comfort during the meal, so cushions should be put on the chairs of the male guests. Near the seat of the host, place a small table containing a basin, jug and hand towel. Just before the Seder service starts, the jug can be filled with water for the washing of the hands during the service.

The Symbolic Foods
To the man of the house falls the duty of arranging the symbolic foods on the table, and full details of the correct order are given in the Haggadah. (There should be a Haggadah for each guest round the

table.) However, the different dishes will have to be prepared by the housewife beforehand. One can buy dishes specially designed to hold each of the different foods: otherwise each can be put in a separate glass dish arranged on a flat platter. They are:

1. *A Roasted Shankbone of a Lamb*
This recalls the lamb that the Jews were told to sacrifice on the night before they left Egypt. Very often a cooked chicken's neck is substituted. This is 'roasted' by holding for one minute in the flames of a gas cooker, or browning under an electric grill.

2. *A Roasted Egg*
This is symbolic of the festival offering brought into the Temple at this season. The egg is hard-boiled then 'roasted' like the shankbone.

3. *A Root of Horseradish*
This symbolizes the bitter life the Jews endured during their slavery.

4. *A Dish of Salt Water*
This is thought to recall the tears the Jews shed during captivity.

5. *A Sprig of Parsley or Watercress*
This is said by some to symbolize the 'springtime' of new hope, when the Jews went towards their promised land.

6. *Charoseth*
This recalls the mortar with which the Jews were forced to make bricks when they built the cities of Pithom and Ramses for their Egyptian taskmasters. Charoseth is a mixture of minced apples, walnuts, cinnamon and wine, mixed to a paste-like consistency (see recipe). Enough should be made to last for both Sedarim.

In addition, the husband arranges on the table three matzot, covered with a special cloth or 'matzo decke' which has a separate pocket for each matzo, and is embroidered like the 'challah decke' used on Friday night. The three matzot are frequently referred to as the Cohen, Levi and Yisrael. The middle matzo will be broken during the service, and part of it will become the 'Afikomen' which is hidden by the head of the house, and searched for by the children after the meal.

All the crockery and silverware should be ready on a side table or trolley, together with prepared food and condiments. Below I give four suggested menus for the Seder meal—two meat and two milk. Some communities traditionally start with a dish of eggs in salt water. How these are prepared depends on family custom, some people slicing the eggs into the salt water and other families serving them whole. In general, however, for each guest allow one hard-boiled egg, $\frac{1}{4}$ pint (125ml/$\frac{2}{3}$ cup) water and $\frac{1}{2}$ level teaspoon salt.

If there are more than six guests, it is advisable to have one bottle of wine at each end of the table so that the glasses can be swiftly refilled during the Seder service.

All these preparations should be completed before the candles are lit at the commencement of the festival. On the final day of Passover, as soon as the festival has ended, the Passover pots can be put away, and 'chametz' brought out once more. The house then slips into its normal routine for another year.

Passover Foods

Matzo (together with matzo meal of varying textures that is made from it) is the main ingredient of Passover cookery. The first matzo, or unleavened bread, was baked by the Jews on the night they left Egypt. In Egypt they had learned to bake a bread leavened with yeast—a discovery that originated in the Nile Delta. On this occasion however, they rolled out their unrisen dough, and baked it on 'gridirons' laid over the heated coals of a fire.

The 'kremslach' or matzo pancakes, which vary from simple 'hot cakes' of meal, egg and water to sweetened fritters with fruit, recall the meal cakes that were offered as sacrifices in Bible times. The custom of making 'eingemachtes'—rich preserves of dried fruits or beetroot—is of more recent origin, and symbolizes the sweetness of the land to which the Jews turned their eyes when they left Egyptian slavery.

Seder Menus

Note: Substitute ingredients specially packed for Passover where necessary.

Milk meal (1)
Wine; Matzot; Charoseth; Eggs in Salt Water
Halibut in Egg and Lemon Sauce
Salmon and Salads
New Potatoes
Rum and Apple Flan
Coffee

Milk meal (2)
Wine; Matzot; Charoseth; Eggs in Salt Water
Golden Vegetable Soup
Halibut in Egg and Lemon Sauce
Gefüllte Fish
Savoury Gefüllte Fish
Chopped Fried Fish
Coleslaw Salad
Cauliflower, Olive and Pimento Salad
Green Salad
Banana and Apricot Pavlova
Raspberry Sorbet
Assorted Passover Biscuits
Coffee

Meat meal (1)
Wine; Matzot; Charoseth; Eggs in Salt Water
Gefüllte Fish, Horseradish Sauce
Chicken Casserole, Roast Potatoes, Baby Carrots and Cauliflower
Pineapple Pyramids; Passover Liqueur
Passover Ring Sponge
Coffee

Meat meal (2)
Wine; Matzot; Charoseth; Eggs in Salt Water
Champignons à la Grècque (use lemon juice not vinegar)
Daube Marseillaise (Chuck)
Glazed Carrots
Aubergines (Eggplant) stuffed with Chicken Livers,
New Potatoes
Chicory Salad in the French manner
Morello Cherry Compote
Orange Liqueur Whip
Coffee

Passover Jams and Preserves

Lemon Curd

Lemon curd keeps for six weeks in the refrigerator. It is often made with the egg yolks left over from baking biscuits, such as cinnamon balls and macaroons.

3 large lemons
3 eggs; or 4 egg yolks; or 1 whole egg plus 3 yolks (whichever is most convenient)
½ lb (200g/1 cup) sugar
4 oz (100g/½ cup) unsalted butter

Grate the rind of two lemons and squeeze the juice of all three. Allow to infuse together all morning if possible. Put the sugar in a bowl in a warm oven to heat through, while you melt the butter in a basin standing in a pan of boiling water. Add the sugar and the strained juice. When the sugar mixture is smooth, pour a little over the beaten eggs, then return to the pan and stir with a wooden spoon until the mixture just coats the back of the spoon (it thickens as it cools). Pour into hot, dry jars (most easily warmed by standing in a warm oven (Gas No. ½, 250°F, 130°C) for 10 minutes. Cover with wax discs. Leave till cold, then cover with tinfoil and refrigerate. Makes 1½ lb (¾kg).

Beetroot Eingemachtes

This traditional beetroot conserve must be cooked until it goes brown—a sign that the sugar in the beets has caramelized, giving the jam its inimitable flavour.

2 lb (1kg) cooked beets; or 2½ lb (1kg/200g) raw beets cooked in boiling water for half an hour and then skinned when cool
2 lb (1kg/4½ cups) granulated sugar
3 unpeeled lemons
½ oz (15g/2 tbsp) ginger
6 fl oz (150ml/¾ cup) water
4 oz (100g/1 cup) split blanched almonds

Cut the cooked beets into slivers each ¼ in (½ cm) wide and 1–2 in (2½–5 cm) long. Put into a heavy pan with the sugar and the water. Stir until the sugar dissolves, then simmer uncovered for one hour. Meanwhile, wash the lemons well, slice and cut into pith-free segments. Add to the beets and cook for a further hour. At this stage the beets will look slightly brown and transparent. Finally, add the nuts and ginger and cook for a further 15 minutes. (At all times the contents of the pan must be barely bubbling.) The preserve thickens as it cools. Ladle the hot jam into warm jars which have been heated for 10 minutes in a low oven (Gas No. ½, 250°F, 130°C). Cover with wax discs. When quite cold, cover with cellophane or foil covers and tie down with rubber bands. Makes nearly 4 lb (2kg) jam.

Apricot Eingemachtes

1 lb (½kg/3 cups) dried apricots
2 pints (1 litre/5 cups) water
2 lb (1kg/4½ cups) sugar
4 fl oz (100ml/½ cup) lemon juice (about 2½ lemons)
2 oz (50g/½ cup) slivered blanched almonds

The night before, put the fruit in the preserving pan and cover with the water. Next day, bring to the boil, then simmer very gently until the fruit is quite tender—about 10 minutes. Do not allow to boil too hard or if possible partially cover the pan. When the fruit is quite tender, add 2 lb (1kg) sugar, stir until the sugar is dissolved, add the lemon juice, then boil hard until the jam sets—about half an hour. (The simplest test: Chill a saucer in the freezer; take out and put a teaspoon of jam on it, then leave a minute. If set, the blob will wrinkle slightly when pushed with the forefinger.) After 20 minutes' boiling, add the almonds. Pot in warm, dry jars (leave in warm oven whilst jam is boiling); cover with wax discs when hot, and foil or jampot covers when cold. Makes 4 lb (nearly 2kg).

Lemon and Walnut Eingemachtes

A thick conserve, which used to be eaten with a spoon, washed down with lemon tea. It is delicious on matzo crackers.

4 oz (100g/1 cup) walnut halves
12 oz (300g/1½ cups) sugar
¼ pint (125ml/⅔ cup) water
2 large lemons

Place the walnuts in cold water and bring to the boil. Strain after 1 minute and set aside. Remove the peel and pith from the lemons but do not discard. Cut lemons into segments, removing all the membranes and pips. Tie peel, pith, membranes and pips into a little muslin bag. Place sugar in water in a large, heavy pan and heat gently until the sugar is completely dissolved. Add the scalded walnuts, prepared lemon segments and the muslin bag. Boil gently, stirring occasionally, for about 20 minutes or until setting point is reached (test as for **Apricot Eingemachtes**). Remove the pan from the heat and allow the contents to cool slightly (about 10 minutes) before potting into small, clean warmed jars. Cover down when cold. Yields about 1 lb (480g).

Charoseth

The quantity given will be sufficient for two Sedarim. Charoseth is not eaten on any other occasion.

3 oz (75g/¾ cup) walnuts
¼ large cooking apple
Kosher wine to moisten
2 level teasp sugar
2 level teasp cinnamon

Mince the walnuts and the apple. Moisten with the kosher wine and flavour with cinnamon and sugar. The consistency should be that of mortar.

Passover Baking

POINTERS TO SUCCESS

1. Use eggs at room temperature, not straight from the refrigerator—they will whisk to a much greater volume than when chilled.
2. As dampness may cause heaviness, make sure that both matzo meal and potato flour are absolutely dry by leaving the packages in an airing

cupboard or warming drawer of the cooker for 24 hours before use.
3. To avoid any chance of cakes sticking in the tins, if available, use silicone lining paper as the commercial bakers do. Prepare the tins before preparing the cake mixture as whisked sponges lose volume if allowed to stand before baking.
4. To allow for loss of heat when the oven is opened, preheat it one Gas No., 25°F, 10°C higher than is indicated in the recipe. Turn down to the correct temperature when the cake is put in. This is a necessary precaution with a delicately-structured cake like a Passover sponge.
5. When whisking egg white, never leave the electric mixer unattended. Overbeaten whites collapse into a liquid state again and cannot be reconstituted.
6. Always use a metal spoon for folding the dry ingredients into the egg mixture. A wooden spoon would crush out the air which has been beaten in.

Note:
To change medium matzo meal into fine meal, or fine meal into cake meal, put in an electric grinder or liquidizer for 5 seconds. To change medium meal directly into cake meal, grind or liquidize for 10 seconds.

Several days beforehand, it is wise to plan exactly what confectionery is to be made at home. As some recipes need all whites and others all yolks, if possible select those recipes to make that will use up an equal quantity of both. Any left-over egg whites can be stored tightly-covered in the refrigerator for use later in the week, but left-over egg yolks should be used within 24 hours.

Biscuits (Cookies) that use both the Whites and the Yolks

Sugared Almond Sticks

3 oz (75g/¾ cup) ground almonds
2 oz (50g/¼ cup) potato flour and 2 oz (50g/7 tbsp) cake or fine meal
2 oz (50g/¼ cup) caster (superfine) sugar
4 oz (100g/½ cup) butter
1 egg yolk and 1 egg white
Few drops almond essence (extract)
Topping:
1 oz (25g/¼ cup) flaked almonds
1 oz (25g/2 tbsp) caster (superfine) sugar

Mix together the potato flour, almonds, meal and sugar. Rub in the butter as for pastry, then mix to a dough with the yolk and essence. Divide into 6 portions. Roll each portion on a lightly sugared board into a 12 in (30 cm) long sausage. Lay the 6 'sausages' side by side and brush the tops generously with the slightly beaten egg white, then sprinkle with the mixed almonds and sugar. Cut across all the strips to make biscuits 1½ in (4 cm) long. Separate the cut pieces and place on ungreased baking sheets. Bake in a moderate oven (Gas No. 4, 350°F, 180°C) for 18 minutes until a light golden brown. Makes about 36.

Coconutties

4 oz (100g) plain (semi-sweet) Passover chocolate
2 oz (50g/¼ cup) butter (or margarine)
4 oz (100g/1⅓ cups) desiccated (dried and shredded) coconut
3 oz (75g/⅓ cup) caster (superfine) sugar
2 oz (50g/½ cup) chopped toasted almonds
1 egg

Line a tin 7 or 8 in (18–20 cm) square with greased greaseproof paper. Break the chocolate into a bowl, standing in a pan of steaming water until melted. Pour the chocolate into the lined tin and spread evenly. Leave to set. In a small pan, melt the butter slowly, then stir in the sugar, the browned nuts and coconut. Add the beaten egg and mix well. Spread over the chocolate in the tin and bake in a moderate oven (Gas No. 4, 350°F, 180°C) for 25 minutes or until golden brown. Allow to go quite cold before cutting into fingers. Makes about 20.

Prelatoes

Light and crisp sponge biscuits, excellent for the base of a trifle.

3 large eggs
2½ oz (65g/⅓ cup) caster (superfine) sugar
1 oz (25g/3 tbsp) potato flour
1½ oz (40g/5 tbsp) cake or fine meal
2 teasp vanilla sugar

Separate the eggs and cream together the yolks and sugar till white and fluffy. Beat in the flavouring. Beat the whites till they form stiff, glossy peaks. Sift together potato flour and meal. Stir a little of the egg white into the yolks and fold in the flour. Finally fold in the remaining egg white. The mixture should be firm but fluffy. Using a ½ in (1 cm) plain pipe, pipe into finger lengths or rounds (or drop from a teaspoon in rounds) on a greased and potato-floured tin. Dust with caster sugar. Bake in a moderate oven (Gas No. 4, 350°F, 180°C) for 5–7 minutes, or until a pale golden brown. Makes about 24.

Passover Crunchies

3 oz (75g/½ cup) potato flour
3 oz (75g/⅔ cup) cake meal
2 oz (50g/½ cup) ground almonds
4 oz (100g/½ cup) caster (superfine) sugar
Pkt (⅔ oz/20g/2 tbsp) vanilla sugar (if available)
Juice of ½ lemon
6 oz (150g/¾ cup) butter
2 egg yolks
2 egg whites

Cream the fat and sugar until light in colour, then beat in the juice, vanilla sugar, and egg yolks. Fold in the mixed flour, meal and ground almonds. The mixture can then be used in either of the following ways:

1. Beat the 2 whites until foamy. Have ready a bowl of desiccated coconut or chopped walnuts or almonds. Take a tablespoon of the mixture, form into a rough ball, drop into the egg white and then into the chopped nuts. Arrange well apart on greased trays and flatten slightly with the base of a glass. Bake in a moderate oven (Gas No. 4, 350°F, 180°C) for 12 minutes. Makes about 24.
2. Put the mixture into a piping bag fitted with a coarse rose tube. Pipe into rosettes, sticks or rings. Scatter with almond nibs. Bake at Gas No. 5, 375°F, 190°C, for 8–10 minutes until golden brown. Makes about 36.

Biscuits (Cookies) made with Yolks alone

Coconut Pyramids

4 egg yolks; or 2 whole eggs
½ lb (200g/3 cups) desiccated (dried and shredded) coconut
4 oz (100g/½ cup) caster (superfine) sugar
Juice and rind of ½ lemon

Beat the yolks and sugar until creamy, then stir in the lemon juice, rind and coconut. Form into pyramids, using a moist egg cup. Bake at Gas No. 5, 375°F, 190°C, 18–20 minutes until golden brown. Makes about 24.

Chocolate Walnut Truffles

6 oz (150g) plain (semi-sweet) chocolate
2 oz (50g/¼ cup) butter
2 egg yolks
3 oz (75g/¾ cup) sifted icing (confectioners') sugar
2 teasp rum or brandy
1 oz (25g/¼ cup) ground almonds
2 oz (50g/½ cup) walnuts
Cocoa, icing (confectioners') sugar, desiccated (dried and shredded) coconut

In a basin standing in a pan of very hot water, melt the butter and broken chocolate. When quite smooth, drop in the egg yolks, and stir until slightly thickened. Take off heat and add rum, icing sugar, almonds, and the finely chopped walnuts. Chill for half an hour until firm enough to handle. Form into balls the size of a marble, using the palm of the hand. Roll in cocoa, or in icing sugar, or in desiccated coconut. Leave in tin in refrigerator until required. When needed, leave at room temperature for half an hour. Makes 25–30.

Biscuits (Cookies) made with Whites alone

Almond Macaroons

5 oz (125g/1¼ cups) ground almonds (hazelnuts can also be used)
5 oz (125g/⅔ cup) caster (superfine) sugar
2 large egg whites
18 split almonds
Few drops vanilla essence (extract)

Put the unbeaten egg whites into a bowl, add the mixed almonds and sugar, a tablespoon at a time, beating well after each addition. Beat in the essence. Line biscuit tins with silicone paper or greased paper. Using either a teaspoon or a metal pipe in a nylon piping bag, drop little bulbs of the mixture onto the trays. Press a half split almond onto the top, flattening the macaroon slightly. Sprinkle each biscuit lightly with caster sugar. Bake in a moderate oven (Gas No. 4, 350°F, 180°C) for 25 minutes or until golden brown. Store in an airtight tin. Makes 18.

Coconut Kisses

The chocolate bits remain whole even after baking.

2 egg whites
4 oz (100g/1 cup) icing (confectioners') sugar
2 oz (50g/¾ cup) desiccated (dried and shredded) coconut
4 oz (100g) plain (semi-sweet) chocolate

Beat the whites until they form stiff peaks, then beat in the icing sugar gradually, beating until stiff after each addition. Fold in the coconut and the chocolate chopped into bits (roughly ¼ in/½ cm cubes). Put in little heaps on an oiled baking sheet, allowing 2 in (5 cm) between kisses. Bake in a slow moderate oven (Gas No. 2, 300°F, 150°C) for 30 minutes, or until crisp to the touch, and easily lifted off the tray. Makes about 20.

Cinnamon Balls

Bake only as long as directed to ensure that the biscuits remain soft and moist inside.

2 egg whites
4 oz (100g/½ cup) caster (superfine) sugar
½ lb (200g/2 cups) ground almonds
1 level tbsp cinnamon

Beat the whites till they form stiff peaks. Fold in all the remaining ingredients. Form into balls with wetted hands. Bake on a greased tray at Gas No. 3, 325°F, 170°C, for 25 minutes, or until just firm to the touch. Roll in icing (confectioners') sugar whilst warm, and then when cold. Makes about 24.

Date and Walnut Kisses

2 egg whites
4 oz (100g/1 cup) sifted icing (confectioners') sugar
¼ lb (100g/1 cup) walnuts
¼ lb (100g/1 cup) blanched almonds
¼ lb (100g/⅔ cup) pitted dates

Roughly chop the dates and nuts. Beat the whites until they form stiff, glossy peaks; then beat in the sugar, a tablespoon at a time, beating until stiff after each addition. Fold in nuts and dates. Drop in little heaps on a greased baking tin. Bake at Gas No. 2, 300°F, 150°C, for 30 minutes, until crisp to the touch and pale gold. Makes about 24.

Florentines

2 oz (50g/¼ cup) butter
2 oz (50g/¼ cup) caster (superfine) sugar
2 teasp cream
2 oz (50g/½ cup) chopped walnuts
2 oz (50g/½ cup) chopped almonds
2 oz (50g/½ cup) sultanas (white raisins)

Bring the butter, sugar and cream to boiling point—do not boil. Add the almonds, walnuts and sultanas. Place in small teaspoonfuls on silicone paper. Bake at Gas No. 4, 350°F, 180°C, for 10 minutes. Finish by coating underside in chocolate, or leave plain. Makes 20.

Passover Cakes

A sponge cake is lightened by the expansion, in the heat of the oven, of the air which is entrapped in the beaten eggs. Whether the whole eggs are beaten together, or the yolks and whites are beaten separately, it is essential that they be beaten to the correct stage. This varies according to the specific recipe, but the wording used is always the same:

Stiff, glossy peaks of egg whites. Withdraw the beaters—the egg whites will stand up straight without tilting to one side or the other. The texture is shiny. When overbeaten the texture becomes dull and like cotton-wool in appearance.

Thick and white yolks and sugar. Lift the beater and allow some of the mixture to fall back onto the surface. This should retain its shape for a few seconds before disappearing. The mixture lightens considerably in appearance. The same test can be applied when the yolks and whites are beaten together with the sugar, whether by electric whisk or by hand over hot water.

Note: All whisked sponges should be left in the baking tin, resting on a wire cooling tray, until completely cold, so that the delicate structure has set before the cake is turned out.

Passover Plava

After many years of experimentation I have found that this particular recipe gives the most consistently successful results. The cake itself stays moist for several days. Use a cake tin approx 2 in (5 cm) deep.

For 9 in (23 cm) cake or two 7 in (18 cm) cakes
5 large eggs
10 oz (250g/1¼ cups) caster (superfine) sugar
3 oz (75g/⅔ cup) cake meal
3 oz (75g/½ cup) potato flour
1 tbsp lemon juice

For 7 in (18 cm) cake
3 large eggs
6 oz (150g/¾ cup) caster (superfine) sugar
2 oz (50g/7 tbsp) cake meal
2 oz (50g/⅓ cup) potato flour
2 teasp lemon juice

Separate the yolks from the whites. Divide sugar into two equal quantities. Put one amount of sugar into bowl with the yolks and beat until thick and white. (If an electric beater is not available, stand the eggs and sugar in a bowl over a pan of very hot water and whisk until thick and white.) Beat in the juice. In another bowl, beat whites until they form stiff, glossy peaks then beat in the sugar until a firm meringue is formed. Fold into first mixture. Finally fold in the sifted meal and potato flour. Spoon into the cake tin which has been oiled and then sprinkled with sugar. Level the surface. Sprinkle a thin layer of caster sugar over top.

To bake: 9 in (23 cm) cake at Gas No. 4, 350°F, 180°C, for 1 hour 10 minutes.
7 in (18 cm) cake at Gas No. 4, 350°F, 180°C, for 45 minutes.

VARIATIONS

Raspberry Sponge: Make the 7 in (18 cm) cake; fold in 1 tablespoon of Passover raspberry jam after the meal and flour have been added. Sprinkle the sugared surface of the uncooked cake with 2 level tablespoons of finely-chopped blanched almonds. Bake as above.

Almond Sponge: A deliciously moist cake. Make in exactly the same way as the 7 in (18 cm) plava, folding in 3 oz (75g/¾ cup) ground almonds with the sifted meal and potato flour.

Traditional Passover Sponge

This cake is excellent if a more shallow cake is required. If preferred the sugar quantity can be cut to 14 oz (350g/2 cups).

10 large eggs; or 12 standard eggs
1 lb (450g/2$\frac{1}{4}$ cups) caster (superfine) sugar
5 oz (125g/1 cup + 2 tbsp) cake meal or fine matzo meal
$\frac{1}{4}$ lb (100g/$\frac{2}{3}$ cup) potato flour
Juice of 1 lemon

Conventional method: Whisk the yolks until they are creamy and light in colour then add the sugar gradually, whisking until the mixture forms a thick glossy ribbon as it falls back into the bowl from the beaters. Beat in the lemon juice. Sift the potato flour and meal together three times. Whisk the whites until they form stiff but glossy peaks. Carefully fold the meal into the yolk mixture, then cut and fold in the whites using a metal spoon and an 'over-and-over' cutting action rather than a 'round-and-round' stirring which tends to press out the air. Spoon the mixture into the prepared tins and sprinkle the surface with 3 teaspoons caster sugar.

New method: This is an easier method for a beginner. Beat the whites with a pinch of salt until they form stiff, glossy peaks (leave the yolk in each half shell). Now add the yolks one at a time, alternately with a tablespoon of the sugar, beating well after each addition. When all the sugar and yolks are in, beat a little longer until the mixture is thick and mousse-like. Finally beat in the lemon juice and fold in the potato flour and meal as in the first method.

To bake:
1. Divide between two greaseproof paper lined baking tins, each approximately 10 × 7 × 3 in (25 × 18 × 8 cm). Bake at Gas No. 4, 350°F, 180°C, for 1 hour.
or
2. Spoon into three 8 in (20 cm) lined cake tins. Bake at Gas No. 4, 350°F, 180°C, for half an hour and then at Gas No. 3, 325°F, 170°C, for a further 15 minutes.
or
3. Divide between two 9 in (23 cm) ring tins. Bake at Gas No. 3, 325°F, 170°C, for 1$\frac{1}{4}$ hours. Leave all the cakes in the tin to cool completely before turning out on to a cooling tray. Store in airtight tins. The sponge cakes can be split and filled as follows:

Lemon Curd: Cream 2 oz (50g/$\frac{1}{4}$ cup) butter with 3 oz (75g/$\frac{3}{4}$ cup) sifted icing sugar. Beat in 2 tablespoons lemon curd.

Chocolate Butter Cream: Cream 2 oz (50g/$\frac{1}{4}$ cup) butter until soft. Beat in 4 oz (100g/1 cup) sifted icing (confectioners') sugar, alternately with 2 oz (50g) kosher chocolate which has been melted in 2 tablespoons strong coffee (made with 2 teaspoons instant coffee).

Mocha Sponge

This is a chocolate sponge which can be served plain or filled with chocolate butter cream (given above), coffee cream or mocha whipped cream (both given below).

1$\frac{1}{2}$ oz (40g/$\frac{1}{4}$ cup) potato flour
$\frac{1}{2}$ oz (15g/2 tbsp) Passover cocoa
1 oz (25g/$\frac{1}{4}$ cup) cake meal
4 eggs
6 oz (150g/$\frac{3}{4}$ cup) caster (superfine) sugar
1 tbsp hot coffee

Use the conventional method described above, sifting the cocoa with meal and potato flour. Add the hot coffee before folding in the egg whites. Bake in a 9 in (23 cm) loose-bottomed tin, which has been greased, then dusted out with cake meal. Bake at Gas No. 4, 350°F, 180°C, for half an hour, then at Gas No. 3, 325°F, 170°C, for 20 minutes. Turn oven to lowest setting and leave cake for a further 10 minutes, then turn off heat altogether and leave cake in for 10 minutes before removing.

Coffee Butter Cream: Beat 4 oz (100g/$\frac{1}{2}$ cup) butter until creamy then beat in 6 oz (150g/1$\frac{1}{2}$ cups) icing (confectioners') sugar alternately with 2 level teaspoons instant coffee dissolved in 2 teaspoons hot water (allow coffee to cool before using).

Mocha Whipped Cream: If kosher cream is available this filling may be used instead. Whip 5 fl oz (125ml/$\frac{2}{3}$ cup) of double (heavy) cream until it begins to thicken, then beat in 1 tablespoon cold strong coffee and 2 teaspoons caster (superfine) sugar. Whisk until the cream holds its shape; but beware of overbeating, which will cause it to curdle.

The topping: The cake can be dusted with icing (confectioners') sugar or: Melt 4 oz (100g) plain (semi-sweet) chocolate with 2 oz (50g/$\frac{1}{4}$ cup) butter in a basin standing in a pan of boiling water. Stir until smooth and liquid, then pour over cake. Decorate with chopped walnuts. Leave 2 or 3 hours at least in a cool place before serving.

Passover Ring Sponge

This is a fine-textured sponge, which can be served plain, dusted with icing (confectioners') sugar; or it can be split and filled with canned or frozen fruit and cream; or with lemon curd blended with twice its volume of whipped cream; or with plain apricot conserve.

4 oz (100g/1 cup + 2 tbsp) sifted cake meal (or fine matzo meal if not available)
1$\frac{1}{2}$ oz (40g/$\frac{1}{4}$ cup) potato flour
Pinch of salt
7 oz (175g/1 cup) caster (superfine) sugar
5 eggs
2 fl oz (50ml/4 tbsp) oil
1 teasp lemon juice
2 fl oz (50ml/4 tbsp) orange juice
1 teasp orange rind

Oil a 9 in (23 cm) tube or ring tin. Sift the cake meal, potato flour, salt and 5 oz (125g/$\frac{2}{3}$ cup) of the sugar into a bowl. Blend the egg yolks, oil, lemon juice and orange juice. Add the rind, and then stir this mixture into the dry ingredients. Beat well with a wooden spoon to form a smooth, slack batter. Whisk the egg whites until they form stiff peaks, then whisk in remaining 2 oz (50g/$\frac{1}{3}$ cup) sugar a level tablespoonful at a time, beating after each addition until the mixture forms stiff peaks. Use a metal spoon to fold the meringue into the batter until well blended. Turn the mixture into the tin and bake in a fairly slow oven (Gas No. 3, 325°F, 170°C) for 1$\frac{1}{4}$ hours. Turn the cooked cake upside down on a wire rack and leave until it is quite cold. Loosen the edges lightly with the tip of a knife and slide the cake out of the tin. Store in an airtight tin. This cake will keep fresh for the whole Passover week—if it survives that long!

Almond Madeira Cake

The French call this 'Pain de Gênes', and it will keep fresh for a week. For success it is essential that the potato flour used be absolutely dry.

4 oz (100g/$\frac{1}{2}$ cup) butter
5 oz (125g/$\frac{2}{3}$ cup) caster (superfine) sugar
4 oz (100g/1 cup) ground almonds
2 oz (50g/$\frac{1}{3}$ cup) potato flour
3 egg yolks
2 tbsp orange juice or orange-flavoured liqueur
1 teasp orange rind
3 egg whites

Cream butter till like the mayonnaise, then beat in 4 oz (100g/$\frac{1}{2}$ cup) of sugar and cream again. Work in orange rind and ground almonds, then beat in yolks and juice or liqueur. Beat whites to a meringue then beat in the remaining 1 oz (25g/2 tbsp) sugar. Fold into first mixture and finally stir in well-dried potato flour. Put into an oiled and bottom-lined 8 or 9 in (20–23 cm) round cake tin. Bake at Gas No. 3, 325°F, 170°C, for 45 minutes to 1 hour, or until firm to the touch. Serve plain or with dusting of icing sugar.

Orange Walnut Torte

A deliciously flavoured cake, which can be served plain, topped with a water icing flavoured with lemon juice or rum, or split and filled with rum-flavoured whipped cream. Half quantities make one 7–8 in (18–20 cm) cake.

6 eggs, separated
7 oz (175g/1 cup) caster (superfine) sugar
7 oz (175g/1$\frac{3}{4}$ cups) ground walnuts
Grated rind and juice of a small orange
5 level tbsp cake meal (or fine meal if unavailable)

Separate the eggs and put in two separate bowls. Divide the sugar in two equal portions. Beat one portion of sugar into the yolks until thick and mousse-like. (If no electric beater is available, do this over hot water.) Beat in the rind and juice. Beat whites with a pinch of salt until they form stiff, glossy peaks, then beat in the second portion of sugar a tablespoonful at a time, beating after each addition. Finally fold the meringue into the yolks. Mix together the ground nuts and meal, then fold into the egg mixture. Spoon into two 7 in (18 cm) or one 9 in (23 cm) or 10 in (25 cm) loose-bottomed cake tin which has been oiled, then sprinkled with meal. Smooth the top of the mixture level, then sprinkle lightly with caster sugar (omit if to be iced). Bake in a moderate oven (Gas No. 4, 350°F, 180°C) for 1 hour 10 minutes, or until firm to the touch and slightly shrunken from the sides. Allow to cool in tin on cooling rack for 30 minutes, then ease out.

VARIATION

Use ground hazelnuts instead of almonds and flavour with lemon juice and rind.

Passover Desserts

The traditional 'afters' for a Passover meal consist of some form of fresh or dried fruit compote, served with a slice of sponge cake. Fresh fruit salads are also welcome at this time of rich food, especially if enhanced with a small glass of Passover liqueur or rum. The recipes that follow are for more special meals during the Festival.

Note: Frozen fruit can be used at Passover, providing it has been frozen without sugar.

Rum and Apple Flan

The 'pastry' for this flan is made from sponge cake or prelato (passover ladyfinger) crumbs. I find this is much more successful than conventional pastry made with meal. Margarine can be substituted for a meat meal, but the flavour is less delicate. It is advisable to make and bake the flan in an oven-to-table glass dish as it is too delicate to turn out.

3 oz (75g/1¼ cups) sponge cake or prelato (passover ladyfinger) crumbs
2 oz (50g/¼ cup) butter
2 oz (50g/¼ cup) caster (superfine) sugar
½ teasp cinnamon

Cream the butter, sugar and cinnamon, then work in the crumbs. Spread over the bottom and sides of an 8 in (20 cm) glass pie dish. Put in a quick moderate oven (Gas No. 5, 375°F, 190°C) for 10 minutes or until golden brown. Leave to cool.

Filling:
1½ lb(¾kg) cooking apples, peeled, cored and sliced
2 tbsp apricot jam
1 oz (25g/2 tbsp) butter
4 oz (100g/½ cup) sugar
Grated rind and juice of half a lemon
1–2 tbsp brandy or rum (optional)

Melt butter in a pan, then add the apples in layers, alternately with the sugar, lemon rind and juice and apricot jam. Put on the lid and cook gently until the apples are tender. Cool, then stir in spirit. Spoon into the baked crust and top with unsweetened whipped cream, spiked with toasted almonds. If cream is not available sprinkle with toasted coconut. Serves 6.

Raspberry or Cherry Frangipane Flan

Flan Case: made as in preceding recipe, left uncooked
1 tbsp icing (confectioners') sugar
Filling:
½ lb (200g) unsweetened frozen raspberries or 1 lb (½kg) unsweetened frozen cherries
Sponge:
2 oz (50g/¼ cup) butter
2 oz (50g/¼ cup) caster (superfine) sugar
1 egg
2 oz (50g/½ cup) ground almonds
2 level teasp potato flour

Beat all the sponge ingredients together until smooth. Sift a tablespoon of icing sugar over the flan case, then arrange the fruit on top and cover with the sponge. Bake in a moderate oven (Gas No. 4, 350°F, 180°C) for 30–40 minutes or until golden brown. Serve warm or cold sifted with icing sugar, or covered with a thin layer of lemon water icing. Serves 6.

Lemon Meringue Flan

Flan case made as in Rum and Apple Flan
Filling:
6 oz (150g/¾ cup) sugar
3 oz (75g/⅓ cup) butter
3 fl oz (75ml) lemon juice (2 medium lemons)
2 teasp grated lemon rind
3 egg yolks

In a small, heavy saucepan, melt butter then stir in sugar till dissolved. Add lemon juice. Pour a little of mixture over yolks beaten in basin, then return to pan. Cook very carefully, stirring constantly until mixture coats back of spoon (if nervous about mixture overheating, cook in double saucepan but it will take longer). Cool lemon filling, then pour into pie dish.

Meringue:
3 egg whites
Pinch of salt
6 oz (150g/¾ cup) caster (superfine) sugar
1 rounded teasp potato flour

Beat whites until stiff with pinch of salt. Gradually add sugar and potato flour (blended together) a tablespoonful at a time, beating after each addition until a solid meringue is formed. Spoon over filling, sealing meringue to edges of pie. Bake in a slow oven (Gas No. 2, 300°F, 150°C) for half an hour or until meringue is crisp on surface. Serve cold. Serves 6–8.

Strawberry Sponge Flan

Raspberries or loganberries can be substituted if preferred. If possible use an 8 in (20 cm) non-stick sponge flan tin (shaped to form a depression when the flan is turned out). Otherwise use an 8 in (20 cm) sandwich tin greased and dusted with caster (superfine) sugar.

2 large eggs, separated
3 oz (75g/⅓ cup) caster (superfine) sugar
1 oz (25g/2 tbsp) each of potato flour and cake or fine matzo meal
1 tbsp hot water
½ oz (15g/1 tbsp) butter (or 1 tbsp oil for a meat meal)

Turn on the oven to Gas No. 5, 375°F, 190°C. Put the water and fat in it to heat. Beat the whites until they form stiff, glossy peaks, then drop in 1 yolk and half the sugar. Beat until blended and thick (about 1 minute), then repeat with the remaining yolk and sugar. Fold the sifted meal and potato flour into the egg mixture followed by the hot water and fat. Spoon into the flan tin and cook at Gas No. 5, 375°F, 190°C, for 15 minutes, or until firm to gentle touch. Leave 5 minutes then ease out onto a cooling tray.

Filling:

1 Passover lemon or strawberry jelly (gelatin mix)
Juice of a lemon
1 tbsp apricot jam
½ lb (200g) frozen strawberries
2 bananas
1 oz (25g/2 tbsp) caster (superfine) sugar

Sprinkle the strawberries with caster sugar. Dissolve the jelly in ½ pint (250ml/1¼ cups) hot water over gentle heat (don't boil or jelly won't set). Put into a measure, add lemon juice and jam and enough additional water (or syrup from canned fruit) to make ¾ pint (375ml/2 cups). Put the cooled sponge flan onto a serving dish, and spoon a quarter of the hot jelly over it, and chill. Put the remaining jelly to chill also in the refrigerator until it is just beginning to set. When it is as thick as unbeaten egg white, mix gently with the sugared fruit and the sliced bananas. Spoon on top of the sponge and allow to set. Serve plain or with whipped cream. Serves 6–8.

VARIATION

Peach, Apricot or Pineapple Flan: Substitute the drained contents of a can of fruit for the sugared soft fruit. Use the syrup as part of the liquid for the jelly.

(*Note:* Do *not* use fresh pineapple—the enzymes it contains will prevent the jelly from setting.)

Lemon and Banana Meringue Baskets

This meringue sets with a crisp outside and a marsh-mallow inside. Any kind of fruit and cream mixture can be used to fill the baskets.

Lemon Curd:
4 egg yolks
½ lb (200g/1 cup) sugar
4 oz (100g/½ cup) unsalted butter
3 large lemons

Grate the rind of 2 lemons and squeeze the juice of all 3. Infuse if possible for several hours. Put the sugar in a bowl of water in a warm oven to heat through whilst you melt the butter in a basin standing in a pan of boiling water. Add the sugar and the strained juice. When the sugar mixture is smooth, pour a little over the beaten egg, then return to the pan and stir with a wooden spoon until the mixture just coats the back of the spoon (it thickens as it cools). Pour into hot dry jars (most easily warmed by standing in a warm oven for 10 minutes). Cover with wax discs. Leave till cold, then cover with foil and refrigerate. Makes 1½ lb (¾kg).

Meringue:
4 egg whites
8 oz (200g/1 cup) caster (superfine) sugar
1 teasp each of potato flour and lemon juice
Pinch of salt

Put whites into mixer bowl with a pinch of salt and whisk until meringue forms stiff peaks. Meanwhile, blend sugar and potato flour, then start adding to the meringue a tablespoon at a time, beating until stiff after each addition. This should take 5 minutes. Finally beat in lemon juice. Cover a greased tin with greased greaseproof paper. Pipe or spoon meringue into cups about 3 in (8 cm) in diameter. Have oven heated to Gas No. 2, 300°F, 150°C, turn down to Gas No. 1, 275°F, 140°C, and leave for 30–40 minutes or until crisp to the touch. Remove from tray. Store until needed.

To serve: Blend ½ cup of curd with 5 fl oz (125ml) double (heavy) cream, whipped until thick. Slice bananas into bottom of each cup. Spoon filling on top. Decorate if liked with chopped walnuts. Chill for at least an hour. Serves 10–12.

Orange Liqueur Whip

A variation on the zabaione theme. Leave for several hours before serving, to allow the flavours to develop.

6 egg yolks
6 teasp caster (superfine) sugar
3 tbsp orange juice
2 teasp lemon juice
Grated rind of ½ orange and ½ lemon
3 tbsp Passover liqueur (orange-flavoured, if possible)

Beat the yolks and sugar with an electric blender until thick and white, then beat in the orange juice, lemon juice, rinds and liqueur. Transfer to a basin standing in a pan of almost boiling water. Continue to whisk vigorously until the mixture fluffs up and has the texture of a whisked sponge or mousse. Immediately remove from heat and stand in a basin of cold water. Continue to whisk until cool. Spoon into 6 glasses. Serve cold.

Banana Soufflé

A delicious ending to a light meal, this is especially tasty when served with an orange and pineapple fruit salad.

6 large ripe bananas
4 oz (100g/½ cup) caster (superfine) sugar
Juice of 1 orange
Grated rind of 1 lemon and 2 teasp juice
3 large egg whites
2 tbsp chopped almonds, fried until golden with nut of butter

Preheat the oven (Gas No. 6, 400°F, 200°C). Purée the bananas either in a blender or through a sieve, then beat in 3 oz (75g/⅜ cup) of sugar, juices and rind, and the toasted nuts. Beat the egg whites until they form stiff peaks, then beat in the remaining amount of sugar. Fold into bananas. Have ready a buttered round dish, approximately 8 in (20 cm) in diameter, and 4 in (10 cm) deep. Sprinkle with caster sugar. Spoon in the soufflé mixture, and level off. Turn oven down to Gas No. 5, 375°F, 190°C, put in the soufflé and bake for 30 minutes. Serve at once. Serves 6.

Bananas in Wine Sauce

6–8 stubby under-ripe bananas
4 oz (100g/½ cup) caster (superfine) sugar
½ pint (250ml/1¼ cups) Israeli burgundy
½ teasp cinnamon
Coconut, chopped nuts or cream for decoration

Peel, string and cut the bananas in half, lengthwise. Dissolve the sugar in the wine in a wide frying pan. Add the cinnamon and bring slowly to the boil. Lay the bananas in the wine syrup, side by side, and allow them to simmer for 5 minutes, turning once. Lift out the bananas and arrange in a glass serving dish. Simmer the wine until it is thick and syrupy (for a further 10 minutes). Pour over the bananas and chill thoroughly. To serve for a meat meal, sprinkle with the chopped nuts or toasted coconut; for a milk meal, decorate with whipped cream. Serve with plain sponge cake or biscuits. Serves 8.

Mocha Mousse

This dessert is rich, so set and serve it in coffee cups.

4 oz (100g) plain (semi-sweet) Passover chocolate
3 large eggs, separated
2 level teasp instant coffee
1 tbsp Passover brandy or rum
Sufficient crushed prelatoes (ladyfingers) or stale sponge cake crumbs to come to a depth of ½ in (1 cm) in each cup
3 tbsp kosher wine
Chopped toasted almonds

Divide the crumbs between the cups and soak each serving with 2 teaspoons kosher wine. Break up the chocolate and stand in a basin over very hot water. Stir until smooth and melted, then remove from the heat. Immediately, drop in the egg yolks and beat vigorously until the mixture thickens slightly. Stir in the coffee and rum or brandy. Beat the whites until they form soft (slightly floppy) peaks. Stir one quarter of the beaten whites into the chocolate mixture, then fold in the remainder. Divide the mixture between the cups. Top with the toasted almonds. Allow to set for several hours. Serves 6.

Passover Pouring Custard

Excellent to serve with stewed or fresh fruit salads. This is very useful when cream is not available. It can also be used to top trifle.

2 whole eggs
¾ pint (375ml/2 cups) milk
2 oz (50g/¼ cup) caster (superfine) sugar
2 level teasp potato flour
1 teasp vanilla sugar (if available)

Using blender, blend eggs, potato flour and sugar for 15 seconds. Heat milk until it steams, then add to other ingredients. Return to pan. Cook gently, stirring until bubbles disappear—the custard will have thickened. Serve hot or cold (pouring custard).

Savoury Dishes

Most of the soup, meat and fish dishes used during the year, can be prepared during Passover, provided that they are not thickened with flour or cornflour (cornstarch). All the clear soups, chicken and borscht in particular, can be used as well as those cream soups such as 'Crème du Jour' and 'Golden Vegetable Soup' that are thickened with potato. All the traditional fish dishes can be served, and salmon is especially popular as a Seder dish. However, there are certain recipes traditional at this season, and others which I have developed that are worth restating here.

Matzo Meal Pancakes (Kremslach)

These are probably similar to the meal cakes that were offered as a sacrifice in the Temple at Jerusalem.

2 eggs
1 level teasp salt
1 level tbsp caster (superfine) sugar
$\frac{1}{4}$ pint (125ml/$\frac{2}{3}$ cup) warm water
3 oz (75g/6 level tbsp) fine meal

Beat the eggs and 2 tablespoons of the water until thick. Gradually, add the meal and the sugar and enough additional water to make a thick batter that just drops from the spoon. Fry in oil $\frac{1}{4}$ in ($\frac{1}{2}$ cm) deep or a mixture of 2 oz (50g/$\frac{1}{4}$ cup) butter and 1 tablespoon oil until golden brown and puffy. Turn and cook the other side. Serve hot off the pan, plain or with cinnamon sugar. Serves 4.

Matzo Brei

There are many variations of this Passover 'French toast'. My family likes the soaked matzo just fried in butter without egg—it's a matter of choice.

2 whole matzot
2 eggs
Pinch each of salt and pepper

Break matzo into bite-size pieces, and put in a bowl, covered with cold water. Soak three minutes, then squeeze out excess water. Add the matzo to the beaten, seasoned egg. Fry in hot butter first on one side and then the other. Serves 3–4.

Halibut in Egg and Lemon Sauce

This delicious fish dish will keep for three or four days under refrigeration, and in any case tastes better the day after it has been made. If it is to be served as an entrée rather than a main course, the fish should be cut into 6 rather than 4 pieces, as halibut is a very substantial fish.

4 halibut steaks (approx $1\frac{1}{2}$ lb/$\frac{3}{4}$kg in all)
1 large onion, thinly sliced
6 level tbsp sugar
2 level teasp salt
Pinch of white pepper
Water to cover the fish (approx $\frac{3}{4}$ pint/375ml/2 cups)

In a saucepan or lidded frying pan wide enough to hold all the fish in one layer, bring the water, the onion and the seasonings to the boil (adding the sugar at this stage greatly improves the taste of the fish, without noticeably sweetening it). Put in the washed and salted steaks, bring the liquid back to the boil, then lower the heat so that the liquid is barely bubbling. Partially cover the pan and simmer very gently for 20 minutes. Lift out the fish with a slotted spoon or fish slice, draining any liquid back into the pan. Place the fish in an oval entrée dish about $1\frac{1}{2}$ in (4 cm) in depth. Remove the skin but leave the bone. Leave to cool while you make the sauce.

Sauce:

2 large eggs
8 fl oz (200ml/1 cup) fish liquor
Juice of 2 lemons (3 fl oz/75ml)
1 level teasp potato starch

After the fish has been removed, boil the fish liquor for 3 minutes to concentrate the flavour, then strain it and measure out 8 fl oz (200ml/1 cup). Beat the eggs thoroughly with a rotary whisk, then stir in the fish liquor and the potato starch (which has been mixed to a cream with the minimum of cold water). Put this liquid into a thick-bottomed saucepan and cook gently over low heat until the sauce thickens to the consistency of a coating custard—you will need to stir it constantly. Do not let it boil, or the eggs may curdle. Taste and add extra juice, if necessary, to make the sauce equally sweet and sour. Pour the sauce over the fish, coating it completely. Leave in a cool place overnight, covered with foil. Serve garnished with parsley. Makes 4 generous helpings.

Baked Halibut on a Vegetable Bed

1½–2 lb (¾–1kg) halibut
1 oz (25g/2 tbsp) butter
Vegetable bed:
4 oz (100g/2 cups) mushrooms
4 large tomatoes, peeled and chopped
1 small onion, finely chopped
1 level tbsp parsley
1 oz (25g/2 tbsp) butter
Pinch sugar
1 level teasp salt
Pinch of black pepper
½ clove garlic, crushed
4 tbsp dry Passover wine or juice of a large lemon

Melt butter in small pan and cook the onion until soft and golden, then add the thinly sliced mushrooms and cook a further 2 minutes. Finally, add tomatoes, wine, salt, pepper, sugar and garlic and cook until a thick sauce is formed. Stir in the parsley and lay sauce down centre of buttered, 1 in (3 cm) deep baking dish just large enough to hold the fish. Lay halibut steaks on top. Rinse out frying pan and melt a further ounce (25g/2 tbsp) of butter, then paint over top of fish. Grill gently 10–12 minutes until a rich brown. Serves 4–6.

Meat Balls in a Sweet-Sour Sauce

As soaked bread cannot be used to lighten the traditional minced (ground) beef mixture it is a good idea to add a grated potato instead. The meat mixture can then be used as required, and is especially nice as stuffing for aubergines (eggplant), peppers or tomatoes.

Meat balls:
1½ lb (¾kg) minced shoulder steak (ground beef)
½ onion, finely grated
2 level teasp salt
Good pinch white pepper
1 medium potato, grated and drained for 10 min
2 level tbsp medium meal
1 level tbsp chicken fat or corn oil margarine
2 beaten eggs
2 tbsp oil for frying

Mix all the ingredients together—the mixture should be just firm enough to form into balls. Leave for ½ hour. Form into balls, and fry in 2 tablespoons hot oil on both sides until a rich golden brown. Arrange side by side in a shallow casserole.

Sweet-sour sauce:
1 onion, finely sliced
1 can Passover tomato and mushroom sauce
Juice of ½ lemon
2 level teasp sugar
1 bayleaf
1 crushed clove garlic
1 glass Israeli burgundy (or 4 tbsp water or meat stock)

In the same oil used to fry the meat balls, fry the onion until golden brown. Pour in the tomato and mushroom sauce, lemon juice, sugar, bayleaf and garlic, and thin the sauce with the wine, water or stock. (*Note:* If canned tomato and mushroom sauce is not available, use 8 fl oz (200ml/1 cup) Passover tomato soup instead.) Pour sauce over the meat balls. Cover loosely with foil and transfer to a moderate oven (Gas No. 3, 325°F, 170°C). Cook for 1½ hours, basting occasionally. If the sauce starts to boil, turn the oven down to Gas No. 2, 300°F, 150°C. Can be reheated. Serves 6.

Steak Braised in Wine

The wine both tenderizes the meat and flavours the sauce.

1½ lb (¾kg) first cut shoulder steak, cut ½ in (1 cm) thick and then cut in 4 or 5 portions; or 4–6 slices blade steak
1 large onion
3 tomatoes, peeled and sliced
½ cup thin gravy or stock
2 tbsp oil
½ cup (4 fl oz/100ml) red wine (optional)
1 clove garlic
Salt, pepper, sugar

Heat the fat in a heavy pan or casserole. Put in the sliced onion, and cook gently till soft and golden. Remove. In the same fat quickly brown the well dried meat. Remove steaks. Put onion back, then add wine (if used) and allow to come to the boil, then add stock, tomatoes, garlic and seasonings. Lay steaks on top. Put in a slow oven (Gas No. 2, 300°F, 150°C) for 2 hours, until meat is tender and gravy thickened. Serves 4–6, depending on amount of meat.

Beefsteak Pie

An enriched mashed potato topping makes this a perfect mid-week Passover main dish.

2 lb (1kg) braising or stewing steak
2 large onions
1 tbsp brown sugar
2 tbsp oil
3 level teasp salt, pepper
Water or stock to cover

Cut the meat into ½ in (1 cm) cubes. Brown in hot fat both sides. Then add the onions and sugar and cook until the onions are brown. Then barely cover the meat with water, or stock, add the salt and pepper and simmer until quite tender (about 2 hours).

The crust: Boil 5 large potatoes until tender, then strain and return to the pan, and mash over a gentle heat with a generous tablespoon of chicken fat, salt and pepper. Remove from heat and add 2 well-beaten eggs and a teaspoon of chopped parsley. Use this mixture to line the bottom and sides of a deep casserole, previously well-greased. Pour in the hot stew and smooth the remaining potato mixture on the top. Brush over with a little egg. Put in quick oven (Gas No. 6, 400°F, 200°C) for 15–20 minutes or until a rich brown. Serves 6 generously.

Passover Potato Latkes

4 large potatoes (16 fl oz/375ml/2 cups pulp when drained)
2 eggs
4 level tbsp cake or fine meal
1 level teasp salt
Pinch of pepper

Grate potatoes, leave to drain 15 minutes. Beat eggs with seasonings then stir in potatoes and matzo cake meal. Fry at once in ¼ in (½ cm) deep hot fat till a rich golden brown, turning once. Flatten the batter as you put it by tablespoon into the fat, which should sizzle moderately as it goes in. Serves 4–6.

Entertaining

The tradition of hospitality to 'the stranger within the gates' has been part of the Jewish way of family life from the very dawn of our recorded history.

Indeed, from the famous occasion when Abraham ordered Sara to 'make ready three measures of fine meal, knead it and make cakes' for three strangers he saw coming out of the desert, it has been the custom even in the most humble of households and in the most difficult of circumstances, to welcome guests to the family table.

It was when times were particularly troublesome that the necessity for the 'mitzvah' (or divine command) of hospitality was most urgent. An interesting picture of the ways European Jews in the early Middle Ages kept open doors for their persecuted fellow-religionists can be found in *The Rabbi of Bacharach* by Heinrich Heine. In that story, there was a place at the family's Passover table which was left for the Jew who might be pursued by 'blood libel' persecutors, but the tradition continued all through those centuries when the Jews lived in tight little isolated communities, though it was constantly re-interpreted according to the customs of the countries where they lived. In Russia, the samovar was kept ready for a glass of lemon tea, accompanied by a 'kichel' (oil and sugar biscuit) or slice of 'plava' (sponge cake) or ginger cake. In the Austro-Hungarian Empire there was a glass of 'schnapps', or a cup of coffee with kuchen or strudel. In Germany, there would be cheese cake or kugelhupf and a glass of beer (for Jews were great brewers until driven from the craft). American Jews who took customs of 'der heim' to the New World were soon quick to adopt more modern modes of entertaining, such as the brunch, the dinner party or the buffet supper.

It is interesting to trace the new trends in Jewish hospitality that have developed since the end of the Second World War. At first, after the war, particularly in the United Kingdom, the warmth of one's welcome was equated with the amount of sugar-rich confections that could be crammed onto the table. But a later, more diet-conscious generation, soon turned to dinner and supper-parties, with the emphasis on foods which contained more protein. This was an innovation in the pattern of Jewish entertaining customs, for in the nineteenth century, though guests were often invited to join the family table, particularly on the Sabbath and holy days, they were never invited to a meal that had been specifically prepared for them, unless there was a wedding or a barmitzvah to be celebrated.

Today the Jewish hostess has to face entirely new situations. No longer do we live and move in the limited social circles—usually family-centred—of earlier generations, but find our friends in ever-widening spheres. And at the moment in our history when careers after marriage and increasing involvement in community life and social welfare leave even less time for 'ancillary' activities, the Jewish woman is expected to entertain in a more sophisticated fashion than ever before, paying attention to the flowers, the décor and the table accoutrements as well as to the food that she sets before her guests.

To be able to welcome an increasing number of guests into one's home, and yet spend less time on preparing for their reception, I think it is essential to mobilize all the weapons of modern kitchen technology, such as the refrigerator, the freezer, the blender, the electric mixer, the dishwasher, stove-to-table ware—even mini-care cloths and napkins—and combine their use with a less formal approach to entertaining. In fact, it means putting a modern interpretation on the traditions of the past, so that entertaining becomes an extension of ordinary family living, with an extra place set once more at the table, and the family circle widened to welcome our friends, be it for coffee, drinks or a casserole and salad supper. Of course there are always those occasions when more formal manners must prevail, when, for example, a dinner party must be arranged. So in the sections that follow, I have set out what I consider to be the most satisfactory ways of continuing the tradition of Jewish hospitality in the present day. These are the methods I have tried and tested over the years, and which have met with the approval of my guests. I hope they meet with the approval of yours.

The Dinner Party

The dinner party is perhaps the most satisfying way of entertaining a small group of people. Carefully chosen and cooked food is served in the maximum of comfort, in an aesthetically pleasing setting, so that conditions are perfect for relaxation and conversation.

The number of guests: In the average home, a maximum of 10 guests is perhaps the most that can be seated round one table and served a hot meal in comfort. More guests can be accommodated if smaller tables are used; but this then becomes a more formal occasion. For the purposes of this section, I have catered for 8 to 10.

The setting: A beautifully-set table can enhance a meal as much as the quality of the food. Indeed some of the most successful hostesses I know have built their reputation on serving simple but beautifully presented food at a table set with carefully chosen linen and accessories. It is important that the chairs be comfortable and that a minimum of 21 in (53 cm) of table space be allowed for each place setting.

The service: Unless this is a formal dinner party, it is usual for the hostess to serve, assisted by a member of the family (husband, or teenage son or daughter), or by one waitress. The hostess usually serves the main course (preferably from a hot plate set on a sideboard or serving trolley), and the guests help themselves to vegetables and salads. If the food is carried to each guest, then two waitresses will be needed for the 10 guests. It is usual to have the first course on the table before the guests sit down (unless it is a hot soup), and the dessert laid on a trolley or sideboard for service by the hostess.

The food: Today it is fashionable to serve no more than 3 courses, or 4 on special occasions. It is important to contrast hot food with cold, crisp with soft, and spicy with bland. Colour is also vital as a monochrome meal can be excessively dull. In planning the menu, consider also practical details. If there is no one to dish up in the kitchen, have only one hot course, and that chosen so that it needs no last minute attention. Choose recipes that can be kept hot without spoiling, as guests are not always as prompt as they might be. In general, plan the menu round seasonal food as it will then be in its prime. Do not serve too many exotic or unusual dishes in the same menu or they will cancel each other out.

Pre-preparation: Even the working hostess can serve a superb dinner party if she plans the menu so that the preparation can be 'staggered' over several cooking sessions. Freeze as much of the 'makings' as possible—for example, pastry cases, sauces, dessert components, though avoid a completely frozen menu as this can be deadly dull. Use the refrigerator also to store those foods, particularly soups, casseroles and desserts, which improve overnight.

Once the menu has been planned, compile a master shopping list, and then divide it into different types of food—greengrocer, grocery, delicatessen, etc. Make sure there is room cleared in the refrigerator and freezer for all the food that will be required.

Make a rough time-table, both for shopping and preparation of the different components of the meal. This is most reassuring and avoids last minute crises. Check all the items that are necessary for the table setting, so that these can be washed and polished well beforehand, and the table set early in the day. It is best to buy flowers the day beforehand and soak them overnight, then arrange them early on the day, otherwise you won't have either time or patience to do the job later on.

Plan to have at least two hours free in the afternoon either to have your hair set or combed out, or to rest *in bed* and relax completely. Unless one has staff to do most of the preparation (and certainly the cooking) I do not think it is practical for the working hostess to plan a dinner party on a weekday.

Drinks before dinner: A maximum of two drinks before dinner ensures that the guests will still be able to appreciate the nuances of flavour in the food. More will certainly dull the palate. I do not believe in serving elaborate canapés or appetizers unless these are planned as a first course in themselves. Rather serve appetite-provoking foods such as sour cucumbers or olives. For a hot meal, I think it is also wise to be specific as to the time at which dinner is to be served. The best formula is to state 'come at 8 for 8.30', allowing thirty minutes' leeway for guests to arrive, meet their fellow guests and relax over a drink.

Drinks during the meal: This is always the province of the host, who pours the wine himself; for non-wine drinkers it is wise to have a selection of chilled soft drinks at hand.

Coffee after the meal: The tray for coffee should be prepared beforehand, and the coffee pot itself left to warm during the meal. It is a matter of preference whether the coffee is served at table or in the living-room, though if conversation is flourishing round the table it is best not to interrupt it by moving to another room. With the coffee, serve petits fours or sweetmeats such as nougat, bitter chocolate, mints, crystallized ginger or Turkish delight, which will round off the meal rather than overload it.

Note on cooking green vegetables for a party: Because it is impossible to gauge the exact moment at which green vegetables are to be served at a dinner party, it is wiser to follow the French method of pre-cooking them by first blanching the vegetables in a large amount of boiling water and then refreshing them in cold water to set the colour. This not only ensures that the vegetables are cooked 'à point' until tender but still firm, but also that the colour remains a brilliant green. After this preliminary treatment the vegetables can be reheated in butter, margarine or sauce, and will taste freshly cooked. This method is not suitable for regular use as the food value is not as good as when cooked by the conventional 'short boil' method in a minimum of water. Explicit instructions for the different vegetables are given in the menus that follow.

Note on quantities: In the recipes that follow amounts are given that will serve a maximum of 10 guests. Where two desserts are offered, one will normally serve 6 full portions, but taken in partnership with another dessert, it will be ample on this occasion for the larger number.

The menus that follow have all been served by me over a period of years. They have been chosen because they represent my philosophy of dinner party planning as set out above. Further dinner party menus can be found in the section on 'Festival Foods'.

Dairy Menus

To serve 8 *or* 10 *guests*

Dinner Party Menu No. 1 (*October to April*)

Avocado on the Half Shell with Fish Salad
Truite aux Amandes, New Potatoes, Cauliflower au Gratin
Orange and Chicory Salad
Savarin au Kirsch or Tarte Normande

Avocado on the Half Shell with Fish Salad

Make sure the avocados are slightly soft to gentle pressure all over, but are not squelchy in any way. The tartly-flavoured fish salad makes a delicious contrast with the bland oiliness of the avocado. It is wise to have melon or grapefruit on the half shell available should any guest not like the avocado. Alternatively, serve them the fish salad on a bed of shredded lettuce in a stemmed glass.

4 or 5 avocados
1 tbsp lemon juice
1 lb (½kg) halibut or haddock cooked in the following:
  Cold water to cover fish
  4 slices onion
  1 level teasp salt
  Pinch of pepper
  1 level teasp sugar

Simmer fish, covered, for 20 minutes, cool for 5 minutes, then lift out to drain. Remove skin and bone, and flake.

Pink Dressing:
10 fl oz (250ml/1¼ cups) soured cream
2 level tbsp tomato ketchup
Juice of ½ lemon
Few dashes Worcestershire sauce
Salt and pepper to taste
¼ large green pepper, finely diced

Mix all ingredients together, then mix with cold fish. Chill for at least an hour.

OR

Green Dressing:
5 fl oz (125ml/⅔ cup) soured cream and same amount of mayonnaise
2 generous tbsp chopped parsley
Pinch of garlic salt, black pepper and salt
2 white stalks of celery, chopped or 2 tbsp chopped walnuts

Put parsley, mayonnaise and seasonings in blender till parsley is finely chopped. Stir in soured cream, nuts or celery. Mix with fish.

To serve: An hour before dinner chill avocados. Cut avocados in half and remove stone. Sprinkle cavity with lemon juice. Fill with salad and garnish with gherkin. Serves 8–10.

Truite aux Amandes

Follow recipe on p. 48, allowing 1 trout per serving. Fry in 2 or 3 batches, according to the size of the frying pan. Keep hot in a low oven (Gas No. 2, 300°F, 150°C) on a baking tin, or heatproof flat serving dish. When ready to serve, make double the sauce recipe, spoon a little over the fish and serve the remainder in a sauce boat.

New Potatoes

Cook 3 lb (1½kg) potatoes before the guests arrive. Drain and cool. Melt 2 oz (50g/¼ cup) butter in a heatproof serving dish. Add 1 tablespoon chopped parsley and the drained potatoes, toss well and rcheat for 15 minutes at Gas No. 2, 300°F, 150°C.

Cauliflower au Gratin

A most delicious dish when it is made with really fresh cauliflower cooked until tender but still slightly firm. The dish reheats well.

Two 8 in (20 cm) cauliflowers, tough stalk removed and divided into flowerets

Plunge the washed cauliflower into a large pan, three-quarters full of boiling water, with 3 level teaspoons salt. Boil steadily, uncovered, for 9–12 minutes or until the stalk feels just tender when pierced with a sharp knife—it's safest to taste a piece. Lift carefully from the water to prevent crushing and put into a colander. Plunge into a basin of cold water. Leave for 3 minutes, then lift out and allow to drain. It is now ready for the sauce.

Sauce Mornay:
1½ pints (750ml/4 cups) milk
2 oz (50g/¼ cup) butter
2 oz (50g/½ cup) flour
½ level teasp salt
4 oz (100g/1 cup) sharp cheese, coarsely grated
Pinch of nutmeg and cayenne
Topping:
3 tbsp fine dry crumbs
3 tbsp grated cheese
2 oz (50g/¼ cup) melted butter

Heat the milk in a saucepan until it steams then pour it into a jug. Rinse the pan under the cold tap, then put in the butter. Melt over a gentle heat then stir in the flour. Allow to bubble for 2 minutes, then add the hot milk all at once, and whisk vigorously with a balloon whisk until smooth and bubbly. Add the seasoning and simmer for 3 minutes. Remove from the heat and stir in the cheese.

Have ready a buttered baking dish approximately 10 in (25 cm) in diameter and 2 in (5 cm) deep (or use a rectangular dish of similar depth). Lightly cover the bottom with sauce, then arrange the cauliflower on top. Mask completely with the remainder of the sauce. Mix the dry crumbs and cheese and sprinkle evenly on top. Finally pour over the melted butter. Leave covered loosely with greaseproof paper until ready to bake.

To bake: Cook in a moderately hot oven (Gas No. 5, 375°F, 190°C) for 30 minutes, until bubbly and golden brown. Keep hot at Gas No. 2, 300°F, 150°C, until required. Serves 8–10.

Orange and Chicory Salad

8 small heads of chicory, cut lengthwise in 4
2 large oranges
1 bunch of watercress
Dressing:
2 tbsp mayonnaise
2 tbsp sour cream (sweet cream may be substituted with a squeeze of lemon)
2 tbsp orange juice

Blend together dressing ingredients until the consistency of pouring cream. Peel the oranges with a very sharp knife, lifting off the pith and revealing the flesh itself, then cut between the skin so that each segment of orange falls out. Arrange the chicory and orange in a fairly shallow bowl and toss in the dressing. Edge the dish with watercress. Chill for an hour. Serves 8–10.

Savarin au Kirsch

A light, yeast sponge, soaked in kirsch-flavoured syrup, served with fruit and cream. The savarin can be baked days or weeks in advance and frozen. On the day, it is put back into the tin, foil-covered and reheated in a moderate oven (Gas No. 4, 350°F, 180°C) for 15–20 minutes or until warm to the touch. It is then treated as though freshly baked.

¼ oz (10g/½ cake) fresh yeast; or 1 teaspoon dried yeast
2½ fl oz (65ml/5 tbsp) warm milk
2 level teasp caster (superfine) sugar
Put all ingredients in a bowl and leave in a warm place till frothy (about 10 min).
1 large egg
4 oz (100g/1 cup) plain flour
2 oz (50g/¼ cup) soft butter
1 level teasp salt
½ teasp vanilla essence (extract)

Add the second lot of ingredients to the yeast mixture and beat for 3 minutes by spoon or mixer until smooth—the mixture should fall in 'sheets' from the spoon. Pour the mixture into a 25 fl oz (625ml/3 cups) capacity well-greased ring tin—which it will half fill. Put the filled tin in a greased polythene bag (pedal bin liner size) and leave for half an hour in a warm place until the mixture has risen level with the top of the tin. Bake in a quick moderate oven (Gas No. 6, 400°F, 200°C) for 25 minutes until a rich brown.

The syrup: While the savarin is cooking, dissolve 6 oz (150g/¾ cup) granulated sugar in 8 fl oz (200ml/1 cup) water and boil gently for 5 minutes. Stir in 5 tablespoons kirsch (or rum). Leave the cooked savarin in the tin for 5 minutes then turn out and place, puffy side up, in a shallow round casserole. Pour the warm syrup all over, then leave until it has absorbed it completely, basting occasionally. This may take up to an hour.

To serve: Turn right side up on serving dish, and fill centre with 8 fl oz (200ml/1 cup) cream, whipped and combined with fruit. The following combinations are particularly delicious:
Whipped cream topped with barely-thawed raspberry or strawberry purée;
Canned pineapple, folded into whipped cream which has had 2 or 3 tablespoons of the pineapple syrup whipped into it;
Well-drained, canned morello (sour red) cherries.
Serves 8–10.

Tarte Normande

Follow recipe on p. 152.

Dinner Party No. 2 (*June to August*)

Gnocchi alla Romana
Poached Salmon, Young Peas, New Potatoes
Mixed Green Salad
Danish Cucumber Salad
Green and Regular Mayonnaise
Raspberry and Banana Pavlova
Chestnut Ice-cream, Prelatoes (Passover ladyfingers)

Gnocchi alla Romana

Delicate 'dumplings', baked with cheese to make a light yet satisfying first course. The gnocchi mixture can be made one day and poached the next, and the whole dish can be prepared except for the final reheating, early in the day. Be sure to use a dry, low fat curd cheese—a rich cream cheese is not suitable.

12 oz (300g/1½ cups) dry curd cheese
3 oz (75g/⅓ cup) melted butter
9 level tbsp finely-grated cheese
3 oz (75g/¾ cup) plain flour
Good pinch of salt and ground nutmeg
4 egg yolks

Stir the yolks into the cheese, then beat in all the remaining ingredients. Put into a large piping bag fitted with a ½ in (1 cm) plain tube. Pipe 1 in (3 cm) lengths of the mixture into a large pan of boiling salted water. Do this in several batches so that each batch has room to swell. After 6 minutes, lift the gnocchi from the water and drain on paper towels. Arrange in one large or eight individual buttered gratin dishes.

To serve: Melt a further 3 oz (75g/⅓ cup) butter and sprinkle over the gnocchi, then add a good layer of grated cheese. Heat through in a moderate oven for 10–15 minutes, then finish under the grill. Serves 8–10.

Poached Salmon

Poach a 3 lb (1½kg) cut of fresh salmon according to the directions for poaching a cut of salmon to be served cold on p. 45. Do this the day before the party. An hour before serving, lift it from the cooking liquor, skin and bone the fish and cut into serving portions. These are most simply and effectively presented on a bed of crisp lettuce arranged on a flat platter. Garnish each portion with a twist of cucumber and a segment of lemon. Foil-wrap tightly until required; if additional help is available it is better to garnish the salmon just before serving. Serves 8–10.

New Potatoes

Allow 3 per serving. Can be cooked and skinned before dinner, then reheated gently in butter until steaming again.

New Peas

At this season peas can be served fresh, but unless they are small and prime, it's better to use frozen petits pois.

3 lb (1½kg) fresh green peas (about 2 lb/1kg shelled weight)
For finishing:
1 level tbsp granulated sugar
Pinch of pepper
2 oz (50g/¼ cup) softened butter
2 teasp fresh chopped mint

Drop the peas into a gallon (4 litre) pan, three-quarters full of water, salted with 3 level teaspoons salt. Boil for 7 minutes, or until almost tender but still a little chewy, then stand in colander in cold water for 2 minutes, to set the colour.

To serve: Ten minutes before serving, put the peas in a pan over gentle heat to evaporate any moisture then add the sugar, pepper, butter and mint. Put on the lid and allow to steam through for 10 minutes to finish the cooking. Serve as soon as possible. Serves 8–10.

Mixed Green Salad

Follow recipe on p. 105. Dress at the table.

Danish Cucumber Salad

Follow recipe on p. 108. Use same amount of dressing but a very large cucumber. Follow the recipes for **Mayonnaise** and **Green Mayonnaise** on pp. 111–12.

Raspberry and Banana Pavlova

Follow the recipe for **Fresh Raspberry Pavlova** on p. 132, but add 2 sliced bananas to the crushed fruit.

Chestnut Ice-cream

Follow the recipe on p. 135. Offer as an alternative to the Pavlova, garnishing with a little very slightly sweetened whipped cream. Serve with Prelatoes (Passover ladyfingers) (p. 241) or bought sponge fingers.

Dinner Party Menu No. 3 (*All seasons*)

Chatzilim, Toast Fingers and Butter, Black Olives and Cucumber Garnish
Fried Trout with Anchovy Butter, Parsley Potatoes, French Beans Amandine
Chicory Salad in the French Manner
Chestnut Pavé
Chilled Zabaione with Raspberries

Chatzilim (*Poor Man's Caviare*)

A delicious Middle Eastern 'starter' to serve like a pâté with toast and butter, or as stuffing for tomatoes.

3 large (1½ lb/¾kg) fat aubergines (eggplant)
1 clove garlic, crushed
1 tbsp finely-chopped onion
Juice of ½ lemon
2 tbsp olive oil
1 level teasp salt
¼ teasp black pepper
2 tbsp finely-chopped parsley
1 tbsp finely-chopped green pepper (optional)

Grill the aubergines for 20 minutes until quite tender when pierced with a knife. Allow to cool for a few minutes, then scoop out the flesh with a knife. Chop all the remaining ingredients into it, add the olive oil and lemon juice last. Put into a dish rather like chopped herring. Garnish with black olives and cucumber slices. Serves 8–10.

Fried Trout with Anchovy Sauce

8–10 trout (approx ½ lb/200g each), washed and salted
3 oz (75g/¾ cup) seasoned flour (for coating the fish)
4 oz (100g/½ cup) butter
2 tbsp oil for frying

Have ready a heavy frying pan wide enough to hold at least 3 trout side by side. Heat the empty pan for 2 or 3 minutes, then put in half the butter and oil. Whilst this heats slowly, toss each fish in the seasoned flour, patting it so that only a thin layer remains. As soon as the butter begins to foam, lay in as many fish as will fit side by side. Cook at a steady but moderate bubble for 5 minutes by which time the underside will be a rich brown. Turn and cook the second side. Transfer to a heatproof dish and keep hot in a low oven (Gas No. 2, 300°F, 150°C) until required. If fat is overbrowned remove.

Add fresh butter and oil and repeat the process. Keep hot till required (Gas No. 2, 300°F, 150°C), maximum 30 minutes.

Sauce (this can be made ahead and reheated):
3 oz (75g/$\frac{1}{3}$ cup) unsalted butter
1 can flat anchovy fillets
6 fl oz (150ml/$\frac{3}{4}$ cup) white wine or Cinzano Bianco
Juice of 1 lemon
1 level tbsp chopped parsley
1 level teasp chopped fresh mint

Melt the butter in a small pan and add the chopped anchovy fillets. Stir until they melt into the butter (about 3 minutes), then add the wine or Cinzano and simmer for 5 minutes. Stir in the lemon juice and herbs. Serves 8–10.

French Beans Amandine

Frozen beans can be cooked as directed and cooled, then reheated with the toasted almonds.

2 pkt frozen haricots verts (whole green beans)
$\frac{1}{2}$ pint (250ml/1$\frac{1}{4}$ cups) water
1 tbsp chopped shallots or spring onions (scallions)
Pinch of salt
1 oz (25g/2 tbsp) butter
2 oz (50g/$\frac{1}{2}$ cup) split or slivered almonds, toasted on a buttered tray in a slow moderate oven (Gas No. 3, 325°F, 170°C) until golden brown

In a wide, lidded saucepan, bring to the boil the water, shallots or spring onions, the salt and butter. Add the partially thawed beans. Cover and bubble steadily for 5–6 minutes, tossing occasionally, until tender. Remove lid and boil off any remaining liquid. If to be reheated, turn out in one layer on a cold dish.

To reheat: Put with the almonds, cover and heat until steaming. Serves 8–10.

Chicory Salad in the French Manner

Follow the recipe on p. 105 using 4 large or 8 small heads of chicory.

Chestnut Pavé

A delectable dessert that can be made and frozen in advance, or refrigerated for several days before use.

17 oz (500g) can sweetened chestnut purée
4 oz (100g/$\frac{1}{2}$ cup) butter
4 oz (100g) plain (semi-sweet) chocolate
28–30 crisp sponge fingers (about 2 pkt)
$\frac{1}{4}$ pint (125ml/$\frac{2}{3}$ cup) strong hot coffee (made with 4 level teasp instant coffee)
1 tbsp rum, brandy or Tia Maria liqueur (optional)
5 fl oz (125ml/$\frac{2}{3}$ cup) cream whipped and sweetened with 2 level teasp caster (superfine) sugar and flavoured with 1 tbsp same liqueur used in coffee

Put the broken-up chocolate in a basin standing over a pan of very hot water and leave to melt. Cream the butter then beat in the soft chocolate followed by the sweetened chestnut purée. Have ready a 2 lb (1kg) loaf tin (approx 9 × 5 × 3 in/ 23 × 13 × 8 cm) or an 8 in (20 cm) round tin about 3 in (8 cm) deep. Lightly grease the tin and then line the bottom with foil or greaseproof paper.

To assemble: Divide the sponge fingers into three groups. Dip the first group quickly in and out of the hot, flavoured coffee, then lay on the bottom of the chosen tin. Spread with half the chestnut cream, repeat with the second portion of biscuits and cream and finally lay the remaining soaked biscuits on top. The mixture can now be foil-covered and frozen, or refrigerated for up to a week.

To serve: Run a knife round the tin to loosen the filling, then turn the cake out onto a serving dish. Mask with the flavoured whipped cream and decorate as required. Serves 8–10.

Zabaione with Raspberries (*To be served cold*)

If possible make early on the day it is to be served, though it will keep without separating overnight, if refrigerated.

8 large egg yolks
4 oz (100g/$\frac{1}{2}$ cup) caster (superfine) sugar
3 fl oz (75ml/6 tbsp) white wine and 1 fl oz (25ml/2 tbsp) brandy or Grand Marnier
1 egg white
2 level teasp sugar
$\frac{1}{2}$ lb (200g) fresh or frozen raspberries

By hand or machine, beat the yolks and sugar until thick and white, then beat in the liquids. Transfer to a basin over a pan of almost boiling water. Continue to whisk vigorously until the mixture fluffs up and has the texture of a whisked sponge or mousse. (It should *just* hold the weight of the mixture dropped off the whisk.) Immediately this stage is reached, take off the heat and stand in a pan of cold water. Keep on whisking gently until it cools. Beat the white until it holds stiff peaks, then beat in the sugar. Fold into the cooled zabaione. Spoon into wineglasses or similar small containers. Top with raspberries. Makes up to 10 glasses.

Dinner Party Menu No. 4 (*May to July*)

Melon and Grape Cocktail
Salmon Steaks in Sour Cream Sauce,
Plain Boiled New Potatoes
Tossed Green Salad
Strawberries in the Venetian Manner or
Gooseberry Fool

Melon and Grape Cocktail

This makes a refreshing starter before a rich main course. Israeli honeydew melons are in season at this time; it is nice to serve two contrasting colours of melon. Follow recipe on p. 22 using 1 large honeydew and one Ogen or canteloupe melon and the same amount of dressing.

Salmon Steaks in Sour Cream Sauce

A really beautiful dish both to look at and to taste. For party purposes the dish can be prepared just before guests arrive and reheated according to the instructions given.

8–10 centre-cut salmon steaks about $\frac{3}{4}$ in ($1\frac{1}{2}$ cm) thick
1 level teasp paprika
2 oz (50g/$\frac{1}{2}$ cup) flour
4 oz (100g/$\frac{1}{2}$ cup) butter
$\frac{1}{4}$ pint (125ml/$\frac{2}{3}$ cup) dry white wine
10 fl oz (250ml/$1\frac{1}{4}$ cups) soured cream
Salt and pepper to taste

Mix the flour and paprika, then coat the washed and salted steaks. Fry for 5 minutes on each side in gently bubbling butter. By this time the fish should be golden brown and flake easily when pierced with a fork. Remove the fish to an entrée dish. Put in the oven at 'warm' and keep hot (if for long, covered with foil). Pour the wine into the buttery juices and bubble for 5 minutes until there is about 4 fl oz (100ml/$\frac{1}{2}$ cup) liquid left (it will cover a 9 in/23 cm frying pan to a depth of $\frac{1}{4}$ in/$\frac{1}{2}$ cm). Pour the cream into the pan and swirl gently until steaming—do not allow to boil. Taste and add salt and white pepper, then pour over the salmon. Serve at once.

Note: For a party, fry fish and keep warm. Add wine and reduce, stir in cream. Just before serving, reheat sauce until steaming, then pour over fish. Serves 8–10.

Tossed Green Salad

Use a mixture of greens in season, two different kinds of lettuce, a bunch of watercress, some slivers of fresh cucumber. Dress at the table with **French Dressing for Green Salads** on p. 113.

Strawberries in the Venetian Manner

This is the way to treat really superb young strawberries that are fully ripe.

$2\frac{1}{2}$–3 lb ($1\frac{1}{2}$kg/3 pints) strawberries
Juice of 2 lemons or small oranges
Caster (superfine) sugar
Pouring cream

Arrange the strawberries in a fairly shallow dish. Chill half an hour. At the table pour over orange juice (for slightly tart fruit) or lemon juice (for very sweet fruit), and serve caster sugar and pouring cream. Serves 8–10.

Gooseberry Fool

This can be made with fresh gooseberries or home-made frozen gooseberry purée. Follow recipe on p. 129.

Meat Menus

To serve 8 *to* 10 *guests.*

Dinner Party Menu No. 1 (*July to October*)

Champignons à la Grècque, Warm Rolls
Braised Stuffed Veal, Wine Sauce
Tomato and Pimento Rice
Courgettes Niçoise
Peaches in Wine
Liqueur Fruit Flan

Champignons à la Grècque

Serve these delicately flavoured mushrooms in small shallow dishes with a large teaspoon. Make 24 *hours in advance to savour them at their best.*

1½ lb (¾kg) button mushrooms
6 tbsp olive oil
6 tbsp water
2 tbsp lemon juice
2 tbsp wine vinegar
2 teasp tomato purée
12 peppercorns, crushed
12 coriander seeds, crushed
1 clove garlic, crushed
1 large bayleaf
Good pinch of fennel
Large sprig each of parsley and thyme (or pinch of dry thyme)
½ teasp salt
½ teasp sugar
10 grinds of black pepper

Wipe mushrooms with damp cloth and cut stalks level with caps. Put all remaining ingredients into pan, bring to boil, cover and simmer for 5 minutes. Uncover, put in mushrooms (sliced only if too large), spoon liquid over them, cover and simmer for 8–10 minutes, or until just tender. Remove mushrooms to serving dish, using slotted spoon. Boil juice down till thick (there should be about 4 or 5 tablespoons). Strain over mushrooms and leave overnight. Serve in little saucers or gratin dishes. Serves 8 generously as a first course, 12 as part of an hors-d'œuvre.

Braised Stuffed Veal

Braise a 4 lb (2kg) shoulder of veal according to the recipe on p. 70. Just before dinner, slice the veal and arrange on a heatproof platter. Tightly foil cover and keep hot in a low oven (Gas No. 1, 275°F, 140°C). Just before serving spoon a little of the gravy over the veal and serve the remainder separately.

Tomato and Pimento Rice

A variation of pilaff that goes particularly well with veal.

12 oz (300g/1½ cups) long grain rice
3 tbsp oil
1¼ pint (625ml/3 cups) chicken soup or stock
½ pint (250ml/1¼ cups) tomato juice
2 onions, finely chopped
1 clove garlic, crushed
1 teasp salt
¼ teasp black pepper
½ teasp sugar
½ small can pimentos

Fry the garlic and onion gently in the fat until golden, then put in the rice and continue frying gently until it turns golden and absorbs the fat. Add the hot chicken stock and tomato juice with the seasoning. Put in a moderate oven (Gas No. 4, 350°F, 180°C) for 30 minutes stirring once. Ten minutes before the end of the cooking time, add the pimentos cut in strips. Serves 8–10.

Courgettes (Zucchini) Niçoise

A really tasty vegetable that can be reheated and needs no last minute attention. Double the quantities on p. 96.

Peaches in Wine

A cool, refreshing finish to the meal. Follow the recipe on p. 124 but use 1 peach per guest. For the syrup use 6 oz (150g/¾ cup) sugar, 6 tablespoons lemon juice, 6 tablespoons water and 8 fl oz (200ml/1 cup) Sauterne. Serve plain.

Liqueur Fruit Flan

Follow the recipe on p. 151. Use margarine in the pastry and canned or fresh poached fruit in season.

Dinner Party Menu No. 2 (*November to January*)

Individual Salade Niçoise
Veal Basquaise
Savoury Noodles
Chanucah Pudding with Wine Sauce
Oranges Vénitienne

Individual Salade Niçoise

2 crisp lettuce
2 cans tuna fish
1 can flat fillets of anchovy
5 tomatoes
4 hard-boiled eggs
1 lb (½kg) frozen haricot verts (whole green beans), cooked
4 oz (100g) black olives
Dressing:
¼ pint (125ml/⅔ cup) oil (preferably olive)
3 tbsp wine vinegar
1 tbsp lemon juice
½ clove garlic, crushed
1 level teasp dry mustard
2 level teasp sugar (optional)
1 level teasp salt
10 grinds black pepper
1 level tbsp mixed chopped fresh herbs such as chives, parsley, chervil

Make the dressing by mixing seasonings and herbs, adding vinegar and finally oil and lemon juice. Shake or whisk until thickened.

To assemble: Line the bottom of each salad bowl with the torn lettuce leaves. Arrange the tuna (in small chunks) in the centre, and all the remaining ingredients in pattern around. Have the dressing on the table for each guest to spoon a little over salad. Serves 8–10.

Veal Basquaise

8–10 boned veal chops
Seasoned flour
8 fl oz (200ml) Graves
Oil for frying
Ratatouille:
2 medium aubergines, peeled and cubed
2 large green peppers, seeded and diced
6 tomatoes, well drained if canned
2 large onions, thinly sliced
1 large clove garlic, mashed to a paste
3 fl oz (75ml/⅓ cup) oil
1 teasp each of sugar and salt
2 teasp oregano
10 grinds black pepper

Fry onions in oil in covered pan till golden. Uncover, add garlic, peppers, aubergines, tomatoes. Season with salt, pepper, sugar and herbs. Cover and simmer 1 hour, until soft. Meanwhile, dip veal in seasoned flour and fry gently in a little oil till golden brown on both sides. Remove to baking dish. Pour the wine into the pan where the veal was fried, stir well to release the sediment, and simmer for 3 minutes—the sauce should be a lovely golden brown. Pour over the meat. Foil-cover and cook in a slow oven (Gas No. 2, 300°F, 150°C) for 1 hour.

To serve: Arrange the ratatouille in a ring in a serving dish and place the chops in the centre. Thicken the juices by stirring in 1 level tablespoon cornflour. Bubble 3 minutes. Serve separately. Serves 8–10.

Savoury Noodles

Use double the recipe on p. 104.

Chanucah Pudding with Wine Sauce

Follow the recipe in 'Festival Foods', p. 230. If you want to flame the pudding, heat 2 tablespoons brandy or whisky either in a ladle held over a flame or poured into a tiny pan. Set alight, pour over the pudding and bring into the room in triumph!

Oranges Vénitienne

This is an ideal sweet to serve when the large Jaffa oranges are in season. It is extremely refreshing after a highly-seasoned meal. Follow the recipe on p. 123.

Dinner Party Menu No. 3 (*June to September*)

Aubergines (Eggplant) Stuffed with Chicken Liver
Daube Marseillaise
Glazed Carrots, New Potatoes
Poached Peaches in Apricot Syrup
Orange Meringue Pie

Aubergines (Eggplant) Stuffed with Chicken Liver

A starter that needs no last minute attention.

5 large boat-shaped aubergines (eggplant)
1 medium onion, finely chopped
10 oz (250g) chicken livers (about 8), cut in sixths (koshered)
Oil for frying
1 oz (25g/2 tbsp) chicken fat
2 level teasp finely-chopped parsley
1 level teasp salt and 10 grinds black pepper
Crushed potato crisps (chips) or dried breadcrumbs tossed in a nut of margarine

Cut each aubergine in half lengthwise; make criss-cross cuts on flesh, sprinkle lightly with cooking salt and leave for 1 hour, then squeeze lightly to remove bitter juices, and wipe surface well. In frying pan, put oil to a depth of $\frac{3}{8}$ in (1 cm). Fry the aubergines, first for 2 minutes on skin side then gently for about 5 minutes on flesh side until golden brown. They should feel tender when pierced with a knife. Leave until cool enough to handle, then scoop out flesh, leaving enough to keep skin firm. (It will probably be necessary to add more oil to pan, as aubergines soak it up alarmingly.) To same pan add chicken fat. Cook onion until soft and golden, then add koshered chicken livers and cook gently (another 3 minutes). Add mashed or chopped aubergine flesh and stir to blend, seasoning with salt, pepper and parsley. Arrange aubergine skins on heatproof platter or oven tray. Divide filling between them. Sprinkle with crushed potato crisps or breadcrumbs tossed in the melted margarine. Reheat in a quick moderate oven (Gas No. 5, 375°F, 190°C) for 15 minutes until piping hot and crisp. Serves 8–10.

Daube Marseillaise (*Beef Braised in Wine*)

Bola (chuck) is marinated in wine which give it the moistness this kosher cut usually lacks.

4 lb (2kg) corner of bola or chuck
The marinade:
The thinly-sliced peel of an orange
12 peppercorns, slightly crushed with the end of a rolling pin
A sprig of fresh rosemary or a teasp of dried rosemary
2 fat bayleaves and a large sprig of parsley
½ bottle of red or white dry wine such as Burgundy or Graves
1 onion and 1 carrot, thinly sliced

Twenty-four hours before you intend to cook the beef, heat the marinade ingredients to boiling point then allow to go quite cold. (I do this in the same cast-iron enamelled casserole in which I intend to cook the meat.) Put the joint into the marinade and leave in a cool place until cooking time. Baste the meat several times with the juices, and turn it so that the marinade can soak in.

To cook: Have ready a large onion and carrot, finely sliced, a sliced green pepper (optional), and 1 level teaspoon powdered bouquet garni or a sprig of parsley and a bayleaf. Lift the meat from the marinade and dry it thoroughly using paper towels. This is essential so that it will brown. Strain the marinade into a small bowl. Wash out the casserole and in it heat 2 tablespoons oil or 1 tablespoon chicken fat. Put the meat into the hot fat and cook it at a moderate sizzle, turning to brown it on all sides. Towards the end of the browning time, slip the carrot and onion under the meat and continue to cook until they are limp and brown. Dust the meat with a little paprika pepper, salt and black pepper. Add the sliced pepper (if used), then pour in the marinade. Cover and bring to the boil, then transfer to a slow oven (Gas No. 2, 300°F, 150°C) and cook at a gentle simmer for 3 hours. If you like a rich, deep gravy, add 2 teaspoons of tomato purée half-way through the cooking time. When the meat is cooked—it will 'give' when pressed—lift it on to a heatproof plate, turn the oven down to 'warm' and deal with the gravy. This can be liquidized, then reheated, or it can be sieved and thickened with 2 teaspoons cornflour (cornstarch).

To serve: Cut the meat in slices about ⅜ in (1 cm) thick and place in overlapping rows on a flat meat plate. Pour the sauce over. Sprinkle with chopped parsley, or garnish with glazed carrots. Serves 8–10.

Glazed Carrots

Follow the recipe on p. 95 but use 1½ lb (¾kg) carrots, 1 level tablespoon sugar, 1½ teaspoons salt and 1 oz (2 tbsp) margarine.

Poached Peaches in Apricot Syrup

Double the recipe on p. 121 allowing 1 peach per guest. This is a splendid recipe for slightly under-ripe fruit.

Orange Meringue Pie

Follow the recipe on p. 151 but make the pastry with margarine.

Dinner Party Menu No. 4 (*October to April*)

Herbed Tomato Soup with Little Meat Balls
Savoury Veal Chops
New Potatoes, Aubergines (Eggplant) Sautés
Orange Sorbet
Spicy Raisin Pie

Herbed Tomato Soup with Little Meat Balls

Meat Balls:
1 lb (½kg) minced (ground) beef
½ grated onion
1 beaten egg
1 teasp salt
Pinch of pepper
2 level tbsp medium matzo meal

Mix all together. Make into 25–30 tiny meatballs.

Soup:
1 oz (25g/2 tbsp) margarine
1 tbsp oil
2 medium onions
1 small clove garlic, crushed
1 level teasp each of oregano and basil
Large can (28 oz/700g) whole tomatoes in juice
1 teasp salt
3 tbsp tomato purée
1 bayleaf
3 pints (1½ litres/7½ cups) strong beef stock, either consommé (ideal) or cubes
1 level tbsp sugar
2 level tbsp cornflour (cornstarch)

Melt margarine and oil and add the sliced onion, garlic and well-drained tomatoes (reserving juice), and salt and sugar. Cover and stew for 1 hour. Sieve and return to the pan with purée, bayleaf, stock and juice from the tomatoes. Bring to boil, then put in meat balls. Simmer for half an hour, then refrigerate. Next day, remove any fat. Mix the cornflour with 3 tablespoons water and add to soup. Simmer for 3 minutes. Serves 8–10.

Savoury Veal Chops

Follow the recipe on p. 71 but use 1 large first cut veal chop per person and the following ingredients:

2 level tbsp chicken fat; or 2 oz (50g/¼ cup) margarine and 1 tbsp oil
6 tbsp spring onions (scallions)
2 cloves garlic
½ pint (250ml/1¼ cups) white vermouth
1 level tbsp tomato purée
8 fl oz (200ml/1 cup) thin gravy or chicken stock

Aubergines (Eggplant) Sautés

Double the recipe on p. 94. This dish can be reheated.

Orange Sorbet

Follow the recipe on p. 137.

Spicy Raisin Pie

Follow the recipe on p. 148 using margarine rather than butter.

Two Soufflés

I have not included these two recipes in any of the preceding menus because I do not think it is wise to attempt them for a formal dinner as it is impossible to ensure that the guests are ready at the same time as the soufflé. However, they are perfect for a special dinner for 4 or 6 close friends so I give full instructions below.

Cheese Soufflé

The classic Cheese Soufflé is ideal as a quick supper for four or an unusual entrée for six. (Larger size soufflés are very hard to handle.) The cheese usually specified is Gruyère. In this country I have only been able to buy processed Gruyère in a kosher pack, so kosher Gouda which has been left uncovered to harden in the refrigerator and then coarsely grated, must be used. The eggs should be large and include an extra white, which makes the soufflé fluffy and creamy.

The soufflé dish need not be tied with a band of paper as long as it is deep enough. I use an ordinary round ovenproof glass casserole (3 in/8 cm deep and 8 in/20 cm from rim to rim).

The oven should be set at Gas No. 6, 400°F, 200°C, and then turned down only when the soufflé is safely on the shelf. This allows for the inevitable heat loss in opening the oven door.

The time lag between piling the finished soufflé into the dish and putting it in the oven can be up to one hour (protect the mixture from draughts by covering it with a bowl). This avoids the need for last minute egg white beating before guests arrive. However, once the soufflé is ready it must be served at once.

2 oz (50g/¼ cup) butter
1½ oz (40g/⅓ cup) flour
½ pint (250ml/1¼ cups) boiling milk
½ level teasp salt
8 grinds black pepper
½ level teasp mustard
Pinch of cayenne pepper
Pinch of ground nutmeg
4 large egg yolks
5 large whites
3 oz (75g/¾ cup) coarsely-grated cheese

Put the milk into a heavy-bottomed 8 in (20 cm) pan and bring to the boil. Immediately pour it into a jug. Rinse out the pan and in it melt the butter, then stir in the flour. Allow to bubble together for 2 minutes, then take off the heat and pour in the milk all at once. Immediately beat the sauce with a small balloon whisk until it is smooth and thickened, then add all the seasonings. Put back on a moderate heat and allow to bubble for one minute, still keeping the sauce moving with the whisk (it will be very thick). Take it off the heat. Have ready the bowl in which you will beat the egg-whites. Separate the eggs and drop the yolks one at a time into the sauce, stirring after each addition, while you drop the whites into the bowl. (The extra white can be one you have in stock in the refrigerator, or a fresh one—in that case, the unused egg yolk should be put in a tiny airtight plastic container and refrigerated. Use it within 24 hours.) Beat the whites with a pinch of salt until they form stiff but glossy peaks when the beaters are withdrawn. Take a quarter of the meringue and stir it into the egg-yolk mixture. Stir in also all but a tablespoonful of the grated cheese. Now drop the remaining meringue on top of the yolk mixture and fold it in with a metal spoon so that the mixture is blended to an even colour but the minimum of air is knocked out in the process. Now coax this fluffy mass into a buttered soufflé dish. With the flat of the knife, trace a line round the edge of the soufflé 1 in (2½ cm) from the edge of the dish rim. (This facilitates the rise.) Sprinkle with the remaining cheese. Put in the preheated oven (Gas No. 6, 400°F, 200°C) and immediately turn it down to Gas No. 5, 375°F, 190°C. It will be ready to eat in 35 minutes. It should be crusty golden brown on top and stand 2 in (5 cm) above the rim of the dish. Serves 4–6.

Soufflé au Grand Marnier

2 level tbsp flour
¼ pint (125ml/⅔ cup) cold milk
3 oz (75g/⅓ cup) caster (superfine) sugar
1 oz (25g/2 tbsp) butter
1 teasp vanilla essence (extract)
Grated rind of a smooth-skinned orange
4 egg yolks and 5 egg whites
3 sponge fingers or stale macaroons
4 tbsp orange-flavoured liqueur—Grand Marnier, Curaçao or Cointreau
2 tbsp water

In a large, heavy-based saucepan, blend the sugar and flour, then slowly stir in the cold milk and grated orange rind. Cook gently until the mixture bubbles then boil for 30 seconds, still stirring, and turn off the heat. Add vanilla. Stir whilst it cools for 2 minutes, then drop in the yolks one at a time, whisking to blend after each addition, and dropping the egg whites into a large mixing bowl. Stir in half the butter and dot the remainder on top of the sauce to prevent it 'skinning' whilst you complete the preparation. Roughly crumble biscuits (cookies); soak them in 2 tablespoons of the liqueur mixed with the water. Beat the 5 whites with a pinch of salt until they form stiff, glossy peaks, then beat in 1 level tablespoon caster sugar. Have the oven heated to Gas No. 6, 400°F, 200°C. Stir the remaining 2 tablespoons of liqueur into the sauce, then stir in a quarter of the meringue. Fold in the remainder. Spoon half the soufflé into an 8 in (20 cm) round soufflé or glass dish, 3 in (8 cm) deep (previously buttered and sugared well). Lay the soaked biscuits on top and spoon the remainder of the soufflé over them. Smooth level and put in the oven. Turn down to Gas No. 5, 375°F, 190°C, and bake for 35 minutes. Serve at once. This makes 6 reasonable portions.

The Supper Party

For 14 *to* 16 *guests.*

This is one of my favourite ways of entertaining, for it is more informal than a dinner party and often more satisfying socially for close friends than a cocktail or drinks party.

The set-up: The cold food is placed on one table, the hot food on a hot plate (preferably on a sideboard or serving table); the sweets on a trolley. Guests help themselves, and then sit informally at card or other small tables. These can be set with silverware or it can be collected with the food and plates at the table. There are no place cards.

The menu and service: Usually the food consists of hot casseroles or cold cuts with salads and rice or pasta accompaniment, followed by a selection of desserts. A 'hold in the hand' first course is offered with the pre-dinner drinks. Some suggestions for such savoury 'starters': guacamole; Mexican cheese; calamata olives; celery filled with savoury cream cheese; cheese, pineapple and cherry kebabs; gaffelbitter, tomato and gherkin kebabs; tiny chopped fish balls, cheese or mushroom bites.

Guests serve themselves with the main course, and then the sweets trolley is wheeled round to them, together with coffee. Accompanying drinks are served by the host as they eat.

Assistance: Minimum help would be one person in the kitchen during service of the main course, ready to help with desserts and coffee later.

Pre-preparations: This kind of entertaining lends itself particularly to freezing in advance. Only salads and fresh fruit desserts need to be made on the day of the party.

Both meat and dairy menus can be served successfully, though one hot dish at least should always be included in the menu for variety. Equally important is to contrast crunchy foods with smooth ones, bland flavours with highly-spiced mixtures. Whilst a supper party menu can be similar in form to a dinner party—with informal service making the main distinction—it can successfully be based quite simply on pizzas or savoury quiches or indeed on a variety of cheese, cheese dips and pickled and spiced fish, followed by a simple dessert, or Danish pastries and fruit.

Supper Party Menu No. 1

Moussaka
Chicken Blintzes or Individual Chicken Pies
Pilaff in the Greek Fashion
Chicory Salad in the French Manner
Spiced Peaches, Pickled Cucumbers
Tarte Montmorency
Orange and Ginger Salad

Moussaka

5 lb (2½kg) medium aubergines (eggplant)
2 medium onions, finely chopped
6 tbsp oil or margarine
3 lb (1½kg) minced fresh lamb or veal
8 fl oz (200ml/1 cup) dry white wine (chicken stock can be substituted)
Large can tomatoes, well drained
2 generous tbsp chopped parsley
1 level tbsp salt
½ teasp ground black pepper
2 tbsp dried fines herbes or oregano
4 heaped tbsp dry breadcrumbs
Oil (preferably olive) for frying the aubergines

Bechamel sauce:

2½ pint (1¼ litres/6¼ cups) chicken stock—use 4 bouillon cubes
4 oz (100g/1 cup) cornflour (cornstarch) mixed with a little of the chicken stock to form a liquid
1 level teasp ground nutmeg
4 oz (100g/½ cup) margarine
3 fl oz (75ml/⅓ cup) sherry
4 egg yolks

Wash the aubergines, then cut in long, slanting slices, each ⅓ in (1 cm) thick, sprinkle with salt in a colander and leave for one hour, then rinse and dry with paper towels.

To prepare the meat sauce: Sauté the finely-chopped onion in the oil or margarine until soft. Add the raw meat and cook, stirring with a fork until the meat loses its redness. Add the wine, tomatoes, parsley, herbs, salt and pepper. Cover and simmer for 45 minutes. Add the breadcrumbs and stir well. Whilst the meat is simmering, fry the aubergines in shallow hot oil until golden brown on both sides, lift out and drain thoroughly on crumpled paper (tissue or kitchen). This draining process is important.

The bechamel sauce: Put the cornflour in a bowl with about 6 tablespoons of the chicken stock and mix to a thin cream. Bring the remaining stock to the boil, then pour on to the cornflour, stirring constantly. Return to the pan, and bubble 3 minutes, then add the margarine (cut in little pieces), sherry and nutmeg. The sauce should now be thick and shiny. In the cornflour basin, beat the yolks thoroughly, then add to the hot sauce, stirring all the time.

To assemble the Moussaka: Grease 2 ovenproof dishes approximately 9 × 13 × 2 in (23 × 33 × 5 cm) (or use 4 foil ones). Sprinkle with a few dried breadcrumbs. Arrange half the aubergine slices to cover the bottom of the dish then spread with the meat sauce. Cover with the remaining aubergines. Finally, pour bechamel sauce over the aubergines to cover the contents completely. Bake in a moderate oven (Gas No. 4, 350°F, 180°C) for 45 minutes. Serves 12 for a main dish, 16 for an entrée. Reheats well.

Chicken Blintzes

Treble recipe on p. 87.

Individual Chicken Pies

If you prefer, make 3 large plate pies instead of individual ones which are more trouble—but more fun!

1 small fowl (about 4 lb/2kg net weight)
1 medium onion, finely chopped
1¼ pint (625ml/3 cups) stock from the chicken
4 tbsp sherry
2 oz (50g/¼ cup) margarine or chicken fat
1 tbsp oil
2 oz (50g/½ cup) plain flour
1 level teasp salt and pinch of white pepper
1 level tbsp chopped parsley
1–2 canned pimentos
1 lb (½kg) frozen peas, cooked
¼ lb (100g) mushrooms, cooked in a squeeze of lemon juice and a nut of margarine
2–3 pkt puff pastry or piecrust mix (1–1½ lb/½–¾kg)

First cook the fowl. Put it in the soup pan, barely covered with cold water. Add a whole onion, 1 large sliced carrot, 2 sliced stalks of celery, 2 teaspoons salt, few black peppercorns, and a sprig of parsley. Bring slowly to the boil, skim off the froth, cover and simmer very, very gently for 2 hours. Test to see that the leg feels tender; if not, cook another half an hour or until it is tender. (Remember the flesh will be recooked in the pie so should be firmer than usual.) Lift out the bird, drain well, cover and refrigerate. Boil the stock down to half, strain and refrigerate also. Next day: remove any fat from the soup—this can be used for making the sauce if required.

To make the pie filling: Cut off then discard ¼ in (½ cm) stalk from each washed mushroom then slice the mushrooms thinly. Sprinkle with a squeeze of lemon juice then simmer, covered, for 5 minutes in the melted margarine. In the meantime, melt the 2 oz (50g/¼ cup) margarine or chicken fat with the oil and in it cook the chopped onion till golden and soft (about 5 min). Add the flour, stir well and simmer for 2 minutes, then add the hot chicken broth, and whisk until the sauce thickens. Then add the sherry, flesh of the bird (cut in small cubes), the cubed pimento, peas, the chopped parsley and the mushrooms with their juice. Season to taste. Allow the filling to cool, whilst you roll out the pastry. The pastry should be rolled out as thin as a penny, and bases cut to fit 2 or 3 pie plates or 18–20 patty tins. Spoon in filling, cover with pastry cut to fit and brush tops with a beaten egg before baking. Bake individual pies at Gas No. 8, 450°F, 230°C, for 20 minutes, and larger pies at Gas No. 8 for 10 minutes and at Gas No. 7, 425°F, 220°C, for a further 15–20 minutes or until a rich brown. Serves 12–15.

Pilaff in the Greek Fashion

Make double the recipe on p. 103.

Chicory Salad in the French Manner

Make double the quantity of recipe on p. 105.

Spiced Peaches

A most delicious sweet-sour relish. Make the day beforehand to allow the flavours to permeate the peaches.

2 large cans peach halves (16 halves)
8 fl oz (200ml/1 cup) peach syrup from can
8 fl oz (200ml/1 cup) vinegar
1–3 in (8 cm) stick cinnamon or pinch ground cinnamon
4 oz (100g/½ cup) sugar
Whole cloves

Stud each peach half with 3 cloves. Simmer the remaining ingredients for 3–4 minutes. Add peach halves. Cool, then store in syrup overnight. Serve drained halves with meat or fish. Serves 16.

Pickled Cucumbers

Follow the recipe on p. 221 or buy from the delicatessen. Allow half a cucumber per person.

Tarte Montmorency

8 oz (200g/2 cups) self-raising flour
Pinch of salt
5 oz (125g/$\frac{2}{3}$ cup) margarine
2 oz (50g/$\frac{1}{4}$ cup) caster (superfine) sugar
1 egg

Make by rubbing-in method. Chill for 1 hour.

Filling:
2 lb (1kg) raw pitted morello (sour red) or black cherries or well-drained canned cherries, sufficient to cover base of flan in one layer ($1\frac{1}{2}$–2 cans)
1 oz (25g/$\frac{1}{4}$ cup) icing (confectioners') sugar
Almond sponge:
4 oz (100g/$\frac{1}{2}$ cup) margarine
4 oz (100g/$\frac{1}{2}$ cup) caster (superfine) sugar
2 eggs
4 oz (100g/1 cup) ground almonds
Few drops almond essence (extract)
1 level tbsp flour

Roll out pastry to fit 11 or 12 in (28–30 cm) flan case. Prick base all over and sprinkle with the icing sugar. Arrange the cherries in a single layer, very close together. Make the almond sponge by beating together the margarine, sugar, eggs, the almond essence, the almonds and flour until smooth (about 3 minutes). Spread over cherries. Bake at Gas No. 5, 375°F, 190°C, for 15 minutes then at Gas No. 4, 350°F, 180°C, for 30 minutes, or until the topping has set into a sponge that feels springy to the touch. The flan may be iced with glacé icing, or it can be served dusted with sifted icing sugar; or it can be dusted thickly with icing sugar then put back at Gas No. 8, 450°F, 230°C until the icing sugar melts into a golden brown glaze. Watch it! Serves 12.

Orange and Ginger Salad

Make double the quantity of recipe on p. 123.

Supper Party Menu No. 2

Holishkes
Gevikelte Kraut
Turkey Vol au Vents
Hot Dogs
Rice, Tomato and Pimento Salad
Chicory and Cucumber Salad
Kirschen (Cherry) Strudel
Citrus Fruit Salad

Holishkes

Make double the quantity of the recipe on p. 227.

Gevikelte Kraut

Make double the quantity of the recipe on p. 227.

Turkey Vol au Vents

Use 3 in (8 cm) cooked puff pastry cases. Allow $1\frac{1}{2}$ per person. For the filling use recipe for Individual Chicken Pies p. 269, substituting turkey breast for chicken. Heat cooked cases in moderate oven (Gas No. 4, 350°F, 180°C) for 15 minutes then add spoonful of hot filling. Serve as soon as possible.

Hot Dogs

Simmer saveloys in boiling water to cover for 5 minutes, then leave covered in steaming water until required, then drain and serve. Allow 3 cocktail-size hot dogs per person.

Rice, Tomato and Pimento Salad

Make double the quantity of the recipe on p. 110.

Chicory and Cucumber Salad

Use the Herb Dressing on p. 113, *doubling the quantity.*

6 pieces Belgian chicory
2 bunches watercress
1 cucumber, thinly sliced and salted for 15 minutes
1 green pepper, chopped

Cut chicory in ½ in (1 cm) slices, and blend with all other ingredients. Chill well. Toss at dinner table with herb dressing. Serves 12–15 as side salad.

Kirschen (Cherry) Strudel

Make double the quantity of the recipe on p. 179.

Citrus Fruit Salad

Make treble the quantity of the recipe on p. 122.

Supper Party Menu No. 3

Moussaka
Oven Fried Chicken
Korean Rice
Cyprus Tomato Salad
Spiced Peaches
Pickled Cucumbers
Lemon Meringue Pie
Oranges in Curaçao Syrup
Myer's Punch

Moussaka

Follow recipe on p. 268.

Oven-Fried Chicken

Make double the recipe on p. 80.

Korean Rice

3 tbsp salad oil
12 oz (300g/1½ cups) par-cooked long grain rice
½ lb (200g) raw minced (ground) beef
½ onion
¼ lb (100g) mushrooms, sliced
3 level tbsp sesame seeds, toasted in moderate oven till golden (about 10 min)
1 tbsp soy sauce
½ level teasp paprika
2 level teasp salt
2 pints (1 litre/5 cups) stock made with water and 2 beef cubes

If possible, use an 'oven-to-table' casserole with a ground base that can go on top of the stove; otherwise, fry the rice in a frying pan, then transfer to the oven to cook. Set the oven at Gas No. 4, 350°F, 180°C, and toast some sesame seeds on a tray for 10 minutes, until golden brown. Meanwhile, gently heat 2 tablespoons of the oil then add the onion and mushrooms and cook until the onion is soft and a rich gold. Add the rice and cook for 5 minutes, until it is dry-looking and brown. Add the meat and the extra tablespoon of oil and cook until the meat loses its redness. Now add the soy sauce, the paprika, salt, and the stock. Finally stir in the toasted sesame seeds. Transfer to the oven (Gas No. 4, 350°F, 180°C) and cook for 30 minutes until the rice is tender and has absorbed the liquid.

Cyprus Tomato Salad

Make double the recipe on p. 107.

Spiced Peaches and Pickled Cucumbers

Follow recipes on p. 269 and 221.

Lemon Meringue Pie

Make double the recipe on p. 151. Makes one 12 in (30 cm) flan or two 7 in (18 cm) flans.

Oranges in Curaçao Syrup

Double the recipe on p. 122.

Myer's Punch

½ bottle orange cordial
¼ bottle lime juice cordial
1 tbsp Angostura bitters
4 fl oz (100ml/½ cup) gin
1 liqueur glass of liqueur
4 large bottles fizzy lemonade (approx)

Pour ingredients in order given into very large bowl. When ready to serve, dilute to taste with chilled lemonade. Garnish with orange and lemon slices, cucumber slices, sprigs of mint and seeded green grapes. Serves approx 12–15.

Supper Party Menu No. 4

Meat Strudel
Boeuf Bourguignon
Savoury Lokshen
Hot Dogs
Spiced Peaches
Pickled Cucumbers
Chicory Salad in the French Manner
Aloha Pineapple Pie
Apple Grillage Flan
Fresh Apricot Compote

Meat Strudel

Make double the quantity of the recipe on p. 141.

Boeuf Bourguignon

4 lb (2kg) bola (chuck), cut ½ in (1 cm) thick
2 tbsp chicken fat or meat dripping
2 onions, finely chopped
4 level tbsp flour
1 pint (500ml/2½ cups) meat stock—from cubes
Sprig of parsley and 2 bayleaves
1 can button mushrooms
1 tbsp chopped parsley
Marinade:
2 large onions, thinly sliced
4 tbsp corn oil
Sprig of parsley
4 bayleaves
½ pint (250ml/1¼ cups) Burgundy
Salt and pepper

About 6 hours before you intend to prepare the casserole, cut the slices of bola into 2 in (5 cm) squares and place in a bowl. Add the thinly-sliced onion, oil, the herbs and wine, and sprinkle with salt and pepper. Leave for 3 hours. Melt fat or meat dripping in a heavy casserole, and thoroughly brown 2 finely-chopped onions. Have the meat well drained and dried by placing on paper towels. Add the meat to the onions, then sprinkle with the flour, so that it draws in any remaining fat. Shake the pan well to keep the browning even, then add stock and strained marinade (discard flavourings) together with a fresh bunch of parsley and 2 bay-leaves. Cover and simmer very, very gently for 2 hours, or until tender. Just before serving, add the drained button mushrooms and the parsley. Serves 12.

Savoury Lokshen

Make treble the quantity of the recipe on p. 104.

Hot Dogs

Follow instructions on p. 270.

Spiced Peaches and Pickled Cucumbers

Follow the recipes on p. 269 and p. 221. Allow ½ cucumber per person.

Chicory Salad in the French Manner

Make double the quantity of the recipe on p. 105.

Aloha Pineapple Pie

Make double the recipe on p. 151 using pastry made with margarine, make one 12 in (30 cm) pie, or two 7 in (18 cm) pies.

Apple Grillage Flan

8 oz (200g/2 cups) plain flour
Pinch of salt
5 oz (125g/⅔ cup) margarine
2 oz (50g/¼ cup) caster (superfine) sugar
1 egg

Make by rubbing in method. Chill for 1 hour.

Filling:
3 lb (1½kg) baking apples (weight unpeeled)
4 tbsp apricot jam
½ lb (200g/1 cup) brown sugar
2 oz (50g/¼ cup) margarine
Juice of 1 lemon
Ground almonds or hazelnuts

Melt margarine in heavy-bottomed pan. Add peeled, cored and thinly-sliced apples. Cook covered until almost soft. Stir in sugar, jam and lemon juice. Allow to go cold. Roll out pastry to fit an 11 in (28 cm) or 12 in (30 cm) flan ring, and prick the base. Sprinkle thinly with ground almonds or hazel nuts. Spoon in the apple filling and smooth level. Cover with a trelliswork of pastry strips cut ½ in (1 cm) wide and painted with beaten egg. Bake at Gas No. 5, 375°F, 190°C, for 35 minutes, or until golden brown. Serves 12. Serve cold. Keeps well overnight.

Fresh Apricot Compote

Make double the quantity of the recipe on p. 121.

Supper Party Menu No. 5

Sauté de Veau Marengo
Scalloped Chicken
Savoury Rice
Pastales
Green Bean Salad
Peaches in Wine
Black Cherry Sponge Flan

Sauté de Veau Marengo

A rich and subtly-flavoured casserole. Ask the butcher to bone and cut the veal into 2 in (5 cm) squares.

4 lb (2kg) veal
¼ pint (125ml/⅔ cup) oil
3 large onion, finely chopped
¾ pint (375ml/2 cups) of dry white wine such as Graves
1½ pints (750ml/4 cups) chicken soup or stock from cubes
2 tbsp flour
½–¾ lb (200g–300g) white baby mushrooms, sliced
3 cloves garlic, crushed
Large sprig of parsley
1 level tbsp of salt
Black pepper
Large can (approx 28 oz/700g) of tomatoes, drained
1 tbsp sugar

You may find it easier to fry the meat in two pans, then combine it in one casserole for the actual cooking. Melt the oil in a heavy frying pan, and put in the veal, a quarter at a time, cooking quickly until brown. Half-way through add the onions and continue cooking. Sprinkle with flour and cook until it browns a little, then add the wine and bubble for 3 minutes to concentrate the flavour. Put into a large casserole. Add the remaining ingredients (except mushrooms) to the frying pan, and scrape it well to get any delicious sediment into the sauce, then bring to the boil. Pour over the meat, cover and simmer until tender (about 1½ hours) in the oven (Gas No. 2, 300°F, 150°C). Twenty minutes before the end of the cooking time, remove the lid and add the raw mushrooms. The sauce should be creamy; if a little too thin, leave uncovered for the remainder of the cooking time. Serves 14–16.

Scalloped Chicken

Layers of tender bird, rich sauce and herb stuffing, baked en casserole.

6 lb (3kg) fowl, net weight
1 carrot
1 onion
2 teasp salt
Water to cover
Stuffing:
1 large loaf stale bread
Few sprigs parsley
1 medium onion
2 stalks celery
4 oz (100g/½ cup) margarine
1 teasp salt
Dash pepper
1 teasp mixed herbs
Gravy:
5 oz (125g/⅔ cup) chicken fat or soft margarine
5 oz (125g/1¼ cups) flour
2½ pint (1¼ litres/6 cups) chicken stock
2 level teasp salt
4 eggs
Topping:
1 cup dry crumbs
2 oz (50g/¼ cup) margarine

Put whole chicken in pan with carrot, onion, salt and water. Bring to boil, reduce heat and simmer 2½ hours, or until very tender. Let bird cool in stock then remove flesh from bones in large pieces.

The stuffing: Cut away crusts and crumble bread in blender. Chop parsley, onion and celery and cook in margarine until tender (5 minutes). Add to breadcrumbs with stock, salt, pepper, herbs and 4 tablespoons chicken soup.

The gravy: Melt fat, add flour, then hot stock, whisking till thick and bubbly. Beat eggs in bowl, add a little hot sauce then tip into pan, and cook over low heat (3–4 minutes) stirring all the time. Do not boil.

To assemble: Grease 2 casseroles. Put in stuffing, then half of the gravy, then chicken and finally remaining gravy. Toss crumbs in melted margarine and put on top. Bake 20 minutes in a moderate oven (Gas No. 5, 375°F, 190°C) until piping hot. Serves 12.

Savoury Rice

Treble the quantity for the recipe on p. 102.

Pastales

Follow the recipe on p. 222.

Green Bean Salad

Make double the quantity of the recipe on p. 106.

Peaches in Wine

Follow the recipe on p. 124. Allow one peach per guest and the following quantity of syrup: 8 oz (200g/1 cup) sugar; 4 oz (100ml/8 tbsp) lemon juice; 4 oz (100ml/8 tbsp) water; 10 fl oz (250ml/1¼ cups) Sauterne.

Black Cherry Sponge Flan

Make double quantity of the recipe on p. 125. Either make two 7 in (18 cm) flans, or one 12 in (30 cm) flan.

Supper Party Menu No. 6

Cold Roast Turkey
Cranberry Jelly
Spiced Peaches
Chicken Liver Sauté with Rice
Aubergine Casserole Provençale
Piquante String Beans
Chocolate Rum Pavé
Pineapple Pyramids

Cold Roast Turkey

Follow the instructions for roasting a turkey on p. 90. Stuff the neck with helzel stuffing which will slice well when the bird is cold. Do not stuff the body cavity, but put a lump of margarine and a bunch of parsley inside, together with a peeled cooking apple and an onion.

Spiced Peaches

Follow recipe on p. 269.

Chicken Liver Sauté with Rice

1½–2 lb (¾–1kg) chicken livers
8 tbsp oil
4 tbsp chicken fat or margarine
2 large green peppers, seeded and chopped
2 large onions, finely chopped
1 lb (½kg) fresh mushrooms, sliced
½ pint (250ml/1¼ cups) beef or chicken bouillon (made with cube)
6 fl oz (150ml/¾ cup) dry sherry
1 level tbsp cornflour (cornstarch)
4 tbsp toasted flaked almonds
1½ lb (¾kg/4 cups) rice cooked in 10 cups chicken stock (see Savoury Rice p. 102–3)

Heat the oil and chicken fat or margarine, then put in onions and peppers and cook gently until the onion is limp and golden. Add the sliced mushrooms and cook for a further 3 minutes, or until softened. Grill chicken livers to kosher then put into pan together with bouillon and sherry. Mix well with the vegetables, bring to simmering point, cover and cook very gently for 10 minutes. Uncover and stir in cornflour mixed to a cream with 2 tablespoons water. Bubble for 3 minutes then taste and season with salt and black pepper.

To serve: Arrange rice on large oval platter, and put chicken liver mixture in centre. Scatter with toasted almonds. Serves 14–16.

Aubergine (Eggplant) Casserole Provençale

For a party it is more convenient to use canned aubergines au naturel (in own juice). If these are not available, substitute 3 lb ($1\frac{1}{2}$kg) fresh aubergines, sliced $\frac{3}{8}$ in ($\frac{1}{2}$ cm) thick, salted for an hour, then dried and sautéd until golden and tender in hot oil. Drain well before use.

2 onions, finely chopped
2 medium cans (15 oz/375g) or 1 large can (28 oz/700g) peeled plum tomatoes
2 cloves garlic, crushed
2 teasp oregano
2 teasp basil
2 teasp sugar
Crushed cornflake or coating crumbs
1 oz (25g/2 tbsp) margarine
1 tbsp oil
2 cans aubergines (eggplant) au naturel
Salt and black pepper

Sauté onion in margarine and oil till soft and pale gold, then add tomatoes, sugar, oregano, crushed clove, salt and pepper, simmer till thick and not watery. Grease a 12 × 9 in (30 × 23 cm) casserole very well. Arrange sliced aubergines in layers, alternately with tomato mixture, seasoning well. Finally, top with crushed crumbs and dot with margarine. Bake in a moderate oven (Gas No. 4, 350°F, 180°C) till golden (about 20 minutes). Serves 12 as an entrée.

Piquant String Beans

Make double the quantity of the recipe on p. 110.

Chocolate Rum Pavé

$\frac{1}{4}$ pint (125ml/$\frac{2}{3}$ cup) strong coffee made with 2 level teasp instant coffee
1 tbsp rum
30 boudoir biscuits (ladyfingers)
Mocha Cream:
6 oz (150g/$\frac{3}{4}$ cup) margarine
6 oz (150g/$1\frac{1}{2}$ cups) sifted icing (confectioners') sugar
4 egg yolks
6 oz (150g) semi-sweet dessert chocolate (Bournville or Menier)
1 level tbsp cocoa
1 tbsp rum

Line a loaf tin 9 × 5 × 3 in (23 × 13 × 8 cm) with a strip of foil. Beat margarine until like mayonnaise, then beat in icing sugar a heaped tablespoon at a time. Beat in yolks, rum and cocoa. Add chocolate which has been melted until liquid in a basin standing in a pan of very hot water.

Divide the biscuits into 3 sets of 10. Dip the first lot in and out of the rum-flavoured coffee then arrange down the tin. Arrange one third of the chocolate cream on top, then repeat with the second layer of biscuits and cream. Cover with the final layer of biscuits and pipe or swirl the remaining chocolate cream on top. Freeze for at least 24 hours.

To serve: Turn out of tin onto serving dish, then decorate with cherries and chopped walnuts. Serve chilled but not frozen. Serves 12–16.

Pineapple Pyramids

Make double the quantity of the recipe on p. 123.

Supper Party Menu No. 7

Chicken à la King
Oven-cooked Savoury Rice
Sweet and Sour Beef
Crispy Fried Noodles
French Bean, Corn, Olive and Pimento Salad
Spiced Peaches
Apfel Strudel
Chilled Lemon Soufflé

Chicken à la King

This same recipe can be presented in many different ways. For this menu it is served on a bed of rice. (*See suggestions below.*)

1 large fowl (about 5 lb/2½kg net weight), covered in cold water
1 large onion
2 large carrots, sliced
2 squashy tomatoes
2 level teasp salt
¼ teasp powdered bouquet garni

Simmer all ingredients either top-of-stove or (preferably) in the oven for 2 hours or until fowl is tender. Lift from stock, drain well, and when no longer steaming, carefully wrap in foil. Refrigerate overnight together with the stock. Next day, remove all the fat from the stock.

Sauce:
1½ pint (750ml/4 cups) stock (from fowl)
4 oz (100g/½ cup) chicken fat or margarine
1 chopped onion
4 oz (100g/1 cup) flour
3 level teasp salt
¼ teasp white pepper
½ lb (200g/4 cups) button mushrooms cooked for 3 min in the juice of ½ lemon, a nut of margarine and 4 tbsp boiling water, in a covered pan
4 canned pimentos, diced
1 tbsp dried peppers or 1 large fresh green pepper, diced
2 tbsp sherry
4 egg yolks

Bring the stock to the boil in a large, heavy-bottomed pan. Turn into a bowl. In the same pan, melt the fat or margarine and simmer the chopped onion until tender but unbrowned (about 5 minutes). Stir in the flour and bubble for 2 minutes. Add the hot stock, the seasonings and the pimentos, then whisk until smooth and thickened. Add the cooked mushrooms (and their juice) and the dried or fresh peppers. Leave to bubble gently for 10 minutes. Beat the egg yolks in a bowl, spoon on some of the hot sauce and stir well, then return this mixture to the pan. Allow to steam for 5 minutes. Taste and add the sherry. Fold in the chicken flesh. For a casserole dish, the chicken should be taken off the bone in 'bite-sized' pieces; for patties or blintzes or pies, it should be cut into chunky dice.

How to use it:

In patty cases: Reheat the baked cases for 5 minutes in a moderate oven. Reheat the chicken filling until steaming; spoon into the cases, cover with the 'lid' of the case and reheat for a further 5 minutes.

In blintzes: Allow mixture to go quite cold. Use to stuff the cold pancakes. Fry in oil and a little chicken fat until crispy and brown on both sides (about 5 minutes in all).

On rice or pasta: Reheat, preferably in the oven in a covered casserole at Gas No. 4, 350°F, 180°C, for 20 minutes. Spoon over the rice or pasta at table.

In a casserole: Turn into 2 greased casseroles. Top with dried breadcrumbs and dot with margarine. Bake in a quick moderate oven (Gas No. 5, 375°F, 190°C) for 20 minutes until bubbly and golden.

In a pie: Allow to go quite cold. Line two 9 in (23 cm) pie dishes with puff pastry. Spoon in the mixture. Cover with a top crust and brush with the yolk of an egg mixed with 2 teaspoons oil. Bake in a hot oven (Gas No. 7, 425°F, 220°C) for 25 minutes until well risen and a rich brown. Serves 14–16.

Oven-Cooked Savoury Rice

Make double the quantity of the recipe on pp. 102–3.

Sweet and Sour Beef

Make double the quantity of the recipe on p. 60.

French Bean, Corn, Olive and Pimento Salad

3 pkt haricot verts (whole green beans)
2 cans (12 oz/300g) corn
Small can pimentos
4 oz (100g) black olives
2 tbsp chopped onion
Dressing:
6 tbsp oil
3 tbsp wine vinegar
Black pepper
2 level teasp salt
2 level teasp sugar (optional)

Boil beans uncovered in large pan of boiling water until bite tender (about 8 minutes). Turn into colander and run cold water over for 2 minutes. Drain well. Blend with drained corn, diced pimento and stoned olives cut in 4. Beat wine vinegar and seasonings together then add oil. Beat till thickened then blend into vegetables. Chill for several hours. Serves 14–16.

Crispy Fried Noodles

Fry earlier in the day and heat through in a moderate oven.

½ lb (200g/3 cups) broad egg noodles

Cook noodles in boiling salted water until par-cooked (about 5 minutes). Drain, rinse in cold water, then dry very thoroughly on towels. Fry in small amounts in deep hot fat until golden brown. Drain on paper, sprinkle with salt. Serves 12 at buffet supper.

Spiced Peaches

Follow recipe on p. 269.

Apfel Strudel

Make double the quantity of the recipe on p. 178.

Chilled Lemon Soufflé

Make double the quantity of the recipe on p. 127.

Coffee and . . .

One of my favourite formulae for entertaining is the evening coffee party for 8–10 guests. This is particularly suitable for the working hostess, for it can consist entirely of cheese, delicatessen and pastries; or include home-made items such as hot breads, quiches and dips according to the time at her disposal.

Here are some suggestions:
A Cheeseboard with Crispbread, French Bread and hot Herb Bread, or Butterfingers
A Variety of Quiches
Swiss Cheese Flan
Hot Cheese Crisps
Pizzas
Low calorie nibbles such as slivers of green pepper, slices of cucumber, cauliflowerets; crisp cos (iceberg) lettuces; celery and carrot sticks which have been chilled for an hour in icy water
Coleslaw
Mexican Cheese Dip
Liptauer Cheese
Schmaltz Herring Hors-d'œuvre
Pickled Herring Hors-d'œuvre
Chopped Herring Salad
Pavlovas of any variety
Apfelschnitten and Cream
Cherry or Plum Kuchen and Cream
Raspberry Round
Quarksahne Schnitten
Coffee with slightly whipped cream

In summer:
Sangria
Wine Cup

To freeze ahead:
Herb Bread
Quiches
Swiss Cheese Flan
Pizza
Pavlovas, Apfelschnitten, Fruit Kuchen, Raspberry Round
Cooked Pastry
Quarksahne Schnitten

Hot Herb Bread

2 French loaves
6 oz (150g/¾ cup) butter
1 level tbsp of a mixture of fresh herbs (e.g. parsley, chives, basil)
¼ teasp paprika
10 grinds black pepper
2 teasp lemon juice

Cut the bread into slices, ⅛ in (¼ cm) thick, but stop at the base of the bread, so the loaf is left intact. Beat the butter to a soft cream with the seasonings, then use to spread on both sides of each slice. Spread any remaining butter on top of the loaves. Wrap each loaf completely in foil. Bake in a quick oven (Gas No. 6, 400°F, 200°C) for 20 minutes, then fold foil back to brown the crust for a further 5 minutes. Serve on long wooden platters, still in the loaf. Serves 10–12.

To freeze: Wrap tightly in heavy-duty foil, ready for the oven. *Storage time:* Up to 1 week. The crust begins to shell off after this time.

To thaw and crispen: Place frozen, wrapped in foil, in a moderately hot oven (Gas No. 6, 400°F, 200°C). A French loaf takes 30 minutes to thaw and heat through. Turn back foil to crispen for last 5 minutes.

Butterfingers

An unsweetened scone mixture forms the basis of these fluffy tender rolls with a crunchy buttery crust. Of American origin, they are delicious served with hors-d'œuvres, salads or cheese platter.

Bare 4 oz (100g/½ cup) butter
1 level tbsp sugar
9 oz (225g/2¼ cups) plain flour and 3 level teasp baking powder; or 9 oz (225g/2¼ cups) self-raising flour and 1 level teasp baking powder
1½ level teasp salt
8 fl oz (200ml/1 cup) milk

Heat oven to Gas No. 8, 450°F, 230°C. Put butter in pan 13 × 9½ × 2 in (33 × 24 × 5 cm) and leave in oven till melted then remove. Sift all dry ingredients together then stir in milk with a fork until dough just clings together. Turn onto well-floured board. Roll over to coat with flour, then knead lightly 10 times. Roll out ½ in (1 cm) thick into a rectangle, 12 × 8 in (30 × 20 cm). With floured knife cut dough in half lengthwise, then cut each half crosswise into 12 strips (24 in all). Dip cut strips into butter, lifting with both hands, then put back in buttery pan. Bake at Gas No. 8, 450°F, 230°C, 15–20 minutes until golden brown. Makes 24.

VARIATION
Add ½ cup grated cheese or ¼ cup minced chives or parsley to dry ingredients.

Swiss Cheese Flan

Pastry:
6 oz (150g/1½ cups) flour
3 oz (75g/⅓ cup) fat
1 egg
Filling:
8 oz (200g/2 cups) Gruyère or Emmenthaler cheese; or 8 oz (200g/2 cups) mature Gouda, grated
1 level tbsp flour
3 eggs, well beaten
Salt and pepper
1 large onion, finely chopped and sautéd in 1 oz (25g/2 tbsp) butter
8 fl oz (200ml/1 cup) single (light) cream
¼ teasp nutmeg

Roll out the pastry and use to fill 9 in (23 cm) sandwich tin or flan ring. With a fork, lightly toss cheese with flour. Spread on bottom of pricked pastry shell and cover with onions. Beat eggs and cream together and season lightly with salt and pepper. Pour over grated cheese. Sprinkle surface with nutmeg. Bake at Gas No. 6, 400°F, 200°C, for 15 minutes then reduce heat to Gas No. 3, 325°F, 170°C, and continue baking for 30 minutes. Serve warm. Serves 8 generously.

Hot Cheese Crisps

These savoury fried sandwiches have butter spread on the outside of the bread rather than on the pan; this gives a crisp, easily digested coating; for greater simplicity use sliced cheese spread with mustard or pickles instead of the cooked filling below. The filling will keep for 1 *week at least under refrigeration.*

8 oz (200g/2 cups) sharp cheese, grated
1 oz (25g/2 tbsp) butter
1 level teasp finely-chopped onion
2 level teasp sugar
2 tbsp vinegar
Pinch of salt
1 level tbsp flour
5 fl oz (125ml/⅔ cup) evaporated milk or single (light) cream
Dash cayenne pepper
16 slices bread
¼ lb (100g/½ cup) soft butter

Melt nut of butter, add onion and cook gently for 2 minutes. Then stir in sugar and flour, vinegar, milk and pepper and whisk over gentle heat until thickened. Add cheese, turn off heat and mix well until cheese is melted. Cool. Use to fill sandwiches. Brush outside of each sandwich thickly with soft butter. Then cook gently in hot ungreased heavy frying pan until golden brown. Cut in 2 and serve warm garnished with olives, gherkins, etc., on cocktail sticks. Serves 8.

Pizzas

Base:

½ lb (200g/2 cups) strong (bread) flour
2 level teasp salt
½ oz (15g/1 cake) fresh yeast; or 2 level teasp dried yeast
1 level teasp sugar
1 tbsp oil
½ egg; or 1 standard egg
4 fl oz (100ml/½ cup) warm water

Heat the water until it feels as warm as a baby's bath. Put into a large bowl. Add one third of the flour, all the sugar and the fresh or dried yeast. Mix until smooth, cover with a tea-towel and leave 20 minutes or until frothy. Add all the remaining flour, salt, oil and egg. Knead until smooth and silky, then put into an oiled plastic bag and refrigerate overnight, or up to 48 hours.

Topping:

2 tbsp olive oil
1 can (15 oz/375g) plum tomatoes
1 onion, finely chopped
1 bayleaf
1 level teasp each of sugar and salt
10 grinds black pepper
½ level teasp oregano or mixed Italian herbs
¼ lb (100g/1 cup) Cheddar cheese, cut in matchsticks
1 can anchovies, split lengthwise

Cook the chopped onion in the oil until softened and golden brown (about 5 minutes). Add all the remaining ingredients except the cheese and anchovies, and simmer, uncovered, until the mixture is ketchup-thick (about 15 minutes). Cool.

Two hours before the pizza is required, roll the dough into two circles about 8 in (20 cm) in diameter, and put in well-oiled sandwich tins or round baking dishes (there must be room for the pizza to expand sideways in the oven). Put each round in an oiled plastic bag to rise in a warm kitchen. Half an hour before serving, spread the sauce on the dough, cover with the cheese and criss-cross with the anchovies. Drizzle a little extra oil over the top. Bake in a hot oven (Gas No. 7, 425°F, 220°C) for 15–20 minutes or until well risen and brown at the edges. Serves 8–10. (See also **Party Pizza** on p. 143.)

Coleslaw

1 cabbage
2 carrots, grated
4 tbsp wine vinegar
1 level tbsp caster (superfine) sugar
Salt and freshly-ground black pepper
6 tbsp mayonnaise
5 fl oz (125ml/⅔ cup) soured cream
Chives

Shred the cabbage, either on the electric mixer-shredder or on a mandolin. Crisp cabbage in salted cold water for one hour (put in refrigerator). Drain and dry thoroughly. Mix together vinegar, sugar, salt and pepper in a salad bowl and allow the cabbage to marinate in this dressing for one hour. Add chives, combine mayonnaise and soured cream and pour over the cabbage mixture. Toss lightly and adjust seasonings. Serves 10–12.

Raspberry or Strawberry Round

Pastry:
4 oz (100g/1 cup) plain flour
2½ oz (65g/⅓ cup) butter
1½ oz (40g/⅓ cup) icing (confectioners') sugar
1 egg yolk
Topping:
1–1½ lb (680g) choice berries
1 tbsp raspberry jam
2 tbsp redcurrant jelly
5 fl oz (125ml/⅔ cup) cream, whipped

Put all the pastry ingredients in the mixer and blend slowly until a smooth dough forms. Chill 1 hour, then roll out ¼ in (½ cm) thick into an 8 in (20 cm) round (use a pan lid as a cutter). Transfer on to a baking sheet and prick all over with a fork. Bake in a moderate oven (Gas No. 4, 350°F, 180°C) for 20 minutes or until golden. Cool, then put on a flat serving dish. Spread thinly with raspberry jam. Cover completely with fresh berries. Melt 2 tablespoons redcurrant jelly in a small pan and when liquid, spoon gently over the berries. Chill until set; decorate with whipped cream. Serves 8. (*Note:* This pastry is very crisp and does not go soggy for several hours when topped with fruit so the cake can safely be made in the morning to serve at night. The rounds of pastry will freeze.)

Quarksahne Schnitten (*Cream Cheese Slice*)

A true continental torte, consisting of a very light sponge filled with a cream cheese mousse and morello (sour red) cherries.

3 eggs
3 tbsp cold water
5 oz (125g/⅔ cup) caster (superfine) sugar
Few drops vanilla essence (extract)
2 oz (50g/½ cup) self-raising flour
2 oz (50g/½ cup) cornflour (cornstarch)

Beat whites and water until stiff and fluffy, add the sugar and vanilla gradually, beating until stiff after each addition. Fold in the yolks, then the flour and cornflour. Bake in a 12 in (30 cm) spring form, or flan tin, or two 9 in (23 cm) sandwich tins at Gas No. 4, 350°F, 180°C, for about 25 minutes, depending on depth of mixture.

Filling:
1½ lb (680g) stewed morello (sour red) cherries (or 1 can), thickened by boiling for 3 min with 2 level tbsp cornflour (cornstarch)
4 oz (100g/½ cup) sugar
1 lb (480g/2 cups) cream cheese
1 lemon jelly (gelatin mix), dissolved in the minimum of water (3 tbsp)
5 fl oz (125ml/⅔ cup) sour cream
5 fl oz (125ml/⅔ cup) whipped cream

Blend the sugar, cheese, dissolved jelly and sour cream. Leave until half set. Split cake and spread with cheese mixture, then top with cherries. Cover top of cake with fresh whipped cream. Serve in slices. Serves 8–10. (*Note:* The sponge by itself is delicious as base for fruit flan but should be soaked with syrup or liqueur beforehand.)

Sangria

½ lb (200g/1 cup) granulated sugar
10 fl oz (250ml/1¼ cups) water
1 orange and 2 lemons, sliced with peel and then cut in 4
1 stick cinnamon
1 small can pineapple titbits (optional)
1 bottle full-bodied red wine such as Burgundy
Soda water
1 wine glass brandy (optional but nice)

Boil the sugar and water for 5 minutes to make a syrup. Cool for 10 minutes then pour over the cut-up fruit in a large bowl. Leave for at least 2 hours in cool place.

To serve: Fill a jug one quarter full of ice and add half the fruit and half of the syrup. Add half the wine, stir very thoroughly then top up with soda. Repeat with second jugful. Serves 10.

Wine Cup

2 bottles white wine (Yugoslav Riesling type)
1 bottle (2½ cups) apple juice
1 lemon, peeled like an apple, but peel left anchored at bottom of fruit
1 small can pineapple titbits
1 glass each vodka and orange liqueur (optional)
Fresh mint in season

Blend all ingredients, floating the lemon in the liquid. Serve well chilled. Serves approx 10–12 with two 4 fl oz (100ml) glasses each.

Join us for Drinks

The informal 'drinks' party can be a most delightful way of entertaining a large group of friends—particularly if one moves in several 'worlds', and wants to have the opportunity of mixing them.

The time: Morning from 11 a.m.–1 p.m. (12–2 p.m. if you are providing a 'fork' meal); or evenings from 6–8 p.m. is probably the best. Two hours seems to me the maximum time that one can comfortably stand and chat—after that the party can sink under waves of guest-exhaustion!

The help: This depends on the formality of the occasion. The *drinks* must be the concern of at least one person—either a professional barman or a son of the house. The food can either be passed round by waitresses, or be scattered on tables with easy access, with young members of the family passing round the hot food. It is essential to have at least some help both for food preparation before guests arrive, and to heat food as it is required. Many 'freelance' waitresses will help with both food preparation and service, and they will advise you on the number of staff you require according to the size of the guest list.

The ambiance: It is essential to clear the room of all 'loose' furniture, restricting what there is to the wall area. Have the minimum of chairs (for elderly guests), as you want people to circulate freely in the room. It is essential to have enough guests to comfortably fill the room, leaving enough space for them to move around from one group to another.

The drink: I think it is simpler to have one basic drink—such as a champagne cocktail, alcoholic punch or 'black velvet' (stout and champagne), with short drinks and fruit juices for those who specifically ask for them.

The food: This can be as simple or as complicated as you prefer; but whatever you serve must be 'bite-size' and easily held in the hand. A combination of cold and hot foods is most satisfying; with something sweet or fruity offered towards the end of the party. Many of the 'makings' of this kind of party can be frozen well in advance.

Drinks for 50

It is impossible to be exact, but from experience I would recommend the following quantities for a drinks party based on champagne cocktails (brandy with a sugar lump, topped up with champagne and garnished with maraschino cherries):

12 bottles champagne or other sparkling wine
1 bottle 3-star brandy
1 bottle Angostura bitters
1 lb (480g) pkt sugarlumps
1 jar maraschino cherries
6 oranges (garnishes)
12 bottles ginger ale
12 bottles bitter lemon
6 bottles tonic water
6 cans beer
2 bottles cordial
2 × 43 oz (1075ml) cans tomato juice
Soda water
7 dozen champagne flutes (borrow from wine merchant)

Also
1 bottle whisky
1 bottle gin
1 bottle vodka
1 bottle brandy
Large pack cocktail sticks
8 dozen cocktail-size paper napkins
Large pack medium-sized dish papers

Suggestions for Dairy Cocktail Foods

Choose from a selection of the following:

Canapé Toppings or Spreads:
Avocado and Cream Cheese
Mexican Cheese
Liptauer Cheese
Guacamole
Smoked Salmon with Lemon
Pineapple and Cream Cheese
Walnut and Cream Cheese
Gaffelbitter, Tomato and Cucumber
Chopped Herring Salad
Egg and Olive Butter
Smoked Salmon Pâté
Smoked Trout Mousse
Smoked Salmon Roulades filled with Trout Mousse
Celery Stuffed with Cream Cheese
Asparagus Rolls
Fried Cocktail Nuts
Cocktail Fish Balls
Cheese and Fruit Kebabs

Hot Titbits:
Cheese and Olive Tartlets
Petites Quiches Lorraines
Cheese Bites
Sherried Mushroom Bites
Individual Party Pizzas

Patty Case (Bouchée) Fillings:
Salmon
Mushroom
Cheese

Note: Quantities are for 50 when 4 or 5 varieties of canapés and 2 or 3 hot foods, with chopped fish balls are served.

Canapés

Serve canapés on crisp crackers (not cheese-flavoured) or crackers and buttered French bread slices. Allow six ½lb (225g) packets crisp crackers or 2 packets crisp crackers and 4 French loaves.

(F) denotes food can be frozen in advance.

Avocado and Cream Cheese (F)

1 large ripe avocado
4 oz (100g/½ cup) cream cheese
2 tbsp mayonnaise
1 tbsp French dressing
½ lemon
Salt and pepper to taste
1 level tbsp snipped chives

Put all in blender till smooth. Pipe on crackers.

Mexican Cheese

A crunchy tangy mixture that is universally popular. Make at least 24 hours before required. It will keep a week in the refrigerator.

½ lb (200g/1 cup) cream cheese
2 oz (50g/¼ cup) butter
½ large green pepper
6 cocktail gherkins
Green part of 2 spring onions (scallions); or
  2 tbsp chives
Sprig parsley
1 tbsp mayonnaise
1 tbsp French dressing
½ teasp salt
1 tbsp top milk (light cream or half-and-half)

Put all seasonings in blender until liquid. Add butter and cream cheese and blend until smooth. Add sliced gherkins and green pepper. Blend only until gherkins are still visible. Without blender, chop finely the pepper, gherkins, spring onions or chives, and parsley, and blend into cheese mixed with all remaining ingredients.

Liptauer Cheese (F)

8 oz (200g/1 cup) cream cheese
2 oz (50g/¼ cup) butter
2 teasp anchovy paste
1 level tbsp chopped capers
2 teasp prepared mustard
1 level tbsp paprika
Pepper and celery salt
1 tbsp chopped chives

Cream butter, then beat in cheese and all remaining ingredients. Taste. Leave for several hours to develop flavour.

Guacamole

This Mexican delicacy is probably best served as a 'dip' with crisps, though it can be used to top tomato slices on bread.

1 large avocado
Good sprinkle garlic salt
2 tomatoes, peeled and finely-chopped
¼ onion, finely-chopped
12 coriander seeds, ground in pepper mill
1 tbsp olive oil
Juice of ½ lemon
Salt and black pepper to taste

Mash the avocado with a silver or stainless steel fork, then beat in the olive oil and lemon juice followed by all the remaining ingredients. Put in a dish, closely wrap and chill for several hours before serving as a dip.

Smoked Salmon with Lemon

Sprinkle slices of smoked salmon with lemon juice and a little black pepper. Cut to fit crackers or bread slices. Garnish with thin section of lemon or sliced fresh cucumber. Allow 1½ lb (680g) salmon.

Pineapple and Cream Cheese (F)

Use ½ lb (200g/1 cup) cream cheese blended with 1 small can crushed pineapple and 1–2 tablespoons mayonnaise.

Walnut and Cream Cheese (F)

Use ½ lb (200g/1 cup) cream cheese blended with 2 oz (50g/½ cup) finely-chopped walnuts and 2 tablespoons mayonnaise.

Gaffelbitter, Tomato and Cucumber

Allow 3 large cans gaffelbitter. On each biscuit place first a slice of fresh cucumber then tomato and finally 1 drained piece of gaffelbitter.

Chopped Herring Salad

Double the quantity of recipe p. 19. Serve on buttered black bread. Garnish with finely grated hard-boiled egg (allow one 2 lb (1kg) black bread, 2 hard-boiled eggs for garnish).

Egg and Olive Butter

Mash 6 hard-boiled eggs with 1 oz (25g/2 tbsp) butter, 2 tablespoons mayonnaise and 2 oz (50g/½ cup) finely-chopped stuffed olives. Garnish with anchovies.

Smoked Salmon Pâté (F)

Double the recipe on p. 17. Frozen smoked salmon or cheaper fresh varieties can be used for this delicious spread; particularly nice on fingers of black bread.

Smoked Trout Mousse (F)

2 medium smoked trout (skinned and boned)
4 oz (100g/½ cup) single cream cheese
5 fl oz (125ml/⅔ cup) soured cream
1 teasp horseradish relish or pinch of cayenne
1 oz (25g/2 tbsp) butter
2 teasp parsley
Juice of ½ lemon (1 tbsp)
Black pepper

Put soured cream, cream cheese, lemon juice and parsley into blender, followed by the trout flesh and soft butter. Blend until smooth. Then add the seasonings, and blend again until smooth. Turn into a small dish and chill for 1 hour, or put into individual cocottes to serve as an hors-d'œuvre; can be piped either for canapés or smoked salmon roulades.

Smoked Salmon Roulades with Trout Mousse

Very extravagant but delicious; make little rolls of smoked salmon, like 'brandy snaps', then pipe with the trout mousse. Spear closed with cocktail sticks. Alternatively an asparagus tip can be used to fill the roll. Allow 1½ lb (¾kg) salmon.

Celery Stuffed with Cream Cheese or Other Spreads

Use ½ lb (200g/1 cup) plain cream cheese blended with 2 tablespoons mayonnaise; or avocado and cream cheese, Liptauer cheese or Mexican cheese, to fill 1 in (3 cm) lengths of crisp white celery. Spear with a cocktail stick. Allow 2 celery.

Asparagus Rolls (F)

Very thin slices of brown bread are decrusted and buttered. Place one canned asparagus tip on edge, dot with mayonnaise and roll up. Place rolls close together on tray, cover with wet greaseproof paper and chill for 2 or 3 hours, overnight if convenient, in which case overwrap with foil. Allow 4 Hovis or other small brown loaves and 4 small cans asparagus tips.

Fried Cocktail Nuts

4 oz (100g/½ cup) butter
1 tbsp oil
1 lb (½kg/3 cups) cashew nuts mixed with almonds

Put the butter into a heavy pan with the oil. Heat the fat until, when a nut is put in, bubbles form around it. Place the nuts in the hot fat, and let them cook gently, turning them with a slotted spoon until they are a rich even brown. Then lift out to drain on crumpled tissue paper, put in a bowl, sprinkle with cooking salt, and when cold, store in an airtight tin.

Cocktail Fish Balls (F)

Treble the **Gefüllte Fish Mix** on p. 40. It is most easily mixed in a large plastic bowl. Use a large vegetable piping bag without a pipe. Fill with some of the mix, then pipe out in blobs the size of a walnut. Roll between the palms into little balls. Put about 20 balls at a time into a plastic bag containing 2 tablespoons flour. Shake until the balls are evenly coated. Fry in deep hot fat (360°F, 180°C or hot enough to brown a 1 in (3 cm) cube of bread in 40 seconds). Fry quickly until golden brown, then drain on crumpled tissue. Repeat until all the balls are fried. When the balls are quite cold put into plastic bags and freeze until required.

To serve: Spread the frozen balls onto an oven tray and heat in a moderate oven (Gas No. 4, 350°F, 180°C) until crisp to the touch (about 5 minutes). Serve warm or cold. This quantity will make 150 cocktail fishballs. Serve plain or with double the **Tartare Sauce Recipe,** p. 113.

Cheese and Fruit Kebabs

Buy ½ lb (200g/2 cups) red cheese and ½ lb (200g/2 cups) white or pale cheese; cut in ½ in (1 cm) cubes (this can be done the day before if cheese is kept in airtight container). Drain a can of mandarins and pineapple titbits; quarter 4 oz (100g/¾ cup) glacé (candied) cherries; arrange alternate cubes of cheese and fruit on cocktail sticks. Arrange on flat trays, or spear, hedgehog fashion, into grapefruit.

Hot Titbits

Cheese and Olive Tartlets (F)

Use either baked tartlets which have been frozen, then fill and bake for 15–20 minutes (Gas No. 4, 350°F, 180°C), or use raw cases, and bake for the same time in a hotter oven (Gas No. 6, 400°F, 200°C).

4 dozen flaky or puff pastry lined patty tins (made from 1½ lb/¾kg pastry)
2 oz (50g/¼ cup) butter
4 well-beaten eggs
12 oz (300g/3 cups) finely-grated Cheddar cheese
6 tbsp fresh breadcrumbs
4 fl oz (100ml/½ cup) top milk or evaporated milk
1 teasp mustard
Pinch of cayenne pepper
4 oz (100g/1 cup) sliced stuffed olives

Make the filling by melting the butter, and stirring in all the remaining ingredients. Fill the well-pricked cases with the filling, put in a quick oven (Gas No. 6, 400°F, 200°C) for 15–20 minutes, or until golden brown and firm to the touch. Makes 48.

Petites Quiches Lorraines (F)

A slightly creamier version without the breadcrumbs, which may be varied with mushrooms, onions, black olives or anchovies.

Shortcrust pastry (made from 1 lb/480g/4 cups plain flour, 10 oz/250g/1¼ cups butter or margarine, 2 level teasp icing (confectioners') sugar, 2 egg yolks and 3 fl oz/75ml water, 2 teasp vinegar)
6 oz (150g/1½ cups) finely-grated cheese
4 oz (100g/½ cup) butter
4 eggs
10 fl oz (250ml/1¼ cups) creamy milk (light cream)
Good pinch of salt, black pepper
2 level tbsp chives

Roll chilled pastry to fit 48 patty tins. Prick well. Beat eggs thoroughly, then add cheese, seasonings and milk. When ready to bake, place a small nut of butter in the bottom of each pastry case. Three-quarters fill with cheese mixture. Bake in a quick oven (Gas No. 6, 400°F, 200°C) for 10–15 minutes, or until pastry is golden and filling is puffed. Makes 48.

VARIATIONS
At bottom of patty case put 1 teaspoon chopped sautéd mushrooms or onions, chopped anchovies or sliced stoned black olives.

Savoury Bites (F)

These can be made with a cheese, mushroom or herb filling.

2 lb (1kg) bought puff or home-made rough puff pastry (double the recipe on p. 140)

To shape the puffs: Roll out the pastry to the thickness of a knife blade. Cut into rounds of 2 in (5 cm) diameter. Put a teaspoon of filling in the centre, fold over and seal into a crescent. This can be done two days before, providing the puffs are then foil-covered and refrigerated, most conveniently on the ungreased baking trays, or the puffs can be frozen uncooked. Just before baking in a hot oven (Gas No. 8, 450°F, 230°C) for 15 minutes, brush with beaten egg and scatter with sesame seeds. Serve warm. Makes approx 72–80 puffs.

Cheese Filling:
1 lb (480g/4 cups) sharp cheese, finely grated
3 large eggs (save ½ egg for gilding puffs)
Blend thoroughly together to make a firm but moist paste.

Mushroom Filling:
2 oz (50g/¼ cup) butter
2 oz (50g/½ cup) flour
1 pint (500ml/2½ cups) milk
Salt and white pepper
Pinch of powdered mace or nutmeg
2 tbsp dry sherry
1 lb (480g) mushrooms
Juice of 1 lemon
3 fl oz (75ml/⅓ cup) water and a nut of butter

First cook the mushrooms: Chop the rinsed mushrooms coarsely. Add to a pan containing the water, lemon juice and nut of butter. Cover and simmer for 3 minutes. Uncover and cook to evaporate most of the liquid.

Sauce: Bring the milk to the boil, then pour into a measuring jug. Rinse out the pan and melt the butter. Stir in the flour and cook for a minute, then add the hot milk all at once off the heat, and whisk until smooth. Return to the heat and bubble for 3 minutes. Season with salt, pepper and mace, then stir in the mushrooms and sherry. Allow to cool to lukewarm before using.

Herb Filling:
12 oz (300g/1½ cups) cooking curd cream cheese
8 oz (200g/2 cups) grated hard cheese
2 large eggs (save some for gilding puffs)
1 tbsp very finely-chopped onion
1 crushed clove of garlic; or a pinch of ready chopped garlic
2 level tbsp finely-chopped parsley
Salt and black pepper to taste
Sesame seeds
A little beaten egg

Mix the cheeses together, beat the egg and add the seasonings. Combine the two mixtures. The mixture should be the consistency of a thick, moist paste.

Individual Party Pizzas (F)

Double the recipe for **Party Pizza** on p. 143, but roll out the pastry and cut to fill 48 tartlet cases. Prick well, then bake at Gas No. 7, 425°F, 220°C, for 12 minutes or until set and coloured, then freeze or store in a tin for up to a week. Fill and top as directed and bake at Gas No. 7, 425°F, 220°C, for 15 minutes. Alternatively, the filling and topping can be arranged in well-pricked, unbaked cases then baked at Gas No. 7, 425°F, 220°C for 20 minutes. Makes 50.

Patty Case Fillings

Heat baked puff pastry cases (bouchées) in moderate oven (Gas No. 4, 350°F, 180°C) till piping hot (about 5 minutes). Add hot filling (most safely reheated over boiling water), and return to oven for further 5 minutes. Serve at once, or turn oven to 'warm' to keep hot without drying out. Makes 80 cocktail size patty cases.

Salmon Filling: (F)
1½ lb (680g) flaked canned or fresh salmon
¼ teasp cayenne pepper
1 tbsp lemon juice

Sauce:
2 oz (50g/¼ cup) butter
2 oz (50g/½ cup) flour
1 pint (500ml/2½ cups) milk
Salt and white pepper
Pinch of powdered mace or nutmeg

Bring milk to the boil, then pour into a jug. Rinse out the pan, melt butter and add flour and cook for 2 minutes without browning. Remove from the heat. Add the hot milk all at once, whisking well. Add seasonings and simmer for 5 minutes on a very low heat. Whisk in canned or fresh salmon, cayenne pepper and lemon juice.

Cheese Filling: (*F*)
2 egg yolks
8 oz (200g/2 cups) coarsely-grated cheese
2 oz (50g/¼ cup) butter
3 oz (75g/¾ cup) flour
1 pint (500ml/2½ cups) creamy milk (light cream)
1 teasp salt
⅛ teasp white pepper
Pinch each of nutmeg and cayenne pepper

Bring milk to the boil, then pour into a jug. Rinse out the pan, melt butter and add flour and cook for 2 minutes without browning. Remove from the heat. Add the hot milk all at once, whisking well. Add seasonings and simmer for 5 minutes on a very low heat. Take off the heat and drop egg yolks into the centre then immediately whisk in, followed by the cheese. Finally beat in a further 2 oz (50g/¼ cup) butter. If you wish to make the sauce ahead of time, dot it with butter and leave. When you wish to reheat it, whisk in the butter and you will find no skin has formed on the top as the melting butter will have protected it.

The sauce should be very thick.

Sherried Mushroom Filling (*F*): Use same mushroom mixture as for 'bites'.

Suggestions for Meat Cocktail Foods

Cocktail Chicken Blintzes
Meat Strudel
Deep-fried Chicken Portions
Latkes on a Stick
Tongue Sandwiches
Chicken Sandwiches
Turkey Sandwiches
Tongue and Gherkin Cornucopias
Chicken Liver Pâte on Pickled Cucumber Slices
Pâté Maison
Pineapple or Melon 'Kebabs' with Grapes and Cherries
Chicken Patties (Bouchées)

Note: Quantities are for 50 when 6–8 different items are served.

Cocktail Chicken Blintzes (F)

Double the recipe for **Chicken Blintzes** on p. 87. Refrigerate or freeze until required. Cut each blintze into 4 or 6 little blintzes and fry in deep hot fat until golden brown. Makes 100 blintzes.

Meat Strudel (F)

Double the recipe on p. 141. Reheat. Cut into 1 in (3 cm) wide slices and spear on cocktail sticks.

Deep-fried Chicken Portions

These need to be prepared by trained help as the chicken must be boned out into bite-sized pieces. Follow the recipe on p. 80 using five 3½ lb (1½kg) birds. Serve hot with napkins to hold.

Latkes on a Stick

Again, this needs someone to cook them freshly. Treble the recipe on p. 230. Drop teaspoonsful of the mixture into deep hot fat and cook until a rich brown. Drain on crumpled paper, then serve on cocktail sticks. Makes 75–100.

Tongue Sandwiches (F)

These are most delicious served on black or rye (lighter brown) bread, spread lightly with rendered chicken fat and seasoned with mustard or sweet fruity pickles. Allow 1 lb (480g) thinly-sliced tongue, 2 loaves.

Chicken Sandwiches

Use a capon, simmered until tender, or cooked as for **To Roast A Bird To Be Served Cold** on p. 79. Both methods give juicy cold flesh. Serve on white bread (challah for preference), spread with chicken fat, then a crisp lettuce leaf, a slice of bird and a touch of mustard. Allow one 6 lb (3kg) capon or two 3½ lb (1½kg) chickens.

Turkey Sandwiches

Use turkey breast on white bread, spread with chicken fat, top the turkey with cranberry jelly.

Tongue and Gherkin Cornucopias

Use thin slices of black bread spread with chicken fat. Twist a slice of tongue into a cornet shape and put a slice of gherkin inside. If unsteady, anchor to the bread with a cocktail stick. Allow 1 lb (480g) thinly-sliced tongue, small jar of gherkins.

Chicken Liver Pâté

Double the recipe for **Chicken Liver Pâté in the Jewish Fashion** on p. 17. Arrange teaspoonsful on slices of pickled cucumber.

Pâté Maison (F)

Double the recipe on p. 17 but use ½ lb (200g) each chicken livers and koshered calves' livers. Use as a spread on bread or crackers, topped with fresh cucumber.

Pineapple or Melon Kebabs with Grapes and Cherries

Spear alternate slices of peeled fresh pineapple or melon with seedless or seeded grapes and halved candied cherries on cocktail sticks. Anchor into whole grapefruit.

Chicken Patties (Bouchées)

Use **Chicken à la King** (p. 276). Heat 48 cocktail size patty cases for 5 minutes in moderate oven. Add hot filling. Reheat a further 5 minutes, then serve or turn oven to 'warm' and keep hot until required.

Quantities for 50

There are many occasions when it is necessary to produce food in quantity whether it be for community or fund-raising functions or for family celebrations. Provided one has reliable recipes and quantities, there are only two major points to keep in mind:

1. Large-scale cooking requires not only more ingredients but also more time than cooking for the family. It is essential to remember this when organizing preparation time and calculating the number of helpers that will be required. If plenty of time is allowed for a planning session—when recipes are chosen, shopping lists prepared and the time-table planned, the actual cooking will be most enjoyable—rather like playing in an orchestra instead of performing solo.
2. Correct equipment will greatly speed the preparation. This means that large enough pans and baking dishes should be borrowed or bought and that knives should be well-sharpened beforehand.

Below, I give a selection of simple but useful recipes for use when catering for 50 people. They can be prepared by any proficient home cook. There are also tables of quantities for common foods and drinks to help in calculating how much food will be required.

Rice

Savoury Rice (50 *servings*)

3 lb (1½kg/7 cups) long grain rice
6 pints (3 litres/15 cups) water
8 chicken bouillon cubes
8 tbsp oil

Bring water, with stock cubes and oil, to the boil, scatter in rice and bring back to boil, stirring. Cover, lower heat to fast simmer, then cook without removing lid or stirring for 15–20 minutes when all the liquid should be absorbed and the rice tender and separate. Remove from heat and serve. *To keep hot:* Transfer rice to shallow serving pans, and keep in a warm place until served.

Note: For parboiled long grain rice: Increase liquid by one quarter and allow 3–5 minutes extra cooking time. There will be a slightly larger yield.

Mexican Rice (50 *servings*)

This makes an excellent main dish for a ladies' luncheon. Serve it with saveloys and frozen peas.

3 lb (1½kg/7 cups) savoury rice
5 green peppers
1 fat celery (about 4 cups diced)
8 onions
½ lb (200g/1 cup) margarine and 1 cup oil
6 lb (3kg) lean minced (ground) beef
8 pints (20 cups) canned tomatoes
8 oz (200g/1 cup) canned tomato purée
4 oz (100g/½ cup) sugar
5 cloves garlic
2 level tbsp salt
1 level teasp pepper
2 level tbsp paprika

Follow directions for cooking **Mexican Rice** in family quantity on p. 57.

Coffee

Fresh Coffee (50 8 *oz cups*, 64 *coffee cups*)

2 gal (8 litres/40 cups) boiling water
1 lb (480g/4 cups) ground coffee
8 fl oz (200ml/1 cup) cold water

Bring water to boil in large pan or urn with tap. Put the ground coffee into a muslin bag with the cold water. Put into the pan, cover and bring very slowly back to the boil—this should take 15 minutes. Do not let the coffee boil; once bubbles start to break the surface, turn off the heat. Remove bag and stir well. Coffee can now be poured into jugs and served black or with cream.

VARIATIONS

With hot milk: Use 11 pints (5½ litres/27½ cups) water to brew coffee. Combine with 5 pints (2½ litres/12½ cups) hot milk.

With instant coffee: Use 5 oz (125g/3 cups) coffee, dissolved in 2 gal (8 litres/40 cups) boiling water.

Meat

Sweet and Sour Beef (50 *portions*)

This is an excellent dish as the meat mixture can be frozen ahead. On the day it is to be served add the vinegar and pineapple mixture and bring to the boil to thicken. Alternatively, the meat can be cooked and refrigerated overnight then thickened the next day.

6 onions
1 celery
6 oz (150g/¾ cup) margarine and 6 fl oz (150ml/¾ cup) oil
5 × 20 oz (580g) cans pineapple titbits
16 lb (8kg) braising steak
4 level tbsp salt
1 level teasp black pepper
6 tbsp soy sauce
4 pints (2 litres/10 cups) beef stock
8 tbsp tomato ketchup
8 fl oz (200ml/1 cup) vinegar
5 oz (125g/1¼ cups) cornflour (cornstarch)
Pineapple juice made up to 4 pints (2 litres/10 cups) with water

Follow directions for **Sweet and Sour Beef** on p. 60.

Meat Balls in Tomato Sauce (50 *portions*)

10 lb (5kg) minced shoulder steak (ground beef)
5 oz (125g/⅔ cup) margarine
1 level teasp salt
1 teasp white pepper
10 eggs
5 onions (1½–2 lb/680g–1kg)
10 oz (250g/1¼ cups) medium matzo meal

Put onions, eggs and seasonings in blender until smooth. Alternatively, grate onions and add to eggs beaten with seasonings. Add meat, soft margarine and meal, and blend thoroughly either by hand or electric mixer at low speed. Leave for 1 hour, then form into balls with wetted hands. Simmer in sauce as follows:

Tomato Sauce:
3 large onions, sliced
5 tbsp oil
3 × 28 oz (780g) cans whole tomatoes
15 oz (375g) can tomato purée
3 level tbsp brown sugar
1 teasp white pepper
3 bayleaves
1 pint (500 ml/2½ cups) water
4 beef stock cubes
2 level tbsp salt
Juice of 2 lemons

Put sliced onions into cold oil, then heat gently and cook until softened and transparent. Add sieved or liquidized tomatoes and all remaining ingredients. Bring to boil. Drop in meat balls. Cover and simmer for 1 hour. Serve with 3 lb (1½kg) rice cooked as for **Savoury Rice** on p. 288.

Beef and Wine Casserole (50 *portions*)

A really savoury dish that can also be used with a top crust or with dumplings. Can be frozen.

12 lb (6kg) lean beef (such as shoulder steak) cut into 1½ in (4 cm) cubes
2½ level tbsp salt
½ level teasp black pepper
6 tbsp oil
5 tbsp chicken fat; or 3 oz (75g/6 tbsp) margarine
4 large onions, finely chopped
4 large carrots, peeled and cubed
1 celery, sliced
4 cloves garlic
5 oz (125g/1¼ cups) flour
2½ pints (1¼ litres/6 cups) beef stock
1½ bottles dry red wine
1 small can (5 oz/125g) tomato purée
Bunch of parsley
4 large bayleaves

Sprinkle the meat with the salt and pepper. Heat the oil and brown the meat quickly on all sides. In another pan heat the chicken fat or margarine and gently sauté the onion, carrot, celery and garlic until golden brown. Carefully drain both the meat and vegetables and arrange either in oven dishes 2 in (5 cm) deep or in one or two large pans. Put the remaining fat together and stir in the flour. Bubble for 2 or 3 minutes, then add the beef stock and wine, followed by all the remaining ingredients. Pour over the meat mixture, dividing it in two if in two pans. Cover and simmer very slowly for 2½ hours top-of-stove or in a slow oven (Gas No. 2, 300°F, 150°C) for the same time.

Hungarian Goulash (50 *portions*)

12 lb (6kg) braising or stewing steak, cubed
1½ lb (¾kg) onions, chopped
8 oz (200g/1 cup) cooking fat; or 6 fl oz (150ml/¾ cup) oil
1 level tbsp dry mustard
4 level tbsp paprika pepper
4 level tbsp salt
5 oz (125g/⅔ cup) brown sugar
5 fl oz (125ml/⅔ cup) Worcestershire sauce
2 tbsp vinegar
1½ pints (750ml/4 cups) tomato ketchup
5 pints (2½ litres/12½ cups) water
Thickening:
½ lb (200g/2 cups) cornflour (cornstarch), mixed to a smooth liquid with 1½ pints (750ml/4 cups) water

Brown the beef and the onion in the fat. Add all the remaining ingredients except the thickening. Simmer in a covered container, 2½–3 hours or until meat is tender. Stir in cornflour mixture, bring back to boil and simmer three minutes. Serve over cooked noodles.

Holishkes (50 *portions*, 2 *holishkes each*)

Can be prepared the day before and reheated.

8 lb (4kg) raw minced (ground) beef
1 pkt (11–12 oz/275g–300g/1½ cups) medium matzo meal
4 large onions
2 level tbsp salt
6 large eggs
6 large cabbages
Sauce:
5 × 28 oz (780g) cans tomatoes
1 lb (480g/2 cups) brown sugar
1 level tbsp citric acid (sour salt); or 12 fl oz (300ml/1½ cups) cider vinegar
2 level tbsp salt

Plunge cabbages in boiling water, bring back to boil, simmer 5 minutes then plunge into cold water. Strip off leaves, cutting out tough stalk portions. Mix all meat ingredients together. Place 1 tablespoon of the mixture on each leaf, then fold in sides, roll up, and gently squeeze in palm to seal. Lay side by side in baking tins. Combine all sauce ingredients and pour over so that cabbage is barely covered. Cover tightly with foil. Cook for 2 hours at Gas No. 2, 300°F, 150°C, then uncover and cook a further half an hour at Gas No. 4, 350°F, 180°C. Reheat, covered, in a moderate oven (Gas No. 4, 350°F, 180°C) for half an hour until bubbly. Serve with savoury rice or baked potatoes.

Chicken Marengo (50 *portions*)

10 steam roasters (each 4½ lb/2kg net)
½ lb (200g/1 cup) fat
½ lb (200g/2 cups) flour
3 lb (1½kg) onions
6 pints (3 litres/15 cups) stock made from boiling birds
1½ pints (750ml/4 cups) white wine
4 cloves garlic
10 oz (250g) canned tomato purée
8 bayleaves
Large bunch parsley
2 oz (50g/¼ cup) brown sugar
3 lb (1½kg) mushrooms

Boil chickens (follow instructions to boil a fowl for chicken soup p. 27, multiplying ingredients by 10). Reserve stock. (If there are several hostesses, this could be done by them at home.) Remove flesh, cut in big cubes.

To make sauce: Melt fat (it can be white fat or chicken fat) and cook finely chopped onion until soft and golden. Add flour and simmer for 3 minutes, then add hot stock, wine, purée, bayleaves and sugar. Simmer for 10 minutes. Refrigerate overnight.

To cook mushrooms: Cover bottom of pan with water to depth of ½ in (1 cm). Add mushrooms, thinly sliced. Sprinkle with salt, cover, bring to boil and simmer 5 minutes. Reserve with liquor.

To serve dish: Add mushrooms and their cooking liquid, chicken and chopped parsley to sauce. Allow to reheat thoroughly. Serve with savoury rice or boiled noodles.

Fish

Fried Fish Patties (Gefüllte Fish) (50 *portions of 1 patty each*)

Follow method for Gefüllte Fish Mix on p. 40 but use the following quantities:

4 lb (2kg) haddock fillet
4 lb (2kg) cod fillet
8 large eggs
2 large onions
2 level tbsp salt
1 level teasp white pepper
2 level tbsp sugar
4 tbsp oil
½ lb (200g/2 cups) medium matzo meal

Note: If blender is used for egg, onion and seasonings, add no extra water. If onion is minced, add approximately ½ pint (250ml/1¼ cups) water, or until mixture is soft enough to shape into balls. Fry in oil that almost covers balls. If equipment is available, deep fry for speed.

Gefüllte Fish Provençale (50 *portions*—1 *patty each*)

Follow method for **Gefüllte Fish Provençale** on p. 41. Use same quantities of mixture as for **Fried Fish Patties** above, and use the following quantities of sauce:

6 × 28 oz (780g) can tomatoes (sieved or liquidized)
5 oz (125g) can tomato purée
6 tbsp oil
5 green peppers, seeded and thinly sliced
6 medium onions, finely chopped
1½ level tbsp each salt and sugar
3 tbsp lemon juice
1 level teasp pepper

Sephardi Cheese Cakes (Savoury) (50 *servings*, 2 *puffs per person*)

Delicious little puffs that can be served as a main course for a dairy lunch.

2½ lb (1¼kg) puff pastry (use frozen vegetarian for simplicity)
2 lb (1kg/8 cups) cooking (Cheddar) cheese, finely grated
4 large eggs
1 level teasp salt

Grate cheese, if possible on electric grater. Beat eggs. Reserve 2 tablespoons for gilding puffs. Add remainder of eggs to cheese with salt to make a sticky paste. Roll pastry to the thickness of a knife blade, then cut with 2½ in (6 cm) plain cutters into approx 100 rounds. Damp edges of each round, place a teaspoon of filling in centre, fold over to form a half moon. Arrange on damp trays. Just before cooking brush with beaten egg. Bake in hot oven (Gas No. 7, 425°F, 220°C) for 10–15 minutes. Serve warm.

Noodle and Kaese Casserole (50 *portions*)

This delicious entrée can be served with salad or to accompany fish. If large shallow baking tins (approx 2 in/5 cm deep) are not available, use foil containers instead.

4 lb (2kg/24 cups) broad egg noodles
4 pints (2 litres/10 cups) soured cream
4 lb (2kg/8 cups) curd (cream) cheese
4 level teasp salt
1 level teasp black pepper
8 level tbsp chopped fresh chives or parsley
2 dozen eggs, separated
1 lb (½kg/2 cups) butter

Boil the noodles according to packet directions and drain. Pour hot water over them to remove any excess starch. Drain again and mix with the sour cream, cheese, beaten yolks, herbs and seasonings. Fold in the egg whites, beaten until they hold stiff, glossy peaks. Melt the butter. Pour half into the bottom of a shallow container approx 24 × 20 in (60 × 50 cm) or 2 smaller containers. Add noodle mixture. Pour remaining butter over the top. Bake in a quick moderate oven (Gas No. 5, 375°F, 190°C) for 45 minutes until puffed and golden. Cut in squares to serve.

Salads

Corn Salad (50 *servings*)

12 cans corn
1 large onion, finely chopped
6 level tbsp chopped parsley
8 fl oz (200ml/1 cup) French dressing
8 fl oz (200ml/1 cup) mayonnaise

Blend French dressing with parsley and chopped onion. Stir into well-drained corn. Refrigerate for at least an hour. Just before serving, blend with mayonnaise.

Potato Salad (50 *servings*)

12 × 19 oz (550g) cans potatoes
1 pint (500ml/2½ cups) French dressing
2 pints (1 litre/5 cups) mayonnaise
1 onion, finely chopped (optional)
10 tbsp chopped parsley

Drain potatoes and cube. Put into the French dressing and leave half an hour. Drain off remaining dressing and blend into mayonnaise together with onion and most of parsley. Fold in the potatoes. Chill for an hour if possible. Serve garnished with remaining parsley.

Cyprus Tomato Salad (50 *servings*)

Make according to the instructions for family quantity on p. 107 but use the following ingredients:

8 large cucumbers
8 lb (4kg) firm tomatoes
8 large green peppers
8 tbsp chopped parsley
$1\frac{1}{2}$ lb ($\frac{3}{4}$kg/6 cups) black olives for garnish (optional)

Dressing:
$1\frac{1}{2}$ pints (750ml/$3\frac{3}{4}$ cups) olive oil
$\frac{3}{4}$ pint (375ml/2 cups) lemon juice
2 level tbsp salt and caster (superfine) sugar
1 level teasp black pepper
1 level teasp garlic salt

French Dressing ($1\frac{1}{2}$ *pints* (4 *cups*) *for* 50)

4 cut cloves of garlic (optional)
2 level tbsp caster (superfine) sugar
1 level teasp white pepper
1 level tbsp dry mustard
2 level tbsp salt
$\frac{1}{2}$ pint (250ml/$1\frac{1}{4}$ cups) vinegar (wine or cider)
1 pint (500ml/$2\frac{1}{2}$ cups)oil

Put all the ingredients into a large jar and shake till thickened. If more convenient, whisk together. Remove garlic before use.

Mayonnaise (*Approx* $4\frac{1}{2}$ *pints*/$2\frac{1}{4}$ *l*/$11\frac{1}{4}$ *cups*)

Follow directions for making mayonnaise on p. 000 but use the following quantities:
12 egg yolks
3 level tbsp salt and sugar
2 level teasp paprika pepper
2 level tbsp dry mustard
4 fl oz (100ml/$\frac{1}{2}$ cup) vinegar (cider or wine)
4 pints (2 l/10 cups) salad oil

Note: Once an emulsion has been formed, oil may be added, 4 fl oz (100ml/$\frac{1}{2}$ cup) at a time. If necessary, thin with boiling water to consistency required.

Cold Sweets

Ice-cream with Sauce

This is a delicious and economical sweet to serve in quantity. For amount of ice-cream to allow see p. 296.

Note: After a meat meal, use parve ice-cream and margarine in sauce. All the sauces below will yield enough for 50 servings.

Chocolate Sauce (50 *servings*)

$1\frac{1}{2}$ lb ($\frac{3}{4}$kg) plain dark (semi-sweet) chocolate
$1\frac{1}{2}$ pints (750ml/$3\frac{3}{4}$ cups) water
$1\frac{1}{2}$ lb ($\frac{3}{4}$kg/3 cups) sugar
6 oz (150g/$\frac{3}{4}$ cup) butter
Vanilla essence (extract) to taste

Put the chocolate, water and sugar into a pan, dissolve over gentle heat and slowly bring to boil. Boil for 7 minutes, then remove from heat. Stir in butter and vanilla essence. Serve hot or cold.

Butterscotch Sauce (50 *servings*)

6 oz (150g/$\frac{3}{4}$ cup) butter
$\frac{3}{4}$ pint (375ml/2 cups) water
3 lb ($1\frac{1}{2}$kg/6 cups) brown sugar
Vanilla essence (extract) to taste

Place all ingredients in a strong pan. Dissolve slowly, bring to boil and simmer for 4 minutes. Cool.

Pineapple Sauce (50 *servings*)

4 × 20 oz (600g) cans pineapple pieces
12 fl oz (300ml/$1\frac{1}{2}$ cups) orange cordial
3 tbsp lemon juice
5 oz (125g/$\frac{2}{3}$ cup) sugar
5 level tbsp cornflour (cornstarch)

Mix together sugar and cornflour then blend with cordial, lemon juice and syrup strained from fruit. Bring to boil, stirring constantly, then simmer 3 minutes. Add finely cut-up pineapple. Leave to go cold.

Chocolate Mousse (50 *servings*)

An excellent parve sweet. Set in paper cases, or serve by the spoonful with fruit salad. Make exactly as for **Chocolate Mousse** on p. 128 but with the following quantities:

2½ lb (1¼kg) plain (semi-sweet) chocolate
30 eggs
5 level tbsp instant coffee
¼ pint (125ml/⅔ cup) rum, crème de menthe, brandy, Cointreau or orange juice
½ lb (200g/2 cups) toasted almonds or chopped walnuts for garnish

Fruit Salad (50 *servings*)

3 lb (1½kg) crisp apples, peeled and sliced
3 × 28 oz (780g) cans pears
2 × 28 oz (780g) cans sliced peaches
2 × 28 oz (780g) cans pineapple pieces; or 2 large fresh pineapples
2 × 15½ oz (400g) cans black cherries
10 oranges
12 bananas
2 lb (1kg) seedless grapes
Syrup:
Juice strained from cans
1–2 lb (1kg) can apricot jam
Juice of 4 lemons

Simmer syrup with apricot jam until smooth, then stir in lemon juice and any juice from fruit preparation. Add to prepared fruit. Leave for several hours.

Dessert Squares

For service on a large scale, it is convenient to bake pies and puddings in rectangular tins. It is then easy to portion them correctly.

All the recipes below are baked in tins approx 12 × 10 × 1 in (30 × 25 × 3 cm). This gives a yield of 25 portions. To make 50 portions, simply double the recipe and use two tins of the same size. *Note:* All these desserts can be frozen in advance.

Canadian Apple Slice (25 *portions*)

Pastry:
1 lb (480g/4 cups) self-raising flour; or 1 lb (480g/4 cups) plain flour and 4 level teasp baking powder
9 oz (225g/1¼ cups) margarine
2 large eggs
Juice of 1 lemon
2 oz (50g/½ cup) icing (confectioners') sugar

Reserve one egg white for glazing the top. Put all the remaining ingredients in the mixer and rub in gently until a dough is formed. Divide into two balls, foil-wrap and chill whilst the filling is prepared, then roll out first ball to fit a tin 12 × 10 × 1 in (30 × 25 × 3 cm).

Filling:
3 lb (1½kg) apples
8 oz (250g/1 cup) sugar
2 level teasp cinnamon

Peel apples and grate into a bowl, then stir in sugar and cinnamon. Immediately spread onto pastry and cover with another layer of pastry rolled to fit from second ball. Press gently down onto apples and lightly mark into 25 squares. Beat the reserved egg white until frothy, then paint all over the top. Sprinkle with a thin layer of granulated sugar. Bake in a moderate oven (Gas No. 5, 375°F, 190°C) for 45 minutes or until golden brown and crisp. Cut into squares. Serve warm or cold.

Peach Slice (25 *portions*)

Pastry:
10 oz (250g/2½ cups) plain flour
6 oz (150g/¾ cup) butter (or butter and margarine, half-and-half)
3 oz (75g/⅓ cup) caster (superfine) sugar
1 oz (25g/¼ cup) ground almonds
Grated rind of ½ lemon
3 tbsp single (light) cream or top milk
1 egg yolk
1 egg white for glazing

Mix flour, sugar, lemon and ground almonds; rub in fat, then mix to dough with cream and egg. Knead into a ball, divide in two and chill until firm enough to handle.

Filling:
6 large peaches (about 2 lb/1kg)
5 oz (125g/⅔ cup) fine brown sugar
1 level tbsp cornflour (cornstarch)
1 level teasp cinnamon
Juice of 1 lemon

Leave each peach in pan of boiling water for 1 minute; lift out with slotted spoon, and peel when cold enough to handle. Halve, then slice ⅛ in (½ cm) thick, put in bowl and blend with lemon juice. In another bowl mix the sugar, cornflour and cinnamon. Roll half the pastry to fit a tin approx 12 × 10 × 1 in (30 × 25 × 3 cm). Blend the mixture with the peaches, then spoon evenly into the tin. Top with the remaining pastry, rolled to fit. Paint with slightly beaten egg white and scatter with granulated sugar. Bake at Gas No. 5, 375°F, 190°C, for 45 minutes. Freezes well. Makes 25 slices.

Swedish Gâteau (25 *portions*)

An easy way to serve fruit-topped sponge, it makes a beautiful centre piece for a buffet.

6 oz (150g/¾ cup) margarine
8 oz (200g/1 cup) sugar
8 oz (200g/2 cups) self-raising flour
3 eggs
6 tbsp water

Put all ingredients in bowl and beat for 3 minutes until smooth. Bake in a rectangular tin approx 12 × 10 × 1 in (30 × 25 × 3 cm) for 40 minutes at Gas No. 4, 350°F, 180°C. When cool, soak with a little canned fruit syrup and sherry, then cover with rows of well-drained fruit, e.g. mandarins, black cherries and pineapple. Make a glaze by boiling 10 fluid ozs (1¼ cups) of the strained fruit syrup with 2 oz (250g/¼ cup) sugar, then thicken it with 1 level tablespoon cornflour, mixed with 4 more tablespoons of the fruit syrup. When the glaze has thickened and cleared (after 3 minutes' boiling), add a squeeze of lemon juice and allow to cool till it stops steaming, then spoon over the fruit. For nicest results, use the syrup from a light-coloured fruit (such as mandarins) so that the glaze will not hide the colour of the fruit. Cut into squares.

Fruit Cake Squares (25 *portions*)

An economical but tasty cake that is good to serve with a fruit salad.

1 lb (480g/4 cups) self-raising flour; or 1 lb (480g/4 cups) plain flour and 4 level teasp baking powder
2 level teasp mixed sweet spice
½ lb (200g/1 cup) best quality margarine
½ lb (200g/1 cup) caster (superfine) sugar
Grated rind of 1 large lemon
1 lb (480g/3 cups) mixed dried fruit
4 eggs
6 tbsp milk (or 5 eggs plus 2 tbsp water or sherry after meat meal)
2 oz (50g/½ cup) slivered almonds

Grease a tin 12 × 10 × 2 in (30 × 25 × 5 cm). Put all ingredients into a bowl and blend until smooth and creamy (about 3 minutes). Turn into tin and smooth level. Scatter with almonds. Bake in moderate oven (Gas No. 4, 350°F, 180°C) for 45–60 minutes, or until golden brown and firm to gentle pressure. When cold, cut into 25 squares.

See also **Spice is Nice** section on p. 168.

Table of Quantities to Serve 50

Food	Serving per Person	To Order
Bread and Rolls		
Crisp rolls	1–1½	4½–6½ doz
Large loaf	1–2 slices	2–3 loaves
Drinks		
Cocoa	8 fl oz (200ml) cup	8 oz (200ml/2½ cups)
Coffee (ground)	6½ fl oz (165ml) cup	1–1¼ lb (500g–600g/4–5 cups)
Coffee (instant)	6½ fl oz (165ml) cup	5 oz (125g/3 cups)
Tea (amount will vary with quality and blend)	8 fl oz (200ml) cup (from teapots)	6 oz (150g/2 cups)
Tomato juice	3 fl oz (75ml/⅓ cup)	7½ pints (3¾ litres/18 cups)
Rice and Pasta		
Noodles	5 oz (125g/½ cup) (cooked)	4 lb (2kg/24 cups)
Macaroni or Spaghetti	5 oz (125g/½ cup) (cooked)	4–5 lb (2–2½kg/20–25 cups)
Rice	5 oz (125g/¼ cup) (cooked)	3 lb (1½kg/7 cups)
Dairy Products		
Butter for table	1–1½ pats	1–1½ lb (¾kg/2–3 cups)
Butter for sandwiches	2 teasp	1 lb (480g/2 cups)
Cream for coffee	1 tbsp	1½ pints (750ml/4 cups)
Cream, whipping (for garnish)	1 tbsp	¾ pint (375ml/2 cups)
Cottage cheese	Scant 3 oz (75g/⅓ cup)	10 lb (5kg/20 cups)
Cheese for sandwiches	1¼ oz (35g/¼ cup)	4 lb (2kg/8 cups)
Eggs	1–2	50–100
Ice-cream, bulk	1 scoop	1½ gal (6 litres/30 cups)
Ice-cream, bricks	About ⅐ brick	7–8 family bricks
Milk (for tea)	Approx 1 fl oz (25ml/2 tbsp)	3 pints (1½ litres/7½ cups)
Milk (for coffee)	⅓ cup	5 pints (2½ litres/12½ cups)

Food	Serving per Person	To Order
Fruits		
Prunes	3 oz (75g) (cooked)	5½ lb (2¾kg)
Apples (stewed)	3 oz (75g) (raw)	15 lb (7½kg)
Apples (for 8 in/20 cm pie)	6–7 servings per pie	15 lb (7½kg)
Canned Fruit	4 oz (100g)	2 × A10 cans
Fruit Juice (canned)	4 fl oz (100ml)	4 × 46 fl oz (1150 ml) cans
Meats	**Cooked Weight**	
Chuck or Bola (braised)	3 oz (75g)	20–22 lb (10–11kg)
Minced (ground) meat for patties	3½ oz (90g)	14 lb (7kg)
Standing rib roast	3 oz (75g)	25–28 lb (12½–14kg)
Stew (with vegetables)	5½ oz (140g)	15 lb (7½kg)
Braising steak, sliced	3½ oz (90g)	16 lb (8kg)
Veal chops (3 to lb/480g)	1 each	17 lb (8½kg)
Lamb chops (4 to lb/480g)	2 each	25 lb (12½kg)
Salami	2 oz (50g)	6½ lb (3kg)
Saveloys (12 to lb/480g)	2 each	8–10 lb (4–5kg)
Poultry		
Chicken, casseroled	¼ chicken	40 lb (20kg) (8 hens, 5–6 lb/2½–3kg each)
Chicken, fried	¼–½ chicken	13–25 fryers, 2½–3 lb (1–1½kg) each
Turkey, roast	2½ oz (65g)	35–40 lb (17–20kg)
Fish		
Fish fillets	4 oz (100g)	12½ lb (6kg)
Vegetables		
Canned	4 oz (100g)	2 × A10 cans
Frozen	2½–3 oz (65–75g)	7½–10 lb (3½–5kg)
Lettuce for salad	1½–2 oz (40–50g)	8–10 heads
Lettuce for garnish		4–5 heads
Potatoes, baked	6 oz (150g)	20 lb (10kg)
Potatoes, to mash	4 oz (100g)	12 lb (6kg)
Potatoes, chips (French fries)	About 4½ oz (115g)	12–15 lb (6–7½kg)
Potato crisps (chips)	¾–1 oz (20–25g)	2½–3 lb (1¼–1½kg)
Tomatoes, sliced	3 oz (75g)	10–12 lb (5–6kg)
Miscellaneous		
Mixed nuts		1½ lb (¾kg/6 cups)
Honey	2 tbsp	5 lb (2½kg/7½ cups)
Jam	2 tbsp	5 lb (2½kg)
Sugar, lump	1–2 cubes	1½ lb (¾kg/5 cups)
Sugar, granulated	2 teasp	1 lb (½kg/2 cups)
Sugar, brown	2 teasp	1 lb (½kg/2¼ cups)

Food	Serving per Person	To Order
Desserts		
Cakes	2½ oz (65g)	2 tins, each approx 12 × 10 in (30 × 25 cm) (25 pieces each)
Fruit Cake	2½ oz (65g)	8 lb (4kg)
Pies, 8 inch		8 pies
Pastry (2 crust) 12 oz (300g) per pie		6 lb (3kg)
Pastry (1 crust) 6½ oz (165g) per pie		3¼ lb (1½kg)
Salads		
Vegetable (e.g. coleslaw)	5 fl oz (125ml)	1½ gal (6 litres/30 cups)
Potato	4 fl oz (100ml)	1¼ gal (5 litres/25 cups)
Soups		
Cream soup	5 fl oz (125ml)	1½ gal (6 litres/30 cups)
Clear soup	8 fl oz (200ml)	2¼ gal (9 litres/45 cups)
Gravy	3–4 tbsp	5–6½ pints (2½ litres/12½–17½ cups)
Sauce, thickened for meat	2 tbsp	2½ pints (1¼ litres/6¼ cups)
Mayonnaise	1½ tbsp	2 pints (1 litre/5 cups)

Index

B